The Decision-Making Network

The Decision-Making Network
An Introduction to Criminal Justice

SECOND EDITION

Risdon N. Slate
Professor of Criminology
Florida Southern College

Patrick R. Anderson
Emeritus Professor of Criminology
Florida Southern College

Lisa M. Carter
Assistant Professor of Criminology
Florida Southern College

Carolina Academic Press
Durham, North Carolina

Library of Congress Cataloging-in-Publication Data

Names: Slate, Risdon N., author. | Anderson, Patrick R., 1943- author.
Title: The decision-making network : an introduction to criminal justice / Risdon N. Slate, Patrick R. Anderson, and Lisa Carter.
Description: Second Edition. | Durham : Carolina Academic Press, [2018] | Revised edition of The decision-making network, c2011. | Includes bibliographical references and index.
Identifiers: LCCN 2017055508 | ISBN 9781531002985 (alk. paper)
Subjects: LCSH: Criminal justice, Administration of--United States.
Classification: LCC HV9950 .A56 2018 | DDC 364.973--dc23
LC record available at https://lccn.loc.gov/2017055508

Carolina Academic Press, LLC
700 Kent Street
Durham, North Carolina 27701
Telephone (919) 489-7486
Fax (919) 493-5668
www.cap-press.com

Printed in the United States of America

To Claudia, Virginia, Teddy, and all those who seek justice in or out of uniform.
Risdon N. Slate

To Family, Colleagues, and Students.
Patrick R. Anderson

To Karl, my family, and all those who strive to work for a fair and just system.
Lisa M. Carter

Contents

Table of Cases

Tables and Figures

Tables

Figures

Preface

This book attempts to explain the criminal justice decision-making network in America. Our approach is to examine the decisions that go into criminal justice. We examine how crimes are defined by the legislature and what importance is placed on various criminal acts. We describe the decisions made by police, prosecutors, defense attorneys, judges, correctional officials, and politicians ... all the decisions that affect the individual who is caught in the arms of the law.

Criminal justice decisions do not occur in a vacuum. The values in our democratic society underpin each decision. For example, our Founding Fathers could not have fathomed the technological advances seen within modern day society. Yet the Bill of Rights, over 200 years old, has essentially stood the test of time and guides criminal justice decision making today. We explain that context in light of the founding documents of our society, specifically the United States Constitution, and the applications of those documents made by the United States Supreme Court.

This is not a new approach. Donald J. Newman and Patrick R. Anderson have previously used it, separately and together. Most recently, Risdon N. Slate joined Anderson as a co-author; this volume, with the addition of Lisa Carter, adds a fresh perspective and reflects a further refinement of the decision-making network in keeping with the evolution of crime control in America.

In the past, issues of importance provided context for the book. Today the same is true, but many of the issues have changed. Criminal justice decision makers face the issues of terrorism, border security, legal status of immigrants, efforts to legalize marijuana, human trafficking, the criminalization of mental illness, various technological advances, the expanded use of DNA, a proliferation of guns, and workplace stress. Racial and ethnic divisions within society remain, and female crime is on the rise.

America has always faced issues of the day, but at different times one or the other becomes more pronounced. What remain constant, at least we would hope, are the underlying principles and values of our free society, but even those are altered by events. Interrogation techniques by criminal justice professionals were refined by the Supreme Court decision, *Miranda v. Arizona,* in the 1960s. But the "War on Terror" of the first decade in the 21st century brought about a number of measures to enhance public safety and constrain civil liberties and led to the establishment of our largest federal agency—The Department of Homeland Security. We continue the assessment of the evolution of this experiment called America and attempt to help students understand how crises sometimes drive policy and how new challenges to our understanding of the Constitution affect the practices of justice.

This book assumes that other, more advanced, courses exist in a criminal justice curriculum. We do not attempt to provide an exhaustive description of all of the intricacies of criminal justice. Rather we attempt to provide the broad sweep of criminal justice decisions, to whet the appetite of the reader for more detailed information, while at the same time providing a good overall understanding of the decision-making network. Thank you for using our work.

Acknowledgments

We wish to express our thanks and appreciation to several friends and colleagues who have encouraged, cajoled, and otherwise contributed to our work on this book. Our fellow professors and writers, James M. Denham and Chastity Blankenship remain unfailing friends. Claudia Slate also provided support and invaluable editing skills. We appreciate the vision of Anne B. Kerr who has fostered and maintained an environment conducive to pursuing and engaging in scholarship and the support of Kyle Fedler and Brad Hollingshead for helping to bring that to fruition.

We are also indebted to Betsy Matthews of Eastern Kentucky University for sharing her expertise on juvenile justice with us by writing a superb chapter on that topic for our book. We thank the many students who have, through the years, challenged us to express ourselves clearly and succinctly, to tolerate divergent views, and to keep our priority on equipping them to think sensibly and with appreciation for the complexities of criminal justice. Several outstanding students have contributed to the development of some material in the book, including Kaitlyn Leroux, Sierra Weld, and Jaimee Rudick.

Current graduate student at Seattle University, Lauren Morgan, wrote an outstanding piece on Criminal Justice Theory for the book. We also consulted with some of our past students, now in the professional work of criminal justice, and we have included comments and essays from them in this text, such as those from Booker T. Hodges and Larinda Slater. In addition, prosecutor Will Jay made significant written contributions to the manuscript, as well as reviewed pertinent portions of the text.

We are also grateful to Gary Gross and Robin Tillett at the Lakeland Police Department for their assistance in providing photographs to us for use in the text, as well as Plant City Police Department, and Editor of the Lakeland Ledger newspaper—Lenore Devore. The Florida Department of Corrections assisted us as well.

Friends and consummate professionals have contributed to our understanding of the "real life" criminal justice profession. These include Bill LePere, Chuck Cepak, Gary Cox, Brian Garrett, Bill Carew, and Gina Enriquez. Evidence of their input can be seen at various places in the text. Others when called upon to render advice or assistance were there in a pinch, including Jimmy Stein, Perry Rosen, and Sharon Chamard of the University of Alaska Anchorage. Lastly, the team at Carolina Academic Press has been wonderful to work with on this project. We appreciate the leadership and vision of Scott Sipe and Beth Hall; the painstaking attention to detail and hard work by TJ Smithers and earlier on by Ryland Bowman helped to ensure the production of a quality product. We also thank Susan Trimble for her cover design of the book and Davis Alderson for his production of the instructor's manual.

The Decision-Making Network

Chapter 1

The Nature and Extent of Crime in the United States

Image by sculpies at istockphoto.com.

Seeking Justice: How Much Crime?

"When you can measure what you are speaking about, and express it in numbers, then you know something about it; but when you cannot measure it, when you cannot express it in numbers, your knowledge is of a meager and unsatisfactory kind."

—Lord Kelvin, Scottish Mathematician of the 1800s[1]

About This Chapter

This chapter discusses the definition and measurement of crime in the United States. To the victim of crime, or anyone touched by crime, statistics are irrelevant. A criminal event is hurtful, often tragic, and always intensively personal. A crime statistic is cold and impersonal as an expression of the harm done. How can one assess the worth of a stolen family heirloom, put a price tag on the loss of a child's innocence, calculate the value of a loved one's lost life or health, or evaluate the erosion of one's personal security? Crime rates and other data pale to insignificance in the face of the personal trauma associated with the socio-political event we call crime. To the victim of a crime, discussions about the increase or decrease in crime rates are meaningless; for that person, crime has increased substantially.

Statistical contradictions leave us to question: How are we going to understand and evaluate American criminal justice if we do not know the truth about the nature and amount of crime in America? How do we study criminal justice? How are laws made? What is crime? How much crime do we truly have? How do we measure crime? What factors influence crime? How does crime affect American society and what does it cost? What do we expect the criminal justice system to accomplish? What purposes do criminal justice decision-makers achieve or attempt to achieve? What should Americans expect from criminal justice agencies? If crime is truly a permanent factor in our lives, regardless of its extent or form, then how can we best seek and serve justice?

The purpose of this book is to help you think about crime in more informed ways. Whether the amount of crime is increasing or decreasing is important to criminal justice policy makers and others. When one asks, "how much crime do we have?" or "what can be done about crime?" We hope your first response is "It depends on what you mean by crime." Crime is not an encompassing term. Shoplifting, armed robbery, and treason are all crimes, but have little or nothing in common beyond that categorization. Also, is it a crime if only the perpetrator is aware of the illegal act and no one is apprehended?

Likewise, one should use statistics carefully. Conclusions should not be made too rapidly, too casually. Success or failure of any crime strategy should not be claimed based on any single measure of crime. Official crime statistics may be better measures of police activity than criminal activity, as we will show. And, for all of the people who work in criminal justice agencies, who serve justice, the intensely personal nature of crime should never be forgotten.

The American System of Government

There are myriad influences on the criminal justice process that take us back to the very founding of our country and the system of government that was established there. Founding Fathers James Madison, John Jay, and Alexander Hamilton, recoiling from the centralized British government's monarchy, wrote newspaper articles under assumed names (fearing harsh punishment or even death from the English) encouraging the colonists to break from the Brits and form a new kind of government. The founding fathers did not have a great deal of faith in the competency of the common man to decide what was best for him, so they did not advocate setting up a pure **democracy**—direct rule by the people. Instead, they encouraged the establishment of a **Republic**—representative government. The closest average citizens would typically come in this new federal government to the making of laws would be by contacting their district's member of the United States House of Representatives with their concerns. In fact, our current system only encompasses a few elements of a pure democracy—propositions, initiatives, and referendums. Even under the American system, the founding fathers continued to fear tyrannical centralized power. So they established a system of separation of powers and checks and balances to be shared among three co-equal branches of government—the *legislative, executive, and judicial* branches. Some argue today that our media can also be considered a fourth branch of government as it operates to keep the other branches in check, as seen for example with the *Washington Post*'s reporting of the Watergate break-in story concerning the executive branch and President Nixon. The founding fathers also believed that **factions** (interest groups) with competing views would serve to balance each other out in vying to influence legislation and the political agenda. In building this new government, surely the founding fathers experienced difficulty in establishing a framework that would stand the test of time. Consider lobbying today, for example, in Critical Thinking 1.1.

Critical Thinking 1.1 The Case of Lobbying

The founding fathers likely could not have fathomed the recent U.S. Supreme Court decision, *Citizens United v. Federal Election Commission* (2010), which held that corporate entities have a First Amendment right to fund political speech by saying: "Government may not suppress political speech based on the speaker's corporate identity. No sufficient governmental interest justifies limits on the political speech of nonprofit or for-profit corporations" (p. 6).[2] In response to the decision, President Obama remarked, this "gives the special interests and their lobbyists even more power in Washington—while undermining the influence of average Americans who make small contributions to support their preferred candidates."[3] The president later said, "[T]he Supreme Court reversed a century of law to open the floodgates for special interests—including foreign corporations—to spend without limit in our elections. Well I don't think American elections should be bankrolled by America's most powerful interests, or worse, by foreign entities."[4] Thus, the ability to influence legislation and the laws may depend on the bankroll of advocates for or against any legislation. In other words, the more dollars you have the more influence on politicians you have. Consider, for example, the National Rifle Association (NRA) reportedly spent more than $36 miilion in the 2016 election cycle, and more than $21 million of that was aimed at helping the Trump campaign, with $12 million focused on anti-Hillary Clinton ads. **Should it be one person, one vote? Or, should it be one dollar, one vote?**[5]

While the founding fathers envisioned co-equal branches of government, Justice John Marshall in *Marbury v. Madison* (1803) brilliantly carved out the U.S. Supreme

Court as the ultimate arbiter of constitutional conflicts between the branches of government by establishing **judicial review.**[6] The Constitution is to reign supreme, and the U.S. Supreme Court will be the ultimate decider of constitutional conflicts between the branches of government.[7]

Crime Is What the Authorities Say It Is

We use the term "crime" casually in conversation ("Defriending someone on Facebook is a crime"), but technically **crime** is what a legislature defines as crime. Certain forms of deviance have more or less consistently been defined as crime throughout history, for example, theft, murder, and kidnapping. These crimes are part of the **common law**, the body of law that has existed for centuries by general agreement without necessarily being codified in written form. But in the modern world behavior is not a crime until or unless the legislature passes a statute precisely describing the forbidden behavior and setting a maximum punishment for violators. There is a Latin phrase, ***nullum crimen, nullum poena, sine lege***, that means "no crime, no punishment, without legislation," and it appears with each legislative term the volume of criminal statutes expands. With the rise of each new social problem, some Americans respond by demanding "There ought to be a law!"—about drug use, abortion, gun possession, and a great deal more. Although nearly unanimous agreement exists as to whether some behaviors should be defined legally as criminal, there is much controversy regarding others. See **Critical Thinking 1.2.**

Critical Thinking 1.2 Creating and Eradicating Crime

In Los Angeles authorities have said it is illegal to bathe two babies at the same time in the same tub, and it is legal for a husband to beat his wife with a strap less than two inches wide. It is not a crime if the wife consents to her husband using a bigger strap. In Arkansas, such beatings by husbands of their wives are legal as long as they are not done more than once a month. In Michigan, a woman is forbidden to cut her own hair without her husband's permission. In South Dakota, a woman over 50 years old is not permitted to walk outside of her home and strike up a conversation with a married male age twenty or older.[8] At the federal level, there are various examples of obsolete laws remaining on the books. Such statutes include specifications that it is a crime to poll military personnel prior to an election, to use the Smokey Bear character without authorization, to install a toilet that exceeds too much water per flush, to write a check for less than one dollar, and to provide for the interstate transportation of dentures. While the legislature is responsible for enacting laws, it also falls under the purview of the legislative branch, respecting the separation of powers, to repeal laws as well.[9] Of course some laws remain on the books but seldom if ever are enforced unless needed to rid the community of a nuisance who cannot otherwise be thwarted. We refer to these rarely if ever enforced laws as "**a law**," while "**the law**" pertains to those laws that are on the books and enforced on a regular basis.

Blue Laws (blue is believed to imply a rigidly moral puritanical stance);[10] yet others claim the description is based on the blue paper the law is written on.[11] Recent examples of blue law controversies have emerged in New York and New Jersey regarding Sunday sales of certain items such as alcohol, frying pans, and nails.[12]

An example of the interface between the enforcement of enacted laws and the legislative repeal of such laws is evident in South Carolina where, in the 1980s, Sunday closing laws (Blue Laws) were on the statute books. Certain types of stores could not legally be open on Sunday and certain items were unlawful to sell on Sunday. Although the Blue Laws were on the books statewide, merchants in the tourist meccas of Charleston and Myrtle Beach ignored the laws, opened their stores and sold whatever items they desired. Law enforcement in these cities elected not to enforce the Blue Laws. Storeowners in the capitol city of Columbia learned of the Sunday openings and sales in Charleston and Myrtle Beach and decided to follow suit to market their wares and increase their profits. However, Richland County Sheriff Frank Powell chose to enforce the state law forbidding Sunday sales. Hardware items were not allowed to be sold on Sunday under the Blue Laws. So Sheriff Powell used undercover officers to go through checkout lines and purchase items such as hammers and nails on Sunday. Once the cashier rang the item(s) up and the deal was closed, undercover agents would produce their law enforcement credentials and place the cashier under arrest. Many of the employees arrested were young high school or college students who were now facing criminal records.

The merchants in Columbia felt undermined as their competitors in the tourist attraction areas were making out like bandits with their sales. This, combined with the potentially damaging criminal records for the mainly young cashiers, led to a media frenzy. Sheriff Powell would not back down, indicating that as the chief law enforcement officer for his county that he was bound to follow the law although his counterparts (sheriffs in Charleston and Horry County—Myrtle Beach) did not sense such an obligation. Powell contended that his job was to enforce the law and it was up to the legislature to make the law or to strike the law from the books.[13] What resulted from the media and public pressure was the convening of an emergency session of the legislature and a repeal of the statewide Blue Laws in South Carolina. A provision was even included in the emergency legislation that allowed for the expungement of criminal records for any of the illegal Sunday sales. The moral of this story is that if one wants to get an unpopular law changed, just enforce it, and it is up to the legislature to repeal it.

Do you think Sheriff Powell handled this matter correctly? What about the sheriffs in Charleston and Myrtle Beach? Was a costly emergency convening of the legislature the appropriate way to handle this matter? Con-

sidering the perspectives of a South Carolina voter, an arrested cashier, a parent of an arrested cashier, a minister in favor of Sunday closing laws, a sheriff, and a legislator, what do you think would have been the most appropriate manner to resolve this matter?

The Case of Prostitution and Marijuana

Howard Becker indicated that "deviance ... is created by society.... Social groups create deviance by making the rules whose infraction constitutes deviance, and by applying those rules to particular people and labeling them as outsiders."[14] What his assessment particularly addresses is both the law enactment and the law enforcement processes. As we have previously discussed, laws are made (law enactment) in America primarily via a representative government process. Through this process, interest groups (or competing factions) bring their items to the agenda for legislators to consider. Of course, what is considered deviant (illegal) can vary from time to time and place to place, and can be heavily influenced by a number of factors. Also, even when a particular act is considered to be illegal there may be selective enforcement of the law that favors some and criminalizes others.

While prostitution is not legal in Las Vegas, it is legal sixty miles outside of the city in Nye County.[15] Brothels such as the Cherry Patch, Sheri's Ranch, and Chicken Ranch have websites, accept credit cards, and are open 365 days a year, seven days a week, and 24 hours a day.[16] Nevada's infamous Mustang Ranch brothel was seized by the federal government for tax evasion in a bankruptcy proceeding and actually owned for a short while by the government before it was auctioned off.[17] Why might the residents of Nye County, Nevada, and lawmakers consider prostitution to be legal there, as cities such as Amsterdam in the Netherlands do, while the rest of the United States outside Nevada outlaws prostitution and law enforcement often targets call girls, pimps, and johns in highly publicized after-the-fact undercover sting operations?

Consider the case of marijuana and the personality of Harry J. Anslinger. Anslinger, a former prohibition agent and railroad police officer, ascended to the directorship of the Federal Bureau of Narcotics (FBN) (what is known as the Drug Enforcement Administration [DEA] today) in 1930. Inheriting an agency on the heels of the Great Depression that was facing severe budget cuts resulting in loss of personnel, offices, and equipment, Anslinger struggled to make his agency necessary. Prior to 1937, marijuana was legal in America. However, Anslinger and his cronies began to decry the evils of marijuana smoking and to incorporate a racist slant to their urgings. Anslinger maintained, "the primary reason to outlaw marijuana is its effect on the degenerate races." He said "[r]eefer makes darkies think they're as good as white men." He described the majority of marijuana smokers as "Negroes, Hispanics, Filipinos, and entertainers. Their Satanic music, jazz, and swing result from marijuana use. This marijuana causes white women to seek sexual relations with Negroes, entertainers, and any others."[18] Anslinger even told of two black youths at a jazz club in Minnesota who lured a white female inside with marijuana only to have their way with her and impregnate her. Anslinger would even testify before Congress using anecdotal sensationalized newspaper headlines erroneously making the case that half of all violent crimes committed by minorities in America were induced by smoking marijuana.[19] He was quick to link marijuana smoking to violent crime by blacks, particularly crimes perpetrated on white women.

Keeping in mind how lawmaking can be influenced, it has been promulgated that a sinister conspiracy transpired in the outlawing of marijuana. It has been maintained that Andrew Mellon, Secretary of the Treasury and an uncle-in-law of Anslinger, got Anslinger his job with the FBN. Reportedly, Mellon was the principal financial operative in support of a multi-million dollar enterprise between newspaper magnate William Randolph Hearst and the DuPont Company. The project conjoined DuPont's chemical pulping procedure with Hearst's forests full of pulpwood trees and his pulp mills. This allowed Hearst to create newsprint at a much cheaper rate than his competitors were able. A threat purportedly emerged when it was discovered that hemp (while hemp and marijuana are varieties of the same plant, smoking hemp does not make one high) could be processed by newly developed hemp pulping machines more cheaply by competitors and undermine the DuPont-Hearst money-making association. As these forces (Mellon, Anslinger, DuPont, and Hearst) allegedly converged, marijuana was outlawed by Congress in 1937 with passage of the Marihuana Tax Act.[20]

The 1930s movie *Reefer Madness* has also been touted as a government propaganda film to show the evils of marijuana smoking depicting individuals smoking marijuana and running over a pedestrian with a car, shooting and killing someone, committing suicide by jumping out of a window, and being rendered insane. Although a distributor of the film, Dwain Esper, testified before the Arizona Supreme Court that the movie was sponsored by the United States government, it has been maintained that such government involvement is a fallacy. Even so, the movie has been revitalized and has become a cult classic, often played at midnight movies. While *Reefer Madness* was intended to be exploitive and decry the evils of marijuana smoking, it is today viewed by most with hilarity.[21]

Communities generally receive the kind of law enforcement that they desire. James Q. Wilson's research has demonstrated that styles of law enforcement can be influenced by community characteristics.[22] A recent Gallup poll found that more Americans than ever (60 percent) support legalization of marijuana, a 16% increase since 2010.[23] While potential conflicts with state and federal law remained, voters in Denver, Colorado, (giving new meaning to "the mile high city") went to the polls to become the first major jurisdiction in the United States to legalize possession of small quantities of recreational marijuana by the citizenry.[24] In addition to Colorado, seven other states

(Alaska, California, Massachusetts*, Maine*, Nevada*, Oregon, Washington), and the District of Columbia have now legalized the use of recreational marijuana (* denotes that these states have passed laws legalizing marijuana that have yet to come into effect at the time of publication).[25] Even where recreational marijuana is legalized in America, there are often impediments to its use. In some of these places marijuana use in public is outlawed or buying or selling marijuana is prohibited. Some states leave it up to local jurisdictions to determine whether use of recreational marijuana is permissible.[26]

The pure democracy elements previously mentioned of proposition (any ballot measure voted on by the citizenry, and this can include initiatives or referendums), initiative (upon acquiring an authorized amount of citizens' signatures a measure can be placed on the ballot for voter consideration), and referendum (voters elect to reject or approve existing law at the ballot box)[27] have largely been used to legalize medical marijuana in this country and in some instances even recreational marijuana. Twenty-nine states, including the eight states that have legalized recreational marijuana, and the District of Columbia have legalized medical marijuana (additional states include: Arizona, Arkansas, Connecticut, Delaware, Florida, Hawaii, Illinois, Maryland, Michigan, Minnesota, Montana, New Hampshire, New Jersey, New Mexico, New York, North Dakota, Ohio, Pennsylvania, Rhode Island, Vermont, and West Virginia).[28]

Marijuana remains illegal at the federal level. While President Obama's administration refrained from the enforcement of marijuana laws, it remains to be determined how the Trump administration will respond. Prior to becoming president, Donald Trump stated that he thought medical marijuana should remain legal and that the status of recreational marijuana should be resolved by the states. However, in terms of marijuana, members of his cabinet who are strictly opposed to drugs surround Trump.[29] For example, Trump's U.S. Attorney General Jeff Sessions (former U.S. Senator from Alabama) was denied a federal judgeship in the 1980s and has been criticized for racism. Sessions acknowledged in the congressional record for his failed judicial confirmation that he had indicated "that he thought [the Ku Klux Klan and] its members were OK until he learned that they smoked marijuana," though he maintained that he had been joking.[30]

President-elect Trump indicated support for medical marijuana and said recreational marijuana should be left up to the states.[31] After taking office, Trump's then Press Secretary, Sean Spicer, indicated that President Trump is not opposed to medical marijuana; however, a crack down from the federal level is expected on recreational marijuana—even in those states that have legalized it. This comes as the majority of Americans (59%) believe that marijuana should be legal, and 71 percent are opposed to a federal crackdown. Politicians in affected states have vowed to fight such a prohibition.[32] "[T]he Trump administration and Attorney General Jeff Sessions [have] promised to crack down on federal marijuana crimes[.] During his confirmation, then-Senator Sessions pointed out that if legislators did not like this approach, they should change the laws accordingly."[33] U.S. Congressman Thomas Garrett of Virginia, a Republican and former prosecutor, has put forth a bill that would allow states to make their own decisions about the legality of marijuana without interference from the federal government.[34] More recently, U.S. Senator Cory Booker has offered a similar bill that goes even further by including a mechanism for expungement of federal marijuana convictions and withholding federal funding from those states that have not legalized marijuana if racially disproportionate arrest and incarceration rates for marijuana are present.[35] Thus, as this book goes to press, the future of marijuana enforcement remains in question in America. U.S. Attorney General Jeff Sessions has rescinded the Obama-era directive to U.S. Attorneys not to interfere with legalized marijuana, which means much will depend on the discretion of federal prosecutors across the country. There is even speculation this decision by Sessions may lead to even more legalization of marijuana.[36] **How is the controversy surrounding the enforcement of marijuana laws somewhat analogous to the previous discussion concerning enforcement of Blue Laws? What is the current legal status of marijuana nationally, in your state? Do you agree with its legal status?**

Former Minnesota governor, Jesse Ventura, has criticized President Trump for ignoring the will of the people regarding legalization of recreational marijuana and has suggested that private prisons helped bankroll Trump's presidential campaign and are strategically positioned to benefit from federal enforcement of marijuana laws.[37] Stocks have been soaring for GeoGroup and CoreCivic, private prison corporations that each contributed $250,000 to the Trump campaign and anticipate amped up enforcement of immigration laws.[38]

The potential economic boost to the country if marijuana were legalized has been likened to that of the lifting of the prohibition on alcohol by President Franklin Delano Roosevelt. Economists such as Jeffrey Miron of Harvard University maintain that the legalization of marijuana in the United States would produce somewhere between $10 and $14 billion in tax revenues and savings annually; this is a conclusion reportedly supported by the now deceased Milton Friedman (a former economic advisor to President Ronald Reagan and Nobel Prize recipient) as well;[39] sales of marijuana in the United States are projected to reach nearly $23 billion by the year 2020.[40] Within the first nine months of 2016, Colorado's marijuana industry had generated in excess of $134 million in taxes with some revenue earmarked to build housing for an increasing homeless population. Some monies from marijuana sales have also been allocated to provide funds for healthcare, substance abuse treatment and prevention programs, law enforcement, college scholarships, playgrounds, and even an anti-bullying program in schools.[41] Investment in marijuana-related stocks is even possible with such companies as GW Phar-

"Snoop"

maceuticals and Insys Therapeutics.[42] Celebrities are even establishing their own brands of marijuana products for sale. For example, Snoop Dogg has a line called Leafs by Snoop, country singer Willie Nelson has Willie's Reserve, and rapper Wiz Khalifa has Khalifa Kush.[43]

Research indicated that for the first time ever, based on 2015 data, motorists killed in vehicle crashes in America were "more likely to be on drugs than drunk. Forty-three percent of drivers tested in [these] fatal crashes ... had used a legal or illegal drug, [while] 37 percent tested above the legal limit for alcohol." More than a third of the drugged drivers killed in crashes had marijuana in their system; Colorado saw a 48 percent increase in marijuana-related fatal crashes after legalizing recreational use of the drug. Furthermore, in 2015, in excess of 33,000 persons died from opioid (heroin and prescription drug abuse) overdoses, which almost surpassed the total of persons killed in crashes—35,095. While all states ban driving under the influence of alcohol or drugs, drug testing is less precise and standardized than alcohol screenings. Drugs can have varying impacts on individuals, and many officers are not properly trained to detect those under the influence of drugs.[44]

Glaring racial disparities have also been reported in the enforcement of marijuana laws in the United States. Under apartheid in 1993 in South Africa, 851 black males per 100,000 population were incarcerated; in America, "in 2004[,] under marijuana prohibition we incarcerated 4,919 black males per 100,000."[45] In 2007, 782,000 U.S. citizens were arrested for marijuana-related crimes (9 out of 10 of them for possession—not distribution or smuggling), with somewhere between 60,000 to 85,000 of these Americans incarcerated in jail or prison.[46] In 2015, almost half of all drug possession arrests (in excess of 574,000) were for possession of marijuana. Violent crimes (murder, non-negligent manslaughter, rape, robbery, and aggravated assault) resulted in 505,681 arrests total. In other words, law enforcement made more arrests for simple possession of marijuana than for all violent crimes combined during this same period. Based on sufficient data from 39 states, it was determined that black adults were more than four times more likely to be arrested for marijuana possession than whites, even though the marijuana usage rates between the two races is essentially the same.[47] Even in states such as Colorado and Washington that have legalized recreational marijuana, partaking of marijuana in public can result in arrest. Arrests for blacks in these states for such offenses are higher than for whites.[48]

Should the influences on such legislation be considered? Should the economic impact of such prohibitions matter when considering whether various acts defined as illegal should be made legal? Should what is popular, as seen in polls, ever matter when determining what is prohibited and what is not?

Law and Criminal Justice in a Democratic Society

Former United States Senator Sam Ervin once said "In a free society you have to take some risks. If you lock everybody up, or even if you lock up everybody you think might commit a crime, you'll be pretty safe, but you won't be free."[49] Within a democratic society a crucial balance must be struck between maintaining public safety while respecting civil liberties. As noted by historian James Truslow Adams, " 'We must rule or be ruled,' because unless the crime problem is brought under control, social order will sooner or later give way to chaos, opening the way for 'the dictator who inevitably "saves society" when social insubordination and disintegration have become intolerable.' " While Adams may have overstated the presence of societal breakdown and tyranny at the time of his writings during America's Great Depression, he perceived the real susceptibility "of democratic rights and freedoms to demagogic appeals for 'law and order.' "[50] See **Field Practice 1.1.**

Field Practice 1.1 Crisis Driving Policy

9/11 and Homeland Security

Samuel Walker has indicated that celebrated, sensationalized cases, which are the exception rather than the rule, tend to drive crime policy.[51] In essence, crises drive policies. No better large-scale example of this phenomenon can be seen than in the establishment of the Department of Homeland Security and implementation of various security procedures after the horrific hijackings of airliners and crashes into the World Trade Center, the Pentagon, and a Pennsylvania field on September 11, 2001. In the face of the threat on American soil, the Department of Homeland Security was formed just over a year (November 25, 2002) after the terrorist attacks. It is now the largest federal justice organization, with twenty-two federal agencies created or merged into the Department of Homeland Security. Among the larger agencies now encompassed by the Department of Homeland Security are the Transportation Security Administration (TSA), the Coast Guard, the Secret Service, Customs, the Immigration and Naturalization Service, Border Patrol, and the Federal Emergency Management Agency (FEMA).[52] As of 2016, there were over 240,000 Department of Homeland Security (DHS) employees.[53] The DHS budget for fiscal year 2016 was $41.2 billion,[54] and a budget of $40.6 billion with an additional $6.7 billion for disaster relief was proposed for fiscal year 2017.[55]

Striking the balance between public safety and civil liberties has been a challenge in the face of the terrorist attacks and attempted attacks. Some of the controversial matters connected to the war on terror are the following: the housing of terrorist suspects and enemy combatants at Guantanamo Bay and on ships and secret locations, publicized abuses at Abu Ghraib prison, the potential use of military tribunals, the use of waterboarding as an interrogation technique, and escalation of police surveillance and intelligence gathering methods.

The Crime Rate: Up or Down?

One would be hard pressed to find many people who would not believe that each year brings more crime to America's cities and communities. Likewise, the general perception of many people in the United States is that we do not use imprisonment enough as a criminal sanction, that serious offenders are handled leniently by soft-hearted judges, that prisoners are released very soon after their incarceration, and that the American criminal justice system is ineffective in curbing crime. Recent election cycles in the United States have spawned rhetoric about getting "tough on crime," reducing crime, and making streets and playgrounds safe, as though we are experiencing an ever-increasing spiral of crimes and have done little to stem the tide.[56]

Recent statistical reports argue to the contrary. An almost 40 percent decrease in the violent crime rate has been realized since its peak in the early 1990s, and the last president to see a murder rate this low in America was Lyndon Johnson in the 1960s.[57] The first years that crime rates fell since the mid-1980s were in 1994 and 1995. Even in 2016, property and violent crimes remain at record lows for the nation and, with rare exception (see FBI data from 2011, 2012, 2015, and 2016), have been declining for the past twenty years.[58] Cooperative efforts of federal, state, and local law enforcement agencies have been credited for this reduction. All the while, with some fluctuations, the number of adults under correctional supervision has remained high in the United States.

In 2015, even with crime rates falling and arrest rates down, 6,741,400 people were under some form of correctional supervision, including probation, prison, jail, and parole. The majority of those persons were under probation supervision. This translates into 1 in 37 U.S. adult residents under some form of correctional supervision, and this translates into the lowest rate of correctional supervision since 1994 when 1 in 38 adults were under such correctional control.[59]

Both community supervision and incarcerated populations in America reflected reductions in 2015. At year-end 2015, the population of persons under community supervision (4,650,900) dropped to its lowest level since 2000 (4,564,900). In addition, the 2015 incarcerated population (2,173,800) hit its lowest level since 2004 (2,136,600).[60]

Even so, the United States reportedly has the highest incarceration rate in the world, locking up 698 per 100,000 persons compared to Rwanda at 492 per 100,000, the Russian Federation at 446 per 100,000, and Brazil at 301 per 100,000.[61] In fact, when broken down by U.S. state and territory, the District of Columbia followed by Louisiana has the highest incarceration rate in the world. In addition to DC and Louisiana, 28 states (Georgia, Oklahoma, Alabama, South Dakota, Arizona, Texas, Florida, Tennessee, Mississippi, Missouri, Virginia, Kentucky, Arkansas, Delaware, Alaska, Pennsylvania, New Mexico, Wyoming, South Carolina, Nevada, Indiana, Idaho, Wisconsin, North Carolina, Ohio, West Virginia, Colorado, and Illinois) had higher incarceration rates as of June 16, 2016, than any country in the world. The first country besides the United States to materialize on the list was Turkmenistan, followed by the states of Maryland, Nebraska, Oregon, Montana, Iowa, and North Dakota. Then, in order of per capita incarceration rates, El Salvador, Hawaii, Cuba, Connecticut, Washington, Thailand, New Hampshire, Russian Federation, New Jersey, Rwanda, New York, Panama, Utah, Minnesota, Rhode Island, Maine, Costa Rica, Puerto Rico, Vermont, Massachusetts, and Brazil emerged.[62]

One in five persons locked up in America are there for a drug offense.[63] This translates to over half of all persons in custody in the federal system being in on drug offenses, with the next closest offense in that system being for weapons offenses (15.9%). Also, in 2014, the majority of offenders in the state system (53.2%) were imprisoned for violent acts, followed by property offenses (19.3%), drug offenses (15.7%), and public order violations (11%).[64] Furthermore, based on 2010 census data, whites comprise 64% of the U.S. population and roughly 40% of the incarcerated population; blacks make up 13% of the country's population and 39% of those in prisons and jails; and Latinos constitute 16% of the U.S. population and 19% of those incarcerated in America.[65]

Recent rates of imprisonment in America ranged from 52 per 100,000 for white women, 63 for Latina women, 103 for black women, 457 for white men, and 1,043 for Latino men, to 2,613 per 100,000 for black men. This results in the likelihood of imprisonment of U.S. residents born in 2001 of 1 in 9 for all men, 1 in 56 for all women, 1 in 3 for black men, 1 in 6 for Latino men, 1 in 17 for white men, 1 in 18 for black women, 1 in 45 for Latina women, and 1 in 111 for white women.[66] Thus, being white can prove to be advantageous in America. Furthermore, of the 159,520 persons serving life sentences in America, 47.2% of these individuals are black, 34.7% white, and 16% Latino.[67]

The cost for corrections operations at the state level has ranged from $6.7 billion to a high of $51.9 billion in 2013.[68] According to the U.S. Department of Education, as of 2016, "23 states increased per capita spending on corrections at more than double the rate of increases in per-pupil P–12 spending. Seven states—Idaho, Michigan, Montana, North Dakota, South Carolina, South Dakota, and West Virginia—increased their corrections budgets more than five times as fast as they did their allocations for P–12 public education.... Since 1990, state and local spending on higher education has been largely flat while spending on corrections has increased 89 percent."[69] The report went on to indicate that "[t]he United States has only 5 percent of the world's population yet more than 20 percent of the world's incarcerated population. According to the Bureau of Justice Statistics, two-thirds of state prison inmates have not completed high school. One study also shows young black men between the ages of 20 and 24 who do not have a high school diploma or an equivalent credential have a greater chance of being incarcerated than employed. Researchers have estimated that a 10 percent increase in high school graduation rates results in a 9 percent decline in criminal arrest rates."[70]

"Key findings from the report include:

- Over the past three decades, between 1979–80 and 2012–13, state and local expenditures for P–12 education doubled from $258 to $534 billion, while total state and local expenditures for corrections quadrupled from $17 to $71 billion.
- All states had lower expenditure growth rates for P–12 education than for corrections, and in the majority of the states, the rate of increase for corrections spending was more than 100 percentage points higher than the growth rate for education spending.
- Even when adjusted for population changes, growth in corrections expenditures outpaced P–12 expenditures in all but two states (New Hampshire and Massachusetts).
- Over the roughly two decades, between 1989–1990 and 2012–2013, state and local appropriations for public colleges and universities remained flat, while funding for corrections increased by nearly 90 percent.
- On average, state and local higher education funding per full-time equivalent student fell by 28 percent, while per capita spending on corrections increased by 44 percent."[71]

America's imprisonment binge has seen a 500% increase in the last forty years largely based on modifications of sentencing policies and laws, not changes in crime rates.[72] Of course, the dissemination of misinformation can have a significant impact on public perceptions of crime. For example, President Donald Trump announced, "the murder rate is the highest it's been in ... 45 to 47 years."[73] Although there was slight upward movement in the homicide rate between 2014 and moving into 2016, the homicide rate is nowhere near the peak levels witnessed in the 1990s; Trump is absolutely incorrect.[74] Reportedly, "[t]he U.S. homicide rate declined by nearly half (49%), from 9.3 homicides per 100,000 U.S. residents in 1992 to 4.7 in 2011, falling to the lowest level since 1963."[75] The rate remained at 4.7 for 2012, 4.5 for 2013, 4.4 for 2014, and saw the uptick beginning in 2015 with a murder rate of 4.9 per 100,000. Thus, according to the FBI, the murder rate is almost at its lowest point in the past 47 years.[76]

In spite of our proclivity to bring persons under control of the criminal justice system, a recent Gallup poll found that almost half of all respondents (45%) do not feel that the U.S. criminal justice system is tough enough on crime. The majority of Republicans and Independents leaning Republican (65%) and whites (53%) agreed that the U.S. is too weak on crime.[77]

Types of Crime

Someone may ask, "How much crime occurs in the United States?" The proper response to this question may well be: "It depends on what you mean by crime." The sheer volume of laws makes general use of the word "crime" too broad. Also, qualitative differences are lost between specific criminal acts, such as disorderly conduct and forcible rape, when they are lumped under a single heading. Categories of crimes help us distinguish between the wide range of behaviors that are labeled as crime.[78] See **Table 1.1** for a preliminary list of crime categories.

This list is by no means all the crimes on the books, but rather a representative sample of the categories of the very long list of behaviors our society calls crimes. The seriousness of any type of crime—the degree of its threat to our social order—can be debated endlessly. Thus, we can debate whether murder is a worse crime than irresponsible toxic waste disposal, which may increase disease resulting in the death of persons in a more indirect fashion, or whether crimes against individual persons (assault with a whiskey bottle, for instance) are more threatening to our social system than "crimes against the people" (manufacture of hazardous products, or unfair credit policies, for instance). Which is worse, to steal money from a person's wallet or to profit from all the residents of a community through illegal price fixing of a commodity? Such questions are unlikely to be resolved by debate, yet the controversy goes on. Proposals are made to "decriminalize" certain behaviors, such as possession and sale of marijuana, and to "criminalize" or more seriously punish other types of conduct, like pollution or abortion, which until recently have not been viewed as serious threats to our way of life.

Common Law and Modern Crime

The ranking of crimes by degree of seriousness is not simply a debater's exercise. Distinctions between classes of crimes have been recognized throughout history. Our present-day criminal codes and corresponding sentencing structures owe much of their content to origins in common law. Our written criminal codes retain many of the ancient and very serious bans on forms of conduct, behaviors considered "evil in themselves" (***mala in se***) such as murder. We have added less dramatic crimes peculiar to different stages of our modern urban industrial development, crimes that have no exact counterparts in common law, such as drug abuse or illegal toxic waste

Table 1.1 Categories of Crime

Crimes against persons	Murder Assault and battery Sexual battery Kidnapping Extortion
Crimes against public morality	Fornication and illicit cohabitation Adultery Incest Prostitution Gambling Intoxication Drug abuse Profanity Indecent exposure Pornography
Crimes against justice and public administration	Bribery Perjury Obstruction of justice Resisting arrest Escape Criminal contempt
Victimless crimes	Gambling Illegal sex acts between consenting adults Drug abuse
Crimes against property and habitation	Larceny (theft) Burglary Arson
Crimes against public order	Disorderly conduct Breach of peace Vagrancy
White-collar crimes	Tax fraud Bankruptcy fraud Insider trading Computer crimes Insurance fraud
Crimes committed by government authorities	Civil rights violations Police brutality Political bribe taking Genocide Torture

disposal. These are offenses created by legislation rather than history (***mala prohibita***). With few exceptions, *mala in se* offenses are considered by most people as more serious than *mala prohibita* offenses, and both categories contain finer distinctions of seriousness, including major differences between heavily penalized felonies and less severely treated misdemeanors.

Felonies and Misdemeanors

Written criminal codes in all jurisdictions distinguish between felonies and misdemeanors and sometimes lesser offenses called "violations" or "infractions." A **felony** is considered to be a serious crime with a correspondingly harsh penalty such as imprisonment for more than one year, or even death, and also including such civil penalties as loss of voting privileges or professional licensure after conviction. A **misdemeanor** is a minor offense, less serious than a felony, subject to penalties such as a fine or a jail term of a year or less.

Most felony convictions take place in state courts, not federal courts.[79] In 2016, there were 1,351,000 state prison inmates, 211,000 inmates in federal prisons, and 646,000 housed in local jails (195,000 of those had been convicted, and 451,000 had not been convicted).[80] Estimates are that that 90 to 95% of all criminal cases are plea bargained each year in state and federal courts.[81] Of course, the percentage of plea bargains varies from year to year. For example, in fiscal year 2012, 97% of all federal convictions were the result of guilty pleas.[82] However, in fiscal year 2015, the federal courts closed 74,990 cases involving defendants and 92.8% pled guilty or were found guilty at trial.[83]

Immigration cases in the federal courts, as of fiscal year 2012, had increased by 97% in the past decade.[84] Immigration issues may very well continue to rise in the courts under the Trump administration. While federal offenders are generally considered more sophisticated than state criminals, due to the caliber of crimes they commit, almost half of federal offenders (49.9%) sentenced in fiscal year 2012 had not finished high school.[85] Roughly 16% of state prisoners have attained a high school diploma.[86]

See **Table 1.2** for a list of 2015 felony and misdemeanor arrests compiled by the FBI.[87]

Both felonies and misdemeanors are graded by degrees of seriousness. Often this grading is expressed in **degrees of crime**. For example, a criminal code provides a variety of categories for the felony of murder. **Murder in the first degree** is defined as an act that is carried out after premeditation and planning. An important exception to this general rule is a killing that is not specifically planned but occurs during the commission of a serious felony, such as armed robbery. This is called "**felony murder**." **Second-degree murder** is any other murder than first-degree or felony murder. That is, no premeditation or malice aforethought existed, but the offender acted in a dangerous way without regard for human life. For instance, a person may wish to beat someone else severely, "within an inch of his (or her) life," as the saying goes, but the victim dies as a result of the beating. Such a murder is substantially different from one in which the offender planned for weeks or months to carry out a cold-blooded killing. In practice, second-degree murder convictions sometimes result from first-degree prosecutions that the jury determines do not deserve the harsh penalty—often death—of a first-degree conviction.

Manslaughter is also a form of murder which is not accompanied by malice or premeditation, but a sudden eruption of passion during the course of an argument, resulting in the killing of a person. The unintentional killing of a person during the commission of a minor crime, during a negligent auto accident, or through other forms of negligence may also be considered manslaughter.

Table 1.2 Estimated Number of Crimes Cleared by Arrest in United States, 2015[1]

TOTAL	10,797,088
PART I INDEX CRIMES	
Murder and nonnegligent manslaughter	11,092
Rape[2]	22,863
Robbery	95,572
Aggravated assault	376,154
(Violent crime[3]	505,681)
Burglary	216,010
Larceny-theft	1,160,390
Motor vehicle theft	77,979
Arson	8,834
(Property crime[3]	1,463,213)
PART II INDEX CRIMES	
Other assaults	1,081,019
Forgery and counterfeiting	55,333
Fraud	133,138
Embezzlement	15,909
Stolen property; buying, receiving, possessing	88,576
Vandalism	191,015
Weapons; carrying, possessing, etc.	145,358
Prostitution and commercialized vice	41,877
Sex offenses (except rape and prostitution)	51,388
Drug abuse violations	1,488,707
Gambling	4,825
Offenses against the family and children	94,837
Driving under the influence	1,089,171
Liquor laws	266,250
Drunkenness	405,880
Disorderly conduct	386,078
Vagrancy	25,151
All other offenses	3,218,880
Suspicion	1,389
Curfew and loitering law violations	44,802

Source: https://ucr.fbi.gov/crime-in-the-u.s/2015/crime-in-the-u.s.-2015/tables/table-29.

[1] Does not include suspicion.

[2] The rape figure in this table is an aggregate total of the data submitted based on both the legacy and revised Uniform Crime Reporting definitions.

[3] Violent crimes are offenses of murder and nonnegligent manslaughter, rape, robbery, and aggravated assault. Property crimes are offenses of burglary, larceny-theft, motor vehicle theft, and arson.

Beginning in 2013, rape is defined for Summary UCR purposes as, "Penetration, no matter how slight, of the vagina or anus with any body part or object, or oral penetration by a sex organ of another person, without the consent of the victim." The new definition updated the 80-year-old historical definition of rape which was "carnal knowledge of a female forcibly and against her will." Effectively, the revised definition expands rape to include both male and female victims and offenders, and reflects the various forms of sexual penetration understood to be rape, especially nonconsenting acts of sodomy, and sexual assaults with objects. Source: https://ucr.fbi.gov/crime-in-the-u.s/2013/crime-in-the-u.s.-2013/rape-addendum/rape_addendum_final.

Just the Facts ...

A 74-year-old man suffered a seizure which caused him to lose control of the car he was driving in Brooklyn, New York. He veered onto a sidewalk, killing a pregnant woman and her unborn child. He was charged with two counts of manslaughter.

So, we can see that even a specific crime, in this case murder, has various degrees of seriousness. Similar differences are found regarding virtually all crimes.

Some crimes may cross the felony-misdemeanor line as their contexts or consequences become more or less serious. **Aggravated assault** is often defined as assault with a weapon with intent to do great bodily harm. **Simple assault**, on the other hand, is a misdemeanor covering common fistfights.

Sometimes the distinction between felony and misdemeanor involving the same criminal conduct is determined by consequences, such as the loss suffered by the victim. **Grand larceny** is a felony because of the amount of money or property stolen; **petty (petit) larceny**—stealing smaller amounts—is usually a misdemeanor.

In some instances, the degree of the crime is determined by the intent of the perpetrator, which, unless the person confesses, can only be inferred from his or her behavior. Thus, whether a homicide is murder, killing by reckless conduct, negligent homicide, or some lesser degree of manslaughter, depends on proof of the mental state of the actor—that is, the extent to which the criminal consequences were intended and willful, or careless and negligent.

Elements of a Crime

Modern law contains six basic elements, or principles, in addition to common law classifications and felony-misdemeanor distinctions.[88] First, ***nullum crimen, nulla poena, sine lege***, as has been previously stated, means that there can be no crime or punishment unless a specific law prohibits a behavior and provides a punishment for it. Also, the U.S. Constitution prohibits ***ex post facto*** (after the fact) laws, or laws which define crimes retroactively. In order to be a crime, an act must be illegal at the time it is committed. The principle of ***actus reus***, or wrongful act, must also be present. That is, crime requires more than evil thoughts, it requires an act, a specific act of commission or omission by a person.

Mens rea must exist, or a guilty mind stemming from a criminal intent of the act. An act cannot generally be considered to be criminal unless the accused intended to commit the prohibited act. A person who was insane, therefore, at the time of the act cannot form the intent necessary for criminal responsibility.

Actus reus and ***mens rea*** must both be present—the act and the intent must be fused together before a person may be punished by society. A person cannot be punished for merely entertaining an evil intention, or for the commission of an unavoidable act.

Harm must also be caused by an act. Person, property, or reputation must be harmed before an act can be considered a crime. Or the interests of society in order, safety, peace, morality, or health must be harmed.

Finally, **causation** must be established. That is, the harm must be caused by an act. For instance, a death must be caused by the actions of an accused person before that person can be found guilty of murder. When these principles exist, or these elements are demonstrated, then a crime has been committed.

Measuring Crime

The crime rate in the United States is generally accepted to be among the highest, if not *the* highest, of all industrial, urbanized societies in the world. The high rate applies not only to such traditional crimes as homicide, robbery, burglary, and common forms of theft, but also to corporate crimes and crimes by prominent and trusted government officials. This said, however, accurate data to substantiate or dispute this view do not exist. Most countries do not make the same serious attempt to accurately measure crime as the United States does. And many other countries are not open to a free press which will report whatever data exist, good and bad, to the public. Likewise, no two countries define crime the same way, so comparisons between countries' crime rates are difficult.

Despite our sophisticated census measurements and our ability to produce impressive economic and marketing data, the unfortunate fact is that no reliable method of counting offenses or offenders exists. The criminal justice system is operating in a sea of law violations whose tides and depths are not fully known. Among other things, this means that no precise base exists from which to measure the effectiveness of different crime control techniques, especially when dealing with unreported crimes for which no currently available data are reliable. We can only speculate about the incidence of vice offenses like gambling or prostitution, and very little information is available about offenses known only to their perpetrators. There is no way of determining, for example, how many Americans illegally carry concealed weapons, though the number surely is far greater than indicated by the number of persons arrested for this crime, nor can we determine how many people possess and use illegal drugs.

The two primary programs to measure crime in the United States are the **Uniform Crime Reports** (**UCRs**)[89] and the **National Crime Victimization Survey** (**NCVS**).[90] Each is sponsored by the U.S. government, and each has strengths and weaknesses.

Uniform Crime Reports

In 1927, the International Association of Chiefs of Police (IACP) began to develop a system to gather statistics on crimes known to the police. By 1929, the IACP had studied the state criminal codes and record-keeping practices in use. Seven offenses, divided between violent and property crimes, were chosen to serve as a crime index

Figure 1.1 2015 Crime Clock Statistics

A Violent Crime occurred every	**26.3 seconds**
One Murder every	33.5 minutes
One Rape every	4.2 minutes
One Robbery every	1.6 minutes
One Aggravated Assault every	41.3 seconds
A Property Crime every	**3.9 seconds**
One Burglary every	20.0 seconds
One Larceny-theft every	5.5 seconds
One Motor Vehicle Theft every	44.6 seconds

FBI Uniform Crime Reports 2015. Source: https://ucr.fbi.gov/crime-in-the-u.s/2015/crime-in-the-u.s.-2015/resource-pages/crime-clock.

for measuring the fluctuations in the amount and rate of crime, and an eighth, arson, was added in 1979. See **Figure 1.1.**

These **index crimes** are referred to as **Part I offenses** by the UCR, but a number of additional crimes which the police routinely respond to have been added. These are called **Part II offenses.** See **Table 1.3** for a list of both Part I and Part II offenses. As seen in **Table 1.3**, offenses in Uniform Crime Reporting are divided into two groupings, Part I and Part II.[91] Information on the volume of Part I offenses known to law enforcement, those cleared by arrest or exceptional means, and the number of persons arrested is reported monthly. Only arrest data are reported for Part II offenses. The eight Part I offenses are comprised of four violent crimes and four property crimes.

In 1930, Congress enacted legislation authorizing the Attorney General of the United States to gather crime statistics, and the Attorney General in turn designated the Federal Bureau of Investigation (FBI) to administer the program. Interestingly, none of the offenses measured is under FBI jurisdiction. Crime data are reported to the Federal Bureau of Investigation directly by police agencies or through state-level agencies which then report to the FBI. The FBI tabulates and publishes the data in a volume called *Crime in the United States* each year. This report is more commonly referred to as the *Uniform Crime Reports*, or UCRs.

Data on Part I crimes include ***crimes known to the police*** and crimes ***cleared by arrest or exceptional means*** (see **Table 1.3**). These data tell us more about what the police know and do than about criminal activity. That is, police learn of some crimes either through their own investigations or by the reports of victims or others. Then, after they know about those specific crimes, the police clear by arrest a certain percent of them. If reported crimes are later discovered through investigation to be unfounded, or false, they are not included in the reports.

Crimes ***cleared by arrest*** are counted as those for which one or more persons are arrested for the offense and then turned over to the prosecutor for further action. Crimes cleared by exceptional means include those cleared by the death of the offender through suicide, or justifiable killing by police, victims, or others. Additional exceptional means are defined as the victim's refusal to cooperate in the prosecution of the

Table 1.3 Percent of Offenses Cleared by Arrest or Exceptional Means, 2015

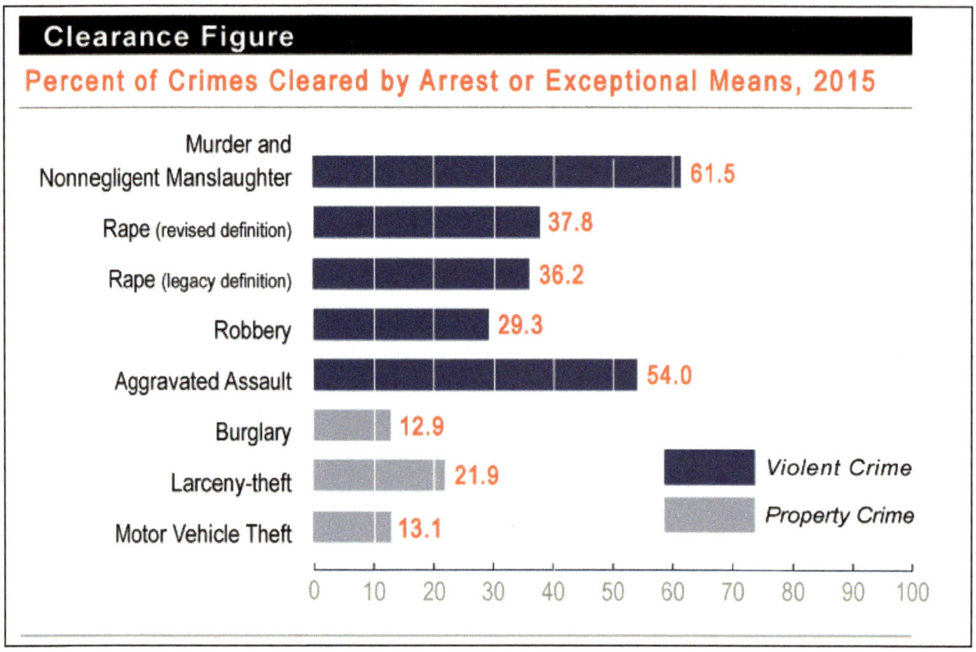

This figure shows the percentages of violent and property crimes cleared by arrest or exceptional means in 2015. Among violent crimes, the individual offenses and their respective clearance percentages are murder and nonnegligent manslaughter, 61.5 percent; rape (revised definition), 37.8 percent; rape (legacy definition) 36.2 percent; robbery, 29.3 percent; and aggravated assault, 54.0 percent. Of property crimes, the individual offenses and their respective clearance percentages are burglary, 12.9 percent; larceny-theft, 21.9 percent; and motor vehicle theft, 13.1 percent. Crime in the United States (2015) FBI: UCR. Accessed May 9, 2017: https://ucr.fbi.gov/crime-in-the-u.s/2015/crime-in-the-u.s.-2015/offenses-known-to-law-enforcement/clearances/national-data.

offender, or cases in which the charges are dropped because the offender is being prosecuted for other charges, or crimes for which the person arrested and prosecuted were acquitted by a jury but the police are still satisfied they arrested the guilty person. The UCR also includes details about the person arrested, including age, race, and gender.

The Crime Rate

Beyond offenses known to the police and cleared by arrest or exceptional means, reports from police departments to the FBI and compiled in the UCR are used to compute the **crime rate**, the statistic which is used to demonstrate overall fluctuations in the incidence of crime. The UCR crime rate for all crimes, or for any specific crime, is computed by dividing the number of crimes reported to the police by the total population and then multiplying by 100,000.

For instance, in 2015 the total number of all Part I index crimes known to the over 15,000 law enforcement agencies participating in the UCR program was 1,197,704 (violent crimes) and 7,993,631 (property crimes, not including arson). The population covered by the reporting agencies was estimated to be 321,418,820.[92] So the total violent crime rate was 372.6 per 100,000 in 2015.[93]

$$\frac{1{,}197{,}704}{321{,}418{,}820} \times 100{,}000 = 372.6 \text{ per } 100{,}000$$

The property crime rate for 2015 was estimated to be 2,487 per 100,000 population.

Likewise, the same agencies reported 1,579,527 burglaries. So, the rate for burglary was 491.4 per 100,000,[94] computed as follows.

$$\frac{1{,}579{,}527}{321{,}418{,}820} \times 100{,}000 = 491.4 \text{ per } 100{,}000$$

The crime rate per 100,000 has become a popular statistic to show crime trends over time. The crime rate tells more than just the total number of crimes known to the police. The crime rate is also used to show differences between neighborhoods, cities, states, and regions of the country. In addition to providing details about crimes known to the police in the various regions of the country, the UCRs also provide analyses of crimes by month, urban and rural comparisons, types of weapons used if any, type and value of property stolen and recovered, crime on college and university campuses, and more. Data are also collected about law enforcement personnel, including the number of officers killed in the line of duty.

Only arrest data are compiled for Part II offenses, but as with Part I offenders, details are tabulated by age, race, gender, and suburban or rural setting. And the rates for states and cities are included.

Weaknesses of the Uniform Crime Reports

The UCR is a major source of U.S. crime statistics, which are used widely by scholars, policy makers, and criminal justice administrators. The press and politicians often quote them as gospel truth. The scope of crime data gathering in the United States is indeed impressive, but these data do not tell the whole story about the extent of crime. The UCR exhibits several weaknesses.[95]

First, UCR data tell more about police activity than criminal activity since they measure the amount of crime police know about and the number of arrests police make. Local police are not always involved in crime investigations. For instance, police may not know about arsons if the fire department does not refer such cases to the police. Also, local police agencies do not typically investigate federal offenses, Securities and Exchange Commission violations, or offenses handled by the Federal Trade Commission. It is also important to note that the FBI index does not include such crimes as extortion, kidnapping, racketeering, terrorism, or many white-collar crimes. Of course, even crimes for which local police have responsibility are not always known to the police since the crimes were not reported to the police or police did not uncover the crimes through investigatory techniques or otherwise.

Figure 1.2 Part I Index Crimes Cleared by Arrest in 2015

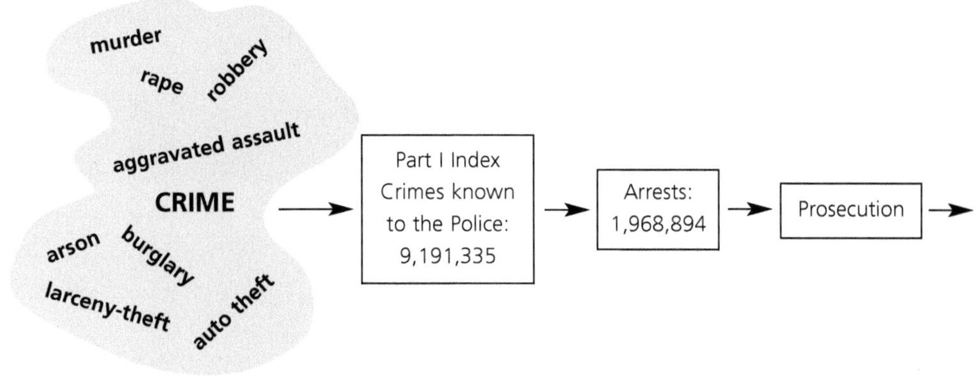

Victims do not always report crimes, even Part I crimes, to the police. Studies have indicated that forcible rape, for example, is one of the most underreported of serious felonies. As we will see, other crimes are grossly underreported as well.

In addition, the FBI index employs the Hierarchy Rule by counting only the most serious crime in cases involving multiple offenses. Thus, for example, if an offender steals an automobile to make an escape after robbing a convenience store and then kills a person while escaping, the robbery and auto theft are not reported and only the homicide is counted in the index.[96]

Finally, police are not required to report to any central source the numbers and types of crimes that come to their attention. Citizens, as victims of crime, are likewise not required to report their own victimization. Even so, the FBI regularly receives, on a voluntary basis, crime data from about 18,000 or so law enforcement departments.[97] While this is not exhaustive of all law enforcement agencies, it does add to our overall understanding of the crime problem in America.

National Crime Victimization Survey

Despite incomplete coverage, the FBI reports probably are still the best available source of crime data covering the nation as a whole. Crimes known to the police, of course, provide a very important category of baseline data. But what about the crimes not reported? Everyone in the field of criminal justice, including the police, knows a large but murky number of unreported crimes exist. Even when Part I index crimes from 2015 and the percentage cleared by arrest or exceptional means as previously depicted in **Table 1.3** are considered, law enforcement is doing good if 20 percent of crimes known to police are solved; it becomes apparent that a significant amount of crimes go unreported and unsolved. See **Figure 1.2**, which results in about a 21.4% arrest rate for index crimes in 2015.[98] It has been called the **"dark figure of crime"**: offenses known only to perpetrators and victims, and others perhaps, but not the police, are estimated to constitute over 50 percent of crime.[99]

In 1973, in an attempt to learn more about crimes, unreported crimes, and crime victims, the **National Crime Victimization Survey** (NCVS) was established by Congress.[100] During 2015, approximately 95,760 households and 163,880 individuals (older than 12 years old) were interviewed for the NCVS. Subjects were interviewed about their victimization regarding nonfatal violent crimes (rape, robbery, and aggravated and simple assault) and property crimes (burglary, motor vehicle theft, and theft).[101] Truman and Morgan refer to the above referenced "dark figure of crime" in their NCVS analysis of victimization data.[102] They also note that, in 2015, 47 percent of violent victimizations and 55 percent of serious violent victimizations (rape or sexual assault, robbery, and aggravated assault) were reported to police. However, they found that property victimizations reported to police declined from 37 to 35 percent. The data are collected annually and published by the Bureau of Justice Statistics (BJS) in reports entitled *Criminal Victimization*.[103]

The NCVS asks about crimes suffered by individuals and households in the previous six months, whether or not they were reported to the police. It specifically asks about all the index crimes, except murder and arson, collecting data about the victims (age, race, gender, marital status, income, and educational level), the offenders (age, race, gender, victim-offender relationship), and the crimes (time, place, use of weapons, injury, loss). Also, the NCVS asks for reasons why victims did not report their victimization to the police, their experiences with criminal justice agencies, possible substance abuse by the offenders, and the nature of any defensive measures taken by the victims.

Victims of crimes of violence who report the crime to the police often say they wish to stop or prevent this incident (such as robbery or assault) and to prevent future acts of violence by the perpetrator against the victim. Respondents frequently indicate the rationale for reporting both violent and property crimes is merely the fact that the act constituted a crime. Victims of property crimes who report the crime to the police often state that they did so to simply to get their stolen property back and a few specify they alert police to facilitate insurance loss claims.[104]

Why Victims Do Not Report Crimes to the Police

A large number of crime victims choose not to involve the police. This is particularly true for property crimes. A substantial portion of persons reveal they do not report crimes because the offender failed to successfully complete the crime or that the object taken was recovered. Many people who have things stolen prefer merely to take the loss rather than participate in a time-consuming police process. This changes if the lost property is valuable and they have theft insurance covering stolen items and their insurance companies require a police report to verify any loss prior to paying a claim. But people also choose not to report their victimization for a variety of other reasons. Sometimes victims consider the events to be private in nature, something they can handle privately without involving criminal justice agencies. Other times victims do not believe the police will be successful in finding the stolen property or the thieves; victims may feel the police do not want to be bothered or are biased. This lack of confidence in police ability is particularly acute in poor neighborhoods and in areas where police-community relations are strained. Still other victims do not wish to involve the police because they fear reprisals from the criminals.[105] Finally, some victims do not wish to have the police investigating anything or anybody close to them for fear that they themselves may come under investigation.[106]

The frequency of unreported crimes against persons, even violent crimes, is explained by respondents to the NCVS in a variety of ways. Perhaps the most commonly underreported crime of violence is rape, for according to the latest victimization study approximately 59 percent of rape victims do not report what happened to the police.[107] Date rape and rape within families are generally known to be underreported, and those victims do not report in part because of the private, personal nature of the crime. But many rape victims also remain silent for fear of retaliation by the known rapist, or where the rapist is a stranger, the fear or shame associated with a police investigation or possible trial intimidates the victim.[108]

The same level of underreporting is true for simple assault, with about 59 percent of victims choosing not to inform police.[109] Assault victims often consider it a private matter, while victims of robbery frequently report that they feel the police will not effectively deal with the problem.[110] This lack of confidence in criminal justice agencies to deal effectively with crime is a matter of concern to policy makers and practitioners alike. Also, considerable amounts of domestic assaults fail to be reported, and even when reported, victims lose confidence in the police if the victim's safety is not enhanced after the reported violence.

Self-Report Surveys

One attempt to measure the number of criminals is through **self-report surveys.** Just as victim surveys ask people if they have been victims of crime, self-report surveys ask respondents if they themselves have committed crimes. Generally, most of the crimes revealed are non-violent in nature—like marijuana use.[111]

The two most common self-report surveys are aimed at students (the National Youth Survey and the Monitoring the Future project), but such surveys can be administered to any population. Obviously, the truthfulness of responses to self-incriminating questions is always suspect, even with promises of confidentiality or with anonymous data-retrieval methods. Some may fear reprisal if they acknowledge wrongdoing and others may embellish the magnitude of their acts to appear worse than they really were. As such, a high percentage of respondents anonymously admit to committing undetected crimes, some of which are quite serious. Typically, when self-report surveys are administered to any population (even non-criminals) around 70 percent of those surveyed admit having committed a felony.[112] Even if, as some claim, people sometimes say on self-report surveys they have done things that they have not in fact done, the fact remains that a very sizable portion of the population has admittedly committed crimes that did not result in arrest and did not end up in official statistics such as the UCR.

Counting Criminals

Statistical measures of crime in our society, whether from police reports or victim studies, indicate the actual number of criminal offenders only in a very general way. The frequency of homicides may come closest to revealing the number of murderers, since, except for comparatively rare mass killings, murder is usually a single perpetrator-single victim crime. In contrast, one thief may be responsible for dozens of robberies, burglaries, or larcenies. A crime cleared by arrest in the FBI reports is just this, a crime for which an arrest was made, not the number of crimes committed by the criminal or the number of criminals arrested. One burglary arrest may clear a large number of crimes. Even in these FBI data a large discrepancy exists between crimes reported and crimes cleared. In fact, because so few property crimes are solved by arrest, the major message of these data is that most crimes are unsolved—that, on the basis of probability of arrest, crime does pay.

Statistics on crimes or criminals are normally based on measurement over a period of time, usually a year. It is no doubt useful to tabulate crimes in this way, but the number of criminals accumulates. Last year's murderers are joined by those who killed this year, and to these will be added successive future killers. The year 2015, as previously noted, produced 14,392 murders ("non-negligent" homicides). But even assuming all the perpetrators were caught and sent to prison, since few murderers are executed, proper nutrition and state-provided medical care make it possible for homicide offenders to live out full lifespans, the cumulative number of murderers is just that much greater.

Crimes other than murder and sentences shorter than life cause criminal populations to accumulate, both in prison and on the street, posing a perplexing question: Is a person who once committed a crime always a criminal? Despite some legislative attempts to expunge criminal records of former offenders who have completed their sentences and have remained law-abiding for a number of years, police intelligence units often keep track of known former criminals.[113] Roundup investigations are not uncommon, particularly when serious or heinous crimes have been committed. And even those few prisoners who receive pardons may be known as "ex-cons" for the rest of their lives.

No accurate census of the number of current and former criminals is currently available in our society. Various states and the federal government have extensive fingerprint banks, but these contain prints of suspects released without prosecution, including those arrested by mistake, and prints of others not caught up in the criminal justice system. Retrieval or expungement of fingerprints and other arrest records of those totally innocent or improperly accused is nearly impossible, even upon court order and with a willing police agency. Thus no one knows how many persons convicted of serious crimes—felonies—are alive in our society right now.

Of the three methods for gathering and disseminating crime data previously discussed (official data—the UCR, victimization surveys, and self-reports), there is no single best method for obtaining a true picture of crime. However, the three methods together make for a more accurate representation of crime within our society.

Cohort Measurement

Full computerization of criminal justice processing of persons at all stages in the system is increasingly viewed as the only satisfactory solution to meet the need for complete and accurate data. The tracking of specific persons across the entire criminal process is sometimes known as **cohort analysis.** ("Cohort" here means all persons arrested on a given day or during a given week.) This technique, pioneered by Marvin Wolfgang, begins with a sample of perhaps 10,000 persons arrested for felonies in a specific time period and follows their paths and branchings as they are processed deeper into the system or diverted out of it.[114] This technique requires data flow (i.e., data on individuals A, B, and C from one decision point to another, not just arrest or charging summaries) and can answer questions in ways not possible with only summarized tabulations. But most criminal justice systems currently lack the facilities required for cohort analysis.

In recent years a high priority has been given to the development of criminal justice reporting systems, but despite strong federal pressure and significant amounts of federal funds granted to the states, data reporting systems in many jurisdictions are still primitive. For example, researchers at Claremont McKenna College looked at the number of incidents of crime reported to police in a year nationally. They considered five Part I Index crimes (the four violent crime categories and burglary). The researchers found that of these incidents, 3,509,036 were reported to police. However, if 50 percent or more of crimes are not known to police, then estimates of the amount of these crimes could be at least 7,018,072 (although murder tends to be more likely known to police, though smaller in numbers, than these other categories of crime). While the discrepancies in crime data may vary from year-to-year, the reality is that generally the one who commits a crime is often not likely to come to the attention of authorities, has a slim chance of going to prison, and would seemingly be highly unlucky if he or she did. See **Figure 1.3.**[115]

Figure 1.3 Criminal Justice Funnel

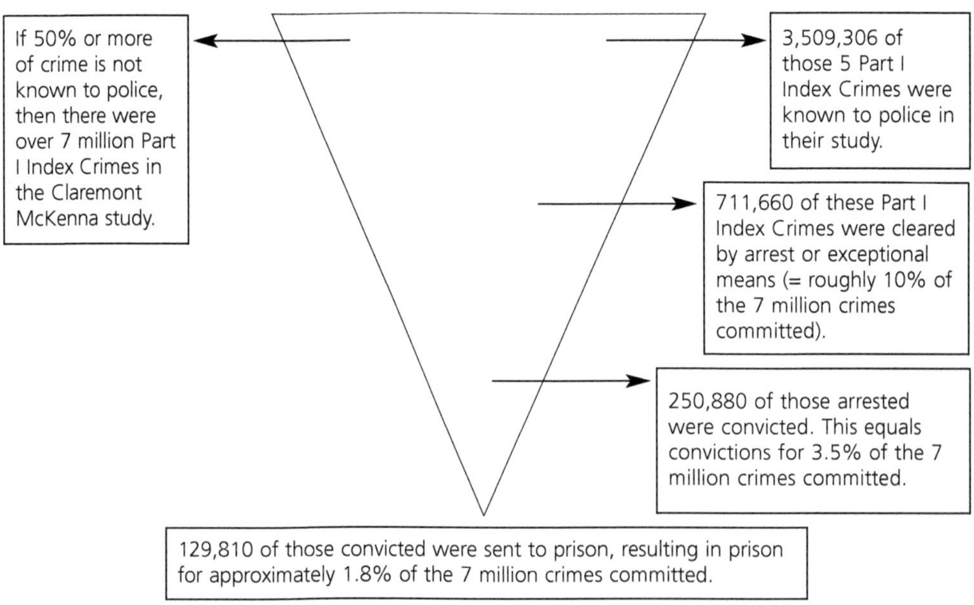

Implications for Criminal Justice

The Need for Accurate Crime Data

If crime control efforts are to be accurately evaluated, there is a need for good, easily retrievable data covering the entire spectrum of the criminal justice process, not just crimes reported to the police. Important questions are being asked today about various post-crime matters. For instance, what are the primary predictors of who is a good risk to be released from jail prior to the trial? What is the ratio of acquittals to convictions in trials? How many people on probation and parole are re-arrested? What is the effectiveness of prison sentences, fines, probation, or other sentences? Which prisoners are the least likely to re-offend upon release?

Adequate statistics are needed by all criminal justice agencies to support sensible budget forecasts and to accurately assess the current achievements or failures of these agencies. Furthermore, such statistics are essential for planning innovative projects and assessing experimental programs. Most criminal justice agencies keep some form of **summary data** on persons processed. Summary data are kept by a simple tabulation, known as **gatekeeping**, similar to the tabulation used by a prison when counting the number of prisoners who come in and go out. By tabulating the number of people handled routinely by a criminal justice agency, a more accurate picture of agency practice is established and future crime projections are garnered.

It is probable that accurate gatekeeping is found only in correctional agencies, where it is both a matter of legal accountability and a necessity for feeding and housing inmates. Reports of the arrest activities of police are required as a part of the booking procedure, but prearrest contact with citizens and suspects is not always a matter of record. Another gap in gatekeeping data may be found in prosecutors' offices and trial courts, which do not always maintain statistical reports.

Obstacles to Collection of Accurate Crime Data

Many obstacles to collecting even rudimentary crime statistics exist. Criminal justice is composed of relatively independent agencies, each with its own reporting forms, data needs, and traditional ways of doing things. Some agencies are municipal, some are county, and others are statewide. Criminal justice agencies rely on different budgets and many are indifferent to gathering information for anything other than immediate and local use.[116]

The entire criminal justice system is not only public; it is politically volatile as well. The result is that most criminal statistics are potentially embarrassing to past claims of agency effectiveness. As noted by the quote from Lord Kelvin that opened this chapter, numbers often influence policymakers. Consider, for example, Critical Thinking 1.3.

Critical Thinking 1.3 Manipulating Crime Statistics

Police departments in New York City and Philadelphia have been caught for fudging crime statistics. In New York, it was their own officers that reported that crime data was manipulated, particularly on Part I index crimes, and victims were encouraged by officers to downgrade their victimizations so that they would not be classified as Part I index crimes to demonstrate a declining crime rate. Likewise, in Philadelphia, sting operations, whereby undercover agents would pose as victims, were implemented to attack the misrepresentation of a downward trend for Part I index data.[117]

What benefits could be wrought by police departments for indicating a declining crime rate? Could demonstration of a downward crime rate ever potentially hurt police departments? What other measures might police departments put in place to combat statistical misrepresentations of crime rates?

Accurate crime data would show that most crimes are not even known by police and of those that are known most are *not* solved by arrest; prosecutors often accept guilty pleas to lesser offenses than are really committed; judges too often show disparity in their sentences; and few offenders are rehabilitated in correctional programs. Inevitably, some agencies, when offered elaborate computer devices that could provide full and accurate statistics, but which would also open their records to public accounting, show little enthusiasm for new reporting systems.

Increasing pressures for more accurate crime data along with the creation of large, secure, available data banks may indicate that a much clearer picture of our crime problem is developing. As with many technological revolutions, there is a danger that too much will be promised by, and too much expected from, electronic techniques. However elaborate, these devices will simply measure crime and evaluate programs; it is unlikely that they will do much to relieve the crime problem. Computers may be valuable aids in quickly identifying suspects, in suggesting ways to reduce delays in the courts, or, in their most sophisticated form, in providing data about associational patterns from which criminal conspiracies can be inferred. But it is unlikely that they will be able to identify specific causal factors in criminality, for our knowledge of the origins of criminal behavior is so fragmentary that we are unable to formulate many basic questions. Computers can respond only to precise questions; they cannot theorize or conceptualize on their own. Theoretical underpinnings for crime causation will be addressed in Chapter 2.

Also, the uncertainty of crime data makes it difficult for criminal justice agencies to sensibly anticipate trends and future needs. In this regard, criminal justice is unlike other bureaucratic endeavors. Educational systems, for instance, can anticipate with some accuracy the numbers of students to be enrolled from one year to the next. And private corporations go to great effort to control their supplies of raw materials, labor, transportation, and support. But criminal justice agencies operate in relative darkness in terms of available data.

Difficulties in gathering data also point to another set of questions regarding criminal justice. What do we expect the agencies of criminal justice to accomplish? If we have difficulty determining how much crime exists from one time to another, or from one jurisdiction to another, how then can we place realistic expectations on the agents of justice? See **Critical Thinking 1.4.**

Critical Thinking 1.4 A "Crime Wave" or Effective Law Enforcement?

Leaders of a local victims' rights organization met with the Chief of Police to discuss the problem of rape in the city. The victims' advocates expressed concern that only a fraction of rape victims reported the crimes to the police. Some scholars had estimated that as many as eight rapes occurred for every one reported to the police, and several reasons for this underreporting were identified. Rape victims, it was said, were reluctant to report the crime to police because the police department and prosecutors who were assigned to rape cases were men who did not treat rape victims with sympathy and understanding. Also, it was pointed out that rape victims were not informed about how to report the crime to police, and were often afraid of retaliation or of being publicly embarrassed by police actions or trial.

The police chief responded to the concerns expressed and began to work on the problem. He called for a meeting with the mayor and the state's attorney, the prosecutor. Together they devised a plan of action. First, the police chief selected three women detectives to work in the rape unit. They were trained in crisis intervention and taught to handle rape investigations with tact and skill. Also, the prosecutor assigned specially trained prosecutors to rape cases. And the victims' rights group provided trained counselors to give rape victims moral support through the entire process, including any possible court appearances.

Second, after the first step was accomplished, the Chief of Police began a public campaign to encourage rape victims to report the crimes to the police. A special "hot line" telephone number was established, and posters were printed and placed throughout the city to inform people that the new rape intervention program was in place. The telephone number was publicized on television and radio.

Almost immediately the number of rapes reported to the police increased, and by the end of the first year the number of reported rapes doubled. Soon, reports from victims of rape and sexual assault consumed the full time of several police officers and prosecutors, and the victims' rights advocates had to recruit and train additional counselors to assist them.

The next year, when year-end crime statistics were reported by the police department, a local television station's news department noticed the dramatic increase in reported rapes, calling the increase a "crime wave." The police chief's record was shown in graphs which demonstrated the relatively low number of rapes reported during his early years, and the dramatic increase during the past two years. Ignored was the correlation between more aggressive tactics to reach out to crime victims and the increase in reports to the police and hence, crime statistics.

A local politician who had announced his intention to run for Chief of Police in opposition to the incumbent began to make public accusations of poor leadership in the criminal justice agencies. He charged that the current police chief was "asleep at the switch" while the citizens of the city were "terrorized by crime in the streets." He cited the dramatic increase in rapes as evidence. The police chief was angered by the charges, and privately told a friend, "If we had done nothing about the rape issue, the statistics would not have changed a bit from one year to the next, and I would have been considered a successful police administrator, I guess."

1. Since official crime statistics show the number of crimes known to the police, and arrests, is it possible for a "high crime" location to actually be one with good, effective law enforcement?
2. Was the police chief correct when he said he would have been better off by doing nothing about the rape problem in his city and instead allowing the existing problem to continue at previous levels of occurrence?
3. What steps would you take to help the public understand that crime statistics reflect police activity as much as they do criminal activity?

The Costs of Crime and Security in America

Crime in America is very costly. Accurate measures of the economic costs are difficult to obtain, but by all accounts the total dollar impact of the incidence of crime places it at the top of all social problems facing American society.

"[Preventing one theft] is the equivalent of freeing up: 30 minutes of a judge's time, 3 hours of a prosecutor's time, 3 hours of a public defender's time, 5 hours of staff time (for court, prosecution, and public defense), and $100 of capital, supplies, and equipment," said Hunt. "Crime prevention or reduction may allow judges, attorneys, their staff and others to transfer their time to other cases to the benefit of taxpayers and society as a whole." Avery Appelman added that the findings are important because they can allow city officials to really understand the true cost of certain crime prevention programs and better allocate appropriate funds.[118]

Some economic costs of crime are relatively easy to compute. "Shrinkage" refers to the portion of inventory that gets stolen or lost. For instance, businesses calculate losses from employee theft ($18 billion in 2014) and shoplifting ($15.7 billion in 2015), as well as the costs of defensive measures such as security personnel. Those costs are generally added to the total costs of goods to be sold and passed along to the consumer. For example, in 2014 it is estimated that each American household had an annual amount of $403.00 from shrinkage passed along to it.[119]

The cost of private security measures such as alarm systems, security guards, armored vehicles, and locks has been said to be as much as $64 billion a year.[120] Additionally, the costs associated with supporting federal, state, and local criminal justice can be computed, but not easily. In any jurisdiction, criminal justice may be one of the largest and most pervasive public expenditures. It has been estimated that over $200 billion a year is spent on the American criminal justice system. Police protection in the U.S. has been reported to cost approximately $100 billion annually, and an additional $69 billion is spent on prisons. Court costs, including prosecution and public defenders' agencies, range to almost $47 billion a year.[121]

Looking at data from every state, the Rand Corporation assessed the average cost to taxpayers nationally to process seven major crimes. The researchers found that the cost to the judicial system for each reported homicide is between $22,000 and $44,000, with the cost of each rape or sexual assault between $2,000 to $5,000, for every robbery it was between $600 and $1,300, for aggravated assaults it was between $800 and $2,100, with each larceny it was between $300 and $600, for burglaries it was between $200 and $600 each, and the costs to the judicial system for each motor vehicle theft was between $200 and $400.[122] **Of course, these figures can be multiplied by the crimes known to police previously addressed in the Uniform Crime Reports for a more expansive view of the costs of crime.**

Most of the money spent on the criminal justice system in America is spent at the local level, with the exception of state prisons.[123] According to the Vera Institute in their study of state correctional institutions, the average annual cost per inmate was $31,286, ranging from an annual cost per inmate in Kentucky of $14,603 to $60,076 in New York.[124] Thus, based on the average annual cost per inmate of $31,286 in the study, the average daily cost of incarcerating an inmate would be $85.71. Overall costs for your state's correctional system or the annual cost per inmate for your state may be accessed at http://archive.vera.org/sites/default/files/resources/downloads/price-of-prisons-updated-version-021914.pdf. The Vera Institute concluded that the total cost to taxpayers of prisons in forty states was $39 billion.[125] Since only forty states participated in the analysis, when it is considered that the 2015 fiscal year budget request for federal prisons and detention is in excess of $8 billion dollars,[126] the money allotted for prisons in this country is well beyond $40 billion dollars for a state prison growth industry that has witnessed an increase in the number of those incarcerated in the past four decades of over 700 percent.[127]

Furthermore, according to the Centers for Disease Control and Prevention, "[t]he annual cost of alcohol-related crashes totals more than $44 billion" in the United States.[128] Estimates for the typical cost for the perpetrator of a drunk driving conviction, without hitting anything or hurting anyone, range from $10,000 to $20,000.[129]

White-collar crime is considered by some to be more costly than street crime in America.[130] Losses from white-collar crime have been estimated at up to $1.7 trillion a year,[131] with fraud associated with defective products ($700 billion annually), healthcare ($80 billion annually), insurance ($80 billion annually), computers ($67 billion annually), commodities and securities ($40 billion annually), telemarketing ($40 billion annually), automobile repair ($22 billion annually), and checks ($10 billion annually).[132] According to the Department of Justice, identity theft affected 17.6 million persons and cost $15.4 billion in 2014.[133] Of course, while the media is loaded with discussions of whether the crime rate is up or down, those analyses are typically limited to an assessment of the Part I index crimes contained in the Uniform Crime Reports. None of the white-collar crimes mentioned above would be included in such an examination.

Estimates of the cost of crime range from 2% to 6% of the gross domestic product, and it has been estimated that the total aggregate burden of crime on society in America is over $1 trillion annually.[134] This includes over $600 billion in losses related to property crime, approximately $575 billion connected to fatalities and injuries linked to crime, and in excess of $90 billion due to victim crime prevention efforts and lost time on the job as a result of crime have been translated into lost opportunity costs. Violent crime has been identified as the culprit for 14% of medical expenditures for injury-related treatment of victims and up to 20% of mental healthcare spending. Wages lost from violent crime are said to equal one percent of all earnings in America, and the quality of life of families victimized by personal crimes, as measured by lifestyle modifications and pain and suffering, is projected to be decreased by two percent.[135]

How can the costs of presidential travel and protection be accurately projected? For example, it is estimated that New York City has expended $1 million a day in costs to provide security for Donald Trump and his family when in New York; this is in addition to expenditures by the federal government for Secret Service protection.[136] Expenditure on Barack Obama's travel and protection while president averaged $12.7 million a year; estimates are that in the first 30 days of his presidency, over $10 million was spent for Donald Trump to make three weekend trips to his Mar-a-Lago Club in Palm Beach, Florida. This is not to mention trips by his sons, Don Jr. and Eric, with Secret Service protection, to the United Arab Emirates for the grand opening of the Trump brand's "Beverly Hills of Dubai" golf course and a business trip for Eric to Uruguay.[137]

Also, if President Trump is to make good on his promise to build that wall on our southern border to keep out illegal immigrants, regardless of who pays for it, the structure will likely cost at least $25 billion.[138] Furthermore, if President Trump's deportation plan comes to fruition, estimated costs are anywhere from $100 to $300 billion.[139]

Incidents leading to protests are often driven by crises, are unpredictable, and can be costly. For example, unanticipated costs were incurred by the City of Baltimore after Black Lives Matter protests of the death of Freddie Gray while in police custody led to an estimated $20 million in expenditures for law enforcement and to clean up the city.[140] Similarly, unplanned policing costs in excess of $22 million were seen in North Dakota regarding Dakota Access pipeline protests, with an additional expense of nearly $9 million required for the National Guard there.[141]

Image by Oleg Albinsky at istockphoto.com

Of course, the total costs of juvenile delinquency programs and institutions, drug and alcohol rehabilitation programs, and a host of other crime-related efforts defy accurate computation. Not all economic costs are easily computed. Much of the cost associated with child abuse and domestic violence may not be evident until years later when children who have been physically or sexually abused themselves become abusive with their own children, thereby perpetuating a cycle of violence. Other costs are intangible, like the lost quality of life resulting from an injury or death of a family member due to crime.

Other costs are also illusive. For instance, how can we compute the loss of contributions to taxes, Social Security, and the gross national product resulting from time prisoners spend incarcerated? Each free citizen must pay additional taxes to compensate for those losses. Also, with the great difference between crimes reported and crimes actually committed, the problem of computing economic impact is even further complicated. But even if accurate economic cost measures were devised, the full story of the costs of crime would not be told. How can you compute the psychological, social, and relational costs which result from victimization? How can the total costs of corporate crimes such as price fixing and false advertising be accurately counted? Crime is very expensive, and non-economic costs are equally difficult to measure, yet they exist as well, and are best understood as the costs of the fear of crime.

Image by sturti at istockphoto.com.

The Fear of Crime

Many Americans express fear of crime when they are asked about it. In a 2016 Gallup Poll, it was discovered that the majority of Americans surveyed worry a great deal about crime and violence, representing a 15-year high for this category. Those 55 years and older, with a high school degree or less, and incomes less than $30,000 were most apt to express this fear.[142] A separate 2016 Gallup Poll survey asked if respondents "Is there any area near where you live—that is, within a mile—where you would be afraid to walk alone at night." Thirty-five percent of those responding answered in the affirmative.[143]

While 35% percent of Americans polled worried about being a victim of terrorism in 2016 more so than being mugged (30%), the crimes Americans most feared were being a victim of identity theft (70%) or credit card hacking (69%); 64% feared having their email passwords or electronic records hacked into. Forty-three percent of respondents feared having their unoccupied home burglarized, and the same percentage feared having their vehicle stolen or broken into.[144] People hear of others' victimization and this feeds their own fear. During political campaigns the fear of crime is emphasized to give voters an added impetus to vote for or against candidates for public office.

Also, the fear of crime crosses racial and ethnic lines. The race-card perception that white citizens are afraid primarily of black citizens is not altogether accurate. Such perceptions have been labeled racist. But similar fears are expressed by African Americans who fear victimization by fellow African Americans. In fact, approximately two-thirds of whites and African Americans have been found to exhibit the same fear reaction when shown a photograph of a black face.[145] In actuality, persons are much more likely to be victimized by someone of their own race. For example, approximately 90 percent of homicides in the U.S. are said to be **intra-racial** (with victim and perpetrator of the same race), not **inter-racial** (with the victim and murderer not of the same race). Furthermore, blacks have been found to be six times more likely than whites to be a victim of homicide.[146]

The Study of Criminal Justice

The many parts of our criminal justice network pose tough problems which make it difficult to understand the network, to be able to ask sensible questions about it, and to suggest feasible changes or reforms for better crime control. The study of only a single agency such as the police or a single decision point like sentencing provides at best only fragmentary information about criminal justice; at worst, it may distort the overall aims and objectives of crime control. At the same time, it is obvious that a broad, total system overview cannot be completed quickly or easily. After all, there are 51 separate jurisdictions in the country (the states and the federal system), and although they are more alike than different, there are variations in practices and policies from place to place. Since all these variations cannot be discussed in detail, we concentrate on the common decision points, common agencies, and common ways of controlling crime while remaining fully aware that local practices may vary.

Such a generalized approach is not without shortcomings, however. We are unable to provide, in a single volume, a detailed analysis of every part and every issue relevant to criminal justice; thus, we will focus on the mainstream, normal, daily (almost mundane) decision stages in the process of solving crimes and dealing with suspects, defendants, and convicted offenders. We recognize that other approaches exist and that each has merit. Where possible, we include the valuable contributions of those approaches and supply the reader with any insights to be learned from them.

Summary

As we conclude this chapter, it should be considered that irrational fears, such as the fear of identity theft, may drive criminal justice policy. For example, a statute was enacted in Michigan to go after identity thieves. The problem, of course, is that such measures may be used to overreach and go after others. Leon Walker logged onto his wife's e-mail account, using her password, via a laptop computer he shared with her in their home. He discovered that she was having an extra-marital affair, and she filed for divorce. However, Leon was charged with a felony for his actions by a statute aimed at thwarting identity theft, and he faces the possibility of five years in prison. The case will likely hinge on whether his wife had a reasonable expectation of privacy for any material she had on the laptop.[147] As we will see with further exploration, what is considered private can vary from time to time and place to place.

If you were a juror in this case, how would you decide this matter? Why?

Chapter 2

The Ideological Framework of Crime Control and Explanations for Crime

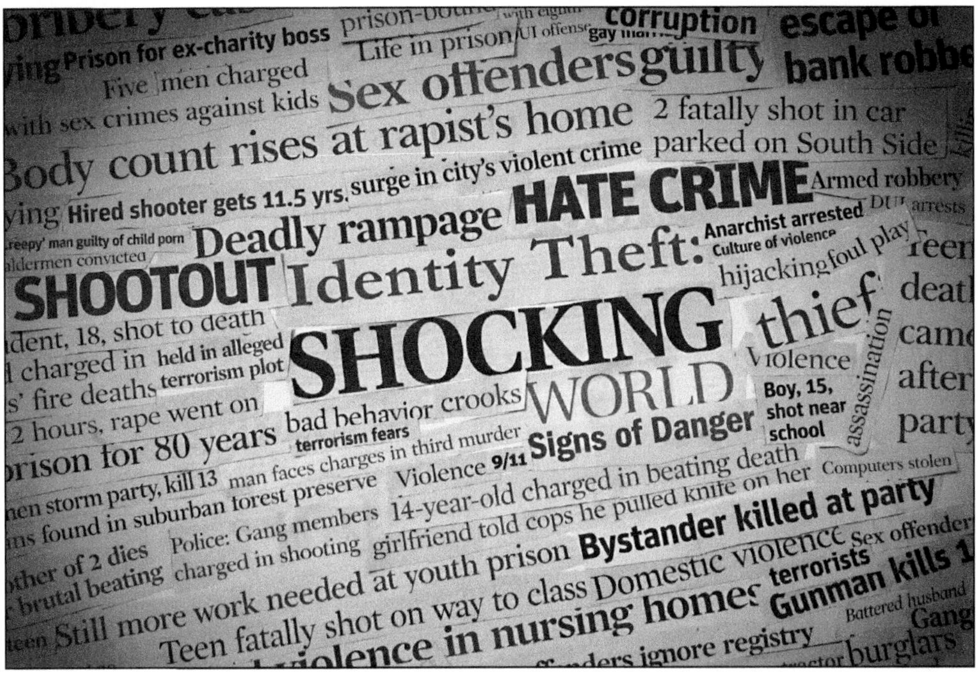

Image by Allkindza at istockphoto.com.

> *"Many writers claim that nearly all crime is caused by economic conditions, or in other words that poverty is practically the whole cause of crime. Endless statistics have been gathered on this subject which seem to show conclusively that property crimes are largely the result of the unequal distribution of wealth. But crime of any class cannot be safely ascribed to a single cause. Life is too complex, heredity is too variant and imperfect, too many separate things contribute to human behavior, to make it possible to trace all actions to a single cause."*[1]
>
> —Clarence Darrow

Seeking Justice

On the day Donald Trump was inaugurated as the 45th president of the United States, seventeen stories involving the criminal justice system from one newspaper reported the following. (1) David Broxterman, a professor at Polk State College, was found guilty for fraudulently maintaining that he had earned a Ph.D. in organizational management to procure a job at the school. He was unable to produce a copy of his dissertation. A registrar from the school where he allegedly obtained the Ph.D. testified that the transcript of his academic achievements and the diploma were not like ones issued by the school; in fact, the word "board" was misspelled on the made-up diploma. Broxterman faced 30 years in prison.[2] Broxterman's actual sentence is listed below.[3] (2) A newly elected state attorney praised the local mental health court for linking persons with mental illnesses who encounter the criminal justice system to treatment, which will hopefully prevent them from recycling through the system. He also indicated that the death penalty as carried out in Florida will be changing based on the U.S. Supreme Court having ruled Florida's practices unconstitutional. Namely, judges should not make factual decisions that should be left to a jury. Further, the Florida Supreme Court ruled that the death penalty decisions should be unanimous on the part of jurors and not via a simple majority vote as had been done in the past.

(3) The local sheriff's office had to close a thoroughfare after a semi-truck struck and killed a pedestrian walking home at night from a bar. (4) A local police department worked for tips at a Bob Evans restaurant to benefit the Special Olympics. (5) A former police chief was appointed as a city manager. (6) Four officers were tapped for officer of the year recognition, and a police chief was sworn in as president of a county police association. (7) A question is asked of the newspaper readership if social media is to blame for terror attacks. (8) The suspect in the slaying of Orlando Police Lt. Debra Clayton cusses the judge in court at his initial appearance and claims he will act as his own legal counsel.

(9) Thomas Daughtery was 17 years old when he and two friends spent an evening attacking homeless men in Ft. Lauderdale, Florida, with a golf club, baseball bat, and a rake. Daughtery was sentenced to life, but his sentence was reduced to 40 years in 2012 due to his juvenile status when Mr. Norris Gaynor was attacked. However, Daughtery will now get a new trial because the judge erred in rendering the jury instructions.

(10) In Riviera Beach, Florida, a woman was taken for a mental health evaluation and will likely be charged with animal cruelty for throwing a dog from a bridge because she reportedly believed dogs could fly. (11) The Florida Highway patrol investigated the death of a construction worker struck by a cement truck. (12) A teenager killed by police in Salinas, California, had a knife.

(13) A defendant was sentenced to 35 years in prison for his part in breaking and entering into an off-campus apartment of a Florida Atlantic University student and killing him in 2015. (14) A suspect in a cold case was arrested in Jamaica as a result of DNA evidence that linked him to the kidnapping, armed robbery, sexual battery, and murder of a Miami Beach female by the name of Mercedes Perez in 1990.

(15) Risk factors for approximately 60% of Louisiana police recruits post-Katrina include possible drug use, unpaid child support, and domestic abuse. (16) According to police, four persons were killed in an SUV crash in Springfield, Massachusetts,

with one survivor in critical condition. (17) Lawyers for the families of terror victims blame both Twitter and Facebook for allowing terrorists to recruit followers, intimidate enemies, and raise money.

All these stories were reported on one day, January 19, 2017, by one newspaper.[4] **What did your hometown newspaper report that day?**

About This Chapter

The local newspapers in virtually every community, as well as local television news programs and social media, daily describe a variety of crimes. Burglaries, rape, robberies, and murder, as well as white-collar crimes, drug busts, drunk driving—every kind of crime is brought to our attention every day. Many of us speculate about why people commit crimes. It seems everyone has an opinion.

Specifically, two types of questions are raised: What causes people to commit crimes? What can be done about crime? Indeed, these are two questions central to the subject of criminal justice. Why do people commit crimes? Can you conceive of a set of circumstances which would prompt you to enter a store with a gun, order the clerk to hand over the cash, and threaten everyone there with death? According to the FBI, there were 4,939 bank robberies in 2015, with an average "take" of $3,884, and the average take in convenience store robberies was reported by the FBI to be $623,[5] with many stores using surveillance cameras and limiting the amount of cash in the register as prevention measures.[6] What motivates a person to commit such relatively unprofitable crimes, knowing the risks to life, limb, and liberty?

The companion question, "What can be done about crime?" also confronts us each day. Because news reporting focuses on the dramatic, and crime is among the more "newsworthy" events of the day, most of us have a strong sense that crime is increasing, that something must be done about it. People feel a sense of urgency about crime, even a fear of crime. During election seasons, which come like clockwork every 2 years, proposals are made by incumbent and aspiring office-holders to curb crime. Political aspirants are expected to propose solutions, congressional representatives and Senators must express their positions, presidents and governors must establish crime policies, and mayors and sheriffs must tell us how they intend to reduce crime. Even city council, county commission, and school board candidates feel the need to demonstrate superior qualifications to deal with the crime problem. But even though most people express with conviction preconceived solutions to the problem of crime, how to deal with it is no easier to answer than why people commit criminal acts.

In this book we are concerned with crime control in a democratic society, our own. Our perceptions of police, prosecutors, courts, and prisons reflect the context of our own history. Our crime control efforts must be evaluated in terms of the personal freedoms guaranteed by our Constitution, in reference to our fundamental political ideology, and in light of all the cherished values of our way of life. Neither arrest nor punishment of offenders can be viewed in a vacuum. No matter that we have a serious crime problem, what we do about it must be measured not only in terms of effectiveness, but by the way our procedures conform to our beliefs in liberty and personal freedom.

This chapter focuses on these beliefs and values. And, in order to provide a context for examining the ways American beliefs and values sometimes conflict with the practical world of criminal justice, we present two models of criminal justice: the crime control (conservative) model and the due process (liberal) model. Not only does our criminal justice system come from the political soil of our country—it also engages Americans in political debate. No issues are more political than those related to criminal justice practice and philosophy. Questions about the causes of and solutions to crime are often addressed in a context of fear, hysteria, political opportunism, and sensationalism.

After a discussion of the democratic values which underlie American criminal justice, this chapter provides a broad overview of criminological theory, exploring how scholars have explained crime and its control. Some criminal justice practitioners might argue that by the time perpetrators of crime encounter them, knowing the causes is too late. However, we consider the circumstances that might possibly explain how persons might be propelled into criminal activity as we look to the future of perhaps preventing some crimes from ever occurring.

Crime Control in a Democracy

Observers inside and outside the criminal justice network have often found reason to denounce American criminal justice as ineffective, unjust, or corrupt. It is easy to point to high crime rates and to ridicule the clumsiness and inefficiency of many of our crime control agencies. Examples of cruelty, indifference, incompetence, and corruption abound. This kind of criticism becomes especially intense when a so-called crime wave occurs or when particularly bad crimes are not solved.

Demands for quicker arrests, for swifter and surer trials and punishments, rest on the assumption that *effectiveness*—catching criminals and punishing them—is the only purpose of our crime control efforts. This is superficial, for American crime control philosophy is much more complex. If the sole objective of crime control, subject to no checks or balances, was arrest followed by severe punishment, this could be accomplished easily. Widespread use of electronic eavesdropping could provide police with a much longer list of suspects. Mandatory use of lie detectors or truth serum would convict many more criminals and eliminate the need for jury trials. Experiments with water boarding, chemotherapy, or psychosurgery might be more effective than the present methods of probation, jail, and prison in restraining criminals and preventing crime.

However, even the strongest advocate of "law and order" is likely to retreat in the face of the full implications of unrestrained wiretapping, sweep searches, widespread preventive detention, long sentences, chemical or surgical manipulation of offenders, and dungeon-like prisons. Most of us will accept the fact that there are certain tech-

Image by Junial Enterprises at fotolia.com.

niques, procedures, and devices more repugnant to our national ideals than inefficiency in law enforcement.

Even in our own system we can find some awful practices that, as Justice Frankfurter put it, "shock the conscience."[7] To control the misuse of state power, we have a series of complex checks and balances in our criminal justice system. The complexity is not accidental, nor does it result from mere historical drift. Rather, the taproots of our criminal justice system are deep in an ideology based on personal freedom and the fundamental worth and dignity of people.

Ideological Framework of Crime Control

The origins of our political order, expressed in the Declaration of Independence, the Bill of Rights, the Constitution (see **Table 2.1**), and the other great documents of our history, rest mainly on the desire to build safeguards that limit the power of the state to intervene in the lives of its citizens. Almost any statement in the Bill of Rights, and several amendments to the Constitution, relate directly to our criminal justice process. Historically, a relatively high proportion of Supreme Court decisions apply constitutional restraints to uncontrolled crime control efforts.

It is thus fundamental to our ideals and to our system of government that a higher allegiance to principles of individual liberty, fairness, and due process of law must check and control law enforcement efforts, trial court procedures, and correctional treatment. Improper methods of catching criminals, no matter how effective, must not threaten the freedom of society at large.[8]

Constitutional Amendments 1, 4, 5, 6, 8, and 14 set specific standards for criminal justice administration. The First Amendment allows for freedom of speech, expression,

Table 2.1 The U.S. Constitution and Criminal Justice

We the People of the United States, in Order to form a more perfect Union, establish Justice, insure domestic Tranquility, provide for the common defence, promote the general Welfare, and secure the Blessings of Liberty to ourselves and our Posterity, do ordain and establish this Constitution for the United States of America.

Article I

Sec. 8: To provide for the punishment of counterfeiting ... to constitute tribunals inferior to the Supreme Court ... to define and punish piracies and felonies....

Sec. 9: The privilege of the writ of habeas corpus.... No bill of attainder or ex post facto law shall be passed.

Article II

Sec. 2: The President ... shall have the power to grant reprieves and pardons ... except in cases of impeachment.

Article III

Sec. 2: The trial of all crimes ... shall be by jury; and such trials shall be held in the state where the said crimes shall have been committed....

Article IV

Sec. 2: A person charged in any state with treason, felony, or other crime, who shall flee from justice, and be found in another state, shall on demand of the executive authority of the state from which he fled, be delivered up, to be removed to the state having jurisdiction of the crime.

Amendments to the U.S. Constitution

I. Congress shall make no law respecting an establishment of religion, or prohibiting the free exercise thereof; or abridging the freedom of speech, or of the press; or the right of the people peaceably to assemble, and to petition the government for a redress of grievances.

IV. The right of people to be secure in their persons, houses, papers, and effects, against unreasonable searches and seizures, shall not be violated, and no warrants shall be issued, but upon probable cause supported by oath or affirmation, and particularly describing the place to be searched, and the persons or things to be seized.

V. No person shall be held to answer for a capital, or otherwise infamous crime, unless on a presentment or indictment of a grand jury ... nor shall any person be subject for the same offense to be twice in jeopardy of life or limbs; nor shall he be compelled in any criminal case to be a witness against himself, nor be deprived of life, liberty, or property, without due process of law....

VI. In all criminal prosecutions, the accused shall enjoy the right to expedient public trial, by an impartial jury of the state and district wherein the crime shall have been committed ... to be confronted with the witnesses against him, to have compulsory process for obtaining witnesses in his favor, and to have the assistance of Counsel for his defense.

VIII. Excessive bail shall not be required, nor excessive fines imposed, nor cruel and unusual punishment inflicted.

XIII. Sec. 1: Neither slavery nor involuntary servitude, except as punishment for crime if the party shall have been duly convicted, shall exist within the United States....

XIV. Sec. 1: ... No state shall ... deprive any person of life, liberty, or property, without due process of law; nor deny to any person within this jurisdiction equal protection of laws.

and assembly, whereby law enforcement officers may find themselves in the unenviable role of protecting speech they do not agree with. For example, officers may disagree with NFL football players out of protest taking a knee during the singing of the National Anthem at football games. However, the officers may protect them in doing so in accordance with the First Amendment. Likewise, officers may detest Confederate monuments but prevent the unauthorized defacing of such objects. The Dallas Police Department had reportedly established a supportive relationship with the Black Live Matter movement, five of their police officers died at the hands of a sniper while trying to provide protection for peaceful protests in Dallas in July of 2016.[9]

The Fourth Amendment prohibits illegal searches; the Fifth Amendment protects citizens from self-incrimination and double jeopardy; the Sixth Amendment guarantees the right to trial by jury, the right to legal counsel, and the right to compel witnesses to testify on one's behalf in a court of law; the Eighth Amendment prohibits excessive bail and cruel and unusual punishment; and the Fourteenth Amendment forbids us to deprive anyone of life, liberty, or property without due process of law. The Supreme Court interprets each of these amendments so as to apply constitutional protections to day-by-day situations. These foundation blocks of our democratic society are directly applicable to crime control and express our ideological principles.

"A fair trial" is fine as a general value, but it requires careful interpretation as to the kinds of evidence allowed, the permissible techniques of gathering evidence, the acceptable composition of juries, pre-trial publicity, whether a change of venue is warranted, and a great many other issues. The continuous honing of the law, the sifting and winnowing of standards, shapes criminal justice. This process sometimes curbs law enforcement, as in the series of Supreme Court decisions which limited the methods police may use to secure confessions from suspects.[10] This process also sometimes gives impetus to new programs and proposals, as in the series of Supreme Court decisions during the 1960s and 1970s expanding the rights of poor defendants to the assistance of lawyers.[11]

It is not possible to provide here an exhaustive list of all our ideological principles, but it is important to note some of the most basic of these, for they are applied in one way or another at every step in the decision network of the American criminal justice process. Most expressions of our basic values are phrased in broad terms, often vague in language but firm in intent. Each requires careful judicial interpretation as to how it applies to situations arising in the daily activities of the police, prosecutors, courts, and correctional agencies.

The principles that are fundamental to our criminal justice system and that act to curb efficiency in crime control are legion. It should be clear from those listed that our process of criminal justice exists within a complex set of values, expectations, and desires that preclude simplistic solutions to crime control problems. Merely to demand greater police efficiency, to call for a "get-tough" policy of enforcement, or to suggest that technological innovations turned loose will reduce crime is to ignore the complexity of the problems. Demands for greater effectiveness of police, prosecutors, courts, and correctional agencies are appropriate, but it must be clearly understood that there are other demands for fairness, propriety, and equal protection that also must be met if we are to retain our identity as a free and humane society.

Due Process of Law

The Fourteenth Amendment to the Constitution states that no person shall be deprived of liberty, life, or property without **due process of law**. The scope of due process is broad and necessarily continuously interpreted and refined by appellate court decisions. Currently, though its boundaries are not fixed, it means that the state cannot intervene arbitrarily or capriciously in the lives of its citizens, even those convicted of and sentenced for crimes.[12] Officials must have some appropriate amount and proper kind of evidence before a suspect can be arrested, charged with a crime, convicted, sentenced, and punished or rehabilitated.

More rigid procedural requirements are generally required *before* conviction than *after*. The fullest measure of due process, though rarely fully actualized, is required and given at *trial*. A citizen accused of a crime is accorded rights that include notice of specific charges and, at the apex, a trial by a jury of peers. Due process also includes the rights of a defendant to confront accusers, to rebut evidence, to be taken before judicial authority for consideration of bail, to be publicly tried, and to be treated fairly and humanely. The dimensions of due process continue to be litigated, and the number of decision points in the criminal procedure where full due process applies encompasses every stage of criminal justice decision making.

Fundamental Fairness

In general, our society holds a strong belief that crime control efforts must be fair even if enforcement efficiency is impaired or guilty people are freed. The principle is clear. Accused persons are entitled not only to a trial, but specifically to a *fair* trial; confessions may be used to convict an individual by the person's own words, but these confessions must be obtained in a *fair* manner. A suspect may be placed in a police lineup, but must be exhibited *fairly*; for example, the suspect cannot be the only one handcuffed and dressed in an orange jumpsuit.

The **balance of advantage** between the state and the accused is also a part of fairness that has become increasingly important. It is clear that both the police and the prosecutor have tremendous resources for investigation and the accumulation of evidence, resources that are not available to most suspects and defendants. One trend to balance this difference is to provide more resources for defendants, particularly for those who are poor, friendless, and powerless. Various court decisions have extended to the poor the right to have a defense counsel, paid at state expense. Other decisions have allowed the accused greater access to the state's evidence before trial and have provided trial transcripts to assist poor defendants in appeals.

Whether a fully equal balance between the accused and the state will ever be achieved is doubtful. It is unlikely, for example, that any defendant will be given the full investigatory power of a police department. But various programs have been developed to make the system fairer for the accused and to achieve equity between wealthy and powerful defendants and their impoverished counterparts. All these issues will be discussed more fully in the chapters that follow.

Propriety

Not only must criminal justice exhibit *fairness* in its functioning, but proper enforcement of the law also requires that evidence be obtained by the state in a *proper* fashion. The *quantity* of evidence alone is not enough for arrest or conviction—the *quality* of evidence is also important. This is known as **propriety**. In our society, we place restrictions on the way crimes can be solved, the *way* evidence can be gathered, and the *manner* in which offenders can be treated. We cannot entrap (trick) innocent persons; wiretaps must be judicially approved; searches must be properly conducted. Our belief in the need for proper criminal justice is reflected in the *exclusionary rule.*[13] This rule prohibits the use at trial of improperly obtained evidence, whether that evidence was obtained from an improper search or an improperly conducted interrogation.

Freedom from Cruel and Unusual Punishment

The Eighth Amendment to the Constitution guarantees freedom from cruel and unusual punishment and places a limitation on the way we treat even the worst among us. The authors of this amendment were aware of the brutal methods used to punish people in European countries: dismemberment, flogging, and burning at the stake, among other practices. We have practically eliminated corporal punishment in criminal justice, at least officially. We no longer beat, brand, or maim offenders.

The outer boundaries of cruel and unusual punishment remain highly controversial. In 1972 the U.S. Supreme Court placed a moratorium on capital punishment.[14] Some people believe the death penalty is cruel and unusual punishment: cruel, in that it is cruel to put persons to death, and unusual in that it is rarely imposed at all, and then usually imposed disproportionately against the poor and minorities. But freedom from cruel and unusual punishment is not only an issue in regard to capital punishment. Prison authorities were free through much of our history to set prison punishment policy as they deemed necessary. Sweat boxes, isolation, bread and water diets, flogging, and other cruel practices were allowed, or at least tolerated. As will be discussed in Chapter 12, the courts turned a deaf ear and a blind eye to such abuses under what has been called the "hands-off" policy of the courts until roughly the 1960s. That means the appellate courts permitted other agencies of criminal justice to operate autonomously without interference.

Current death penalty statutes and prison procedures include provisions which attempt to avoid the Eighth Amendment prohibitions against cruel and unusual punishments. Likewise, appellate courts no longer refrain from deciding prison issues on the grounds that wardens have been delegated full power to set prison rules and conditions by legislation. Certain fundamental rights are retained by prisoners, and their effective demand for these rights has become one of the most important and most controversial issues in criminal justice administration. Chief among those rights is the Eighth Amendment right to be free from cruel and unusual punishment.

Equal Protection

It is a constitutional principle that the law be applied equally and impartially to everyone—rich and poor, black and white, the powerful and the helpless. The idea has often been violated in the past (the monetary basis of bail is a clear example of economic discrimination), and it has been the subject of a great many challenges. This principle of equal protection has been affirmed often in recent years by legislatures and appellate courts in issues ranging from representative and fair jury selection to racial disparity in prison populations.

Rule of Law

The rule of law principle means our system is supposed to be one ruled by the written law, not by the whims of individuals. This principle is closely related to the principle of equal protection. In theory, statutes forbid criminal conduct, courts interpret and apply these laws, and criminal justice agencies—the police, prosecutors, judges, and correctional personnel—carry out the legislative requirements without further interpretation. In fact, however, criminal justice does not, and probably cannot, work in such an automatic fashion.

All criminal justice personnel exercise discretion in applying the law.[15] Often, as with prosecutors and correctional authorities, such discretion—the authority to choose among alternative actions or not to act at all—is recognized by tradition or by legislative delegation. In other instances, as with the police, no formal discretionary authority exists. Nevertheless, no police agency has sufficient resources to investigate all crimes or to detect and arrest all violators of laws. Nor is this actually desired in daily operation. Police have literally thousands of citizen contacts in which arrests could be made but where, for a variety of reasons, the arrests are not carried out. Likewise, prosecutors often choose among different but possible charges to level against defendants or decide in certain cases not to charge at all. Also, not all people who are actually guilty are so found by judges or juries, and, in sentencing, a judge, unless bound by sentencing guidelines, usually has a number of alternative punishments from fines to imprisonment among which to choose.

In actual operation, criminal justice is individualized; that is, choices are made in each case, within limits. Laws are not automatically applied. Given the nature of the crime problem, the resources available for crime control, and the often conflicting purposes of criminal justice administration, discretion in the application of criminal law is inevitable.

Perhaps it is also desirable. Full enforcement of all laws would, in the words of Judge Charles Breitel, be "ordered but intolerable."[16] Currently there are various proposals to curb and to control discretion and in some cases, as with mandatory sentences, to eliminate it altogether. The effective control of discretion and attempts to monitor its proper use are other issues of great importance today in criminal justice administration.

Presumption of Innocence

If a number of ordinary American citizens were asked to express in a single phrase the basic underlying philosophy of criminal justice, a common response would no doubt be the presumption of innocence: that a person is presumed innocent until proven guilty. There is little question that this is a very strongly held value. Yet in actual operation, it presents the system with a paradox. The criminal justice process begins and proceeds on an increasing belief in a person's *guilt*.[17] When the police arrest a suspect, their function in the arrest depends on a reasonable belief that the suspect has committed a crime. Similarly, as the arrested person proceeds through the system, evidence of guilt is accumulated.

The fullest adherence to the principle of presumption of innocence, perhaps the only place it exists at all, occurs during trial. This is when strict rules place the burden of proof of guilt on the state.

Models of Criminal Justice

Herbert L. Packer has described two models for criminal justice decision-making which are recognized by practitioners and scholars of criminal justice: the crime control model and the due process model (see **Table 2.2**).[18] Samuel Walker describes two "theologies" of criminal justice, conservative theology and liberal theology, which in some ways parallel Packer's models.[19] Walker claims conservatives and liberals have ideas about crime based on faith rather than fact. Conservatives believe, for instance, that the death penalty deters crime despite a lack of conclusive evidence to support their belief. Liberals, on the other hand, support rehabilitation programs for offenders despite the evidence that such programs do not always work. According to Walker, such blind belief in the absence of factual evidence is similar to religious belief, and hence his use of the term "theology."

Other models exist, but for the purpose of this text we will focus on the ones suggested by Parker and Walker. We caution, however, that although the application of models to the criminal process has the advantage of providing broad, sweeping views of the total system, there is a danger of overgeneralization, of distorting reality into simple yes or no, good or bad views. It is well to keep in mind that the purpose of the models discussed below is to attempt to clarify the assumptions that underlie criminal justice actions (policies) and to examine the conclusion which those assumptions led us to if they are fully accepted.[20]

Table 2.2 Crime Control versus Due Process Models of Criminal Justice

Conservative Crime Control Model	Liberal Due Process Model
"Get tough on crime" "Lock 'em up" "Unleash the police and prosecutors" Criminal sanctions resemble parental discipline Abolish "loopholes" in criminal justice Punishment-deterrence Quick, efficient processing of guilty persons Most important functions of criminal justice include: • Repression of criminal conduct • High rate of apprehension and conviction • Speed and finality of criminal justice processing Assembly-line conveyer belt justice Presumption of guilt Factual guilt	Criminal justice resembles a classroom Emphasis on causes of crime Due process of law Criminal justice should be an obstacle course Quality, not quantity, of arrests and convictions Control the police and prosecutors Individual rights Legal guilt

The Crime Control Model

According to Samuel Walker, crime control theology is expressed in the dual slogans, "Get tough on crime" and "Lock 'em up." In this view, criminal law makes up an important set of boundaries which mark the limits of behavior. Crime can be controlled by reshaping individuals. Walker writes:

> The world of crime control is modeled on an idealized image of the patriarchal family. Criminal sanctions resemble parental discipline. Minor misbehavior is greeted with a gentle warning; a second misstep earns a sterner reprimand. More serious wrongdoing is answered with severe punishment. The point is to teach the wisdom of correct behavior by handing out progressively harsher sanctions and threatening even more unpleasant punishment if the behavior continues. Communication of this message is the essence of deterrence theory. Many people were raised in this way and raise their own children in the same manner. Their personal experience tells them it works, and they assume that society should work the same way. Conservative thinking about crime is closely related to conservative ideas about the problem of permissiveness.[21]

Such an idealized world is not accurately reflected in either the real world of families or of criminal justice, according to Walker. Incorrigible children do not get the message, they do not accept the authority of parents or criminal justice, and punishment fails to deter.

Conservatives explain this by claiming that the structure of discipline has broken down because of loopholes in the justice system, such as the exclusionary rule, the insanity defense, the *Miranda* warning, and plea bargaining. Also, they claim, if the certainty of punishment were assured, people would get the message and would be deterred from committing crimes. And if punishment were made stronger through mandatory sentences, use of the death penalty, and longer prison terms, punishments would provide a strong deterrence.[22]

Packer's crime control model pictures the system as essentially geared to quick, efficient processing of guilty persons. When the administrative fact-finders (police and prosecutors, primarily) are allowed to exercise discretion within the boundaries of good will and reason, then criminals can be discovered, apprehended, convicted, and incarcerated. This model is based on the proposition that the most important function of criminal justice is the repression of criminal conduct by producing a high rate of apprehension and conviction and doing so with maximum speed and finality.

Speed of processing criminals is created through informality and uniformity, a process which seeks to be "swift and sure." Any delay in criminal justice processing is seen as contributing to the public's lack of respect for criminal justice. The police and prosecutors must be unfettered to exercise their discretion and to respond to the huge number of criminal events that come to their attention as efficiently as possible.

Finality is created by minimizing the occasions for challenging or derailing the process. The criminal event must be repressed, disposed of, closed. The volume of cases dictates the need to finalize cases in as efficient a manner as possible. Because of the limited resources and the enormous number of criminal events, it is necessary to assure high rates of arrest, quickly eliminate the innocent, and then convict as many offenders as possible, preferably by guilty pleas. In order to accomplish these goals, administrative fact-finders must utilize discretion (informality), treat all cases and offenders the same (uniformity), and be unencumbered by unnecessary rules and restrictions.

In the crime control model, criminal justice is seen as a factory, taking the raw materials (the criminals) and processing them along in such a way that they, and hence their crimes, are controlled. This **assembly-line conveyor belt** image of justice shows an endless stream of cases moving constantly to workers who stand at fixed stations and process the cases one step closer to being closed files. Each successive stage of this screening procedure—prearrest investigation, arrest, postarrest investigation, preparation for trial, trial or entry of plea, conviction, disposition—involves a series of routine operations. Cases must be passed along to a successful conclusion.[23]

Efficiency in processing the large numbers of cases ingested by the criminal justice network is the primary concern of the crime control model. If errors happen—and the crime control model optimistically points to the improbability of error—then such deviation is normal in the same way that a factory expects some standard deviation in its products. Whereas the factory builds in a quality control mechanism and expects a tolerable level of deviation, however, the primary concern of criminal justice as the crime control model sees it is the efficient functioning of the process. If efficiency demands that certain short-cuts be made that may result in less reliability in the fact-finding process, or put another way, if occasionally a truly innocent person is caught up in the "justice production line" and is thereby wrongly processed as criminal, well ... although an unfortunate set of circumstances, the crime control model would be tolerant of such an error up to the point that the probability of mistakes would interfere with its goal of crime control.

Packer points out that this model rests on a *presumption of guilt*, not as a judicial norm, but as an operational prediction of outcome.[24] That is, cases in which it appears that the persons apprehended are not likely the offenders are thrown away, discarded as quickly as possible. The probably innocent are thereby screened out. Then the probably guilty are processed along the "justice conveyer belt." This model places confidence in the police and prosecutors, believing they have adequate screening abilities to guarantee reliable fact-finding and thereby to accurately identify the guilty individuals.

It is important to this model, therefore, to place as few restrictions as possible on the police and prosecutors, except where the reliability of their conclusions might be enhanced. If they do their work properly and efficiently, the final stop on the "justice assembly line" will be a negotiated plea and a sanction that is agreed to by both the state and the offender. The crime control model, therefore, offers "two possibilities: (1) exoneration of the suspect or (2) the entry of a plea of guilty."[25]

The Due Process Model

According to Walker, the due process theology also has an idealized view of the world. This view sees crime as resulting from bad influences from the peer groups or neighborhoods, and from social factors such as discrimination and lack of economic opportunity. If conservatives view the world as a large family, Walker says, liberals view it as a big classroom:

> Rehabilitation, the core liberal policy, involves instructing the criminal offender in the ways of correct behavior.... A fundamental article of faith in liberal crime control theology is the belief that people can be reshaped. Much liberal thinking in this area is directed toward a search for an effective rehabilitation program. The history of prison and correctional reform is the story of a continuing search for the Holy Grail of rehabilitation.... Faith continues to survive in the face of repeated failure.[26]

Although liberals reject the conservatives' emphasis on individual choice and responsibility in criminal behavior, rehabilitation programs are designed to assist individuals make better choices, that is, noncriminal choices of behavior.[27]

The liberal approach described by Packer in his due process model does not reject the need to control crime, but instead places more emphasis on the formal structure of law than on the ability of police and prosecutors to be able to accurately determine exactly what took place in an alleged criminal event. According to Packer, the due process model resembles a factory that places greater emphasis on quality control than on efficiency. The result, both for the factory and criminal justice, may be reduced quantitative output, but the quality of the goods improves.[28] The due process model sees police and prosecutors as needing to be regulated and controlled lest they infringe on the rights of the individual citizen.

The due process model places a higher value on individual rights, on controlling and limiting the power of the state *vis á vis* the individual citizen. Therefore, if the crime control model resembles an assembly line, the due process model looks very much like an **obstacle course.** Rather than allowing for unrestrained actions on the part of the representatives of the state, the due process model places constitutional rules and prohibitions on the process that obstructs the power the state can exercise in regard to its citizens. The due process model presents formidable impediments to processing an accused person. The accused person has a full opportunity to discredit the case against him or her, and that only then is the factual case heard publicly by an impartial tribunal.[29]

This obstacle course perception of the criminal process is based on realities just as valid as the assembly line analogy, although it is less frequently encountered in practice since most people have developed a great confidence in police and prosecutors to determine the facts in a case. But the due process model stresses the fallibility of the system and the possibility of error. Packer himself considers people to be notoriously poor observers of disturbing events. Indeed, the more emotion-arousing the context, the greater the possibility that recollection will be incorrect. Packer points out that confessions and admissions by persons in police custody may not be completely voluntary and witnesses may be biased. With these considerations in mind, therefore, the due process model rejects informal fact-finding as too unreliable.

The due process model views maximum efficiency on the part of the criminal justice system as leading to increased tyranny. The effective work of criminal justice means stigma and loss of liberty for the person found guilty, and this represents the most significant power the state can exert against an individual. That makes it imperative that the criminal justice process be subjected to controls, safeguards which prevent it from operating at absolute efficiency. In the due process model, efficiency is sacrificed in order to prevent the official repression of the individual by the oppressive, coercive power of the state. From its perspective, it is better that a hundred guilty persons be set free because of the effective exercise of procedural safeguards than for a single innocent person to be wrongly convicted.[30]

Whereas the crime control model rests on the presumption of guilt, the due process model considers guilt to be the matter in question. Not only must an accused person be determined guilty factually, by sufficient evidence, but he or she must be found guilty according to proper procedures, by properly competent authorities, and in accordance with the various rules designed to protect citizens in the arms of the law and to safeguard the integrity of the process. Packer states:

> the tribunal that convicts him must have the power to deal with his kind of case ("jurisdiction") and must be geographically appropriate ("venue"); too long a time must not have elapsed since the offense was committed ("statute of limitations"); he must not have been previously convicted or acquitted of the same or a substantially similar offense ("double jeopardy"); he must not fall within a category of persons, such as children or the insane, who are legally immune to conviction ("criminal responsibility"); and so on. None

> of these requirements has anything to do with the factual question of whether the person did or did not engage in the conduct that is charged as the offense against him; yet favorable answers to any of them will mean that he is legally innocent.[31]

Thus **legal guilt**, as opposed to factual guilt, must be determined quite separate from the police and prosecutors who clearly are unable or unwilling to apply these guilt-defeating doctrines.

This is the source of great consternation to the police or prosecutors, or both, who have worked the cases. But the larger consequence of the due process model has been that illegally obtained evidence does not make its way into court, and that convictions may be reversed where procedural safeguards have been violated. Therefore, not only are criminal offenders held accountable before the law, but so also the police and prosecutors.

The Search for Justice and for Less Crime

Most of the problems faced by criminal justice are as old as humanity. Moreover, the same basic problems that faced our forbearers are likely to be confronted by our children. Obviously, we have not effectively prevented, controlled, or diminished crime. We have not made the same kind of breakthroughs in crime control or prevention comparable to those in medicine or physical science or technology, where advances have become common. Such comparisons may be unfair, however, for crime is not a disease, nor is crime control a science in the same sense as physics or biochemistry.

In the United States, a free society built on principles of justice and freedom, we expect even more from crime control. Prevention and effective law enforcement, although important, are not the sole determinants of appropriate criminal justice efforts. Whatever preventive or control measures are taken must be consistent with our sense of justice. And this term—justice—is as elusive of definition, as difficult to measure or evaluate, as any concept in our language.

From our origins as a colonial people to the present day, American history can be characterized as a search for justice. We have slowly and often painfully constructed a Constitution, a government, and a highly intricate set of administrative machinery intended to maximize liberty, afford wide opportunities for the pursuit of happiness, and protect the civil liberties of all our citizens. But we have not yet fully achieved these goals.

We have at times supported repressive institutions, like slavery, that in hindsight seem unbelievable and that took a civil war to change, only to be followed by Jim Crow segregation laws. Rejecting aristocracy, we still developed a class-entrenched society. Our treatment of all minorities (racial, political, sexual, and economic) has been less than consistent with our ideals. In terms of our pursuit of justice, U.S. Senator Jim Webb maintains "If the laws against drug use were uniformly enforced ...

half of Hollywood would be in jail instead of half of Harlem."[32] Our history is littered with examples of injustice and only too frequently with cases of corruption in our own institutions. Yet the search for justice continues.

Few will deny that we have progressed from the days of the Salem witch trials or the frontier justice of Judge Roy Bean. We have introduced higher standards of propriety in processing suspects and defendants; we have become more humane in the treatment of most offenders. Nowhere have we fully achieved our ideals of equal protection under the law, due process, and effective and humane treatment of violators. But progress has been made and is ongoing.

The study of criminal justice, therefore, presents a complex challenge to us all. The fact that university courses on criminal justice have expanded to virtually every campus in the United States is an indication of the seriousness with which the subject is considered in academia. In addition to courses taught in departments of criminal justice or criminology, several academic disciplines within the university offer their own insights into the subject: sociology, political science, psychology. This multidisciplinary interest reflects the variety of approaches available for the study of criminal justice. These multidisciplinary perspectives, as we shall see, have also influenced how the causes of crime are viewed.

Implications of Criminological Theory for Criminal Justice

Throughout history, theorists have attempted to determine the causes and solutions to crime, in an effort to reduce or eliminate it. Yet, criminal justice policy and practice is established seemingly without regard to criminological theory because theories contradict each other, and no one theory has been proven right. Some crime policies deal with individual offenders, seeking to apprehend, restrain, incarcerate, deter, or rehabilitate them by locking them up. Other approaches may attempt to address the social causes and the social environment of crime and may attempt to change society. Advocates of some crime policies may attempt to change the laws by decriminalizing certain offenses so as to remove them from the jurisdiction of the criminal justice system, while advocates of other policies may attempt to criminalize additional behaviors in order to bring about a desired improvement in the overall social environment.

Police practice is based on a belief that criminals choose to commit crimes and will choose not to commit further crimes if the proper punishments are imposed. However, most police officers and officials acknowledge the harmful effects of living in crime-laden communities. Indeed, many police officers are themselves products of those same areas, and understand the pressures inherent in lower-class environments. But the law and police practice leave little room for social engineering.

Prosecutors are often influenced by theoretical aspects of criminal behavior in making charging decisions. An offender who clearly needs alcohol rehabilitation, psychological counseling, or some other treatment may find the prosecutor willing to defer prosecution, or even to drop charges completely when the offender agrees to seek help for the problems which have caused the criminal acts. But, especially in serious crimes such as murder, regardless of the presumed causes of the crime, free-will choices on the part of the offender are usually assumed and the prosecution seeks to punish the behavior, not rehabilitate the offender, to deter other such potential crimes in the society at large.

American law, as established in the U.S. Constitution, emphasizes punishment for crimes. Punishments are provided to deter potential criminals without regard to the biological or social causes of crime. Nowhere in the Constitution does the word "rehabilitation" appear, nor does the Constitution address the causes of crime.

Prisons, probation and parole agencies, and other so-called correctional agencies may be suited to respond to the presumed theoretical causes of criminal behavior. Prisons may have group counseling, drug and alcohol rehabilitation, vocational training, and a host of other programs designed to assist a person overcome the adverse social conditions which led to the life of crime. But little evidence exists to demonstrate that such programs provide effective solutions—recidivism rates remain high despite such well-meaning programs.

The juvenile justice system is perhaps better suited to apply solutions to the causes of delinquency. Juvenile offenders are still young, impressionable, changeable—perhaps that is the time to exert a maximum effort to identify the causes of delinquency and treat them.

The difficulty is that little consensus exists as to the causes of crime and delinquency. And where consensus may exist, crime policies responding adequately to the perceived causes are difficult to institute if they are at odds with the established order of criminal justice practice. The political context of criminal justice today places an emphasis on punishment as deterrence; anything less is rejected as being "soft on crime."

However, crime policies can be responsive to the findings of criminological theory. Modern police, courts, and correctional administrators can develop programs and policies which are both consistent with scientific findings and effective in satisfying the loud insistence that a war on crime be waged.

As seen in **Table 2.3**,[33] criminologists have tended to view behavior along a continuum of responsibility, from individuals having full responsibility for their actions to persons being perceived as having no responsibility for their actions whatsoever. **Table 2.3** summarizes the major criminological theories presented in this chapter. These theories are divided into two primary groups: classical criminology and positive criminology.

Classical Criminology

Classical criminology, as it is commonly understood, has its roots in the eighteenth century writings of Italian mathematician **Cesare Beccaria** (1738–1794). Beccaria's

Table 2.3 Continuum on Responsibility

Classical School	Neoclassical School	Positive School
Free Will Fully Responsible	Soft Determinism Responsibility Mitigated by Circumstances	Hard Determinism Not Responsible

Classical Criminology
Historical: Cesare Beccaria (1738–1794): Law and government should serve the goals of society. Law can be moral. Contemporary: Criminals are responsible for their crimes. Consistent and vigorous punishment will deter further crimes.

Positive Criminology		
Biological Determinism	Psychological Explanation	Sociological Determinism
Historical: Cesare Lombroso (1835–1909): Introduced scientific method to criminological study. His study of human physique led him to believe that criminal behavior is the result of biological conditions. Francis Gall (1758–1828): Espoused phrenology. William Sheldon (1898–1977): Body types determine behavior, temperament, and personality. **Contemporary biological research:** C. Ray Jeffery: Focus is on the brain and central nervous system, and on hormones. Behavior is seen as the result of complex interactions between genetics and the environment.	Alfred Binet (1857–1911): Used task-related skills to measure intelligence. H. H. Goddard: Linked feeble-mindedness and crime. Travis Hirschi/Michael Hindelang: Supported the IQ-delinquency link. Personality disorders: Behaviors outside of normal definitions are ascribed to psychological or emotional disturbances.	Clifford Shaw/Henry McKay—*The Chicago school and social disorganization*: Using a mapping system, studied the characteristics of neighborhoods classified as high and low in delinquency. Conclusions: Delinquency rate is influenced by a socially disorganized environment and the conditions of poverty. Edwin H. Sutherland—*Differential association*: Techniques, motives, and rationalizations for crime are learned behaviors. Ronald Akers—*Social learning theory*: Crime is learned, depending on the rewards and punishments attached to it by reference groups. Albert K. Cohen—*Middle-class measuring rod*: Delinquency is a product of collective consensus among lower-class boys against middle-class values. Delinquency is a means to develop positive self-concepts through antisocial values. Walter Miller—*Lower-class focal concerns*: Delinquent boys are competent youngsters whose needs are not met through socially accepted channels, who seek status and a sense of belonging among their peers. Robert K. Merton—*Social structure and anomie*: People substitute unacceptable goals and means when they are unable to achieve society's institutional goals. Robert A. Cloward/Lloyd E. Ohlin—*Differential opportunity theory*: Blocked opportunity causes delinquency, expanded opportunity should lower delinquency. Travis Hirschi—*Control theory*: People with strong social bonds are less prone to criminal activity. Edwin Lemert—*Labeling theory*: Two types of deviance: primary behavior caused by biological or social conditions: secondary behavior which comes from a person having a self-image as a deviant. George Vold/Austin Turk—*Conflict theory*: Members of society who are the most powerful influence the law and criminal justice system; members of the lowest classes are powerless and are most often legislated against, and hence are most often labeled as criminal. *Radical/Marxist criminology*: Crime is a product of the struggle between the classes within society.

Source: Patrick R. Anderson and Donald J. Newman, *Introduction to Criminal Justice*, 6th ed. (New York: McGraw Hill, 1998), 62.

treatise, ***On Crimes and Punishments*** (1764)[34] is perhaps the best known among students of criminology of any publication from that era. The influence of the philosophy found in that work, as well as in other works of that genre, had a profound influence on the language of both the Declaration of Independence and the United States Constitution.

Cesare Beccaria (1739–1794)

On Crime and Punishments (1764)

A GENERAL THEOREM: In order for punishment not to be, in every instance, an act of violence of one or of many against a private citizen, it must be essentially public, prompt, necessary, the least possible in the given circumstances, proportionate to the crimes, dictated by the laws.

Beccaria's writings are representative of his age, often referred to as the Age of Enlightenment. The intellectual climate in the *Age of Enlightenment* encouraged revolutionary ideas. New social structures emerged which obliterated the ancient domination of the European monarchies. The French Revolution, and the American Revolution, brought about new governments and new types of governments. Great European philosophers, including Hobbes, Locke, and Hume—the "Social Contract Writers"[35]—espoused the idea that people should be served by government rather than government served by people. The social contract between people and their governments meant that individuals were required to relinquish only the amount of freedom necessary to protect the rights of other people, the aim of such an arrangement being to produce the greatest happiness for the greatest number of people. Citizens would relinquish the right to punish to the state, and the state would be in place to protect the lives and property of its citizens.

According to the philosophy underlying the social contract, laws should be written in such a way that people would willingly accept and obey them. The power of the government should be restrained and limited so as to eliminate the possibility of a recurrence of the excesses of the *Church Age*. Examine the **Critical Thinking 2.1** exercise below.

Critical Thinking 2.1 Would Laws Abolishing Abortion Be Obeyed?

Perhaps no social issue is as loaded with emotional feeling as abortion. Public opinion polls show that most people in America support a woman's choice in abortion, certainly in cases arising from rape, incest, or when the woman's health is at risk. Many would say a woman has an absolute right to choose. However, some who wish to abolish abortion completely in American society wish to use the law to enforce their belief. They call those who would favor a woman's right to choose abortion, murderers. Since 1993, at least 11 people have been killed in attacks on abortion clinics. There are even those such as Robert Dear, Jr. who opened fire with an assault rifle at a Planned Parenthood clinic in Colorado Springs in 2015, injuring nine people and killing three. He was in an hours-long standoff with police, and he was talking about "no more baby parts" after being apprehended and interviewed by the police.[36] They wish to pass laws which would criminalize abortion, to overturn the *Roe v. Wade* Supreme Court decision, which legalized what was up to that time a back alley, dangerous practice. Women seeking abortions could only secure the procedure illegally, prior to *Roe v. Wade* (1973), and many did. Researchers contend that legalized abortion in the United States has actually contributed to a significant lessening of the crime rate. The contention is that many of these children, if their mothers were forced to bring them to term, would be born into dire circumstances thereby increasing their likelihood of engaging in criminality.[37]

1. Do you think having legalized abortion in place can reduce the crime rate? If so, is that a valid reason for keeping abortion legal?
2. In your opinion, if the anti-abortion view were to win, and laws were passed to abolish the practice and place any medical practitioner in prison who participated in abortions, would the laws have enough support among the entire public to be obeyed?
3. When public opinion is narrowly divided about whether a behavior should be outlawed, should the government pass legislation one way or the other? Or, should the law be limited in its content to only those behaviors which have overwhelming consensus?
4. Has the existence of a law prohibiting behavior, for instance, underage drinking, kept you from participating in that behavior?
5. Conduct further research on Scott Roeder and distinguish how while his motivations for engaging in criminality may be similar, his approach is markedly different from Martin Luther King, Jr.'s, discussed later in this chapter.
6. Where in the Constitution is the right to privacy found? Apply the previously discussed categories of judicial activism and judicial restraint, as well as Cardozo's methodology. to the *Roe v. Wade* decision.

Much of what was written by Beccaria was a reaction against the legal and social abuses of the Church Age in Europe, during which a person could be tortured, drawn and quartered, burned at the stake, dismembered, or branded, among other terrible punishments, for such offenses as blasphemy. Beccaria argued against that kind of cruelty, and his book, written anonymously, was in fact condemned by the Catholic Church in 1766.

During the European Church Age, confessions were extracted from people through torture, and the belief was that God would intervene on behalf of truly innocent individuals to rescue them from the fate of false confessions forced from their lips through those methods. Beccaria argued that such a system of "justice" was irrational. Beccaria sought to eliminate torture as an interrogation tool, to limit the amount of punishment the state could impose, and to "let the punishment fit the crime."

The privileged classes, including the clergy, had developed ways to circumvent the law and the harsh consequences of unlawful behavior. For example, church and legal authorities were immune from legal punishment for their crimes. Among the common people, respect for the law diminished, and even disappeared. The Age of Enlightenment writers in general espoused the belief that in order to have a meaningful legal system, the people being governed must be in agreement with and in control of their government—this is known as *government by the consent of the governed.* In such a system the law would be established by the people and the power of the government would be restrained by the same system of law that defined illegal behavior. Also, in this view, law and government should serve utilitarian purposes. That is, laws should be designed to promote the general welfare, to benefit the greatest number of people, to lead toward the greatest good and happiness possible.

The basic premise of Beccaria's schema is that everyone has total **free will**, equal rational choice, and freely chooses their behavior, good or bad. The theory is based on the pleasure/pain principle with the underlying belief that humans are pleasure seeking and want to avoid pain. In fact, **Jeremy Bentham** (1748–1832) developed the **hedonistic calculus**, which was devised to determine the amount of pleasure derived from a particular act, and this was aligned with a statutory schema to indicate the amount of pain necessary to stop the act from occurring. Thus, it is believed that the reason persons perpetrate crimes is because such actions bring them pleasure.

Then, for Beccaria, to prevent crime a punishment a little greater than the pleasure derived from the commission of an act must be swiftly and certainly imposed to thwart future criminal activity. The proportionality of fitting the punishment to the crime was essential, Beccaria believed, to ensuring allegiance to the social contract. With an emphasis on public punishments for deterrent effect, if the punishment were too severe, citizens observing an overly harsh punishment may question the legitimacy of the social contract and why they should comport their behavior to its dictates.

Beccaria controversially advocated limiting the discretion of judges and believed that there was class bias in the application of the law. He was so much concerned about the preferential treatment of the wealthy over the poor in the criminal justice process that he indicated that when there were class differences between the victim and the offender that half of the jury should be comprised of the victim's class and that the other half should be made up of members who were of the offender's class. Even though a proponent of punishment, Beccaria, aware of the inequities (the rich being favored over the poor) in the imposition of punishment, was opposed to the death penalty, believing that life imprisonment would actually result in more suffering.

The beauty of the Classical School is to treat everyone the same in terms of the application of the law. The tragic flaw of the Classical School of criminology revolves around its focus on the act and not the intent. Over time, the Classical School's functionality began to give way as various circumstances began to arise in which acts occurred but evidence of persons freely choosing to perpetrate the acts was non-existent or suspect. Thus, it began to be called into question if indeed everyone was the same.

Neoclassical School of Criminology

During the roughly 100 years between the founding of the Classical School of Criminology and the emergence of the Positive School of Criminology, the Neoclassical School of Criminology developed. The Neoclassical School emerged in an effort to make the Classical School administratively workable. Situations kept arising that did not fit neatly within the premise of the Classical School, that individuals who perpetrate crime do so under all circumstances of their own free will. The basic premise remained that yes there is free will, but sometimes circumstances that may negate or lessen someone's responsibility for the commission of an act may exist.

For example, we have a separate system for processing juveniles because we recognize that they typically do not have the same reasoning capability as adults. Neoclassicalists acknowledged that not all behavior is based on rational choice, that insanity and coercion could cause the commission of crime. *Actus reus* (guilty act) was not sufficient to define a crime; *mens rea* (guilty state of mind) must also be present. The Classical School would not consider intent, as everyone was believed to freely choose to commit crime. But the Neoclassical School allows for the sifting through the circumstances to determine if individuals truly, freely chose to commit criminal acts.

Actors within criminal justice (police, prosecutors, defense attorneys, judges, correctional officials, etc.) armed with discretion, the very thing that Beccaria wanted to avoid in his quest to treat everyone fairly, must sort through the circumstances and decide who should be processed and how through the criminal justice system. A problem with this individualized process is that, if left unchecked, it can lead to discrimination via race or class, according to gender or sexual preference, immigration status, or any number of factors.[38]

Positive Criminology

Positive criminology is usually understood to represent the systematic empirical study of crime and criminals, the search for causes and cures for crime, and, ultimately, the control of crime and the preservation of social order. Its proponents understand conformity to the social order to be normal and deviance from social conformity to be abnormal, or pathological. The individual criminal is assumed to be fundamentally different from non-criminals in detectable, and thus curable, ways. The positive criminologist studies biological, psychological, and sociological factors that contribute to criminal behavior. Forces outside the offender's control propel him/her to crime. This is a hard deterministic approach whereby the offender can be likened to a billiard ball sitting on a pool table struck by the cue ball and potentially other balls and propelled around by forces (biological, psychological, sociological, economic, and/or legal) outside of his control. The focus of the **Positive School** is to deal with the force(s) that caused the aberrant behavior.

Biological Determinism

The school of positive criminology owes much of its heritage to **Cesare Lombroso** (1835–1909), **Enrico Ferri** (1856–1929), and **Raffaele Garofalo** (1852–1934).[39] However, perhaps no name in the history of criminology is as familiar as Lombroso. Indeed, when one discusses the positivist tradition in crime-related studies, immediate reference is made to Lombroso, even to the point of calling him the "father of modern criminology."

Just the Facts: Cesare Lombroso (1835–1909)

"This was not merely an idea, but a revelation. At the sight of that skull, I seemed to see all of a sudden, lighted up as a vast plain under a flaming sky, the problem of the nature of the criminal—an atavistic being who reproduces in his person the ferocious instincts of primitive humanity and the inferior animals. Thus were explained anatomically the enormous jaws, high cheekbones, prominent superciliary arches, solitary lines in the palms, extreme size of the orbits, handle-shaped or sessile ears found in criminals, savages, and apes, insensibility to pain, extremely acute sight, tattooing, excessive idleness, love of orgies, and the irresistible craving for evil for its own sake, the desire not only to extinguish life in the victim, but to mutilate the corpse, tear its flesh, and drink its blood."

For Lombroso, a surgeon, the study of the criminal entailed a physiological examination of the human body. As the excerpt from his book, *L'Uomo Delinquente* (1876), details, Lombroso was aroused by his study of the physiques of criminals, and especially of their skulls. His studies of insanity, as well as his studies of Italian soldiers, led him to conclude that criminals were fundamentally different from non-criminals in observable, physiological ways. The evolutionary theories of Charles Darwin, more than any other thinker of his age, had a profound impact on scientific views of human nature and the scientific study of people. In Lombroso's view, criminals were not as evolved as non-criminals. Criminals were characterized by animalistic, amoral behavior. They did not choose to commit crimes, as Beccaria stated, but their criminal behavior was innate—a result of biological conditions beyond their control. Lombroso believed that criminals were **atavistic**, that is, throwbacks to a more primitive stage of human development.

In such a context, humans were not seen as willful creatures capable of doing whatever they choose; instead, they were viewed like other animals, their behavior determined by pre-existing conditions, breeding, and natural selection. This school of thought is called **biological determinism**.

Although among contemporary criminologists virtually none of Lombroso's conclusions about criminals are still accepted, he is largely responsible for introducing the **scientific method** to the study of crime. He changed the focus of crime studies from the classical school's philosophical emphasis on the law to a scientific emphasis on criminal behavior. And, of course, Lombroso is a patriarch of the view that human behavior is biologically determined.

Later biological determinism theories have focused on studies of physical stigmata, or body types, genes, and chromosomes, as well as of differences in the brain and central nervous system. Such studies have differed in the parts of the human body thought to contain the key to understanding human behavior, but all of them take as their starting points the idea that behavior has its genesis in conditions caused by the biological makeup of the individual, conditions which are inherited.

Phrenology

Among the earliest approaches to biological determinism was **phrenology**, often referred to as the "lumps on the head" theory, which was first publicly espoused by **Francis Gall** (1758–1828). As a young medical student, Gall noticed that some of his fellow students had distinctive head shapes. He began to examine every skull he could in an attempt to discover why some people seemed to have "such different faces and such different natures; why one was deceitful, another frank, a third virtuous."[40] He studied heads in medical laboratories, prisons, and lunatic asylums. Gall concluded that differences in head shapes and bumps on the head demonstrate corresponding parts of the brain which were housed in those compartments of the skull. He developed a system to show the relationship between head shapes, or knobs, and behavior and character traits.

Gall's studies were widely publicized in Europe and his theories became extremely popular. The American phrenologist **Charles Caldwell** published *Elements of Phrenology* in 1824, which reported three compartments of the brain, "one the seat of the active propensities, another of moral sentiment, and the third of the intellectual faculties."[41]

Body Types

Body types, the early focus of Lombroso's attention, were also seen as determinants of criminal behavior by William H. Sheldon. In the 1940s, Sheldon conducted physical studies of delinquent boys in a small institution for delinquents in Boston. He observed three basic body types among males and concluded each had corresponding behavior and temperament characteristics, or personalities.[42]

Sheldon classified the body types as **endomorph**, **mesomorph**, and **ectomorph**. People with endomorph body types are rotund and heavy with jovial and outgoing personalities. People with mesomorph body types are muscular and well proportioned, with competitive, aggressive, and driven personalities. And people with ectomorph body types tend to be slender and frail, with introverted, aloof, and withdrawn behaviors. Sheldon classified individuals according to a 10-point endomorph-mesomorph-ectomorph scale. No one was completely, perfectly any one of the body types, but had various qualities of each. Sheldon concluded that criminals tended to be mesomorphic in body build.

Later studies of the relationship between body build and delinquency have to a certain degree supported the general hypothesis of Sheldon's theory.[43] However, a direct link between body build and criminality has not been proven. The sample sizes in Sheldon's research were quite small. Also, the extent to which delinquency is due to social factors, not body build, is not adequately explained. And not only criminals tend to have mesomorphic body types, but police do as well. These and other flaws have been pointed out, but among the theory's proponents the focus on biological factors in behavior persists.

XYY Chromosomes

Abnormalities in sex chromosome associations introduced genetic research to the study of crime.[44] The normal female has XX sex chromosomes, the normal male XY. Studies of prisoners revealed that a statistically significant number of prisoners had an XYY chromosome abnormality. Since the Y chromosome determines maleness, the idea developed that the extra Y chromosome constituted a "supermale," a person more aggressive and therefore potentially criminal.

The **XYY male** was said to be about 6 inches taller, at 6 feet 1 inch, than the average male. The early view was that the extra Y chromosome meant more testosterone and therefore more violence and aggression. Also, the extra Y chromosome was considered to be related to lower IQ. However, as research continued, these findings were largely refuted. XYY males have been shown to be less aggressive, not more, to have lower criminal rates, not higher, and to be less likely to commit crimes against persons than the XY male.

But research always points the way toward gaining new knowledge and insights. The existence of chromosomal abnormalities among prisoners has opened the window of exploration into genetic influences on criminal behavior beyond that of chromosomes themselves.

More Recent Biological Research

Because much of the early research into biological influences on criminal behavior was disproven, this approach was largely rejected by criminologists through much of the twentieth century. However, with advances in medical science, and with the remarkable growth of technological approaches to curing disease, biological theories concerning behavior have re-emerged stronger than ever. Heredity is a significant causative factor in diseases as diverse as alcoholism, cancer, and heart disease, as well as in violent behavior, including crime. Studies also show that nutrition and early childhood care affect behavior patterns for years after their actual occurrence.

C. Ray Jeffery was a leading proponent of the focus on the influence of genes in behavior through pathway mechanisms such as the brain, brain chemistry, and hormonal systems, all in interaction with one another and with the environment. The brain has major centers for the control of emotional and motivational behavior, as well as for the control of rational behavior and decision making. Behavior is a product of the interaction of the millions of neurons in the brain. The brain sciences, and the joining of psychology, biochemistry, neurology, and psychiatry have created an interdisciplinary approach to a theory of human behavior.[45]

In this view, human behavior is not a simple response to free-will, rational decisions. Behavior is the product of extremely complex interactions between genetics and the environment. Jeffery points out that there is no crime gene lurking in the human body which springs into action causing a person to pounce on another to rape or pillage. Genes do not cause crime. Rather, genes influence **biological traits.** Those traits may be recessive; that is, they may remain in the background, invisible and inactive, until or unless they are triggered. Likewise, behavior may be attributable to genetics in much the same way propensities to cancer, heart disease, diabetes, or any number of mental conditions may be.

Psychological Explanations of Crime

Psychological terminology is found in both biological and sociological approaches to crime causation, but in addition to studies of the brain and central nervous system mentioned above, pure psychological theories about crime have focused on intelligence, personality disorders, and insanity.

Intelligence

The relationship between **intelligence quotient** (IQ) and crime was explored throughout the twentieth century. For much of the century, the primary concern insofar as criminal behavior was concerned was to identify the "subnormals" and "feebleminded" so as to isolate them and keep them from breeding additional offspring considered undesirable.

The link between **feeblemindedness** and crime was popularized by **H. H. Goddard,**[46] who administered IQ tests to all inmates at the New Jersey Training School for the Feeble Minded at Vineland. He found no inmate with an IQ over 75, so that figure was set as the upper limit for feeblemindedness. Psychologists also administered the tests to a great number of other people in prisons, jails, and other public institutions.

The results, showing that about 70 percent of the criminals were feebleminded, seemed to support the notion of a feeblemindedness-crime link.

But later, during World War I, Goddard administered the same tests to draftees and discovered approximately the same proportion of feebleminded individuals in that population, a finding he could not adequately explain. He then changed his mind about his conclusions and the proposals to incarcerate all feebleminded persons and prevent them from reproducing.[47]

That was not the last word on the issue, however. In 1977, **Travis Hirschi** and **Michael Hindelang** supported the IQ-delinquency link anew in a review of scientific research on the subject in which they reported an average gap of 8 points in the IQs of delinquents and nondelinquents.[48] They reported that low IQ is at least as relevant to official delinquency reports as social class or race. They also concluded that IQ is directly related to self-reported delinquency rates, and that lower-class delinquents are more likely to have low IQs than lower-class nondelinquents. They were less certain about IQ and adult criminality, and they suggested that low IQ might be connected to school failure, which in turn might lead to truancy, vandalism, and other forms of juvenile delinquency which in turn could lead to more serious forms of criminality. Adult criminal acts often require more thought and planning; therefore a low-IQ connection to adult crime is less evident.

Considerable controversy still surrounds claims of an IQ-crime link. Research which measures the IQs of prisoners is suspect since low IQ may be a better explanation of why a person was caught rather than why he or she committed a crime. Convicted criminals and delinquents probably do not constitute a representative sample of the overall offender population; the best and brightest may not get caught, prosecuted, and convicted. However, some crimes—stock fraud, embezzlement, complex white-collar crimes, swindles, or fraud, for instance—may require a higher-than-average IQ.

Personality Disorders

Psychologists sometimes use terms like abnormality, mental disorder, behavior disorder, mental illness, psychological problem, or emotional disturbance to describe behaviors which appear to be outside normal definitions. One such behavior is the **anti-social personality** disorder. Approximately 2 or 3 percent of the male population, and less than 1 percent of the female population, is believed to have this disorder. Sometimes this is known as the **psychopathic**, or **sociopathic**, personality. Such a person may appear to be charming and pleasant, but their lack of guilt, shame, remorse, love, or empathy leads to exploitive and manipulative relationships. They are often arrogant, have inflated opinions of themselves, and blame others for any problems or misdeeds.[49]

Other personality disorders stem from **substance abuse**, such as drug or alcohol dependency or intoxication. Although some crimes are committed by people under the influence of drugs, such as crack cocaine, other crimes are committed by people under the urgent need for the drug. Heroin addiction, for instance, condemns the addict to a constant physiological need for the drug, which since it is illegal, leads the person to find illegal means to obtain the drug. But the substance which by far influences the most crimes in America is alcohol. The first effect alcohol has on a person's psychological state is to depress inhibitions, and in some people violence is a result.[50]

Sociological Explanations of Crime

Sociology is concerned with the social environment in its search for explanations for crime and primarily focused on the environment, the social context of crime. This approach identifies factors in the social environment which are believed to contribute to a person's behavior—the family, peer group, economic conditions, success opportunities, school, and all the other myriad influences into which a person is born. Factors outside the individual are seen to exert powerful influences on the individual, influences beyond a person's will, which cause delinquency and crime. This approach is known as **sociological determinism.**

The Chicago School and Social Disorganization

The environmental approach had its genesis in the studies conducted by a group of University of Chicago sociologists on behalf of the Institute for Juvenile Research in Chicago in the late 1920s and is sometimes referred to as the Chicago School of criminology. It is most commonly associated with the work of **Clifford Shaw** and **Henry McKay**, among others.[51]

Using police reports and official data, these researchers mapped delinquency by plotting police reports and juvenile court referrals on a map of Chicago (see **Figure 2.1**). They then drew concentric circles from the center of the city on the map. This technique is referred to as a "**mapping system.**" They next studied Chicago neighborhoods to discover what characteristics distinguished high- and low-delinquency areas. And by intensively studying the people in those neighborhoods, by virtually living with them, the researchers were able to observe the everyday lives of individuals in their natural environments, much like botanists study flora and fauna in their natural habitats. For this reason the technique is sometimes called the "**ecological approach.**"

Juvenile referrals were discovered to be highest in neighborhoods of rapid change, poor housing, poverty, tuberculosis, adult crime, and mental disorders. These neighborhoods were closest to the center of the city, and delinquency tended to decline with distance from that core. Over time, the maps and charts of delinquency in the Chicago area showed a consistent pattern of crime and other social problems in inner-city areas despite rapid changes in the ethnic populations living there.

The delinquency-prone areas were characterized by deteriorating homes and encroaching factories and businesses. Immigrants tended to settle there first because

Figure 2.1 Zone Rates of Male Juvenile Delinquents, Chicago 1927–1933

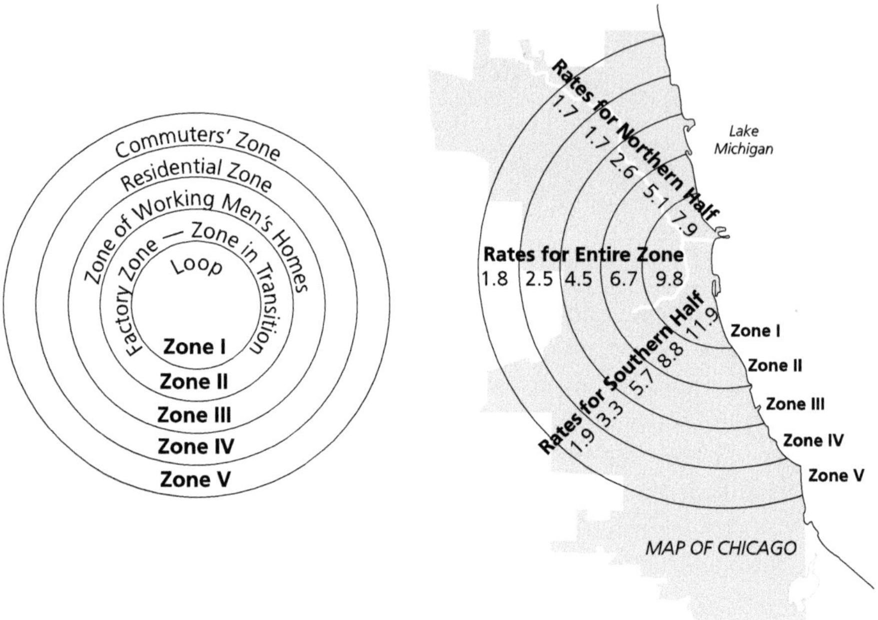

Source: Clifford R. Shaw and Henry D. McKay, *Juvenile Delinquency and Urban Areas* (Chicago: University of Chicago Press, 1969), pp. 51, 69.

of the cheap housing and close proximity to factories where employment could be found. Then, as they were able, these immigrants moved into the next zone, called the "workingmen's neighborhood," and as affluence allowed, later moved into more stable, wealthy, and crime-free, neighborhoods. The further out from the core, inner-city area, the less delinquency, crime, and other social problems the researchers discovered. And each group of immigrants moving out of the core city was replaced by new immigrants moving in for the same reasons as their predecessors and facing the same problems.

Shaw and McKay concluded that delinquents were essentially normal adolescents who were adversely influenced by the criminogenic influences of their socially disorganized environments, especially youth gangs. This concept of **social disorganization** greatly influenced the study of crime and delinquency, focusing on poverty and unemployment as contributing causes of delinquency. The foremost contribution the Chicago school made to criminology was to relate crime to lower-class issues and connect causally the conditions of poverty which contribute to delinquency and crime.

Official data (police reports) reinforce the relationship between social class and crime, leading to the perception that crime is largely a lower-class phenomenon. This may be because crimes known to the police and arrest data appear to cluster in poverty areas, areas that the police patrol more intensively than middle- or upper-class neigh-

Image by katifcam at istockphoto.com

borhoods. Lower-class crimes are more likely to result in arrest since they include such high-visibility activities as muggings, assaults, public drunkenness, and other so-called "street crimes" that are readily discovered and punished. If the scientist uses official data as a starting point to study crime, therefore, the conclusion that crime is a lower-class activity is inescapable, and this view has dominated much of sociological theory about crime. See **Critical Thinking 2.2** below. Should one's environment be considered when meting out punishment?

Critical Thinking 2.2 Applying Criminological Theory to the Criminal Justice Process—You Be the Jury

The Matter of Jermaine Julian

Jermaine Julian faced the death penalty in 2009 in Tampa, Florida, for robbing, shooting, and killing a man associated with a reputed "drug house." A local deputy referred to such a killing as "misdemeanor murder," because it did the community a favor by getting rid of a nuisance. Speculation ensued as to why the federal government would seek the death penalty in such a case. It was suggested that this was consistent with the Bush administration's policy to be tough on black-on-black crime.

From 1980 to 2000, the years that Jermaine Julian grew up in his neighborhood (Florence Villa in Water Haven, Florida), the racial composition was over 86% black; the percentage of high school graduates over age 25 ranged from 45% to 60%; the percentage of renters in his neighborhood ranged from 45% to 53%; the median household income for his community ranged from $9,901 (1979) to $19,934 (1999); in 1989, 36.9% of residents in his community were considered to be below poverty level, with 26.3% deemed so in 1999.

A review of police reports revealed that from 1991 until 2003 (676 weeks) there were 2,559 known police calls for violent crimes to his community, which translates into 3.78 violent crimes a week. There were also 857 police responses in this community to drug- and weapon-related crimes for a total of 127 drug/weapon crimes a week. This means there were 5.05 violent/weapon/drug crimes responded to per week by the police in Jermaine Julian's neighborhood during his formative years, not to mention all the crime that took place that the police did not know about. There were also indications that Julian grew up without a father, his mother had drug problems, and he was left to fend for the survival of himself and his younger siblings.

How does Jermain Julian's neighborhood compare to the area you grew up? Check out your census tract and compare it to the above figures. What theories from this chapter would you offer to support Jermaine Julian's case or to detract from it? Should one's environment matter in determining responsibility for crime—guilt—sentence? Would you have voted for the death penalty in this case based on the above information? Do you think Jermaine Julian received the death penalty in this case? Why or why not?[52]

Differential Association

One of the more famous scholars to emerge from the Chicago school was **Edwin H. Sutherland.**[53] Sutherland used the Chicago school methods—statistical data analysis and the case history (or life story)—and expanded his data base to include the newly introduced Uniform Crime Reports (UCRs), which the FBI began publishing on a yearly basis in the early 1930s.

In 1937, he published *The Professional Thief,*[54] a book written in collaboration with Chic Conwell, himself a professional thief. Based on lengthy interviews with, and written answers to questions by, thieves, the book explored the professional world of theft, stealing as a business, crime mobs, the "fix," and criminal rackets, as well as attitudes of thieves toward the law and society. Sutherland stated in the book, "The essential characteristics of the profession of theft ... are technical skill, status, consensus, differential association, and organization."[55]

Sutherland developed this concept of **differential association** into a theory which he discussed in his 1939 book, *Criminology,*[56] and which he subsequently revised in 1947. The theory, briefly stated, is as follows:

1. Criminal behavior is learned; it is not inherited, nor is it invented, but is acquired through training.
2. Criminal behavior is learned in interaction with other persons in a process of communication; that communication may be either verbal or "the communication of gestures."

3. The principal part of the learning of criminal behavior occurs within intimate personal groups; secondary sources such as movies, books, or newspapers are relatively unimportant.
4. When criminal behavior is learned, the learning includes (a) techniques of committing the crime, which are sometimes very complicated and other times very simple, and (b) the specific motives, drives, rationalizations, and attitudes that cause people to commit crimes.
5. People are surrounded by other people who view the legal code either as rules to be obeyed or rules to be violated. The individual's own orientation toward obeying or breaking the law results from the favorable or unfavorable view he or she has toward the legal code.
6. A person becomes delinquent because he or she defines the law as something to be violated rather than to be obeyed; that way of defining the law comes from the type of culture and the personal associations which have influenced the person most heavily.
7. Different personal associations may vary in frequency (how often do you see this person), duration (how long has this relationship existed), priority (how important is this association to you—most important), and intensity (is this a casual or intense relationship); but criminal behaviors which begin in childhood through the influence of associations with significant others persist throughout life.
8. The process of learning criminal behavior or rejecting it by association with those who exhibit criminal or anticriminal patterns of behavior involves the same mechanisms as any other type of learning; it is not merely imitation, but becomes internalized in much the same way a person learns how to lay bricks.
9. While criminal behavior is an expression of general human needs and values, it is not explained by them since noncriminal behavior is an expression of those same needs and values; that is, both thieves and honest laborers attempt to secure money to meet their personal needs. The sources of criminal and noncriminal behaviors lie in a different area.

The essence of the theory is that individuals associate with may rub off on them, an admonition often offered by parents. Succinctly, the theory can be summarized in the following fashion: if you lay down with dogs, you're liable to get up with fleas.

Social Learning Theory

In a significant restructuring of differential association theory, **Ronald Akers** combined it with the psychological theory of operant conditioning.[57] Akers contended that behavior is shaped by behavioral reinforcers, either positive (rewards) or negative (punishment). These reinforcers can come from direct nonsocial sources such as the physiological effects of alcohol or drugs, but usually they come from social sources such as family and peer groups from which most behavior is learned. Akers stated that both conforming and nonconforming behaviors are acquired through the process of learning definitions of behaviors as good or bad, justified or not justified. And, as with all learning as understood by operant conditioning theory, criminal behavior is learned depending on the rewards and punishments attached to it by the significant groups with which people interact. This is known as **social learning theory**.

Middle-Class Measuring Rod

Albert K. Cohen's book, *Delinquent Boys* (1955),[58] advanced the notion that lower-class values and lifestyles differ significantly from those of the middle class. It claimed that much juvenile delinquency is the result of the frustration experienced by lower-class boys who are measured against the **middle-class measuring rod**.

Cohen listed the middle-class values as:

(1) drive and ambition;

(2) individual responsibility;

(3) achievement and success in every area of endeavor;

(4) deferred gratification;

(5) long-range planning and budgeting;

(6) courtesy and self-control, especially with strangers;

(7) control of verbal or physical violence and aggression;

(8) "wholesome" recreation, such as a hobby;

(9) respect for the property of others.

According to Cohen, the failure to adhere to those values, and the failure to perform well in the middle-class dominated school system, leads lower-class boys to reject those values and the school system and to act out against them. In that sense, delinquency is a product of a collective consensus among lower-class boys.

The delinquent gang, for Cohen, was characterized by apparently senseless acts by mean boys. But he also considered acts such as vandalism, terrorism on the playground, and defecating on the teacher's desk to be expressions of hostility to bolster the poor self-image of the "street corner" boys who committed them. And he saw much delinquent gang behavior as negativistic, direct attacks on middle-class values.

Lower-Class Focal Concerns

Walter Miller's work among lower-class people in Boston led to a different set of conclusions.[59] Although he also considered lower-class delinquent gang behavior as anti-middle-class, he saw it as normal and useful in the lower-class context. He identified categories of attributes, or roles, it promoted for the male gang member:

> the ability to handle *trouble*, which for lower-class males means being able to handle run-ins with police and other authorities, as well as being able to fight, drink, and engage in sexual activity.

being *tough*, or engaging in masculine bravado, means showing strength, sexual skills, tattoos, the lack of emotion.

being *smart*, which means to have street savvy, including the ability to outwit someone, to hustle unsuspecting "johns," or to "play the game."

finding life *exciting*, which means heightened adventure, the thrill found in alcohol, sex, gambling, and other behaviors which come before and after prolonged periods of inactivity, called "hanging out."

finding life *fateful*. Fate refers to the belief that one is unable to control events, that strong forces of destiny or magic take one's future out of one's hands.

being *autonomous*, the very desirable ability to be independent of controls, especially those of a spouse or a boss.

These **lower-class focal concerns**, according to Miller, flourish in the female-based households which predominate in poor families. Boys need to belong, to have status among their peers. These needs are met in the street-corner gang. The delinquent boys, therefore, are not emotionally disturbed or inferior, but represent competent youngsters whose needs are not met in middle-class ways, who do not have proper male role models to help them succeed in mainstream society.

Social Structure and Anomie

Émile Durkheim, a French sociologist introduced the term **anomie** in his book, *The Division of Labor in Society* (1893), and later used it in his book, *Suicide* (1897).[60] Durkheim had studied the French and American cultures after the Industrial Revolution and had noted that economic crises and a general breakdown of normal societal conditions created a "deregulation" of social and moral rules. This deregulation, which he called "anomie," could lead to all sorts of social deviance, including suicide and crime. Durkheim believed that normally society could perform a regulating function; it was only in periods of rapid societal and economic and fluctuation that this state of flux, anomie, would emerge.

In *The Division of Labor in Society*, Durkheim distinguished *mechanical society* from *organic society*. Mechanical societies tend not to have an extensive division of labor, are composed of common laborers, are generally homogeneous, and are found in rural communities. Current-day examples of mechanical societies might be found in textile mill villages and coal mining towns. Organic societies are more complex in terms of the labor pool and tend to be associated with urban, heterogeneous environments.

Certain types of punishments may work better in one environment than another. For example, in rural, mechanical societies public humiliation and shaming have traditionally been used to try to deter deviant behavior. Even today in small-town newspapers, minor infractions are reported for the locals to see. The individual receives the punishment from the criminal justice system and is also held out for potential public scorn. Gossip can be another extra-legal means for attempting to keep people in line. This approach would not work in an organic society. What would happen, for example, if we began to try to list every seat belt and no valid license violation in Miami, New York City, San Diego, and Minneapolis in the newspaper?

Durkheim was among the first in the study of criminology to indicate that crime was normal and that punishment was a necessity in a society. He maintained that punishment was a means of ensuring *social solidarity*. Persons who abide by the social contract feel self-righteous when transgressors are caught and punished. Individuals feel better about themselves when they have been doing what they are supposed to do and those who have not are made to answer for their misdeeds. If too many persons were blatantly succeeding by violating the law, such as a drug dealer with no legitimate job and a fancy car, others may begin to question their own allegiance to the social contract and begin to pursue a life of crime themselves.

Durkheim believed that a society without crime would be over controlled, something Durkheim did not conceive could possibly exist. Such a dictatorial environment would thwart any chance for societal advancement and progress. In other words, Durkheim actually perceived crime and criminals as potentially having positive attributes. He maintained that positive social change could be brought about by those considered criminals within society, that sometimes "the good ones go to jail."[61]

He would consider personalities such as Mahatma Gandhi, Jonathan Swift, Nelson Mandela, and Martin Luther King, Jr., all of whom were considered criminals at one time or another and locked up. Durkheim considered such reformers as boundary testers. These would be the individuals on the fringes that would be there to test the limits, ensuring that society would not become too restrictive.

Robert K. Merton's 1938 article, "Social Structure and Anomie," was published in the *American Sociological Review* during the Great Depression. It is the most frequently cited article in sociological or criminological textbooks.[62] Merton observed the collapsing social conditions brought about by severe economic conditions, and rejecting the notion that crime is an intrinsic and individual behavior, looked beyond the immediate personal environment of criminals to the broader context of social structure and anomie for explanations.

Merton borrowed the term **anomie** from Durkheim. Anomie is understood to be the condition which exists when norms no longer control people's behavior. When people no longer have clear rules, when normlessness exists, controls on behaviors and aspirations cease to exist. Merton maintained that anomie is especially likely in a society such as the United States, where there is unequal opportunity and an emphasis on material success, and claimed it can explain a broad range of socially deviant behavior.

In Merton's view, American society has established institutionalized goals, usually understood to be financial success, which society emphasizes and reinforces. Then, socially structured avenues to achieve those goals exist, called "means." When materialistic goals are overemphasized and extolled to the population at large, but the means to achieve them are unavailable to a considerable part of that same population, then anomie is likely. The people whose paths to material success are blocked experience **strain**, and must either adjust their aspirations downward or devise alternative

Table 2.4 Robert Merton's Five Modes of Adaptation

Modes of Adaptation	Cultural Goals	Institutionalized Means
Conformity	+	+
Innovation	+	−
Ritualism	−	+
Retreatism	−	−
Rebellion	±	±

Source: Robert Merton, "Social Structure and Anomie," in *Social Theory and Social Structure* (Glencoe, IL: Free Press, 1957).

routes to achieve the goals. Merton viewed anomie as a permanent fixture in such an environment and believed deviant behavior would be widespread.

Merton described five **modes of adaptation** to achieve goals (see **Table 2.4**):

Conformity is the path taken by most people, according to Merton, even if they realize that the means to achieve their goals are restricted. However, the remaining four modes present alternatives to conformity which may lead to various forms of deviance, including crime.

Innovation occurs when a person accepts a goal, but rejects the accepted, legitimate means to achieve the goal. For instance, if a child wants a new bicycle, legitimate means to obtain it exist: asking grandparents for a bicycle at Christmas, saving money from one's allowance or part-time jobs, etc. If those means are not available, or if the child is not sufficiently committed to them, then alternative—innovative—means may be chosen, such as theft.

Ritualism refers to the person who continues to follow the institutionalized means of achieving goals, hard work and thrift, but who has lost sight of the goals, or has rejected them. This may describe the so-called rat race, in which people work diligently in socially approved ways but have no hope of success in achieving their goals, or no longer identify with long-term goals. Although they know that they will never get rich under the current system, they do not want to lose what little they have.

Retreatism occurs when both goals and means are rejected. The retreatist response to an inability to reach goals is to drop out, to quit trying. This may lead to extreme retreatist behavior such as alcoholism, drug addiction, or vagrancy.

Rebellion is an option for people who reject the approved goals and means to achieve them for new goals and means. Rebels and revolutionaries are disgruntled individuals who view accepted goals as unattainable or undesirable and socially approved means of reaching them as demeaning or unworkable. Therefore, these persons substitute new, socially unacceptable goals and means, such as the redistribution of wealth through a socialist political structure. (See **Field Practice 2.1.**)

Field Practice 2.1 The Unabomber, Dylann Roof, and Omar Mateen as Models of Retreatism and Rebellion

Harvard-educated Theodore J. Kaczynski, with a Ph.D. in mathematics, and a former professor at the University of California, Berkeley, was arrested in April of 1996 as the suspected "Unabomber." He was responsible for mailing letter bombs to unsuspecting victims who were maimed, and sometimes killed, when they opened otherwise innocent-looking mail packages. But long before the arrest, federal agents had developed a profile of the person they were searching for, a profile based on the best analysis of crime files available. The agents anticipated the Unabomber would be creative, male, middle-aged, and a loner. He was also expected to be conservative, based on his preference for print media over television for the publication of his "Manifesto." That Manifesto proved to be Kaczynski's undoing, but the profile proved to be accurate.[63]

Merton would no doubt label Kaczynski as both retreatist and rebellious. (Likewise, Timothy McVeigh, who blew up the Federal Building in Oklahoma City, after his disillusionment with the government beginning with his military service in Iraq and the siege by federal agents on the Branch Davidian compound in Waco, could also be labeled as retreatist and rebellious.)

Dylann Roof flunked ninth grade twice before dropping out of school; he was described by a high school authority as "very transient." He reportedly lived an existence fueled by alcohol and drugs. In pictures, he is seen wearing a #88 shirt, denoting the fact he had 88 Facebook friends. Roof maintained his concerns about racial conflicts were awakened within him by the Trayvon Martin case, as he wrongly believed that hundreds of black-on-white murders were occurring and being ignored. He was described as paranoid and narcissistic by a former FBI profiler; even though he lived an "unfulfilled life," the profiler contended that Roof viewed himself as superior and others (blacks) as inferior. In his nearly 2,500-word manifesto, Roof explained why he chose Charleston and why he was the lone one to carry out the horrific shooting. He wrote: "I chose Charleston because it is most historic city in my state, and at one time had the highest ratio of blacks to whites in the country. We have no skinheads, no real KKK, no one doing anything but talking on the internet. Well someone has to have the bravery to take it to the real world, and I guess that has to be me." His actions left nine people dead in the historically black Emanuel A.M.E. Church in Charleston.[64] **Do you think Merton's retreatist and rebellious categories fit Dylann Roof?**

Omar Mateen, a 29-year-old American born citizen, whose family had immigrated from Afghanistan, walked into the Pulse nightclub (a gay club) in Orlando, Florida, on June 12, 2016, and began a shooting rampage, leaving 49 dead, plus the gunman, and more than 50 persons wounded. During contact with police, Mateen claimed allegiance to ISIS (Islamic State in Iraq and Syria), and that organization has reportedly praised his actions. Mateen has been labeled as a homegrown, self-radicalized terrorist with no known direct ties to other terrorists. While he had trouble fitting in and succeeding in the workplace, and had been interviewed on three previous occasions by the FBI, James Comey, FBI Director, said there was no indication that Mateen was a "credible threat" prior to the shootings. Rumors circulated, with people coming forward to indicate that Mateen had visited the Pulse nightclub on multiple times prior to the 12th, used gay dating apps, his own ex-wife reportedly suggested he had gay tendencies, and one person claimed to be Matteen's gay lover after the shootings. However, the FBI found no evidence to support any of those claims.[65] In terms of a possible motive, Mateen did tell a police negotiator by phone during the siege "You have to tell the U.S. government to stop bombing. They are killing too many children. They are killing too many women, okay." He indicated his actions were a protest against Islamic State targets in Syria and Iraq.[66]

Can you identify other alleged terrorist suspects that could fit possibly into the category of retreatism and rebellion identified by Robert Merton? How so?

Merton's theory has gained great popularity, as evidenced by the frequent references to it in sociological literature. This was largely due to its focus on issues larger than personal environment—to its focus on the overarching social structure which influences behavior, and which especially serves to disenfranchise large numbers of poor people.

More recently, however, a seemingly new twist has been placed on the influence of the class structure on criminal behavior. Where above Merton's "innovation" category represents a means by which persons may resort to crime when their legitimate avenues to goals are blocked perhaps due to the lack of financial resources, the phenomenon of affluenza has been offered as an explanation for criminal behavior. It is suggested that those who have been pampered and are accustomed to the finer things in life, the affluent, know no boundaries and can just throw money at their problems/victims to make them go away. Ethan Couch could be considered the poster boy for this defense. A psychologist, G. Dick Miller, used these arguments and indicated that Couch's parents raised him to believe "that other people were beneath him and have no worth." While affluenza is not a recognized medical malady, the affluenza defense was used in his case. Ethan Couch, who was 16 years old at the time of the crash, was charged with "four counts of intoxication manslaughter and two counts of intoxication assault." His blood alcohol level was three times the legal limit. He admitted his guilt and was sentenced to 10 years' probation and time served in a rehabilitation center. With the assistance of his mother, Couch violated his probation and fled to Mexico. This resulted in the imposition of 720 days of incarceration for Ethan Couch, 180 days for each person killed. Couch's attorneys have appealed the criminal sentence.[67]

Differential Opportunity Theory

Cloward and Ohlin took Merton's concept of illegitimate means, and Sutherland's theory of differential association, as the background of what they called **differential opportunity theory**, which they proposed in *Delinquency and Opportunity: A Theory of Delinquent Gangs* (1960).[68] Essentially, this theory states that blocked opportunities to achieve economic goals cause feelings of frustration and poor self-images, and those feelings in turn lead to delinquent gangs of juveniles.

Cloward and Ohlin contended that opportunities to commit illegal acts are distributed unevenly throughout society, just as opportunities to participate in conformist behavior are. They identified three types of lower-class gangs: criminal, conflict, and drug-oriented or retreatist.

According to differential opportunity theory, *criminal gangs* emerge in neighborhoods where adult, organized, long-term criminal behavior exists. Adult criminals are the tutors and role models for adolescent gang members. Gang behavior is stable and theft-oriented; crime is supposed to be businesslike and disciplined, not violent and irrational.

Conflict gangs emerge where no such adult criminal role models exist, where conditions of poverty are greater, and where neighborhoods are less stable and more transient. *Blocked opportunities* lead to frustration and then to violence. Conflict gangs seek to obtain through violence that which they cannot obtain legitimately and which they do not have the opportunity to achieve through nonviolent ways. These gangs lack the stable system of social control evident in criminal gangs. Cloward and Ohlin point out that when a social street worker attaches to a conflict gang, gang violence diminishes due to the recognition by gang members that they are no longer rejected, that they can begin to gain access to legitimate success opportunities.

Some gangs are dominated by drug use. These Cloward and Ohlin labeled *retreatist*, or *drug-oriented*, *gangs*. Sometimes members of criminal gangs or conflict gangs gravitate toward retreatist gangs, making those youths "double failures," unable to achieve success either by legitimate means or illegitimate means. These gangs are characterized by "street-corner boys" who have scaled down their aspirations and have dropped out of active involvement in any goal-directed behavior.

Cloward and Ohlin advocated the expansion of opportunity structures in American society. And many of the social programs which emerged at the national level in the 1960s were spawned by the widespread reading of *Delinquency and Opportunity*. If blocked opportunities cause delinquency, then many of those concerned about juvenile delinquency believed that expanded opportunities should lower delinquency rates.

Control Theory

A **control theory** about crime and delinquency was developed by **Travis Hirschi** in his book, *Causes of Delinquency* (1969).[69] Hirschi stated that people's tendency to commit deviant acts is controlled by social bonds, bonds consisting of attachment, commitment, involvement, and belief.

Attachment means strong ties to parents and friends, including a good peer group, as well as to teachers and others in school. Strong attachments to significant people like family members, friends, and teachers (or a significant person from some other area of one's life) can help one resist criminal tendencies.

Commitment to conventional lines of action helps a person resist unconventional, or criminal, lines of action. For instance, a conventional way to obtain wanted merchandise is to work to earn money with which to purchase goods. To the extent to which a person is committed to following conventional lines of action he or she is able to resist the temptation to take a "short cut," or the "easy way," to obtaining goods through crime. Jackson Toby's 1957 "stakes in conformity" is really a precursor to Hirschi's commitment concept. Toby maintained that some individuals risk a great deal more than others by acting out.[70] For example, college students desirous of careers in the criminal justice system would want to strive to avoid a criminal conviction. For others, when you have nothing, you have nothing to lose.

Involvement in conventional activities keeps a person busy so that no time is available for mischief. "The idle mind is the devil's workshop," the old saying goes, and when a person is involved in school, church, hobbies, clubs, scouts, teams, or work activities, then temptations stemming from idleness do not survive.

Belief, for Hirschi, involves not only religious belief, but also the acceptance of commonly held values. Among those values is respect for the feelings and property of others, and belief in obeying the law and social norms. To have a true allegiance to something, one needs to believe in it.

Control theory demonstrates the qualities of life that help bond a person to his or her society, and therefore control his or her behavior. People with strong bonds are less likely to commit criminal acts than those with weak bonds. And Hirschi has not only demonstrated the value of the family, school, and other kinds of social groupings in the formation of conventional or criminal behavior; he has provided some direction for corrective and preventive efforts to help control behavior. Note also that all these controls posited by Hirschi are extra-legal variables, outside the legal system. These controls are the first line of defense against deviant behavior. When the bonds to these controls are eroded or non-existent then interventions by the criminal justice system are more likely to occur.

Techniques of Neutralization

Gresham Sykes and **David Matza** developed **techniques of neutralization** which can be considered rationalizations for perpetrating crime and allowing the offender not to have a negative self-perception. Their five techniques included the following:

- Appeal to higher loyalties (I robbed for the gang.)
- Condemn the condemners (The police are crooks.)

- Denial of injury (They could afford it; no one really got hurt.)
- Denial of the victim (He had it coming; he knew the risks involved.)
- Denial of responsibility (Socio-economic, biological, or psychological factors made me do it.)[71]

Labeling Theory

Labeling theory looks beyond the criminal act to the process of defining the act criminal. It examines the process by which persons become labeled as criminals, delinquents, or deviants. And it attempts to explain how labeling influences a person who has been labeled.

Edwin Lemert is the recognized proponent of this view,[72] although **Howard Becker** and **John Kitsuse** are also identified with the theory.[73] Lemert asserted that two types of deviant acts occur, primary and secondary deviance. **Primary deviance** is that behavior which may be caused by biological or social conditions, or may be minor violations of the law such as childhood pranks. Primary deviants are able to avoid a criminal self-image by having such readymade explanations for their behavior. **Secondary deviance** is that behavior which comes after a person has developed a self-image as deviant, when crime or delinquency becomes incorporated into his or her identity or lifestyle.

Labeling theory assumes that no act is inherently criminal, that the label placed on the behavior and on the actor by the social audience determines whether or not an act or actor is criminal. Labeling theory has two aspects. *First*, labeling affects the person(s) labeled, and *second*, it affects the person(s) assigning the label. The first effect involves the process of "self-fulfilling prophecy," the process by which a person acts according to his or her self-perceptions. A person is given the status of criminal, or delinquent, a stigmatizing label which results in degradation, incarceration, and isolation. The person is subjected to treatment which causes him or her to become the thing he or she is described as being. In short, if you see yourself as a criminal, you will behave as a criminal, and finally you will become a criminal. And then you will join with others who have been labeled similarly and develop a criminal subculture. For the labeling theorist, the self-image is a product of assigned labels, and people tend to act out, or fulfill, the labels assigned to them, especially if those labels are internalized, made part of the *persona*. And the label is more important than the act the label describes. The harmful effect of labeling a person criminal occurs whether or not that person actually committed a crime.

The second effect involves the **social audience**, or those in a position to assign labels. The social audience includes family, peer, schools, psychologists, neighbors, and the criminal justice system. Consider the negative labels that can be assigned by parents and school officials: unwanted child, slow learner, disruptive child, behavior problem, unruly, disobedient, disrespectful, etc. Or consider negative labels that can be assigned by psychologists: emotionally disturbed, mentally retarded, passive-aggressive, etc. These labels, and their positive counterparts, can affect not just the person labeled if the labels are accepted, believed, and internalized, but also the social audience. People behave differently toward a labeled person; they respond to the label rather than to the person.

Labels assigned by criminal justice are uniformly negative, and can be circular, making it difficult to escape them:

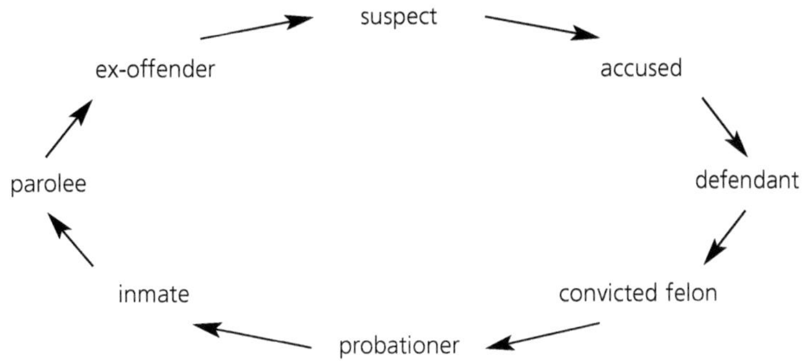

None of these improves a person's self-image, and none is considered desirable by the social audience—which in this case would be everyone not so labeled who hears the term. What would happen if a young woman said, "Mother, please say hello to my new boyfriend, Sam. He is a convicted felon." Mother would undoubtedly respond to the label before she did to Sam. The same principle applies to employers, police, school officials, and others in the social audience.

Labeling theory claims that labeling is especially powerful in regard to children and adolescents, and among those who are wrestling with their own self-concepts. And labeling is more likely to be applied to lower-class persons. Labels may impel an individual into delinquency; the labeling process can actually help create delinquency and criminality by harshly and publicly degrading a person, forcing him or her to retreat from the mainstream of society.

Proponents of labeling theory demonstrate that labelers tend to be white, middle-class, authority figures. Labeled criminals and delinquents tend to be poor, minority ethnicity, and powerless. Labeling theory has focused attention on the social audience as well as on the offender. And it has contributed to the view that social class is related to perceived criminality, whether or not the people so labeled are actually criminals, and to an understanding of the process by which individuals become criminals. The intersection between criminological theory and popular culture is sometimes reflected in music.

Intersection between Popular Culture and Criminological Theory

See Merle Haggard for an example of an attempt at Travis Hirschi's familial and religious control:

http://www.youtube.com/watch?v=jxQbvSjQy9A&feature=related; http://www.cowboylyrics.com/lyrics/haggard-merle/mama-tried-507.html

See Todd Snider for an example of Jackson Toby's "stakes in conformity" theory of having nothing to lose:

http://www.youtube.com/watch?v=lmCrU_RjoZg; http://www.cowboylyrics.com/lyrics/snider-todd/looking-for-a-job-17321.html

See Merle Haggard for an example of the detriments of labeling theory:

http://www.youtube.com/watch?v=UO67h_359wM; http://www.cowboylyrics.com/lyrics/haggard-merle/branded-man-503.html

What lyrics from songs can you identify as being reflective of crime and criminological theory?

Conflict Theory

Conflict theory is related to labeling theory in that it looks beyond the simple identification of criminals in society to the processes by which laws are made and certain lawbreakers are identified as criminals. But where labeling theory emphasizes the social audience as a causative factor in criminality, conflict theory shifts the focus even further from the individual offender to the established social order, to the power structure which writes into the criminal law its own interests, its own values. **George Vold** and **Austin Turk** are major spokespersons for this approach.[74]

Conflict theory concludes that criminal laws and criminal justice agency policies are established and influenced by political pressures. Those pressures are based in economics and comprise the predominant influence on the making of laws and the practices of the police, the courts, and corrections agencies. According to conflict theory, those members of society who are higher up the ladder of social class are the most powerful, exert the greatest influence on social policies, and impose their values on the rest of society. Those members of society who are lowest on the ladder of social class are powerless. They find themselves the targets of the criminal justice system and are unable to influence the law or that system; therefore, they are most often legislated against, and their behavior is most often labeled as criminal.

Turk maintains that two methods are used by the powerful to control the less powerful. The *first* is *coercion*, or the use of force to control the population and make it conform to the requirements of the law. The more this type of control is used by the authorities, the more difficult it is to control a society, and the greater the likelihood of higher crime rates among the less powerful.

The *second* form of control is found in the *law* itself. The law may assume a great deal of importance, even more importance than the people whose behavior it regulates. In Turk's view, the law consists of lists of undesirable behaviors, along with their corresponding punishments, as well as procedures for the criminal justice system to follow. Turk also introduced the concept of "living time," which refers to generational transitions or the process by which older generations of people die out, leaving younger generations made up of people who have experienced only the existing legal order and therefore have less reason to resist the law or to question existing social structures. Turk believed that during such "living times" the relationship between the powerful and the less powerful is less conflict-oriented, thus leading to less crime.

Turk claimed that crime is higher among the less powerful when the power of the controlling groups is greatest. He also thought that if the less powerful were to become organized, conflict with the authorities would become greater, and the likelihood of higher crime rates would increase as well.

Radical/Marxist Criminology

Radical/Marxist criminology focuses attention on the people who have the political and economic power to define crime for the rest of society. Labeling and conflict theory both focus criminological inquiry away from the individual offender toward the impact of criminal justice itself, and away from individual deviant behavior toward the wider quest of the social origins of crime. Radical/Marxist theory explains crime and delinquency as a product of a struggle between the classes within society, between the "haves" and the "have nots," and especially between those who own the means of production (the *bourgeoisie*) and those who do not (the *proletariat*).

The language is borrowed from the writings of Karl Marx, as is the critique of capitalist social and legal structures, although Marx himself did not write much at all specifically about crime in capitalist society. What little he did say revolved around his discussion of the *lumpenproletariat*. Marx maintained that this group would constitute the underemployed (like pulling up to a fast-food drive-in window and having your professor ask you if you would like fries with that) and the unemployed. Burdened with economic disadvantages in the *lumpenproletariat*, the criminal element would most likely exist within a capitalistic society according to Marx.

This view explains crime, therefore, as a product of the economic system of capitalism and the social class system it establishes. Criminal justice is seen as a tool of the capitalist class—the rich and powerful people who own industry and have money—to influence legislation and control the lower classes. Since most crime, according to official data, is committed by the poor against other poor people and is very visible, the attention of the poor is drawn away from the less visible exploitation they experience at the hands of the rich. In other words, the condition of being relatively powerless is viewed by these criminologists as a possible cause of crime.

Radical/Marxist criminology also discusses crime from another point of view. For example, **William Chambliss**[75] stated that crime is a rational reaction to the life conditions of a person's social class and that the criminal law expands as the gap between the *bourgeoisie* and the *proletariat* widens so as to coerce the proletariat into submission. **Richard Quinney**[76] expanded on this to identify two broad categories of criminality: **crimes of domination and repression**, and **crimes of accommodation and resistance.** Crimes of the first type are committed by the agents of the capitalist class in order to maintain capitalist supremacy. Crime control policies are used by the capitalist class to suppress the lower classes, and crime control agencies may even break the law in order to maintain order. Quinney also argued that crimes of economic domination are committed by the powerful to preserve the capitalist system. These would include white-collar crimes, environmental pollution, and organized crime.

Crimes of accommodation and resistance, on the other hand, are committed by the working classes in order to survive in the oppressive capitalist system. These would include burglary, robbery, and drug dealing, committed by poor people to obtain the goods and services they are unable to provide for themselves through legitimate, legal means. Crimes such as murder, assault, and rape arise out of the frustration and rage resulting from the inequality in capitalist society.

Law Enactment versus Law Enforcement

Certainly, conflict and radical/Marxist theorists maintain that law enactment (how laws are made) and law enforcement (how laws are enforced) are two distinct processes that must be considered separately. As Anatole France once said, "The law, in its majestic equality, forbids the rich as well as the poor to sleep under bridges, to beg in the streets, and to steal bread."[77] Of course, while on the surface the law appears fair, as everyone is treated the same—as Beccaria envisioned, the problem is that some among the impoverished may out of necessity find themselves in violation of the law while the rich would not have to resort to such means for shelter and sustenance. Thus, an unequal law, even if equally enforced, can favor one group over another. Again, the tragic flaw of the Classical School not considering intent emerges, as does the contention that while Beccaria honed in on limiting potentially class-biased judicial discretion he mistakenly never questioned and accepted as gospel the lawmakers' decisions of the day. This genre of theorists (conflict, radical/Marxist) would maintain that both those making the laws and those enforcing the laws must be scrutinized. They maintain it creates less strain to prosecute the politically weak and powerless than it does to bring the affluent to justice (providing laws have been made to define the actions of the wealthy as criminal).

A rallying cry for being leery of this interface between big business, lobbying, and the legislative process can be seen in the article by Mark Dowie entitled "Pinto Madness."[78] Consider the following in **Field Practice 2.2.**

Field Practice 2.2 Influencing Lawmakers

As documented by Dowie, in 1972 executives at Ford Motor Company knowingly left an automobile on the highway, the Ford Pinto, that could kill with an exploding gas tank. Instead of recalling the vehicle and replacing an $11.00 gasket on the fuel tank, the executives performed a cost/benefit analysis, decided to take their chances, believing it was more cost effective to leave the automobile on the highway. The executives even circulated memoranda estimating that a human life was worth $200,000 back then, figuring in burn unit and funeral expenses for those who would be scarred and/or killed in the fiery crashes. Ford also managed to lobby the legislature and prevent legislation from being passed that would have made it criminal homicide for an automobile manufacturer to knowingly put an automobile on the highway that would kill. Dowie asked at the end of his article how long Ford Motor Company would have found it beneficial to leave the Pinto on the highway were Henry Ford II and Lee Iacocca serving twenty years in federal prison for homicide.

While the current number of lobbyists in Washington is down from previous years, in 2015 the total spending by the 11,514 active lobbyists was almost $3.22 billion.[79] Compare this number of lobbyists to the 50 U.S. Senators and 435 members of the U.S. House of Representatives, and that translates to about 24 lobbyists for every federal lawmaker. According to Professor Allan Cigler, "The growth of lobbying makes even worse than it is already the balance between those with resources and those without resources."[80]

What is your opinion of the often-used business principle of cost-benefit analysis? Compare the Ford Pinto matter to the British Petroleum (BP) oil rig explosion and oil spill in the Gulf of Mexico. Reportedly, criminal and civil investigations are being undertaken concerning BP.[81] What would you estimate the chances of criminal charges being issued against BP to be? What percentage of politicians do you think receive contributions from big oil companies like BP? Are lobbyists more restricted these days in terms of being able to influence politicians? Should they be? Should the law-making process be a concern of those who enforce the law (police officers) or apply the law (judges)? How many of you can name the representative from your home district in the U.S. Congress? How many chief executive officers can do so? How many people sleeping under bridges can?

Above the Law

William Chambliss, in an article entitled *State-Organized Crime*, depicts how governments can operate above the law—carrying out actions that if perpetrated by citizens would be considered criminal but operating as if the law does not apply to government officials.[82] This is particularly poignant considering that the United States has yet to sign on as a member nation of the International Criminal Court (ICC). The court was established in 2002 and could potentially prosecute war crimes. Over 100 countries have ratified the treaty establishing the court.[83]

Why might the United States not want to become a participating member nation of the ICC? Should actions by any government's officials, including the United States', be fair game for scrutiny and prosecution on the world stage?

Criminal Justice Theory

Lauren Morgan of Seattle University discusses "criminal justice theory," which expounds on elements of law enactment and enforcement and conflict and critical criminology, not on crime rates and causation so much. **Criminal Justice Theory** is an essential part of understanding the roles and functions of various sub-systems in the criminal justice field and for the overall knowledge of the ways policies and practices are guided by the criminal justice system.[84] The goal of criminal justice theory is to apply certain principles of police, courts, and corrections to underpinning theoretical concepts to engender meaningful discussion and actual deliberations on criminal justice interests and careers as opposed to the criminological theories which aim their focus primarily on crime and crime rates.[85] Kraska claims that numerous theoretical orientations are recognizable in the criminal justice field and that while all of the frameworks provide their distinct set of principles, each can be appropriate to explain policy and practice in their own right (2006).[86] *Theorizing Criminal Justice: Eight Essential Orientations* highlights eight theoretical orientations, which Kraska and Brent argue are habitually used in the criminal justice field (2011).[87] These orientations are as follows: rational-legalism, systems, crime control vs. due process, politics, the social-construction of reality, growth complex, oppression, and late-modernity. Within these eight frameworks, Kraska and Brent acknowledge that two are more obviously recognizable because the field has historically been preoccupied on the dialectic they create; namely systems and oppression orientations. The pressures created by the opposite views these two frameworks hold are commonplace in the criminal justice system. Each framework is acknowledged differently as a factor guiding certain practices in the criminal justice field, and each can be used to influence reform and policy implications for the future. Similar to conflict theory in criminology, the focus of these orientations is to highlight contemporary social conflict. For example, in the oppression view, the focus is on power and coercion, placing major emphasis on the role of social threat in the miscarriage of criminal justice laws and practices. Social threat refers to those who are viewed as minorities and consequently are treated as lesser with little power to refute their imperfect status; this can lead to criminalization and penalization by means of our laws and criminal justice practices.[88] I use the example of the drug war and mass incarceration to explain how each theoretical framework can be employed differently when attempting to make sense of criminal justice practice.

Rational-Legalism View:

From the rational-legalism view, criminal justice is centered on keeping people safe and secure from criminal "others."[89] Rooted in Beccaria's rational choice/deterrence model, this perspective suggests that criminal justice processes are based on the "rule of law" and that criminal justice policy should aim to punish criminals by preventing further harm to society and deterring other individuals from committing similar crimes. Using the rational-legalism view, the strict drugs laws resulting in mass incarceration were aimed to reduce crime and illegal activity. Based on this theory, individuals have rationally weighed the consequences of illegal drug crimes and understand the punishment (i.e., longs periods of incarceration).

Systems View:

The systems perspective steps back and views the criminal justice structure as a whole.[90] Therefore, the systems approach is a very macro-level analysis and looks at police, courts, and corrections as interrelated agencies that work together to create our criminal justice system. From this view, drug offenders respond to incarceration and harsher penalties more readily, and policy makers believe that prisons are an effective use of community resources and therefore a good use for those who have committed drug offenses.

Crime Control vs. Due Process View:

This approach looks at the criminal justice system as a pendulum that switches back and forth between crime control and due process depending on the government, era, and polity of the time.[91] This approach rests on what the government is currently defining as criminal behavior. Crime control emphasizes the reduction of crime and the due process model stresses the importance of protecting individuals from injustice. Mass incarceration swings towards the crime control model, where drug crimes are considered a major threat to the social order, the correction of the drug "problem" rests on administrative controls, and where to regain social order we must have high rates of apprehension and conviction.

Politics View:

Many argue that the politics theory is a significant way mass incarceration and the drug war came to the forefront.[92] The politics lens views criminal justice action from a political orientation generating interests to generate problems, conflict, and overall disorder leading to a need for change, new policy, and correction. Under this lens criminal justice practices can also be influenced by cultural, societal, and media factors, which shape political figures and their motives.[93] From this view, it can be noted that certain stances taken in regards to police, courts, and corrections are endorsed for gaining political wealth. Politicians will regularly blow up issues in crime control to gain political capital, and an exemplary example of this can be seen in the declaration of the war on drugs by Nixon in 1971.[94]

Social Constructionist View:

The social constructionist lens views criminal justice policy and practice as a socially constructed reality and consequently, these realities must be answered through crime control methods.[95] Through this lens reality is not viewed as a given but rather a made-up reality through the use of media, politics, symbols, and moral panics. Media reports of certain stories like that of basketball star Len Bias, who the media reported dying of a "crack death" and the reports of crack-addicted babies when there was no data confirming it is things that lead individuals to believe there is a problem and that it needs to be corrected.[96] The compelling rhetoric of harm and the effects of ignoring these issues are brought to light and subsequently policies and movements are enacted from these constructed problems.

Growth Complex View:

Under the growth complex orientation, the criminal justice system has the primary motive to follow self-serving schemas to maintain survival and economic growth.[97] According to this framework, incarcerating individuals at an increased rate will provide additional employment opportunities in correctional facilities and be beneficial to the growth of the prison industry.

Oppression View:

In the oppression framework, we look to disparities and historical functions of the criminal justice system to make sense of past and current behavior.[98] The oppression framework can be considered as a function of oppression, which formally means to press against, in regards to those of peripheral status in society (i.e., those of different race, gender, and societal backgrounds). The dramatic effects of mass incarceration are among us now and are centered on the "war on drugs" and "get tough" policies. These laws were aimed at minority groups and led to increased arrests and prosecutions for minor drug offenses. Many look at mass incarceration as the "re-racialization" of U.S. society and another attempt to oppress the minority group of African Americans, similar to what we saw during slavery and the Jim Crow laws.[99]

Late-Modernity View:

The late-modern orientation is more complex than the other orientations, including different characteristics that are synonymous with the previous frameworks. The late-modernity orientation looks at criminal justice actions through a larger, macro lens, incorporating the political, social, and cultural settings of an ever-changing society.[100] In his book *The Culture of Control: Crime and Social Order in Contemporary Society*, Garland emphasizes that criminal justice does not function entirely out of its own entity but as a reflection of the sociocultural order of "late modernity."[101] Therefore, mass incarceration and increasingly punitive drug laws would be the result of a crime control setting. The laws and policies constructed during and after the war on drugs were reflective of the cultural sensibilities of the time.

Contemporary Theories

Recent inquiries in terms of criminological theory and explanations for crime causation have focused on criminogenic risk factors, gender-based, life-course, and victimization assessments. For example, research has indicated that the more of these eight criminogenic risk factors (history of antisocial behavior; antisocial personality pattern; antisocial cognition; antisocial attitudes; family and/or marital discord; poor school or work performance; few leisure or recreation activities; substance abuse) one has, the more likely one is to have adverse encounters with the criminal justice system. Persons with mental illnesses tend to have more of the criminogenic risk factors than those without mental illnesses, increasing the likelihood of such contacts for them.[102] Gender theories have shed light on the male-dominated aspects of society and criminal justice. Particular emphasis has been placed on paternalism, sexism, and chivalry.[103] Life-course analyses recognize the ebb and flow of much criminal activity over life spans, as teens are prone to act out, with criminal activity typically peaking in late adolescence and declining over time.[104] (This approach will be discussed in more detail in Chapter 13 on juvenile justice.)

Pathways Perspectives: Theoretical Explanations for Female Criminality

Feminist scholars have argued that classical criminology theories and research have been male-centered. A more specific, gendered approach to crime explanations has been the motivation for conducting research, and a theoretical approach to understanding the causes of female offending has increasingly gained recognition, acceptance, and credibility in the literature over the past several decades.

Noted pioneer in the research examining female offending, Freda Adler (1975) contended that females increasingly committed crimes as their participation and equality in the workforce grew. According to Adler, women would have more opportunities to commit crimes as employment opportunities opened.[105] This approach as an explanation has come to be known as the liberation/emancipation hypothesis. Kathleen Daly has been regarded as a leader in this area of theoretical scholarship with her 1992 publication of "Women's Pathways to Felony Court: Feminist Theories of Lawbreaking and Problems of Representation." In this work Daly, outlined five pathways that led females into crime.[106] Women who left home at an early age, as a result of running away and/or being turned away by family, developed survival skills to meet their needs. Often, these skills involved criminal behaviors such as prostitution. Childhood victimization led some females to partake in drug use as a coping mechanism and resulted in violent behaviors. Her third typology involved battered women, who displayed violent behavior, often towards abusive partners. Drug-involved women were often introduced to offending associated behaviors through their relationships with males. Finally, women became economic offenders motivated by poverty. Until publication of this work, pathways perspectives had not been labeled as a criminological explanation.[107]

The works of Adler, Daly, and others created the foundations of pathway perspectives. In summation, pathways perspective contends that women's maltreatment, resulting from the social and environmental conditions of their existence, should be examined as contributing factors to their entry into crime. Furthermore, females experience these conditions differently from their male counterparts as a result of gendered experiences and opportunities from social structural conditions (i.e., economics).[108] A primary factor of the experiences of women, leading to "pathways" of criminal offending and for some, resulting in imprisonment, is rooted in life histories of various forms of abuse and trauma, which is suffered as a result of those victimizations and lack of power in their social and familial relationships and interactions.[109] Abuse is known to be connected to criminal offending in various ways. Notably, abuse creates a cycle of trauma, leading to street lives—including running away, prostitution, and introduction to drug use, and is often utilized as a coping mechanism to deal with past trauma manifesting itself in current situations. This, in turn, increases the likelihood of women and girls encountering the criminal justice system resulting from their engagement in criminal behaviors.

Contentions of economic marginalization, such as poverty, have been described to understand female involvement in property and work place crimes. Economic stress for women may result with the responsibilities of motherhood. Women may commit economic crimes in order the better support their children, to compensate for low-wage pay, and in some cases, as a result of pay inequalities in the workforce. Referring back to women's issues of substance abuse, economic and property crimes may be committed to support habits related to addictions.

Routine activities theory is a form of rational theory which is somewhat a return to the basic tenets of the Classical School and rational choice. Routine activities theory is a theory of victimization, whereby factors are analyzed to determine under what conditions persons are most likely to be victimized. The contention under the theory is that when suitable targets for victimization, motivated offenders, and a lack of capable guardians of persons or property are present, victimization is likely to occur.[110]

As we close this chapter, consider this headline regarding a Kansas bank robbery: "Sick of living with wife, Kansas man robs bank to go to jail." The perpetrator faced up to 20 years in prison.[111] Thus, **the first question is what is likely wrong with the headline regarding this case.** Secondly, **of the criminological theories discussed throughout this chapter, which one would you contend is most applicable to the circumstances depicted in the headline above?**

Summary

No doubt criminal justice decisions are made in the ideological context and theoretical framework of a democratic society and scientific insights. Whether consciously or not, each actor in the criminal justice network is influenced by that context and framework. The chapters that follow will demonstrate the close connections between theory and practice, the ways in which decision makers, often reliant upon the best science available, strive to live up to our ideals or fall short of doing so.

Chapter 3

The Criminal Justice Decision Network

Image by Jennifer Clark at fotolia.com.

"In the Halls of Justice, the only justice is in the halls."[1]

—Lenny Bruce

Seeking Justice

The many purposes of crime control in our democratic society, pursued within the ideological framework inherent in that democratic society, are addressed through a complex network of decisions made by people who work in criminal justice agencies. That network includes the legislature, appellate courts, chief executives, and the most visible actors, including police, prosecutors, judges, lawyers, juries, and corrections agencies. All criminal justice decisions are interrelated: police actions affect the courts and prisons, and court actions affect the prisons and the police, and prison actions affect both the police and the courts.

The individual regarding whom those decisions are made unifies the decisions into a network. Otherwise, each decision is made by a separate agency whose goals are often separate and sometimes conflicting.

About This Chapter

All the participants in the criminal justice decision network act with the authority of the law. Everyone connected with criminal justice, whatever their roles, are representatives of our government. None is a mere robot, of course, simply and automatically doing whatever state legislatures, Congress, or the Supreme Court orders. All can act with a certain amount of discretion and have the ability to choose among alternative actions in carrying out their jobs. We now examine the steps in the criminal justice process, where opportunities for employing discretion abound.

Steps in the Criminal Justice Process

The complexity of the criminal justice process does not make for a clear picture of a well-defined and manageable system. Criminal justice appears even more disorganized when viewed with its multiple objectives, but it becomes more clearly a system when its actual operation is traced. For the glue which holds it together is the **decision network** which transforms individuals from free citizens into suspects, then into defendants, into convicted offenders, into probationers, and into inmates or parolees, leading, in most instances, to their eventual discharge from sentence and their return to society. The full-scale network includes a number of major decisions made at different times by people in different agencies which link and flow into one another.

Investigation and Arrest

The criminal justice process normally begins when the police set out to **investigate crime**, either because they have received a report that a crime was committed or have observed suspicious behavior on their own. If they discover a crime has occurred, their next action is to determine who the violator was and decide whether to apprehend the individual. This is the **arrest decision**. After an arrest, the individual (now a suspect) is taken into **custody** and "booked," that is, the arrest is registered in a precinct house and the suspect fingerprinted and photographed. The next step, unless all vital information has already been obtained, is **in-custody investigation** which, among other things, may involve interrogation and can require the suspect to appear in a "line-up."

Initial Appearance

After the police have obtained sufficient evidence, the suspect is usually brought to a court for what is called the **initial appearance** before a magistrate. This is to be done "without unreasonable delay."[2] The judge is to make neutral and detached de-

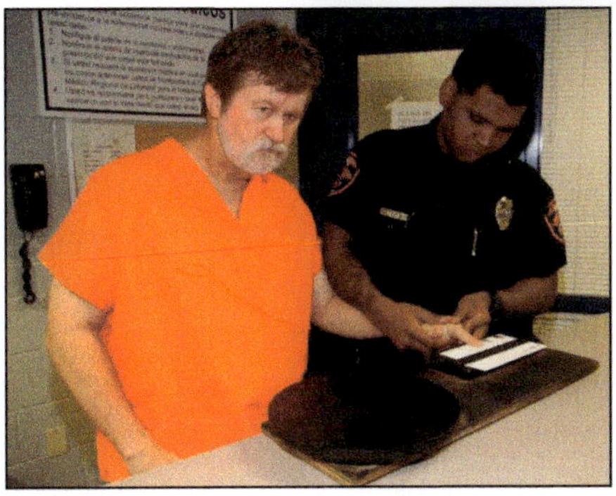

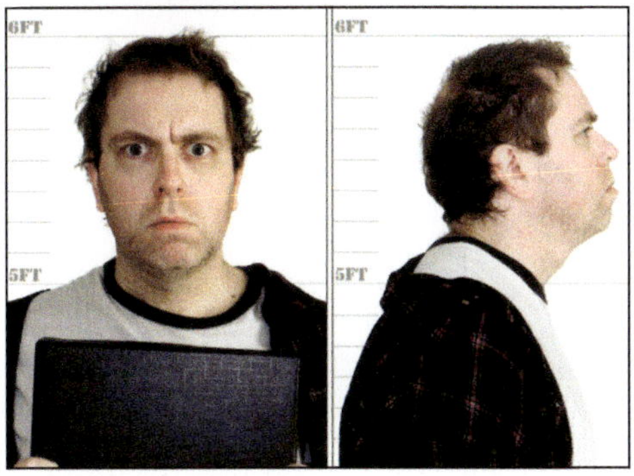

Image (bottom right) by upsidedowndog at istockphoto.com.

termination of whether probable cause exists that a crime was committed and that this person more than likely committed the crime. Many cases are resolved at this point as a result of guilty pleas, dismissals, or withdrawals of charges. If the judge is satisfied regarding the probability of the crime and the accused person's role in it, the question of release pending trial is faced. The judge can set a certain amount of bail or free the person on his or her word of honor to appear for later proceedings ("release on his or her own recognizance"). If the suspect posts bond or is released on recognizance, he or she is then free to return home until summoned for later proceedings.

At virtually all of the early decision points from arrest onward, the suspect has a right to a defense lawyer, provided at state expense if he or she cannot afford to pay for counsel. Prior to formal charges being filed, suspects do not have a right to an attorney at police show-ups or lineups. The popular television show *COPS* often depicts a suspect apprehended in the vicinity of a crime and taken by the police to the victim back at the scene of the crime, maybe in the back of a squad car with a flashlight in the suspect's face, for positive identification (*Kirby v. Illinois*, 1972).[3] This is an example of a show-up and will be discussed further in Chapter 5.

The Charging Decision

While the suspect is free on bail or waiting in jail, the police reports are passed on to the prosecutor, usually referred to as the district attorney or DA. The prosecutor decides as to the specific crime or crimes involved. This decision also involves how many charges to bring, since not infrequently an individual has been arrested for more than one offense. Sometimes a prosecutor decides not to charge any crime, perhaps because the evidence does not seem sufficient to result in conviction, or because the evidence obtained by the police was wrongfully seized and would likely be held inadmissible at trial, or, more rarely, simply because the DA does not wish to prosecute a particular kind of crime. Then the suspect is released from custody. But more commonly the district attorney decides to proceed with the prosecution and, depending upon the provisions in the jurisdiction, may bring a formal charge against the suspect, either via an information or grand jury (to be discussed in Chapter 8).

Arraignment

Once formally charged with a crime the defendant, accompanied by a lawyer, is brought before a court for **arraignment**, which is the point where the charges are read and the defendant is asked to plead to them. If the plea is not guilty, a time is set for the trial and once again bail is reconsidered or the defendant is returned to jail to await trial. If the plea is guilty and the court accepts it, the defendant is can be sent to jail to await sentencing, which may occur sometime after a presentence investigation is conducted by probation officers attached to the court. Sometimes special pleas, such as "not guilty by reason of insanity," are allowed, and the defendant is sent for a mental examination before being returned to the court for trial or sentencing or, if found insane, for commitment to a mental hospital.

Pre-Trial Motions

A number of motions may be entered, usually by the defense, prior to trial. These include motions for a change of venue, disclosure of evidence, a mental health examination of the defendant, and suppression of evidence. The judge's decisions regarding pretrial motions often are pivotal in the final outcome of a case.

Jury Selection

The prosecutor and defense attorneys have the opportunity to examine potential jurors and to either move to accept each juror, or move to challenge, or ask for the exclusion of a potential juror. The trial judge usually allots a certain number of "peremptory" challenges to each side, whereby a person can be excluded from the jury for any reason or no reason, or by the whim of the lawyer. Sometimes in high-profile cases, special jury consultants are hired to help lawyers make decisions about the makeup of a jury.

Trial

Trial judges rule on pretrial motions, make rulings on law, give instructions to juries, decide whether to sustain or overrule objections made by lawyers during testimony of witnesses or submission of evidence, and a great deal more. Defense must decide whether or not the defendant will take the stand to testify in his or her own defense. Prosecutors decide what order in which to present evidence and whether and to what extent to challenge defense motions or witnesses. Indeed, the trial is a complex playing field for strategic, legal, and emotional decision-making.

Sentencing

If the defendant is acquitted (found not guilty) at trial, he or she is freed, as long as there are no other charges pending. If convicted by trial or plea, the defendant (now an offender) is scheduled for sentencing. The judge may order a presentence report from probation officers, which provides a great deal of social, psychological, and financial information about the offender, as well as a victim impact statement, to assist in making a sentencing decision. The judge may hear whatever the offender or the offender's counsel wishes to say. The judge also ordinarily requests a sentence recommendation from the prosecutor. The judge then imposes a sentence on the convicted person.

While sentencing choices vary from one place to another, and from one crime to another, in general the judge may **fine** the offender a set amount of money, order the offender to perform a specified number of **community service** hours, or order **probation**, which is a sentence served in the community under supervision of a probation officer and subject to rules and conditions imposed by the court. The judge may order the offender incarcerated in a local **jail**, usually for a definite amount of time—30, 60, 90 days, 6 months, or any time up to 1 year. Or, the judge may impose incarceration in a **prison** for a term that may be defined by both a minimum and a maximum number of years, or if the law requires it, a mandatory sentence may be imposed.[4]

Prison, Parole, and "Good Time"

The maximum sentence, usually set by a judge at some point within a permissible outer limit fixed by legislation, is the date at which the inmate *must* be released from confinement, not on parole but as discharged from sentence. Inmates who serve their full term are said to "max-out" their sentence without supervision in the community. However, except for those serving short prison terms of 1 or 2 years, most persons (80%) are not mandatorily released from prison; instead they are conditionally released and must comply with rules while on supervised release.

Additionally, in almost all states (except for Hawaii, Montana, and Utah), inmates can earn time off the maximum sentence for good behavior, participation in programs, and, in some instances, automatically while serving their sentence. **"Good time"** provisions vary considerably from one state to another but, in general, these laws can substantially reduce the maximum sentence (and sometimes the minimum period for parole eligibility) of inmates who serve their sentences without causing disruptions in the prison or trouble by fighting, smuggling contraband, or otherwise violating prison regulations.[5]

The actual time served in prison by an inmate is determined through a complex series of decisions. An example might help to clarify this complexity. Assume that a statute provides a sentence of not more than 20 years in prison for an offender convicted of armed robbery. The same, or a related statute, allows the sentencing judge to set a court-imposed maximum at any point up to 20 years, but not beyond this limit. Simultaneously, the law provides that a minimum term may be fixed by the judge, usually at not more than one-third the imposed maximum. In a particular case a sentence of 3 to 10 years would appropriately fall within this penalty structure, which is the term the judge imposes. The sentenced robber could be paroled in 3 years or any time after that up to 10 years. He, or she, could also max-out at 10 years, having completed the full sentence. Good time statutes, however, may reduce the actual maximum by as much as 6 or 7 years so that if the inmate accumulates all possible good time credits, and is not paroled, release will be in 3 or 4 years. Thus the maximum legal sentence of 20 years is reduced by the judge to 10 years and further reduced by good time provisions to 3 or 4 years. Such sentencing schemas have induced many to call for "truth in sentencing" approaches.[6]

While this example may seem complicated, it is actually simple compared to what *could* happen. If parole were granted and later revoked or if some good time credits were disallowed because of misbehavior by the inmate, the calculation of time actually served would be considerably more complicated. And it could be still further tangled by the imposition of consecutive sentences for multiple crimes or a new sentence imposed upon the offender for a crime committed while on parole.

Probation Conditions and Revocation

Offenders can also be sentenced to **probation** outside jail or prison. Probation rules and conditions are fixed by the court. These are generally standard requirements that the probationer keep a curfew, avoid excessive drinking, not associate with known criminals, keep his or her whereabouts known to the probation officer, and otherwise behave in a law-abiding manner. Sometimes special conditions are imposed, such as requiring the offender to seek psychological help, to make restitution to victims, to submit to drug testing, or to carry out other tasks relevant to the particular case. Should the probationer violate any of these conditions (and, in many places, should he or she fail to "cooperate" with probation authorities), probationary status can be revoked by the court and incarceration imposed.

Prison Conditions

Convicted offenders sentenced to prison are classified according to their estimated escape risk, as well as according to whatever educational, vocational, or counseling needs they may have which can be delivered by in-prison services. Generally, both prisons and prisoners are classified in terms of maximum, medium, or minimum security, and many of the conditions of serving time are determined by these classifications: decisions in regard to which type of prison (maximum security, etc.) inmates will be sent to, what kinds of cells and jobs prisoners will be assigned to, and who will be allowed to visit them or send them mail. Some inmates may find themselves placed in minimum-security (the majority, in actual fact) work release or on farms. Other inmates are maintained in fenced, medium-security institutions involved in vocational training, while still others are housed in walled, gun-turreted fortress-like maximum-security prisons, working in such state-use industries as furniture manufacturing or the making of road signs.[7]

Release from Prison and Discharge from Sentence

The next major step in the criminal justice process is release from incarceration or successful completion of a designated period of probation supervision. As mentioned earlier, prison inmates are released in one of three ways: on parole (subject to rules, conditions, and supervision very similar to those imposed on probationers), upon completion of their maximum sentences, or upon completion of their maximum sentences less time off for good behavior. Probationers who successfully complete their terms of supervision and prisoners who max-out are **discharged from sentence** but, of course, still retain their criminal records, which will last all their lives.

Parole terms can be revoked and parolees returned to prison to complete their maximum sentences. In a number of states, supervision is also required of good time releasees, whose releases also may be revoked and the offenders returned to complete their maximum sentences.[8]

Though the criminal justice process ends for a particular offender when he or she is released from state control, a record of conviction and sentence remains, and the effects of that record may continue to be felt by the ex-offender throughout his or her life. While the specific restrictions may vary by jurisdiction and type of crime committed, in many jurisdictions persons convicted of a felony have their rights severely curtailed or even lose them. Examples of possible rights impacted include owning a gun, voting, serving on a jury, and working in certain occupations and professions.[9] Today some jurisdictions have procedures for **restoration of rights.** The ex-offender may apply to a court for such restoration, usually no sooner than five years after discharge from sentence. In some places, there are procedures for **"expunging,"** or erasing or wiping out, records of youthful offenders who have successfully completed sentences and remain law-abiding for a period of time. Restoration or expungement procedures vary and their success has been limited. Some negative aspects of having been convicted of a crime and having served a sentence may be diminished, but the record of having been a prisoner persists.

The decisions described above are made "under color of law." That is, legal authority exists for each decision point. We will now examine the sources of authority for those decisions.

Figure 3.1 The Criminal Justice System's Authority

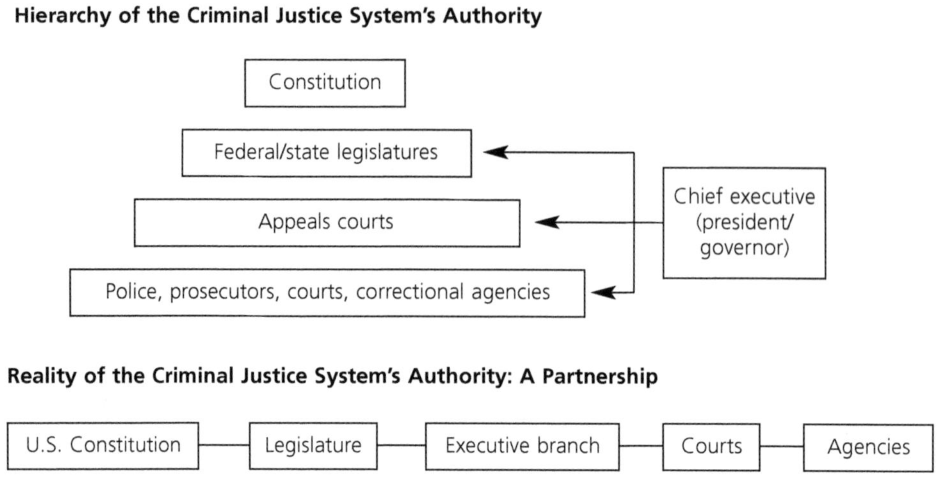

Source: Patrick R. Anderson and Donald J. Newman, *Introduction to Criminal Justice*, 6th ed. (New York: McGraw Hill, 1998), pp. 94–95.

Sources of Authority

Criminal justice decisions are not made in a vacuum—they do not reflect merely the whims of the decision maker. All crime control decisions, and all programs for crime control, rest on government authority. Above all else, the criminal justice system is a legal system. Its sources of authority may be found in the U.S. Constitution and in each of the major branches of our government: executive, legislative, and judicial.

The executive branch (the president, state governors, or city mayors) functions primarily to initiate legislation, appoint administrators, and propose budgets. Sometimes it has a more direct role in the criminal justice system, such as when it pardons prisoners or commutes sentences (that is, lessens them, whereby some inmates may even be released). The legislative branch defines crimes, and the judicial branch decides how the law should be applied. Various agencies in the criminal justice system—police, prosecutors, trial courts, probation offices, prisons, and parole authorities—administer this authority by enforcing the laws; they are in charge of the overall criminal justice process on a daily basis, and in that role are given some rule-making authority.

Traditionally, the criminal justice authority structure has been seen as a hierarchy. (See **Figure 3.1**.) At the very top is the U.S. Constitution. Next is the legislature, which defines crimes, subject to judicial review on constitutional grounds. Appeals courts come next, with the power to interpret and apply statutes to specific criminal cases brought by the operating (or "on-line") agencies. At the bottom of the hierarchy are the police, prosecutors, courts, and correctional agencies, which are expected to do no more than carry out what the legislature and the higher courts demand. In brief, power flows downward from the U.S. Constitution to the legislature which makes the laws, to the judicial branch which interprets them, and finally to the police and other agencies, which, in theory, have no discretion to ignore or modify written laws or court orders. In this model, the chief executive stands somewhere outside criminal justice, feeding ideas, programs, and appointive personnel into it, but chiefly acting indirectly as an influential political leader.

While this sort of hierarchical authority structure does exist, criminal justice actually operates in a more complex, less automatic way. The complete system of criminal law cannot be found simply by looking at statute books. Other parts—appeals courts and enforcement agencies—have lawmaking functions as well.

The usefulness of this mixed-power approach rests on the need to apply legislative language to actual street crime situations. All statutes are necessarily broad and general, whether defining a crime or permitting such procedures as search and trial. It is virtually impossible to provide written laws that cover all the variations of situations that arise. It is equally impossible to specify all the proper (or improper) actions of a police officer, who is constantly confronted with diverse and unpredictable street situations.

To understand how criminal justice works, the role and functions of all actors in the network must be understood. The major sources of authority—U.S. Constitution, legislatures, courts, and agencies—are mutual and simultaneous partners, although not always equal partners, in crime control efforts.

The U.S. Constitution

The U.S. Constitution is the basic document that gives authority to criminal justice agencies. It also sets the outer limits to their efforts, making sure that our system of crime control fits our form of government. However important the other authority pillars of our criminal justice network are, its bedrock is the U.S. Constitution—and, it should be noted, the constitutions of each of the fifty states. In a showdown, the U.S. Constitution takes precedence (with judicial review establishing the U.S. Supreme Court as the ultimate arbiter of constitutional disputes) but states have constitutions too, and most are consistent with the U.S. Constitution (although not always in each particular). Part of the history of our constitutional democracy has involved the long, painful process of conforming state constitutions to the federal document. Indeed, this very issue, the dominance of the federal Constitution over those enacted by each state, was one of the reasons that contributed to our fighting a very bloody war between the states.

In a real sense, criminal justice starts with the Constitution, as we shall see in some of the important Supreme Court cases. Criminal justice ends there as well, with the Court's interpretation and/or application of the Constitution to justice decisions. Various practices of law enforcement, trial court behavior, and prison treatment can be developed by the criminal justice agencies, but ultimately these practices are tested for **constitutional conformity**. If they do not conform, they must be changed: the U.S. Constitution, as interpreted by the U.S. Supreme Court, is the last word.

Legislative Functions

Legislatures exist at all levels of government, from the federal Congress to city councils. Defining crime is limited to Congress (United States Senate and United States House of Representatives), which enacts federal criminal laws, and to state legislatures, responsible for statewide criminal codes. County and city councils have limited authority to enact local **ordinances,**[10] which are civil violations, not crimes, although violators can be fined. City councils cannot define felonies or misdemeanors. Crimes must be illegal acts defined at least statewide. Therefore, in criminal justice terminology, **legislature** refers to Congress or to the state legislatures having crime-defining powers.

Definition of Criminal Conduct

As noted in Chapter 1, crime is what the legislature defines as crime; there are a multitude of influences on legislators, as seen in **Field Practice 3.1.** The primary legislative function is to define criminal conduct and some defenses to criminal charges such as insanity or entrapment. These crimes and defenses are written into laws called **statutes.** Statutes typically specify elements that distinguish different degrees of a crime. For instance, the amount of money stolen is used to distinguish grand from petit larceny. However, even the most specific statute must be interpreted as it applies, or does not apply, to individual cases. Even what seem to be precise definitions can prove to be inadequate in practical situations. For instance, statutes forbid carrying a concealed weapon. What is a weapon? Is a starter pistol a gun? The issue becomes much more complex with statutory definitions of the mental-state elements of crimes, such as "willful intent," "negligence," and "reckless disregard for life."

In spite of these difficulties, our criminal laws must be specific, and terms need to be **strictly construed** (that is, read just as written) by courts. Statutes that are not specific may, upon judicial review, be held unconstitutional on grounds of vagueness. It is an important principle in our society that all definitions of criminal conduct be clear so that everyone may know the limits of criminal law. Yet in many criminal codes there are offenses that are not precisely defined; these often include public-order misdemeanors such as vagrancy, loitering, and unlawful assembly. These are rarely challenged in court because they typically involve the poor and the homeless and because the penalties are less severe than the jail time those charged serve while awaiting trial. Such vague offenses pose tough enforcement problems, and many probably are unconstitutional on the grounds of vagueness. In recent years these and other "victimless" crimes have been frequent targets for legislative repeal.

Legislative attention to crime matters is not frequent, except in rare periods of total penal code revision. However, even after revision, most jurisdictions every year see some new crimes added to the penal code or old crimes modified in some way. There are numerous reasons for this. In some cases, the legislature is attempting to resolve conflicting court interpretations of crimes or defenses. In others, a new or overlooked or controversial form of misconduct may be brought to legislative attention, thus creating a new crime. By legislation or citizen-initiated ballot measures, as discussed in Chapter 1, various jurisdictions have, for example, sought and brought about the legalization of medical and recreational marijuana.

Field Practice 3.1 Crisis Driving Policy

The Influence of Politics, the Media, and Popular Culture on the Creation of Legislation

Example 1: The Matter of Carlie Brucia

Carlie Brucia was an 11-year-old who was abducted, raped, and murdered by Joseph P. Smith in Sarasota, Florida, in 2004. Her abduction by Smith was captured on a carwash surveillance camera. Smith was on state probation in Florida at the time for drug charges. He could have technically had his probation violated for failure to pay court costs associated with his conditions of probation, but he remained under probation in the community. After the abduction of Carlie Brucia, Smith was jailed on unrelated drug possession charges and subsequently charged, convicted, and sentenced to death for the murder of Carlie Brucia. In the media frenzy surrounding the case, U.S. Congresswoman Katherine Harris, gearing up for a run for the U.S. Senate, introduced federal legislation which she referred to as Carlie's Law. The essence of the proposed law was to expand the reasons for revoking federal probation and sending violators to prison. The law when passed only targeted sex offenders and did not focus on other felons who could violate their probation. Even had the law been in place at the time Joseph P. Smith's probation violation occurred prior to Carlie's abduction it would not have applied to him, because he was on state probation in Florida, not federal probation. The law when passed did not bear Carlie's name.[11]

Example 2: The Matter of Jessica Lunsford

John Couey was convicted for the abduction, rape, and murder of 9-year-old Jessica Lunsford. She was abducted by Couey from her bedroom in the trailer that she shared with her father and his parents. Her father, Mark Lunsford, reportedly after giving her a hug and a kiss to put her to bed, spent the evening at his girlfriend's home. Upon his return the next morning, he unlocked the back door and came in to find the alarm clock blaring in her room, but Jessica was gone. Upon checking with his own father and finding no answers about her whereabouts, Mark Lunsford checked the front door and found it and the screen door unlocked. He called 911. The pieces of the puzzle would begin to be assembled.

John Couey was a registered sex offender who had ditched his counseling sessions and relocated without notifying his parole officer. In fact, unknown to authorities, he lived very near the Lunsfords. Jessica's body would be found buried behind the house Couey lived in approximately 150 yards from Jessica's home. "Jessica was found wrapped in two black garbage bags and duct tape, sitting with her knees to her chest and holding the stuffed purple dolphin her father had won her at the state fair. Her hands were bound in front of her body with speaker wire. Two fingers poked a hole through the bags, scratching the sandy dirt that buried her alive."[12] Much media attention was drawn to the case, and Couey was ultimately convicted and sentenced to death, only to die from cancer while still in custody.[13] Mark Lunsford has become an outspoken proponent of combating sex offenders and legislation has been passed that still has an impact today.

While it is unclear whether John Couey ever met Jessica Lunsford at her school, he had done some construction work there in the past.[14] Under the media and public scrutiny the legislature acted to prevent similar tragedies in the future by passing Jessica's Law in Florida.[15] One of the provisions in the law provides that all school employees be fingerprinted and all persons contracted to do work on school premises have criminal background checks performed on them. Anyone with a conviction for a crime on a list of over 50 crimes under the law is forbidden from being on school grounds and coming into contact with children.[16] Included among the crimes are commission of a theft in excess of $3,000, any theft from someone 65 years old or older, dealing in stolen property, aggravated assault, and aggravated battery.[17] How long ago the crime was committed does not matter. Thus, a crime committed forty years ago in one's youth, such as a barroom fight, could be reason for dismissal. The costs of implementing the fingerprinting and background checks are roughly $60 per person. For example, one district estimated it would cost over $700,000 to comply with the law, and there are 66 other counties in Florida that must be in compliance as well.[18] Mark Lunsford's advocacy has contributed to similar laws being passed in over 30 states.

At the time, then-Florida Republican legislator and former prosecutor Mike Weinstein indicated, "The emotion and publicity and political science that comes into play after a horrific situation tends to create an overreaction." Jessica's death prompted cities and counties to implement barriers to sex offenders living and working near bus stops, churches, playgrounds, and schools. Five years after the death of Jessica Lunsford, registered sex offenders in Florida have increased almost 50 percent, yet the number of sexual offenses against children has been declining since the 1990s. While living restrictions have forced a number of sex offenders into homelessness, with dozens even being supervised while living under the Julia Tuttle Causeway in Miami, according to professor Jill Levenson, "[t]here is no empirical support that restrictions on where sex offenders live prevents sexual abuse or re-offending." In fact, Jennifer Dritt, Executive Director of the Florida Council Against Sexual Violence, has said "[m]ost sexual offenders are not strangers across the street. The overwhelming majority are those with familial authority." As noted by another Florida lawmaker, Rich Glorioso, "Sometimes we focus on where those people live." "Where they are sleeping last night really isn't the issue. It's what they are doing when they are awake." He plans to introduce legislation that would include a "circle of safety" in areas where children are present by requiring that sex offenders not be able to loiter within 300 feet of such locations. The legislator had also hoped to include a provision that would not permit locales to be more restrictive than the 1,000-feet barrier allowed under state law of keeping sex offenders from living and working where children are present. However, due to political pressure, he dropped that proviso.[19]

More recently, California's version of Jessica's Law came under attack for the residency requirement that sex offenders not live within 2,000 feet of any public or private park or school. The residency requirement was challenged as to whether or not such a provision violates constitutional protections concerning interstate travel and property. The California Supreme Court remanded that decision back to lower courts to determine such issues on a case-by-case basis.[20]

Determination of Appropriate Sentences

Legislatures react to particularly serious crimes, or perhaps to a so-called crime wave, by creating new statutes, increasing penalties for particular offenses, or both. For example, in recent years a number of state legislatures have increased penalties for driving while intoxicated and expanded scrutiny of sex offenders' activities on the Internet. Of course, unintended consequences sometimes result.

An important legislative function is to determine the appropriate sentences for crimes. Many recent code revisions have been undertaken because of the need to modify sentencing provisions, reconciling what often were clearly inequitable penalties.

The lawmaking function of legislatures is not always the rational procedure it is widely assumed to be. Legislators are first and foremost politicians who represent a wide variety of interests. They are often pressured by various political groups, lobbyists, and mail, including electronic mail, campaigns, and sometimes by public demonstrations. Although most legislative activity has little to do with crime and public interest in the revision of an insignificant statute may be minimal, the crime-defining (or -repealing) function occasionally becomes a hot political issue. Continued controversies regarding overturning the 1973 Supreme Court ruling legalizing abortion illustrate the intensity of public feeling and the political implications of each legislator's actions in connection with this question, as observed during passage of President Obama's healthcare bill when Congressman Bart Stupak was called "baby-killer" from the House floor by a fellow representative from another party.[21]

Expression of Public Morality

Many legislators feel duty-bound to express standards of public morality, even though they realize that laws that attempt to legislate morality are impossible to fully enforce. Many criminal codes contain proscriptions against adultery, fornication, and other consensual sexual conduct; public drunkenness; gambling; and other behavior deemed immoral. At best these laws can be enforced only loosely. In some cases, there may be no serious legislative intent that they be enforced at all. Why have these laws at all then? Many legislators evidently feel a political need to publicly take a vigorous stance now and then against what many pressure groups feel to be rampant immoral conduct. Also, despite the impossibility of full enforcement and the tacit understanding that full enforcement is not intended, these laws have a suppressant effect on behaviors that are not necessarily seen as criminal but are nonetheless discouraged by society. That is, the law makes a statement of moral standards and for many people it encourages (rewards) moral conformity, and may discourage engagement in such conduct simply because there is a law on the books against it.

Repeal of Laws

It is comparatively easy for a legislator to win passage of a statute establishing a new "crime" on the basis of high principle; it is very difficult to **repeal** such a law. A number of so-called **blue laws**, as discussed in Chapter 1, still exist in some states, sometimes because their repeal has been overlooked, but also because motions to repeal them may be politically damaging. Few legislators, for example, wish to be identified as supporters of adultery. It is true that a number of victimless crimes, primarily sexual misconduct statutes, have disappeared from legislation in recent years. But usually this was achieved by omission during total code revision, when the responsibility for repeal[22] did not attach to any single legislator, whereby potentially damaging floor debates over any particular activity is avoided. However, reasons exist in addition to fear of political retaliation for not repealing criminal laws, even ancient blue laws. The proliferation of criminal statutes can be advantageous to the state in providing the technical means for "getting" certain dangerous or notorious offenders who cannot be arrested for the worst of their crimes. This has been called the "**Al Capone theory of lawmaking,**"[23] because the famous mobster was successfully prosecuted for tax law violations when he could not be charged with more serious crimes, such as murder. Several decades ago Thurman W. Arnold wrote: "Substantive criminal law for the most part consists not in a set of rules to be enforced, but in an arsenal of weapons to be used against such persons as the police or prosecutors may deem to be a menace to public safety."

It is generally desirable for criminal laws to be worded precisely, not only to avoid a constitutional challenge on grounds of vagueness, but also to minimize uncertainty regarding arrest, charging, and adjudication decisions. Occasionally, however, legislation is drafted in deliberately ambiguous terms. One reason for this is the difficulty in specifying all possible varieties of conduct in certain crime categories. For example, few legislators doubt that sexual molestation of children is and must be considered a serious crime. The difficulty, however, arises in wording statutes to fully cover the range of conduct to be outlawed. Making "carnal knowledge and abuse of a minor" a felony leaves a great deal of interpretation to enforcement agencies and courts.

Another reason for occasional ambiguity is to prevent the introduction of technicalities, or "loopholes," by which serious or professional criminals can avoid prosecution. Gambling statutes in some jurisdictions are examples of this. Most often the legislature's purpose in outlawing gambling is to curb professional gambling or the bookmaking activities of organized criminals rather than to hinder neighborhood poker games or church bingo. To avoid the difficulty of distinguishing professional from amateur and friendly gambling, the statute may be written to forbid all gambling, with a tacit expectation that the law will be enforced sensibly—implying that enforcement officials will concentrate on bookies, numbers games, and other forms of professional gambling rather than poker games in the locker room of the country club.

Definition of Procedural Law

In addition to defining crimes and fixing penalties, legislatures also establish some criminal justice procedures. In most jurisdictions, statutes delimit the conditions under which arrests can be made with or without warrants, standards for the amount of force that may be used in making arrests, and requirements for using search warrants or wiretaps. Legislatures have been less precise in defining such procedures than in drafting substantive criminal laws. The basic reason is the nearly impossible task of spelling out in specific detail all the conditions necessary to cover the variety of enforcement situations confronted in the criminal justice system's daily operations. In most cases, no attempt is made to legislate specific conditions for arrest. Rather, the effort goes toward stating in general terms that the officers making the arrest must have probable cause or a reasonable belief that a felony has been committed and that the person being arrested is responsible for the act. Or, if the offense is a misdemeanor, the law may require that the arresting officer have witnessed the offense for an arrest to take place. Similarly, only such force as is necessary may be used to make an arrest, and warrants can be issued only on probable cause. The determination of probable cause or reasonableness is determined first by the police officer at the scene, then by litigation at the trial court level, and finally, if necessary, by appellate review.

Generally, legislative procedural laws have been limited to police activities and the trial court stages of the criminal justice process up to and including sentencing. Legislatures have done little about post-sentencing procedures, preferring instead to create correctional agencies and to delegate almost complete authority to them, subject only to constitutional restrictions against cruel and unusual punishment.

Some legislatures take a more active interest in all procedural matters, including those for processing inmates, probationers, and parolees. Similarly, there are statutes spelling out criteria for wiretaps, for preventive detention, for procedures to be followed in parole revocation, and for other operational decisions.

Budgetary Appropriations

Authorizing budgets for crime control efforts is a very important legislative function. Not only is this a power where legislative authority is supreme but, by granting or withholding funds, legislatures can limit the exercise of agency discretion. The director of a correctional system, for example, will find the ability to make changes in the agency largely a function of the budget for the agency approved by the legislature. The director may be powerless to make any modifications that cost money when funds are not allocated and, indeed, may be forced to cut existing programs when budgets are reduced.

Although legislatures become more liberal with funds when the crime problem assumes greater political significance, few agencies are adequately staffed and supported. One of the complex problems of budgeting is that some criminal justice agencies are locally autonomous, whereas others are statewide in their jurisdiction, and still others are federal. Local expenditures are primarily for police, county budgets support jails and courts, and state monies fund prison systems. Discrepancies in funding may exist within criminal justice because different legislative bodies with different tax bases are responsible for the monetary support of the different parts.

Other Powers of the Legislature

It is obvious that legislatures play an important part in criminal justice. Criminal justice starts with legislatures setting the limits of criminal justice intervention and providing the monetary support. Legislatures also have additional powers that impact on criminal justice. For example, the investigatory power of legislative committees is a function that occasionally assumes major significance.[24] And legislatures have impeachment power over certain criminal justice participants, although impeachment is a cumbersome and rarely used procedure.

Finally, the functions of legislatures vary from one place to another, and in some instances unique powers exist. For example, in South Carolina and Virginia the legislature elects state supreme court justices.[25] Legislatures may also have the authority to approve or reject executive appointments to courts and agencies.[26]

Executive Authority

The chief executive of any jurisdiction (the president of the United States, the governor of a state, and to a lesser extent the mayor of a city) has a number of important functions in criminal justice. Some executives become directly involved; others act in a subtle or indirect fashion, perhaps with equal effect. Executive functions fall into four major categories enabling the executive to:

1. *Appoint personnel*, including judges, boards and commissions, and directors of major criminal justice agencies.
2. *Introduce legislation*, requests for new programs, and submission of executive budgets.
3. *Direct intervention* into the criminal justice process through powers of pardon or commutation, the creation of investigatory commissions, the appointment of special prosecutors, and the removal of incompetent or corrupt officeholders.
4. *Give direction* to crime control efforts by proposal, persuasion, and skillful application of political pressure using the power and prestige of his or her office.

The effectiveness of the executive in shaping criminal justice depends in part on individual style and the extent of interest a particular individual holding the executive office shows in crime control matters. Some executives have strong opinions about certain issues, such as the death penalty, and may push vigorously to exert a personal influence on the legislature, the courts, and the agencies. This type of executive may propose sweeping legislative reforms to fulfill campaign promises, or may do so simply out of personal conviction. Another executive may exhibit a quite different style, allowing maximum legislative autonomy and waiting to react to legislation as it reaches his or her desk.

The function of the executive also varies according to the opportunities available, particularly with respect to the appointment of personnel. In some jurisdictions, the executive has no authority to appoint judges or prosecutors except on an interim basis because these are elective offices. In others, the chief executive may be able to appoint judges at all court levels as vacancies occur. And in some states, prosecuting attorneys[27] and public defenders[28] can be appointed by the governor. Similarly, the executive may be able to appoint parole board members, a police commissioner, a director of corrections, and perhaps even wardens and some lower-echelon personnel. In some states, however, agency heads or parole board members have civil service tenure or overlapping term appointments that can be filled by the executive only when vacancies occur by retirement or resignation or when terms expire.[29]

The governor may use pardon and commutation powers frequently in some jurisdictions, particularly where long sentences are commonly imposed. In others, the use of pardons may be rare, limited to a few "Christmas commutations" and exceptionally meritorious cases.[30]

One important function of executive power is the **veto**, an example of the checks and balances built into our system of government. Even if rarely used, the veto tends to restrain legislative excesses. The executive may veto any legislation, whether it deals with definitions of crime or fund allocations. Though the veto ultimately may be overridden (usually a two-thirds vote of the legislative bodies is required to do so), this is a difficult and cumbersome process, particularly if there is no single-party domination of the legislature. Vetoes have been overridden by legislative coalitions, but the threat of executive veto remains a potent force for influencing legislative deliberation. Its power is more than an inconvenient obstruction to easy passage of laws. The exercise of veto power usually attracts widespread publicity, crystallizing public support for or against the measure under consideration and thereby focusing political attention on individual legislators, who may find themselves pitting their own popularity against that of the president, a governor, or a mayor.

Appellate Court Authority

As noted previously, the relationship between appellate courts and legislatures has been long, stormy, and controversial. An important form of check and balance in our system of government is the power, derived from the **supremacy clause**[31] of the

U.S. Constitution, of judicial review to revoke legislation found to be unconstitutional. Thus, in constitutional matters, the Supreme Court is the highest authority in the land.[32]

Appellate courts do not conduct trials. They act only on appeals of lower-court decisions. The appellate process relies on the records of lower-court proceedings, responding to briefs submitted by petitioners and government lawyers. Higher courts normally do not deal directly with defendants, nor do they (except in very unusual cases) review the factual evidence brought out at trials. Instead, they decide points of law, determine the applicability of statutes to the particular cases in question, examine transcripts for prejudicial errors, re-examine denials of motions to suppress evidence, and so on. Appellate courts have the authority to reverse convictions or to remand cases back to the lower courts for retrial or other action.

All jurisdictions have levels of courts, topped by the supreme court of each state.[33] At the top of the nation's judicial system is the U.S. Supreme Court. A jurisdiction may have intermediate appellate courts (most commonly found in large states and in the federal system) that hear appeals arising from trial courts within a particular region of the state, encompassing a number of counties, or, in the federal system, appeals from district courts. The decisions of these intermediate courts can in turn be appealed to the supreme court of the jurisdiction and in some state cases even beyond this, rising eventually for potential review by the U.S. Supreme Court.[34]

Power to Select Cases for Review

The appellate process is complex and costly, particularly when a case appealed through state channels moves into the federal appellate process.[35] The right to appellate review of a lower-court holding is by no means automatic; sufficient arguments must be made to convince the appellate court that the appeal is "meritorious," i.e., that it is not based on frivolous claims. The U.S. Supreme Court has original jurisdiction (meaning a case may come directly to the Court without passing through a lower court) in limited circumstances.[36] The U.S. Supreme Court (and the supreme courts of some states), via discretionary review, has the power to select among the petitions it receives to determine those it will act on—it may decide not to consider a case at all. Once arrived at this level, a case is presented to the Supreme Court by a *writ of certiorari*—a request for review—and the Court may deny this review without giving reasons. Denial of *certiorari* may not mean the justices find the case lacks merit, but rather that they do not think its implications are broad enough to affect the law of the land; or denial may indicate that the Court does not wish to consider such matters at this time.[37]

Agency Authority

Each of the criminal justice agencies, those agencies engaged in day-to-day criminal justice operations, has rule-making powers and a good deal of independence in decision making too. The outer limits of police, prosecution, judicial, and correctional authority are set by legislation and modified by appellate courts, but within these boundaries the range of decision alternatives—the discretional power left to the agencies—is great indeed. In fact, such discretional power may be even more important than the impact of legislatures or appellate courts in determining what criminal justice is like in daily operation.

Legislative delegation is the most familiar source of discretionary authority. For example, it is usual for prison systems and parole boards to have broadly delegated authority over their functions. Often there is little legislative direction beyond the creation and funding for a department of corrections for the "care and treatment" of prisoners, and perhaps providing for a parole board given the power to "make rules and specify procedures for the release of inmates prior to the expiration of their terms."

Police Authority

Police comprise the largest component of the criminal justice network. In terms of both citizen and suspect contact, they are more directly involved than any other agency. And in most cases the criminal justice process begins with the police in a number of ways:

1. A complaint or call for help made to the police.
2. Routine police patrols, other forms of surveillance, and the stopping and questioning of suspicious people.
3. Police searches for violations, as in placing wiretaps on the phones of suspected gangsters or the use of undercover cops to investigate the drug subculture.

Yet with minor exceptions, police agencies have *no formally delegated or traditional discretion* with respect to enforcing criminal laws. In theory, the police have a mandate to equally and impartially enforce every criminal law, to keep the peace, search out crime, and, when evidence warrants, to take all violators into custody. But as every observer of police activity has pointed out, and as most citizens know, full enforcement is a myth. Selective enforcement is the rule. **Police discretion** (judgment as to alternatives in enforcement) is exercised by the police agencies as a whole and by each individual police officer. Reasons for police discretion range from community expectations of "sensible" enforcement to police efforts to achieve desired purposes without using the entire justice process—for example, simply disposing of a marijuana cigarette without further processing or warning rather than arresting those violating minor laws.

The specters of corruption and discrimination are present whenever discretion exists, but this potential misuse of authority is characteristic of all criminal justice decisions. Why does the myth of full police enforcement of laws continue to persist although the police themselves, courts, prosecutors, researchers, legal scholars, and many other people are aware of the discretionary way they use their power? The primary reason is that legislatures and courts have refused to sanction police discretion, which in turn puts police officials in a defensive position. Without an express delegation of authority, the police official who admits to discretionary practices is put in the untenable position of appearing to overrule the legislature and courts. Admitting to such practices also requires the police to confront the most complex and difficult task of all in criminal justice administration: defining, defending, and monitoring criteria for discretion.

Officially recognized or not, there is little doubt that the discretionary practices of police are critical to criminal justice. Some police departments attempt to develop policy guidelines for the exercise of discretion. In some instances, methods of monitoring officer discretion have been tested, for example, by requiring written reports of all citizen contacts whether or not they result in arrest. In general, however, without firm guidelines, the criteria for the actual exercise of police discretion remain obscure, resulting in what Professor Joseph Goldstein many years ago labeled a complex of "low-visibility" decisions.[38]

Prosecutor's Authority

The discretion of the prosecutor is probably as broad as that of any participant in criminal justice. It is noteworthy that this discretion is more often "recognized" than delegated by the legislature. The origin of the prosecutor's broad powers is in common law antecedents in both English and French legal history.[39] Regardless of its origins or antecedents, however, such discretion is intrinsic to the task of screening the hundreds of cases brought to prosecutorial attention each year.

Prosecutorial discretion is clearly broad in scope, ranging from the power of ***nolle prosequi*** (a decision to not prosecute and dismiss charges even after charges have been brought, sometimes abbreviated to *nol pros*) to the selection of specific charges to be leveled against any defendant. In some jurisdictions there are legislative attempts to develop appropriate checks on the DA's authority. This may be done by requiring written reasons for *nol pros* decisions or by requiring the district attorney to continue to prosecute once an indictment is issued. In general, however, checks on the wide discretionary authority of the prosecutor have been ineffective. In some states the attorney general may have some "supervisory" authority over local prosecutors or may have concurrent jurisdiction to prosecute, but this power to intervene is rarely used.

The prosecutorial process is really a series of decisions, ranging from deciding whether to prosecute at all to determining the number of and specific charges to be presented to a grand jury or a judge. Decisions not to prosecute are virtually uncontrollable, short of evidence of corruption or other forms of malfeasance on the part of the district attorney. Decisions to proceed to prosecution, however, are subject to screening by grand juries or judges via preliminary hearing and/or information. These procedures are designed to test whether there is probable cause to hold the defendant for trial and can serve as a check on the prosecutor's discretion.

The district attorney establishes broad enforcement and prosecutorial policies in addition to functioning as a decision maker in each individual case. For example, the police may notice that the prosecutor consistently dismisses bad check cases whenever restitution is made to the victim. In this manner, without directly saying so, the prosecutor establishes enforcement policies regarding such offenses. Why should the police bother to arrest anyone in such cases when it is known the prosecutor will refuse to charge? And the police may decide that proper police procedures need not be followed in certain cases if it is known the DA will overlook the use of improper procedures.

Prosecutors' policies may be stated explicitly, either in oral directives to chiefs of subdivisions or by memoranda distributed to all assistants. Policies issued in these ways may state standards for determining whether evidence is admissible at trial, the appropriate charges to be leveled in certain kinds of cases, or even procedures and guidelines for plea bargaining. Such discretion is justified and generally supported. Just because a crime has been committed, it does not follow that there must necessarily be a prosecution. The district attorney determines whether acts fall within the literal letter of the law and whether they should as a matter of public policy be prosecuted or not.

> Florida's '10-20-Life' law [was] a law that require[d] courts to impose a minimum sentence of 10 years, 20 years, or 25 years to life for certain felony convictions involving the use or attempted use of a firearm or destructive device.... Under the '10-20-life' law, courts must impose a:
>
> 1. 10-year prison sentence on anyone convicted of committing or attempting to commit any of the above felonies (with certain exceptions), while armed with a firearm or destructive device;
>
> 2. 20-year prison term if the accused fired the firearm; and
>
> 3. 25-year to life term if the accused discharged the firearm and killed or seriously hurt someone.[40]

Such a law is known as a mandatory-minimum and is aimed at limiting judicial discretion. The law has since been repealed, giving judges more leeway in sentencing. "The 2008 case of Orville Lee E. Wollard III of Davenport, is often cited by those who pushed for repeal. Mr. Wollard is serving 20 years in state prison for firing a warning shot inside his home to scare away his teenage daughter's unwelcome 17-year-old boyfriend; the shot was meant to scare the teen, and no one was hurt.... Wollard was convicted of aggravated assault with a firearm, and a judge had no choice but to throw the book at him." Loren Elliott (February 25, 2016) "Good Riddance to Bad Law, 10-20-Life," *Miami Herald.* Accessed May 2, 2017: http://www.miamiherald.com/opinion/editorials/article62557122.html.

However, to demonstrate the awesome discretion of prosecutors, consider the particulars of the following case from the same county, Polk, as Mr. Wollard, with the same elected prosecutor in charge.

A middle-aged married couple had a few too many drinks one night and got into a heated argument. The wife told her spouse, "I could kill you in your sleep." The husband drunkenly replied, "Well, why don't you do it now?" He then went and retrieved his loaded .22-caliber pistol and handed it to her. He stepped back a few paces, and she fired; missed him. Her second shot glanced off top of his ear and the bullet knocked him down on the floor. When he staggered to his feet, there was blood; he went into the bathroom to tend to his wound. Within moments, the police arrived as the result of a neighbor's call. The wife's booking information card reads "aggravated battery deadly weapon." Both the wife's charge and Mr. Wollard's constitute felonies to which 10-20-Life applied. In fact, the wife's charge of a battery is even worse, as a battery implies offensive touching, whereas assault is merely threatening. However, via prosecutorial discretion, the female pleaded to a lesser charge and was placed on probation. A prosecutor could well do what a judge could not. A prosecutor was not mandated by law to charge a person with a mandatory minimum crime, but, if the prosecutor did, judges were bound to follow the law.

Should prosecutors have more power than judges in such matters? What reasons can you think of for resolving the female's case in such a manner and not Mr. Wollard's? Is this an example of fair and equitable justice? Do you like the concept of mandatory minimums?

Of course, as is often the case with legal authority, once a general rule is declared, and exceptions to that rule can often be found. While prosecutors do seem to have unbridled discretion, their decisions do not always go unchecked. Certainly, an elected prosecutor can be voted out of office by the electorate if they are not satisfied with his or her work product. Also, consider the examples given in **Critical Thinking 3.1.**

Critical Thinking 3.1 Checking the Prosecutor's Discretion

District Attorney Mike Nifong, who was determined to have lied about withholding DNA evidence that could have assisted in exonerating three Duke University lacrosse players, was disbarred by a disciplinary panel. Nifong subsequently resigned from his prosecutorial role; he was sentenced to one out of a possible 30 days in jail.[41] Speculation is that Duke University settled with the three wrongly accused lacrosse players and that the total settlement may have exceeded $50 million.[42]

Following the fatal shooting of Michael Brown by Officer Darren Wilson in Ferguson, Missouri, over 115,000 signatures were collected in an online petition to remove the prosecutor from the potential criminal case regarding Wilson. Among the concerns were that the prosecutor was biased in favor of white police officers. It was even suggested that the governor, Jay Nixon, had the authority under a Missouri emergency powers statute to remove the prosecutor and replace him. However, the governor, even in the face of opposition, rioting, and looting, refused to do so.[43] **If you were Governor Nixon, would you have intervened in this situation?**

An elected state attorney (prosecutor), Aramis Ayala, in Orlando, Florida, publicly announced outside the Orange County Courthouse that she would not seek the death penalty in a high-profile case involving Markeith Loyd, who reportedly killed his pregnant ex-girlfriend and Orlando Police Lt. Debra Clayton. Furthermore, Ayala indicated that her office would not seek the death penalty in any case. Governor Rick Scott reassigned the *Loyd* case to another elected prosecutor in another circuit and has subsequently reassigned 22 more cases to that prosecutor's office. Scott's rationale is that the prosecutor is elected to uphold the laws of the state of Florida, and he expressed concern for the victims and their families. The governor used executive orders to reassign the cases. The matter has been litigated in the courts to determine if the governor has the legal authority for this intervention. Ayala filed a federal lawsuit contesting the governor's actions. Meanwhile, Governor Scott won the first battle in state court, as a judge refused to delay the transfer of cases to the other circuit. However, more than 100 law professors and legal experts questioned Governor Scott's authority.[44]

Should the Florida governor be able to legally intervene? Do you believe the governor would have done so if the announcement by Ayala had not been publicly made? What if she had been more discreet about her position?

The Florida Supreme Court ultimately determined that Governor Scott did have the authority to intervene, as the elected prosecutor was not adhering to the letter of the law by refusing carte blanche to seek the death penalty in any cases. Ayala has interpreted the decision by the Court to mean that she needs to make determinations on seeking the death penalty on a case-by-case basis. She, therefore, indicated that she will set up a commission made up of assistant state attorneys to review cases to see whether a death sentence should be pursued.[45] Obviously, any controversies regarding the process may end up back in court for resolution.

Trial Court as a Criminal Justice Agency

Although it has the title "court," in operational terms the trial court, presided over by a judge, is an agency for the processing of accused offenders and the sentencing of those convicted of criminal activities. In one sense, the police and the prosecutor move cases along the assembly line of justice and the court stamps individuals "convicted" and moves them along to the correctional agencies.

In addition to formal duties at trial and sentencing, a judge is responsible for court personnel, from clerks to possibly probation officers. Not only is the judge given *discretion by statute*, but he or she may also have the authority to *delegate discretion* to particular members of the court staff such as probation officers who conduct presentence investigations.

The legislative delegation of sentencing discretion to trial judges is normally quite specific. Except in those cases where statutes fix **mandatory sentences** (discussed previously) for certain crime (life imprisonment for first-degree murder, for example) or restrictive sentencing guidelines are in place, judges are usually granted the authority to choose among several sentencing alternatives. Generally, judges are delegated discretion to choose *types of sentences* (fines, probation, or imprisonment), to set some *conditions of sentences* (particularly rules of probation), and to fix minimum or maximum *lengths of prison sentences* within the outer limits set by statute via sentencing guidelines.

In making a finding of guilt or innocence at trial, the discretion of the judge is less liberal than at sentencing. At trial, it is assumed judges will rely on the impartial analyses of evidence and will arrive at their decisions on a purely professional basis using their skills as lawyers and jurists. Dismissals or acquittals on other than evidentiary grounds are not part of a judge's delegated powers, although in practice such things occasionally occur. Conviction on insufficient evidence is, of course, improper and subject to appellate reversal.

Relationships among Criminal Justice Agencies

Social scientists interested in studying complex organizations have argued that criminal justice is not a "system" at all because it has no core organization. Rather it is a series of processes by which people are passed through a series of separate agencies that, though related through the process, are structurally independent. In a traditional sense of "system," this is accurate. The agencies of crime control are indeed separate and distinct from one another, without the common organization chart usually found in industrial, military, and other large bureaucracies. Yet the term "criminal justice system" has come into general usage with a full awareness that it is different in a variety of ways from more traditional systems, complex organizations, or even administrative agencies.

The organization of criminal justice agencies differs from more traditional, "monolithic" complex organizations in at least six major dimensions:

1. Non-interchangeable personnel and absence of central authority
2. Separate, unrelated budgets
3. Differing jurisdictional boundaries
4. Separate labor pools, with personnel in each agency recruited from different professions or occupations
5. Differing patterns of personnel selection from one agency to another (and sometimes between the same type of agency in different jurisdictions)
6. Variations in the amount of citizen involvement in agency decision making

Some of the major conflicts in crime control can be attributed to these variations in the way agencies are organized, funded, and staffed. And rooted in this structure, or lack of it, are a number of problems that tend to obstruct easy changes or improvements. But this is not the whole story.

Another way to depict the criminal justice process is as an ever-narrowing funnel which screens offenders, as depicted in Chapter 1. Each agency of criminal justice is connected by decisions made in a specific crime event. Out of the large, unknown mass of crimes, some are brought to police attention either through police initiative or, more likely, through citizen reports and complaints. Then, of those crimes known to the police, a lesser number result in an arrest. Following that, fewer still are prosecuted, an even lesser number are convicted, and finally a yet smaller number are incarcerated. The actions of the prosecutor, necessarily, depend on actions taken by police. Corrections agencies are totally dependent on both police and court actions. So, each agency is autonomous, but each also is connected to the others.

Social Values Served by Variations in Criminal Justice Organization

The hodgepodge structure and diverse staffing patterns of criminal justice agencies compound inefficiency, create stresses and tensions in and between those agencies, and make it difficult to suggest workable reforms. From the standpoint of efficiency, it would be more businesslike to merge all the agencies and offices into a unified whole, perhaps even to "federalize" all police, prosecutors, judges, and correctional services, and to set common personnel standards and requirements.

Yet efficiency is only one goal of our criminal justice system. Just as the governmental separation of the powers of the legislative, judicial, and executive branches supports our political philosophy of pluralism and freedom, so the mixture of agency organizations and personnel standards serves certain other values that we espouse as well.

At best, we give reluctant support to crime control efforts because we must. We want safety and domestic order, but we also fear the enforcement power of the state and wish to maintain a degree of community control over the way the law is administered. As attractive as a federally controlled criminal justice system may appear from an efficiency viewpoint, any proposals in this direction tend to conflict with preferences for home rule and local autonomy in the staffing and funding of agencies.

Likewise, the professionalization of criminal justice roles requires the removal of some jobs from patronage. If newly elected or appointed agency administrators replace personnel with their own close associates or supporters, without the neutrality of civil service protection or standards of professionalism and experience, justice decisions become suspect.

The differences in jurisdictions, budgets, methods of role selection, and degrees of lay involvement in agencies serve multiple purposes. The principle of home rule is maintained by the local staffing patterns used in the selection of most police officers, prosecutors, and judges. But centralism exists in prison systems, where problems are beyond the coping capacity of local jurisdictions. Most prosecutors, judges, and chief executives are chosen by ballot. But educational prerequisites and competitive examinations remove incumbents from direct political whim or threat. Juries continue to function and lay police volunteers are useful, but the trend toward professionalism goes on. The result is a mixture of lay and expert decision makers across the criminal justice process, in some instances working side by side in a single agency.

A careful analysis of criminal justice clearly shows that its basic structure, cumbersome and inefficient though it may be, nevertheless serves values that are central to a democratic society. A more uniform, better organized system would probably be achieved only by diminishing citizen control and forfeiting local autonomy and some individual rights. We are evidently unwilling to pay this price, in part because there is no assurance that a single, national criminal justice system would be more effective, nor that it would necessarily be more honest and just. We view with deep suspicion centralized police power—by which we mean the authority of all criminal justice agencies to compel conformity. And while we recognize the need for police, courts, and prisons, we have too many historical and contemporary examples of totalitarian police states to relinquish altogether the checks and balances that exist on that power in this country. The complex relationships among criminal justice agencies and the separation of sources of power may not be perfect from any single perspective, but these arrangements serve many different ideals, each in its own way fitting notions of a proper form of justice for our society.

Summary

Each major branch of our government contributes to the crime control effort. The U.S. Constitution is our most fundamental source of criminal justice authority. Federal and state legislatures create substantive and procedural criminal law and approve budgetary appropriations for the fight against crime. Occasionally legislators are called upon to investigate, impeach, and try public officials accused of crimes while in office. The executive branch (headed by the U.S. president, state governors, or city mayors) contributes to crime control by nominating officials or groups to positions in the criminal justice decision network, by introducing proposals for new legislation to deal with crime and criminal justice, and by exercising the power to commute sentences or to pardon prisoners. The judicial branch accepts pleas, conducts trials, and decides disputed points of law and the constitutionality of statutes. The judiciary also sentences criminals within legislative limits. The administrative agencies of the criminal justice system (police, prosecutors, trial courts, prisons, etc.) conduct the day-to-day operations of the criminal justice decision network and therefore have wide discretionary powers.

This chapter deals with the relative independence each criminal justice agency has in regard to the others. There is no common hierarchical link or command among them so that, except indirectly, neither a judge, nor a prosecutor, nor a prison warden can tell the police what to do or not to do, and vice versa. In short, there is no operational boss of the criminal justice decision network as a whole—no person, office, or commission to oversee the entire process. Legislatures can commit or withhold criminal justice agency funds, appellate courts can overrule lower-court decisions, trial judges can acquit suspects and bawl police out for not getting proper evidence. But the parts of the criminal justice decision network do not make up a unitary whole, like branches of a corporation or units in a military organization. The criminal justice agencies are separate entities with separate budgets and distinct jurisdictional boundaries. In addition, each agency recruits, trains, and promotes its personnel differently, and the amount of citizen input or participation varies with different agencies and at different stages of the criminal justice process.

Each official within criminal justice has a certain amount of discretionary power, that is, the power to decide between alternative courses of action. Control and regulation of discretionary practices is one of the most important problems in criminal justice administration.

We now turn to the evolution of policing in American society. Various eras of American policing will be discussed, as will innovative developments and organizational solutions.

Chapter 4

Policing in American Society

Image courtesy of Tampa Police Department.

"Justice Oliver Wendell Holmes, Jr. said that no formulation of legal rules, in the criminal law or elsewhere, can be effective to the degree that it is at cross-purposes with the beliefs and expectations of the community. But one difficulty in applying this standard lies in the accurate identification of what the prevailing consensus of those beliefs and expectations is."[1]

Seeking Justice

Contained within this chapter is a discussion of how issues of race and justice have been handled historically. The intersection of American history and racial conflicts with authorities remain evident today. This is reflected in the discussion that follows.

When Do Black Lives Matter?
Statement from a Police Administrator

American history is full of events that have changed the direction of our country. One of those such events occurred on February 26, 2012, when a self-proclaimed neighborhood watchman shot and killed an unarmed teenager who was walking through a neighborhood. The killing of Trayvon Martin by George Zimmerman would set in motion the founding of the Black Lives Matter (BLM) movement. Ironically, the BLM movement would get started due to the actions of a private citizen and not a law enforcement officer. Many people may not realize this as the sole focus of the BLM movement seems to focus on interactions between law enforcement officers and African Americans. When I first heard about the BLM movement I was hopeful that those involved would focus on all black lives and not just those lost in encounters with law enforcement officers.

As an African American who served as president of a local branch of the NAACP and as a peace officer, I have seen my share of black lives taken. I was hopeful that the movement would live up to its name. Unfortunately, it seems as though the BLM movement is only focused on those black lives that are lost during encounters with law enforcement and not those lost in our urban centers. I have seen highways, interstates, and city streets shut down by those supportive of the BLM movement after a black life has been lost as the result of an encounter with law enforcement. I have yet to see this occur when a black life is lost during urban street violence—even in instances where infants or toddlers are killed. So I ask the question, when do Black Lives Matter?

The BLM movement will be around for a while I predict and those in the majority community should not be dismissive of the issues that prompted the formulation of the movement. As our country continues to diversify, we will have to confront challenges around the issues of race. If we are to thrive as a nation, we must meet these challenges head on and overcome them.[2]

Image by Nikola Nastasic at istockphoto.com.

In addition to the cost from damages allegedly brought on by BLM demonstrators discussed in Chapter 1, former Chicago Superintendent of Police, Garry McCarthy, has gone further by maintaining that the BLM group has actually contributed to more black deaths by preventing the police from doing their job.[3] "The bulk of the deaths and shooting incidents, which jumped from 2,426 in 2015 to 3,550 [in 2016], occurred in ... all poor and predominantly black areas where gangs are most active."[4]

> "McCarthy was superintendent at the time of the 2014 death of Laquan McDonald, a 17-year-old who was shot by police. Dashboard camera footage of McDonald's death contradicted the officers' accounts of the incident, which contended that McDonald had come at them with a knife. The resulting protests after the footage was released helped to fuel the then-growing Black Lives Matter movement. An officer in the shooting has been charged with murder. McCarthy was fired by Mayor Rahm Emanuel earlier this year."[5]

The statement from the Black Lives Matter website http://blacklivesmatter.com/ about the movement contends,

> "Black Lives Matter is a unique contribution that goes beyond extrajudicial killings of Black people by police and vigilantes. It goes beyond the narrow nationalism that can be prevalent within some Black communities, which merely call on Black people to love Black, live Black and buy Black, keeping straight cis Black men in the front of the movement while our sisters, queer and **trans** and **disabled** folk take up roles in the background or not at all. Black Lives Matter affirms the lives of Black queer and trans folks, disabled folks, **Black undocumented folks**, folks with **records**, **women** and **all Black lives** along the gender spectrum. It centers those that have been marginalized within Black liberation movements. It is a tactic to (re)build the Black liberation movement."[6]

Of course, what continues to primarily thrust BLM into the media spotlight are protests and demonstrations regarding contentious interactions between blacks and law enforcement. In 2016, 135 law enforcement officers reportedly suffered line-of-duty deaths, with almost half of these officers being shot and killed and 21 of them murdered in ambush-style shootings like the one in Dallas.[7] Furthermore, 34 police canines lost their lives while on duty in 2016 as well.[8]

In fact, BLM released a statement on their website about the police officers shot and killed in Dallas. The message indicated,

> In the last few days, this country witnessed the recorded murders of Alton Sterling and Philando Castile at the hands of police, the latest victims in this country's failed policing system. As we have done for decades, we marched and protested to highlight the urgent need to transform policing in America, to call for justice, transparency and accountability, and to demand that Black Lives Matter.
>
> In Dallas, many gathered to do the same, joining in a day of action with friends, family, and co-workers. Their efforts were cut short when a lone gunman targeted and attacked 11 police officers, killing five. This is a tragedy—both for those who have been impacted by yesterday's attack and

Black Lives Matter.

> for our democracy. There are some who would use these events to stifle a movement for change and quicken the demise of a vibrant discourse on the human rights of Black Americans. We should reject all of this. Black activists have raised the call for an end to violence, not an escalation of it. Yesterday's attack was the result of the actions of a lone gunman. To assign the actions of one person to an entire movement is dangerous and irresponsible. We continue our efforts to bring about a better world for all of us.[9]

A review of the Black Lives Matter website and Facebook page reveals a who's who list of perceived injustices, in addition to Sterling and Castile, indicated above, represented by the handling of: Trayvon Martin, Freddie Gray, Walter Scott, Sandra Bland, Eric Garner, Joyce Curnell, and Dontay Ivy, to name a few. As of July 1, 2015, according to the U.S. Census Bureau, the demographic makeup by race in this country was 77.1% white, 13.3% black, and 17.6% Hispanic.[10] However, the number of fatal shootings by the police in terms of race of the civilians shot and killed has been disproportionate to their make-up in the population as reflected in recent data. In 2015, of the 991 fatal shootings by police, 49.9% of those killed by police were white, 26% were black, and 17.3% were Hispanic. Similarly, in 2016, 963 persons were fatally shot by police, and 48.2% of those victims were white, 24.1% were black, and 16.6% were Hispanic.[11] Furthermore, approximately 25% of those killed by police in both 2015 and 2016 were identified as having a mental illness.

Such disparities, as reflected above, have led to questioning perceived injustices within the justice system. Some make the argument in response to Black Lives Matter that "all lives matter." However, Carla Shedd of Columbia University maintains that such an approach can actually be racist, and Texas A&M sociology professor Joe Feagin argues such a slogan serves to "ignore the black lives movement."[12] As reflected on the Black Lives Matter Facebook page, "If I say my house is on fire and you say 'all houses matter,' well that may be true, but all houses aren't on fire right now. My house is."

Some police departments are expanding their community outreach to be inclusive of Black Lives Matter groups. Wichita police planned and successfully carried out a barbeque with BLM members.[13]

What are your thoughts on the Black Lives Matter Movement and its interaction with law enforcement and the justice system? In 2016, civilians were seven times more likely to be killed by police than civilians were likely to kill police officers. Any death by force is tragic. Who are the persons named above as part of the rallying cry for the Black Lives Movement? Should police be held to a higher standard than citizens?

About This Chapter

How did the police come to be, and what is the legacy of American policing? What techniques do police traditionally employ to handle citizen complaints? Can police departments be better organized so as to better serve the public and solve crime-related problems? This chapter attempts to answer these questions.

History of the Police

Many of our perceptions of how police functioned in the past and even today have been created by novels, television, and the movies. Many of us recognize *Training Day*, *True Detective*, *CSI*, *Criminal Minds*, *Crime and Punishment*, *The Shield*, *Blue Bloods*, and *Law and Order: Special Victims Unit* as representing stereotypes of various stages of police development. Yet what the police *actually* do and what they are properly expected to accomplish in American society often differs significantly from these popular representations.

Most of us have had dealings with the police. We have called on them for assistance, received a speeding ticket, or perhaps we have been arrested. And, depending on the nature of our personal experiences with them, each of us has formed opinions about the police. Although the cowboy sheriff, the FBI agent, or the big city TV cops color our understanding, we need to acknowledge the fictional nature of much of the popular depiction of American police. Indeed, before we can understand policing in America, we must understand its history. In many ways the current structure and practice of police may be traced to various stages of development in the past.

English Antecedents

Policing as we know it did not originate in America. Like much of our common law tradition, many of our modern police practices had their origins in early English history. Before the Norman Conquest (in 1066) there were no police *per se*. Every citizen was held responsible for aiding neighbors who might be plagued by outlaws and thieves. This was known as the **pledge** system. People were pledged to help protect their neighbors, and in turn their neighbors were pledged to help protect them.[14]

In early England, ten families (called a **tithing**) were bound together by the pledge, each promising to cooperate in policing their own problems. Ten tithings were grouped into a **hundred**, directed by a **constable** (appointed by the local nobleman) who, in effect, became the first police officer, that is, the first official with law enforcement responsibility greater than simply helping neighbors.

Just as the tithings were grouped into hundreds, after nearly a century the hundreds were grouped into **shires**, which were similar to our counties. For each shire the king appointed a supervisor, whose duty was to ensure that order would be kept. The supervisor was known as a **shire reeve** and was the forerunner of our modern **sheriff.**

A century later (in the 1300s), a **watch system** was created to protect the larger cities and towns. Appointed night watchmen patrolled the cities at night to be on the lookout for thieves and disturbances and to act as fire watches. Theoretically, all male residents were to take their turns as unpaid watchmen. However, the affluent were able to pay others to perform the service. These watchmen reported to the constable, who became the central law enforcement officer.

In the early 1300s, the office of justice of the peace was created to assist the shire reeve in controlling his territory. The local constable and the shire reeve became assistants to the justice of the peace, supervised the night watchmen, served warrants, and took prisoners into custody for appearance before justice of the peace courts. This was the first formal relationship between the police and the judiciary and this system continues to the present day.[15]

Originally constables were appointed from the gentry, and the position was more or less honorary. Since constables could not function solely on their own, they hired assistants. The constables' assistants became the first paid police officers. By the seventeenth century, a combination of night watchmen, constables and their assistants, and justices of the peace made up the first criminal justice system. Then as now, the sheriff functioned as the chief enforcement officer in rural areas and small towns.[16]

Henry Fielding is credited with establishing the **Bow Street Runners** in the mid-1700s. He served as a magistrate on Bow Street and established ties with community pawnbrokers. He created a network whereby pawnbrokers would report to him receipt of stolen property, and he and his investigators (runners) would track down the thieves and return the property to its rightful owners. Fielding is credited as having created the first official crime reports. In 1798, Patrick Coloquhoun, a London magistrate, created what some consider to be England's first civil police department. It was modeled after the Bow Street Runners and was publicly financed to patrol the Thames River.[17]

With the industrial revolution came the first large cities (built around the factories) throughout England. For the first time congested, urban populations required more sophisticated policing activities than could be provided by a constable and watchman. In 1829, the British Home Secretary **Sir Robert Peel** organized the first metropolitan police force in London. This force was composed of over one thousand men and was structured along semi-military lines. Orders originated at the top of the organization and were passed down through a chain of command. Standard procedures were established and standards of behavior were imposed.

For the first time, police officers in England wore uniforms but were not, and generally still are not, armed. These early police were directed by two judges who eventually came to be known as "commissioners." Police officers in England are still called "Bobbies" in honor of Sir Robert Peel, although in Peel's lifetime the term was a derogatory one stemming from the British suspicion of police intrusion on their privacy. Indeed, so much resistance to the new police presence existed that those early police officers were required to adhere to rigorous standards of personal behavior and appearance. Peel's experiment in London was so successful in combating crime that by 1856 every borough and shire (county) in England was required to form its own police force.[18]

The Beginnings of American Police

The history of police in the United States is incoherent and nonlinear.[19] Our Founding Fathers evidently feared a strong, centralized police apparatus more than they feared crime, for by leaving policing to local governments they guaranteed that police would be dispersed, unorganized, and ineffective.[20] To a great extent, colonial America's policing followed the British model. The county sheriff was the most important law enforcement agent as long as the colonies remained small and primarily rural. The sheriff had many duties other than apprehending criminals. In fact, at first sheriffs had no patrol function, but acted only upon complaints of citizens. Sheriffs were paid by a **fee system**, that is, they were given a fixed amount for every arrest made or subpoena served and for each court appearance. The primary function of sheriffs was tax collecting, rather than law enforcement, and since the sheriffs received higher fees based on the taxes they collected, law enforcement was not one of their primary concerns.

In some areas a **town marshal** was named, who often called on **vigilante** groups (or "posses") to assist him in his law enforcement duties. But as cities grew, marshals and posses found it increasingly difficult to enforce the law effectively. Police became more highly organized only with the emergence of major cities in the eastern part of the United States.

The history of American policing is typically traced through three stages: the **political era**, in which police represented local politicians who put them in power; the **reform** or **professional era** (includes **incident-driven policing**—in which police emphasized patrol and responses to calls for police action) whereby police came under broad public scrutiny and many abuses were uncovered and addressed; and the **community problem-solving era**, a contemporary direction for policing, in which police became more proactive, addressing the root causes of crime rather than only responding to incidents of crime.[21]

The effects of **race**—especially slavery, segregation, and discrimination—in the American police legacy must be understood.[22] No history of the police can be useful in understanding the present state of American policing, nor help in objectively assessing the profession's future directions, without acknowledging its racist influences.[23] We will describe the three primary developmental stages of police work in the United States in this chapter (see **Figure 4.1**), but we will also include the important issue of race.

Figure 4.1 The Evolution of American Police

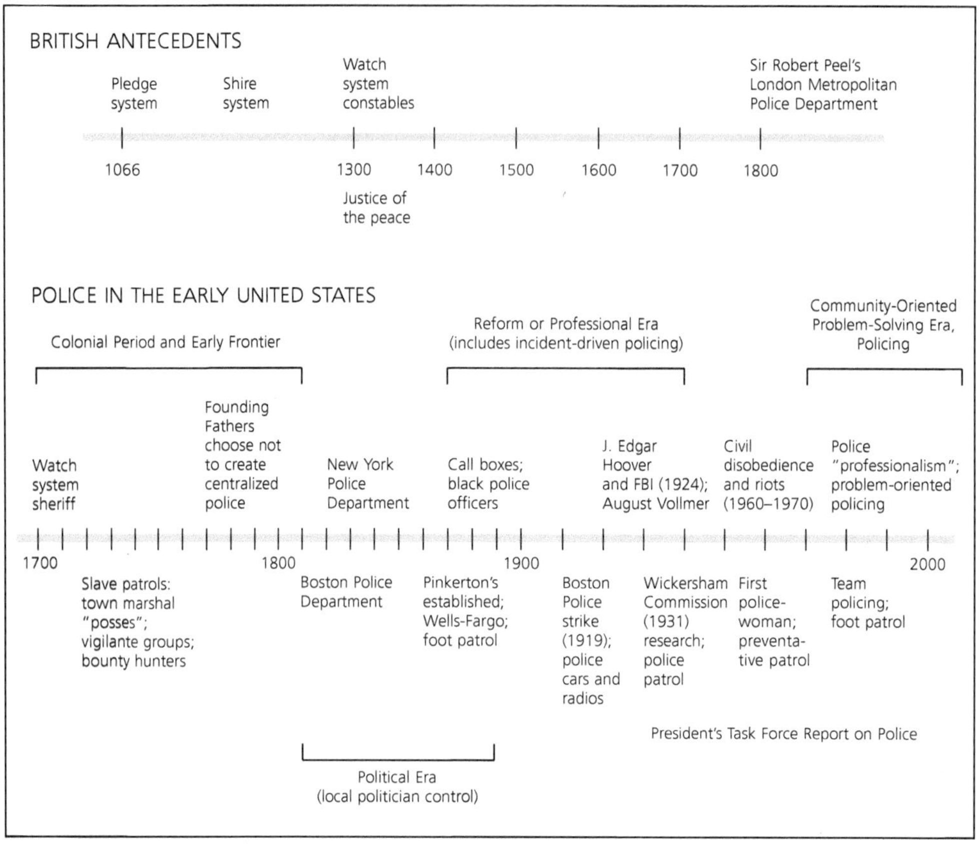

Source: Patrick R. Anderson and Donald J. Newman, *Introduction to Criminal Justice*, 6th ed. (New York: McGraw Hill, 1998), p. 121.

The Political Era

As the thirteen American colonies developed independently, and then as additional states were added, each area developed its police organizations without a clear national model for police. For instance, police in Louisiana, which were greatly influenced by French culture, developed distinctly from police in the Southwest, and both were different from police in northern cities.

Geography, and the cultural influences unique to each geographic area, resulted in some differences. But the political structures in various areas became a dominant influence. American police in the nineteenth century represented the local politicians who placed them in power and gave them their resources and authority. Those local politicians were uniformly male and white. This segment of American policing is referred to as the **political era** and roughly covers the time period from 1840 to the early 1900s.

Northern Cities

The political era was most clearly evident in America's northern cities that developed rapidly around industries. Immigrant workers, freed slaves, and poor whites from the South came to the cities in search of work and better lives. Poverty, pollution, substandard and crowded housing, and traffic congestion led to disorganization and crime. The many problems of fast-growing cities created a need for order, control, and law.

In northern cities, the local **ward boss** and the local political machine recruited police. As representatives of the local political powers, the police provided a variety of services to citizens such as collecting garbage, operating soup lines, and finding work and lodging for recent immigrants. And, importantly, the police helped the local politicians maintain their positions by encouraging citizens to vote for them, discouraging any opposition or any voting for opposition candidates, and occasionally even rigging elections. If new local politicians were elected, the police were replaced as well. Cities were divided into precincts and each police precinct operated autonomously under the direction of the ward leaders. Precincts hired, fired, managed, and deployed personnel, usually on foot patrols (walking a beat), and in this decentralized fashion responded to the demands of local citizens.

This is not to say that the police in America's northern cities in the nineteenth century did not work to prevent crime and maintain order—they did both. While on foot patrol, they handled disorderly conduct and other minor problems as well as responded to more major crimes. While on patrol they were often alone, cut off from communication with other officers and without supervision. Unfortunately, although police worked at close quarters with the community and provided many useful services to its members, the lack of supervision sometimes led to corrupt practices such as taking bribes and frequently led to racial discrimination and violence. Night sticks were used to enforce "curbstone justice," while the image of the bungling *Keystone Kops* often fit the reality.[24]

Boston created the first "professional" police department in 1838, and New York City established its own in 1844, using Peel's London Metropolitan Police as a model. Philadelphia followed in 1854.[25] Slowly, night watchmen were replaced by **police officers**, and sheriffs were relegated largely to serving court orders and running local jails and lockups. The marshal system moved westward with the frontier, eventually disappearing, except in the federal system where marshals still play a law enforcement role, usually by serving federal arrest warrants and transporting and protecting prisoners and witnesses. For example, the U.S. Marshals Service has established fugitive task forces in every state, coordinating federal, state, and local resources to apprehend individuals wanted on warrants from any court level[26] (see also **Critical Thinking 4.1** on the United States Federal Witness Protection Program).[27] In the mid-1800s, the Boston police set up the first detective bureau, replacing amateur bounty-hunters as the chief searchers for criminals.[28]

Critical Thinking 4.1 The Witness Protection Program

Sometimes the best way to catch a crook is with another crook. It is estimated that over 97% of persons in the federal witness protection program (formerly known as the Federal Witness Security Program or WITSEC) have extensive criminal histories. Sammy "the Bull" Gravano, who was involved in nineteen murders, including his own brother-in-law's death, entered WITSEC and testified against John Gotti, who had embarrassed the federal government by having jurors bribed. In exchange, Gravano only served five years in prison, received a new identity, plastic surgery, and governmental protection. He ultimately ditched the protection, resumed criminal activity, and was sent to prison for spearheading an ecstasy drug ring in Arizona. This has been a problem that has plagued WITSEC since its inception. There have been a number of participants equipped with their new identities that have absconded from the program and gone on violent crime sprees. This coupled with the fact that hefty bounties are being placed on some of those wanted by the federal government (i.e., $25 million for the capture of Osama bin Laden or $2 million for the apprehension and conviction of drug kingpin Pablo Escobar) there are questions about the motivations and even the veracity of some of those who may seek to enter WITSEC for protection. (It should also be noted that bounties are not just placed on the heads of fugitives from justice, but can also be placed by criminals on law enforcement personnel. For example, Carl Williams, who headed the Narcotics Division in Jamaica, had a $1 million price tag placed on his head by drug runners while in charge of drug enforcement in that country.[29] He is currently pursuing his Ph.D. in criminal justice.)

Should WITSEC participants be allowed to walk away from governmental protection? Shouldn't authorities continue to know their whereabouts even if they no longer desire protection? How could this be arranged? If the government placed a one-million-dollar price tag on your head, do you think someone might come forth and identify you as someone they saw down at the docks off-loading cocaine?

Slavery and the South

The local political structure in the South was different than that in the northern cities. In the South, the institution of slavery existed. Some police historians contend that American policing began in the Southern **"slave patrols"** of the 1740s.[30] The fear of slave revolts among plantation owners and the rest of the Southern white populace led to the enactment of laws providing for the surveillance of all blacks, free and slave. The slave patrols had complete power to break open houses, punish runaway slaves, whip any slave who interfered with or resisted arrest, and arrest and take any slave suspected of any crime before the closest magistrate. The slave patrols enforced the Southern laws that forbade blacks to move freely, keep guns, or strike a white person.

Southern states had no monopoly on racism, however, and the oppression of blacks was not limited to states or cities where slavery was legal. The major cities in the north experienced many large-scale race riots during the nineteenth century, and overt hostility and hatred toward blacks was common. The north also had its own version of slavery in the early nineteenth century, and the police were responsible for enforcing the slave laws.[31] Throughout the nineteenth and early twentieth centuries states such as Illinois, Ohio, Indiana, Iowa, and California did not allow blacks to testify in court if whites were involved in the case. Oregon forbade blacks to own real estate, file lawsuits, or make contracts. Massachusetts outlawed interracial marriage and enforced segregation in hotels, restaurants, public transportation, and theaters.[32] Freed slaves had to register and carry "freedom papers" which could be inspected in any city north or south or by any suspicious white.[33] In such an environment, as was commonplace across many occupations, virtually no African American police existed anywhere in the United States; little attention was given by police to the needs of areas populated by racial minorities.

Attempts at Integration and Assimilation

After the Civil War, change came very slowly. A few black police began to appear in Houston, Selma, and Raleigh in the 1870s. In New Orleans, which was predominantly black by 1870, the five-member police board, with three black members, had appointed a police force that included 177 blacks.[34] The first African American police officer in the north was appointed in Chicago in 1872, followed by Washington, DC (1874), Indianapolis (1876), Cleveland (1881), Philadelphia (1881), and Boston (1885).[35]

When African Americans were appointed as police officers in Philadelphia, several white officers quit in protest. There, as elsewhere, the black officers were assigned in or near black neighborhoods and were restricted as to what they could do. In Miami, black police were called "patrolmen" and whites were called "policemen," in St. Louis black officers worked "black beats," and in Los Angeles they were assigned to a special "black watch."[36] As late as 1961, many police departments throughout the United States restricted the power of black police to make arrests, generally forbidding them from arresting white suspects.[37]

Policing has not been without its own reported pockets of resistance to racial equality. In 1941, in *An American Dilemma*, Gunnar Myrdal offered the following observation.

> In many, but not all, Southern communities, Negroes complain indignantly about police brutality. It is part of the policeman's philosophy that Negro criminals or suspects, or any Negro who shows signs of insubordination, should be punished bodily, and that this is a device for keeping the 'Negro in his place' generally.

However, career lawman and then Los Angeles Police Chief William Parker maintained that public understanding of police work is severely impacted by "the criticism of the police by certain minority groups in order to distract attention from the high incidence of criminal activity within those groups and the practice of the media in magnifying police failures and in minimizing their successes or accomplishments."[38]

Stetson Kennedy, who infiltrated the Ku Klux Klan, serving as an undercover informant on Klan activities for federal agents, reports in his book *The Klan Unmasked* of attending Klan rallies and observing the police blue and deputy sheriff khaki pants legs underneath the Klan robes of hooded Klansmen who were also sworn law enforcement officers.[39] In an article entitled "Khaki, Blue and Black," David Shipler acknowledges that "[n]ot every white police officer is a bigot and not every police force is a bastion of racism." He notes that on the heels of the Rodney King verdict "[s]ome departments have made strides in promoting blacks, teaching tolerance and engaging minority communities in monitoring police work." However, Shipler maintains that intensive work remains to be done to overcome continuing biases. He points to the tarnished reputation of the Los Angeles Police Department following well-publicized incidents of police brutality, but he also provides the example of white Harris County, Texas (Houston) sheriff's deputies who elected to promote a celebration of James Earl Ray, the assassin of Martin Luther King, Jr., instead of acknowledging the King holiday. Ku Klux Klan literature was also sent to the department's African American Liaison for deputies.[40] Similarly, a mug shot of Martin Luther King, Jr. from his arrest in 1956 for his involvement in the Montgomery, Alabama, bus boycott was discovered in a Montgomery County sheriff's storage room in July 2004 with the word "DEAD" and "4-4-68" scribbled with an ink pen on the photograph.[41]

The present justice system is impacted by the past, and, often without recourse, "the current system disproportionately ensnares poor individuals and minorities."[42] Community aspects, as reflected in socio-economic status and racial composition, often commingle with suspect characteristics to predict use of forceful authority by the police and arrest. Threats by law enforcement and arrests have been found to more likely occur in minority communities, and the significance of a suspect's race in predicting police use of deadly force seems to fluctuate across the social context of communities and cities.[43]

Despite the election of Barack Obama as the president of the United States, it appears that race still matters. In a survey by the National Organization of Black Law Enforcement Executives (NOBLE), the following question was posed: "In the Age of Barack Obama, is race still relevant?" The majority of respondents replied, "Yes, nothing has really changed." Thirty-nine percent said, "Yes, but only as relevant as you allow it," and seven percent replied, "No we have achieved a color blind society."[44]

The Frontier

As the American frontier became populated, criminal activity followed. Before areas west of the Mississippi River gained statehood, lawlessness was widespread. Vigilantes took matters in their own hands, chasing and capturing criminals and often shooting or hanging them shortly after capture. As towns developed, sheriffs were chosen to bring law and order out of the chaos. Sometimes former outlaws were chosen for the job because of their toughness and their reputation for violence, which was seen as useful to deter crime. With no training or paid helpers, the local sheriff named local men to a "posse" to respond as needed to chase cattle thieves, bank robbers, and other outlaws.

The local western sheriff represented a limited geographic area and was responsible to a small number of constituents in that area. Therefore, when outlaws moved between jurisdictions, or eluded capture and left the area, it became difficult to control crime. Without state government and police, all law enforcement stopped at the local level.

Two famous private policing agencies can trace their reputations to the Old West. Perhaps the best known of the private agencies is the earliest, **Pinkerton's**, which was founded in Chicago in 1850 by Allan Pinkerton, a Scottish immigrant and Chicago detective. Pinkerton agents worked with railroad companies whose trains cut across boundaries of local law officials in the west and were thus vulnerable to crime. Pinkerton agents were credited with hunting and capturing famous outlaws. They were also used in the late 1800s to help put down striking workers.

Fact

The term "Private Eye" can be traced to a Pinkerton advertisement, which shows an unblinking eye with the caption "We Never Sleep."

Another well-known private agency is **Wells-Fargo**, a banking company begun by Henry Wells and William Fargo in 1852, whose stage coach line carried millions of dollars in gold dust from California to the East Coast during the nineteenth century. Because of the constant threat of bandits, Wells-Fargo structured its own security force, which included treasure boxes ("safes") and armed guards for all shipments. When thefts occurred, specially trained agents hunted the bandits down ruthlessly.[45] See **Critical Thinking 4.2.**

Critical Thinking 4.2 Why Do We Need Private Police?

It's easy to see how the private companies were important in the Old West, but why are they important today?

Both Pinkerton's and Wells-Fargo are still vibrant companies, and they are not the only private police agencies today. Many others have emerged, which provide private security guards, alarm systems, armored vehicles with armed guards, protected delivery of valuables, vaults, and a great many other such services. Additionally, private corporations, retail stores, educational institutions, warehouses, shipyards, healthcare facilities, financial institutions, and a host of other private concerns hire their own private security personnel.[46] For example, railroad police in accordance with applicable state laws, have arrest powers throughout the United States on crimes related to railroad commerce.[47] Additionally, there are the private investigators who advertise in the yellow pages of most telephone books and who conduct "confidential investigations." Significantly more money is spent in the United States on private than on public policing, and the growth of private police forces is exceeding the growth of those in the public sector.[48]

Furthermore, municipalities today, in the face of severe budget cuts, are finding it cheaper to hire private police over publicly paid police to keep the peace. The city of Oakland, California, found it one-fifth as expensive to pay private guards instead of public police officers to roam crime-plagued neighborhoods. Similar practices have been employed in Los Angeles, Chicago, and New Orleans.[49]

Serious problems have existed—and still exist—between public and private police. Today, an estimated two million people are employed by private police forces, or by private security agencies,[50] and sometimes they are resented by city or county police for interfering with police investigations. Not without justification (a proportion of private security personnel are not of the caliber to make it as police officers), many public police officers refer to private agents as "Rent-a-Cops," a term intended to be derogatory. Although many states have recently passed legislation requiring the licensing of private police companies and the training and background investigations of private agents, still many private cops are not trained or otherwise properly equipped to carry a gun and enforce law and order, even on private property.[51]

1. Why are private police still being hired today?
2. Why might some "public" police sometimes object to private police?
3. What do you believe is the future for private policing?

A different type of law enforcement officer was needed, one with broader jurisdiction, and not just one for companies who could afford their own private police. **Federal marshals** were appointed and sent to western territories with wide ranging jurisdiction, but once statehood was achieved, law enforcement became the responsibility of local and state government. For instance, the **Texas Rangers** were organized to enforce the law in Texas and became an effective force in apprehending and executing cattle thieves, robbers, and murderers.

The Reform Era

American policing was disjointed, with little information passed from one jurisdiction to another. Critics pointed out that the decentralized nature of its authority contributed to a lack of leadership and discipline. They noted that the police were more the private servants and cronies of local political bosses than anything else, and that they spent much of their time running political errands and guarding private plants, docks, or railway stations. They charged that police chiefs were figurehead lackeys of local political machine bosses—lackeys who showed little policing know-how and had little authority.[52] Lingering racial imbalances and prejudices, dissatisfaction with abuses of power, corruption, and political favoritism on the part of the police led to pressures from inside and outside police departments for reform, and police work entered a **reform era** from the early 1900s into the 1970s.

Prior to that, various technological improvements such as **call boxes** were being introduced into urban policing, beginning around the 1850s. Similar to a wall telephone, call boxes were placed at strategic locations on an officer's beat to allow him to maintain contact with precinct headquarters and to provide a means of monitoring a police officer's location and movements. In addition to this early technological advance, structural changes were introduced, such as police administrative boards, which were created in many cities in an effort to cut down on police corruption and to curb political influence.

At first such reforms met with little success. But the need for change became increasingly clear. For example, there was a long, bloody, and costly **police strike** in Boston in 1919. The police there, dissatisfied with their salaries, attempted to become affiliated with the American Federation of Labor (AFL). They were opposed by the city and they struck on September 9, 1919. Looting broke out and rioting occurred. Governor Calvin Coolidge called in the state militia to take over the city, the police received little public support, and the strike was broken. These events stirred an interest among the public in police behavior and from some a call for reform was heard.

Another important stimulus was the **Federal Bureau of Investigation (FBI)**. **J. Edgar Hoover** became the director in 1924 at a time when it was a discredited and corrupt agency. He attempted to transform the FBI into a prestigious agency with a sterling reputation for honesty and integrity. He raised eligibility standards for and implemented training of agents, required agents to dress in suits and to wear hats, and made other changes in an attempt to establish the bureau's reputation for professionalism. He kept his agents out of narcotics investigations, which could have had a corrupting influence on them, and utilized a powerful public relations approach, creating the image of an incorruptible crime-fighting organization always presented by the media in the most favorable light.[53] Local police who were poorly dressed and equipped, without training or standards for conduct, had their first role-model for professionalism as measured in those terms.

In the aftermath of the Boston strike, various crime commissions, including some on the national level, began to investigate the extent of American crime and the ability of the police to deal with it. Probably the best known of these was the **Wickersham Commission**, created by President Herbert Hoover in 1931.[54] This commission pointed out that there was no intensive effort made to educate, train, or discipline police officers or to eliminate those who were incompetent. The commission also noted that with few exceptions police forces suffered from inadequate methods of communication and had poor equipment. While the Wickersham Commission received a great deal of attention, its report was issued at the beginning of the Great Depression. As a result, local funds needed to implement its suggested reforms generally did not materialize.

The move toward modern police professionalism was also sparked by a number of early pioneers in policing, in particular **August Vollmer**. Vollmer was police chief in Berkeley, California, and he instituted university training as an important part of the development of the young officer cadre of his police. One of Vollmer's students,

Orlando W. Wilson, pioneered in the use of advanced training for officers in Wichita, Kansas, and later in Chicago.[55]

The work of Vollmer, Wilson, and others did a great deal to upgrade the standards of American policing. With their innovations and the introduction of various **technological advances** (including the radio, the patrol car, the two-way radio, and new techniques in forensic science and criminalistics), major police agencies rapidly moved toward the scientific control of crime.

It should be noted, however, that early reform efforts did not significantly address the residual effects of racism and sexism. Police agencies began to establish standards for police recruits and improved police salaries and benefits. Some departments stated height and weight requirements. But, standards developed for physical strength and agility were developed and used to exclude women from being accepted into police work. Written civil service examinations were culturally skewed, which put people denied access to quality education at a disadvantage, often eliminating African Americans from consideration. And background investigations of police applicants also created another obstacle for a number of blacks since many departments eliminated people with arrest records, those who had changed jobs too often, or those who had associated with known criminals. The net result was that minorities were largely excluded from police work throughout much of the twentieth century.[56]

Americans became painfully aware of this discrimination during the 1960s. Cities faced racial tensions which erupted into riots. These were riots the police were not only unprepared to prevent or suppress but which some observers claimed the police precipitated. No major American city had even half the percentage of nonwhite police as in the cities' general populations.[57] The National Advisory Commission on Civil Disorders found that many of the riots studied followed incidents of police brutality. An atmosphere of hostility between blacks and whites was reinforced by the widespread belief among blacks that the police used a double standard in dealing with minority communities, and that white society created the black ghetto, white police maintained it, and white institutions condoned its continued existence.[58]

Since the late 1960s, a number of reforms have been instituted that were designed to reduce the tensions between police and inner-city blacks and other minorities. More African American officers patrol the streets, and strict rules are in place against police brutality, discourtesy, the use of weapons, and verbal harassment. More needs to be done, to be sure, but police work today is finally becoming more representative of the heterogeneity of American society.

In addition to the changes already mentioned, the reform era produced several other effects.[59] Police departments were restructured in a quasi-military fashion, so that they became hierarchical organizations with centralized authority, which passed directives down through a chain of command. Officers were selected and promoted according to merit-oriented, civil service, competitive, bureaucratic procedures. Police work became routine, impersonal, and "professional" crime fighting. Serious crimes were treated with a new importance, both by chiefs at the top of the organization, who used the focus on them to garner public support and respect, and by the officers at the bottom of the organization, who could achieve rapid advancement for "good busts," or serious crime arrests.

Incident-Driven Policing

More than anything else, the police patrol car and the telephone revolutionized police work. The patrol car provided police with the ability to respond immediately to citizen calls, and the telephone gave the public immediate access to the police. This led to **incident-driven policing** and is part of the **reform era** of policing.

Incident-driven policing is described by John Eck and William Spelman as a series of actions taken by police officers who respond to dispatcher calls following a citizen call to the police station.[60] The officer arrives at the address given to the dispatcher by the citizen caller, talks to the caller and others who may have information, and then tries to resolve the complaint. Depending on the type of complaint, the officer may try to negotiate a resolution without creating an official record. If a criminal report must be made, the officer usually records the complaint on an official police report form and passes it on to detectives without making an arrest. But if the offender is present or if people at the site become hostile and unruly, the officer may invoke the criminal law and make an arrest. Indeed, just the threat of arrest usually helps the officer reach a negotiated settlement. Then, once the call has been handled, the officer returns to patrolling the streets until the next call comes from dispatch.[61]

Incident-driven policing is also called **reactive policing** in that incidents that have already happened make up the work loads of police officers and detectives. Of course, not all police work is of this nature. There is also **proactive policing**, in which vice and crime prevention officers actively seek out problems before, or without, specific citizen complaints. But proactive policing generally comprised a small percentage of the overall police effort throughout the twentieth century and in many jurisdictions still.

Incident-driven policing involves both police officers and detectives gathering information from victims, witnesses, and other citizens that can help resolve the problem, or help make an arrest. Also, incident-driven policing relies heavily on the fact that officers and detectives have the criminal law power of arrest as their primary tool in resolving problems. Officers on patrol are the front-line troops of incident-driven policing and civilian-clad detectives make up the second wave in crime control efforts.

Police Patrol

The cop on the beat has been, and continues to be, the mainstay of policing.[62] The patrol function is so fundamental to law enforcement that the need for it seems beyond dispute. As both a concept and a technique, patrol remains basic to all but the most specialized police agencies, such as the FBI. Indeed, to many citizens, the ever-present force of officers dispersed throughout the community, in uniform and armed, on-call 24 hours a day, is policing. All other police activities are service functions, seen by many people as necessary but as secondary in importance to working the beat.[63]

This attitude is a bit extreme, yet there is some truth to it. The patrol officer is the generalist of law enforcement. He or she exercises a vast amount of police discretion and is the most visible embodiment of authority, of law and order, in our communities. And there is little doubt that the success or failure of law enforcement, no matter what test is applied, depends in great part on the quality of patrol officers and the ways in which they are used by their commanders.[64]

In contrast to the village constable of yesteryear, who walked a beat and came to know the citizens of his small area, the typical patrol officer covers a beat in a marked, radio-equipped patrol car. **Preventive patrol** became a popular policing technique—that is, police officers cruising in squad cars through the community as an omnipresent deterrence to potential criminals. Already by the 1950s preventive patrol was well entrenched. As the National Advisory Commission on Civil Disorders commented, "The patrolman comes to see the city through a windshield and hear about it over the police radio."[65] Not all patrolling today is done in cars, however. See **Field Practice 4.1** below.

Field Practice 4.1 Police out of the Cruiser

Some characteristics of the police presence hearken back to the time of the village constable. **Foot patrols**, which we will also discuss later in this chapter, have been reintroduced to certain areas of some cities.[66] **Police on horseback** are familiar sights in some of our larger cities and common in our most desolate outlands, providing an opportunity for better interaction with the citizenry.[67]

Image by R. N. Slate.

Other forms of patrol exist as well, some that do not involve car patrols. Occasionally officers use **motorcycles** or small motorbikes. In some communities, officers patrol waterfronts and parks with dogs (called K-9 squads), and large police agencies often utilize both fixed-wing **planes and helicopters** on patrol. Depending on location and need, some police agencies use boats for **river and harbor patrol. Bicycle patrols** have allowed officers to get out of the patrol cars and once again begin to develop more personal relationships with the citizenry, while maintaining their mobility. In a way, this is a move back to more simple times, but the bicycle patrols have been found to be extremely effective. The **Segway** has also found a significant place in patrol work in metropolitan areas, airports, and other areas. The officers, standing on the Segway platform, are able to see over pedestrian traffic and are able to conserve their energy, otherwise expended by walking, for potential difficult encounters.[68]

What experiences have you had with officers through various means of patrol? Which methods of patrol do you prefer as a citizen? Which would you prefer if you were an officer? Which do you think police officers in general prefer? Explain your answers.

Patrol officers represent the full authority of police power and are expected to perform all the functions involved in general law enforcement as well as to achieve specific objectives set by their own departments. Patrol, in all forms, has three primary purposes: (1) answering calls for assistance; (2) the maintenance of a police presence in the community; and (3) the probing of suspicious circumstances.[69]

In precincts characterized by high crime rates and other social problems, patrolling officers may spend most of their on-duty time responding to calls. In smaller communities and less busy precincts—and even in high-crime areas at certain times—calls for assistance may be infrequent, leaving much uncommitted time for officers to patrol the area.[70]

The pattern followed during any particular police patrol depends on a variety of factors. In some cases the routes to be followed by tactical units may be prescribed by patrol regulations and monitored by a supervising sergeant. In this way, police departments try to achieve the deterrent function of making the police presence known in the area being patrolled.

Although there may be regulations requiring a precinct to be "fully covered" during each tour of duty, the actual routes taken by cruising patrol cars are more commonly left to the discretion of individual officers. Indeed, it is expected that an experienced officer will vary the patterns of patrol, selecting areas of emphasis based on current conditions in the precinct, a knowledge of "trouble spots," and past experiences with incidents occurring at particular checkpoints. See **Field Practice 4.2** for example.

Field Practice 4.2 Snapshots of Police Patrol

Crime Scenes

A police officer and her partner jointly worked out a series of major checkpoints on their patrol route which they were careful to drive to at staggered, unpredictable times. These checkpoints included an alley containing rear doors to a number of warehouses, a schoolyard where youth gangs were known to congregate, a subway station where a homicide had occurred some two years earlier, an isolated bus stop, and a pawn shop that had often been burglarized in the past. When not responding to calls, their patrol duties were otherwise random within their precinct, but these checkpoints were always visited at least twice during each tour of duty.

Of course patrol patterns are broken when unusual circumstances are observed and must be investigated, when suspicious characters are stopped for questioning, and when calls for assistance are received. The motorized beat officer is constantly within radio range of a police dispatcher and, in fact, the **dispatcher-patrol officer relationship** is central to policing.

Often the information communicated to patrol officers is brief to the point of being cryptic: "Investigate family trouble"; "Prowler on the roof"; "See the man at Broad and Tenth"; "Investigate burglary"; and so forth. Sometimes the calls are urgent, and the dispatcher gives some indication of danger: "A man with a gun"; "Shots fired"; "Robbery in progress"; or, the one most likely to elicit the most rapid response, "Officer in trouble" or "Officer down."

The dispatcher-patrol officer relationship is an equation of discretion. The dispatcher uses discretion in deciding whether to send a car on a call at all and, if so, whether to assign to the call a degree of urgency. In turn the patrol officers who receive the call must decide whether to respond and, if so, in what manner. In some dispatch situations the police respond in an urgent manner, driving rapidly to the scene, often using the emergency lights or siren. In other dispatcher responses they respond in a clearly routine manner, observing all the traffic rules and laws on the way to the scene, and even looking for a parking space. Some dispatches have such a low priority that officers may deliberately waste time responding, their attitude being: "It'll probably turn out to be nothing"; "No need to rush"; "We'll never catch him"; "If we go slow, that'll be over before we get there."[71]

Are crimes deterred merely by the visible presence of police in an area? If so, the aggressive presence of police who are known to be constantly checking, probing, and inquiring should have an even greater impact.[72] And it would seem that increasing the numbers of officers in any patrol area, to the point of saturating it with police, while increasing the vigor with which suspicious circumstances are investigated and suspicious persons are questioned, would reduce crime rates.

In 1972, the Kansas City Police Department in conjunction with the Police Foundation undertook the year-long patrol experiment to study exactly these questions.

Under controlled conditions, the impact of different levels of patrol on crime and perceptions relating to crime were compared. Precincts across the city were divided into three groups. One area received the same type and level of patrol it had received in the past; another received no routine patrol (cars from other precincts responded to distress calls in this district); the third area received two to three times its normal patrol assignment.

The major conclusion of the study was that routine preventive patrol in marked police cars has little value in preventing crime or making citizens feel safe. Many police scholars and administrators concluded that patrol, no matter how it is used, does not result in less crime or caught criminals. In other words, the police presence does not deter.[73] One noted police scholar stated that "it makes about as much sense to have police patrol routinely in cars to fight crime as it does to have firemen patrol routinely in fire trucks to fight fire."[74]

The Kansas City experiment has been vigorously criticized for several reasons. For example, the Kansas City police department found it difficult to maintain the experimental conditions, and some critics pointed out that a number of cities patrolled their streets more heavily than even the highest-level experimental zone in the study. The results of the experiment did cast considerable doubt on past claims of the effectiveness of patrol practices, crystallizing into skepticism on the part of many police administrators.

Although patrol in general is at least a questionable use of police resources according to many criminologists, most police departments still support the tactic, and even the most vocal critic of patrol must acknowledge that the police presence in the community enhances response to citizen needs. The presence of police in the community, in highly visible venues, makes it easier for a citizen to call for help or to otherwise obtain police assistance even for non-crime related matters. But as for crime prevention and other purposes, the assumption of patrol is that crime could happen anywhere and that the police must be present throughout any given community in order to be effective. Some researchers argue that this is a fallacy, that patrol is effective when, rather than patrolling an entire beat, police pay special attention to a small number of locations that have a high risk of crime.[75]

Patrolling Known "Hot Spots" of Criminal Activity

Most areas in many cities experience relatively few serious crimes. Indeed, more than half of all requests for police response originate in only 3% of addresses within a jurisdiction.[76] This fact clearly leads to the conclusion that police patrol could be concentrated in a few locations, thereby providing a more efficient and effective use of police resources. The main weakness of the Kansas City study, according to Sherman and Weisburd, is that the zones used in the statistical analysis were too large and that patrol was not targeted to needed areas. They sought to correct these shortcomings in a patrol experiment in Minneapolis.

The Minneapolis study focused on 100 small geographic locations in the city which had experienced high levels of police activity in previous years. Half of those locations were targeted for increased police presence (the experimental group), and half were kept at the same patrol level (the control group) for comparison purposes. The six-month study measured a police presence 2.6 times greater in the experimental hot spots than in the control hot spots. The results show that increases in police presence in crime hot spots resulted in fewer calls for police response. Police patrol, when properly and scientifically employed, can serve to reduce crime in certain hot spots, therefore. The presence of police seems to have a deterrent effect on would-be criminals.[77]

Some police officers in Minneapolis found the hot spot patrol distasteful and repetitious. Preventing crime is not as exciting as catching criminals after a crime has occurred. One solution to this problem is for police to rove from one hot spot to another, keeping both the boredom at a minimum and the potential offenders unsure as to where and when the police will appear.[78]

Aggressive Preventive Patrol

Sometimes police patrol is not performed in a reactive, wait-for-a-call manner. Officers occasionally are instructed to engage in aggressive preventive patrol—that is, to take the offensive against possible crime, to be more vigorous in probing, stopping, questioning, and frisking suspects, almost at random. Not all aggressive patrols are random or preventive. Sometimes officers are ordered to round up suspects aggressively in the wake of serious, high-publicity crimes. See **Critical Thinking 4.3.**

Critical Thinking 4.3 Does Aggressive Preventive Patrol Reduce Crime or Just Make People Mad?

After a series of apparently random and motiveless murders in Los Angeles, the police dispatchers used the code word "Zebra" to notify officers on patrol of other similar killings. Based on the testimony of some witnesses who noticed "suspicious circumstances" at the site of some of these murders, the police intelligence unit came to the conclusion that the Zebra killers were two or three young black males. The victims had all been white. Based on this information, the chief of patrol issued instructions to his officers to stop and question all youthful black males whenever they were encountered by patrols.[79]

In Detroit, after a series of rapes and murders of women, police stopped, searched, and arrested about 1,000 people randomly. For a while, all young black males walking the streets of the city involved were stopped, told to "spread-eagle" their hands and feet and lean against a wall or across a car, and then they were frisked and questioned by teams of police.

In Baltimore, after two armed men killed one policeman and seriously wounded another, police officers searched more than 300 homes, most belonging to African Americans, looking for the gunman. The searches were often made in the middle of the night and were based almost entirely on anonymous tips. This caused an uproar in the community. The home invasions by the police "could" happen in prosperous suburban (white) neighborhoods, but the innocent victims knew only that wholesale raids do not happen elsewhere and did happen to them.[80]

1. After reading the three examples of aggressive patrol techniques, discuss whether or not any valid reasons exist for such tactics.
2. What would be the reaction if police searched student housing on your campus in the manner described above? Do the ends of "getting the weapon and junk off the streets" justify the means? Is this reactive or proactive policing? Is the technique legal?
3. Do you believe police would have been equally aggressive if the victims had been black and the suspect white? The "suspicious circumstances" required for a stop appear here to be racially defined. Is this proper? legal? understandable?
4. Is it possible, in your opinion, that some police officers could conduct aggressive preventive patrol in a polite, non-threatening manner while other police officers may perform the same function in a way that would create a hostile response?[81]

Common street crimes—assaults, muggings, traffic in narcotics, rapes, and even many homicides—do not occur in equal distribution throughout a community. In metropolitan areas particularly, police can easily identify high-crime neighborhoods with such accuracy that incidents of various types of offenses can be predicted on a weekly or monthly basis, and sometimes even daily. Residents in these areas understandably demand protection and insist that the police do something to make their neighborhoods safe.

The police are also subject to outside pressures—from political figures, citizen action groups, the press, and other sources—to "clean up" the city and to crack down on lawbreakers. In addition, it is often demanded that police prevent crimes as well as solve them. In these circumstances, the continued existence of high-crime pockets becomes frustrating. No matter that the root causes of such crimes may be well beyond the ability of the police to relieve—the urgency of the situation demands action, and aggressive patrol is the result. The police simply take techniques such as field interrogation, which have proven efficient in more orderly circumstances, and apply them intensively and at random.

However, as will be discussed in more detail in the next chapter, citizens have a constitutional right to be free from "unreasonable searches and seizures," and aggressive patrol tactics may violate that right. Although the police do not deny the extralegal nature of aggressive patrolling, they often justify its use on the grounds that there are no alternatives. Brief stops to identify persons in the neighborhood fix those individuals in time and place and become "intelligence" information that may be used later if a crime is reported. Frisks and searches "get the weapons and drugs off the street," ostensibly preventing more serious crimes. Furthermore, the saturation of a neighborhood with officers, the police claim, acts to deter potential violators.

Detectives

Most city police departments of any size have detective units, distinct from but in close working relationships with the patrol force. In specialized instances, like the FBI and similar governmental enforcement agencies that have no routine patrol functions, both frontline officers and most of their superiors are detectives.

Detectives assigned to specialized units like vice squads or organized crime intelligence units may perform many duties similar to those of patrol officers. They may be assigned to stake out premises, street corners, hotel lobbies, or other suspicious sites, keeping them under surveillance for extensive periods of time. Or they may be required to tail suspects, to act as bodyguards for dignitaries, or to go out and look for crimes in the community like patrol officers do.

Detective work often entails visiting the scene of a crime to look for clues, interrogating victims and interviewing witnesses, and making a record of the nature of the loss and the harm done. Contrary to popular conceptions, there is ordinarily little a detective can do at the scene of a crime, for there is rarely much fresh information to be gathered at such a site after the initial visit by the patrol officers. With serious crimes, such as murders, bombings, and even some cybercrimes, detectives may call on crime laboratory experts to dust for fingerprints, analyze bloodstains, recover and analyze bomb fragments, or otherwise collect physical evidence that eventually may be used against the perpetrator. In more routine, less serious offenses, however, detectives normally can do little more than look around and make a record of the crime, often primarily to help victims fill out their insurance claims.

The greatest tool of detective work, and the technique most commonly employed, is interrogation. Usually detectives simply question crime victims and any witnesses to confirm information already gathered by the patrol officers who first arrived on the scene. But occasionally detectives also carry out post-arrest interrogations of suspects—almost exclusively a detective function.[82]

In general, detectives occupy a higher status and enjoy more prestige than uniformed officers, both within and outside the police department.[83] This does not necessarily mean that a detective occupies a higher rank than a patrol officer; in fact, rank in the paramilitary structure of most police agencies has little to do with whether an officer is a member of the patrol force or a detective in a special investigating unit. Typically in large departments, patrol officers of different ranks from rookie through various "grades" to sergeant, lieutenant, captain, and so forth, are under the command of a chief of patrol. In terms of functions, working conditions, privileges, and prestige, becoming a detective at any rank is ordinarily considered a promotion. Detective status is normally earned after an officer has served on patrol or in some other uniformed capacity.

Detectives are distributed within police organizations in a variety of ways, depending on the administrative preferences of top police officials. In some police departments, especially smaller ones, it is customary to have generalist detectives assigned to perform a wide range of investigative duties, primarily follow-up investigations of cases originated by patrol officers.

If a city is large enough and presents sufficiently complex enforcement problems, specialized detective units (intelligence, vice, burglary, homicide, robbery, and similar crime-specific squads) may be distributed throughout the detective divisions and housed in decentralized offices. A step between generalist and specialist in some departments is to just specialize in "property crimes" or in "crimes against persons."[84]

Of all police activities, that of the detective has been the most romanticized, to the point where common notions about detective work have almost nothing to do with the reality. A "mystique" exists about police detectives which consists of nonsense written and televised and sometimes affects the detectives' own behavior and obscures their real role.[85]

In the wealth of research studies and extensive commentary on policing that has accumulated since the mid-1960s, the work of detectives has been neglected. Most police research concentrates on "basic" policing, which encompasses police practices, management, the issue of discretion in general, the selection of recruits and training patterns, the relationship of police administrators to line-and-staff departmental problems, and such important issues as the relationship of police authorities to political leaders in the community. The place and use of detectives and the entire matter of crime investigation beyond patrol, have only recently begun to attract the professional interest they deserve. The first major study of detectives in the United States was conducted by staff members of the Rand Corporation in the 1970s.

The Rand Study

The Rand Study was based on observations of detective operations in 25 police agencies and a survey of detective practices in an additional 156 departments.[86] Several instructive lessons are among numerous findings of this research.

The research findings belie all the popular conceptions of detective work. For example, the Rand analysis showed that an investigator's time is largely consumed reviewing reports, documenting files, and attempting to locate and interview victims in cases that experience indicates will never be solved. Furthermore, even for cases where a suspect is identified, a detective spends much more time in post-clearance processing than in actually determining the perpetrator.

The public in general and criminal juries in particular expect detectives to employ elaborate scientific investigative devices, like fingerprints, DNA prints, lie detectors, ballistics reports, and spectrographic analyses of physical evidence. Of course, much of this insistence is based on unrealistic expectations created by television and movies; the Rand report showed that more than half of all serious reported crimes received only superficial attention from investigators. Latent fingerprints, voice patterns, bloodstain analysis, and the like rarely provided the basis for identifying a suspect. This puts the detective in a bind. Juries have been found to be reluctant to convict in cases where there are no fingerprints or other bits of "hard" scientific evidence, and crime victims often feel cheated if a detective fails to look for physical "clues."

The Rand Study showed that the most important determinants of whether a case is solved are the amount of time between the commission of the crime and police notification, and the completeness of information given by the victim to the patrol officers responding to the complaint initially. If the needed information is not quickly and accurately obtained at that point, the perpetrator will likely never be identified. Even in cases in which the officers responding to the call receive no on-scene identification of the offender, any subsequent arrest is usually the result of routine police procedures rather than the work of detectives.

One exception would be detective "strike forces," units of detectives assigned temporarily to contend with a specific problem (such as a rash of armed robberies), which have significant potential to make arrests when concentrated on a few difficult target offenses which they are uniquely qualified to investigate. Another exception occurs when detectives of adjacent and allied agencies communicate on a regular basis—comparing notes and cases. It is a common occurrence that an arrest in one agency results in the clearance of cases in surrounding agencies as well.[87]

The Rand report reached several controversial conclusions, and it is not without its critics, particularly with respect to the researchers' methodology.[88] But other police scholars agree with the Rand Study. For example, it has been reported that the vast majority of crimes, about 95%, are solved because a patrol officer caught the offender at the scene, or because a witness tells the detective who the offender was, or due to routine clerical work such as tracing a license tag. Perhaps only about 3% of crimes involve extraordinary efforts on the part of detectives, a far cry from public perception.[89]

For many knowledgeable police administrators, however, the Rand report's conclusions do not differ from their own experiences. Many observers accept the necessity of destroying the mystique surrounding detective work before realistic improvements can be expected, and studies more recent than the one by Rand Corporation agree on that point.[90]

Effectiveness of Incident-Driven Policing

The effectiveness of incident-driven policing has traditionally been measured by **clearance rates**, the proportion of crimes reported to the police that result in arrest. Another measure is **response time**, always considered an important element in solving crimes, but used to measure how quickly police officers arrive at the scene of the complaint or crime.

Careful allocation of patrol officers in the community can result in rapid response time, and clearance rates for many street crimes, but this also has kept police in a reactive, rather than preventive, or proactive role. Police may become attached to the squad car, reluctant to leave it for any reason for fear of missing a call, or perhaps missing an opportunity to make a "good collar." The underlying causes of crime are not easily addressed under this philosophy. Relationships with citizens are not usually cultivated by police whose normal interaction with citizens occurs only after a complaint or crime. Therefore, police have not been successful in developing the kind of information and relationships that allow them to get ahead of the crime problem, to take actions which can lessen the incidence of crime rather than take action only after the incidence of crimes.

Whether the patrol of "hot spots" and aggressive preventive patrol are effective tools of law enforcement is debatable. Rather than deterring crime, such vigorous patrol techniques sometimes merely displace the crime from one area to another.[91] This **displacement effect** of patrol practices does not actually reduce crime or prevent crime but just moves it around. As police put pressure on offenders in one location, those same offenders sometimes merely relocate their activities to an area which is less aggressively policed, until or unless the police reassert an aggressive presence in the new location. Not all criminal activity is merely displaced by police practices,[92] but even if some criminal behavior is moved around by enhanced police tactics it is reduced in that specific location.

One of the major difficulties caused by aggressive patrol is the negative effects its use has on police-community relationships, which may far outweigh any gains made by seizing contraband or weapons.[93] And the final costs of unfettered aggressive patrol and widespread arrests for investigation may be greater even than simple feelings of community hostility toward police. Excesses in the patrol function may, in fact, precipitate riots and mass disorders. The National Advisory Commission on Civil Disorders mentioned earlier pointed to both aggressive patrol practices and the increasing "motorization" of police as contributing to ghetto tensions and the outbreak of civil disorder.[94]

Incident-driven policing is considered by many criminologists to be obsolete as a problem solving technique, although police will always be expected to respond to victims and complaints, and rightly so. But effective police tactics can no longer be restricted to preventive patrol, fast response to calls, and investigating criminal events after the fact. Those traditional tactics are ineffective in preventing or solving most crimes. In fact, fast response is needed by law enforcement for life-threatening calls, while not-in-progress or calls that are not jeopardizing to life are likely to get slower response today.[95] Innovations such as scientific crime analysis, differential police response, and investigative case management have helped police manage their time better, to implement these tactics more efficiently. But the tactics have not helped to reduce or solve crimes. Most police activity is not directly related to crime in the sense most of us understand that term.[96] Police are expected to fill a much larger role, and crime itself can no longer be the sole concern of the police.

The result is that, borrowing from business and psychological models, some police departments have begun to move away from their traditional incident-driven methods and toward participant management, where officers have a say in structuring their own jobs and duties. A new world of police work is emerging, one that recognizes the police do much more than just fight crime. The police today face problems no one else can solve, that are often not directly crime-related, and that require new methods.

The traditional staples, especially patrol, continue to characterize contemporary police work. Responding to pressures from communities and pressures from a new generation of police, police administrators have increasingly experimented with new techniques and programs, many of which are designed to correct the chasm between the community and the police which has occurred in recent decades. See **Critical Thinking 4.4.**

Critical Thinking 4.4 What Are the Police Expected to Do?

Every police department in America is faced with high expectations from citizens. Regardless of the time of day, the weather, or the inconvenience, citizens expect the police to respond to calls for assistance. "Where are the police when you need them?" People want immediate help when needed, but otherwise are just as happy not to see police. Here are some of our expectations of the police:

To prevent and control "serious crime," that is, any conduct widely recognized as threatening our lives or property.

To assist and protect victims of crime, especially those in danger of physical harm.

To protect constitutional guarantees, including those of free speech and assembly.

To facilitate the movement of people and vehicles.

To assist persons who are intoxicated, addicted, mentally ill, physically disabled, old, young, and others who cannot care for themselves.

To resolve conflict between individuals, groups, and anyone in conflict with the government.

To identify problems before they become more serious for individuals, police, or the government.

To create and maintain a feeling of security in the community.[97]

1. What do you think the major expectations placed on the police should be?
2. Do we expect too much from the police?
3. How would you prioritize the above list of expectations the public generally has for the police in society?

LPD Chief Giddens

A New Generation of Police: Community-Oriented Policing

Police today increasingly view crime as a problem to be solved, not merely as an event to which the police react. In this view the community is seen as a partner in solving the crime problem, not as on-lookers, witnesses, or information sources to be interviewed after the criminal event. The community is seen as constituency, a public to be informed about police matters and prepared to help police deal with the complex crime problem. This view of policing calls for a different type of police officer than was common a generation ago. Some law enforcement agencies buy toys during the holidays for underprivileged kids. Other departments like St. Louis have tried to rebuild fractured relations with the community after Ferguson by acquiring an ice cream truck and distributing ice cream to children in the community. Similar gestures have been seen with police agencies in Salisbury, NC, Columbia, SC, Milwaukee, WI, and Cleveland, OH.[98]

During the 1970s and 1980s, police departments faced external pressures from communities to change their daily activities, and this emerged into the **era of community-oriented policing**. Many communities, especially minority communities, demanded that police become more involved in the life of those communities in order to identify ways to serve them better. The use of unnecessary force by police was bitterly criticized. In response, police administrators first attempted to include citizens on "review boards" and to create community relations units to deal with conflicts and violence. But officers resisted civilian review, and communities placed no confidence in the community relations units.

Police administrators have come to realize that the traditional, rigid organizational structure of police departments is not capable of meeting community demands. Despite that structure, police officers exercise a broad, unregulated discretionary power, which has always been tacitly accepted as necessary by police administrators. But when those administrators began attempting to define that discretionary power through policies and structured procedures, they found themselves at a loss to prescribe the proper responses to the varied situations police officers encounter. They were unable to write rules for appropriate, creative police responses. Moreover, police administrators have increasingly become aware that a new generation of police officers is less willing than its predecessors to submit to hierarchical authoritative organizational structures. They have found that incident-driven police work fails to motivate many officers because the officers find the opportunities for meaningful work limited, they do not feel a sense of responsibility for the outcome of their work, and they do not receive feedback about how well they are doing their jobs. The police organizations have found they need to reform to meet these needs of modern police officers.[99]

So some police administrators attempted to bring officers into the communities they served through **team policing.** This approach placed small groups of officers in storefront, neighborhood-centered stations. It encouraged contact between police and citizens, and helped develop relationships between police and neighborhood residents and merchants.[100] Police team members were generalists who could investigate any crime, and participant management was the order of the day.

Team policing was not a widespread success, partly because of resistance to change on the part of entrenched police organizations,[101] but three tactics it implemented have survived; **foot patrols**, **community watch programs**, and **storefront police stations.** Police were present in the community at all times, giving them constant communication and contact with citizens.[102] See **Field Practice 4.3.** This exposure in turn led to additional neighborhood demands to expand the scope of police work. People in the community expressed concern about broken windows, unruly youths, and public drunks as well as burglaries and other traditional crimes.

Field Practice 4.3 Foot Patrols—Walking the Beat

Foot patrols had been abandoned during the 1960s when the rush to motorized patrols was in full swing because they were considered too geographically limited. Officers on foot were clustered together in neighborhoods and could not be moved quickly in response to emergencies, and this was interpreted as a wasteful use of personnel. But foot patrols have advantages which were being overlooked. Two professors at Michigan State University compared perceptions of safety between citizens protected by foot patrols and those protected by motorized patrols. They found that people felt much safer with foot patrols, although the actual impact of using such patrols on the incidence of crime was not as clearly demonstrated.[103]

Following lessons learned from team policing, community-oriented policing and problem-oriented policing developed. Both of these approaches center on removing the police from the isolation of patrol cars and placing them among the people in the community in intimate, continuous ways. The majority of large police departments—including those in Boston, Houston, San Francisco, and New York—began Community Patrol Officer Programs (CPOP).[104]

Community-oriented policing has been advocated by Professors James Q. Wilson and George L. Kelling, who admit that the popularity among police chiefs that the concept enjoys "is as great as the ambiguity of the idea."[105] Indeed, the concept can encompass a variety of ideas and programs, but the significant contribution it has made is that it puts police officers in closer proximity to the people they serve, thereby changing the perceptions police often have about people in high-crime areas. This in turn can lead to a moderation of the "them versus us" attitude so often felt by both sides in such areas, allowing community-oriented policing to be a success.

Professor Herman Goldstein is identified as the developer of the **problem-oriented approach to policing.** These three examples were offered by Goldstein as illustrations of the approach. Like parables, they give us an insight into today's new world of policing.[106] See **Field Practice 4.4.**

Field Practice 4.4 Problem-Oriented Policing Examples

Lansing, Michigan

Officer Donald Christy knew his work was cut out for him in the nine-block area of Lansing, Michigan, he was assigned to as a CPOP officer in a departmental experiment with the new technique. At first disheartened by the sight of crack houses and blighted streets, Christy took pains to get on a first-name basis with many of the area's 700 residents and learn what neighborhood problems concerned them most. Those conversations led him to recognize, he says, "that the good people far out-numbered the bad." Meanwhile, he organized a volunteer community cleanup, which filled 30 Dumpsters with litter; arranged federal funding for floral plantings; and even held a contest to choose a name for the neighborhood: Sparrow Estates.

His unconventional approach to policing paid big dividends. Residents began to give Christy tips that helped him drive away criminals. Indoor dealers found themselves evicted by absentee landlords. "You can walk around the block now without fear of being attacked," says Ralph Casler, a retired mechanic who has lived in the area for 30 years. Says Christy, "I haven't made an arrest in eight months."

Officer Christy considers this to be a good thing.

Gainesville, Florida

After frequent news stories about the rash of armed robberies of convenience stores had appeared on television and in the local newspaper, Gainesville police conducted a detailed analysis of the problem. They assigned an officer to perform a national search for knowledge about the problem and strategies to deal with it. This analysis led them to focus attention on characteristics of the stores, especially whether they had one clerk or two on duty at the time of the robbery. They concluded that stores with only one clerk on duty at night were more vulnerable to robbery during the night hours.

Although the store management did not agree with police findings, the police department was able to secure independent research confirming the police conclusion that the presence of two clerks was the primary factor in deterring convenience store robberies in Gainesville. The nationwide study of the problem also discovered several communities which had reached the same conclusion and had enacted ordinances which required convenience stores to have more than one clerk on duty at night.

With these precedents and local data the police approached the city council with the proposal that a local regulation be established which requires two clerks on duty in convenience stores during certain hours. This was challenged in the courts, but the regulation was upheld, in large measure because of the careful analysis of the problem which the police documented. And, a follow-up study revealed that convenience store robberies dropped by 65% immediately after the new ordinance was adopted.

Philadelphia, Pennsylvania

The sergeant was very dissatisfied with the responses of his officers and the dispatchers to such a large waste of police resources on "unfounded" complaints. The sergeant decided to respond to a complaint at a bar with his officers the next time his officers were dispatched. When the call came, he also found that there was no loud music and no disorderliness. He asked dispatch for the name of the complainant and was told that policy did not require recording the source of complaints for this type of call. At the sergeant's request the dispatcher took the name and address of the complainant the next time the call was made. As it turned out, apparently the same woman had made all of the calls.

The sergeant approached the woman and offered to help her with her concerns. Studies with a decibel meter revealed the bar was operating within the noise control ordinance. He found that it was not the noise which was the source of irritation as much as it was the vibration created by jukebox speakers which were attached to a common wall. The sergeant made arrangements with the bar operators to move the speakers to another wall and for the woman and the bar operators to communicate with each other directly. The woman was pleased, the bar owner was pleased, and the calls to the police stopped.

Problem-oriented policing in the three previous cases involved a process of (1) identifying the problem, (2) analyzing the problem, and (3) developing an effective response to the problem. In Lansing, Officer Christy engaged community residents in problem identification and solutions, helping them to establish community identity. In the Gainesville case, top-level police management along with governmental leaders performed the three steps. In the Philadelphia case, a street-level police officer carried them out.

The first step, identifying the problem, requires the police to develop a series of questions regarding the actors involved in the problem. The actors include victims, offenders, and witnesses and other "third parties." Then, a series of inquiries about the incidents that make up the problem must be developed, for example, inquiries into the sequence of events, the physical context of the events, and the effects of the events. Finally, the police examine the responses to the problem by the police themselves and by other community institutions.

After the problem has been identified and the appropriate questions have been developed, an in-depth analysis is carried out. The sources of information for this step include relevant literature, police officers, official police reports and other data, other government agencies, the community at large, even the problem makers themselves, the suspected offenders. Also, the analysis can include inquiries outside the local region or state to see how other communities have dealt with similar problems. Analysis is a difficult and time-consuming process and requires the best investigative efforts the officer or department can put into it to ensure that it is sufficiently thorough.

Then, after the problem has been identified and analyzed, the final step is developing alternative strategies to cope with, or developing tailor-made responses to, the problem. This can challenge the ingenuity and creativity of the top-level and street-level police involved. In some cases proposed solutions may eliminate the problem, significantly reduce it, or minimize the harm it causes. In other situations it may lead to better police techniques for dealing with the problem or maybe even to a decision to remove the matter from police consideration.

As with any innovative technique, the degree of success enjoyed by those introduced by police agencies varies. Jerome Skolnick and David Bayley studied innovative police practices in six American cities and concluded, in part, that the quality of leadership within a police department is critically important to the success or failure of innovative programs. With proper leadership, the community support and the political environment needed to improve the chances of their successful implementation can be achieved.

However, not all things are in the hands of police officers. With the overwhelming presence of handheld devices like cell phones, YouTube, surveillance cameras, police radio scanners, and the like, many other people have access to police encounters and police information. Police information is no longer considered to be confidential, with so much access and scrutiny by the public.

Summary

We have explored some of the history of the American system of policing, from its English antecedents to contemporary approaches to problem solving and crisis response. In a cursory way we have explored the evolution of American police through the political era, with its precinct ward bosses in the north and slave patrols in the South. We have discussed the racism and political patronage associated with much of the history of policing in the United States. We have also described the reform era, the role of police "patriarchs" like Peel, Vollmer, Wilson, and Hoover, and the impact of the Wickersham Commission report. We have attempted to explain private policing, detectives, and community-oriented policing, among other specialized issues. And we have discussed the controversies and problems surrounding such traditional police activities as patrol.

Police, we have seen, do much more than merely enforce the law. In many ways, we can conclude, the police task is too large, too difficult, too complex for any single agency. Perhaps the emergence of private police with very narrow responsibilities—guarding a warehouse, delivering a valuable package, monitoring conversations, watching for shoplifters—has occurred for this very reason.

Likewise, we have seen that normal police practices seldom match the stereotypes promoted by television or the movies. Popular art seldom portrays real culture accurately and, as pointed out in this chapter, that is particularly true in the case of police detectives.

The advent and impact of contemporary police practices, especially of community-oriented policing and problem-oriented policing, provide the prospect of better days ahead for police. With new approaches that place officers among the citizens they serve, in personal and helpful contexts, perhaps a new era of effective police work is now beginning. But whatever the techniques employed, the police can expect to continue facing a variety of situations, for it is certain they will continue to be involved in handling whatever crises occur.

We began this chapter with a discussion of the Black Lives Matter movement and its interactions with the justice system in America. These contacts are symbolic of a historic undercurrent involving race and policing in this country. **In terms of the three distinct eras of policing discussed in this chapter, under which era would you classify the approach utilized by the Wichita Police Department as described at the beginning of this chapter? Why?**

We now turn to the day-to-day decisions faced by police officers. The influences on officers from constitutional restraints and procedural requirements are examined. Much of this structure for police emerges through court decisions, as will be seen in Chapter 5.

Chapter 5

Police Decisions: Detection, Arrest, and In-Custody Investigation

Image by Acerebel at istockphoto.com.

"No system worth preserving should have to fear that if an accused is permitted to consult with a lawyer, he will become aware of, and exercise [his constitutional] rights. If the exercise of constitutional rights will thwart the effectiveness of a system of law enforcement, then there is something very wrong with that system."[1]

—Justice Arthur Goldberg

Seeking Justice

Upon receiving a call from a dispatcher, Officer Bill Smith arrived on the scene of a crime in progress. As he approached the scene his adrenaline was pumping, his senses alert, and his responsibilities numerous. He knew he was expected to solve the problem, to protect and serve the community. As an enforcer who might have to resort to deadly force, Officer Smith was also required to respect the rights of suspects. He had vast discretion at his disposal, which might be affected by the public visibility of the event, departmental priorities and orientation, and any number of factors not easily articulated. His decisions and actions could come under public and media scrutiny later. When other services fail in a community, it is often the police who must intervene. The police have been referred to as "street corner psychiatrists." Officer Smith must literally be a walking Constitution. His training will guide him as he enters the scene. Besides his standard issue weaponry, he is armed with laws made by legislators and interpretations of those laws and the Constitution by the Supreme Court.

The pressures are great and contribute to high stress levels for police personnel that will be discussed in Chapter 14. Split-second decisions made by Officer Smith today may be picked apart in the hallowed splendor of a courtroom months or years later. This protector, this server, this enforcer is governed by forces essentially outside of his control. The U.S. Supreme Court, whose members have life tenure, interpret the Constitution and the laws and have an extensive impact on training in police academies and on police enforcement of the law. Life tenure supposedly provides for independence of thought by the judiciary. This is certainly a perk that police officers, armed with immense responsibility, do not have. Therefore, this chapter will place particular emphasis on how the Court impacts police decision making.

About This Chapter

Chapter 4 described the history of the police and how police history has molded the role the police play in today's society. This chapter examines the day-to-day practice of policing. Perceptions about police sadly come from media portrayals of law enforcement.[2] It is difficult for outsiders to understand the complexity and, at times, the monotony of law enforcement. Police are the gatekeepers of the criminal justice system.[3] The choices police make directly and indirectly determine the pressure placed on jails, courts, prisons, probation, and parole. These entities, particularly the courts, can have a significant impact on how the police do their job. Furthermore, the manner in which the police use their power affects the creation and maintenance of order. Integral to order maintenance in democratic societies is the rule of law, which defines how police power is to be implemented. Decisions to investigate, arrest, detain, search, interrogate, release, and use force come with a tremendous responsibility. While policing requires the use of personal discretion, the actions of police are constrained by a variety of factors.

Specifically, this chapter focuses on answers to the following questions: What options are available to police investigating crime? What constitutional values and procedural rules affect police choices from the arsenal of investigative techniques available to them? How do police decide when, in what way, and against whom to assert their authority?

Identifying Crime

The criminal justice process usually begins when the police suspect that a crime has been committed, is being committed, or is about to be committed. Then the situation is investigated to verify or dispel this suspicion. There are three major ways in which police suspicion is aroused: when (1) a victim or other witness complains; (2) an officer on patrol observes suspicious activity; or (3) police actively search out crime. The first two ways involve reactive policing. The third way, searching out crime, involves proactive policing.[4] Both reactive and proactive policing were discussed in Chapter 4.

Initial Complaint

The first way police learn about a crime is when a victim or witness contacts the police to report the crime, known as an *initial complaint.* As discussed in Chapter 4, responding to citizen complaints is incident-driven policing, the most common function of police patrol. Normally all complaints trigger investigations, which vary in intensity depending on the type of crime reported, the apparent credibility of the complainant, and other specifics of each situation.

Police Observation

Police also observe what happens on the street while on routine patrol. An officer working a beat, in a patrol car, on foot patrol, or occasionally at a fixed post, may observe some occurrence—a person running from a warehouse in the early hours of the morning, a "clean" automobile with "dirty" license plates, or a similar unusual situation—that in his or her experience may indicate the commission of a crime and justify further investigation. Or the officer on patrol may witness an actual crime or what appears to be a crime being committed.

Searching Out Crime

Even when no complaints of crimes have been made by witnesses or police have made no observations of suspicious activities while on routine patrol, the police may decide to go out and look for specific criminal activity. This *proactive* investigation originates in the belief, sometimes supported by informer tips but more frequently based simply on knowledge of local conditions, that certain types of crimes are occurring or will occur in the community. These investigations are usually directed toward so-called victimless crimes such as organized gambling, prostitution, the sale of narcotics, and other vice offenses, but they may include looking for criminal conspiracies ranging from robbery plots by professional criminals to meetings of "political terrorists." Large police agencies often have specialized detective units—vice squads, organized crime intelligence units, and the like—for the investigation of these types of offenses and the observation and surveillance of persons believed to be involved in vice, rackets, or conspiracies.

Many crimes are very serious. Actual victims are harmed by narcotics pushers, terrorists, and others engaged in criminal conspiracies. Conspiracies are crimes without specific complainants usually and are ordinarily not discovered on routine patrol. The conspiracies themselves often have to be searched out, as do the conspirators, particularly those in charge of narcotics manufacturing and distribution, gangs of professional bank or jewelry store robbers, terrorists groups, or the like. Uncovering these crimes and arresting these criminals poses a big challenge to police enforcement efforts. The methods used by the police to discover such crimes and to make arrests connected with them are controversial.[5]

Investigating Crime

Police have a wide variety of techniques to choose from to investigate or seek out possible criminal activities, depending on the quality of their information, the extent of community pressure for enforcement of particular laws, and the kinds of offenses toward which investigation is directed.[6] Decisions police make are controlled also by the values expressed in the U.S. Constitution as interpreted by the U.S. Supreme Court, and as the complexity of American society increases, so does the complexity of interpretation of constitutional values. Investigations may involve field interrogation, frisk, searches, electronic eavesdropping, sting operations, monitoring e-mail or text messages, and digital forms of communication, as well as undercover infiltration of ongoing criminal activities.

Field Interrogation

Observation of suspicious persons or unusual activity generally leads officers to investigate further. This often means they stop and question the individuals whose actions aroused their suspicions and/or others in the area. This is known as field interrogation. The police ask those they have stopped for identification and briefly question them about their actions. Such field interrogation may confirm police suspicions, so that an arrest or further investigation results, or it may simply produce a satisfactory explanation by the person, so that he or she is allowed to move on.

The legality and appropriateness of field interrogation is sometimes controversial and misunderstood.[7] Normally the police rely on the cooperation of those they stop, and, when officers inquire about a person's presence or behavior, the encounter is easily resolved by a satisfactory reply. In such cases police should be polite and courteous. But what happens when a person refuses to stop or to answer any questions? Should the officers drop the matter and leave the person alone, or does the refusal to cooperate coupled with the original suspicious circumstances constitute sufficient reason to proceed with an arrest?

Legislative or appellate court authorization of field interrogation practices do not always spell out exactly what authority does exist and leaves some room for discretion by police officers. The law is often silent concerning police authority to stop and question pedestrians in the absence of reasonable suspicion or evidence sufficient for arrest.

In general, the authority of the police to stop people briefly for questioning is covered by the notion of *reasonable suspicion.* What is reasonable? Police officers may vary in what they consider to be suspicious, but a reasonable suspicion has been defined generally as a police officer having at least 20 percent certainty that criminal activity is afoot.[8] If the officers have such reasonable grounds to suspect that a person has committed, is committing, or is about to commit a crime, or that the individual is a wanted criminal, they may stop the suspect for questioning. How the suspect responds may give rise to further action of the police under the totality of the circumstances and according to the street smarts and training of the officer. Police may pursue and apprehend persons in suspicious circumstances, such as a person who fled a high-crime area known for narcotics upon seeing police,[9] a person fitting the profile of a drug courier,[10] or suspects sought for previously committed felonies.[11]

Police may also stop and question witnesses near the scene of certain crimes. Usually this is not problematic. As the U.S. Supreme Court has stated: "[i]t is an act of responsible citizenship for individuals to give whatever information they may have to aid in law enforcement."[12] In many circumstances citizens are only too happy to cooperate with police who are investigating a crime to which they may have been a witness or have pertinent information. But if a citizen is not cooperative or attempts to avoid police questioning, this may give rise to sufficient suspicion on the part of the police to use their power to stop, question, and possibly further intrude into a citizen's life.

But such authority is not always sufficiently detailed, and even the constitutionality of laws that do permit the police to stop suspicious-looking individuals is not always clear. An individual certainly has a right to be left alone. In a California case called "The Walker," a man had been arrested and detained 15 times over a two-year period for violating a statute that required persons who "wander or loiter" the streets to provide "credible and reliable" identification to a police officer when asked to do so. The man, Edward Lawson, was stopped by police frequently because he "looked suspicious" and "out-of-place." He was black, wore a dreadlock hairstyle, and often walked through all-white neighborhoods. When stopped, he either could not or would not provide appropriate identification. There were no allegations that Lawson committed any crime other than failing to provide identification. He brought legal action against the arresting police officers, and he sought an injunction to restrain enforcement of the statute, asking, in fact, that the statute be declared unconstitutional. The Supreme Court agreed with Lawson. Justice Sandra Day O'Connor, writing for the majority, held the statute to be unconstitutionally vague, since it gave virtually unlimited discretion to the police to determine in any given case whether the statutory requirements were being met.[13]

However, a person's right to be left alone must be balanced when the government has a legitimate governmental interest. In 2004, the U.S. Supreme Court ruled in favor of a Nevada statute requiring a person in a public place to identify him/her self to a police officer in uniform upon request for the reasonable furtherance of public safety requirements.[14] Field interrogation, one of the most important tactics of police, remains an area of continuing controversy.

Frisk

Frisk involves a "pat-down" search of the suspect only for the purpose of detecting weapons, not for discovering contraband (illegal items). The scope of a frisk is much more limited than a full-scale search, and a frisk can occur only under specified conditions where the officer has reason to believe he/she or the public is potentially "in danger of life or limb." A frisk does not automatically follow a stop. Answers to questions posed by a police officer may satisfy the officer's suspicions and allay any fears that a person is in any way dangerous or criminal. However, under certain circumstances a police officer may frisk a person following a valid stop when a police officer has reasonable suspicion to believe that someone may be armed with a weapon.

A police officer often uses his or her "street smarts" in deciding whether to stop and question, and more importantly, frisk, a person. The officer's perception of suspicious and possibly dangerous situations is based on that officer's experience. Experienced officers may find their suspicions aroused by circumstances that would not give pause to the ordinary citizen. But this use of street smarts often has a dubious legal status. Police, in contrast to other participants in the criminal justice process such as prosecuting attorneys and judges, often use abilities not generally recognized or justified on the basis of formal education, training, or state certification, so that their actions based on those abilities can be called into question.

One such instance arose in a case known as ***Terry v. Ohio***, which established the parameters for police stop and frisk of citizens in America. Detective McFadden, a policeman for 39 years, was on afternoon patrol in Cleveland, Ohio, when he observed two men standing at a corner. One would walk past a store, look in the window, go a short distance, and then return to the window for another look. The other man would then repeat the same pattern. After this took place a dozen times the men walked off together. Officer McFadden came to the conclusion that the men were "casing" the store for a possible robbery. He followed them, and when they stopped to confer with another man, he approached and asked all of them their names. When they mumbled in response, his suspicions were raised even more, and when he began to feel the three men posed a threat, he turned one of the men around, patted him down, and found a .38 caliber revolver in his overcoat pocket. Frisking the other two, the officer found another gun. He took the men with the guns into custody, and they were charged with carrying concealed weapons. Later, McFadden's decision to stop and frisk on the basis of suspicion alone was called into question as the two arrested men contested the constitutionality of their arrest.

The case made it to the U.S. Supreme Court, and the Court found in favor of Detective McFadden, declaring that the behavior of the three men did warrant further investigation. The Court wrote, "It would have been poor police work indeed for an officer with 39 years' experience in the detection of thievery from stores in this same neighborhood to have failed to investigate this behavior further."[15]

The Court also affirmed Officer McFadden's frisk of the men, declaring that a police officer is justified in making certain "that the person with whom he is dealing

Frisk—Plant City PD

is not armed with a weapon that could unexpectedly and fatally be used against him." The mumbled responses from the three men to McFadden did not dispel the detective's fears regarding safety. He interpreted the men's defensiveness and body language as potentially threatening to him. The sole justification of such a frisk is the protection of the police officer or others, and in this particular case the frisk was limited in scope to the outer clothing; McFadden did not place his hands inside pockets, or under the suspects' outer garments, until he felt the weapons. The intrusion had been carefully limited.[16]

Another legal problem with frisking arises when evidence of a crime other than possession of a concealed weapon is discovered. Court decisions in these cases usually depend on the way the pat-down was conducted. While a police officer's decision to frisk a suspect must be driven by concerns for safety and cannot be mere fishing expeditions aimed at looking for any evidence of a crime, a police officer is permitted to seize illegal items during a frisk for weapons if the items are discoverable via "plain touch." If the items are apparent, not hidden inside clothing or requiring an officer to manipulate the suspect beyond the frisk for weapons, the officer may seize the evidence and make an arrest. The court said an officer may use such evidence to justify an arrest. "If a police officer lawfully pats down a suspect's outer clothing and feels an object whose contour or mass makes its identity immediately apparent" as contraband, seizure by the police may legally occur. This case has come to be known as the "plain touch" or "plain feel" case to clarify a police officer's frisk powers. However, in the *Dickerson* case the cocaine seized by the officer as the result of the frisk for weapons was not allowed into evidence because the cocaine was not immediately apparent as contraband to the officer upon the initial pat down; it required further manipulation, squeezing, and searching.[17]

Search

The Fourth Amendment to the U.S. Constitution gives the clearest statement regarding a police officer's decision to search a person or place. Written in 1791, the amendment specifies: "The right of the people to be secure in their persons, houses, papers, and effects, against unreasonable searches and seizures, shall not be violated, and no Warrants shall issue, but upon probable cause, supported by Oath or affirmation, and particularly describing the place to be searched, and the persons or things to be seized." Of course, what constitutes an unreasonable search and seizure has been open to interpretation over the years. Guidance for such police decisions is often provided by the Court.

As indicated above, in the Fourth Amendment, a seizure can be of a person or a thing. An arrest constitutes a seizure and will be discussed later in this chapter. However, things or property can also be seized. This can even include the seizure of money and goods (automobiles, boats, houses, etc.) believed to be obtained through criminal activity. This type of seizure is also known as asset forfeiture. Unless defendants can demonstrate they obtained the items in question legally, then they are subject to seizure. In fact, 26 states permit police organizations to keep all the proceeds obtained from asset forfeiture. Sixteen states allow law enforcement agencies to keep a portion of such proceeds, sometimes sharing with victims' organizations. States often share their windfalls with federal prosecutors, and the Department of Justice has indicated that $4.2 billion annually has been garnered from the program. Only eight states do not allow the police to be legally involved in asset forfeiture.[18] In *Kaley v. U.S.* (2014), the U.S. Supreme Court held that defendants' assets could be frozen with a grand jury finding of probable cause for an indictment, prior to conviction, which could even affect defendants' abilities to hire an attorney.[19]

Search is an important investigatory technique that can be used at any time, before or after the arrest of a suspect, so long as the requirements of the Fourth Amendment are met. Following a lawful arrest, a suspect may be searched without a warrant.[20] Indeed, part of the booking process of a person entered into jail after an arrest is that everything is removed from pockets and clothing, and a person is thoroughly searched.

Search prior to arrest requires the consent of the person searched, exigent circumstances, probable cause, or a search warrant issued by a judge based on the sworn statement of an officer or citizen complaint based on probable cause, which has been defined as a belief that more than likely (50.01 percent chance or better) the incriminating evidence desired will be found on the person or at the place specified.[21] The search warrant instructs police to search for and return to the court specific items to be used in the prosecution of a person. Sometimes exigent (emergency) circumstances cause a police officer to believe that it is not possible to obtain a search warrant and that a search without a warrant is justified. (See **Critical Thinking 5.1.**[22]) This decision is almost always challenged in court, so it is always best for law enforcement to rely on judges for the establishment of probable cause and the issuance of search warrants, as reliance on them shifts the responsibility from law enforcement to judges who are considered the experts in this matter. However, due to circumstances, most searches take place without warrants.[23]

Critical Thinking 5.1 Exigent Circumstances: The Case of the Bloody Glove

Exigent circumstances are "[t]hose circumstances that would cause a reasonable person to believe that entry (or other relevant prompt action) was necessary to prevent physical harm to the officers or other persons, the destruction of relevant evidence, the escape of a suspect, or some other consequence improperly frustrating legitimate law enforcement efforts" (*United States v. McConney* [1984]). Such emergency conditions when met can legally justify searches and govern issuance of *Miranda* warnings (covered later in this chapter).

Los Angeles Police Department detective, Mark Fuhrman, after leaving the bloody crime scene with the lifeless bodies of Nicole Brown Simpson and Ronald Goldman, detected a speck of blood with his flashlight near the bottom of the driver's door of a white Ford Bronco parked outside the Rockingham residence of former football star O.J. Simpson. Detective Fuhrman decided to scale the fence, without judicial consent, maintaining that fear for the safety of possible residents at Mr. Simpson's and/or a potential hostage situation constituted exigent circumstances and justified immediate action. Fuhrman's actions were later challenged at a preliminary hearing and efforts were made to suppress evidence of a bloody glove that was reportedly found by Officer Fuhrman inside a back gate at O.J.'s.

What do you think the court decided and why?

Illustration Two: A Police Chase ... Shots Fired

Two officers, X and Y, were sitting in a doughnut shop at the end of their shift. A Be On the Look Out (BOLO) bulletin came over their radios concerning a robbery suspect speeding away from the police. They jump in their respective cruisers with a description of the getaway car. Officer X saw the car abandoned on the side of the road and a man running from the car into the woods. Officer X stopped his car and gave pursuit on foot. Officer Y arrived on the scene only to see Officer X entering the woods in pursuit of the suspect. Shots are fired, and Officer Y is unable to reach his comrade via the radio. Officer Y manages to sneak up on the suspect, and, with gun drawn, Officer Y places him in handcuffs and demanded to know the whereabouts of Officer X.

Is Officer Y required to read the *Miranda* warnings to the suspect before making this inquiry?

The Exclusionary Rule

Although the protection from unreasonable search and seizure was established in 1791, when the Fourth Amendment to the United States Constitution was ratified, it was largely ignored for many years. Many searches and seizures would be considered unreasonable by today's standards that were conducted by law enforcement authorities and produced evidence used in trials to gain convictions. In fact, the Fourth Amendment prohibition against unreasonable search and seizure in the United States was not taken seriously by federal agents until 1914, when the U.S. Supreme Court decided ***Weeks v. United States***, which established the *exclusionary rule* and its applicability to federal agents (see *Boyd v. United States*, 116 U.S. 616, 1886). The exclusionary rule prohibits the use in trials of illegally obtained evidence, that is, evidence obtained through illegal searches and seizures. For almost a century now the exclusionary rule has been a source of debate and disagreement among criminal justice professionals. Some states just ignored the *Weeks* decision.[24]

In *Wolf v. Colorado* (1949) the Supreme Court made a legislative tally and found that thirty states rejected the *Weeks* doctrine and only seventeen states embraced the doctrine. In other words, the majority of states did not require that the exclusionary rule be applied to the actions of state and local law enforcement officers. While evidence seized inappropriately by federal agents could be suppressed and excluded from trial, the Court held that states were not required to exclude evidence similarly obtained by state and local agents even if the evidence would have been excluded had federal agents' actions resulted in the seizure.[25]

This translated into what is known as the **silver platter doctrine** from 1914 until 1960, whereby federal agents could use evidence provided to them by state and local law enforcement agents in federal courts that would have been illegal had the federal agents procured the evidence in the same manner. The contingency was that the federal agent(s) were not to have conspired with the state and local agents for the production of the evidence. This meant that state and local agents could hand over what could have been illegally seized evidence in state prosecutions on a "silver platter" to federal agents for use in federal courts. The silver platter doctrine was not erased until 1960 in *Elkins v. U.S.* This case ended the practice of using illegally seized evidence in federal prosecutions regardless the origin of the evidence from federal, state, or local law enforcement agents.[26]

The exclusionary rule was designed by judges to deter police misconduct.[27] Today, the exclusionary rule has been applied as a constitutional requirement in all states as well as in federal jurisdictions.

The exclusionary rule was expanded and clarified further in a major Supreme Court decision, ***Mapp v. Ohio***. The story is as follows: Don King, the boxing promoter, had his home bombed, and the police were looking for the suspect.[28] Three Cleveland police officers arrived at the home of a woman named Dolree Mapp, acting on information that a person was hiding there who was wanted for questioning in connection with the bombing and also that the home contained gambling paraphernalia. Ms. Mapp, after conferring by phone with her attorney, refused to admit the police officers. The three officers placed the house under surveillance until joined some three hours later by four additional officers. They approached the house and forcibly entered it. In the meantime, Mapp's attorney arrived, but the police would not allow him to enter the house or confer with Mapp. When Mapp demanded to see a search warrant, the officers held out a paper they claimed was a warrant and Mapp seized it and placed it inside her blouse. After a struggle the police recovered the paper, which apparently was not really a warrant, and handcuffed Mapp because she had resisted their recovery efforts. She was forcibly taken upstairs to her bedroom and restrained while police searched the entire house. In the basement they discovered and confiscated obscene materials concealed in a trunk, possession of which later became the basis of the charge for which Mapp was convicted.

A number of states did not deem the Fourth Amendment's prohibition against unreasonable searches and seizures applicable to state and local law enforcement agents until the landmark decision in *Mapp v. Ohio* (1961). The judicially created **incorporation doctrine** has been used as a means for the Court to apply fundamental rights enunciated in the federal constitution to the states via the Fourteenth Amendment (see Justice Black's discussion of the incorporation doctrine in *Gideon v. Wainwright*, 372 U.S. 335 [1963] at 341–342). As seen with the evolution of what is considered unreasonable search and seizure from *Weeks* to *Wolf* to *Elkins* to *Mapp* and to inventions that could not have been fathomed in 1791, such as the automobile, airplane, telephone, and computer, this *illustrates* the importance of the members of the U.S. Supreme Court as they strive to make a document, the Bill of Rights, written over 200 years ago, adaptable and applicable to more modern innovations.

At the time of the Mapp search and arrest, Ohio did not follow **the exclusionary rule** that would require that evidence improperly seized be excluded at trial. She was convicted based on that evidence and later appealed her conviction claiming the search had been illegal. In the *Mapp* decision, the Supreme Court stated, "We hold that all evidence obtained by searches and seizures in violation of the Constitution is, by that same authority, inadmissible in a state court." If a criminal goes free because "the constable has blundered," then, the Court wrote, "The criminal goes free, if he must, but it is the law that sets him free. Nothing can destroy a government more quickly than its failure to observe its own laws."[29]

Under the **"fruit of the poisonous tree doctrine"** it followed that if the evidence (fruit) seized by the police were the product of illegal action by the police (poisonous tree) then anything that evolved from that action would need to be considered tainted and should be excluded or suppressed from use at trial.[30] In general, police and prosecutors strongly criticized the exclusionary rule as acting to "handcuff" the police in their law enforcement objectives and maintaining it would invalidate many searches.[31] Over time, a series of U.S. Supreme Court cases began to carve exceptions to the exclusionary rule, which served to lessen this perceived negative impact of the exclusionary rule. The Court fashioned a **"good faith exception"** to the rule by determining that the results of a search conducted by police who in good faith believed they acted properly should be admissible at trial and that only evidence seized when the police knowingly acted improperly in obtaining it should be excluded. (Also, see other exceptions within the endnote.)[32]

Search remains a difficult decision for police. Two hundred years ago the Founding Fathers could not have imagined the complexities of our modern technologically advanced society. Police practice and the law have to keep up with changing conditions. Several issues have been raised during recent decades which have stretched legal reasoning and directed police decisions regarding search. For instance, can a police officer search a hotel room occupied by a person who is not currently available based on the hotel clerk's permission? No, according to the Supreme Court in *Stoner* v. *California*, a hotel's clerk's interests in a hotel resident's Fourth Amendment rights to be free from unreasonable searches and seizures are not the same as those of the room's occupant. Therefore, in the absence of a search warrant or exigent circumstances, a hotel clerk cannot consent to a search of a room rented by someone else, even if the renter is a robbery suspect.[33]

The guiding principles of the *Stoner* case also apply to landlord-lessee relationships, where **"common authority"** over an area to be searched has been found to be a crucial consideration in several cases. The question in *U.S. v. Matlock* was, can police search a residence shared by two unrelated persons? In this case Mr. Matlock and Ms. Graff were living together in a house when Matlock was arrested in the front yard. He was not asked for consent to search the residence. Ms. Graff consented to allow the officers to search the premises even though they did not have a search warrant. They found almost $5,000 in cash inside a closet within a bedroom shared by Graff and Matlock, and the court determined Ms. Graff had common authority over the area searched. Therefore, the search was considered legitimate and the monetary evidence allowed.[34]

What happens if one resident consents to a search and the other does not? In *Georgia v. Randolph*, when the police arrived and asked for consent to search, one of the residents consented to the search and the other inhabitant (the suspect) refused to consent to the search. The Court clarified if one of the inhabitants with common authority refuses the search then the search cannot take place at that time. Of course, if probable cause exists and can be articulated for the search, it may be possible to obtain a search warrant for the premises.[35]

The concept of common authority applies to roommates as well. For example, if a person shares an apartment with another roommate, in any areas within that apartment where there is common authority, the roommate may legally consent to a search by police if the other roommate is not there to deny consent. For example, if one roommate placed illegal drugs in the refrigerator that both use, the roommate can consent to a police search of that refrigerator. However, if each roommate has separate, private bedrooms, then the roommate cannot legally consent to a police search of the other's bedroom, as one roommate does not share common authority over the roommate's bedroom. So, the concept of common authority matters a great deal when police decide whether it is proper to search an area or not. Sometimes it may be unclear whether a particular area in an apartment or house is commonly used, but the Court indicated as long as law enforcement reasonably believes under the totality of the circumstances that the person who authorized the search has common authority the search is valid.[36]

A common practice among colleges and universities is to require students who live on campus to sign a housing agreement, which is a document that when signed constitutes a formal, legal, and binding agreement between the student and the educational institution. For example, a clause within such an agreement might indicate "I understand that College/University personnel will need to gain access to my room for various reasons during the academic year. The reasons include, but are not limited to, making repairs, health and fire safety inspections, safety inspections during break periods, or for violations of policy as outlined in the Student Code of Conduct. Whenever possible, advance notice of entry will be given, but is not required."

Whatever contraband is discovered from such entries into dorm rooms as described above can be used to establish probable cause for the police to request and obtain a search warrant. The key is that the police cannot have participated in or initiated the initial entry into the dorm room that resulted in the discovery of the contraband. Searches and seizures by private persons are not governed by the Fourth Amendment. Therefore, student X could break into student Y's dorm room; steal half a kilo of cocaine, and alert police to the remaining half kilo left in the dorm room. This could conceivably lead to issuance of a search warrant for the dorm room. The only repercussions for student X might possibly be criminal charges for breaking and entering and for possession of cocaine, as he is not a government agent and is therefore not obligated to uphold student Y's Fourth Amendment rights.[37]

One's reasonable expectation of privacy, a value in a democratic society and implicit in the Bill of Rights, impacts the government's ability to intrude into people's lives. Generally, the more public or mobile an act or event, the less one has of a reasonable expectation of privacy.

Search of persons, premises, and vehicles is an extremely complex and controversial investigatory technique, yet one considered essential by most police agencies. Where the scene of an arrest is a suspect's home, searches undertaken without warrants must be limited to those areas immediately adjacent to where the arrest occurred. The reasoning behind this is that police must be allowed to search places within the suspect's reach in order to prevent him or her from grabbing a weapon or destroying evidence. Searching the rest of the home would require consent, a warrant, or exigent circumstances.[38]

Search of Motor Vehicles

Automobile searches have been treated somewhat differently from searching premises, giving a wider scope to warrantless motor vehicle searches. Drivers are more readily able to flee or discard evidence before warrants could be obtained, so officers do have more leeway in decisions about searches under such circumstances.[39] The same is true for motor homes, as probable cause requirements for warrantless searches of cars also apply to motor homes due to their mobility.[40]

But does this mean that police are permitted to search a vehicle in a traffic stop? Can they search the passenger area or trunk? At the scene of a traffic stop searches undertaken without warrants must also be limited. Generally, police are allowed to search places within the suspect's reach in order to prevent him or her from grabbing a weapon or destroying evidence. Searching the rest of the vehicle would require consent, probable cause, or exigent circumstances. The Court in *New York* v. *Belton* and *U.S.* v. *Ross* expounded on the scope of vehicle searches incident to arrest and when probable cause is present.[41]

What about the search of a U-Haul trailer being pulled behind a car? (See **Critical Thinking 5.2.**)

Critical Thinking 5.2 Request to Search

One of the authors of this textbook, in preparation to pull a U-Haul trailer across country to graduate school, drove his vehicle with the trailer attached to a ballpark beside his house to practice backing the trailer up before the trip. As you might imagine, unbeknownst to the officer, the trailer was mainly loaded with books to assist in the grueling phenomenon that is graduate study. Out of nowhere, a deputy, in a vehicle with lights glaring and siren blaring, approaches and stops the vehicle with the trailer. The deputy asks your author to see his license and registration and asks if he can take a look in the U-Haul trailer. The license and the registration is produced, but your author states that unless the officer has probable cause or a search warrant no consent to a search is given. The officer retreats to his cruiser, radios in, hurriedly returns to the stopped vehicle, throws the license and registration at the author, and announces that he has another pressing call that he must answer. The officer takes off with lights glaring and siren blazing.

What just happened? Should individuals know their rights? Should the subject have consented to the search because he had nothing to hide?

Even the Supreme Court has difficulty spelling out every possible contingency in a police officer's decisions regarding vehicle searches. Sometimes, as in the *Belton* case referenced above, dissenting opinions include questions and issues for the Court to consider on another day. In *Belton*, both Justices Brennan and Marshall asked the question "Does it matter whether the suspect is standing in close proximity to the car when the search is conducted?" (p. 471). They were concerned that a police officer may search a vehicle even when the suspect clearly could not grab a weapon from the vehicle or destroy evidence within the vehicle. Not until 2009 would the Court add further clarity to this question. In 2009, the Court considered the case of a police search of a vehicle after occupants had been arrested. In this case the driver and two other occupants of the stopped vehicle had been handcuffed and secured in separate police vehicles by five officers. Thus, the Court held it was not reasonable to believe that any of the men could have returned to the vehicle to access a weapon or destroy evidence. Furthermore, the purpose of the arrest was for operating a motor vehicle with a suspended license, and there could be no reasonable expectation on the part of the police that evidence related to that crime would be found in the vehicle.[42]

All of these Supreme Court decisions affect the way police are trained and the development of departmental policies. Progressive police departments strive to be sure their officers are properly trained and informed regarding their decisions to search so as to assure the professionalism of the officers as well as to avoid wasting the time of prosecutors and courts in attempting to use improperly obtained evidence at trial.

In 1991, two important cases involving search were decided. The U.S. Supreme Court ruled in *Florida v. Bostick* that evidence seized in a drug sweep of a public bus was admissible. Two police officers boarded a bus heading from Ft. Lauderdale to Miami, clearly identified themselves as police officers, said they were searching for possible drugs, and asked passengers to show identification and submit to a search of their luggage. The officers had no reasonable suspicion that anyone other than Bostick on the bus carried drugs. When Bostick was approached, he voluntarily surrendered his ticket and identification, which raised no suspicion. The officers then asked to search his luggage and explained that he had the right to refuse. Bostick consented (he later disputed this), and the officers found cocaine. They arrested Bostick and charged him with possession of a controlled substance with intent to distribute. He pled guilty but retained the right to appeal the search. In a split decision, the U.S. Supreme Court ruled that Bostick was not "detained" in the bus and therefore could have freely refused the search, the officers were not required to advise him of his right to refuse consent, and that such warrantless searches without probable cause are justified in the effort to fight the war on drugs.[43]

In the second case, *California v. Acevedo*, the U.S. Supreme Court upheld the search of a man's car without a warrant. In this case police had been informed by a federal drug agent that marijuana was being shipped via Federal Express and staked out the Federal Express office. They observed the addressee claim the package, followed him to his apartment, and then observed another man enter the apartment. When the second man came out of the apartment, he was carrying a brown paper bag containing what the officers considered to be a package about the size of one of the marijuana bundles in the Federal Express shipment. The officers did not have time to obtain a search warrant and were afraid the man would leave the scene and dispose of the package, so they stopped him, searched the car, opened the trunk and the bag, and discovered the marijuana. The court ruled that such a search was permissible because

Image by kali9 at istockphoto.com.

the officers had probable cause to believe the package placed in the trunk contained marijuana, even if there was not sufficient probable cause to search the entire car.[44]

Vehicle Stops

Generally, a vehicle stop requires reasonable suspicion by the police of illegal activity. This suspicion may be in the form of an equipment violation such as a broken taillight on an automobile.[45] An exception to the reasonable suspicion requirement for vehicle stops is seen with roadblocks.

Roadblocks

A common practice is for police department traffic units to set up roadblocks or systematic vehicle stops at a set location for the purpose of checking drivers' licenses and vehicle registration, as well as to conduct routine equipment safety checks. Sometimes drivers are found to be driving with suspended or revoked licenses, vehicle registration is found to be elapsed or improper, and occasionally a police officer may detect evidence of alcohol or drug use and proceed with further investigation. Such policy is a reasonable tool in the law enforcement arsenal as long as vehicles are stopped in a non-random fashion and motorists are briefly inconvenienced.[46]

Similarly, interior border checkpoints to detect illegal aliens are seen as worthy of intervention for brief stops without reasonable suspicion being present.[47] Likewise, police checkpoints set up without reasonable suspicion under exigent circumstances surrounding very serious crimes are allowable, such as assisting in the capture of a dangerous offender, attempting to save the life of a kidnap victim, or locating the

Nox. Photo by LPD.

perpetrator of a hit and run accident.[48] Although police may stop a vehicle at a police roadblock, probable cause is legally necessary to search a vehicle prior to arrest, unless consent is given or exigent circumstances exist.[49]

What about the search of a car towed in for the accumulation of overdue parking tickets and impounded? Normally, police conduct an "inventory search" of property inside the car in a police car park, primarily as a safety precaution and to verify any valuables which may be contained. As long as such an inventory search was not done for purposes of a police fishing expedition, the Court has said it is legal, and probable cause is not required for such a procedure.[50] That means any contraband found during the inventory could be legally used against the owner. This tactic is often utilized by authorities to circumvent the establishment of probable cause and still justify a look inside the vehicle.

Police Search Dogs

Police and Homeland Security agents routinely use specially trained dogs in the detection of drugs or explosives. Such use of dogs in police work is not technically considered a search under the Fourth Amendment. An "alert" by a police dog can establish probable cause for an officer to conduct a search. In 2005, the Court ruled that a dog alerting to a specific location where it had detected the scent of an illegal substance during a legal traffic stop was acceptable.[51] Due also to public safety concerns associated with heightened security in airports and the effort to detect illegal drug importation, trained dogs legally sniff for illegal contraband. As long as the duration of such stops is not excessively long and law enforcement agents/dogs are legally in the place where the items are encountered, these intrusions are acceptable.[52]

In *Florida v. Harris* (2012), the U.S. Supreme Court established at a routine traffic stop that if a police canine alerts to an illegal substance in a vehicle—even if the dog has not been trained to detect that specific type of contraband—probable cause existed for a search of Harris' truck. Ingredients for manufacturing of methamphetamine were discovered.[53] In practice, many departments require that the production of a canine for a "sniff" during a routine traffic stop must come to pass within a reasonable amount of time, such as the normal amount of time it would take to write a traffic citation. Of course, a judge or jury may ultimately determine what is "reasonable."

The U.S. Supreme Court distinguishes canine alert in a home from such an alert in a vehicle in the following case. In *Florida v. Jardines* (2013) dealt with a canine alerting to marijuana after "bracketing" outside the front door of Jardines. The alert by the dog led to a search warrant and the obtainment of the marijuana. However, the Court stated, "when it comes to the Fourth Amendment, the home is first among equals. At the amendment's 'very core' stands 'the right of a man to retreat into his own home and there be free from unreasonable governmental intrusion.'... This right would be of little practical value if the State's agents could stand in a home's porch or side garden and trawl for evidence with impunity; the right to retreat would be significantly diminished if the police could enter a man's property to observe his repose from just outside the front window.

We therefore regard the area 'immediately surrounding and associated with the home'—what our cases call the curtilage—as 'part of the home itself for Fourth Amendment purposes.' ... This area around the home is 'intimately linked to the home, both physically and psychologically," and is where "privacy expectations are most heightened.' ... Here there is no doubt that the officers entered it: The front porch is the classic exemplar of an area adjacent to the home and 'to which the activity of home life extends.' ... To find a visitor knocking on the door is routine (even if sometimes unwelcome); to spot that same visitor exploring the front path with a metal detector, or marching his bloodhound into the garden before saying hello and asking permission, would inspire most of us to—well, call the police."[54] Thus, the marijuana seized in this case was illegally seized. Since the police canine was not legally in the place from which the marijuana was sniffed, the previously discussed **fruit of the poisonous tree doctrine** would forbid use of this contraband as evidence against Jardines.

Computer Searches and Seizures

The crucial question that emerges regarding searches and seizures of computers is, do such searches violate the people's Fourth Amendment right to be "secure in their persons, houses, papers and effects against unreasonable searches and seizures"? On the surface, the answer is, of course that is possible. So, what processes should police utilize to both protect the right of people, and at the same time secure and maintain evidence? This is a newly developing area of the law, with little case law to guide the way. Clearly, police can no more seize and examine computer files with abandon any more than they can go into a person's house or files or possessions without first adhering to Fourth Amendment rights; generally, that means securing a warrant from a judge.

Police need to establish probable cause in order to convince a judicial authority to issue a search warrant. This standard of probable cause for a computer search is the same as would be required for any other type of search or seizure. To establish probable cause for a computer search and seizure the suspect needs to be believed to likely be in possession of a computer containing incriminating data, with the computer and data likely to be located at the place specified to be searched in the warrant. In particular, a specific description of the hardware or software to be examined should be offered. Of course, if the information desired is contained on the hard drive of a specific computer then the scope of the search is limited to that particular device. If, however, the desired information is contained on a removable storage device, such as a flash drive, the police may look anywhere within the premises specified in the warrant where the device might be reasonably located (i.e., drawers or cabinets).[55]

Computer searches are governed by the same exceptions to the warrant requirements as other searches. In other words, warrantless searches can be reasonably carried out on computers when there is valid consent, material is in plain view,[56] exigent circumstances exist coupled with probable cause, or the search is contemporaneous to a lawful arrest as limited by *Chimel*.[57]

According to the Department of Justice, other than the exceptions noted above, police should view computers just like any other closed containers such as briefcases or file cabinets. Generally, law enforcement is prohibited from being able to search and seize closed containers without a warrant. However, if an individual has openly made information available, or a computer is stolen, or someone else other than the owner also is permitted to use the computer, then no reasonable expectation of privacy exists, and therefore no Fourth Amendment protections against unreasonable searches and seizures exists.[58]

But, what about e-mails? Is e-mail, mail? Only to be opened by the person it is addressed to and therefore requiring a court order to open? As of 2009, no U.S. Supreme Court decision has specifically considered seizure of e-mails by the government. However, a lower court in 2007 did identify guidelines that an e-mail subscriber must be provided prior notice by the government and an opportunity to challenge the search prior to the seizure. If not, the government must demonstrate that the e-mail subscriber possessed no reasonable expectation of privacy, thereby not maintaining any protection via the Fourth Amendment.[59]

Text messages, twitter, e-mails ... do we all expect such communications to be private? The Supreme Court will likely be the venue where the issue of police access to such communications will be resolved.[60] As telecommunication in society has shifted from analog to digital, new technology enables police officers to investigate cell phone records, text messages, e-mails, and other forms of communication.[61] Although not yet addressed by the U.S. Supreme Court, lower courts have held that cell phone users do not have a reasonable expectation of privacy because, like cordless phones, the signals they transmit over the public airwaves are sometimes intercepted. Even so, government agents currently can only monitor such calls with a warrant. As such, the Communications Assistance for Law Enforcement Act (CALEA) requires the cellular telephone industry to make the monitoring of cell phone calls by government agents easier.[62] While courts have yet to protect the federal government from litigation for warrantless wiretaps, a U.S. District Court recently held that such warrantless monitoring of e-mail and telephonic communications has been authorized by Congress and that telecommunication companies involved in the process at the request of the government are free from legal liability for their involvement in such intrusions.[63] This certainly serves to create an atmosphere that is conducive to such intrusions. Clarity on this issue is likely to be offered by the U.S. Supreme Court in a case entitled Carpenter v. United States, in which the Court agreed on June 5, 2017 to hear in the next term.[64]

Wiretap and Electronic Surveillance

Modern police have many techniques to investigate, observe, and eavesdrop on suspects. For instance, as previously discussed, they can even use dogs to sniff out certain illegal substances in cars or suitcases or any number of other places. Technology for electronic surveillance has advanced far beyond the use of man's best friend, however. Parabolic listening cones can be used outdoors to pick up conversations hundreds of feet away, tiny microphones can broadcast from anywhere, scopes give vision in the dark, heat sensors follow suspects at midnight, and tiny camouflaged television cameras can be strategically placed in the smallest, most innocuous places.

One of the older but still widely used eavesdropping techniques is wiretapping.[65] Even the term, wiretapping, seems archaic in this unhooked era. When telephones first became widely used, police quickly saw what a great source of information was transmitted over the telephone wires. With party lines and nosey operators, privacy considerations seemed irrelevant. So, early in the twentieth century, the basis for determining whether telephone wiretapping was legally permissible or not revolved around whether there had been a constitutional trespass on to a suspect's property to attach the wiretap. In 1928 the Supreme Court ruled that if there was no trespass in order to tap the phone, there was no invasion of privacy. Just as birds were free to sit on telephone lines outside a residence, police were free to tap exposed phone lines.[66] However, by 1967, with the widespread use of telephone booths and the assumed privacy of closing a door while on a public phone, the Court held that a person stepping inside a telephone booth had a reasonable expectation of privacy and that their telephone conversation could not legally be overheard without a warrant regardless of whether a physical trespass had taken place to plant the wiretap.[67] Thus, generally, a warrant is required for a wiretap of a private phone today. Some exceptions apply. For instance, if one party to a conversation consents, a government agent, depending on state law, can use an electronic device to record a telephone conversation,[68] or a supposed friend may allow the police to listen in on telephone conversations.[69]

Typically, after securing a search warrant in a wired context, the police arrange with the telephone company to implant electronic recording devices ("bugs") in the telephone lines of suspects. In this way, they can listen to and record all incoming and outgoing phone conversations. Similar bugs, again used with judicial approval, are sometimes concealed, often quite cleverly, directly in the houses of suspects to pick up and record non-telephone conversations in their homes.

Surveillance cameras are pervasive today in many public places, a fact that has been very useful to police in less celebrated cases and some highly publicized instances. The arrest of Joseph P. Smith in Florida, for instance, was the result of a surveillance camera at a car wash parking lot which recorded Smith abducting Carli Brucia.[70] In the Craigslist Killer case at Boston's Marriott Copley Place, digital closed-circuit cameras detected alleged killer Phillip Markoff, a medical student, enhancing the investigation and leading to his arrest.[71] Surveillance cameras also captured images concerning the London subway bombings in 2005.[72]

The case of Robert Farley provides a prime example of the power of video to solve crime. Robert Farley and his wife planned an overnight New Year's Eve getaway at the Red Rose Inn in Plant City, Florida, with dinner and music included, leaving Robert's 93-year-old father, Walter, back at home. Robert is even seen on video dancing the night away with his wife and singing along with the music of the Temptations to "Papa Was a Rolling Stone." Robert and his wife returned home the next day only to find that Walter had been shot to death. Robert notified police that his father had been killed by an unidentified intruder. Robert seemingly had the perfect alibi. However, police review of the surveillance camera at the inn showed Robert Farley inexplicably leaving the premises during the evening. After subsequent questioning by police, Robert confessed to returning and killing his "crotchety" father, ransacking the house to make it look like a robbery, and even mailing valuables away to be retrieved later.[73]

Clearly, our society is under far greater public surveillance than any of the Founding Fathers could have anticipated. Most of us are often on camera. Many police departments video tape all traffic stops, bookings, searches, lineups, and sometimes, interrogations. Photos uploaded and contained on media-sharing systems can even be seized as evidence for trials, as in the Casey Anthony case.[74]

Sometimes people are observed without their knowledge while using a computer. For example, Polk County, Florida, Sheriff Grady Judd recently announced the apprehension of 39 of 45 suspected child pornographers as the result of a clandestine Internet investigation.[75] Every computer connected to the Internet has a traceable Internet protocol (IP) address in numeric form, and the accessing and sharing of illegal files over the Internet typically is the avenue that alerts law enforcement via digital identifiers to a specific IP address.[76] With the cooperation of Internet service providers, police acquire customer information, obtain search warrants, and assist in the prosecution of sexual predators and others for a variety of criminal activities.

The use of surveillance in general raises two questions: Is the evidence it yields legally admissible in court, and, if so, when and under what conditions? The answers to these issues ultimately depend on whether a constitutionally protected right to privacy exists[77] and how far that right extends. The U.S. Supreme Court considered an illustrative case in which police officers, acting on a tip that someone was growing marijuana, went to his farm, followed a path around a locked gate posted with a "No

Trespassing" sign, and found a field of marijuana over a mile from the farmhouse. The suspect was arrested, but at trial moved to have the case dismissed, arguing that the method of gathering the evidence against him constituted an illegal invasion of his privacy. The lower appellate courts agreed with his position, but the U.S. Supreme Court held the evidence to be admissible under an "open-fields" doctrine, that is, that the Fourth Amendment protects only reasonable expectations of privacy.[78]

Sometimes simple surveillance ("tailing" an individual or "staking out" a residence) or electronic surveillance is used not to gather evidence specifically to be used in court but to accumulate "intelligence" information, which, in its entirety, might be used to determine the extent of or to prove a criminal conspiracy in the future. Occasionally surveillance, whether conducted on an informer's tip or not, pays off with the observation of a crime being committed. And now and then surveillance is carried out by means of unusual assistance rendered to the police.

As electronic eavesdropping techniques have become more sophisticated, they have been heavily litigated. Covert, unobtrusive observation of suspects or premises is difficult to control, as in the case of the police use of a thermal imaging device to detect heat associated with lights used to grow marijuana in a private house, a grow house. Police used the device from the street without entry into the home and gathered information to obtain a search warrant. The Court held "[O]btaining by sense-enhancing technology any information regarding the interior of the home that could not otherwise have been obtained without physical intrusion into a constitutionally protected area constitutes a search[,]" and, under the circumstances, would have required a search warrant.[79]

Police surveillance is of major concern to everyone in our democratic society. The uncontrolled use of eavesdropping and other surveillance techniques would remove Americans' constitutional right to privacy.[80] In general, courts and legislatures have tried to set reasonable limits on surveillance practices, as they have on search practices. Such limits are intended to control police misuse of their power while allowing them to effectively gather evidence of crimes. Simple observation, tailing of suspects, and staking out of locations are usually left to police discretion, subject to court restraints only if the practices border on harassment. The use of electronic surveillance, however, is more stringently regulated, and both appellate courts and legislatures (including Congress) agree that prior judicial approval must be obtained before most mechanical forms of eavesdropping can be employed. Courts enforce this by invoking the **exclusionary rule**, forbidding any evidence obtained without prior judicial approval to be used in legal cases. Legislatures set time limits on wiretapping and require police to clearly identify targets of investigation before proceeding.

Congress has passed legislation providing stricter judicial control over electronic eavesdropping and specifying conditions and criteria limiting both the legitimate purposes and the scope of interceptions.[81] And it should be noted that virtually all of the police techniques used in domestic surveillance are also employed by major governmental powers in international relations.[82] Five weeks after the September 11, 2001, attacks on American soil the Uniting and Strengthening America by Providing Appropriate Tools Required to Intercept and Obstruct Terrorism Act (USA PATRIOT

Act) was passed by Congress to enhance the executive branch's ability to combat terrorism. The PATRIOT Act has expanded the government's ability to investigate and communicate regarding terrorism by monitoring such things as phone calls and e-mail transmissions, but concerns remain that innocent citizens may have their privacy invaded.[83] Governmental requests for wiretaps are rarely refused by the courts. Under the Foreign Surveillance Act (FISA) aimed at combatting terrorism and espionage, for example, since 1979, only .03% of the requests for electronic surveillance have been denied by the secretive FISA court.[84] Reportedly, since 1979, 38,365 FISA applications for surveillance have been approved by the court and only a dozen such warrants have been rejected, with none rejected in 2015. The majority of these requests under FISA are directed at foreigners, but 20% of the warrants have been directed at Americans.[85] Controversy regarding courts rubberstamping wiretap requests and suits regarding the PATRIOT Act will likely continue to emerge and be addressed in the courts.

Cellular Phones

Of course, the Founding Fathers could never have envisioned cellular phones when they pondered construction of the Fourth Amendment. However, the U.S. Supreme Court was faced with what is required for the police to legally search a cellphone in *Riley v. California* (2014). Chief Justice Roberts wrote the opinion for the Court in this case, which dealt with two vehicle stops and police review of driver cellphones. Roberts spoke of balancing an individual's privacy interests with governmental interests and addressed what was reasonable under the circumstances. He noted, "[c]ell phones ... place vast quantities of personal information literally in the hands of individuals." Roberts also said, "many of these devices are in fact minicomputers that also happen to have the capacity to be used as a telephone. They could just as easily be called cameras, video players, rolodexes, calendars, tape recorders, libraries, diaries, albums, televisions, maps, or newspapers."

Roberts also stated, "[o]ne of the most notable distinguishing features of modern cell phones is their immense storage capacity.... Most people cannot lug around every piece of mail they have received for the past several months, every picture they have taken, or every book or article they have read—nor would they have any reason to attempt to do so. And if they did, they would have to drag behind them a trunk of the sort held to require a search warrant ... rather than a container the size of the cigarette package."

He also indicated, "[d]igital data stored on a cell phone cannot itself be used as a weapon to harm an arresting officer or to effectuate the arrestee's escape. Law enforcement officers remain free to examine the physical aspects of a phone to ensure that it will not be used as a weapon—say, to determine whether there is a razor blade hidden between the phone and its case. Once an officer has secured a phone and eliminated any potential physical threats, however, data on the phone can endanger no one." Thus, the Court in *Riley* concluded "[t]he police generally may not, without a warrant, search digital information on a cell phone seized from an individual who has been arrested." Of course, if one voluntarily consents to such a search or exigent circumstances exist, a legal search may occur.[86]

Even if a search warrant is obtained, access to the contents of the phone may be problematic. For example, cell phones equipped with encryption technology or passwords may be difficult to penetrate. This was evident in the government suing Apple, Inc. to unlock the encrypted cellphone of radicalized Syed Rizwan Farook and his wife, Tashfeen Malik, who shot to death fourteen individuals at a center for the disabled in San Bernardino, California. Ultimately, the FBI dropped the suit against Apple, as they were able to crack the code and gain access to the contents of the phone with help from an outside entity. The FBI reportedly paid $1.3 million to an un-named corporation to hack in and ascertain the contents of the phone. Media outlets have sued the government to ascertain who provided the necessary information to crack the code and gain access to the iPhone's contents.[87]

Let's say a man's girlfriend has been murdered, but the man claims he was 100 miles away at the time the horrific act occurred. However, the police know he has a cell phone, and they know they can possibly check his proximity to the location of the murder around the time of death. Unlike *Riley*, which focused on a search of cell phone contents, this scenario focuses on signals transmitted over the public airwaves. This is known as "cell phone pinging," as cell phones typically ping off the nearest cell phone tower when a call is made—which can serve to identify the date, time, and location of a call. While lower federal courts have been divided on whether citizens have a resonable expectation of privacy under such circumstances,[88] and whether a warrant is required, the U.S. Supreme Court heard oral arguments in the fall of 2017 and, as previously mentioned, are expected to render an opinion in 2018 in *Carpenter v. U.S.*

Undercover Operations

A major police investigatory technique is undercover work, in which officers whose identity and profession are concealed join criminal gangs and suspected criminal conspiracies.[89] They pretend to be criminals themselves, in all sorts of settings from drug-dealing to terrorism, and pass along the information they gain to their police colleagues, who then "make the bust," that is, arrest the suspects identified by the undercover cops. Of course, the vulnerability of officers is contingent upon the maintenance of their undercover identities.

Of course, some undercover activities are not as exhilarating and dangerous as others. Even so, they may send a valuable message and promote public safety as reflected in the following efforts regarding texting and driving.

According to the U.S. Department of Transportation (DOT), cellphones are involved in 1.6 million auto crashes annually, resulting in 6,000 deaths. Ninety-eight percent of motorists surveyed informed the DOT that they knew texting while driving was unsafe, but 49% indicated they do it anyway. This has prompted some police departments to place officers in plain clothes at freeway off ramps where panhandlers often congregate. The "undercover" officers hold cardboard signs indicating, "Police [arrows

Photo property of R.N. Slate.
NOTE: This photo is a reenactment. The person in the photo is not an actual police officer.

pointing to officer]. I am not homeless. Looking for seatbelt and cellphone violations." Drivers tend to be oblivious and commit violations within the presence of the cardboard holding officers who in turn radio ahead to waiting officers in marked squad cars. In some jurisdictions, first offense for driving while handling a cellphone can result in a fine of $162, and a second offense can result in a $285 penalty.[90] In a similar operation in Concord, New Hampshire, and undercover police officer poses with a cardboard sign that reads "WWJD?" (What Would Jesus Do?), with crosses drawn on the cardboard and includes the words "REPENT! THE END IS NEAR!" A female driver stopped at a red light grabs her cellphone and takes a picture of the man. Moments later she is pulled over by a policeman in a squad car and ticketed for violating the state's law against using cellphones or other electronic devices while driving.[91]

Nationally, a texting driver is 23 times more likely than a non-texting driver to crash. Specially designed undercover SUVs, which allow state troopers to sit up higher than other drivers and look down into their vehicles to detect distracted driving, are in operation in New York. A distracted driver can lose five points off his or her driver's license for a violation.[92] Tennessee Highway Patrol officers have even used semi-trucks seized via asset forfeiture to provide a vantage point to observe motorists and their texting habits.[93] Similarly, police in Austin, Texas, have been known to ride buses to provide a vantage point for identifying drivers who are texting while driving.[94]

Usually the undercover officers act merely as informants, telling the "visible" police who to look for and where and why to look for them (and unlike citizen informants, who are usually participants in the crimes they are reporting on, the undercover police officers only pretend to be criminals). But sometimes an undercover officer makes the bust himself by "flashing the badge" and arresting the former "colleagues" in crime.

Often from the point of view of police administrators, however, an undercover officer is more valuable if he or she maintains the undercover status and continues to pass along incriminating information. Once the identity of an officer becomes known, as it inevitably does when he or she makes an arrest, the usefulness of the agent is lost, or at the very least severely limited, as an undercover agent.

The extent to which an undercover police officer must become personally involved, or participate, in illegal activity in order to maintain credibility while gathering sufficient evidence to arrest others is a major problem in such operations. Police officers sometimes blend in with the criminal gangs they have infiltrated not only by wearing the appropriate disguises, but by emulating criminal behavior.[95] But should police officers commit crimes in order to enforce the law?

The use of undercover law enforcement techniques is a controversial topic among judges, lawyers, prisoners, arrestees, and the American Civil Liberties Union (ACLU). The work of undercover officers, which are often critical to restoring order in areas where organized and disorganized crime have control over communities, has the potential to violate constitutional limits on police power as delineated in the First, Fourth and Fifth Amendments. It is imperative that law enforcement officials be intimately familiar with the U.S. Supreme Court case law to reduce the risks of violating individuals' rights during an undercover investigation.[96]

Related to the matter of the personal involvement of police officers in crime, is the question of the extent to which undercover officers may "encourage" others to commit offenses in order to make arrests. "Encouragement" involves crimes committed privately with "victims" who are willing participants—usually "vice crimes" such as solicitation by a prostitute, gambling, and the illegal sales of liquor, narcotics, or pornography.[97]

"Encouragement" is a word used to describe the activity of the police or a police agent who (1) acts as a victim; (2) intends, by his or her actions, to encourage a suspect to commit a crime; (3) actually communicates this encouragement to the suspect; and (4) thereby has some influence on the commission of the crime. It does not usually consist of a single act but a series of acts, part of the normal interplay between "victim" and "criminal."[98]

Although encouragement is an important practice, used by national, state, and local law enforcement agencies throughout the country, it has no generally accepted name. At times it is loosely or mistakenly referred to as entrapment, a label properly reserved for outright illegal forms of encouragement. The term "encouragement," although imperfect and perhaps connoting impropriety to some, is intended only to be descriptive, a neutral word neither critical nor complimentary of the practice. But the ambiguousness of the term points to our uneasiness over the propriety of police encouragement of criminal activity.[99]

Sometimes persons arrested in undercover operations claim they were entrapped and that they were not intending to commit a crime until a police officer set a trap for them. Entrapment is a powerful defense and can be used as a defense to a criminal charge in virtually every jurisdiction in America. Usually defendants claim they were entrapped in police decoy and sting operations with police acting as potential victims[100] or setting up "buy-bust or sell-bust schemes." This is most common in cases involving narcotics or prostitution. In such vice crimes police exercise more leeway in their discretion and with greater discretion comes a greater risk of entrapment.[101]

In addition, sometimes police establish bogus fronts for fencing stolen property and after purchasing stolen property from unsuspecting burglars and thieves, they make arrests.[102] Sting operations may also include bogus prizes or awards. For example, Boston police pretended to establish a film company with promises of making respondents to their bogus advertisement famous. Those with outstanding warrants were targeted in the sting. No one met Robert DeNiro; instead of being cast in a movie, approximately 60 persons were arrested.[103]

Police may also collaborate with private citizens in creating opportunities for individuals to commit crime, a well-known example of which is the NBC television show, *To Catch a Predator* (see **Critical Thinking 5.3**).[104] Such operations are not without controversy, not the least of which is whether and to what extent offenders are encouraged, which is legal, or entrapped, which is not.

Dateline NBC television correspondent Chris Hansen has initiated a number of investigations of men reportedly attempting to make contact with underage teenagers for the purpose of engaging in sexual activity with them.[105] In these investigative reports, called *To Catch a Predator*, that have aired on NBC, Hansen has collaborated with law enforcement and Perverted Justice, a non-profit foundation that recruits private citizens to seek out and identify pedophiles and potential predators.[106] NBC pulled the show after a predator caught up in a sting, described below, committed suicide.[107] The show has since morphed into *Crime Watch Daily*, with Chris Hansen at the helm at times with a predator watchdog group by the name of Tetrad Core. In cooperation with police, pictures of underage children are posted on social media to lure predators to a location where Hansen confronts suspects and shames them.[108]

Critical Thinking 5.3 To Catch a Predator

A typical episode would go something like this: Internet contact is established between an adult Perverted Justice member who indicates during a detailed online chat with a suspected predator that she is underage and available for a rendezvous for a sexual liaison. After the online conversation becomes sexual, an address for the meet-up is provided to the male, and the hidden cameras ultimately pick up the arrival of the suspect at a decoy residence. Upon arrival, the Perverted Justice member stays out of reach of the suspect and immediately scampers off to allegedly brush her teeth or perform some other bogus errand. At this juncture, Chris Hansen emerges and the confrontation begins, with the subject twisting in the wind, as he is confronted by Hansen with incriminating statements obtained from his electronic chat with the Perverted Justice member who was not underage after all. Each segment culminates with Hansen identifying himself (if the subjects do not already know his identity), bringing the cameras in and camera operators in view, and the subjects scurrying from the house, often running unknowingly into the arms of waiting law enforcement, who have even been camouflaged as shrubbery to jump on subjects upon exiting the residence and to detain them for processing.

The *To Catch a Predator* show has been criticized for blurring the lines between journalism and law enforcement, with allegations that correspondent Hansen has seemingly directed law enforcement operations. The show has been sued by a former producer, who alleged that Perverted Justice did not maintain accurate records. The sister of a Texas prosecutor by the name of Louis Conradt has also filed a lawsuit against the show as well. Conradt allegedly, according to Perverted Justice, made sexual overtures online. Although he did not go to the decoy house, as camera crews and police closed in on his house, Conradt committed suicide. **What familiarity do you have with this show or *Crime Watch Daily*? Do you believe the tactics used are appropriate? Why or why not?**

Two primary entrapment standards, **subjective** and **objective**, are used today which emerged from the Supreme Court case, *Sorrells v. U.S.* The subjective model focuses on the *defendant's behavior* to assess whether inducements by the police or the predisposition of the defendant resulted in the criminal activity. Police may merely provide an avenue for an already predisposed individual to engage in illegal activity, but, as indicated in *Sorrells*, "it is not permissible to ensnare the innocent and law-abiding into the commission of crime."[109] The objective model for entrapment focuses on the *behavior of police* to determine whether an innocent individual had been compelled by police actions to engage in criminal behavior. In other words, police are not to create criminals, they are to apprehend existing ones; entrapment defenses have been created both judicially and legislatively to combat overzealous police practices and/or gauge the predisposition of suspects.[110] (See **Critical Thinking 5.4**—The Objective[111] and Subjective[112] Tests for Entrapment.)

Critical Thinking 5.4 The Objective and Subjective Test for Entrapment

"I've never had a problem with drugs. I've had problems with the police."

—Keith Richards of the Rolling Stones[113]

The Objective Test for Entrapment

In this decoy case an undercover police officer posed as a vulnerable passed out drunk in a passageway just off a busy sidewalk with money visibly hanging out of a sack. Other officers were strategically secreted to nab passersby who took money from the decoy.

Applying the objective entrapment standard, how do you think the Supreme Court of Hawaii ruled in this case?

The Subjective Test for Entrapment

In *Russell*, the U.S. Supreme Court upon examination concluded that Russell was supplied an ingredient by an undercover federal narcotics agent that was necessary for the manufacture of methamphetamine (meth) in exchange for a cut of the unfinished product. Russell conceded he was predisposed to commit the crime, as he had already been manufacturing meth before the government agent's appearance; however, Russell maintained that the government's involvement in the matter necessitated an acquittal.

Applying the subjective test for entrapment, how do you think the Court ruled in this case?

In *Jacobson*, for over two years the defendant was bombarded by mailings and promotions from U.S. postal inspectors, the Customs Service, and a phony pen pal, representing five bogus agencies, aimed at attempting to entice him into ordering child pornography through the mail. After over 26 months of these mailings, Jacobson—a rural farmer—acquiesced and placed an order for child pornography through the mail.

Applying the subjective test for entrapment, how do you think the Court ruled in this case?

Arrest

Once the police have "probable cause" to believe suspected individuals did indeed commit the crime, arrests can be made. Arrest is the point of "intake" for the criminal justice process—the point at which governmental power actually touches the arrested person and compels him or her to conform to its practices. Arrest is also the point where criminal records are born, for this is the stage where suspects are "booked."

In some instances—say where a suspect has been named by a complainant—police may apprehend the individual through the authority of an arrest warrant. But more commonly, felony arrests are made without warrants. Such arrests are proper if, at the time they are carried out, the arresting officers have probable cause to believe that a felony has been committed (or is being committed) and that the person arrested is the one who committed the crime.

Arrest, properly speaking, involves taking a person into police custody (meaning a person is not free to leave) and transporting the person to a police station where booking (the recording of the arrest) takes place. There are some variations in this procedure and in the requirements for arrest. In some situations, primarily involving minor offenses, the suspect may be issued a citation, an order to appear at a later date, rather than being taken physically into custody. In regard to misdemeanors, as already mentioned, statutory laws, with some exceptions (such as shoplifting and domestic violence) require officers to actually witness the crime being committed—probable or reasonable cause to believe the person committed the crime does not in itself provide sufficient grounds for carrying out a warrantless arrest. And in making felony arrests, police officers may use such force (police use of force will be discussed in Chapter 6) as is necessary to take and maintain custody of suspects.[114]

The issue of probable cause is always a problem in regard to arrest. If the police could not prove they had probable cause to arrest a suspect, they could be held liable for damages in any legal action brought by the person they arrested. Civil juries determine the propriety of police behavior in arrests based on probable cause, not on the guilt or innocence of the suspects involved.[115]

It is commonly assumed that when police arrest a suspect they will accumulate evidence and move the case along to the prosecutor for a charging decision. However, a number of circumstances have been identified under which police arrest with no intention of prosecution. These include arrests of drunks, who are taken into custody for their own protection; street-walking prostitutes detained to "control and contain" the problem; and petty gamblers and liquor law violators where the penalties are small and the inconvenience of arrest is considered sufficient punishment.[116] Where no prosecution is intended, the police need not exercise special care to obtain evidence in ways that would make it admissible at trial. Furthermore, constitutional protections do not matter if a defendant pleads guilty.

In-Custody Interrogation

A suspect arrested for a felony (and for serious misdemeanors) is fingerprinted and photographed during the booking procedure. The detainee is searched and, after appropriate notification of a right to remain silent and to have a lawyer present, an in-custody interrogation can be carried out, during which the suspect is questioned regarding the offense for which he or she was arrested. The detainee may also be questioned in regard to other offenses.[117] The suspect has the right to refuse to answer questions, as guaranteed by the Fifth Amendment to the U.S. Constitution. The particularly guiding provision of the Fifth Amendment specifically states: "No person

Sequence of an Arrest—LPD—*The Ledger*

shall be held to answer for a capital, or otherwise infamous crime ... nor shall be compelled in any criminal case to be a witness against himself, nor be deprived of life, liberty, or property, without due process of law."

Also, if the suspect requests legal assistance, interrogation cannot proceed until he or she has conferred with counsel, unless, for example, the subsequent conversation with the police is initiated by the suspect (*Edwards v. Arizona*, 1981).[118] However, the U.S. Supreme Court recently held that if a "break in custody" goes for more than 14 days between interrogations after a suspect has requested an attorney the *Edwards* rule does not apply and officers may reinitiate questioning.[119] Also, the U.S. Supreme Court has held that although legal counsel has been formally appointed for a suspect this does not mean that the police are prohibited from questioning that suspect without his/her attorney's authorization or the attorney being present. Just because counsel has been appointed it does not automatically follow that an individual has invoked their right to an attorney. Only if the suspect invokes his/her *Miranda* rights would such a custodial interrogation need to legally cease.[120]

It should be noted that the implementation of such rights has not always been standard. Uniform nationwide requirements for notification of rights prior to in-custody interrogation were only established by the U.S. Supreme Court in 1966, in *Miranda v. Arizona*.[121] That case had to do with Ernesto Miranda, who was arrested in Phoenix, Arizona, and charged with kidnapping and rape. He was taken to police headquarters, where he was identified by the complainant. He was interrogated for two hours by detectives who admitted at trial that he was not advised of any right to

Image by RichLegg at istockphoto.com.

have counsel present at the interrogation. Miranda signed a written confession and was subsequently convicted, but appealed; nevertheless, his conviction was upheld by the Arizona Supreme Court. The U.S. Supreme Court, however, reversed the decision, declaring that such confessions are coerced and that interrogations carried out in the course of police investigations without notification of rights or the offer of legal assistance place suspects under "the will of the examiner."

The Supreme Court based its decision on the possibility that coerced confessions may be untrue. Certainly such confessions violate the Fifth Amendment prohibition against self-incrimination. Moreover, interrogations of suspects held in police custody are inherently coercive, so that suspects should (and must) be informed of their legal and constitutional rights, and, even more, those rights should (and must) be honored by the police. Thus, *Miranda* served primarily to protect unsophisticated, uneducated, and disadvantaged suspects from the intimidating practices of police interrogations, since sophisticated criminals have always known and exercised their Fifth Amendment rights and refused to answer any questions without their attorneys' presence.

By the time of the *Miranda* case, police use of confessions to gain convictions of criminals had become a primary tactic in investigations, even to the extent of ignoring more productive avenues of evidence gathering. The Court stated:

> Although confessions may play an important role in some convictions, the cases before us present graphic examples of the overstatement of the "need" for confessions. In each case authorities conducted interrogations ranging up to five days in duration despite the presence, through standard investigation practices, of considerable evidence against each defendant.[122]

The *Miranda* decision has dramatically impacted American police techniques, but from the day it was decided, it was extremely controversial, and bitterly opposed by many law enforcement officials. For one thing, it marked a departure from usual Supreme Court opinions in that it listed specific steps that must be followed by the police prior to in-custody interrogations. Most Court decisions that define the limits of search, arrest, interrogation, or other police procedures are essentially negative in that they forbid particular practices but do not specifically tell the police how to proceed properly. The Court normally prefers to leave the determination of proper practices to the police. For example, it might decide that a search took place under certain conditions that made it illegal under the Fourth Amendment, but, except by inference, not specify the conditions that would have made it legal. In *Miranda*, however, the court not only held the particular conditions of the interrogation to be improper but provided specific steps, the so-called *Miranda* warning, that officers must follow if they wish any custodial confessions by suspects to be accepted as admissible evidence at a trial. The *Miranda* warning requires that before interrogating suspects who are in custody, police must warn them of their Fifth Amendment right to remain silent (not to incriminate themselves), their Sixth Amendment right to have a lawyer present during questioning, and their right to terminate the interrogation at any time; they must also be warned that anything they say can and will be used against them. The primary aim of the *Miranda* decision is to protect one's right against self-incrimination. The purpose of allowing for an attorney's presence is to protect that right.

The actual ***Miranda*** **warning** typically covers the following. "You have the right to remain silent. Anything you say can and will be used against you in a court of law. You have the right to talk to a lawyer and have him present with you when you are being questioned. If you cannot afford to hire a lawyer, one will be appointed to represent you before any questioning, if you wish. You can decide at any time to exercise these rights and not answer any questions or make any statements. Do you understand each of these rights I have explained to you? Having these rights in mind, do you wish to talk to us now?" The U.S. Supreme Court has held that the warnings do not have to be given verbatim; for example, the last two statements are not required by *Miranda*, but most law enforcement agencies include them.[123] Officers often read the warning from a card carried on their person to a suspect in custody. This allows them to retrieve the card and read from it in later court proceedings so as not to be stumped by a zealous defense attorney in the pressurized atmosphere of testifying in court.

Whatever Happened to Ernesto Miranda?

Ernesto Miranda got a new trial after his conviction was overturned in *Miranda v. Arizona,* and he was convicted without the confession. On January 31, 1976, Miranda was stabbed to death in a dispute over less than $3.00 in a card game in a bar in Phoenix, Arizona. Ironically, his assailant was read *Miranda* warnings upon his arrest.[124]

Many police professionals and supporters criticized the *Miranda* decision as going too far, and handcuffing the police in their enforcement efforts, believing that such a rule would make confessions virtually impossible to obtain.[125] Studies of police practices in the years following the *Miranda* decision show that these requirements do not seem to affect the success of interrogation, recovery of stolen property, police clearance rates, or percentage of offenders convicted for serious crimes.[126] *Miranda* warnings are only required to be read to a suspect when there is a custodial interrogation, and a number of cases over the years have whittled away at the significance of the *Miranda* decision. Police do not have to give the *Miranda* warning if public safety is threatened, after a routine traffic stop, or if a police officer is posing as an inmate, and confessions can be allowed if a person claims to be following the advice of God and in other situations.[127] (See **Critical Thinking 5.5**—Scenario 1[128] and Scenario 2,[129] the Functional Equivalent of Interrogation, concerning what constitutes the "functional equivalent" of interrogation.)

Critical Thinking 5.5 Scenario 1 and Scenario 2: The Functional Equivalent of Interrogation

Scenario 1: The Functional Equivalent of Interrogation—You Decide

A defendant accused of murdering a 10-year-old girl alleged that he was denied effective assistance of counsel when, while being transported from the point of arrest to the jurisdiction of the crime, he revealed to the officers the location of the girl's body. The defendant had been given *Miranda* warnings and the officers, though they did not allow his lawyer to accompany him on the trip, promised not to interrogate him during the ride. However, they did talk to him about the crime, playing on his feelings of guilt and inducing him to reveal the location of the body.

Can the defendant's confession legally be used against him?

Obviously, the suspect was in custody, and, although the police were not asking the suspect questions and no actual interrogation was taking place, the Court held that this case represents the functional equivalent of interrogation, as the officers were aware their conversation was likely to illicit a confession. This case is known as the "Christian burial speech." The Supreme Court held this evidence to be inadmissible (*Brewer v. Williams*).

As reflected earlier with Ernesto Miranda, just because a defendant prevails on appeal does not necessarily mean he/she will be set free. The prophetic words of Justice Burger's dissent in *Brewer* would ultimately be actualized on appeal as he described the decision as

> intolerable in any society which purports to call itself an organized society ... it mechanically and blindly keeps reliable evidence from juries whether the claim of constitutional violation involves gross police misconduct or honest human error. Williams is guilty of the savage murder of a small child; no member of the Court contends he is not. While in

> custody, and after no fewer than five warnings of his rights to silence and to counsel, he led police to the place where he had buried the body of his victim. The Court now holds the jury must not be told how the police found the body.... I cannot possibly agree with the Court. (*Brewer v. Williams*, 430 U.S. 387, 415 (1977)).

> On appeal, Williams was given another trial at which time the incriminating statements were not admitted but which resulted in his reconviction anyway. Williams again appealed, and in 1984 the Supreme Court reconsidered the case in the light of the second conviction. With Justice Burger delivering the majority opinion, the conviction was upheld this time, primarily because in the Court's opinion search parties would have discovered the victim's body even without Williams' incriminating statements. This represents **inevitable discovery**, one of the exceptions to the exclusionary rule. In other words, we would have found the body anyway without his confession (*Nix v. Williams*, 467 U.S. 431 (1984)).

Scenario 2: The Functional Equivalent of Interrogation—You Decide

> The suspect, a man named Innis and believed to have murdered a cab driver with a shotgun, was transported to police headquarters by three police officers after having been notified of his *Miranda* rights and after the officers were instructed not to interrogate him during the trip. While in transit, two of the officers, talking to each other and not directly to the suspect (although he could overhear them), discussed the fact that the murder had taken place near a school for handicapped children and expressed fear that one of these children might find the shotgun and injure someone. At this point, Innis offered to lead the officers to where the shotgun was hidden, thereby incriminating himself.

Does this constitute custodial interrogation in violation of *Miranda*?

According to the National Registry of Exonerations, between 1989 and March 2017 there have been 2,000 exonerations of persons wrongly convicted in the United States.[130] There have been at least 349 U.S. citizens that have been acquitted based on DNA evidence.[131] Factors contributing to wrongful convictions were eyewitness misidentification, government misconduct, incentivized informants, inadequate defense, and misapplication of forensic science. Furthermore, it is estimated that over 25% of those wrongly convicted made a false confession or incriminating statement.[132] False confessions are often obtained through psychologically coercive and/or improper interrogation methods.[133] In response to the liability associated with wrongful convictions and mounting public pressure many police departments now electronically record confessions. Such strategies are, in the long run, cost effective, saving taxpayer dollars paid in wrongful conviction lawsuits. However, according to a study by the International Association of Chiefs of Police, electronic recording does stop or reduce false confessions.[134] The Innocence Project counters that electronic recording of interrogations from beginning to end is the single best strategy for preventing wrongful convictions based on false confessions.[135]

Over the years there have been a number of proposals to abolish or otherwise nullify *Miranda*, including suggestions for federal legislation allowing some interrogations to be carried out without the full warning. However, the U.S. Supreme Court has maintained that the *Miranda* warnings are safe from legislative intervention and can only be modified by the Court,[136] something some observers still believe will ultimately happen.

Release from Police Custody

A short time after arrest, suspects must be taken before a magistrate for consideration of bail, what is called the initial appearance. How short the interval must be between arrest and this initial appearance depends on the law and court decisions in each state. Most jurisdictions require a bail hearing, also called a probable cause hearing, be held within a "reasonable time" after arrest, "promptly," or on the first occasion the court is open for business, while in some places, including cases under federal jurisdiction, the initial appearance must be "immediate."

The U.S. Supreme Court has established the standard that a delay of up to 48 hours before such a hearing is presumed reasonable. If the detention of an individual exceeds 48 hours without an initial appearance before a judicial authority, the burden shifts to law enforcement to prove that the delay was reasonable.[137] As with most criminal procedures, this time interval is a controversial matter, for the sooner bail is fixed (assuming the suspect can post bond or is otherwise released by the magistrate) the shorter the opportunity for the police to carry out an in-custody interrogation. Bail will be discussed fully in Chapter 8. (For exceptions to the time of detention allowed before charging a suspect see **Field Practice 5.1.**)[138]

Field Practice 5.1 Worldview

British Detainment of Suspected Terrorists

In the British Terrorism Act of 2006, a provision was established for the detention of suspected terrorists for up to 28 days without charges being filed. This, it was believed, would allow authorities time to gather incriminating information to bring charges. Police groups advocate for a period of up to 90 days detainment without charges being filed to allow for proper investigation.

U.S. Detainment of Suspected Terrorists

The United States can detain terrorism suspects indefinitely without charging them. A congressional resolution passed after September 11th "provided the President all powers necessary and appropriate to protect American citizens from terrorist attacks.... Those powers include the power to detain

> identified and committed enemies..., who associated with al Qaeda ... who took up arms against this Nation in its war against these enemies, and who entered the United States for the avowed purpose of further prosecuting that war by attacking American citizens."

Summary

Police make many decisions in the course of their jobs, some routine and others requiring significant preparation and strategy. Almost all important decisions made by police are spelled out in Supreme Court decisions, which have influenced greatly the manner in which police carry out their duties. For much of our history, the police enjoyed almost total autonomy from appellate court interference. But, as we have seen, a succession of major decisions rendered by the Supreme Court have brought about a greater degree of professionalism and more careful actions by police.

In light of these Court decisions, this chapter examined the major decisions made by police in the course of carrying out their duties of criminal law enforcement. It started with techniques of investigating crime and the problems involved in stopping and questioning suspects, surveillance, and undercover operations. It described the conditions under which a police officer can stop and frisk a suspect.

The chapter discussed the limits on police power to search people and premises and to obtain evidence by means of electronic eavesdropping equipment or access to internet or telephone conversations. The exclusionary rule was explained.

Police arrest decisions were discussed, as well as limits on in-custody interrogation. Entrapment used as a defense against a criminal charge was explained. Finally, the chapter discussed release from police custody by a magistrate within a reasonable period of time, the point at which the flow of police decisions ends.

Even though police decisions are controlled by law and policy, the custom and practice of police invariably raise questions and issues regarding those decisions. The nature of policing a free society leads to gray areas of the propriety of police practices, and it is to those issues we turn next.

Chapter 6

Issues in Contemporary Policing

Image by inhauscreative at istockphoto.com

"Those who cannot remember the past are condemned to repeat it."

—George Santayana[1]

Seeking Justice: Milwaukee Police Decided Not to Arrest Dahmer

Few cases have as clearly and comprehensively represented the extent of police prejudice as that of Jeffrey Dahmer. In the *Dahmer* case, the Milwaukee Police Department (MPD) returned a fourteen-year-old Laotian, Konerak Sinthasomphone, who had escaped from Dahmer and was on the street intoxicated, nude, and experiencing rectal bleeding, to Dahmer at his residence. This was done without the police bothering to attempt to discover that Dahmer was already on probation for sexual abuse of a child.

"Officers joked among themselves about the incident and characterized it as a homosexual lovers' spat.... There is strong evidence to support the allegation that members of the MPD failed to extend the full protection of the law to a citizen because of assumptions police officers made about the citizen's sexual orientation and lifestyle."[2] Dahmer went on to kill Sinthasomphone and at least four others before he was ultimately apprehended, and this has been attributed to a pervasive history and pattern of internal and external discrimination on the basis of race and sexual orientation within and by the MPD.[3]

Two African American women dialed 911 and reported Jeffrey Dahmer, a young white man, to Milwaukee police after they had seen a 14-year-old Laotian boy naked, bleeding, and incoherent in the street near Dahmer's apartment. The women knew the boy had been in Dahmer's apartment and had feared foul play, suspecting something was wrong. Police investigated, questioned Dahmer in his apartment, and dismissed the incident as a domestic dispute between two consenting homosexuals. As soon as the police left and Dahmer was alone with the boy, Konerak Sinthasomphone, Dahmer apparently killed the boy and dismembered his body.

The three officers involved in the case say they acted with sensitivity. They claim they responded to a report of "a naked man down," inspected Sinthasomphone in the street and in Dahmer's apartment, and observed no bleeding from the anus as was later claimed. They said the youth seemed calm and his only wound was a scuffed knee. The officers saw pictures inside Dahmer's apartment of the boy in underwear, but believed he had posed willingly for his friend. They concluded that a caring relationship existed between Dahmer and the boy. After the three officers left Dahmer's apartment, one officer said over the police radio, amid laughter, "Intoxicated Asian, naked male, was returned to his sober boyfriend." The tape of that statement incensed citizens in Milwaukee after the boy's mutilated body was found.

The tapes also revealed that when one of the neighbor women called 911 after the boy had been returned to Dahmer's apartment by the police, the following conversation took place:

> Woman: My daughter and my niece witnessed what was going on. Do you need information or anything from them?
>
> Officer: No, not at all.
>
> Woman: You don't?
>
> Officer: Nope. It's uh, an intoxicated boyfriend of another boyfriend.
>
> Woman: Well, how old was this child?
>
> Officer: It wasn't a child. It was an adult.
>
> Woman: Are you positive? This child doesn't even speak English.
>
> Officer: It's all taken care of ma'am.
>
> Woman: Are you sure?
>
> Officer: Ma'am, I can't make it any more clear. It's all taken care of. He's with his boyfriend at his boyfriend's apartment, where he's got his belongings.

Woman: I mean, are you positive this is an adult?

Officer: Ma'am. Like I explained to you. It's all taken care of. It's as positive as I can be. I can't do anything about somebody's sexual preferences in life.

Woman: I'm not saying anything about that, but it appeared to have been a child.

Officer: No, he's not. OK?

Apparently, by the time of this conversation, Dahmer had killed the boy and dismembered his body. Later, at least 17 murdered and dismembered bodies were traced to Dahmer, who quickly became one of the most notorious serial killers of recent times.

The controversy, however, did not focus on the actions of Dahmer, but on those of the Milwaukee police officers. African American citizens complained bitterly that these police actions were further evidence of racism, that had Dahmer been black and the women reporting the crime white, the police would have treated the events with greater seriousness. They pointed out that a routine computer check was not run on Dahmer, something that would likely have been done for a black male, and which would have revealed the fact that Dahmer was currently on probation after serving 10 months in jail ... for sexual molestation. Likewise, members of the local gay community charged that the callous attitude of the police was consistent with their homophobic biases.[4]

About This Chapter

Decisions made by police are among the most important, difficult, and controversial in all of criminal justice. They can have life or death results, as in the case of Konerak Sinthasomphone, to be sure, but police decisions also affect all of us whether we are conscious of it or not.

Chapter 5 examined police decisions from the point of view of the criminal justice process as a whole. This chapter examines the constraints on the many decisions left to police discretion and the issues that surround and influence police behavior: including propriety of police techniques, police misconduct, and police use of deadly force.

Given the extent and variability of our crime problems, the old truism that the constable's lot is not a happy one is often vividly experienced by police officers, who must balance their concern to meet community demands for vigorous and effective crime control against the legal restraints on their authority. Any action taken by a police officer—and their actions are sometimes based on split-second decisions—is subject to criticism and reprimand. Most of us reluctantly accept the need for police but expect that police interference with our lives will be minimal and police power will not be misused. We want effective crime control tempered by restraint, fairness, and sensible patterns of enforcement.

Police Discretion

We have already noted that the police have many duties in addition to solving crimes and chasing suspects. They are responsible for traffic control, answering emergency calls, guarding dignitaries, settling disputes between neighbors, and many other functions—some far removed from the TV image of cops and robbers. The police have these other duties in good part by default; there is simply no other organization or agency, staffed 24 hours a day, which patrols the streets and is ready to be called on. Often the police are not only the last resort, but the only resort. Missing children, treed cats, vandalized schools, suspicious lurkers, family fights, gutter drunks—all become police problems and, it should be added, take a lot of time and staff to handle.

Police facing such a variety of tasks must use their own judgment when enforcing the law or serving the public. Many situations require immediate decisions by police officers, and this discretion complicates the police task while at the same time causing it to be endlessly interesting.

Evaluating the Police

The diverse demands society makes on the police in turn make it difficult to define the limits of the police role or to establish agreed-upon measures of police effectiveness. Of course the police are expected to solve crimes and arrest the guilty. But is this the major way they should be tested and evaluated? Suppose the police of a certain city solve (by arrest of thieves and recovery of stolen property) a very high percentage of burglaries but find themselves unable to handle the city's traffic flow. This results in traffic being constantly fouled up and a high rate of auto accidents with correspondingly higher-than-average automobile insurance rates for local residents.

Suppose most murders, robberies, and even rapes are solved but vandalism in the schools is rampant. Suppose the police make many mugging arrests but most citizens are still afraid to walk the streets. Or, conversely, suppose foot patrols saturate a community and the constant police presence makes citizens feel safer while, in fact, muggings continue to increase.

Public expectations of police complicate a full understanding of the extent to which police practice lives up to the expectations. To the victim of a house burglary, for instance, the crime is horrendous. His or her personal sanctuary has been invaded and looted! But to the police, burglary is commonplace, old hat, not very serious on their scale of atrocious crimes. Furthermore, the police know only too well that most burglaries are never solved, most loot never recovered. But should they share this information with a victim? Should they downplay the crime and the likelihood of its being solved? Sometimes police detectives go through the motions of crime scene investigation to give the appearance that extra precautions are being taken to apprehend a suspect; for example, they may "throw some powder around"[5] supposedly to detect fingerprints. This is more for the benefit of the victim than with any realistic expectation that uncovered evidence will result in subsequent arrest and successful prosecution.

How police effectiveness is measured is perhaps one of the most subtle, difficult, and, when examined closely, controversial issues in policing. Good police are not simply officers who are neither corrupt nor brutal, but officers who accomplish their tasks efficiently (at reasonable costs) and effectively. The difficulty of determining what effective policing is lies in the nature of the police tasks measured and the methodology employed to measure effectiveness.

Police departments often use the *number of arrests* officers make as the indicator of their effectiveness. Indeed, some police officials set internal departmental arrest quotas for different units to show that the force is working hard and performing effectively. But quiet and safe streets may be a better measure of real police effectiveness—although, unlike arrest quotas, quiet and safe streets may be difficult to measure objectively. Sir Robert Peel, discussed in Chapter 4, for example, believed that the measure of police success can be found in the *absence* of police activity.[6]

In "**Broken Windows**," James Q. Wilson and George Kelling argue that a major purpose of policing is to prevent neighborhood deterioration. They point out that when a window is left unrepaired, other windows are soon broken. Likewise, "social windows" become broken and left unrepaired, such as uncollected litter, vagrancy, vandalism, and public drunkenness. This sets in motion a spiral of neighborhood deterioration, which feeds the fear of crime. People begin to move out, converting family homes into rental property.[7] Houses deteriorate and some are abandoned. Businesses close or relocate. Crime increases. Therefore, a major function of police, according to "broken windows" metaphor, is to stop neighborhood deterioration.[8] Without appropriate intervention, petty crimes may morph into more serious street crimes and other social problems.[9]

"Foot patrol" and experiments exist, in which uniformed police officers walk neighborhood beats in an attempt to diminish citizens' fear of crime and encourage people to use the streets in the hope that because there are more people around street crime will decrease.[10] But whether the measure of police effectiveness is the solving of actual crimes, the reduction of fear of crime, slowing neighborhood decay, the way officers handle emergency responses, or the steps the police can take to prevent community deterioration, there is no common basis for assessing police effectiveness.

Our expectations of effective policing may be unrealistic. The police can and do solve many of the "big" crimes—homicides, kidnappings, bank robberies—but, as seen in Chapter 1, *most other crimes are not solved.* Police agencies monitor car traffic, inspect automobiles, and license drivers, but automobile accidents still occur. Police presence, even in saturation force, has a limited deterrent effect on crimes and may, in fact, serve to escalate the commission of certain kinds of crimes such as riots. We have diverted so many tasks and assigned so many functions to our police that they cannot ever be as effective, on all levels, as we expect them to be. The truth is, the best, most hardworking, highly educated, strongly motivated, honest police force in the world cannot achieve all that is expected of it. The police must make choices.

The Myth of Full Enforcement of the Law

Police activity in criminal law enforcement is a crucial function carried out by individual police officers who must make frequent decisions about whether or how to investigate suspicious circumstances, whether to arrest, when and to what extent to use force, and a great deal more. The decisions which a police officer faces are known primarily only to the police. They are rarely part of public discourse unless a highly publicized event shines a bright light of public awareness on the decisions. Police decisions are reviewed and discussed only in the closed world of policing, and solidarity and secrecy among police officers, along with a corresponding social isolation from others in the community, are well-known characteristics of police work.[11]

Police decisions are not made *in a vacuum*. Policing is often a thankless task. Many police officers are disliked for doing their job effectively, for few people like to be questioned or given traffic citations even when such actions are reasonable and warranted. Although national polls generally show that most citizens have a high opinion of the work of police, members of racial, ethnic, and economic minorities, who have the most contact with police, tend to view them with a high degree of hostility and a lack of confidence.[12] For example, one poll found that 70 percent of blacks reported that "police 'racism against blacks'" was common or fairly common. In another poll, 40 percent of blacks and Hispanics responded affirmatively to the statement that they were "'sometimes afraid that the police will stop and arrest you when you are completely innocent.'" Only 16 percent of whites expressed such a concern.[13]

Policing can be a dangerous business, and police officers believe that they face potential violence in all confrontational situations, even when called on to provide emergency assistance or to perform apparently uncomplicated peace-keeping functions. A speeding car is usually nothing more than a traffic violation, but now and then it holds an armed felon fleeing the scene of a crime or wanted by police elsewhere. All experienced police officers know, and continually repeat to colleagues, stories of other officers hurt or killed in what appeared to be routine, non-threatening calls, stops, or other investigations. This constant awareness of potential violence leads officers to act with what often appears to citizens as undue suspicion and unnecessary caution in situations in which there seems to be no reason for such protective action.[14]

Furthermore, over time a police officer becomes accustomed to crimes and other emergency situations, handling them as routine matters, often to the dismay of victims and witnesses. When the police arrive at a scene to respond to a call or to stop a fight, the victims and suspects are all agitated, fearful, and tense. But the police have seen it all before. Instead of offering sympathy and immediately taking the victim's side, they may seem cool, suspicious, or disinterested.[15]

Faced with these factors, and others, perhaps it is too much to expect police officers to be anything other than dispassionate at the many points in the criminal process at which they have the opportunity to exercise discretion. No doubt much of the misunderstanding about police work stems from a failure to recognize the discretionary nature of the police role in criminal justice. That failure results in unrealistic expectations placed on the police to enforce all laws without fear or favor and to always vigorously and rigidly enforce the law.

Effectiveness on all levels of the broad police task may be too much to ask, but what about the vigorous enforcement of criminal laws? Traffic control is one thing, but "real" police work, defined this way by many police officers, as well as citizens, is catching crooks, protecting the community from the "criminal element." And in doing so, should not the police enforce all criminal laws, evenly and uniformly?

In theory, and indeed according to the laws of most jurisdictions, the police have no authority to choose to enforce some laws and ignore others. Nor can they arrest only some among the individuals they reasonably believe to be guilty of committing crimes while letting others go. To suggest otherwise seems wrong somehow, even when bribery or police corruption are not at issue. Yet police discretion—that is, the choice by police to enforce some laws vigorously and others reluctantly, if at all, and to take into custody only some suspects but to release others—is a reality everywhere in our land.

James Q. Wilson, in his seminal work on police behavior, identifies three styles of policing: "**legalistic**," "**watchman**," and "**service**." Community and political characteristics can influence these various styles of policing. The legalistic style is characterized by strict enforcement of the law with little leeway for discretion. The watchman style embraces selective enforcement of the law with primary emphasis on arrests for mostly serious, violent offenses, and the service style focuses on strict enforcement of the law against outsiders while community residents are handled informally.[16] **How would you categorize the type of enforcement you have received from the police in the area where you grew up? Why? What style of enforcement would you prefer from the police?**

Discretion *Not* to Arrest

Police have the clear authority to investigate crimes and arrest suspects when there is sufficient evidence to do so. However, there is a question of whether they *must* act—*must* investigate or arrest—or instead whether they *may* properly decide, despite adequate evidence, not to follow through. The issue arises from the expectation of full enforcement conflicting with the desire for reasonable use of the criminal process. Is intake into the criminal process mechanical, with police officers mere automatons? Or is their expertise sufficient not merely to justify suspicions, as in Officer McFadden's actions in *Terry v. Ohio*[17] (see Chapter 5), but also to decide when and under what conditions the criminal process should *not* be used? Consider the cases described in the "Snapshots" described below, beginning with **Field Practice 6.1**. Do you consider the decisions described there to be proper police work?

Field Practice 6.1 Police Discretion Not to Enforce the Law

1. Bumper Sticker

One of the authors of the textbook was stopped by a state trooper for doing 85 miles per hour in a 65-mile-per-hour speed limit zone on an interstate highway. The officer asked the author where he was heading in such a hurry and was informed that he was a criminal justice professor headed home after teaching a course at the local college. The officer chose not to give him a speeding ticket and remarked as he turned to leave, "I like your bumper sticker." The professor had a sticker on his bumper which read "State Troopers are your best protection."

Do you think bumper stickers can influence one way or the other whether someone's vehicle is stopped, one is cited, or one is arrested? If so, provide examples.

2. Uncle Charlie

In an unusual ceremony, a 60-year-old police officer in a small town was given an award by the Chamber of Commerce for not having arrested any local resident for a period of 10 years. In accepting his award, the officer said, "There's no need to arrest people you know real well. These things can be handled in other ways and better, too. Most problems can be solved without throwing people in jail. Strangers, now that's another matter. People coming from out of town to commit crimes here will find themselves arrested, and quickly too. But my job is to keep our town a good place to live and when our people get a little wild or silly, why there's plenty of ways they can be straightened out without being put in jail."

Which of James Q. Wilson's styles of enforcement is being exhibited by the officer receiving the award?

Despite the absence of laws permitting police to choose *not* to arrest, studies of actual police practices show that non-arrest is common. This fact reveals an important dimension of the police job not evident from arrest statistics. Based on field observations, research has shown a number of circumstances in which the police do not use their full authority and has identified the reasons for this exercise of discretion.[18] In some of the situations decisions not to arrest are based on police *belief that the legislature did not intend full enforcement*, even though the conduct is outlawed. This is illustrated by decisions not to arrest when:

1. The law is vague, as in complaints regarding obscene materials.
2. The statute appears to have been designed as a device to deal with "nuisance" behavior rather than to call for full criminal processing.
3. Broad statutes have been enacted to cover professional criminal activity but the situation encountered involves no criminal intent, as when legislation prohibits all gambling but the police come upon a friendly poker game.
4. The intent of law is merely to express a moral standard without a real expectation of its full enforcement, such as the prohibition of "normal" adult consensual sexual misconduct.

5. The legislation is out of date, as when "blue laws" (as discussed in Chapter 1) remain on the books because of legislative oversight or traditional reluctance to repeal.[19]

In other circumstances the police may not act because to do so would *strain limited resources*, as when arresting an offender would take up too much police time in filling out reports, clog already overcrowded jails, and overburden prosecutors and courts. Included in these types of situations are:

1. Trivial offenses such as jaywalking or obscenity.
2. Conduct that is felt to be common, even normative, among a particular subgroup of the community although generally prohibited, as in cases of fistfights and family assaults in lower-class neighborhoods.
3. Instances where the victims do not desire prosecution and refuse to sign complaints or testify at trial.
4. Instances where the victims are parties to the offenses, as when the client of a prostitute complains of having been robbed.[20]

Still other circumstances have been identified through research, unrelated to the interpretation of legislative intent or to limited resources, in which the police may decide *not* to arrest even though arrest would be technically correct. These include situations in which:

1. Arrest would be ineffective, as in continuous arrests of skid-row drunks.
2. Arrest would cause loss of public support, as in sudden crackdowns on public gambling or other technically illegal activities that have long been tolerated in a community.
3. Informants or persons who may become states' witnesses to assist long-range enforcement goals are involved.
4. Arrest would cause harm to the offender outweighing any risk from inaction, as when young first offenders or others with good reputations are involved in minor violations.[21]

Obviously, reasons for police inactivity are not all alike or of the same dimensions. Some are self-serving, like rewarding informants. Others rest on an awareness that long-range objectives of crime control may be achieved in ways other than arrest and prosecution, like releasing a first offender with a reprimand rather than giving him or her an arrest record. Some are matters of convenience, such as overlooking trivial offenses. Others rest on police attitudes toward differences in morality and lifestyles exhibited by various social classes and minority groups in the community. Whether these patterns of police discretion are good or bad is open to controversy. They are often what Professor Joseph Goldstein calls "low-visibility" decisions.[22] The range of these decisions is impossible to describe; only illustrations can be given.

Discretion *to* Make an Arrest

The reverse of the type of discretion just discussed involves officers making arrests in situations where common practice normally would be simply to warn or reprimand the suspects. Here the characteristics or behavior of the suspect when stopped, or other circumstances of the incident, including an affront to the officer's dignity or a challenge to his or her authority, or characteristics of the neighborhood may lead to arrest instead of routine dismissal.[23] Consider **Field Practice 6.2.**

Field Practice 6.2 Police Discretion to Make an Arrest

1. Call My Lawyer

On a routine automobile registration check, a police officer asked a driver for his license and registration. The officer noticed a shotgun on the back seat. The driver's registration and license were in order. It was hunting season, a time when this officer customarily merely warned drivers not to carry loaded guns in their automobiles and that all shotguns must be displayed and "broken," that is, opened to show that they are unloaded. However, in this case the driver was surly and arrogant. Before the officer took any action, the driver demanded to see a lawyer and asked why the police wasted taxpayers' time stopping them for no good reason. The officer arrested him for carrying a loaded shotgun in his car.

2. The Gangster

An officer summoned to the scene of an automobile accident noted that one of the drivers involved in the crash was a reputed gang member in the community. Although the accident was minor, this driver was apparently at fault. The officer arrested him for reckless driving, later explaining to his partner that normally he would not have made an arrest, but that it was his private policy to arrest "gangsters" wherever and whenever possible.

The cases in Field Practice 6.2 above demonstrate how police can act on their own prejudices or perhaps take out their own frustrations on a person. The arrest, or ticket, or cuffing is an overt way in which a police officer can demonstrate authority. And that authority is within the officer's power to use.

The major issue is not whether police discretion exists, but how it can be controlled. There is a fine line between prudent **selective enforcement** and **discriminatory enforcement**, which is clearly harmful to our social order. The first step in the control of police discretion is the frank recognition of its existence. The second step is to develop internal police department policies and review procedures and to forbid certain forms of discretionary practice altogether. Recognition and control of discretion are important steps on the road to police professionalism. For until the police themselves come out from behind the mask of full enforcement, until they abandon the pretense of being simple gatekeepers of the law, mere robots carrying out policies made by others, professional recognition will be withheld.

Legislatures sometimes respond to demands from the public to do something dramatic about a certain type of crime by passing laws intended to solve the problem by restricting police discretion. An example of this is legislation regarding domestic violence, which in some jurisdictions requires the police to arrest one party or the other in such cases. Police often do not like this, and no doubt legislation limiting police discretion may be a poor method to fight crime. However, particularly in rural or small-town jurisdictions, officers eventually began to appreciate "mandatory arrest" laws because it allowed them to actually take action in those circumstances where they were dealing with friends or relatives. They could "blame" the new law requiring them to arrest the suspect, get the perpetrator into the system, and interrupt the cycle of violence instead of just coming back to the family fight again the next weekend. The old "discretionary" way of dealing with domestic violence problems was not working—and it placed a lot of responsibility for prosecution of perpetrators on the victims. Taking the discretion away from the officers addressed these and other issues. Similar results have occurred with DUI laws.[24]

Discretion is a vital element of policing. However, until police administrators recognize its dimensions and prepare officers properly, and until the issue of discretion is frankly addressed by legislatures and courts, the true nature of police work cannot be fully understood. Having said this, it must be admitted that controlling discretion is an extremely difficult task that may never be completely realized.

Individual Discretion

At the primary level, discretion involves the choice of alternative actions by individual police officers, including taking *no* action. This is **individual discretion**. Every situation confronted by a patrol officer on a beat and a detective in the course of his or her investigation requires the use of judgment. This is simply another way of saying that discretion is always exercised. Every day, on each tour of duty, police officers must decide where to patrol, what to look for, which suspicious circumstances or persons to investigate, and, having done this, what to do about situations that arise, including those that involve possible criminal behavior. As for detectives, they must decide what priorities to give to investigations (for rarely do detectives work only on a single case), the steps to be followed, the vigor of the pursuit, and, at the end, how to deal with those cases in which criminal guilt is evident. Situations calling for the exercise of police discretion may be established by police commanders or by state statutes, but the precise codification of proper and improper discretionary choices covering all possible situations is virtually impossible.

Command Discretion

A second level of police discretion involves decisions made by the police command staff. **Command discretion** is a critical part of the entire police discretion issue, for it offers a major point for structuring and controlling first-level discretionary practices.[25] Command discretion is implicit in the very structure and organization of a police force. Decisions concerning the training of patrol officers and the development of detective and special units are made by police officials, often with no outside guidance or controls. Determinations must be made about how many officers are to be assigned to the traffic division, to patrol, to the detective unit, to the homicide unit, about the use of a vice squad, the size and purposes of a police intelligence unit, internal security policies, and so on. Normally the size and deployment of different units reflect insofar as possible the nature of the local crime problem and the service needs of the community. Yet exceptions to this rule are not unusual, as when a new commissioner or chief alters organizational patterns even though community problems remain unchanged.

In addition to the organizational pattern of a department, command discretion may be seen in policy manuals, written orders, and operational memoranda from the command staff to line units. Such manuals, orders, and memoranda are intended to establish departmental objectives and standard operating procedures. When these documents are well researched, carefully reasoned, and comprehensive, they provide direction and valuable guidelines for the sensible and effective use of on-the-street discretion. They also provide an appropriate basis for the evaluation of police operations and, as noted earlier, lend credence to police claims of professionalism.

Not all command discretion is the product of careful staff work and systematic review. Police commanders are continuously called on to make discretionary decisions quickly. This is not unlike the patrol officer on the beat. However, unlike the on-the-beat decisions, command decisions are often more visible to members of the press and the public and have a broader impact. Therefore, these decisions can occasionally have far-reaching consequences for law enforcement in the community and for the career of the commissioner or chief making them.

Command decisions can be influenced by public outcries, adverse media coverage, and limited resources. For example, a series of highly publicized recent murders may force elimination of specialized units and/or reduction in personnel in some areas of a police agency to bolster the homicide investigations and demonstrate to the public a concerted effort to find the killer(s).

Control of Police Discretion

Controlling discretion does not mean that it must be eliminated. Police work probably cannot be properly done without officers exercising substantial discretion at the operating level. However, detailed policies covering particular aspects of police functioning are impossible to provide since an infinite number of possible circumstances could occur. Recognizing this difficulty, it would seem desirable that discretion be structured in such a way that *all officers in the same agency are operating on the same wavelength.*

Limits on discretion, therefore, should embody and convey the objectives, priorities, and operating philosophy of the agency. They should be sufficiently specific to enable an officer to make judgments in a wide variety of unpredictable circumstances in a manner that will win the approval of top police administrators. That is, policy should specify when and under what conditions a police officer may shoot. Likewise, policies should require that all police actions will be free of personal prejudices and biases. And, discretionary decisions should be reviewed by supervisors regularly so that officers will know their behavior does not go unnoticed. A reasonable degree of uniformity in handling similar incidences in the community can be achieved if police administrators, police officers, and the public support the limits placed on discretion.[26]

Field Practice 6.3 So You Want to Be a Law Enforcement Officer: In Their Own Words — Booker T. Hodges, Deputy Sheriff, Minnesota

During my undergraduate career I was taught a great deal about theory and history in regards to the criminal justice system. All of the information that I received was valuable, but it only provided the basic information that I needed to survive as a law enforcement officer. You can read all the books and sit in all the lectures that you wish, but until you actually put on a uniform and work in the criminal justice system you will never fully understand how it functions and why it functions the way it does.

My education did not prepare me for the politics, culture, public scrutiny, complex societal issues, and the amount of paperwork that one faces once they become a police officer. Being unprepared early in my career for these issues caused me a great deal of frustration, motivating me to continue my education. I wanted to combine the knowledge that I gained as a police officer with some good old fashioned formal education to allow me to become a better police officer and to better the law enforcement profession as a whole. The better educated criminal justice professionals are the better able they will be to serve the public.

I went back to school and earned a master's degree in public safety administration and I am currently working on my doctorate in public administration. I would encourage those who want to enter the field of criminal justice to realize that what you learn in school will only partially prepare you to work in the field, but it will provide you with a solid base to work from.[27]

The Propriety of Police Techniques

The methods used by police to detect crime and gather evidence against suspects are often controversial. Techniques that violate constitutional rights are clearly improper and, as discussed in Chapter 4, have been condemned by the Supreme Court and limited by the exclusionary rule. Wrongful searches, excessive interrogations, some forms of entrapment, and other practices are now beyond the bounds of proper policing. As Justice Felix Frankfurter once put it, such techniques "shock the conscience"[28] and must be condemned.

A number of policing methods may fall short of clear violations of constitutional provisions yet offend common values. Sometimes it may appear that the techniques routinely employed by the police are as devious as those used by the offenders they are trying to catch—or even more so. However, these techniques are often justified by police officers, who feel that they must "stay one step ahead of the criminals" and that "all's fair" in the detection and apprehension of law violators and in the perpetuation of the image of police effectiveness.

Unusual Techniques: Stings

This eagerness to be, or at least to appear to be, effective is displayed by local police who have to continually develop new law enforcement techniques. Many citizens view avoiding the police as a kind of cat-and-mouse game. The police counter this behavior with their own increasingly ingenious (and sneaky) techniques. Police may use **stings** to detect criminal behavior and bring law violators to justice. See **Field Practice 6.4.**

Field Practice 6.4 Unusual Techniques

"Convinced they were picking up money being given away by a government agency, 76 people were instead picked up by police when they arrived to collect their prize. There was no cash and no agency: It was all an elaborate setup by Fort Lauderdale police to arrest suspects wanted on various warrants.

'These are individuals who were running away from the law, but they came to us freely,' said Sgt. Frank Sousa, a police spokesman. 'They were coming for one reason only: money.'

Dubbed 'Operation Show Me the Money,' the undercover sting took place Wednesday and Thursday at the War Memorial Auditorium. The arrests ranged from people wanted for failure to provide child support to [a fugitive from justice] on a charge of attempted second-degree murder. All the suspects were Fort Lauderdale residents.

'We're always looking for creative ways to reduce crime, and this is one of the most creative operations I've seen,' Sousa said.

Using a bogus agency called the South Florida Stimulus Coalition, police sent out letters promising recipients hundreds of dollars in stimulus money. All the suspects had to do was call a number and set up an appointment to meet at the auditorium's lobby. Officials would not say how many letters were sent out. More than 100 people made appointments and 82 showed up, though only the 76 were arrested, Sousa said.

The ones who did make it to the auditorium were met with a very convincing set. Large banners bearing the fake agency's name flanked the walls while American flags and balloons were sprinkled around the lobby. A table

Image (on right) by rdegrie at istockphoto.com

held fliers and business cards complete with an agency slogan: 'Helping jump-start the economy.'

Undercover officers then verified their identities and made sure the warrants under their names were still standing before taking them into custody, Sousa said.

Though most of the suspects showed up at their appointed times, one man who identified himself only as Rob walked in shortly after a news conference held to announce the sting. 'I'm surprised they did this, and really, I feel humiliated,' said Rob, 21. He wasn't arrested because the warrant against him had been dropped, he said. 'I knew it was something shady, but I've got kids to feed, I needed the money,' he said. He'd been promised $653, according to the coalition's letter."[29]

Police often dub their sting operations with catchy, clever titles such as an undercover prostitution bust called "March Sadness" coinciding with the NCAA Basketball tournament referred to as "March Madness." By posting fake ads on online dating sites, such as backpage.com, officers nabbed 104 suspects and reportedly were looking for women who may have been forced into prostitution due to human trafficking.[30] More and more, law enforcement has focused on the linkage between human trafficking and the illicit sex industry, with warnings, websites, and hotline numbers posted in strip clubs and even airports. An example of such a sign in Pasco County, Florida, indicates the "county's new human traffic ordinance ... 'mandates that all adult establishments must have signage on the bathroom doors of every female bathroom and the dressing rooms.... These signs offer phone numbers and resources to people who feel like they might be victims of human trafficking.' County law requires the signs to be written in English, Spanish and Mandarin Chinese.' "[31] Hostess/strip club-based human trafficking occurs when "traffickers use force, fraud, or coercion to force [persons] to engage in commercial sex acts." Force, fraud, or coercion is not required to constitute trafficking if the victim is under the age of eighteen. Though not engaged in sex acts, there can also be labor trafficking.[32] The Super Bowl has been called the largest human trafficking event in America, as women are made available for those attending game-week festivities.[33]

According to Graeme Newman, the purposes of sting operations are for investigation and the reduction/prevention of specific crimes.

> [W]ith some exceptions, all sting operations contain four basic elements:
>
> 1. an opportunity or enticement to commit a crime, either created or exploited by police.
> 2. a targeted likely offender or group of offenders for a particular crime type.
> 3. an undercover or hidden police officer or surrogate, or some form of deception.
> 4. a "gotcha" climax when the operation ends with arrests.[34]

Newman notes that a variety of methods may be employed in sting operations. Police may utilize disguises to blend in with offenders, particularly seen with officers posing as drug dealers and prostitutes. Officers may set up false storefronts, acting as pawnbrokers, to uncover illegal fencing operations. Police may use professional informants, with leniency considerations regarding potential punishment for previous crimes or financial enticements, to ascertain incriminating information about suspects. Likewise, surrogates can be used, such as juveniles, due to their status, to obtain information about illegal alcohol and cigarette sales, for example.[35]

Sting operations often engage in false advertising to lure miscreants in. Potential prizes may be offered, such as a flat-screen television or lottery winnings. Just as criminals can use the Internet for illegal activity, law enforcement can and does pose as others in juvenile chat rooms and fake online storefronts. Sting operations often employ electronic surveillance, audio, and/or video. Such recordings are used to show persons engaged in criminal activity and typically at the gotcha moment at the time of apprehension. Such depictions are also available and can be used as evidence against any potential claims of entrapment by defendants.[36]

Unusual Techniques: Decoys

Police may use bait cars ("decoy cars" or "gotcha cars") when they know of a hot spot of car theft and the type of car that is most often stolen. Types of bait-car operations range from the simple, when a car is left parked and staked out by police, to the elaborate, when the car is fitted out with tracking devices, or it automatically locks when the thief is inside. There is even a truTV *Bait Car* television series focusing on law enforcement operations with such vehicles in Los Angeles, San Francisco, Atlanta, and Chicago.[37]

Unusual Techniques: Informants

Successful police work, particularly the work of detectives, depends very much on information received from **confidential informants.** And most detectives work hard to build an informant network so that when serious crimes occur they can pass the word to their informants to be on the lookout for leads. Many informants, most in fact, are themselves criminals who are given a break (not arrested) by police in return for future underworld information. Indeed, if informants did *not* have criminal contacts, they would be of little use to the police. Some informants play the role to avoid their own arrest; others are paid, usually from police department funds for this purpose. How much and how often they are paid depends on the importance of the information they pass on and the past reliability of their information.[38]

In general, the police do not like to publicly admit how much of their success is due to informants, paid or otherwise. It is better public relations to maintain an air of mystery about how leads are developed or cases are solved. Yet among themselves, police officers recognize the importance of informants. Indeed, there is a common courtesy displayed by most police agencies: "We lay off informers for other police [the FBI, for example] and they are expected to lay off ours."

Sometimes the police are too vigorous and/or too ruthless in developing informers. Young first-offenders arrested for drug-related crimes who are often very concerned about keeping their arrest secret from parents or others have been recruited by police to lead them to "higher-ups" in the drug trade. Many police informers in the major cities are known addicts and ex-cons. Sometimes police informant activities may lead to injury or death. Many agencies have implemented policies and practices pertaining to the use of informants in order to protect their officers and the departments from the liability that could arise from inappropriate relationships with or other misuse of "civilians" in police investigations.[39]

Consider the matter of Rachel Hoffman. (See Crisis Driving Policy in **Field Practice 6.5** below.)

Field Practice 6.5 Crisis Driving Policy

We're Here to Help You

Rachel Hoffman, who majored in psychology at Florida State University, was accosted by authorities for possession of a quarter-pound of marijuana and six ecstasy pills while already in a court-ordered drug intervention program for marijuana possession. Rachel also had a record of transactions

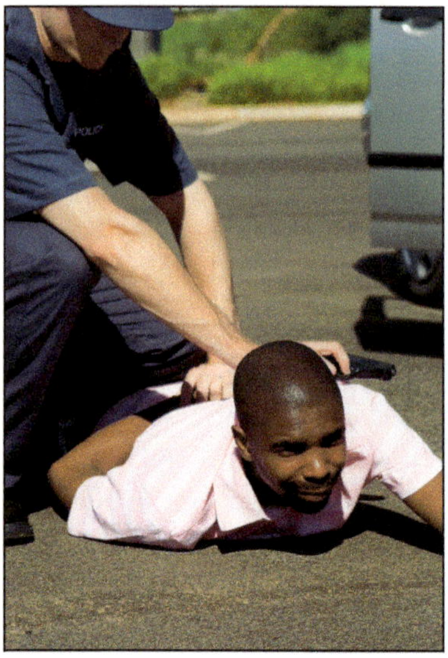

Image by Michale Jung at fotolia.com.

complete with names and amounts in her possession. The police recruited her to be a confidential informant in exchange for not getting busted for her current actions. She was set up by police with $13,000 to buy cocaine, 1,500 ecstasy pills, and a gun from two suspect males. Rachel called the two investigators who were to monitor and notified them that the location of the buy had changed. She was reportedly instructed not to leave her location at the park set up for the buy, but she did. The transaction went bad. She was shot by the gun that she was purchasing and ultimately was found in a ditch wearing a Grateful Dead sweatshirt, dead.

The principal officer handling Rachel Hoffman was terminated, four officers were suspended, and the chief of police was reprimanded. Furthermore, Florida enacted a new state law, the first in the nation of its kind, to regulate relationships and transactions between the police and confidential informants. The law is known as Rachel's Law. Under the law, informants are allowed to consult with an attorney if they ask to do so regarding such relationships. Also, police are not allowed to promise a reduced sentence in exchange for confidential information, and any officers who are involved in recruitment of confidential informants must receive appropriate training.[40]

What would it take for you to agree to be a confidential informant for a law enforcement agency?

Unusual Techniques: Roundup of Chronic Offenders

Once a person has a police record it becomes easier for that person to be arrested. Persons on probation or parole are "known to the police" and generally become primary suspects when new crimes are reported. Police sometimes use what is called a **roundup**, a technique whereby all former offenders known to the police are brought in for questioning even if the police have no direct evidence or information to implicate them in the crime being investigated. Habitual offender units may be in place to locate repeat offenders who meet the ***modus operandi*** (Latin for method of operating) for unsolved crimes that have been reported. The use of this technique may hamper the readjustment efforts of a person who is making every attempt to lead a law-abiding life, or, when the roundup arrest occurs at the person's place of employment, it may result in humiliation or loss of a job. (See **Field Practice 6.6** below.)

Field Practice 6.6 Roundup

A Discouraging Term

Following the rape and murder of a small child, a crime that received extensive newspaper coverage, detectives were sent to interview all "known sex deviates" residing in the community regarding their whereabouts at the time of the crime. There were 117 active records on known sex deviates in police files. Some of those interviewed were on parole for sex crimes, others had completed sex crime sentences years earlier, and about thirty had never been convicted or sentenced although they had been arrested for sex offenses in the past. Following the interrogation of these individuals, the police focused their suspicions on three of them, one of whom eventually confessed to the crime. He was one of the thirty who had been previously arrested but never convicted of a sex offense or any other crime.

Police are generally aware that disproportionate numbers of crimes in any community are committed by a comparatively small number of persistent repeat offenders, or **chronic criminals.** With this in mind police departments sometimes set up habitual offender units to focus on this problem with repeat offenders. (See **Field Practice 6.7** below.)

Field Practice 6.7 Chronic Offenders

We're Behind You

Officers in the habitual offender unit of a police department identified twenty-four male residents of the city who had been arrested for (but not necessarily convicted of) at least three felonies in the past seven years. Ten of the habitual offenders were in prison and parole dates were obtained for each. A surveillance team providing 24-hour coverage was assigned to each of the free fourteen chronic offenders and a team would be assigned to each imprisoned chronic offender on the day of his parole. The teams tailed and watched each habitual offender around the clock. The officers were not particularly concerned if the chronic offender discovered he was under observation. One plainclothes officer explained, "Our job is to prevent as well as bust."

Image by SV Luma at fotolia.com.

Whether any or all of the above-described police techniques are appropriate to use or not is largely a matter of judgment. The judgment used by individual police officers may or may not reflect the values of the community he or she serves. As the police become more open to community involvement through innovative practices such as community-based policing and problem-oriented policing, perhaps the perceived need for questionable practices will disappear. But as long as police work behind a cloak of secrecy, behind the "blue curtain," their controversial practices will continue to exist, often known only to the people directly involved.

High-Speed Pursuit

For years, police movies and television shows have included scenes of high-speed pursuit or police car chases, often as the exciting finish to the story. Viewers have become accustomed to police chase scenes in San Francisco (the hills always provide camera angles that maximize the excitement of cars flying over bumps), Chicago (racing through the supports of an elevated train lend an obstacle course element), and Miami (the avenues along Biscayne Bay add color and beauty). Indeed, such scenes are almost obligatory. But seldom do those glamorous scenes include the more common, and often tragic, elements of actual chases. Viewers do not see the pursuits initiated by traffic offenses, nor do they see the tragic consequences of innocent bystanders placed in danger by them or visit the courtrooms where lawsuits are heard alleging negligence by the police when an innocent person is seriously injured or killed as the result of a chase.

Geoffrey Alpert and Patrick Anderson describe seven possible endings to police high-speed pursuits:

1. The offender stops the car and surrenders.
2. The pursued vehicle crashes into a structure and the offenders are apprehended, escape, or are injured or killed.
3. The pursued vehicle crashes into another vehicle without injuries or death to passengers or bystanders.

4. The pursued vehicle crashes into another vehicle with injuries or death to passengers or bystanders.
5. The pursued vehicle hits a pedestrian (with or without injuries or death).
6. The police use some level of force to stop the pursued vehicle, including firearms, roadblocks, ramming, bumping, boxing, etc.
7. The police car crashes (with or without injuries to officers or civilians).[41]

Of course, the fleeing driver may also escape capture, thereby ending the chase. But if the chase results in anyone's injury or death, one party or the other often brings legal action against the police.

Police are empowered to violate traffic laws in the performance of their duty. This usually means they are exempt from laws related to speed, traffic signs and lights, right-of-way, and so forth. On the other hand, the law and the public require police to drive in such a way as to protect the public, make the roads safe for all persons, and to operate their vehicles in a non-negligent manner.

Why do the police chase suspects? The police mission is to apprehend criminals, so chases are expected. And many officers feel that any law violator *must* be apprehended. Moreover, it is often impossible to find an offender who has fled successfully, even if an accurate description of the car and license plate number is given, so officers choose to pursue immediately. On the other hand, if an officer chooses not to chase, is that a violation of the duty to enforce the law and apprehend criminals? And if the public becomes aware the police do not pursue traffic violators, will that knowledge result in more offenders fleeing? What about the officers' self-images and reputations if they allow law violators to escape? Consider the **Critical Thinking 6.1** exercise below.

Critical Thinking 6.1

As one California police officer lamented, "restricting pursuits to violent felonies is not the solution.... [W]e now have a very restrictive policy. Is the public better served, I'm not sure. Ask the woman who was tied up in the trunk of a car. When the kidnap suspect was about to be pulled over for a traffic violation, he ran. Because of policy the officers did not chase. The woman was later found dead in Los Angeles. She could have been saved. Does she have any less of a right to protection from criminals than you do from a police pursuit?[42]

Do you see any flaws in this officer's reasoning?

The most common interaction between the public and the police has been found to be the result of a traffic stop, which has been said to comprise 40 percent of police-citizen contacts.[43] Furthermore, most chases start after police observe a minor traffic violation,[44] with approximately 35 to 40 percent of all police chases ending in crashes.[45] Research has shown that 50 percent of all police crashes occur within the first two minutes of a chase; by the six-minute mark of police pursuits 70 percent of collisions have transpired.[46] It is estimated that 360 persons are killed annually in high-speed police chases. Innocent bystanders are said to constitute approximately 33 percent of those dying as the result of such chases. Alpert maintains that the number of deaths is actually three or four times greater than current estimates, as bystanders who are killed after police chases cease, even seconds afterward, are not included in the data.[47]

A more recent study has revealed racial disparities in deaths of blacks fleeing the police and bystanders as the result of police pursuits. "Police chases kill roughly 400 people each year." However, "[b]lack people are three times likelier to be killed in police chases.... Blacks have been killed at a disproportionate rate in pursuits every year since 1999. On average, 90 black people were killed each year in police chases, nearly double what would be expected based on their percentage of the population [makeup]. Deadly pursuits of black drivers were twice as likely to start over minor offenses or non-violent crimes.... In daylight, 31% of the drivers involved in deadly police chases were black. In darkness, 21% of the drivers in deadly chases were black.... For every 100,000 black people in the United States, 4 were killed in police chases over the 17 years between 1999 and 2015. For every 100,000 people who are not black, 1.5 were killed.... [C]hases of blacks were 75% more likely to kill a bystander or a fleeing passenger than chases of white drivers." Police have contended that "a suspect's race has no impact on officers' decision[s] to pursue. Instead, they suggest ... that any disparity [is] likely a byproduct of police spending more time in high crime neighborhoods." Police also maintain you don't get pursued if you don't flee. However, critics contend that police seem more willing to take such risks in black neighborhoods. It has been said that "[i]t's an issue of institutionalized racism that communities of color are not valued as much as communities not of color."[48] **How might you explain such discrepancies?**

Police vehicle pursuits have become a contentiously litigated area of the law, and the majority of the states have made it easier for plaintiffs to prevail in lawsuits against police officers and departments by relying upon a mere negligence standard.[49] Often policies are changed after a horrific event.

The costs of high-speed pursuit can be high. The consequences of aggressive police pursuits without policy guidelines and training can be the needless loss of property and life. Some police departments have issued guidelines forbidding prolonged pursuit of traffic violators and have established policies for when to initiate chases and when to break them off. Such policies and practices take into account the individual officer's training and preparation, the conditions of the road and neighborhood, and the events leading up to the chase.[50] Some police departments' policies require the approval for pursuit from a supervisor not involved in the "chase." That supervisor monitors the pursuit and has authority to "call it off" with no questions asked. This takes the ego and emotion of the involved officer(s) out of the decision-making process and provides for a more rational choice about whether or not to pursue a suspect.[51]

A number of police departments across the country have implemented more restrictive pursuit policies. For example, Milwaukee police now require probable cause instead of reasonable suspicion as the standard to engage in vehicle pursuit in violent felony cases. St. Petersburg police allow vehicle pursuit only for forcible and violent felonies.[52] See the Lakeland Police Department's pursuit policy in **Field Practice 6.8** below and note the infractions for which they cannot pursue suspects. **Would you call their policy restrictive?**

Field Practice 6.8 Lakeland, Florida, Police Department's Pursuit Policy

"Since motor vehicle pursuits present a danger to our officers and the public, it is the policy of the Lakeland Police Department to limit the circumstances in which such pursuits take place and to regulate the manner in which they are conducted."

Specifically, the Lakeland Police Department permits officers to chase violent felony suspects, "known" stolen vehicles, and in other cases with supervisor approval. Officers are **not** permitted to pursue non-violent felonies, misdemeanors, criminal traffic offenses, and traffic infractions.

Scott v. Harris (2007)

Departmental policies like Lakeland's are designed to give officers some guidance regarding the decisions to pursue fleeing persons. The U.S. Supreme Court has also considered pursuit issues, particularly in the 2007 case of *Scott v. Harris.*

The facts of the *Scott v. Harris* (2007) case are as follows. In March 2001, a Georgia county deputy clocked a vehicle traveling at 73 miles per hour on a road with a 55-mile-per-hour speed limit. The deputy activated his blue flashing lights and instead of pulling over, the car sped away. The officer began a chase down what is in most portions a two-lane road, at speeds exceeding 85 miles per hour. The deputy radioed his dispatch to report that he was pursuing a fleeing vehicle, and broadcast its license plate number. Deputy Timothy Scott heard the radio communication and joined the pursuit along with other officers. At one point in the chase, the fleeing driver pulled into the parking lot of a shopping center and was nearly boxed in by the various police vehicles. He evaded the trap by making a sharp turn, colliding with Scott's police car, exiting the parking lot, and speeding off once again down a two-lane highway.

Following the shopping center maneuvering, which resulted in slight damage to Scott's police car, Scott took over as the lead pursuit vehicle. Six minutes and nearly 10 miles after the chase had begun, as explained in the case, Scott decided to attempt to terminate the episode by employing a Precision Intervention Technique ('PIT') maneuver, which causes the fleeing vehicle to "spin to a stop." Having radioed his supervisor for permission, Scott was told to "'[g]o ahead and take him out.'" Instead, Scott applied his push bumper to the rear of the fleeing vehicle. As a result, the driver lost control of his vehicle, which left the roadway, ran down an embankment, overturned, and crashed. He was badly injured and was rendered a quadriplegic.[53] The subsequent lawsuit was decided in *Scott v. Harris* (2007).

Scott v. Harris (2007)

Justice Scalia, writing for the majority, stated that

In determining the reasonableness of the manner, "[w]e must balance the nature and quality of the intrusion on the individual's Fourth Amendment interests against the importance of the governmental interests alleged to justify the intrusion."

... Scott's action—ramming [the suspect] off the road—was certain to eliminate the risk that [the suspect] posed to the public, ceasing pursuit was not.

Scalia continued on to say,

... we are loath to lay down a rule requiring the police to allow fleeing suspects to get away whenever they drive so recklessly that they put other people's lives in danger. It is obvious the perverse incentives such a rule would create: Every fleeing motorist would know that escape is within his grasp, if only he accelerates to 90 miles per hour, crosses the double-yellow line a few times, and runs a few red lights.... A police officer's attempt to terminate a dangerous high-speed car chase that threatens the lives of innocent bystanders does not violate the Fourth Amendment, even when it places the fleeing motorist at risk of serious injury or death.... The car chase that [the suspect] initiated in this case posed a substantial and immediate risk of serious physical injury to others; no reasonable jury could conclude otherwise. Scott's attempt to terminate the chase by forcing respondent off the road was reasonable[.][54]

Do you agree? Or do you disagree? Explain how the public safety is both protected and endangered through the actions in this case.

Terminating a Pursuit

The decision of an officer or supervisor to terminate a pursuit for safety reasons is not subject to review. Any unit ordered to terminate pursuit by the Pursuit Supervisor should terminate the pursuit immediately and acknowledge the order by radio. When aerial assistance becomes available, consideration should be given to terminating the pursuit. With the exception of exigent circumstances, units will terminate a pursuit when contact with the Pursuit Supervisor is lost.

Of course, with advances in technology, police departments have various tools in their arsenal in addition to aerial surveillance to prevent or quickly cease vehicle pursuits. For example, officers may fire vehicle-tagging devices onto fleeing cars that will allow monitoring via GPS technology to ascertain a vehicle's location. Use of auto-arrestors allows the police to project electrical impulses to destabilize automobile computer systems. Also, there is the more common device used by police of retractable spiked barrier strips to deflate a fleeing suspect's automobile tires.[55]

Police Misconduct

Police have been known throughout history to engage in wrongful acts, to abuse their power, and to violate the trust placed in them by society. "Without fear or favor" is the motto many police officers recite, but too often they intimidate people for their own profit and overstep their lawful power to use force. Police sometimes use their power to give favorable treatment to certain people for profit.[56]

Police often work in an environment of poverty, frustration, and crime in the inner city. As a result of the elements of danger and authority a sense of isolation emerges for police, which translates into an occupational solidarity, an "us versus them" view of the world.[57] The psychological impact of daily confrontations often causes officers to turn inward, to surround themselves socially with fellow police officers, and to become part of the "blue code," which prohibits one officer from informing on another.[58]

Simmons has identified three principal elements that comprise police culture: the "blue wall of silence" referred to above, ineffective designation and correction of disobedient officers, and the common attitude across different ranks and levels of law enforcement officers that some brutality or violence is a fundamental component of productive law enforcement.[59] A *Harvard Law Review* articles maintains that the "police, through violence, send a twofold message. First, they inform the brutalized that their behavior is unacceptable. Second, they remind the judiciary that the police will fill the punishment gap left by the courts. In other words, because some officers do not trust others within the legal system to achieve moral order, they will do it themselves."[60]

This social world of police and the secrecy which surrounds much of what police do, coupled with the frustration which accompanies the knowledge that many of those they arrest will "get off" with little or no official sanction, sometimes leads to police misconduct. "Street justice" may be administered with the baton, more than necessary force may be used, and trouble may be sought out by misfit officers who are predisposed to brutality. Some officers may also choose to benefit financially in the police world, and many opportunities exist for unscrupulous police. These characteristics of the police culture have resulted in a rift between the community and the police.[61]

Police Brutality

The overwhelming majority police officers in the United States are honorable, naturally decent men and women, who sincerely wish to protect and serve the public. Indeed, much less police brutality occurs than is popularly believed, and only a small percent of citizen complaints of police brutality actually are substantiated.[62] But the work the police do can sometimes brutalize them, making them hard and insensitive.[63]

And sometimes people who already have authoritarian, hostile, suspicious, and prejudiced attitudes are attracted to police work.[64] For those, the working world of policing can exacerbate those characteristics and lead to brutality. (See the **Critical Thinking 6.2** below.)

Critical Thinking 6.2 Police Misconduct/Brutality

1. In the Aftermath of Katrina, New Orleans

Five police officers were charged by a federal Grand Jury in connection with the shooting death of a civilian in the days after Hurricane Katrina. An 11-count indictment against the officers revealed a sequence of events that led to the body of Henry Glover, 31, being found burned in an abandoned car.

The indictment said that the killing occurred four days into the flooding of the city, in the Algiers neighborhood on the west bank of the Mississippi River.... One police officer was charged with shooting Mr. Glover with an assault rifle. As Glover was bleeding to death he was picked up by a citizen named Tanner, who said he drove him to an elementary school that was being used as temporary headquarters for a police special-operations unit. Tanner said he was beaten by police officers and his car was seized, with Mr. Glover inside. The citizen fled the city but returned weeks later, he said, and found his car, with the remains of Mr. Glover inside, burned and parked on a levee behind a police station.

Two police officers were charged with hitting and kicking Tanner and another man who was with him at the elementary school. They were also charged with taking Tanner's car and burning it, along with Glover's body. [Each of the officers] could be facing 60 years imprisonment.

Also, the indictment says a false police report was drawn up by Lt. Robert Italiano, who later left the force, and Lt. Travis McCabe. Both were charged [for] obstruction of justice and making false statements to the FBI.

This gruesome death was one of several that are believed to have occurred at the hands of the New Orleans police, a force that has been troubled for decades. At least eight investigations into actions of the New Orleans Police Department have been conducted by the federal government, including the shootings of civilians on the Danziger Bridge [which] left two dead and four wounded. That shooting resulted in five guilty pleas from current or former police officers.

Accounts in the pleas described police officers shooting a mentally disabled man in the back and then beating him, and also strafing unarmed civilians. The Department of Justice announced that it would conduct a full-scale investigation into the patterns and practices of the police force, a step that usually results in a legally binding blueprint for wholesale reform.[65] Of the ten officers charged in these two incidents, eight were either found guilty or pled guilty. However, due to appeals, Gregory McRae is the only officer who has a conviction that still stands. His sentence was recently reduced from seventeen years to eleven years; he has already served five years in prison. He remains incarcerated on unreasonable seizure of an automobile and use of fire to commit a felony.[66] **What does your research on these incidents suggest led to the convictions of the other officers being overturned?**

2. Chicago's War on Crime

Three decades after criminal suspects interrogated at a South Side police station began complaining that they were being tortured into making confessions, a jury found a former police commander guilty of crimes related to the abuse. He was not convicted of abusing prisoners—crimes for which the statute of limitations had passed—but of perjury and obstruction of justice for lying about the abuse in a civil case.

Chicago's South Side has been scarred by stories of suspects burned, suffocated with typewriter covers, and shocked with electrical devices. The police commander, Mr. Jon Burge, whose name had become a symbol of police brutality, faced punishment.

More than 20 men remained behind bars because of false confessions that grew from abuse. One, Mark Clements, sobbed and said he had spent almost 30 years in prison after being tortured into confessing to four murders. "I sat in a prison cell, and I prayed for this day," he said.

Mr. Burge, 62 and in ill health, was fired from the Chicago Police Department in 1993. He faces up to 45 years in prison. In 2003, Governor George Ryan pardoned four death row inmates who long said they had been abused by Burge and his officers. Then, four years ago, special prosecutors issued a report supporting the accusations that dozens of suspects had made.

At his trial, Burge vehemently denied wrongdoing, and his lawyers described him as a hero whom the city's South Side would be better off to still have on the force. The lawyers said the jury faced a choice between whether to believe the accounts of police officers or the tales of five men the defense team described as a "murderer's row."

Prosecutors portrayed Burge as a brash, boastful officer who attached shock devices to suspects, played Russian roulette by pointing guns at them and expected detectives to adhere to a "code of silence."

"David Weisman, an assistant United States attorney told jurors in closing remarks, 'Chicago police officers are working hard to regain the trust that the defendant took away 20 years ago.'"[67] Jon Burge was convicted and sentenced to four years in prison for lying under oath when he denied that he had participated in torture of black suspects which resulted in coerced confessions. A recent Department of Justice report focused on problems at the Chicago Police Department but has been criticized for not specifically mentioning the torturous acts by police that have reportedly resulted in over 100 million dollars in costs to Chicago taxpayers.[68] **If you had been a rookie police officer and you were assigned to partner with or were supervised by any of the derelict officers discussed above, do you think you would have "gone along to get along," or would you have taken other actions? What actions would be possible for a rookie police officer?**

3. Accountability

The Sarasota County Sheriff's Office arrested Frankie Eugene Bybee, DOB 10/13/70, an 18-year sheriff's office employee, after allegations of harassment led to a criminal investigation and subsequent felony charges.

Bybee's actions were first called into question on December 20, 2016, after the 79-year-old victim reported that Bybee was harassing her. An Internal Affairs (IA) investigation quickly revealed that Bybee befriended the victim after responding to her home for a call for service on October 21, 2016. Bybee began making regular visits to the victim's home while on- and off-duty, and also introduced the victim to several members of his family.

As the investigation began, officials learned that Bybee took possession of the victim's dog while she was hospitalized and received a check for $1,000, in the event that the dog had any medical needs while the victim was away. Bybee deposited the money into his personal bank account and later told detectives that he "rehomed" the dog on Craigslist. The victim told detectives that Bybee only had permission to watch the dog while she was away and was not entitled to keep or sell it. Bybee initiated a relationship with the victim for both his personal and financial gain.

On January 9, 2017, an envelope addressed to Bybee was delivered to the agency's main office, located at 2071 Ringling Blvd., Sarasota. Within the envelope, detectives seized four checks belonging to the victim, made out to Bybee and his three children for a total of $65,000. When shown the checks, the victim stated she did not address or sign them. Bybee was immediately placed on administrative leave. A forensic analysis led latent print examiners to the discovery of Bybee's fingerprint on one of the checks.

Three days later, on January 12, patrol deputies were called to the victim's home where she reported Bybee entered her unlocked front door while wearing dark clothing and blue latex gloves. Bybee mounted the victim and while holding her down, forced prescription medication in her mouth, causing lacerations and abrasions to her face, and bruising to her body. The victim lost consciousness and when she awoke, summoned help. It was determined that her home filled with carbon monoxide after the internal door to her garage was left open and her car was left running. The investigation revealed that Bybee attempted to kill the victim and make it appear to be a suicide.

With signed arrest warrants, detectives today arrested Bybee and booked him into the Sarasota County Jail, where he faces charges of Attempted Murder, Battery on a Victim 65 Years or Older, Burglary of an Occupied Dwelling,

Exploitation of the Elderly, two counts of Grand Theft, Forgery and Petit Theft. Pursuant to Florida statute and in line with the formal process that upholds the rights of sworn personnel facing disciplinary action, Bybee will also be presented with a proposed discipline of termination.

Because Bybee has been employed at the sheriff's office for more than 18 years, we urge anyone who may have been victimized, to contact the Criminal Investigations Section at 941.861.4932 or 941.861.4935. Both the internal affairs and criminal investigations into Bybee's actions will remain open.

"The community should know that the actions of Mr. Bybee are in no way reflective of the nearly 1,000 other men and women who serve the public with honor and integrity," said Sheriff Tom Knight. "It is beyond unacceptable that an individual who works in a position of trust and guardianship to their community, is capable of such heinous crimes. His actions are a disgrace not only to our agency but to law enforcement professionals everywhere. As soon as we learned of these allegations, we took quick action to begin an investigation and in moving forward, will continue to look at the totality of this case. Now that he is off our streets and behind bars, we will let the criminal justice system take its course."

On Monday morning, Sheriff Knight held a news conference immediately following Bybee's arrest. A video of the conference can be viewed on the sheriff's office YouTube channel at www.YouTube.com/SarasotaSheriff.[69] **How would you have dealt with Deputy Bybee? What is his status now? (Bybee's sentence can be found at endnote 69.)**

Whatever its causes, police brutality must be controlled. Civil lawsuits have been a major factor in reforming police practices. Police administrators have created new policies or revised existing ones to discourage police misuse of force.[70] In-service training and improved recruit screening and training increasingly address the proper use of force, especially in the face of civil litigation against police departments.

Police Corruption

Relatively low salaries, high stress, and the perpetual risk of personal harm have all been cited as causes of the continuing problem of police corruption. These factors, coupled with the extensive training required for police and the low esteem many police believe the public holds them in, have contributed to the attitude among some police officers that one way to compensate for these and other debts owed to them by the public is to accept favors and personal rewards.

Favors have historically been offered to police officers. A free cup of coffee, cut-rate dry cleaning, half-price or free meals at restaurants, and discount apartment rents have all been part of police officers' unofficial compensation for decades. Businesses have benefited from such payments by having a police presence. That is, business owners perceive police cars in their parking lots as a deterrent to crime, so as far as they are concerned, if giving a discount or a "freebie" can assure greater police presence, all the better. The implication is clear: Would business owners have less police protection if they did not entice police to frequent their businesses? Police administrators have learned that such "enticements" can lead to corruption, to officers enforcing the law in a biased manner, or even to their soliciting gifts, or "shaking down" citizens for favors.

During the 1970s, in response to wide-spread allegations of police corruption in New York City, the **Knapp Commission** was established to investigate the charges. When the commission's report was published in 1972[71] it concluded that corruption did exist, mostly in the form of accepting bribes. The commission classified corrupt police officers into two categories: "**meat eaters**" and "**grass eaters**." Meat eaters were those officers who aggressively demanded bribes or payoffs and threatened legal action if the favors were not received. Grass eaters were those who merely accepted what came their way as a result of the happenstances of police work without overtly asking or demanding anything. While grass eaters were considered to be more commonplace, they were determined to be more seriously detrimental to policing, as they could evolve into the more aggressive meat eaters.

Others have also identified corrupt police practices and categorized them. Ellwyn Stoddard described police officer corruption, or "blue-coat crime," in terms of:

> "mooching" (receiving food, gifts or discounts);
>
> "chiseling" (demanding gifts, free admissions, or discounts);
>
> "shopping" (taking items from store shelves without paying);
>
> "extortion" (demanding money from citizens stopped for minor traffic violations);
>
> "bribery" (receiving cash or gifts to help a person avoid prosecution in the future or past, called being "on the pad");
>
> "shakedown" (taking expensive items from burglary scenes and reporting it as stolen in the burglary);
>
> "Perjury" (lying or providing an alibi for fellow officers caught breaking the law,
>
> "favoritism" (not enforcing the law for friends or relatives, especially in regard to traffic violations);
>
> "premeditated theft" (making prior arrangements, using tools or keys to gain entrance, to take property).[72]

Lawrence Sherman categorized police departments as: (1) "rotten apples" and "rotten pockets," departments with a few rotten apples who, when they get together and cooperate, become rotten pockets of corruption; (2) "pervasive unorganized corruption," departments with many corrupt officers who act as individuals, not as groups, and (3) "pervasive organized corruption," departments in which almost all of the officers are involved in systematic, organized corruption.[73] See **Field Practice 6.9** below.

Field Practice 6.9 Police Corruption

Motel Heaven

Dispatch received a call from a motel cleaning woman who said she had observed a drug deal taking place in a motel room. The two officers who responded found two men with a large amount of cocaine and a large amount of cash. While one of the officers placed the two suspects in the back of the patrol car and radioed for assistance, the other officer returned to the room alone and stuffed several thousand dollars into his clothing. The two officers split the money evenly, and justified the act by saying, "No one will ever miss the money. It would have just gone into the police vault, and besides, we put our lives on the line every day and deserve some benefits from our thankless job." **Based on your knowledge of what happened in this case, how would you categorize the actions of the officers based on Sherman's previously outlined typology?**

Much police corruption exists in the area of vice crimes—gambling, prostitution, and drugs. A great deal of money is available in vice, along with opportunities for police officers to take payoffs and bribes, or to actively participate in the crimes. Some police officers believe that corruption exists in every department and that it is inevitable.[74] But police corruption can be controlled. Some critics advocate removing the vice crimes from police jurisdiction by decriminalizing those behaviors. Other observers say that the "blue curtain" of secrecy must be eliminated by the creation of citizen oversight committees and more public accountability. Some citizens are taking matters into their own hands and actually actively monitoring and videotaping police activities.[75] But rather than relying on outside forces to address the issue of corruption, police administrators themselves can help control it through the careful screening of police applicants, the thorough training of police recruits, and the active promotion of an atmosphere of police professionalism within their departments.

Many police administrators and line officers have recognized the critical need to "police themselves" or have the media and others police them. For the most part, they have learned that it doesn't pay to try to keep mistakes or outright violations "quiet," but to deal with them openly. This only results in greater public trust. Many communities have successfully worked with their police departments to establish "citizen review" panels or committees. These groups review reports of police use of force, complaints of excessive force, or other concerns about police actions and then provide non-binding recommendations for discipline or redress. Most, if not all of these groups have been found to be more lenient in their assessment of the severity of an alleged violation by an officer than when the same kind of incident is investigated by internal affairs or other similar actions within a police department.[76]

LPD SWAT—*The Ledger*

Police Use of Force

Shows of Force

Part of the militarization of the police is reflected in their use of Special Weapons and Tactics (SWAT) teams. SWAT team officers often roll up on a house "in an armored Humvee, [several officers] poised to leap off the running boards. They [may be] carr[ying] Colt submachine guns, light-mounted AR-15 rifles and Glock .40-caliber sidearms. Many [wear] green body armor and Kevlar helmets. They [come equipped with] a door-breaching shotgun, a battering ram, sledgehammers, Halligan bars for smashing windows, a ballistic shield and a potent flash-bang grenade.... As policing has militarized to fight a faltering war on drugs, few tactics have proved as dangerous as the use of forcible-entry raids to serve narcotics search warrants, which regularly introduce staggering levels of violence into missions that might be accomplished through patient stakeouts or simple knocks at the door.

Thousands of times a year, these "dynamic entry" raids exploit the element of surprise to effect seizures and arrests of neighborhood drug dealers. But they have also led time and again to avoidable deaths, gruesome injuries, demolished property, enduring trauma, blackened reputations, and multimillion-dollar legal settlements at taxpayer expense....

For the most part, governments at all levels have chosen not to quantify the toll by requiring reporting on SWAT operations. But, [a review], which relied on dozens of open-record requests and thousands of pages from police and court files, found that at least 81 civilians and 13 law enforcement officers died in such raids from 2010 through 2016. Scores of others were maimed or wounded.

The casualties have occurred in the execution of no-knock warrants, which give the police prior judicial authority to force entry without notice, as well as warrants that require the police to knock and announce themselves before breaking down doors. Often, there is little difference.

Innocents have died in attacks on wrong addresses, including a 7-year-old girl in Detroit, and collaterally as the police pursued other residents, among them a 68-year-old grandfather in Framingham, Mass. Stray bullets have whizzed through neighboring homes, and in dozens of instances the victims of police gunfire have included the family dog.

Search warrant raids account for a small share of the nearly 1,000 fatalities each year in officer-involved shootings. But what distinguishes them from other risky interactions between the police and citizens, like domestic disputes, hostage-takings, and confrontations with mentally ill people, is that they are initiated by law enforcement.

In a country where four in 10 adults have guns in their homes, the raids incite predictable collisions between forces that hurtle toward each other like speeding cars in a passing lane—officers with a license to invade private homes and residents convinced of their right to self-defense.

After being awakened by the shattering of doors and the detonation of stun grenades, bleary suspects reach for nearby weapons—at times realizing it is the police, at others mistaking them for intruders—and the shooting begins....

The American Civil Liberties Union concluded in a recent study of 20 cities that 42 percent of those subjected to SWAT search warrant raids were black and 12 percent Hispanic. Of the 81 civilian deaths tallied [in the current research], half were members of minority groups....

Researchers found that from 2010 to 2015, an average of least 30 federal civil rights lawsuits were filed a year to protest residential search warrants executed with dynamic entries....

At least seven of the federal lawsuits have been settled for more than $1 million in the last five years. They include a $3.75 million payment in 2016 to the family of Eurie Stamps, the unarmed Framingham grandfather who was accidentally shot while compliant and on his stomach; and $3.4 million in 2013 to the family of Jose Guereña, a 26-year-old former Marine shot more than 20 times as agents broke into his house in Tucson. No drugs were found.

"In each of those cases, as in almost all botched raids, prosecutors declined to press charges against the officers involved.... Oregon is the only state with a law requiring the police to always announce themselves before serving a search warrant." Most states routinely allow no-knock warrants, other states permit police forcible entry under exigent circumstances, and Utah has outlawed forcible entry for suspicion of drug possession; the Florida Supreme Court has stopped the use of no-knock warrants by police noting the "staggering potential for violence to both occupants and police."[77]

Deadly, Lethal Force

In the United States, all official police agency officers are armed. In addition to a shield, or badge, identifying a person as a sworn police officer, each individual officer carries a gun—sometimes, when the officer is in uniform, in the open; at other times, when in plainclothes, concealed. But firepower is omnipresent, and it is not limited to pistols and other handguns. Police cruisers often have shotguns, either kept for easy access in the front seat or stored away in the trunk. All types of modern weaponry, including bean bags, tasers, tear gas launchers, and automatic weapons, are available to municipal, state, and federal police.

Not only are the police armed, but they have the authority, under law, to use force, including **deadly force**, to maintain compliance with our criminal laws. *Most* police officers in most jurisdictions complete their entire careers, in uniform or in plainclothes, *without shooting* or attempting to shoot at any suspects. On the other hand, officers assigned to certain high-crime precincts, usually urban ghettos, often carry their sidearms out of holsters and at the ready, though shooting even in those circumstances is still comparatively rare. No accurate national statistics are collected on the number of civilians killed by police annually. But, we do know, based on the most recent statistics available, almost one out of five persons age 16 or older have at least one face-to-face contact with a police officer annually. Of these contacts, approximately 90 percent of persons acknowledge that law enforcement conducted themselves appropriately. Only in 1.6 percent of these interactions did police reportedly use force or threaten individuals. However, when force was used by police, 80 percent of the recipients of the force reported that it was excessive, and 15 percent of them indicated that they suffered injuries.[78]

"For the most recent period where statistics are available (2003–2009), the BJS found that 4,813 persons 'died during or shortly after law enforcement personnel attempted to arrest or restrain them.... About 60 percent of arrest-related deaths (2,931) were classified as homicides by law enforcement personnel.' However, among these 2,931 homicides by law enforcement personnel, 75.3 percent were reported to have taken place in response to a violent offense—constituting a force-on-force situation, such as an intervention with an ongoing assault, robbery, or murder: 'Arrests for alleged violent crimes were involved in three of every four reported homicides by law enforcement personnel.' Still, 7.9 percent took place in the context of a public-order offense, 2.7 percent involved a drug offense, and among 9.2 percent of all homicides by police no specific context was reported."[79]

Other factors implicated in deaths at the state level are as follows, according to the Bureau of Justice Statistics:

Percent of reported arrest-related deaths, by manner of death, 2003–2009								
Manner of death	2003–2009	2003	2004	2005	2006	2007	2008	2009
All manners	100.0%	100.0%	100.0%	100.0%	100.0%	100.0%	100.0%	100.0%
Homicide —								
by law enforcement	60.9%	60.0%	55.7%	54.7%	62.0%	61.1%	64.2%	68.2%
by other persons	0.6	0.5	0.6	0.6	0.3	0.9	0.5	0.5
Suicide	11.2%	9.6%	12.5%	11.9%	9.3%	10.5%	12.1%	12.9%
Intoxication	10.9%	13.2%	12.3%	13.1%	10.5%	11.9%	8.6%	6.9%
Accidental injury	5.7%	8.5%	6.1%	6.8%	5.4%	4.7%	4.5%	4.0%
Natural causes	5.1%	4.1%	6.8%	4.6%	4.7%	5.6%	5.2%	4.3%
Unknown	5.7%	4.1%	5.9%	8.3%	7.8%	5.2%	4.9%	3.3%
Number of deaths	4,813	627	673	689	721	745	629	729

Department of Justice, Bureau of Justice Statistics, November 2011

Over a three-year time period, 380 law enforcement officers were killed in the line of duty (221 accidentally and 159 as the result of homicide), with 174,760 officers reportedly assaulted.[80] Much has been written about police shootings.[81] While Skolnick and Fyfe have maintained unnecessary force is "usually a training problem,"[82] a number of factors have been associated with police use of deadly force: individual factors such as age of the officer, his or her educational attainment, and race; situational factors such as the physical setting or location of the shooting, events precipitating the incident, the opponent's weapon, and more; organizational factors such as the restrictiveness of department policies and administrative philosophies regarding firearm discharges; and, community-level factors such as population size and violent crime rate. Some of the research focuses on police killings as "justifiable homicides," and there have also been analyses of "suicides by cop."[83] Studies typically exclude information on shots fired which either miss their intended targets or wound, rather than kill them. However, one would assume such shootings should still fall under the heading of use of deadly force.[84]

The Bureau of Justice Statistics was actually requested by Congress to conduct research after highly controversial police incidents with unarmed black men in New York City—Amadou Diallo (who was shot 19 times and killed by police when reaching for his wallet) and Abner Louima, discussed earlier, (who was sodomized with a broken broomstick by an officer in a precinct bathroom).[85] The problems associated with police use of force and the variety of circumstances relating to police shootings, especially as they involve minority citizens and officers, make this subject a very special issue in modern policing. Of those who died in police custody over the three-year period of the Bureau of Justice Statistics study, 44 percent were white, 32 percent were black, and 20 percent were Hispanic.[86]

In a previous study of shootings by New York City police officers over a five-year period, James J. Fyfe found that minority police officers were responsible for a disproportionate number of them. Fyfe's study found that civilian minorities, particularly African Americans and Hispanics, were more likely to be *targets* of police shootings as well. The minority police officers, in Fyfe's study, were also much more likely to be assigned to high-crime ghetto precincts than their white counterparts, which helps to explain the disparity in rates.[87]

Variations in shooting rates by precinct, by day or night, and by other measures correlated with occurrences of violence and violent crimes can explain in a general way squad and shift differences in shooting incidents. Variations in shooting rates by city, however, are harder to explain.[88] Why should cities with comparable crime rates and comparable sizes of police forces show marked variations in police killings? Perhaps, in the past, part of this difference was the result of variations in laws and rules governing police use of deadly force. Until 1985 about half of the states, following English common law traditions,[89] allowed police to shoot and kill any or all felons who were running away to escape arrest. Most *large departments* had policies restricting such use of police force. The other half of the states outlawed the so-called **fleeing-felon rule,**[90] and in 1985 the United States Supreme Court in *Tennessee v. Garner* invalidated the rule for all states as a matter of federal constitutional law and established deadly force law for police formally.

In fact, the legal doctrine regulating use of excessive force by the police in America is rather sparse. Three U.S. Supreme Court cases in particular have addressed the issue: *Garner*, *Graham v. Connor* (1989), and *Scott v. Harris* (2007). All law enforcement uses of force, whether lethal or nonlethal, are to be reasonable. Police use of force is considered a seizure and is governed by the Fourth Amendment to the U.S. Constitution. The ultimate question becomes what constitutes reasonable use of force by the police.

In *Garner*, an unarmed 15-year-old boy was killed by a Memphis police officer. The officer was investigating a prowler report, saw the boy running, and ordered him to halt. When the boy did not stop but began climbing a fence, the policeman shot and killed him. Ten dollars and a purse stolen from the home the boy was running away from were found on the boy's body. The officer testified that he did not believe the boy to be armed but shot him to prevent his "getting away." The Supreme Court held:

> The use of deadly force to prevent the escape of all felony suspects, whatever the circumstances, is constitutionally unreasonable. It is not better that all felony suspects die than that they escape. Where the suspect poses no immediate threat to the officer and no threat to others, the harm resulting from failing to apprehend him does not justify the use of deadly force to do so.[91]

As established in *Garner*, "deadly force is permitted when three conditions are met: (1) it is necessary to prevent escape, (2) warning has been given, if feasible, and

(3) one of the following has occurred: (a) an armed threat against an officer, (b) the officer has probable cause to believe that the suspect has already committed serious physical harm, or (c) the officer has probable cause to believe that the suspect has threatened to commit serious physical harm. Failure to demonstrate any of the three prongs (necessity, warning, and one of the qualifying triggers) means that deadly force is unreasonable."[92]

Police use of deadly force is controlled by police department rules, state statutes, and by Supreme Court decisions like *Garner*, which resulted in a considerable reduction in the police use of deadly force.[93] The most stringent requirements governing police use of their firearms comes from departmental regulations, which are tuned more finely than legislation or court decisions can be. **See Critical Thinking 6.3.**

Police Body Cameras

"Surely, historically the most impactful use of video on the criminal justice process has to be the Rodney King case. Had the Rodney King beating not been videotaped by a citizen bystander the ultimate convictions of two police officers and the civil resolution would likely never have happened. Even with the video evidence there were still experts that testified frame by frame for and against the legitimacy of the force used.

"I teach criminal law and procedure, and some of my students go on to work as police officers. I impress upon my students whether they are citizens who will never work in the criminal justice system or those that will become law enforcement officers that the U.S. Constitution is their friend. Citizens should know their rights, and if police officers abide by the Constitution in carrying out their duties their cases should be rock solid. Use of police body cameras create a win-win situation for protecting the rights of citizens and preserving the integrity of police investigations. I view police body cameras as another tool in the tool-belt of officers for bringing about justice.

"We know that eyewitness testimony is often inaccurate. While police body cameras are not in and of themselves a panacea, they can provide a piece in the puzzle for arriving at accurate decisions. The images caught on camera can be balanced, for example, with eyewitness recollections to possibly corroborate or dispel memories of witnesses.

"Of course, there will be glitches. Sometimes the cameras will malfunction, be damaged during physical confrontations, not provide the whole picture, and may not be turned on at crucial times. However, this is no reason not to employ them in police work. Lastly, some law enforcement authorities are opposed to the use of such cameras, often arguing against them under the guise of protecting the privacy of citizens. [However, video can be redacted and images blurred when necessary.] In the name of transparency and the seeming increasing focus on negative police-citizen interactions, I recommend the use of police body cameras for the benefit of officers and citizens."[94]

Critical Thinking 6.3 Police Use of Deadly Force

1. (White officer shoots black man) "Michael Brown, an unarmed black teenager, was shot and killed on Aug. 9, 2014, by Darren Wilson, a white police officer, in Ferguson, Mo., a suburb of St. Louis. The shooting prompted protests.... On Nov. 24, the St. Louis County prosecutor announced that a grand jury decided not to indict Mr. Wilson. The announcement set off another wave of protests. [More recently], the Justice Department called on Ferguson to overhaul its criminal justice system, declaring that the city had engaged in constitutional violations." A St. Louis County grand jury, made up of nine whites and three blacks, decided in November not to indict Officer Wilson in connection with the shooting of Michael Brown, 18. Its task was to determine whether there was probable cause to believe that Officer Wilson should be charged with a crime, and if so, which one. An indictment would have required nine of the 12 grand jurors to agree."[95] "The most credible eyewitnesses to the shooting death of Michael Brown in Ferguson, Mo., said he had charged toward Police Officer Darren Wilson just before the final, fatal shots, the St. Louis County prosecutor said ... as he sought to explain why a grand jury had not found probable cause to indict the officer."[96] Following buildings being set on fire, looting, and weeks of demonstrations "a scathing report issued [by] the Justice Department called on Ferguson to overhaul its criminal justice system, declaring that the city had engaged in so many constitutional violations that they could be corrected only by abandoning its entire approach to policing, retraining its employees, and establishing new oversight. The report described a city that used its police and courts as moneymaking ventures, a place where officers ... hurled racial slurs, used stun guns without provocation, and treated anyone as suspicious merely for questioning police tactics. Shortly after the report was issued, Thomas Jackson, the embattled police chief, stepped down."[97] **From your review of materials available in the article cited here and online, do you think the right decision was reached by the grand jury in the Michael Brown/Darren Wilson case? How are things in Ferguson today?**

2. (White officer shoots black man) On December 5, 2016, the criminal processing of the death of Walter Scott at the hands of Officer Michael T. Slager resulted in a mistrial due to a hung jury—one lone juror held out coming short of conviction. Prosecutors promised a new trial. "City officials ... agreed to a $6.5 million settlement with Mr. Scott's family, have ... insisted that Mr. Slager was an outlier.... The Justice Department is [also] involved in a ... federal indictment of [Slager for] violating Mr. Scott's civil rights.... Mr. Scott fled from Officer Slager after being stopped for a broken taillight on his vehicle."[98] A video exists showing the incident and Officer Slager reportedly dropping a taser by Mr. Scott's feet after he shot Mr. Scott in the back as he ran away from the officer. See: https://www.nytimes.com/video/us/100000003615939/video-shows-fatal-police-shooting.html. Officer Slager subsequently pled guilty to the federal charges mentioned above. In doing so, he acknowledged that he

had "used deadly force even though it was objectively unreasonable under the circumstances." All pending charges were dropped, including the possible retrial in state court. In a rarity, a conviction was obtained against a police officer. Furthermore, "[u]nder the plea agreement, prosecutors will ask the court to apply sentencing guidelines that in effect would be for a second-degree murder charge." The plea bargain allows the federal prosecutors to encourage the U.S. district court judge "to order ... Slager to spend the rest of his life in prison."[99] **Watch the video referenced above. Do you think Officer Slager was guilty? If you do not yet know, how much time do you think Officer Slager was sentenced for in federal prison? How much time in prison do you think he should have received? (See one of the cites in endnote 99 listed above for his sentence.)**

3. (White female officer shoots black man) On September 16, 2016, Tulsa Police Officer Betty Jo Shelby shot and killed Terence Crutcher. The probable cause affidavit by the District Attorney's (DA) Office with the court indicates that Officer Shelby followed Mr. Crutcher toward his vehicle with his hands up; she ultimately pulls her duty weapon. Another officer joins Officer Shelby and readies his Taser. Reportedly, Mr. Crutcher arrives at the driver's side front window, at which time both officers fire. Crutcher is struck Shelby's shot and dies. Official dashcam video reveals Mr. Crutcher "walking toward [his] vehicle with both hands in the air. The ... helicopter view shows Mr. Crutcher at the driver's side front door ... with his right hand in the air and his left hand unobservable." No weapons were found on Mr. Crutcher, in the vehicle, or anywhere in the vicinity. The DA's office maintained that Officer Shelby "reacted unreasonably" and became "emotionally involved" to the point that she "over reacted"—whereby she was charged with first-degree manslaughter.[100] Shelby also consented to be interviewed by *60 Minutes* prior to trial. See the video and interview, and determine if you think she was justified in the shooting of Mr. Crutcher.[101] **Justified or not justified? A jury has now decided the case (see the decision in the above endnote). Do you agree with their verdict?**

4. (Two black officers shoot white autistic boy) Louisiana Police Officer Derrick Stafford was convicted of manslaughter and attempted manslaughter in the shooting death of a 6-year-old autistic white boy and critically wounding his father. Video of the father inside the vehicle shows his hands raised when the shooting began. The father reported that he did not immediately pull his vehicle over for the officers and fled, because he wanted to catch up with his girlfriend to look after his son if he were arrested.[102] Two other officers at the scene did not fire their weapons as Stafford and Greenhouse did. Stafford received a 40-year prison sentence for his actions; officer Greenhouse awaits trial.[103] **From your assessment of official video from the scene, do you think the actions of the two officers who were charged were justified? What ever happened to Officer Greenhouse? If you were Officer Greenhouse, would you plead guilty in this case? Why or why not? See Officer Greenhouse's fate in one of the cites in endnote 103.**

5. Follow this case: Fifteen-year-old Jordan Edwards, a black teenager, was shot and killed by Balch Springs, Texas, police officer Roy Oliver, who is white, on April 29, 2017. Three days later Oliver's employment with the agency was terminated. A revised statement from the police department after the incident indicated officers had responded to the scene of a party where gunshots were purportedly heard. Officers reportedly heard gun shots ring out with numerous people chaotically exiting the premises. "As officers exited the house, they encountered [a] vehicle backing out onto a main road and driving away despite their attempts to tell the driver to stop." Officer Oliver, as the vehicle was being driven away, fired his rifle into the car driven by Edwards' brother, striking and killing Edwards who was sitting in the front passenger seat. Police had initially stated "the teenagers' vehicle was reversing 'in an aggressive manner' toward officers, but [Chief of Police Jonathan] Haber [has since] said ... that video taken at the scene proved the vehicle was driving away."[104] Within a week, Oliver was charged with murder, and his bail was set at $300,000. He was released on bail.[105] **Do you think Roy Oliver will ever work as a police officer again? Should his personnel record before this incident matter? Do you think he will be convicted of murder? Will he be incarcerated? What do you think should happen? Would a "reasonable" police officer have reacted this way?**

Sometimes, if the misconduct at the local level is so pervasive within criminal justice agencies that it goes beyond isolated propensities to violate civil rights, the United States Department of Justice (DOJ) may conduct investigations and even enter into consent decrees with agencies to monitor compliance with federal dictates. This was done under the Obama administration, for example, emanating out of the Freddie Gray case in Baltimore. This accentuates the battle between the reach of the federal government and the desired autonomy of state and local governments. The Trump administration and U.S. Attorney General Jeff Sessions have expressed desires to back off from consent decrees, not only in Baltimore, but also in Cleveland, Ferguson, Miami, and Newark. As Sessions called for members to undertake a review of current consent decrees, he remarked, "[t]hese are, first and foremost, tasks for state, local, and tribal law enforcement.... It is not the responsibility of the federal government to manage non-federal law enforcement agencies," Sessions wrote in a memo—a federalism-tinged tone that some forecast as the beginning of the end of the department's use of consent decrees. "I think there is concern that good police officers and good departments can be sued by the Department of Justice when you just have individuals within a department that have done wrong," Sessions said in January. "These lawsuits undermine the respect for police officers and create an impression that the entire department is not doing their work consistent with fidelity to law and fairness, and we need to be careful before we do that." Many in the local law enforcement community were heartened by the Attorney General's comments. However, Chiraag Bains, a former federal prosecutor and senior official at the DOJ's Civil Rights Division, maintains that "[i]f the federal government has jurisdiction over anything, it's the enforcement of constitutional rights.... It's not as if DOJ was out there doing (federal investigations) on their own—Congress gave DOJ a mandate to seek judicial relief when it found a pattern and practice of unconstitutional actions." A federal judge ignored Sessions' request to wait for a review of the Baltimore situation and approved a consent decree between the DOJ and the city.[106]

Field Practices 6.10 Crisis Driving Policy: Police-Citizen Collaboration

A fatal shooting of an unarmed African American by a white police officer in Cincinnati led to riots. This was the fifteenth fatal shooting of an African American by Cincinnati police within the past six years. A federal judge appointed a special master in the case and urged all the parties to come together and enter into a collaborative agreement. This constituted a "bottom-up" approach as stakeholders (African American residents, white residents, youth, law enforcement and their families, social service leaders, clergy, business/foundation leaders, educators, and other minorities) came together with the special master and a policing expert who could identify best practices to solidify a cooperative agreement. When signed, the agreement provided for "substantive changes on ways to rally community members through problem-oriented policing, use of force reporting, external criticism of the agreement's execution, collaboration by the parties to maintain fair treatment for all citizens and citizen review processes.... [This] process demonstrates police and citizens can work together to develop policies governing the conduct of the police."[107]

Non-Lethal Force

Non-lethal force was not addressed by *Garner* but would initially be considered by the Court in *Graham v. Connor* (1989). In this case Graham, a diabetic, felt the onset of an insulin reaction. He asked a friend, William Berry, to drive him to a nearby convenience store so he could purchase some orange juice to counteract the reaction. Berry agreed, but when Graham entered the store, he saw a number of people ahead of him in the checkout line. Concerned about the delay, he hurried out of the store and asked Berry to drive him to a friend's house instead.

Connor, an officer of the Charlotte, North Carolina, police department, saw Graham hastily enter and leave the store. The officer became suspicious that something was amiss and followed Berry's car. About one-half mile from the store, he made an investigative stop. Although Berry told Connor that Graham was simply suffering from a "sugar reaction," the officer ordered Berry and Graham to wait while he found out what, if anything, had happened at the convenience store. When Officer Connor returned to his patrol car to call for backup assistance, Graham got out of the car, ran around it twice, and finally sat down on the curb, where he passed out briefly.

In the ensuing confusion, a number of other Charlotte police officers arrived on the scene in response to Officer Connor's request for backup. One of the officers rolled Graham over on the sidewalk and cuffed his hands tightly behind his back, ignoring Berry's pleas to get him some sugar. Another officer said: "I've seen a lot of people with sugar diabetes that never acted like this. Ain't nothing wrong with the M. F. but drunk. Lock the S. B. up." ... Several officers then lifted Graham up from behind, carried him over to Berry's car, and placed him face down on its hood. Regaining consciousness, Graham asked the officers to check in his wallet for a diabetic decal that he carried. In response, one of the officers told him to "shut up" and shoved his face down against the hood of the car. Four officers grabbed Graham and threw him headfirst into the police car. A friend of Graham's brought some orange juice to the car, but the officers refused to let him have it. Finally, Officer Connor received a report that Graham had done nothing wrong at the convenience store, and the officers drove him home and released him.

At some point during his encounter with the police, Graham sustained a broken foot, cuts on his wrists, a bruised forehead, and an injured shoulder; he also claims to have developed a loud ringing in his right ear that continues to this day.[108]

What the Supreme Court Concluded in *Graham v. Connor* (1989)

The Court in *Graham* held "Determining whether the force.... requires careful attention to the facts and circumstances of each particular case, including the severity of the crime at issue, whether the suspect poses an immediate threat to the safety of the officers or others, and whether he is actively resisting arrest or attempting to evade arrest by flight.... [T]he question is whether the totality of the circumstances justifies a particular sort of seizure."[109]

The Court went on to say "[t]he 'reasonableness' of a particular use of force must be judged from the perspective of a reasonable officer on the scene, rather than with the 20/20 vision of hindsight.... 'Not every push or shove, even if it may later seem unnecessary in the peace of a judge's chambers'... violates the Fourth Amendment.... [T]he reasonableness inquiry in an excessive force case is an objective one: the question is whether the officer's actions are 'objectively reasonable' in light of the facts and circumstances confronting them, without regard to their underlying intent or motivation.... The Fourth Amendment inquiry is one of 'objective reasonableness' under the circumstances, and subjective concepts like 'malice' and 'sadism' have no proper place in that inquiry."[110]

Critical Thinking 6.4 A Question of Reasonableness

As is often the case with U.S. Supreme Court cases, we do not know what happens to the parties after the U.S. Supreme Court hears a case and remands it to a lower court for further proceedings. If you were sitting in judgment

would you consider any or all of the actions of the Charlotte police officers reasonable under the circumstances in this case? Explain why or why not.

The *Graham* case demonstrates how inadequately trained police officers can tragically mistake signs of illness. In Graham's case, a diabetic's insulin crisis was mistaken for resistance to arrest or some other crime. Sometimes officers unsure of what they are dealing with escalate matters. Proper training exists for law enforcement to recognize signs and symptoms of illnesses and ascertain techniques for deescalating potentially volatile encounters. In the concluding chapter, we will discuss how specialized training for police is becoming part of police training in many jurisdictions. This training will likely continue to grow in the future as greater numbers of persons, particularly those with mental illnesses who lack access to treatment, are encountering the criminal justice system.

While no complete data on police excessive uses of force exist, through the monitoring of headlines we know it happens, and it shapes our perception of the police. Among the sensationalized cases that have grabbed our attention are: the videotaped Rodney King beating in Los Angeles; a Bay Area Rapid Transit officer's shooting and killing of an unarmed 22-year-old male on a New Year's Day in San Francisco, captured on video; the termination of 4 Philadelphia police officers after 19 officers pulled 3 males from a vehicle and beat them, which was caught on videotape; the indictment of 3 Atlanta police officers for fatally shooting a 92-year old female; and Rafael Perez, who allegedly used his position as a Los Angeles police officer to obtain and sell narcotics, and who informed on other officers, resulting in their prosecution for routinely placing evidence on suspects, coercing confessions via physical violence, and even the commission of homicide.[111] See **Field Practice 6.10.**

The problems of police brutality and racism are powerful and lingering. However, while policing has collectively failed to fully eradicate these elements from its midst, there have been extensive efforts to improve the quality of policing. Over the past forty years or so police have become more diverse, better trained, and more connected with the public. Police today are less violent toward the citizenry than they have been historically, and they are more attuned to constructing and implementing administrative policies. Furthermore, the police have become more accustomed to judicial oversight of their actions. The courts have played an integral role in regulating and advancing police conduct, and the time is ripe for the court to continue to intervene to make certain the advances made in policing do not go by the wayside with diminished executive and legislative oversight.[112]

Much more research and much better national statistics are needed regarding this important aspect of policing. The use of force, including but not limited to deadly force, is the real heart of police authority. It is here that the greatest threat to democratic rights exists; all the rest is shadow and smoke. It is extremely important that we devise ways to control police use of force, for it threatens us all. Yet we must allow force, including deadly force, to be used reasonably, sparingly, and reluctantly to protect us from the predators among us, from the dangerous and demented.

Diversity in Police Agencies

We have seen how police agencies have been slow to permit diversity within their ranks. For many years African Americans were not welcomed in many police departments. For even longer female police officers were not welcomed. Today, both minority and women police officers are common fixtures in the police profession, and few Americans would dispute that they serve admirably. According to the Department of Justice, 27 percent of local police officers are members of racial or ethnic minority groups,[113] and 21 percent of the sworn police force in locales with less than 10,000 population are female officers.[114] It is also estimated that roughly 20 percent of law enforcement agencies target females and minorities in their recruitment strategies, with larger agencies doing a better job of doing so than smaller ones.[115] Now we see the inclusion of gay and lesbian persons in policing.

The Christopher Commission

The Rodney King beating incident at the hands of the Los Angeles Police Department (LAPD) revealed underlying racial tensions among and within police departments. The ensuing Los Angeles riots followed the exposure of the videotaped beating of King. In the wake of those events, the Christopher Commission was established to study underlying causes of the beating and the riots. In addition to racial bias permeating the affairs of the LAPD, both internally and externally, the Commission determined that gender bias as well as discrimination on the basis of sexual orientation was prevalent. The Christopher Commission found a recorded history of discrimination against homosexuals within and by the LAPD.[116] For example, a memorandum issued in 1975 read as follows: "To retain the current trust of the community and the high level of efficiency enjoyed by the Los Angeles Police Department, the disqualification of police applicants based on substantiated homosexual conduct must be continued."[117]

It was also uncovered that as late "as 1988 an LAPD background investigator told a watch commander that he had identified several 'faggots' in his applicant pool and was searching for reasons to disqualify them."[118] Personnel files were frequently flagged by supervisors for further investigation regarding a person's sexual background, while violence and other behavioral issues in an applicant's past would be ignored.[119]

During that time frame Mitch Grobeson graduated first in his class at the LAPD's police academy. When he joined the force there were no openly gay police officers in the LAPD, but after his probationary period his supervisors at the LAPD were made aware of Grobeson's homosexual status after a deputy encountered him in a gay area. From there the harassment commenced.[120] Often condoned by superior officers, LAPD officers refused to back Grobeson up in dangerous situations, singled him out for insults and graffiti, and otherwise discriminated against him. Finally, fellow officers coerced a cocaine addict to file charges against Grobeson. LAPD Chief Gates refused to intervene, would not meet with Grobeson, and provided no protection for employees on the basis of sexual orientation.

Grobeson finally resigned from the LAPD, joined the San Francisco Police Department, and filed the first lawsuit against a police department in the United States alleging discrimination based on sexual orientation. Los Angeles settled the lawsuit, and Grobeson is credited with getting agency policy changed to allow for the active recruitment, selection, and promotion of gays and lesbians throughout the LAPD. In addition, supervisors are now held accountable for not taking measures to check known harassment, and provisions were made for relevant training for the force.[121] The LAPD implemented a policy prohibiting discrimination on the basis of sexual orientation within the ranks.

In view of the blatant discrimination on the basis of sexual orientation found to be permeating the LAPD, the Christopher Commission[122] included that sensitivity training/retraining be implemented for all officers and that the articulated policy of not discriminating in hiring and promotions on the basis of sexual orientation be put into practice within the LAPD, with those throughout the chain of command held accountable if not. Since culmination of the Christopher Commission's initial report, the Police Commission has overridden the LAPD and allowed openly gay and lesbian officers to recruit at public events in furtherance of the stated policy.[123]

Los Angeles, of course, is not alone in its history of discrimination based on sexual preference, racism, and gender. The decision of three Milwaukee police officers to *not* arrest Jeffrey Dahmer caused a great amount of criticism of the police department. But, many citizens believed that the actions of the Milwaukee police officers were typical of police indifference and symptomatic of deeper, troublesome racial and sexual biases. One of the recommendations of the commission that investigated the fiasco in the matter of Jeffrey Dahmer was that the police department become more diverse in its composition and that sexual orientation should not be an impediment to employment on the force.[124] Today, many police departments across the country have Gay Officers Action Leagues (GOAL) for their homosexual officers.[125]

Serving Justice

If police had looked in Dahmer's refrigerator during the incident described at the beginning of this chapter, when they were in his apartment investigating the complaint of the two Milwaukee women, they would have found body parts from some of his prior victims. As soon as the police left and Dahmer was alone with the boy, Konerak Sinthasomphone, Dahmer apparently killed the boy and dismembered his body. Later, after another intended victim narrowly escaped Dahmer's grasp and ran to police, Dahmer was found to be responsible for the murder and dismemberment of at least 17 people.

Racism and homophobia are the public accusations against the Milwaukee police in the Dahmer-Sinthasomphone case. Is this an adequate explanation for the decisions police made? If you had been the officer to respond, what would you have done differently? If you were the chief of police, how would you respond to the public outcry concerning the actions of some of your officers?

The police technique in this case was to interview and investigate. Should officers have done more? Should the presence of photographs of the boy in his underwear trigger a more in-depth investigation? Why do you suppose the officers who responded to the call did not interview the women who had phoned the complaint in to the police dispatcher?

Here, the police were criticized for *not* acting, for turning a blind eye and deaf ear to a crime victim who people in the community knew to be suffering. Often, police are criticized for acting too quickly, too harshly, too aggressively. In this instance, the inaction of the officers led to dire consequences? To what extent should police discretion not to arrest be controlled by police supervision and policies? The discretion was individual, but to what extent should the command structure be held accountable for decisions of officers?

Summary

After police complete a case by making an arrest, additional decisions will be made by criminal justice professionals. We go next to decisions regarding jail, pretrial release or detention, and legal representation. Various concerns will be considered. Is a defendant a flight risk or potentially dangerous if released? Will monetary bail be required? Those detained will be less able to participate in their defense. Probable cause will be required at each stage to continue processing a defendant through the criminal justice process. One's Sixth Amendment right to an attorney will be explored as the differentiation will be made between retained counsel and public defenders.

Chapter 7

Jail, Pretrial Release, and Defense Lawyers

Image by rook76 at fotolia.com.

[I]t [is] more beneficial that many guilty persons should escape unpunished than one innocent person should suffer. The reason is because it is of more importance to [the] community that innocence should be protected than it is that guilt should be punished, for guilt and crimes are so frequent in the world that all of them cannot be punished, and many times they happen in such a manner that it is not of much consequence to the public whether they are punished or not. But when innocence itself is brought to the bar and condemned ... the subject will exclaim, 'It is immaterial to me whether I behave well or ill, for virtue itself is no security.' And if such sentiment as this should take place in the mind of the subject there would be an end to all security whatsoever.

—John Adams

Seeking Justice

The American Bar Association has adopted rules of professional conduct to serve as a guide for states in establishing canons of legal ethics. These model rules of professional conduct cover, among other things, attorney-client relationships, advertising, and disciplinary matters. In terms of attorney-client relationships, Rule 1.6 governs the "confidentiality of information." The rule indicates:

(a) A lawyer shall not reveal information relating to the representation of a client unless the client gives informed consent, the disclosure is impliedly authorized in order to carry out the representation or the disclosure is permitted by paragraph (b).

(b) A lawyer may reveal information relating to the representation of a client to the extent the lawyer reasonably believes necessary:

(1) to prevent reasonably certain death or substantial bodily harm;

(2) to prevent the client from committing a crime or fraud that is reasonably certain to result in substantial injury to the financial interests or property of another and in furtherance of which the client has used or is using the lawyer's services;

(3) to prevent, mitigate or rectify substantial injury to the financial interests or property of another that is reasonably certain to result or has resulted from the client's commission of a crime or fraud in furtherance of which the client has used the lawyer's services;

(4) to secure legal advice about the lawyer's compliance with these Rules;

(5) to establish a claim or defense on behalf of the lawyer in a controversy between the lawyer and the client, to establish a defense to a criminal charge or civil claim against the lawyer based upon conduct in which the client was involved, or to respond to allegations in any proceeding concerning the lawyer's representation of the client;

(6) to comply with other law or a court order.[1]

About This Chapter

Can a defense lawyer make the difference between a guilty and not guilty verdict? Sometimes. Novels, popular movies, television shows, and miniseries, such as *To Kill a Mockingbird*, *A Time to Kill*, *The Accused*, *How to Get Away with Murder*, and *American Crime Story: The People v. O.J. Simpson*, dramatize the charisma and abilities of defense lawyers. But the vast majority of criminal defendants brought before the court are not able to hire any attorney at all. Many private attorneys provide criminal defense services to defendants who can pay, but most defendants are poor and are therefore unable to make bail or to hire a lawyer. Famed defense attorney Gerry Spence has said, "if there is no profit in justice, people are not likely to receive it."[2] Professor Bryan Stevenson has maintained, "[T]hat we have a criminal justice system that treats you better if you're rich and guilty than if you're poor and innocent.[3] **Does the quality of justice a person receives in the United States depend on their economic status? Should it?**

If you were arrested and charged with a crime and were required to post a money bail to gain release until your trial, could you secure the money? Would you be able to hire the best defense lawyer available? How would you pay the attorney? What would you do if you had no money, or property, or any other resources to post bond for pretrial release or to secure the services of a high-powered defense attorney? Do you believe that a defendant's ability to hire an expensive attorney is a factor in the quality of justice?

For the person arrested and brought into the criminal justice network, especially for the first time, entrance into the world of police lockups, court arraignment, and jail detention is frightening. The intimidating surroundings are alien to most of us. No comfort can be found by knowing other people in the same circumstances, nor in a growing familiarity with the routines of life behind bars or with the faces and attitudes of police officers, detention officers, fellow arrestees, judges, or bailiffs. Most people caught up in the criminal justice process are eager to get out of custody and return home to family and friends. A phone call is a welcome opportunity to say to someone, "Get me out of here!"

Likewise, the person in the arms of the law typically needs help—help to obtain release, help to cope with the police investigation, help in the process of bringing the event to a close. "I want a lawyer." That simple statement reveals the detainee's feelings of fear and anxiety, and his or her need to lean on someone, to find comfort, advice, and solace from a knowledgeable professional. If you were brought before the criminal justice system, you too would want a lawyer.

This chapter explains how a person moves through the early stages of court processing after arrest, and covers the important decisions involving detention in jail, release, and the assistance of counsel.

Jails and Lockups

"Go directly to jail. Do not pass GO. Do not collect $200." That famous line from the board game *Monopoly* does not reflect the bitter truth about jails, nor the people locked in them. Jails, and police lockups, serve the single purpose of holding individuals caught in the arms of the law, confining them securely so they cannot freely move about the community. Jails are pervasive in our society.

> The American criminal justice system holds more than 2.3 million people in 1,719 state prisons, 102 federal prisons, 901 juvenile correctional facilities, 3,163 local jails, and 76 Indian Country jails as well as in military prisons, immigration detention facilities, civil commitment centers, and prisons in the U.S. territories.[4]

Jails are typically local county or city institutions for the *temporary detention* of persons awaiting indictment, arraignment, trial, or sentencing, and for persons serving short-term misdemeanant sentences (less than 1 year). In six states (Alaska,

Connecticut, Delaware, Hawaii, Rhode Island, and Vermont) jail administration and operation is under the purview of state government, with Alaska, for example, having fifteen locally run community jails subject to state funding, programming, and monitoring.[5] The equivalent of jails in the federal system exist in federal metropolitan detention centers or federal detention centers.[6] Jails are not to be confused with prisons or correctional institutions, discussed in Chapter 11, which are designed for the confinement of convicted persons sentenced to more than one year.

What's wrong with this newspaper headline?

Convicted Armed Robber Sentenced to 10 Years in Jail

In some cases, jails also hold material witnesses—that is, witnesses to a crime who might flee or move away before the trial if they are not detained—as well as probation violators who have failed on community supervision and parole violators awaiting return to prison. Also, Immigration and Customs Enforcement (ICE) detainees may be held in local facilities. At mid-year 2014, 16,384 immigration detainees, persons being held for U.S. Immigration and Customs Enforcement (ICE) were held in local jails, the lowest number since 2007.[7] Especially in states where prison overcrowding is acute, persons sentenced to prison terms are sometimes held in local jails pending transfer to the prison system when space becomes available there. Holding prisoners for other jurisdictions can be a profitable business. Virtually every city, county, and town in the United States has a facility for the confinement of arrested persons and the incarceration of misdemeanants. Village and town jails often consist of no more than a few cells for locking up six to eight persons.

In 2015, just over 8 percent of jail populations in the U.S. were housed in facilities holding fewer than 100 inmates (based on average daily custodial populations), with large jails (those housing 1,000 inmates or more) accounting for about 45 percent of the (average daily) populations of jails.[8] Furthermore, in 2015 the smallest jails, those housing 49 or fewer inmates, recorded a number of admissions more than 37 times the size of their average daily populations. This suggests that higher admissions and higher turnover rates led to shorter stays of incarceration, resulting in increased pressure to process inmates at admissions and releases.[9]

According to a Bureau of Justice Statistics report, the five largest jail populations in America can be found in Los Angeles, California, 19,185; New York, New York, 10,949; Cook County, Illinois, 9,514; Harris County, Texas, 8,511; and Philadelphia, Pennsylvania, 8,318.[10] Each of these jails contain average daily populations in excess of the 5,000 or so inmates in America's largest prison, Angola (The Louisiana State Penitentiary), in Louisiana.[11]

Jails are by far the most utilized incarceration facilities in the criminal justice system. Of those being held in local jails, about 68% were held for felonies and 32% for misdemeanors or some other violations.[12] Also, as reported by the Bureau of Justice Statistics, 63,478 persons were in various community supervision programs outside of jail facilities, including: electronic monitoring, home detention, day reporting, community service, treatment programs, and other pretrial and work programs. See **Table 7.1**.

Table 7.1 Persons under jail supervision, by confinement status and type of program, midyear 2000 and 2006–2014

Confinement status and type of program	2000	2006	2007	2008	2009	2010	2011	2012	2013	2014*
Total	687,033**	826,041	848,419**	858,385**	837,647**	809,360	798,417	808,622	790,649	808,070
Held in jail[a]	621,149**	765,819**	780,174**	785,533**	767,434**	748,728	735,601	744,524	731,208	744,592
Supervised outside of a jail facility[b]	65,884	60,222	68,245	72,852**	70,213**	60,632	62,816	64,098	59,441	63,478
Weekend programs[c]	14,523**	11,421**	10,473	12,325**	11,212**	9,871	11,369**	10,351	10,950	9,698
Electronic monitoring	10,782**	10,999**	13,121	13,539	11,834**	12,319	11,950**	13,779	12,023**	14,223
Home detention[d]	332	807	512	498	738	736	809	2,129**	1,337**	646
Day reporting	3,969	4,841	6,163**	5,758**	6,492**	5,552**	5,200	3,890	3,683	4,413
Community service	13,592	14,667	15,327	18,475**	17,738**	14,646	11,680	14,761	13,877	14,331
Other pretrial supervision	6,279**	6,409**	11,148**	12,452**	12,439**	9,375	10,464	7,738	7,542	8,634
Other work programs[e]	8,011	8,319**	7,369	5,808	5,912	4,351**	7,165	7,137	5,341**	7,003
Treatment programs[f]	5,714**	1,486**	2,276	2,259	2,082	1,799	2,449	2,164	2,002	2,100
Other	2,682	1,273**	1,857**	1,739	1,766**	1,983**	1,731**	2,149	2,687	2,430

* Comparison year by status and program.
** Difference with comparison year is significant at the 95% confidence level.
[a] Number of inmates held on the last weekday in June.
[b] Number of persons under jail supervision but not confined on the last weekday in June. Excludes persons supervised by a probation or parole agency.
[c] Offenders serve their sentences of confinement on weekends only (i.e., Friday to Sunday).
[d] Includes only persons without electronic monitoring.
[e] Includes persons in work release programs, work gangs, and other alternative work programs.
[f] Includes persons in drug, alcohol, mental health, and other medical treatment.

Source: Bureau of Justice Statistics, Annual Survey of Jails, midyear 2000 and midyear 2006–2014.[13]

Major city jails have large group cells (called bullpens) as well as individual cells, while police stations have **lockups**, small holding cells, for the temporary detention of persons under investigation or being processed for their initial appearance before a magistrate. Police lockups are usually in police offices within sight and sound of the police officers. Persons placed in lockup cells must be screened for medical or psychological problems which may threaten their own safety, and once locked up they should be visually monitored so as to prevent self-inflicted harm.

Jails, in the pure sense, are not correctional facilities. "Every year, [approximately] 641,000 people walk out of *prison* gates, but people go to *jail* ... million[s of] times each year.[14] In fact, there were 10.9 million admissions to jail in the United States in 2015.[15] Rotation in and out of]jail ... is particularly high because most people in jails have not been convicted. Some have just been arrested and will make bail in the next few hours or days, and others are too poor to make bail and must remain behind bars until they are further processed. Only a small number (187,000 on any given day) have been convicted, generally serving misdemeanors sentences under a year."[16] For example, at year-end 2015, roughly 693,300 people were incarcerated in local jails. Of those jailed inmates, approximately 37 percent had been convicted and were awaiting sentence or were serving their sentence in jail. Thus, the majority (roughly 63%) of those held in jails had not been convicted of a crime.[17] See **Table 7.2.** At year-end 2015, roughly 693,300 people were incarcerated in local jails (year-end counts tend to be less than mid-year counts).[18] This number is included in the total of 2,173,800 persons incarcerated in local jails and prisons (state and federal) nationwide at year-end 2015. This total number of those incarcerated is the lowest number for this population since 2004.[19] Also, according to the Bureau of Justice Statistics, per capita jail incarceration rates in the U.S. have been declining since 2008, when 340 per 100,000 were incarcerated, to 2015 when 300 per 100,000 persons are jailed. However, the female inmate population in jails has increased. In 2000, females comprised about 11% of total jail populations; in 2014, they made up about 14% of jail inmates. Males account for about 85% of jail inmates. Male populations have remained stable since 2000—approximately 400 per 100,000 male residents. In terms of race, since 2013, approximately 47% of the jail population is comprised of whites (up from 42% since 2000), 35% are blacks (down from 40% in 2005), 15% are Hispanic (stable since 2000), and 1% are American Indian and Alaskan Natives (doubled since 2000).[20]

Typically jails have little, if any, correctional capability in terms of counseling, recreation, libraries, vocational training, educational programs, and the like. With a very transitory population, jails maximize secure confinement of the greatest number of inmates with the fewest possible detention personnel (officers). Because most of those housed in jail are awaiting disposition of their charges, and are therefore presumed "innocent," correctional programs are inappropriate.

In most urban jurisdictions, persons who are sentenced for misdemeanors are housed in separate local correctional facilities rather than in city or county jails. Often the only sentenced persons housed in the large "holding" jails are those "trusties,"

Table 7.2 Number of confined inmates in local jails, by characteristics, midyear 2000, 2005, and 2010–2014; yearend 2015

	Midyear							
Characteristic	**2000**	**2005**	**2010**	**2011**	**2012**	**2013**	**2014***	**Yearend 2015**
Total	621,100**	747,500	748,700	735,600	744,500	731,200	744,600	693,300 !
Sex								
Male	550,200**	653,000**	656,400**	642,300	645,900	628,900	635,500	594,200 !
Female	71,000**	94,600**	92,400**	93,300**	98,600**	102,400**	109,100	99,100 !
Adult	613,500**	740,800	741,200	729,700	739,100	726,600	740,400	689,900 !
Male	543,100**	646,800**	649,300**	636,900	640,900	624,700	631,600	591,100 !
Female	70,400**	94,000**	91,900**	92,800**	98,100**	101,900**	108,800	98,800 !
Juvenile[a]	7,600**	6,800**	7,600**	5,900**	5,400**	4,600	4,200	3,500 !
Held as adult[b]	6,100**	5,800**	5,600**	4,600**	4,600**	3,500	3,700	3,200 !
Held as juvenile	1,500**	1,000	1,900**	1,400	900	1,100	500	300 !
Race/Hispanic origin[c]								
White	260,500**	331,000**	331,600**	329,400**	341,100	344,900	352,800	335,100 !
Black/ African American	256,300	290,500**	283,200**	276,400**	274,600	261,500	263,800	243,400 !

Table 7.2 Number of confined inmates in local jails, by characteristics, midyear 2000, 2005, and 2010–2014; yearend 2015 *continued*

	Midyear							
Characteristic	**2000**	**2005**	**2010**	**2011**	**2012**	**2013**	**2014***	**Yearend 2015**
Hispanic/ Latino	94,100**	111,900	118,100**	113,900	112,700	107,900	110,600	99,000 !
American Indian/ Alaska Native[d]	5,500**	7,600**	9,900	9,400	9,300	10,200	10,400	8,600 !
Asian/Native Hawaiian/ Other Pacific Islander[d]	4,700**	5,400**	5,100**	5,300**	5,400	5,100**	6,000	5,800 !
Two or more races	...	1,000	800	1,200	1,500**	1,600**	1,000	1,500 !
Conviction status[d,e]								
Convicted	271,300	284,400	291,300**	289,600**	293,100**	278,000	277,100	258,800 !
Unconvicted	349,800**	463,200	457,400	446,000**	451,400**	453,200	467,500	434,600 !

Note: Data are adjusted for nonresponse and rounded to the nearest 100. Detail may not sum to total due to rounding. Midyear estimates are based on the number of inmates confined on the last weekday in June, and year-end estimates are based on the number of inmates confined on December 31. In 2015, the ASJ collected characteristic data at year-end but did not collect details for midyear 2015. See *Jail Inmates at Midyear 2014* for years 2006–2009.

... Not collected.

! Not compared because the jail population goes through seasonal variation, typically with fewer inmates at year-end than at midyear.

* Comparison year for each characteristic.

** Difference with comparison year is significant at the 95% confidence level.

a Persons age 17 or younger.

b Includes juveniles who were tried or awaiting trial as adults.

c Excludes persons of Hispanic or Latino origin, unless specified.

d Reports prior to 2014 combined American Indians and Alaska Natives and Asians, Native Hawaiians, and Other Pacific Islanders into an other race category.

e Includes juveniles who were on trial or awaiting trial as adults.

Source: Bureau of Justice Statistics, Annual Survey of Jails (ASJ), 2000, 2005, and 2010–2015; and Census of Jail Inmates, 2005.[21]

Table 7.3 2017 Jail Population Percentages by Selected Characteristics, Prison Policy Initiative

Offense Characteristics	Not Convicted	Convicted
Violent	31.15%	21%
Property	24.6%	24.5%
Drugs	25%	24.5%
Public Order	17.15%	30%
Other	2.1%	—

that is, privileged convicts, who are assigned to do various operational chores such as laundry, cleaning, and cooking.

The average length of stay in jail increased by over 60% from 1983 to 2013—from 14 days to 23 days; many of these extended stays were for unconvicted persons. Of course, many individuals booked into "jail over the course of a year are released within hours or days, rather than weeks or months."[22] This is especially true of police lockups, where release is often arranged prior to arraignment or transfer to jail, as friends or relatives raise bail or make other release arrangements. Thus, jails are high-volume facilities within the criminal justice process.

A mixture of persons charged with violent and nonviolent crimes, or not charged at all, are housed in the jail or lockup. As seen in **Table 7.3**, the largest percentage of those jailed who had not been convicted were being detained for violent offenses, and public order offenses constituted the greatest percentage of convicted persons who were jailed.[23] represents the variety of people in jail—those already convicted as well as those awaiting various stages in criminal justice processing. Although all the prisoners reside in the same facility, it is very important that a classification procedure be used to separate them so that predators cannot prey on victims. Also, see the purposes of jail in **Table 7.4**.

Unfortunately, through the years jails have been used as dumping grounds for every conceivable human problem. Drunks, vagrants, the homeless, the mentally ill, prostitutes, and every other variety of street people, as well as persons arrested for all types of felony offenses and for every type of misdemeanor, have found their way to local jails. Criminologist John Irwin refers to this phenomenon as jails performing the role of social sanitation, sweeping the unsightly rabble class off the street.[24] See **Field Practice 7.1**.

Field Practice 7.1 In Their Own Words—Larinda Slater, Jail Program Coordinator

After obtaining a bachelor's degree in psychology, I gained employment in an adult male correctional facility. Here, my personal views, integrity, skills,

Table 7.4 Purposes of a Jail

- to receive individuals pending arraignment and hold them awaiting trial, conviction, or sentencing
- to hold probation or parole violators until decisions about revocation can be made
- to hold people who failed to appear after having been released on bail or their own recognizance, called ROR
- to temporarily detain juveniles until they can be transferred to juvenile authorities
- to hold mentally ill persons pending transfer to appropriate health facilities
- to hold individuals for potential immigration violations, those wanted by the military, people in protective custody, those detained for contempt of court, and as material witnesses
- to hold convicted felons until they can be transferred to state or federal correctional authorities
- to hold federal or state prisoners because of crowding in their institutions
- to hold persons serving short-term misdemeanor jail sentences[25]

and abilities were all challenged and tested by the clientele in the institution, where my grades and education were not relevant. My undergraduate studies taught me about the history, statistics, and theories/theorists in the field. We also learned about psychological disorders, state hospitals, and other phenomena. Though we learned about Maslow's hierarchy of needs, cognitive thinking, negative/positive reinforcements and punishments, none of this education was practical or useful when dealing with "real" people, not lab rats. Unfortunately, my educational experience fell short of teaching beyond the "classroom" and it did not adequately prepare me for the "real world." I was void of the essential tools that allow you to deal with human behavior inside of an institution, such as critical/creative thinking skills and interpersonal communication skills.

I was not aware of the merging of the criminal justice and psychology fields. I also learned that the criminal justice system had now become the modern-day state hospital. It was difficult to cope with the substantial number of individuals in jail who were suffering from mental illness. I would encourage those who want to enter the criminal justice field to study psychology as well and to mentally prepare themselves on how to manage individuals who suffer from mental illness. Working in a jail has taught me many things, but one lesson that stands out the most is the importance of knowing your core self so you don't succumb to the psychological pressures in dealing with the realities of serving people with mental illness in a correctional setting. Serving people with mental illness who commit crimes can be difficult but it can also be rewarding.[26]

In virtually any large jail in the United States, especially on a weekend night, the booking area displays an intriguing variety of humanity. Jailers like to say that sooner or later everyone comes to the jail—lawyers, doctors, judges, ministers, teachers, students, laborers, young and old, rich and poor, members of every race, color, and creed. Some are more apt to leave than others; poor people generally contend that jails are built for them, and indeed most people in jail are poor, minorities, and young.

Police have often used jailing as the ultimate exercise of their power. And even though most people taken to the jail are released on bail or their own recognizance almost immediately, for the police officer, placing a person in jail can serve as a kind of closure to an arrest, satisfying the officer's desire to "do something" about the offense in question. In the same way, judges sometimes use the jail as the ultimate device for venting frustration or anger or disappointment in defendants. (See **Critical Thinking 7.1** below.)

Critical Thinking 7.1

In 1923, a judge announced the following sentence on a person convicted in his court:

> I not only sentence you to confinement for thirty days in a bare, narrow cell in a gloomy building, during which time you will be deprived of your family, friends, occupation, earning power, and all other human liberties and privileges; but in addition I sentence you to wallow in a putrid mire demoralizing to body, mind and soul, where every rule of civilization is violated, where you are given every opportunity to deteriorate, but none to improve, and where your tendency to wrong-doing cannot be corrected, but only aggravated.[27]

It seems this judge took pleasure in the miserable conditions in his jail. How would you like to be sentenced to a jail like this?

Jails are typically operated under the authority of law enforcement officials, the chief of police for the city jail and the sheriff for the county jail. This has been the traditional arrangement, but in recent years some jails have been reorganized under a separate department of corrections. Sheriffs and police have been hesitant to relinquish control of jails because they generally do not relish having a separate governmental agency controlling access to detention. Moreover, jails have been a source of revenue for law enforcement agencies, particularly for sheriffs' departments that operate their jails on a fee-per-inmate basis. In some jurisdictions, a significant portion of a sheriff's budget is derived from jail operations. Jail inspectors are usually representatives of the state department of corrections. Although some states have abolished state jail standards,[28] they attempt to "persuade" counties and cities to adopt minimum standards of care and staffing, but by and large jails operate in an autonomous fashion.

Most veteran prisoners will agree that jail time is much more difficult to serve than a prison sentence. While jail terms are usually shorter, typically the jails themselves are not equipped with outside recreation facilities, adequate activities to break the boredom, or adequate sanitary facilities. Jails are often crowded, dirty, unsafe, and populated by an unstable mixture of felons, misdemeanants, and drunks—often those considered the "dregs of society." Jail inmates are usually unclassified by category and housed together, whereas prisons attempt to separate the aggressive from the weak prisoners, the persons with mental illnesses from the general population. In comparison to jails, most prison facilities provide a great deal of stimulation in the form of hobby and craft activities, vocational training, educational opportunities, outdoor activities, movies, and religious programs. Visitor facilities in jails typically are dismal, crowded, and without privacy. In many jails visitors must talk though little speaker boxes in cellblock doors and peer through small, thick Plexiglas windows at the inmates they are visiting. By comparison, medium- or minimum-security prisons are much better.

Based on the most recent data available, the five states with the most jail inmate fatalities were California (132), Florida (87), Texas (76), Georgia (45), and Virginia (38). Approximately 40% of jail inmate deaths occurred in these five states.[29] In 2014, over a third (425 of 1,053) of jail inmate deaths occurred within the first seven days of admission. Suicide was the leading cause of death in local jails and accounted for more than a third (35 percent) of the deaths of jail inmates. From 2013 to 2014, the number of suicides increased 13%, from 328 to 372. In 2014, the suicide rate in local jails was 50 per 100,000 local jail inmates, the highest suicide rate observed since 2000.[30] Inmates most likely to have committed suicide while in jail, based on data from 2000–2014, were white (41%), males (91%), convicted of a crime(s)—72%—(versus those who were not convicted), and were in custody for violent offenses (50%). While jail populations have decreased, the numbers of jail inmate suicides have increased.[31]

Suicides in jail have historically occurred at a rate considerably higher than that of the general population.[32] With the transient nature of jail populations and constraints on thorough classification and categorization of inhabitants, the jail suicide rate of those in custody has been found to be over three times the suicide rate of those in state prison (50 per 100,000 compared to 15 per 100,000).[33] Suicide has been found less likely to occur in the 50 largest jail systems, as the rate of suicide there has previously been determined to be half that of all of the other jails in the country. The nation's smallest jails (50 or fewer persons detained) have been discovered to have suicide rates five times higher than the nation's largest jail complexes (2,000 or more inhabitants).[34] The most recent statistics available reveal that approximately one-third of deaths in jail custody were due to suicide. While data is insufficient at this time, some suggest that alleged sex offenders may be particularly vulnerable to suicide while in custody as well.[35] The stigma and shame associated with such offenders within society and even the inmate subculture likely contributes to their being prone to suicide.

Explaining jail suicide rates is not easy. Jails are often repositories for vulnerable persons with substance abuse and mental health problems who are socially isolated and socially disenfranchised. The loss of freedom, separation from whatever semblance of life on the outside one had, the unknown threatening atmosphere of a jail, and the uncertainty regarding future prospects can prove overwhelming—particularly to those who do not have a familiarity with such confines.[36] Attempts to develop prediction scales and profiles of suicide-prone inmates have had limited utility.[37] The sad fact remains that conditions in older detention facilities especially, such as jails and lockups, are often poor and persons confined in them are desperate. Jails and other detention facilities constructed during the last quarter of the twentieth century have been designed to prevent suicides and other deaths. This has been done to foster more humane and create more healthy environments.

A history of violence and homosexual assaults is well known in jails and lockups, although accurate statistics about them do not exist. Classification by inmate types and constant surveillance by trained officers provide the best protection for people locked in group cells.

Holding a person in custody implies a responsibility to provide care for that person who, by virtue of being incarcerated, is no longer able to fully provide for his or her own needs. When the police agency arrests someone, even for the individual's own protection, the responsibility for that person's safety and health lies with the local unit of government responsible for the detention facility. Therefore, in properly managed jails and lockups, medical screening is provided. Detention personnel are trained to recognize threatening behavioral characteristics, policies require routine standards of care, and officers are trained and equipped to render aid quickly and expertly in any emergency.

For all these reasons, various national organizations have attempted to upgrade jail conditions by instituting accreditation procedures and by publishing minimum desirable standards. For decades, organizations such as the National Sheriffs' Association, the American Correctional Association, and the American Jail Association have published standards for the safe operation of jails that meet constitutional criteria and cover all aspects of jail operation, from security to safety and healthcare.[38]

While suicide may be a leading cause of death in jails, sometimes deaths occur due to actions on the part of staff. Consider Terrill Thomas. He flooded the cell of another inmate in a Milwaukee jail. As punishment, the water to his cell was turned off. Thomas was bipolar and lost 35 pounds over the seven-day time period he was deprived of water. He died on the eighth day in solitary confinement from dehydration. A grand jury is recommending that charges be filed against seven employees.[39] **Follow this case to determine the outcome. Will there also be a civil suit?**

Pretrial Release or Detention

Perhaps nothing in criminal justice is more controversial than the matter of releasing persons after their arrest for a crime, but before their trial. Sometimes a police officer complains: "That crook beat me back to the neighborhood after I arrested him. The paperwork I had to complete took me longer than it took for him to get out of jail!" There are conflicting justifications for pretrial detention and release. This legal area is governed by statutes and Supreme Court decisions, but a certain amount of discretion still exists. The issues raised by pretrial release decisions are difficult to solve.

When the police bring a person they have arrested to jail, for booking, the suspect is to be taken before a magistrate for an **initial appearance**. This presentment before a neutral, detached judicial authority usually occurs within 24 hours of arrest and certainly transpires within 48 hours, unless extenuating circumstances exist.[40] This is the first time the suspect appears before the court. Sometime during this initial period the case materials are turned over to the prosecutor for the consideration of formal charges. At this point in the criminal justice process, the police task is done. Of course, the officers may be required to testify later at a trial, if the case goes that far, but in the majority of instances the police role is over after this initial appearance before a magistrate.

Several matters are resolved at the initial appearance:

1. The defendant is informed of the arrest charges, often by the reading of the complaint, although he or she is not required to plead to them, but may do so to any misdemeanor;
2. The defendant is informed of his or her constitutional rights, including those that pertain to self-incrimination and legal representation (which he or she may already have been advised of by the police);
3. An attorney is assigned to indigent defendants, if they desire one, or the public defender's office is officially notified that the case will proceed to trial;
4. If probable cause is determined not to exist, the matter could be dismissed.

The primary issue resolved, and the one that most immediately affects the person in police custody and charged with a crime, is decided by the judge—that is, whether to release or detain the individual pending further processing. This step is often called, in shorthand, "bail or jail," and the judge's decision depends on many factors.

Police have arrested the person on evidence of criminal behavior. The person may even have been caught in the act of committing the crime. And the prosecutor has stated the intention to prosecute, to secure a conviction either through a guilty plea or a trial. Is it safe to allow the accused to remain in the community at large? What was the nature of the crime? What is in the best interests of the accused?

Some jurisdictions may provide advice and support to judges regarding such decisions and their aftermath. The federal system, with their vast resources, for example, employs federal pretrial service officers that assist with background investigations of persons who appear before the court, make recommendations regarding release, and provide supervision to those released and awaiting trial.[41]

At the beginning of the twenty-first century, more than 300 pretrial service programs were operating in America.[42] If the judge allows the individual to go free pending further processing, it is known as **pretrial release**. If the judge does not allow it, pretrial release has been denied. This is somewhat of a misnomer, as a trial may never take place.

Several pretrial release options are used by judges, making most defendants, regardless of economic status, eligible for release pending trial. (See types of bail below.) Of course, the most commonly known method for pretrial release is **bail**, the posting

Table 7.5 Defendants released pretrial for cases disposed in federal district courts, by offense type, FY 2008–2010

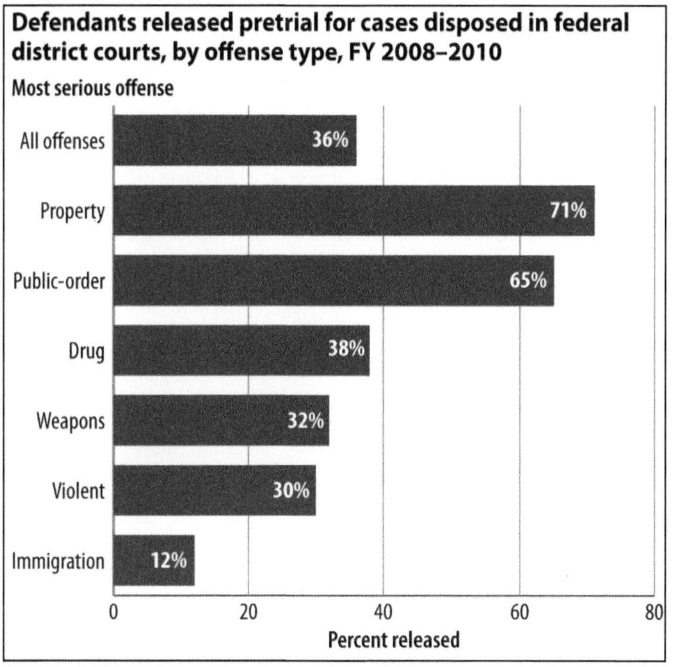

of an amount of money which a judge deems necessary to assure the defendant's later appearance at trial.

During fiscal years 2008 through 2010, 36% of the 283,358 defendants in cases disposed in federal district courts were released prior to case adjudication. The percentages of pretrial release ranged from 12% for defendants brought into federal courts for immigration violations to 71% for defendants charged with property offenses (see **Table 7.5**). Nineteen percent of released defendants committed some form of pretrial misconduct, and technical violations accounted for 90% of these pretrial violations.... Twenty-four percent of these defendants were released at the time of their initial appearance, while another 12% were detained and then released at subsequent court events, including detention or bond hearings. Nonfinancial methods, including release on personal recognizance or unsecured bond, accounted for 73% of pretrial releases in federal courts.[43]

Four different types of money bail (or bond, as it is sometimes called) are used:

1. **Fully secured bond**, or **surety bond**, in which the defendant must post the full amount of bail with the court;
2. **Deposit bond**, or privately secured bail, in which a bail bondsman signs a promissory note for the full amount for the defendant in exchange for a fee of 10 percent of the full amount and some collateral, such as an automobile and/or house, in addition;

Bail Bonds

3. **Cash bond**, or **deposit bail**, in which the court allows the defendant to post 10 percent of the full amount with the court, which is usually refunded when the defendant appears for trial (although, there may be administrative costs even if one is found not guilty, and the full amount is due if the defendant does not show); and
4. **Unsecured bond**, in which the defendant pays no money to the court but is liable for the full amount of bail if he or she fails to appear for trial.

In addition to financial bail, alternative release options exist, including:

1. **Release on recognizance (ROR)**, in which the defendant is released on the promise to appear for trial, discussed later in this chapter.
2. **Conditional release**, in which the court releases the defendant with specific requirements, such as that he or she attend a drug rehabilitation program or meet some other special condition; and two other methods which are not as common:
3. **Third-party custody**, in which the defendant is released into the custody of another individual or agency on the promise that his or her later appearance will be assured; and
4. **Citation release**, in which the arresting officer grants the defendant a release through a written order, or citation, for his or her first court appearance.

In fact, commercial bond agents have become the most prevalent means of pretrial release today. Speculation is that the ability of these bond agents to monitor those released and to be selective in choosing their clientele adds to their success in assuring their clients appear before the court.[44]

Pretrial Release: Bail

Where did pretrial release originate? The exact origin is unknown. However, it is believed to have roots in the historical practices of **hostageship, wergeld, and surety. Hostageship** provided for the replacement of the accused with a willing hostage who could be tried and punished should the accused not appear for trial. **Wergeld** refers to the medieval practice of the accused being able to pay a price to offset his conviction, often associated with a caste-like system, whereby the less one had the less they were worth and the more they would have to pay if adjudged to be the wrongdoer. Wergeld could also be used as a means to ensure in advance the ability to sufficiently repay loans in the event a conviction for fraudulent loans occurred.

Bail has roots in the tradition of **surety**, which has been traced back to 2,500 B.C. and was codified in Roman law around 700 B.C. Under this system, accused persons were required to place some real property as collateral against their failure to appear at a future trial. A third-party, under the surety system, could also vouch for a person borrowing money and promise to cover the loan if a borrower failed to do so. In pre-Norman England, the surety system evolved in to the process where the accused were released unto "bayle" or safekeeping from prison.[45]

In the American experience, the drafters of the U.S. Constitution retained the concept of bail, reacting only against the European practice of setting extreme bail on poor defendants, stating that "excessive bail shall not be required."[46] Prior to the modern era, such a system of placing a surety to guarantee later appearance had greater importance, since defendants could easily "disappear" by departing the jurisdiction involved. Today, however, the ability of the agencies of the criminal justice system to track down and re-apprehend offenders has diminished the possibilities of such successful absconding. Therefore, a large percentage of offenders of every type of offense, as seen in **Table 7.5**, are released prior to trial, and only about 6% of all persons released prior to case disposition remain fugitives a year after their initial release.[47]

Criminal Justice 7.1 Ethics: Controversies Related to Bail

The imposition of money bail in this century has resulted in a burgeoning private business operated by **bail agents**, who for a fee (about 10 percent of the amount of the bail) will secure and post the surety bond that allows the suspect to be released. The bail bond agent assumes responsibility for the person's later appearance at court and keeps the 10% fee. Bail agents often troll for perspective clients at court during first appearances, in the lobbies of jails, and by hanging out by holding cells.[48] As noted by Professor John Goldkamp, "It's really the only place in the criminal justice system where a liberty decision is governed by a profit-making businessman who will or will not take your business."[49]

All forms of discrimination can be and have been practiced by bail bond agents, who have total discretion as to their choice of clients. Greedy practices of bail bonds personnel have been the focus of much of the criticism directed at the bail system, resulting in much of the reform in the bail system that has occurred. A bail bond agent, for instance, is not required to post bond even if the defendant can pay the 10%. Furthermore, bail bond agents have had literally unchecked power to pursue and apprehend bail jumpers, and have disregarded constitutional protections that criminal justice agency personnel must honor, including Fourth Amendment protections, those disallowing kidnapping and transportation of individuals without extradition.

Bounty hunters may be bail agents themselves or they may be contracted to track down and retrieve those who abscond. Bounty hunters have even been glamorized, for example, with production of the *Dog The Bounty Hunter* series on the A&E television network. The authority of bounty hunters to circumvent what have generally been considered rights of the accused is often traced to the U.S. Supreme Court case of *Taylor v. Taintor* (1872).[50] In that case, Justice Swayne delivered the opinion of the Court and wrote:

> When bail is given, the principal is regarded as delivered to the custody of his sureties. Their dominion is a continuance of the original imprisonment. Whenever they choose to do so, they may seize him and deliver him up in their discharge; and if that cannot be done at once, they may imprison him until it can be done. They may exercise their rights in person or by agent. They may pursue him into another state; may arrest him on the Sabbath, and, if necessary, may break and enter his house for that purpose. The seizure is not made by virtue of new process. None is needed. It is likened to the rearrest by the sheriff of an escaping prisoner. In 6 Modern it is said, "*The bail have their principal on a string, and may pull the string whenever they please, and render him in their discharge*"[51] [emphasis added].

Former Supreme Court Justice Arthur Goldberg stated that the bail system "at best ... is a system of checkbook justice; at worst, a highly commercialized racket."[52] However, some researchers contend that via legislation and court cases some states are beginning to rein in the bail bond process and make it more in line with the rule of law.[53] More and more the actions of bail agents and bounty hunters are being distinguished from those of mere private citizens, and the interests of bounty hunters in bringing those on bail to justice are being viewed as more in line with criminal justice professionals who are legally bound to comply with constitutional protections.

Collusion between bail agents and judges in Illinois and sheriffs in Louisiana has been uncovered, and four states (Illinois, Kentucky, Oregon, and Wisconsin) have disallowed commercial bail bond systems, relying upon deposits to courts and/or trusting defendants to return for further processing. In fact, only the United States and the Philippines predominantly use commercial bail bond companies for pretrial release. Even those states that have abolished the use of commercial bail bond agencies, such as Oregon, acknowledge that failures to appear have skyrocketed. Whereas, those supervised by commercial bail bond agents are more likely to show up for court proceedings to begin with and more likely to be apprehended if they abscond than those allowed to be released under other means.[54]

In accordance with U.S. Supreme Court cases, *Stack v. Boyle* (1951) and *U.S. v. Salerno* (1987), effective January 1, 2017, the flight risk and dangerousness of defendants are to be the sole guiding criteria for determining bail decisions. Voters came forth in 2014 and amended the New Jersey Constitution in favor of eliminating cash bail.

Critics of bail maintain it disparages the poor, many of whom are minorities, unable to put together even modest amounts of money for bail. Often for minor offenses, poor defendants languish in jail, severely limited in their contribution to their defense, sometimes losing jobs and having families disrupted. New Jersey's bail system changes closely model the federal system and the District of Columbia—shunning monetary bail. In fact, like the feds, in New Jersey they are striving diligently to make bail decisions within 48 hours. While other states such as Kentucky, previously mentioned, and Colorado have modified their bail systems, New Jersey represents the most radical overhaul.

While bail is still a possibility, in reality judges have all but ended monetary bail in New Jersey. For example, in the first month of January 2017, in 3,382 cases across the state of New Jersey, judges set bail three times. Additionally, during this time frame, 283 defendants were denied bail due to the seriousness of the crime and/or their potential flight risk.

In the past, New Jersey's chief justice indicated one out of eight inmates could not post a $2,500 bail, which would require a 10 percent deposit to a bail bond agent of $250.00, which a number of defendants still could not afford.

The biggest opponents of the new bail system in New Jersey are the bail bond agencies. They have even created a Facebook page: "NJ Bail Reform—Why NJ is Less Safe at the Taxpayers Expense." They contend that hardened violent criminals are being unleashed into the community under the new system. In conclusion, the chief justice, mentioned above, indicated, "[t]here will be a crisis one day, where a single defendant will violate conditions and [do] something that grabs the public's attention."[55] Indeed, as we know, often crisis drives policy. The question will be if there will be enough crises to overturn the policy.

Recently, a federal judge in Houston, Texas, overhauled the Harris County bail system pertaining to minor crimes after determining that it disproportionately impacted poor defendants and was in violation of the U.S. Constitution. The judge "ordered Harris County to stop keeping people who have been arrested on misdemeanor charges in jail because they cannot pay bail." The matter came to the judge's attention "when a woman was arrested on a charge of driving without a license and spent more than two days in jail because she could not post $2,500 in bail." The judge ruled that " 'Harris County's policy is to detain indigent misdemeanor defendants before trial, violating equal protection rights against wealth-based discrimination and violating due process protections against pretrial detention.' [The judge] cited statistics showing that 40 percent of people arrested on misdemeanor charges in the county had been detained until their cases were resolved." Estimates are that as many as 500 individuals with misdemeanor charges are detained in the Harris County Jail on an average night.[56]

The traditional purpose of bail has been to assure the later appearance of defendants at trial, that is, to prevent or discourage flight. This implies that bail should only be set at an amount necessary to achieve this purpose. In ***Stack v. Boyle*** (1951), a landmark Supreme Court decision that reaffirmed the traditional right to freedom before conviction, the Court considered the case of several defendants charged with offenses which carried maximum penalties of not more than a $10,000 fine or more than 5 years in prison. Their bail had been set at $50,000 each. The government argued that previous defendants, charged with similar offenses, had jumped bail set at lower amounts, so that the higher bail in *Stack* was needed to assure the defendants would remain around—in jail—until trial. The Supreme Court disagreed. Justice Felix Frankfurter, joining in the majority decision, stated:

> The practice of admission to bail, as it has evolved in Anglo-American law, is *not a device for keeping persons in jail* upon mere accusation until it is found convenient to give them trial. On the contrary, the spirit of the procedure is to *enable them to stay out of jail* until a trial has found them guilty. Without this conditional privilege, even those wrongly accused are punished by a period of imprisonment while awaiting trial.... Thus, the amount is said to have been fixed not as a reasonable assurance of their presence at the trial, but also as an assurance they would remain in jail ... it is contrary to the whole policy and philosophy of bail[57] [emphasis added].

Although the primary purpose of bail is to prevent flight by setting the amount so high that it would be excessively costly to abscond, there is another motivation. By setting bail so high as to block release, community can be protected from further crimes by defendants while they are awaiting the trial.

Some magistrates have used the bail decision itself as punishment. Judges sometimes set very high bail for alleged drug dealers, for instance, knowing full well that upon release the suspect would travel directly to the closest international airport and leave for a foreign country, never to be seen or heard from again. Nevertheless, the offender had been "punished" since the government kept the bail money. And, of course, setting bail high enough so that a defendant could not meet it meant the accused did jail time *even before trial.* In this way, accused persons whom a magistrate is convinced were guilty but perhaps not convictable by trial standards could be punished before their guilt or innocence was formally determined.

Economic Discrimination and Bail

Whenever and wherever money becomes a factor in criminal justice processing, as it does in the determination of bail and the assessment of fines, the result is obvious discrimination against the poor. In American criminal justice, dealing as it does with ordinary street crime, the fact is that most suspects and defendants are poor. Many, if not most, suspects cannot even afford to pay a bail bonds agent a hundred dollars. Lacking access to this amount or any dollar figure over it thus means pretrial detention is the fate of roughly one out of three accused felons and a proportion of misdemeanants too.[58] Of the 38% detained prior to disposal of their case, five out of six had a bail amount set, but did not post the necessary finances for release.

Failure or inability to post bail can have a particularly adverse impact on the outcome of one's case. Conviction rates are higher for those detained while awaiting case disposition as opposed to those defendants who were released. Roughly 8 out of 10 persons detained while awaiting case disposition were convicted, while 6 out of 10 persons released while awaiting case resolution were convicted. Furthermore, those released while awaiting disposition typically wait longer to have their cases resolved than those detained.[59] A more recent study considered the impact of pretrial detention on state sentencing and found the following. "Compared to defendants released at some point prior to trial, defendants held for the entire pretrial detention period had: four times greater likelihood of being sentenced to jail, three times longer jail sentences, three times greater likelihood of being sentenced to prison, and two times longer prison sentence[s}."[60] It costs almost six times more a day to house someone in jail as it does to release that person.[61]

Money bail has been criticized for being contradictory to the Equal Protection Clause of the Constitution and a violation of the principle of fundamental fairness. Reforms affecting defendants charged in federal courts were made in the **Bail Reform Act of 1966** and the **District of Columbia Bail Agency Act** (1966). Also, changes in Rule 46 ("Release on Bail") of the Federal Rules of Criminal Procedure promoted the position that *pretrial release is preferred*, that alternatives to money bail must be developed, and that pretrial detention is to be reserved for uncommon cases.

The primary inequity in the money bail process is that poor people are detained for failing to have money or property to put up as collateral and that rich people are easily and routinely released without hardship. This inequity was addressed in 1960 in *Bandy v. United States*, in which Justice William O. Douglas considered the question of whether an indigent person should be denied freedom in cases in which a wealthy person would be allowed to go free, simply because the poor person lacks property or money. Justice Douglas concluded that no person should be denied release purely because of indigence and that people should be released on personal recognizance if other considerations support the likelihood that they will return for trial.[62]

Release on Own Recognizance (ROR)

Most persons released prior to trial are not arrested for new crimes while awaiting trial.[63] Between the years of 1954 and 1957, the **Vera Institute** (a privately financed nonprofit foundation for the improvement of criminal justice) conducted studies of bail practices in Philadelphia.[64] These studies showed that only 18% of persons jailed pending trial because they could not afford bail were acquitted, whereas 48% of persons released on bail were acquitted. Further, detained persons received prison sentences two and a half times as frequently as released persons, and released defendants received suspended sentences four times as frequently as jailed defendants.

As a follow-up to the Philadelphia studies, the Vera Institute created an experimental pretrial release program in New York City in the 1960s. This program was known as the **Manhattan Bail Project.**[65] Vera staff investigated indigent arrested persons in regard to their ties to the community (such as length of residence and employment, and family relationships) as indicators of who would not abscond if released after their initial appearances. Based on that information, Vera personnel then convinced magistrates to consider releasing accused persons on their own promise to return for later proceedings (called release on own recognizance or ROR) if they could not meet monetary bail. The project was remarkably successful in that the rate of return for ROR releasees was consistently equal to or better than the return rate for those on monetary bail.

ROR programs based on the Vera model spread across the nation and are now found not only in most large jurisdictions in the United States but around the world wherever bail procedures are used. Recognizance release is one of the most widespread modern reforms in criminal justice. It is remarkable that it was instigated from outside the system by a private foundation rather than by agencies within the criminal justice system itself.

The success of the Manhattan Bail Project also led to the introduction of other types of pretrial release. Many police departments, including the New York City Police Department, instituted a process called **stationhouse release**, in which some suspects are issued citations (something like traffic tickets) to appear in court at a later date, thereby bypassing both formal, in-custody release and the need for an initial appearance. This has even been extended to **field citations**, whereby police officers in the field may give a person a notice to appear for further court processing at a later date, keeping the officer on the street to tend to his or her crime fighting duties without having to use valuable time to return to the station for further processing. Officers may even take photographs and fingerprint suspects in the field, officially recording the police contact without returning to the station. Stationhouse and citation release are typically employed with minor types of offenses.

Field Practice 7.2, "Release on Recognizance" cases represent a normal range of cases wherein a ROR decision is contemplated by a judge.

Field Practice 7.2 Release on Recognizance (ROR)

1. Down and Out

An 18-year-old girl arrested for shoplifting requested release on recognizance, claiming to be indigent. A field investigation showed that she lived with an unemployed boyfriend, had no steady employment, had dropped out of school in the eleventh grade, and was indeed indigent. She had one prior arrest for shoplifting but the charges had been dismissed for reasons not known. On her prior arrest she had posted a bail of $200, and this was returned when the charges were dropped. The ROR investigator recommended pretrial release, but the judge remanded her to the municipal jail to await arraignment.

2. Con Artist

A 40-year-old male was arrested for fraud and forgery. He was accused of posing as a representative of a roofing company, talking some homeowners into ordering new roofing from a fictitious firm and forging a false name to endorse their initial deposit checks. Actually, he was employed half-time as a car salesman, lived in his own home with his wife and three young children, and had one prior conviction for drunk and disorderly behavior, resulting in a fine of $75, which he had paid. An ROR investigation showed him to be unable to post bail without undue hardship to his family. He was a lifelong resident of the city and was well thought of by the car dealer for whom he worked. The magistrate granted pretrial release on recognizance.

3. Slugger

A 20-year-old male accused of mugging an elderly man (robbery in the third degree) requested ROR. An investigation showed that he was employed full time as a movie usher, that he lived with his parents rent-free, and that he had no prior record as an adult. He had been judged delinquent because of chronic truancy when he was 13 years old and had spent one school year in a foster home. Based on residence, employment, and community ties, the field investigator recommended ROR. The magistrate, however, set bail at $5,000, which the defendant could not provide. He was sent to jail to await indictment and arraignment.

Pretrial Release, the Presumption of Innocence, and Community Safety

Pretrial release does not rest on a presumption of innocence. The obviously guilty as well as those who insist on their innocence both have access to it. But the effect of it—whether achieved by bail or other means—may well be to preserve that presumption, even though such a result is neither the formal purpose of release nor the intent of most judges in making their release decisions.

The majority of defendants released on monetary bail or on ROR return for later proceedings without further incident. However, some arrested persons who are dangerous professional criminals might indeed commit additional crimes while on pretrial release. This presents the system with a dilemma: should a greater emphasis be placed on crime control or on individual rights?

This issue, not surprisingly, finds crime control advocates and due process advocates of criminal justice on opposite sides of the argument.[66] See **Critical Thinking 7.2.**

Critical Thinking 7.2 Point/Counterpoint

The Crime Control View of Pretrial Release

Although the importance of pretrial release to the defendant is clear, crime control advocates espouse what they consider to be the more important need for community protection from possible depraved behavior by bailed offenders.

The Bureau of Justice Statistics reports that from 1990 to 2004, rearrest rates for those facing felony charges, released from the nation's largest 75 county jails while awaiting further court processing, ranged from 13 to 21% and felony arrest rates ranged from 10% to 13%.[67] Some crime control advocates argue that these statistics, along with well-publicized crimes committed by defendants released on bail, show the need to emphasize community protection in the pretrial release decision.[68]

Concern over these problems has generated a number of **preventive detention** programs aimed at keeping suspects in custody who might commit crimes while on pretrial release. The Bail Reform Act of 1984 specifies that an individual must be indicted for a violent or "dangerous crime" and have at least one prior conviction for a similar crime, be currently on bail or some other form of community release, such as probation or parole, and should be kept "off the streets."

The Due Process View of Pretrial Release

According to those concerned about the due process issues, pretrial detention is a dismal failure. The truth is that we are unable to predict with any certainty who is likely to commit crimes while on pretrial release and who is not. And additionally, protectors of civil liberties argue, there are major purposes served by pretrial release besides preventing future crimes. Those purposes include allowing the accused to continue with his or her normal activities, including work and family support, as well as allowing the defendant to help prepare a defense to the charges against him or her. Irving J. Klein provides the following illustration of the importance of pretrial release to defendants (who, it should be remembered, are to be presumed innocent until their guilt has been established through legal proceedings):

The reader should imagine him/herself as being arrested for a robbery committed several days before the arrest. Let us further imagine that the reader is innocent and at the time of the robbery was in a crowded bar located on the other side of town from the robbery location, imbibing some spirits with some newfound acquaintances of the night. The reader is processed in the usual police procedure and comes before a magistrate who is determined that no robbers will be tolerated in his/her town. Bail is fixed at $25,000, and you do not have more than $50 to your name and on your person; you have no friends or relatives who have any assets that can be used as collateral for your bail. A lawyer is assigned to defend you, and you protest that you are innocent. The lawyer asks you if you have any witnesses, and you answer that if you could only get out of jail you could locate some of the people who were at the bar on the night of the robbery who would testify that you were at the bar with them when the robbery took place.[69]

In addition, other factors should be considered according to due process advocates, such as the financial burden on society to maintain jails for the purpose of preventive detention, the impact on the family of the detained person, and the costs of the loss of liberty, including the appalling conditions in many jails, which threaten the life and limb of the detainee.[70]

What Do You Think?

1. Do you believe it is appropriate to hold someone in jail because of things we *think* they may do in the future? Do you believe we can accurately predict future criminal behavior?
2. Should the public's safety needs be considered more important than an individual's right to due process?
3. Why do you think detained defendants tend to be convicted more often and sentenced more harshly than those released pending trial?

Right to Bail

Do we have a constitutional right to pretrial release? To make bail if we can? Although the Constitution does not guarantee the *right* to bail, the **Eighth Amendment** to the United States Constitution states that "Excessive bail shall not be required." What is excessive? For most of us a $1,000 bail would be possible to raise; we could call family or friends for help if the amount was beyond our own means. However, what about extremely poor, unemployed, friendless defendants? The U.S. Supreme Court has never explicitly indicated what constitutes excessive bail.

Field Practice 7.3 Bail

A defendant who was considered by the police to be a leader of organized crime was arrested and charged with conspiracy to distribute narcotics. At the initial appearance the judge set bail at $2 million, noting the reputation of the defendant. Most conspiracy charges of crimes less than homicide elicited bail amounts ranging from $500 to $10,000. The defendant appealed and the appellate court ruled that the bail was excessive and reduced it to $50,000, which was still much higher than average. The defendant deposited the full amount in cash and left the courtroom.

Although the U.S. Supreme Court has never held that the Fourteenth Amendment requirements of "due process of law" and "equal protection of the laws" make the "excessive bail" clause applicable to the states, inclusion of the key word "excessive" has had the practical effect of establishing a right to pretrial release on *reasonable* bail that has been generally acknowledged.[71] On the other hand, over the years, the Supreme Court has allowed states to define certain crimes, usually capital offenses such as murder and treason, as "nonbailable" at the discretion of the magistrate, so that most states have developed a list of nonbailable charges. In 1987, the U.S. Supreme Court ruled in ***United States v. Salerno*** that no absolute right to bail exists under the Eighth Amendment.[72]

The Bail Reform Act of 1984: Crisis Driving Policy

After considerable consternation over the perceived problem of crimes committed by persons free on bail, the U.S. Congress in 1984 passed legislation supported by the Reagan administration allowing broad preventive detention of persons perceived to "pose a threat to individuals or to the community."[73] The Bail Reform Act of 1984 is a major departure from the traditionally held view that the purpose of bail is to permit pretrial release.

It has institutionalized the practice of detaining a person perceived to be "dangerous" by setting unattainable bail levels or by denying bail altogether. The constitutionality of the act was upheld in 1987 in ***United States v. Salerno***, in which defendants reputed to be high-ranking organized crime figures were detained pending trial by a judge who held that their release would result in the defendants continuing "business as usual," including murder and other acts of violence. The defendants argued that such a law "authorizes punishment before trial," but then-Chief Justice Rehnquist, speaking for the Supreme Court majority noted:

> When the government proves by clear and convincing evidence that an arrestee presents an identified and articulable threat to an individual or the community, we believe that, consistent with the Due Process Clause, a court may disable the arrestee from executing that threat.[74]

In upholding the act against an Eighth Amendment challenge, Rehnquist further wrote:

> When Congress has mandated detention on the basis of a compelling interest other than prevention of flight, as it does here, the Eighth Amendment does not require release on bail.[75]

Justices Marshall and Brennan, in their dissenting opinion, called the statute "an abhorrent limitation of the presumption of innocence."[76]

The evolution of law in this regard is clear. Under the Bail Reform Act of 1966, a defendant in federal court was *entitled to bail* "unless the court or judge has reason to believe that no one or more conditions of release will reasonably assure that the person will not flee, or pose a danger to any other person or any other community." The Bail Reform Act of 1984 *reversed* that presumption of entitlement. Now the defendant has the burden of proving an entitlement to release on bail based on the criteria of the act.

Release Pending Appeal

After conviction, if defense counsel files notice of appeal of the conviction, the question arises once again as to whether or not the defendant should be granted freedom pending the outcome of the appeal. The same types of release already discussed are generally available to persons so situated, but before granting bail the Bail Reform Act of 1984 mandates that the court must determine the following:

1. The defendant is not likely to flee or pose a danger to the safety of any other person or the community if released.
2. The appeal is not merely for the purpose of delay in serving sentence.
3. The appeal raises a substantial question of law or fact.
4. If that substantial question is determined favorable to the defendant on appeal, that decision is likely to result in reversal or an order for a new trial on all counts for which imprisonment has been imposed.[77]

Key Court Decisions—Bail and Pretrial Release

Stack v. Boyle (1951)

A person arrested for a noncapital offense is entitled to bail. The purpose of bail is not punishment, but to insure the appearance of the accused person in court. This landmark Supreme Court decision that reaffirmed the traditional right to freedom before conviction and established risk of flight as a legitimate criterion for determining bail decisions.

Bandy v. United States (1960)[78]

No person should be held in jail prior to trial purely because of poverty. If other considerations support the likelihood the person will not flee and will appear for trial, then release on "personal recognizance" should be made.

United States v. Salerno (1987)

No constitutional right to bail exists under the Eighth Amendment when the basis of detention is other than prevention of flight. Persons accused of violent crimes, especially those with histories of committing violent crimes, may be held without bail pending trial. Thus, the Bail Reform Act of 1984 was upheld, and dangerousness could now be considered as a factor in making the release decision.

Defense Lawyers

"You are entitled to have an attorney.... If you cannot afford an attorney, one will be appointed to represent you." These are *Miranda* warning words on the right to legal counsel, which police must provide to all arrested suspects prior to their interrogation. They are perhaps better known than the words of the Sixth Amendment to the United States Constitution, which states in part: "In all criminal prosecutions, the accused shall ... have the Assistance of Counsel for his defense."

Lawyers have always been available for those defendants who have the money and resources to employ them, but for much of the history of the United States, lawyers have not been available to poor people. Today, due to U.S. Supreme Court decisions in the 1960s and 1970s, that has changed. Everyone, rich or poor, is entitled to be defended by a defense attorney when charges are brought against him or her, and if the individual cannot pay to hire (retain) an attorney, the state must provide one free of charge under most circumstances.

Key Court Decisions—Right to Free Attorney

The Sixth Amendment to the U.S. Constitution indicates, "In all criminal prosecutions, the accused shall ... have the Assistance of Counsel for his defense." But, what does it mean?

Powell v. Alabama (1932)

In a capital case (facing the death penalty) where the defendant cannot defend himself or herself and where he or she is unable to employ a lawyer, the court should assign counsel for defense. Fundamental fairness and the due process of law require that indigent defendants have free court-appointed lawyers if they cannot otherwise provide for counsel.

Betts v. Brady (1942)

This case reaffirmed *Powell* and concluded that states were not required to appoint counsel for indigent defendants in noncapital cases.

Gideon v. Wainwright (1963)

This decision overruled *Betts*. The right to counsel is extended beyond the special circumstances already enumerated in death penalty issues. The Sixth Amendment requires court-appointed counsel for indigent defendants facing prosecutions for serious crimes (felonies).

***Argersinger v. Hamlin* (1972)**

The right to counsel was extended to misdemeanors where the defendant has the possibility of being sentenced to jail or prison.

***Scott v. Illinois* (1979)**

Legal counsel does not have to be appointed for a criminal defendant where imprisonment is authorized by statute but not imposed.

The Role of the Defense Lawyer

As soon as a person is arrested, and sometimes even before then, he or she needs a defense attorney. As a matter of fact, even the most seasoned offender, accustomed to the maze of decisions about to be made and familiar with the language of criminal justice, turns to a defense attorney as quickly as possible. If such a need does not immediately come to mind, the police routinely remind the suspect, "You have a right to an attorney." And the role of the defense attorney begins almost as soon as an arrest occurs, for the accused needs the assistance of counsel to make sure interrogation and other pretrial, post-arrest procedures are conducted in a fair and constitutional manner.

After that point, the defense counsel role is to review the documents and other evidence the police have accumulated against the accused and to interview or question the arresting officers and others involved in the case. The defense attorney may interview witnesses to the crime and may even conduct an independent investigation.

Important work of the defense attorney is done in conversations with the prosecutor. Defense attorneys usually have dealt previously with the prosecutors assigned to their particular cases. Thus, defense and prosecuting attorneys know each other and can feel each other out for impressions about the strengths of cases.

At bail hearings and in plea negotiations defense attorneys represent the accused. They prepare pretrial motions and often argue them in pretrial conferences and hearings. Then, if all else fails and the cases go to trial, the defense attorneys prepare the defense material for trial, all the while maintaining open ears for any possible opportunities for advantageous plea negotiations with the prosecutors.

At trial, defense attorneys question prospective jurors, cross-examine prosecution witnesses, call defense witnesses, and generally represent the accused. If cases result in conviction, the defense attorneys help those convicted gain the best possible sentences. Then, sometimes appeals may be pursued, which can entail written documents arguing for reversal of the decisions or sentences and may involve appellate attorneys who were not involved with the initial decision or sentence.

Defense attorneys are involved, intimately, in every stage of the criminal justice system beginning with the arrest. Throughout all of the stages of criminal justice decisions they are responsible for protecting the constitutional rights of the accused to be sure their clients are not treated unfairly or improperly. Everyone accused of a crime needs a good defense attorney.

Right to a Free Defense Lawyer: The Evolution of Law

From the very beginning of our system of justice, defendants who were financially able could hire lawyers to represent them at trial. Poor defendants, however, had to rely on whatever provisions regarding state-paid attorneys existed in each jurisdiction. In some states, there were provisions to assign counsel to any defendant unable to afford a lawyer; in others, the assistance of state-paid counsel was limited to very serious cases, usually those involving capital offenses. For many years, the U.S. Supreme Court took the position that this was a "states' rights" issue and that there was no federal constitutional requirement that states must provide counsel.

Then, in 1932, the U.S. Supreme Court considered the appeal of an Alabama court decision known as the "Scottsboro Rape Case," in which nine young black men had been convicted of raping two white women and were subsequently sentenced to death. In ***Powell v. Alabama*** the court held that the advice of counsel was essential as a constitutional matter in such capital cases.[79] Thus, for the first time, in state trials involving a possible death sentence, defense lawyers were required, if requested by defendants, and at state expense if the defendants were too poor to pay an attorney's fees. As stated in the majority opinion by Justice Sutherland,

> Even the intelligent and educated layman has small and sometimes no skill in the science of law. If charged with crime, he is incapable, generally, of determining for himself whether the indictment is good or bad. He is unfamiliar with the rules of evidence. Left without the aid of counsel, he may be put on trial without a proper charge, and convicted upon incompetent evidence, or evidence irrelevant to the issue or otherwise inadmissible. He lacks both the skill and knowledge adequately to prepare his defense, even though he have a perfect one. He requires the guiding hand of counsel at every step in the proceedings against him. Without it, though he be not guilty, he faces the danger of conviction because he does not know how to establish his innocence. If that be true of men of intelligence, how much more true is it of the ignorant and illiterate, or those of feeble intellect.[80]

Powell was an important, but obviously limited, decision. Most felonies were not capital crimes while most criminal defendants are poor. This meant that, even after *Powell*, states could decide whether they wished to provide lawyers for most poor defendants or not. And many did not.

Ten years later, in 1942, in ***Betts v. Brady*** the Supreme Court again held that states, as a matter of federal constitutional rights, did not need to appoint lawyers for the poor in noncapital cases.[81] It was only in 1963, 31 years after *Powell*, that the Supreme Court again confronted a case concerning the right to counsel. That case, ***Gideon v. Wainwright***, has proved to be a landmark decision.[82]

Clarence Earl Gideon was charged in a Florida state court with having broken and entered a poolroom with intent to commit a misdemeanor. That offense was a felony under Florida law. Appearing in court without funds and without counsel, Gideon asked the court to appoint a lawyer to represent him.

The judge said, "Mr. Gideon, I am sorry but I cannot appoint Counsel to represent you in this case. Under the laws of the State of Florida, the only time the Court can appoint Counsel to represent a defendant is when that person is charged with a capital offense. I am sorry, but I will have to deny your request to appoint Counsel to defend you in this case."

Mr. Gideon responded, "The United States Supreme Court says I am entitled to be represented by counsel."

Gideon was not correct about the Supreme Court. He was referring to the Sixth Amendment to the U.S. Constitution, which states in part, "In all criminal prosecutions, the accused shall enjoy the right ... to have the Assistance of Counsel for his defense."

Put on trial before a jury, Gideon conducted his defense about as well as could be expected by an uneducated person. He made an opening statement to the jury, cross-examined the state's witnesses, presented witnesses in his own defense, declined to place himself on the stand, and made a short argument "emphasizing his innocence to the charge contained in the information filed in this case."

The jury returned a verdict of guilty, and the judge sentenced him to serve five years in the state prison. Later, Gideon filed a petition in the Florida Supreme Court attacking his conviction and sentence on the ground that the trial court's refusal to appoint counsel for him denied him rights "guaranteed by the Constitution and the Bill of Rights by the U.S."

However, the conviction was upheld under the Florida law providing for appointed counsel only in capital cases. Gideon then filed a handwritten petition to the U.S. Supreme Court, and prominent attorney Abe Fortas, who would later become a U.S. Supreme Court Justice, was appointed to represent him. Attorney Bruce Jacob prepared and presented the case on behalf of the State of Florida.

The U.S. Supreme Court agreed with Gideon and ordered a new trial. It also required that the Sixth Amendment be applied to the states through the Fourteenth Amendment's requirements of "due process of law" and "equal protection of the laws," and even held the *Gideon* ruling to apply *retroactively* to the states, which resulted in new trials for or the outright releases of thousands of inmates around the country. In addition, the decision increased the rules of criminal procedure that govern the trial process in terms of size and complexity markedly. Gideon's charge was a felony, so the decision in this case was considered applicable to felony cases.

Gideon has resulted in a dramatic expansion of the presence of attorneys at virtually every "critical stage" of judicial decision-making regarding an accused person. Free defense counsel is provided to indigent defendants either through public defender programs, assigned counsel, or contracts between courts and law firms or other legal entities. And although *Gideon* did not assure the presence of *effective* counsel, a vast amount of law on that topic has since emerged.[83] Ineffective assistance of counsel claims have ranged from a defense attorney sleeping during a death penalty case to a defense attorney in another capital case having previously represented the now deceased victim.[84]

Additionally, persons charged with serious misdemeanors were ultimately included in the right-to-counsel rulings, expanding the right to counsel to any defendant who seriously faced the possibility of incarceration even for misdemeanors (*Argersinger v. Hamlin*, 1972).[85] As stated by Justice Douglas in the majority opinion, "absent a knowing and intelligent waiver, no person may be imprisoned for any offense, whether classified as petty, misdemeanor, or felony, unless he was represented by counsel at his trial."[86]

Scott v. Illinois (1979) further clarified under what conditions the right to counsel is applicable. In this case, the defendant, convicted of shoplifting, faced the possibility of a $500.00 fine and/or one year in jail. Upon his conviction, the penalty he ultimately received was a $50.00 fine. The defendant appealed the conviction, maintaining that he was denied legal counsel contrary to the holding in *Argersinger*. The U.S. Supreme Court, with Justice Rehnquist writing for the majority, held, "The Sixth and Fourteenth Amendments require that no indigent criminal defendant be sentenced to a term of imprisonment unless the State has afforded him the right to assistance of appointed counsel in his defense, but do not require a state trial court to appoint counsel for a criminal defendant, such as petitioner [Scott], who is charged with a statutory offense for which imprisonment upon conviction is authorized but not imposed."[87]

In some rather rare instances a defendant may refuse the assistance of court-appointed lawyers, or public defenders, and asks the judge for permission to act as his or her own defense lawyer. Such requests by defendants are often referred to as *Faretta* motions, and this is allowable since the state cannot force an attorney on a defendant who *voluntarily and intelligently waives the right to representation of counsel.* Persons who represent themselves are referred to as *pro se* defendants. *Pro se* defendants have included Dylann Roof (who committed the Charleston, South Carolina, church shooting),[88] Ted Bundy (convicted and executed serial killer), John Allen Muhammad (ultimately deemed responsible for a series of sniper related shootings in Northern Virginia and Maryland), Zacarias Moussaoui (considered the twentieth hijacker from the September 11th attacks), and Colin Ferguson[89] and Scott Panetti, as discussed below. (See Field Practice 7.4.)

The Supreme Court requires trial judges to thoroughly examine defendants in such instances, to encourage them to accept the help of effective counsel, and to make sure the waiver of counsel is voluntarily and knowingly made. The test for the validity of such a waiver is not necessarily the legal skill or knowledge of the defendant but rather his or her understanding of the advantages of counsel. The judge must let the defendant know that it is better to have counsel, that the prosecutor is a lawyer and will have a great advantage over a defendant who does not have a lawyer, and that if technical legal matters arise during the course of the trial the judge may rule against the defendant with no obligation to explain the technicalities to the defendant. If the trial judge feels that a defendant should be allowed to refuse the assistance of counsel, yet the judge does not feel that a fair trial will result without the defendant having some legal assistance, the judge may appoint a standby counsel for the defendant. This counsel will sit with the defendant and be available in the event the defendant may wish to confer and obtain legal advice during the course of the trial.[90]

Field Practice 7.4 Colin Ferguson Defends Himself

Colin Ferguson was convicted in 1995 of shooting and killing six Long Island commuter train passengers and the attempted murder of 19 other wounded passengers, resulting in a sentence of 200 years. Ferguson represented himself at trial, and in his opening statement indicated that the only reason he was indicted on 93 counts was because the incident took place in the year 1993. His closing statement, which victims and family members walked out on, was also bizarre, as he rambled about television violence, the Irish Republican Army, and world hunger.[91]

Scott Panetti's *Pro Se* Defense

"Consider the case of Scott Panetti, a man with schizophrenia. Panetti, who had an extensive history of severe mental illness with 14 hospitalizations in the six years preceding his crime, was tried for the capital murder of his parents-in-law in 1992. Despite testimony that he was highly delusional and unable to rationally consult with his attorney, he was found competent to stand trial. At trial, Panetti represented himself, dressed in a cowboy outfit, and attempted to subpoena Jesus Christ, John F. Kennedy, and Anne Bancroft. He frequently spoke in a rambling, incoherent manner, asking irrational questions and citing biblical passages that had no apparent relevance to his case." Panetti apparently believed that he was being tried because the state was in cahoots with Satan to stop his preaching of the gospel. Nevertheless, the trial proceeded, he was convicted, and sentenced to death, although, his death sentence was ultimately remanded to the trial court for further proceedings on competency grounds.[92]

Who Defends the Poor?

States have developed three primary models for providing legal help for poor defendants. Those are public defender programs, assigned counsel systems, and contract systems.[93]

Public defender programs serve many of the nation's defendants and are the dominant form of legal defense in statewide or local agencies. Other states have public defender systems headed by a person who is responsible for providing defense in the various counties in that state. Many states have local systems that are autonomous. The public defender, much like the assistant state attorney, is usually a government employee.

Assigned counsel systems involve private attorneys who are appointed by a judge to provide legal defense on a case-by-case basis. A minimum fee is usually paid by the state for the legal services. In some jurisdictions, a court administrator oversees the appointment of lawyers and develops standards and guidelines for the program. Assigned counsel systems operate primarily in small counties.

Contract systems involve the government contracting with individual attorneys, bar associations, or private law firms to provide services for a specified dollar amount.

Contract systems are found in both small counties and very large ones. Contract lawyers sometimes handle the overflow cases public defenders do not have the time for and also represent codefendants in cases of conflict of interest.

So you want to be a defense attorney. See aspects of the job outlined in **Critical Thinking 7.3.**

Critical Thinking 7.3 "How Can You Defend Those People?"[94]

According to James Mills, "Criminal law to the defense lawyer does not mean equity or fairness or proper punishment or vengeance. It means getting everything for his client." Mills describes the response by a defense attorney to an inquiry from a non-lawyer friend about how it feels to go to trial with a client he knows is guilty and get the client off.

"Lovely! Perfectly beautiful! You're dancing on air and you say to yourself, 'How could that have happened? I must have done a wonderful job!' It's a euphoric feeling. Just to see the look of shock on the judge's face when the jury foreman says 'Not guilty' is worth something. It's the same sense of greed you get if a horse you bet on comes in at 15 to 1. You've beaten the odds, the knowledgeable opinion, the wise people." He laughs. "The exultation of winning dampens any moral feelings you have."

"But what," he is asked, "if you defend a man who had raped and murdered a 5-year-old girl, and he was acquitted and went free, and a year later was arrested for raping and murdering another 5-year-old girl. Would you defend him again with the same vigor?"

"I'm afraid so."

"Why afraid?"

"Because I think most people would disapprove of that."

"Do you care?"

"No."

"It doesn't concern you?"

"I'm not concerned with the crime committed or the consequences of his going free. If I were, I couldn't practice. I'm concerned with seeing that every client gets as good representation as he could if he had $200,000. I don't want him to get screwed just because there wasn't anyone around to see that he not get screwed. If you're a doctor and Hitler comes to you and says you're the one man in the world who can cure him, you do it."

"How much of that is ego?"

"Ninety-nine percent."[95]

List any negative aspects you find about the criminal defense attorney described by Mills.

Do you see any positive aspects from this defense attorney? If so, what?

"In July 1973, Robert Garrow, a 38-year-old mechanic from Syracuse, New York, killed four persons, apparently at random. The four were camping in the Adirondack Mountains. In early August, following a vigorous manhunt, he was captured by state police and indicted for the murder of a student from Schenectady. At the time of the arrest, no evidence connected Garrow to the other deaths.... The court appointed two Syracuse lawyers, Francis R. Belge and Frank H. Armani, to defend Garrow.

"Some weeks later, during discussions with his two lawyers, Garrow told them that he had raped and killed a woman in a mineshaft. Belge and Armani located the mineshaft and the body of the Illinois woman but did not take their discovery to the police. The body was finally discovered four months later by two children playing in the mine. In September, the lawyers found the second body by following Garrow's directions. This discovery, too, went unreported; the girl's body was uncovered by a student in December.

"Belge and Armani maintained their silence until the following June. Then, to try to show that he was insane, Garrow made statements from the witness stand that implicated him in the other three murders. At a press conference the next day, Belge and Armani outlined for the first time the sequence of events.

"The local community was outraged. The lawyers, however, believed they had honored the letter and spirit of their professional duty in a tough case. 'We both, knowing how the parents feel, wanted to advise them where the bodies were,' Belge said, 'but since it was a privileged communication, we could not reveal any information that was given to us in confidence.'

"The silence was based on the legal code that admonishes the lawyer to 'preserve the confidence and secrets of a client.' The lawyer-client 'privilege' against disclosure of confidences is one of the oldest and most ironclad in the law. If the defendant has no duty to confess his guilt or complicity in a crime, it can make no sense to assert that his lawyer has such a duty. Otherwise, the argument goes, the accused will tell his lawyer at best a deficient version of the facts, and the lawyer cannot as effectively defend the client. This argument frequently seems unconvincing; it certainly did to the people of Syracuse."[96]

The Fifth Amendment of the U.S. Constitution indicates that an individual has the right not to incriminate him or herself. Based on the segment entitled Seeking Justice that opened this chapter, do you believe attorneys Belge and Armani appropriately followed the canon of legal ethics regarding divulging confidences in this case? Why or why not?

Do you agree with that particular standard concerning divulging confidences? Why or why not?

Based on these descriptions, do you think you could work as a criminal defense lawyer? Why or why not?

Summary

Pretrial release consideration and legal representation of poor defendants are two major prerequisites for further processing. The prosecutor now must make important decisions about charging the person in court and decisions about what, if any, charges to bring. And, the negotiations between prosecutor and defense begin in earnest, called plea bargaining. We now turn to those issues.

Chapter 8

The Prosecutor's Decisions and Plea Bargaining

Image by George Wada at fotolia.com.

"Prosecutors could get a grand jury to 'indict a ham sandwich,' if they wanted to."

—Judge Sol Wachtler referring to the sway that prosecutors hold over grand jurors[1]

Seeking Justice: What Is the Role of the Prosecutor?

One Opinion: The Prosecutor Is the Chief Law Enforcement Officer

The prosecutor is expected to marshal society's resources against the threat of crime and to emphasize *law enforcement* by taking cases to court which have a good chance of conviction. The prosecutor is in the best position to study all the relevant facts in a case and decide if the evidence will support a conviction. The prosecutor's own reputation is at stake, since that reputation is based in large measure on the proportion of convictions obtained after charges are filed against a defendant. Thus, the prosecutor should be in total control of the decision to charge.

In addition, the prosecutor is a public figure that is expected to take a visible stand *against* crime and *for* justice and is called upon to make public statements, to propose legislative reforms, or to direct the energies of the law-enforcement machinery of the community. In this sense, the prosecutor is the chief *law-enforcement* person in the community, for without the prosecutor, police arrests would be meaningless.

Another Opinion: The Prosecutor Is a Champion for Individual Rights

The prosecutor's office demands and the public expects that the prosecutor respect the rights of persons accused of crime. It is not realistic to believe that the police will bring only cases that have sufficient evidence to gain conviction at trial. American citizens demand that the prosecutor accord basic fairness to all persons. Prosecutors have a special duty to *protect the innocent* and to *safeguard the rights guaranteed to all*, including those who may be guilty. The public nature of his or her position should be used by the prosecutor to rally citizen support for the values which are evident in the U.S. and state constitutions and to represent the interests of the accused as well as the interests of the state or the police. The prosecutor is not, therefore, a law enforcement agent, but a seeker of justice.

A Third View from the Field, a Former Prosecutor: Prosecutors Are Both Chief Law Enforcement Officers and Champions of Justice

The prosecutor is both the Chief Law Enforcement Officer in a jurisdiction as well as being a Champion for Individual Rights and Justice. The prosecutor is the Chief Law Enforcement Officer because he or she is the most powerful person in the criminal justice system. He or she decides who to charge or seek indictments against, what to charge them with, and how to offer to resolve the cases. Whereas other law enforcement officers investigate and arrest suspects, the prosecutor, in addition to doing that, can formally charge and formally drop charges—the latter being a power no police officer has. While there can be some discussion whether a particular prosecutor is also a champion of justice, there is no doubt as to who is the boss of the criminal justice system.

A good prosecutor should be a champion of justice—it is what is ethically required. No other type of lawyer is obligated to disclose evidence to the opposing side which hurts his own case. Also, a good prosecutor, one who champions justice, is one who tells law enforcement when they are wrong about the law. A good prosecutor is one who trains and educates law enforcement how to avoid violating one's constitutional rights, and thereby threatening not only potential convictions, but justice itself. A good prosecutor is one who tells law enforcement officers to seek the truth, not convictions, because every obvious door that an officer leaves open in the investigation will be slammed shut into his face by a defense attorney. There's nothing inconsistent with being both the boss and a champion of justice.[2]

About This Chapter

After apprehension for a crime by the police and appearance before a magistrate for the bail or jail decision, a trial does not necessarily follow. As a matter of fact, a

Figure 8.1 The Prosecutor's Decisions

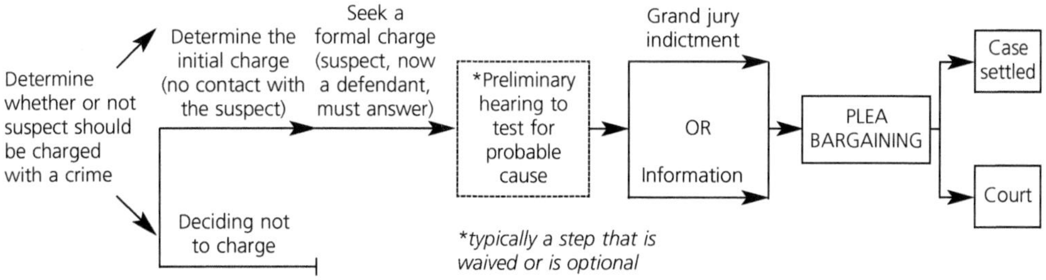

large percentage of arrests do not result in prosecution. The prosecutor, or district attorney, can for any number of reasons—or for no obvious reason—decide not to prosecute. And if the defendant has been arrested for more than one offense, the prosecutor decides which offense to charge once the decision to prosecute has been made. The prosecutor has considerable discretion as to how to proceed against a person caught in the arms of the law. The prosecutor's decisions, outlined in **Figure 8.1**, are discussed first in this chapter. Then, we turn to prosecutors themselves and the forces which motivate their decisions.

Defense attorneys and judges also influence prosecutors' decisions. The most obvious way this influence is seen is in plea bargaining, which will be discussed in detail later in this chapter. Plea bargaining creates heated political discussions, yet it results in unmistakable advantages both to the accused and to society. Without plea bargaining it is doubtful the wheels of justice would continue to roll. Again, plea bargaining is discussed in the final section of this chapter.

The Prosecutor's World

The prosecutor is not a mere automaton, stamping criminal conduct with appropriate statutory labels and proceeding to trial. The prosecutor's discretion is much broader and is based on many considerations beyond legal expertise in fitting charges to different factual situations.

The prosecutor is a political figure as well as a lawyer and, like all politicians, is responsive to community pressures and sensitive to community norms. Political pressures on a prosecutor vary from one jurisdiction to another. He or she usually is required to run for office in partisan or non-partisan elections, as only Alaska, Connecticut, New Jersey, and Washington, DC, use the appointment process.[3] Prosecutors are referred to by different titles across the states, such as: district attorney, commonwealth's attorney, prosecuting attorney, state's attorney, solicitor, deputy attorney general, or district attorney general.[4] **Field Practice 8.1** reveals the role and career prospects of assistant prosecutors hired by the elected or appointed prosecutor in various jurisdictions around the United States.

At the federal level, prosecutors are appointed in similar fashion to federal judges. The president appoints, and the U.S. Senate must confirm the appointment. Unlike federal judges, U.S. Attorneys do not have life tenure and are sometimes removed from office as new presidential administrations come into power.[5]

Field Practice 8.1 Who the Prosecutors Are

Many young attorneys find employment in prosecutors' offices. As lawyers employed by the state or county, they gain invaluable experience. Many gain more experience, more rapidly, while working as an assistant district attorney, than would be possible in a private law firm. Also, the constant exposure to the local courts gives attorneys the personal knowledge of the inner workings of the courts. Some continue their employment in the district attorney's office, becoming career prosecutors. Others move on to private litigation practices after several years' experience as prosecutors, experience that proves to be very valuable in their private practice. Many executive and legislative leaders, as well as judges, have served as prosecutors at some point in their careers. Experience as a prosecutor is a familiar stepping stone to higher office.

The prosecutor's activity is in large part open to public gaze through the press so that the least mistake as well as the most successful exploit is likely to be magnified. And, public sentiment is likely to be a consideration in highly publicized cases.[6] This aspect of the prosecutors' task requires them to be on guard. There is little room for error, and high conviction rates, with little controversy, are important to prosecutors who must enter the political arena for public approval on a regular basis. As such, it is much easier to prosecute a person sleeping under a bridge than to go after a corporation. Perhaps this selectivity in choosing cases to prosecute contributes to the fact that "in most jurisdictions at least 95 percent of all charged crimes never reach trial."[7] Of course, most of these cases are plea bargained, but what of the cases where there is awareness of criminal activity, but no one is ever charged? Prosecutors have to include in their decisions on whether or not to prosecute the impact on resources (time, personnel, etc.), particularly when and if high-powered defendants are pursued. Cases that propel prosecutors into the public spotlight can have a significant impact on their careers, for good or ill. Gil Garcetti's reputation was damaged from the prosecution of O.J. Simpson for murder, as was Mike Nifong's, who botched the prosecution of Duke University lacrosse players for allegedly gang raping an escort service dancer. In such high-profile cases, every action, every decision, every hearing was closely watched by millions of people.

The political powers of a prosecutor are formidable, making the prosecutor an important person in the community. If he or she is not truly independent and professional, the powers of the office can be misused for political and other improper purposes.

Prosecutors often measure their success by the number of convictions they gain. See **Field Practice 8.2**. Indeed, the conviction of people arrested by the police for crimes is what police, victims, and the public usually expect. At the same time, it is generally agreed that the basic duty of the prosecutor is to "seek justice, not merely to convict,"[8] but beyond this, the American Bar Association's Standards posit the "duty to improve the law" and to stimulate efforts to reform criminal justice.[9] However, membership in the ABA is voluntary, and many prosecutors purportedly do not pay the dues to join that association. Therefore, their views are not fully represented by them. It is the state's bar rules that a prosecutor must adhere to, and the standard for maintaining a prosecution varies from place to place but never falls below having probable cause.[10]

Field Practice 8.2 If This Were Baseball, That Is Not a Bad Average

Of all felony defendants who had their cases adjudicated in courts within the nation's 75 largest counties in 2006, 68 percent were convicted, with almost two thirds of them entering guilty pleas (55 percent pled guilty to a felony, and 10 percent pled guilty to a misdemeanor). Twenty-three percent were not convicted or had their cases dismissed, one percent were acquitted, and eight percent had their adjudication deferred or were placed in a diversion program.[11] Of course, part of the reason for the success in the majority of felony cases that are prosecuted may much have to do with the behind-the-scenes selectivity that goes into deciding which cases to prosecute.

Sometimes the prosecutor is also referred to as the "chief law enforcement official" of a district, and in this sense his or her role is seen as proactive (i.e., searching out criminal activity) as well as reactive (i.e., responding via the charging function to cases brought by the police). The prosecutor normally relies on the police or other investigative agencies to uncover illegal acts, but they also have the responsibility to investigate suspected illegal activity when it is not adequately dealt with by other agencies.[12]

The scope of the prosecutor's duties—the community expectations commonly assigned to this role—coupled with broad discretionary authority make this office one of the most powerful and complex in criminal justice. Lawyer, politician, law-enforcement official, administrator, reform advocate, the "architect of fair trials," local "minister of justice"—all are parts of this job. Moreover, elements of the district attorney's role embody expectations expressed in the points of view of both the crime control and due process models discussed in Chapter 2, which complicates any analysis of the role.[13]

The Prosecutor's Discretion

The first formal duty of the prosecutor involves determining whether a defendant should be charged with a crime or not. Even if the evidence clearly indicates the guilt of a suspect, the prosecutor is free to choose whether to prosecute and, if so, what charges to pursue.

Deciding *Not* to Charge

The prosecutor has the discretion not to charge a suspect even though there is sufficient evidence that the suspect has committed a crime. Also, the prosecutor may dismiss charges that have already been brought through the traditional power of ***nolle prosequi***.[14] Studies have shown that a significant number of felony arrests, once the cases have been forwarded to the prosecutors' offices, are rejected by prosecutors and dropped without further action.[15] Several valid reasons exist for a prosecutor to choose not to prosecute a case, including:[16]

Insufficient evidence. A failure to uncover enough evidence to link a suspect to the crime is the most frequently cited reason for the decision not to prosecute. See **Field Practice 8.3** below.

Field Practice 8.3 How Much Evidence Is Enough to Prosecute?

How much evidence is sufficient for a prosecutor? The lowest standard tolerated by ethical rules is probable cause. But a prosecutor also considers whether he or she can prove the case beyond a reasonable doubt to a jury. Some prosecutors use this standard, while others fear substituting their judgment for that of the jury's. Conversely, if a prosecutor brings a defendant to trial even if the prosecutor has reasonable doubt about a defendant's guilt, but is confident a jury would convict, is that proper? These are tough issues without universal agreement, but taxpayers generally expect and respect the prosecutor's expert opinion and sense of justice. Most would not prefer that the prosecutor take any *prima facie* case and "charge 'em all and let the jury sort it out."[17]

Witness problems. Witness problems arise when a witness fails to appear, gives unclear or contradictory statements, refuses to testify, or is unsure of the identity of the offender. Also, a major cause of witness problems is a relationship between the victim and the defendant, a factor which has been shown to dramatically reduce the number of prosecutions and convictions of domestic violence cases. Child victims and witnesses present numerous problems to prosecution as well, for example, see **Field Practice 8.4.**[18]

Field Practice 8.4 Don't Re-Victimize the Victim: The Debra Lafave Case

According to investigators, 23-year-old middle school teacher Debra Lafave and a 14-year-old teen had sex on a couch in her portable classroom, in the townhouse she shared with her then-husband, and in her Isuzu sport utility vehicle. She was arrested in the teen's driveway, where police waited. She was initially charged with sexually assaulting a student. After almost two years of worldwide news coverage, prosecutors dropped charges of lewd and lascivious battery and lewd and lascivious exhibition against Lafave after concluding that the emotional welfare and privacy of the victim was more important than sending Lafave to prison.

Had prosecutors not dropped the charges, Lafave and the former student would have had to go forward with a trial guaranteed to draw media from around the world. The victim ... likely would have had to testify in detail about his sexual encounters with Lafave when he was 14. The prosecutors chose to work out a plea with Lafave and her attorneys.

If convicted, Lafave could have been sent to prison until she was in her 60s. Instead, she will live under the terms of a plea deal in which she will be serving three years of house arrest followed by seven years of probation in exchange for pleading guilty to two counts of lewd and lascivious battery stemming from her conduct in June 2004.

The judge was not happy with the agreement and at first refused to approve it, but the prosecutor prevailed. "The court may be willing to risk the well-being of the victims in this case in order to force it to trial. I am not," he said.

On Tuesday, speaking at length for the first time since her arrest, Lafave apologized. "I only pray the young man and his family will be able to move on with their lives," Lafave said, reading from a piece of yellow paper as her parents and fiancé stood behind her. "His privacy has been violated. His picture has been on the Internet."

The plea deal had the blessing of the victim's mother, who did not want her son to go through a trial in which his identity might be revealed. Martin Lazoritz, chairman of the department of psychiatry at the University of Florida, met with the victim for 90 minutes. He concluded the teen would be "re-victimized by the system" if he had to testify during such a highly publicized trial about his sexual encounters with Lafave.

After the arrest, Lafave had lost her job and divorced. She is classified as a sex offender (see http://offender.fdle.state.fl.us/offender/flyer.do?personId=43558) and can no longer work with or near children or live within 1,000 feet of a school, church, or playground. That order was later modified to allow her some unsupervised contact with children of family and friends with parental consent.[19] She must wear an ankle monitor and adhere to a 10 p.m. curfew. She must undergo psychological therapy for four years and a polygraph test once a year.

A judge, in 2008, allowed her to be released from her house arrest requirements, but she remains on probation.[20]

1. Should concern for the trauma and public exposure of children in a trial, which can sometimes cause as much psychic harm as the actual crime, be considered in this case? Or, should the main concern be for punishing the offender to the maximum?

2. Does the prosecutor's interest in proceeding without trial include concern for public humiliation associated with a public trial which the victim's family wants to avoid?
3. The suspect defendant also would like to avoid the severe effects of conviction of a serious sex crime on a child. Since both sides often are eager to negotiate, is this the best way to achieve justice?

IN THEIR OWN WORDS: According to a former prosecutor and defense attorney: "The bulk of sex crimes involve allegations made by children against someone they know. Whether or not a child will make a good witness and whether or not the litigation process would be good for the child are always major considerations in making a plea offer. If there happened to actually be any corroborating physical evidence or an eye-witness, seldom could the plea bargain not achieve a sentence the public would accept as reasonable. Unfortunately for the state, it's very rare to have more than the child making allegations of sexual crimes in the past and not supported by any physical evidence. As a defense attorney, it is also difficult to recommend that a defendant, even one who claims innocence, go to trial on these types of charges, no matter how bad the state's case is. The reality is that very tough sentences can come with these types of charges. These are not easy cases to prosecute or defend."[21]

The interests of justice. Prosecutors may conclude that certain offenses violate the letter of the law, but not the spirit, such as a case of elderly men betting a few cents in a pinochle game.

Due process problems. Due process problems involve violations of constitutional requirements in obtaining evidence or in securing statements from the accused.

A plea on another charge, or guilty pleas. When the accused is charged in several cases or on several counts, the prosecutor may agree to dismiss or drop some charges in exchange for guilty pleas on others. This is the number one reason for dismissals.

Pretrial diversion. A defendant who voluntarily accepts, for example, commitment to a mental hospital or substance abuse treatment facility may be spared prosecution in criminal court. The prosecutor may conclude that even after a trial the judge may sentence the offender to just such a facility, and by taking this step voluntarily, the court is spared the time necessary for a trial. Sometimes a defendant is already under sentence of a court for previous offenses, perhaps serving the remainder of a prison sentence on parole, or may be on probation for other crimes. In such cases, revocation of probation or parole is easier and more definite than prosecution on new charges.

Referral for other prosecution. Charges may be dropped in one jurisdiction when an accused person is charged with more serious crimes in another jurisdiction and the decision is made to transport him or her to that jurisdiction for processing.

More effective civil sanctions exist. When a case involves someone in a position of trust, such as an accountant or a lawyer, license revocation is a very debilitating punishment. The bar association or the board of accountancy may solve the problem, leaving the criminal sanction unnecessary and redundant.

Deals cut for informers or cooperating state's witnesses. If a person has information that is valuable to the police about criminal activity, the police often encourage the prosecutor to "make a deal," to grant freedom from prosecution in the immediate case in exchange for the defendant remaining in the community and passing information along to the police about past or on-going criminal activities. Sometimes co-defendants offer to testify against their "rap partner," their companion in the crime, if the prosecutor will drop charges against them. In extreme cases, the state will even provide protection and relocation to witness protection programs for people who could legitimately be charged for crimes but who have agreed to become witnesses against more serious offenders, often at great personal risk.

"Deserving" defendants. Charges may be reduced or dropped in such cases as technical violations of regulatory laws by otherwise law-abiding citizens. Or, sometimes youthful first offenders, especially those with good school records and with supportive families, are "*nolle prossed*," the charges are dropped, by sympathetic prosecutors who do not wish to destroy a young person's future opportunities.

Victim participation. Charges are sometimes dismissed or reduced because the victim either precipitated the offense by his or her own conduct or appears unwilling to cooperate fully in the prosecution. Juries are loath to find a person guilty when the victim refuses to testify. Therefore, in a large number of those cases, they choose not to prosecute at all. See **Field Practice 8.5.**

Amends. Charges may be reduced or dismissed when the offender, otherwise not a serious or persistent violator, has made restitution or other amends and the victim is satisfied with the settlement. Often, the victim is satisfied to have their out-of-pocket losses in a property crime reimbursed.

Comparable results. Prosecutors sometimes calculate whether maximum prosecution, seeking the most extreme sentence available in a case, would cost more money to fully prosecute and more time than it seems worth if comparable sentencing results could likely be achieved by lesser charges. Consider the possibility that a person could legitimately be prosecuted for three separate but related offenses. The maximum sentence in the most serious case is seven years in prison. If the defendant is willing to plead guilty to one charge with a sentence of five years, prosecutors are usually willing to *nolle pros* (dismiss) the other charges.

Plea bargaining. Plea bargaining to avoid trial will be discussed at length later in the chapter. Plea bargaining will also be discussed in Chapter 9.

Field Practice 8.5 The Wall of Silence[22]

A "wall of silence" has developed in many inner-city subcultures. The social pressure to not be a rat is just as strong there as it is for cops to not rat each other out. There's a real wall of silence based on the "don't be a rat" philosophy in the inner city. Whether it's a distrust of the police, fear of retaliation, or both, it is not uncommon to have to drop or plea out many very serious crimes because of a lack of cooperation from victims and witnesses. 911 calls to report a shooting and people going to the hospital with bullet wounds don't prove anything if nobody is willing to finger the shooter. Proving a domestic violence case with 911 calls and photographs is easier.

In the 2004 decision of *Crawford v. Washington*,[23] Justice Scalia wrote for the Court that confrontation means confronting a witness in court with cross-examination, rather than a judge deciding what hearsay is reliable enough to come in. This has made it more difficult, but not impossible, for prosecutors to proceed on cases without victims.

The prosecutor's right *not* to prosecute, even with sufficient evidence, is one of the broadest, most powerful examples of discretionary authority in the entire criminal justice system. This traditional discretion, with its origins in early common law, always has been controversial.[24] Many years ago Thurman W. Arnold wrote: "The idea that a prosecuting attorney should be permitted to use his discretion concerning the laws he will enforce and those which he will disregard appears to the ordinary citizen to border on anarchy."[25] Professor Kenneth Culp Davis commented about the frequency of using the discretion not to be lenient as well as the discretion to be lenient. He wrote, "The power to be lenient is the power to discriminate."[26]

However, discretion is not the same as discrimination; to treat everyone the "same" with minimum mandatory sentences, or harsh sentencing guideline calculations, judges are left without discretion. In all decisions in criminal justice, discretion properly used and monitored helps attain justice.[27]

The discretion of the prosecutor to engage in selective enforcement of the law and to prosecute for less than the full extent possible has been repeatedly upheld by appellate courts.[28] The prosecutor still retains the "absolute power" to dismiss cases against defendants, even if a trial court disapproves, according to the U.S. Supreme Court.[29] See **Critical Thinking 8.1** below.

Critical Thinking 8.1 Exploring Ethics: What Should Influence the Prosecutor's Decision Whether or Not to Prosecute?

1. What if a prosecutor knows a person is guilty of a crime but does not have sufficient evidence to support a conviction? Should the case be prosecuted anyway? Why? What would be accomplished?
2. What weight should the prosecutor give to the political advantages or disadvantages in the decision whether to charge? What if the victim, or the offender, is a very prominent and powerful citizen, or if media attention has been drawn to the case? Should this be considered?
3. To what extent should the prosecutor's decision be influenced by a desire to enhance his or her record of convictions? No one likes to lose. What is accomplished by taking a case to a jury which is very difficult to prove?

4. What should the prosecutor do if past juries have consistently failed to convict persons accused of the criminal act in question?

The American Bar Association says that *none* of those matters should influence the decision as to whether or not to prosecute a crime.[30] But, the ABA also says that the decision *should* be influenced by:

1. The prosecutor's doubt that the accused is in fact guilty
2. The extent of the harm caused by the offense
3. The disproportion of the authorized punishment in relation to the particular offense or the offender
4. Possible improper motives of a complainant
5. Reluctance of the victim to testify
6. Cooperation of the accused in the apprehension or conviction of others
7. Availability and likelihood of prosecution by another jurisdiction

---

Applying the Probable Cause Standard

When the prosecutor has sufficient evidence to show probable cause that a defendant is guilty of a crime, a final formal charge may be brought against her or him. For the police, "probable cause" is essentially backward-looking. The officer must have had sufficient evidence in hand to establish probable cause at the time of the arrest of the suspect. If sufficient evidence was not present, the officer may be held liable for damages for what is commonly called "false arrest," but which is, more precisely labeled, a civil action for "false imprisonment" (detaining a person for even a short period of time without proper grounds to do so).

The prosecutor, however, is not interested in justifying past actions but is looking ahead toward the trial at which the higher evidence standard of proof "beyond a reasonable doubt" is necessary for conviction. In this sense, the district attorney's application of probable cause is colored not only by the higher trial standard, but also by such tactical considerations as the credibility of witnesses, the likelihood of a successful defense or of motions to exclude evidence, and the likely effect on the jury of the reputation of the suspect or the victim.

Determining the Initial Charge

If the district attorney decides to proceed to prosecution, the specific charge or charges to bring and how many counts to seek in a formal charge must be decided. If more than one offense is contained in the complaint, or if more than one defendant is involved in the crime, the prosecutor must decide whether to *join* offenses and offenders in a single prosecution, called **joinder**, or to *sever* them for separate charges and trials, called **severance.**[31] If the suspect's record makes it possible to do so, the prosecutor must also decide whether to levy additional charges, such as being a "habitual offender."

In routine cases, the district attorney's initial charging determination is made in the absence of the suspect, who at this point may be out on bail or held in jail awaiting further processing. The prosecutor may interview the arresting officer and perhaps the complainant or available witnesses. Upon request, the prosecutor may talk with the suspect's defense attorney if one has been hired or appointed at this time. In certain cases—generally those involving very serious crimes or famous or notorious suspects, or cases that otherwise have generated a good deal of publicity—the prosecutor may interrogate the suspect. These are comparatively rare occurrences; usually the initial determination to charge or not is made without contact with the suspect.

In some cases, a complaint is made directly to the prosecutor's office, bypassing the police altogether. If the alleged criminal is named by the complainant, the prosecutor may then seek an arrest warrant from a judge and direct the police to take the suspect into custody. Likewise, in cases in which the complainant makes an accusation against a specific suspect directly to the police, the police may obtain an arrest warrant by showing probable cause to a judge and then take the suspect into custody.[32] In such cases, the initial charge is determined by the warrant, but the formal charge will ultimately be made by the prosecutor and may differ as evidence accumulates or dissipates. Even prosecutors may change their minds about how to proceed in a case. See **Field Practice 8.6.**

Field Practice 8.6 The Prosecution of Casey Anthony

In the Florida case of *State v. Casey Anthony*, the prosecutor's decision to seek the death penalty was criticized by the defense as being driven by improper motives. They said the State changed its mind about seeking the death penalty after the remains of the victim were discovered and their client, the child's mother, was charged. Prior to that, the State had filed a notice of intention to *not* seek the death penalty.

Defense lawyers argued that prosecutors were seeking leverage for plea bargaining and seeking to seat "death qualified jurors" who are more prone to convict than other jurors. The defense also maintained that the prosecution was attempting to prevent her attorney, Jose Baez, who was not qualified to handle a death penalty case, from representing her, and insisted there was gender bias against their client.

The remains of the infant victim were discovered close to the Anthony residence and implicated the child's mother. This certainly changed the strengths and weaknesses of the State's and Casey Anthony's cases for the portion of the trial to determine whether the State proved she committed first-degree murder against Caylee Anthony.

The defense had been relying upon the theory that Caylee Anthony had been kidnapped and may possibly still be alive prior to the remains being discovered. In fact, the defense was stating so in the media whenever given the opportunity. It was during that time the prosecutors had stated no death penalty would be sought in the case, hoping the kidnappers would return the child.

Should the State consider the strengths and weaknesses of its case when deciding whether or not to seek the death penalty? Or should it only consider whether there are aggravating factors?[33]

Bringing Formal Charges

Assuming the initial decision is to prosecute, the next step in the charging process is to seek a formal charge that the defendant must answer, either an indictment from a grand jury or the prosecutor's drafting the formal charge in the form of an information. Either one of these mechanisms for formally charging a defendant can be used in conjunction with a preliminary hearing, a formal hearing before a judge to determine if sufficient evidence exists that a crime has been committed and that the accused is guilty.

The use of a preliminary hearing in a number of jurisdictions can be rendered unnecessary if a grand jury indictment or a "bill of information" is received and accepted by the court prior to conducting a preliminary hearing. Furthermore, it is estimated that in the majority of cases defense attorneys waive the preliminary hearing for their clients.[34] Regardless of the mechanisms through which a case proceeds, all three processes are primarily focused on ensuring probable cause is sufficiently present to believe that a particular defendant has committed a crime. The formal charging mechanism from the prosecution to the court will either come in the form of a "true bill" of indictment via the grand jury (if the grand jurors refuse to indict, it is called a "no bill") or through a "bill of information." Thus, the charging document will arrive to the court either as a result of a grand jury indictment or via a bill of information filed by the prosecutor but not by both means.[35]

It should also be noted, in terms of the Fifth Amendment prohibition against double jeopardy, jeopardy does not attach to any of these proceedings. Therefore, even if a prosecutor fails to establish probable cause at a preliminary hearing, in an information, or before a grand jury, he or she may at some future date, providing the statute of limitations for the particular crime has not expired, obtain additional evidence and once again seek to bring the same person to justice.

The Preliminary Hearing

A preliminary hearing is essentially a testing of the evidence to see if probable cause has been established against a suspect. In addition to the probable cause determination, it assists in the discovery of evidence for the defense in a case, as this is an adversarial process. In other words, the defendant and legal counsel can be present and cross-examine witnesses. The prosecutor attempts to put on enough evidence to establish probable cause, and a judge presides over the proceedings. This is unlike grand jury proceedings that almost always take place without the presence of the defense counsel and defendant. Various motions for such things as suppression of evidence can be entertained here and may also be brought up again at trial if one occurs. A case could be dismissed at this stage or charges reduced. However, if a preliminary hearing occurs and probable cause is established, the next logical step is to have the matter bound over for trial either via an information or a grand jury indictment. Just as with grand jury proceedings, most states have determined that preliminary hearings are not required for misdemeanor cases.[36]

Unlike grand jury proceedings,[37] the right to counsel for defendants appearing at a preliminary hearing was established in *Coleman v. Alabama* (1970).[38] The Supreme Court stated that the preliminary hearing is a "critical stage" in criminal justice decisions. The Court stated that a poor defendant needs "the guiding hand of counsel at the preliminary hearing" in order to be protected "against an erroneous or improper prosecution." However, in *Gernstein v. Pugh* (1975), the U.S. Supreme Court held that there is no constitutional requirement for an adversary preliminary hearing after a prosecutor files an information against a defendant. A judicial review (by reading reports/statements) satisfies the Fourth Amendment establishment of probable cause to proceed.

At the preliminary hearing the defendant is not asked to plead to any charge and need do nothing but listen to the evidence presented by the prosecutor. However, independently or through counsel, the defendant may cross-examine state's witnesses and otherwise challenge evidence introduced by the prosecutor. In some jurisdictions, the defendant is allowed to introduce an affirmative defense—for example, an alibi purporting to show that the accused was elsewhere and otherwise engaged when the crime was committed.[39]

Because the defendant has a right to cross-examine state's witnesses, even though he or she may choose not to do so, direct testimony presented at the preliminary hearing may be used at the trial if for a valid reason the witness is unavailable later. This is unlike testimony given to a grand jury, where the defendant has no opportunity to confront and challenge his or her accusers. Also, unlike grand jury proceedings, a defendant may waive (refuse) the preliminary hearing, in effect accepting the charges as drafted by the prosecutor, and moving his or her case along the process.

A variety of reasons may exist for a defendant to waive the preliminary hearing, but there are two major ones: (1) an already firm decision to plead guilty, and (2) a desire to avoid the negative publicity that is likely to follow such a hearing. Typically, only the state's case is presented at a preliminary hearing, whereas evidence in rebuttal is not revealed until the trial, perhaps months later. Even if a defendant is eventually acquitted, extensive damage to the defendant's reputation may flow from the reported testimony of preliminary hearing witnesses. Can you imagine being called a "mad-dog rapist" at a preliminary hearing only to be acquitted months later? A preliminary hearing is open to the public, and the testimony or evidence presented is available to the press and other media, but grand jury proceedings are secret, behind closed doors.

Though these important differences exist between the grand jury and the preliminary hearing, their purposes are identical in the sense that the demonstration of probable cause sufficient to hold the defendant for trial is the prosecutor's goal. Both processes are referred to as pretrial screens designed to act as curbs on police arrests for investigation and to reduce the possibility that the prosecutor will present the wrong charge. As previously discussed, both approaches tend to confirm the initial charging decision of the prosecutor. Like the grand jury, the preliminary hearing most often results in a finding of probable cause.

The Grand Jury Indictment Process

Grand juries are commonly composed of anywhere from 12 to 23 members and may act with a specified quorum of members present. Regulations for indictments vary from state to state, with some states requiring every grand juror present to vote affirmatively for an indictment, and others require a simple majority vote. Some specify that three-fourths of grand jurors must endorse an indictment.[40]

Grand juries do not come together once to hear just one case like trial juries do. Grand juries may meet periodically over several months or up to a year and consider a number of cases being offered by the prosecutor for indictment. Grand jury members are generally selected from some master list, in similar fashion to that of trial jurors. The seating of grand jurors, unlike the selection of trial jurors, does not involve the defense. The prosecutor customarily runs the show, and there is no adversarial use of peremptory challenges and challenges for cause.

Unlike bench and jury trials, grand jury proceedings are secret, not only from the public and the press, but also from the defendant. Defense counsel is almost always without exception excluded from these hearings. A notable exception was found with the impeachment proceedings of former President Bill Clinton, whereby the parties agreed at a grand jury hearing to allow defense counsel to be present, the proceedings to be televised, and a manuscript of the proceedings to be published. With the permission of the trial judge, the transcribed minutes of grand jury deliberations may be shown, in part or in whole, to the defense counsel immediately before or during the trial. However, transcripts are usually made available only if the defendant can show a "particularized need" to obtain the testimony or other evidence presented to the grand jury in order to prepare a defense for a later trial.[41]

After the American Revolution, the grand jury was incorporated into the Constitution as a key part of our system of criminal justice. The Fifth Amendment, normally remembered for its protection against self-incrimination, includes the clause that "No person shall be held to answer for a capital, or otherwise infamous crime, unless on a presentment of a Grand Jury."

Though specified in the Fifth Amendment, the Court in *Hurtado v. California* (1884)[42] held that a grand jury indictment is not constitutionally required. Thus, this component of the Fifth Amendment has not been incorporated to apply to the states.

The federal government is required to prosecute by grand jury. But in the approximately 20 states where it is used today, the grand jury serves two purposes. The first is to screen cases brought by the prosecutor. The other is to conduct independent investigations and inspections of possible criminal conduct in the community even when no defendant is brought to the jury by the prosecutor. If the prosecutor brings a case and the grand jury finds probable cause to believe a crime was committed and that the defendant committed it, grand jury members issue an indictment, a formal charging document.[43]

When a grand jury is assembled for the first purpose, to screen a case for possible formal charging, the district attorney appears before it and requests an indictment. The prosecutor need only show sufficient evidence to convince a majority of the jury's members that there is "probable cause" to hold the defendant for trial. There is no requirement at this stage to reveal all of the state's evidence or bring forth all the witnesses. Furthermore, in most places, evidence presented to the grand jury need not conform to trial standards of admissibility.

While defendants may be asked to appear before grand juries, protected by their right not to incriminate themselves but not advised formally of that right during the proceedings,[44] grand jurors essentially hear only the government's evidence without any opportunity for defense or rebuttal or contradiction. Therefore, it is to be expected that they will honor the prosecutor's request for an indictment in most cases, and it is estimated that they do in over 95 percent of cases. Even when grand jurors refuse to indict, it may still be what the prosecution wants. See **Critical Thinking 8.2** below. It is argued that grand jurors typically rubber stamp whatever the prosecution desires.[45] But it is a cumbersome charging process and is falling into disuse even in those states where it has been the traditional means of charging felonies.

Critical Thinking 8.2 To Convene or Not to Convene

As discussed above, under the Fifth Amendment to the U.S. Constitution it is required to bring all federal charges for a capital or infamous crime to a grand jury to consider an indictment. However, states vary on their requirements for convening a grand jury. For example, Florida only requires the convening of a grand jury in capital felonies (where the state is seeking the death penalty), otherwise use of the grand jury process is optional. Considering the various factors influencing a prosecutor's decision in a high-profile elected position, why might a state prosecutor choose to convene a grand jury for a particular crime when the law does not require him or her to do so?

You Decide:

A person was heard attempting to break in to a vehicle under a homeowner's carport at 3 a.m. The homeowner, who had been victimized four times in the past month, was awakened by the noise and retrieves his gun, emerges from the house chases the would-be burglar down the street, and finally shoots him in the back. The suspected burglar was a sixteen-year-old boy and died with a screw driver in his possession. Public sentiment was mounting in support of both sides on this matter.

Although state law does not require it, if you were the prosecutor, would you convene a grand jury or make the decision on your own as to whether or not to prosecute the homeowner for murder? Why or why not? If a grand jury was convened and you were a member of the grand jury, would you vote to charge the homeowner? Why or why not? If yes, what would you charge the homeowner with and why?

The investigatory role of grand juries is perhaps a more important function: investigating possible crimes, corruption, and assorted wrongdoings of citizens, public officials, and agencies. Generally, investigatory grand juries are assembled for this purpose and are separate entities from charging grand juries, but this is not always the case. All grand juries can pursue almost unlimited investigations if they wish and may level charges on their own motions if they uncover crimes. The investigatory grand jury has traditionally played a particularly important role in organized crime investigations and official inquiries into such matters as police corruption and forceful state reactions to mass disorders, prison riots, and so on. While the charging function of grand juries may be waning, their investigatory functions are likely to remain important within criminal justice. Many jurisdictions that have abandoned the use of grand juries in charging retain them for investigatory purposes.[46]

The Information Process

The major way by which felony charges are formally brought against defendants is by the prosecutor drafting an information, and even those states that require a grand jury indictment for some or all felony cases deem an information sufficient for charging misdemeanants.[47] An information is a formal document noting in statutory language the highest crime charged and the number of charges against the defendant. In some instances, the prosecutor tests the case for probable cause to support the charges at a preliminary hearing before a judge. The information achieves the same purpose as a grand jury indictment, even though it is prepared and tested differently.

The power to charge someone with a crime by way of an information really has no comparison anywhere in the legal system. Just charging someone with a serious crime, such as child molestation, regardless of whether they eventually plead guilty or are convicted at trial, is a bell that can never be "unrung." For example, sex crimes prosecutors routinely have to make judgment calls about which cases to prosecute, and which cases not to prosecute. It is much easier to decide which cases had sufficient evidence to prosecute versus deciding which cases (that could be proven) *should* be prosecuted. Deciding whether an 18- or 19-year-old young man needs to be charged with a sex crime for having consensual sex with his 15-year-old girlfriend is a lot more difficult than deciding whether an uncle who molested his 6-year-old nephew deserved to be charged.[48]

Plea Bargaining

Criminal courts in most jurisdictions are very busy. The number of people arrested and prosecuted is so large, and the availability of defense attorneys to assist an accused person prepare and offer a defense creates a heavy caseload demand on everyone associated with criminal justice—prosecutors, public and private defenders, and judges.

The result of the crowded court calendars, court delays, and clogged caseloads is that most cases do not go to trial at all. Most are "settled" through guilty pleas; pleas arranged between the prosecutor, defense attorney, the accused, and the judge. Guilty pleas are induced through negotiations whereby the defendant pleads guilty to reduced charges in exchange for a lenient sentence, that is, a lighter sentence than the judge would normally give after conviction at trial. This entire process is generally known as plea bargaining or plea negotiation.[49]

A guilty plea is, of course, a form of confession and in some cases it may simply be the result of remorse. In part, confessions can be attributed to careful arrest practices and cautious charging. But a question remains: Why would guilty defendants give up their right to trial, foregoing the test of proof beyond a reasonable doubt and the possibility of a miraculous acquittal? The answer, in short, is that when the defendant pleads guilty it is generally to reduced charges and a more lenient sentence.

Guilty pleas are common everywhere, often exceeding 90 percent of all charged offenders, so that court schedules, staffing, attorney caseloads, and other resources are planned in anticipation of a high rate of pleas. The guilty plea, not the trial, is the chief form of criminal conviction in our society.[50] Despite the extent of its use, plea bargaining is still controversial.

Leniency for Pleading Guilty

Is an offer of leniency in exchange for a guilty plea a proper practice in our system of justice? Notice that this is stated as leniency for a guilty plea, not harshness if convicted after trial. A more severe sentence given to a defendant solely because he or she had demanded a trial is clearly improper; judges who have threatened to "throw the book" at defendants unless they pleaded guilty have been reversed by appellate courts on the grounds that they have "coerced" pleas of guilty. So this fine distinction is made by those judges who wish to support the guilty plea process: leniency if the defendant has "copped out" (pleaded guilty) but no more severe sentence merely because a trial has been demanded. Deceptive, perhaps, but this is the way the issue is usually put. See **Field Practice 8.7** below.

Field Practice 8.7 Leniency and Vindictiveness in the Plea Bargain

It's not unusual in serious cases for plea offers from the state to be contingent on not filing motions, not taking depositions, or not conducting discovery. It is not considered vindictive for prosecutors to do that, and prosecutors routinely make offers like that on cases, for example, with child victims. It is judges who have to be very careful, not only about initiating plea discussions, but about sentencing more harshly after a trial when the judge made an earlier plea offer. If the judge cannot point to specific facts learned during the trial which he or she was unaware of at the time the plea offer was conveyed, the defendant will be entitled to a new sentencing hearing in front of a different judge. The fine line of whether you are punishing people for going to trial or rewarding those who resolve their cases short of trial will always be a source of great debate, but it's indisputable that the American criminal justice system could not survive as we know it without plea bargaining—there are just too many cases.[51]

Many judges feel it is proper to take a guilty plea into account in the sentencing decision. They point out that the costs of a trial are saved, guilty verdicts are assured without a chance of a jury acquittal, some defendants should be "given a break" because they have thrown themselves on the mercy of the court, and the guilty plea confession is the first step on the road to rehabilitation. In addition, some judges feel that the defendant who goes to trial and who takes the stand in his or her own behalf but is convicted anyway has added perjury to the original crime. Those offenders are not considered to be as deserving of leniency as one who has admitted guilt up front. Showing remorse for one's actions, whether genuine or not, is attractive to the puritanical ideals that underpin our criminal justice system and considered conducive to redemption.

The Purposes of Plea Bargaining

Plea bargaining is not new; in all probability it has gone on as long as there have been criminal courts. Out-of-court negotiations and arrangements customarily take place off the record, ***sub rosa***, in the prosecutor's office or in the hallways of the courthouse. Defense lawyers and prosecutors rarely get into arguments about the guilt or innocence of a defendant today; justice is pursued behind the scenes by professionals who do their work and make their decisions within a closed, private system.[52] Plea bargaining provides many advantages for the state and crime victims, and for defendants and their defense attorneys, as well.

Advantages of Plea Bargaining for the State

The guilty plea obviously avoids the time, expense, and work of proving guilt at trial. In most cases, assuming a competent (sane) defendant, the plea assures conviction, whereas the result of a trial, no matter how carefully conducted, is an uncertainty, given the unpredictability of jury decisions. Furthermore, there is or may be a certain psychological satisfaction provided by an offender who admits guilt. A defendant who continues to protest her or his innocence, even though found guilty "beyond a reasonable doubt" after a full and fair trial, may nevertheless leave some doubts about his or her guilt. The propriety of the conviction may be in question. A variety of additional advantages exist for prosecutors, judges, the police and correctional agencies, and even for victims.

Prosecutors

The prosecutor is in a position not simply to apply statutes to facts but also to apply the sentencing laws and consequences to individuals. Criminal laws are by their nature broad and encompassing, but cases are specific and almost infinitely varied. Furthermore, sentencing provisions are often severe because legislators usually have in mind the worst offenders—gangsters, and professional, hardened, or otherwise extremely vicious criminals. In the routine of the typical prosecutor's office, however, this type of violator is comparatively rare.

Most offenders, even those guilty of serious criminal conduct, are not in any sense professional criminals. For instance, in the day-to-day operations of the police and prosecutors, arrested narcotics sellers are rarely professional cocaine dealers, but more likely young people who sold marijuana or a few pills to acquaintances. Technically they are guilty of selling narcotics and face mandatory prison terms, often in the range of 20 years to life. Such harsh sentences have been established by legislatures which seek to deter large-scale trafficking in drugs and to take professional pushers off the streets by sentencing them to long years in prison. Confronted with cases of amateurs charged with selling drugs, only a rare prosecutor or sentencing judge wishes to impose such long sentences. Yet, in some jurisdictions, the sentences are mandatory and the only way they can be avoided, assuming an unwillingness to dismiss the charges entirely, is to reduce the charge of selling drugs to some lesser offense—for example, "possession" of drugs—which would normally involve a lighter sentence, often with an option for probation. See **Critical Thinking 8.3**.

Critical Thinking 8.3 Your Legislature at Work

Plea bargaining is just as much about discussing the strengths and weaknesses of each side's case as it is about what particular sentence this particular defendant deserves. Should an 18-year-old who has consensual sex with his 15-year-old girlfriend get the same sentence as a man who forcibly rapes a woman? Assuming the two people have the same criminal history, the Florida sentencing guidelines say they should both do 94.5–180 months prison. Should someone who's addicted to Oxycontin and forges a prescription for 5 grams of pills and takes them all himself in less than 48 hours be treated the same as someone who forges the same prescription and turns around and sells the pills? Florida law would require both to do a three-year minimum-mandatory prison sentence. Interestingly, it takes possessing 25 pounds of marijuana to get the same three-year sentence—not even Cheech and Chong could go through that as quickly as an addict could go through just 4 grams of painkillers. Supposedly, the purpose of minimum mandatory sentences in drug trafficking cases is to get defendants to do substantial assistance against their suppliers. Pretty hard to do that if you are "supplying" yourself with forged prescriptions.[53]

Usually the prosecutor's motive in plea bargaining is *to get a conviction* and arrive at a sentence appropriate to the actual harm done by the defendant. Also, concessions are often made in cases in which there are codefendants of unequal culpability. For instance, an older experienced robber may have a "lookout," a youthful accomplice with a clean record. Technically both are equally guilty of the crime, but the prosecutor may feel it serves justice to reduce the charges against the young accomplice while making no concession to the experienced robber.

Still another reason for charge reduction is that on-the-nose conviction might preclude some correctional alternative, such as probation, likely to be more effective in the long run than imprisonment. Also, prosecutors may agree to reduce charges in the cases of informers or cooperative state's witnesses in order to assist the police in making "big" cases.

Prosecutors also are amenable to plea bargains in cases where conviction would carry mandatory prison terms which the prosecutors view as excessive punishment. For instance, a state law may require a mandatory prison term for conviction of any felony committed while armed. But sometimes, such as when a prosecutor is faced with a woman charged with aggravated battery resulting from assaulting her drunken husband with a weapon, a reduction in charge may be desirable if the individual is not viewed as a "serious, violent" offender. These bargains are sometimes called *charge bargains* rather than plea bargains.

Prosecutors rarely let judges get involved with plea bargaining when there is any charge bargaining by the prosecutor. Rarely will a prosecutor say: "Ok, I will reduce the charge to x and let the judge sentence your client to whatever." It's usually all or nothing. The defendant either accepts the state's offer or has to roll the dice with a plea to the judge or a trial. On less significant cases, particularly ones without victims, judges are much more likely to interject and play "good cop/bad cop" with the state and make a better offer than the state to move things along.[54]

Judges

For judges the guilty plea, even if not preceded by charge reduction, offers both a rationalization for showing leniency to deserving defendants and an opportunity to do so in a setting ordinarily free from the publicity that attends a trial. Usually, except in cases which gain media attention, bargained justice happens quietly, sometimes behind the closed doors of the judge's chambers. But, judges also must manage a calendar which is often crowded with contested cases. If each case were to be tried in open court, complete with jury selection and all the stages of a trial, judges would be incapable of hearing all of the cases. The backlog would grow and grow. Therefore, judges are especially interested in seeing the parties in any given case reach an agreement which would not take precious court time. Judges sometimes become primary encouragers for the sides to reach some accommodation.

Police and Correctional Agencies

Other important advantages accrue to the prosecutor and judges, but some even apply to the police as well. Most, if not all, complex corollary issues such as the admissibility of evidence or the propriety of police investigation and arrest practices are largely avoided by plea bargains, for instance. Law enforcement officers avoid the onerous duty of long court appearances and escape being challenged by the defense on their methods of arrest, investigation, or interrogation. Indirectly, a defendant pleading guilty may help them solve other crimes by admitting other offenses or may implicate other offenders in a crime. The police, of course, are under pressure to clear their books of unsolved crimes. A defendant who pleads guilty to one count of an offense is more likely to admit other counts and thereby "solve," to police satisfaction at any rate, a series of burglaries or whatever crimes are involved.

From the point of view of correctional treatment authorities, rehabilitation can begin only after the person admits guilt, admits that they have a behavioral problem. The probationer or inmate who steadfastly denies the crime presents a very real dilemma to treatment personnel. Sometimes truly innocent people are wrongfully convicted of crimes,[55] but many offenders continue to deny their guilt when they have clearly committed crimes. The plea bargain requires the person to admit guilt, thereby negating a later claim of innocence in the eyes of correctional personnel.

Furthermore, generally a bargained sentence is shorter than one imposed after trial and a finding of guilt. If bargaining were reduced, sentences would probably increase in length. Longer sentences are unwelcome in most states with already crowded correctional caseloads.

Victims

Advantages of a guilty plea exist for victims as well, as they sometimes are reluctant to be exposed to the publicity and trauma of a trial. They are able to dispense of the formality of testifying in open court. The guilty plea is quick and relatively anonymous. Not only are the details of the crime largely kept from public view, but ordinarily only minimal interference with the daily routine of complainant and witnesses is experienced.

Advantages of Plea Bargaining for the Defendant and Defense Attorney

Plea negotiation, like all bargaining, is a two-way street. While some guilty and remorseful defendants may plead guilty without any concessions being made to them, most defendants expect to receive clear advantages in waiving their right to trial. Apart from such matters as avoiding adverse publicity for themselves and their families in addition to whatever self-satisfaction confession brings, the defendant who pleads guilty is typically most concerned with what will happen following conviction. In pleading guilty, most defendants ordinarily expect a break.[56]

Throwing oneself on the mercy of the court is one thing; arranging for leniency before entering a guilty plea is a more controversial process. Bargaining can take place at various stages. Sometimes plea bargaining occurs after a preliminary hearing and before the trial. Sometimes bargaining occurs prior to filing an information, or after the defense lawyer has seen the evidence against the defendant through discovery or deposition of key witnesses scheduled to testify at trial. The kinds and types of bargains also differ among jurisdictions, just as sentencing provisions vary from one state to another. The major motivation in bargaining by any defendant is to achieve a lenient sentence, but other incentives exist as well.

It's Like Betting on Football

Especially on serious cases, the biggest motivator in people accepting plea bargains is **certainty**—regardless of whether they are actually guilty or innocent. If someone accepts the state's plea offer, he knows what his sentence will be. If someone goes to trial on a serious charge, it's like going to Las Vegas and betting your life. And regardless of the odds of who should win the trial, just like there's a reason they play pro football every Sunday in the fall, there's a reason we actually go to trial instead of just look at who "should" win—juries can do whatever they want with your case at the end of the day.[57]

First offenders are most often interested in plea bargaining, but a defendant who is on probation or parole also has a great interest in bargaining and is usually sophisticated enough to understand how to work the system best. Someone on probation or parole, for instance, may consent to revocation in exchange for dismissal or reduction of charges. Depending on the crime or crimes charged and the sentencing provisions in the state, defendants seek one or more of the following concessions by plea bargaining:

Charge reduction: The defendant agrees to plead to some lesser offense with a correspondingly shorter sentence.

Dismissal of charges: The prosecutor charges only one or two of multiple offenses and dismisses the others. This is sometimes called count bargaining.

Softer label: The charge is altered from one carrying a particularly damaging label that implies depravity on the part of the defendant to one with less negative connotations, for example, rape to assault. See **Field Practice 8.8.**

Sentence promise: The prosecutor promises to recommend probation or a shorter prison term at the time of sentencing.

Field Practice 8.8 The Softer Label

A 24-year-old defendant accused of raping and sodomizing a 19-year-old college coed in a "date rape" episode was indicted for forcible rape, a felony carrying a possible prison sentence of 8 to 25 years. The defendant knows that a conviction for rape can be more stigmatizing for the offender than just about any other crime. The prosecutor knows that "date rape" is often difficult to prove. Through his attorney, the defendant offered to plead guilty to a charge of aggravated assault ("assault with a deadly weapon evincing disregard for human life"), a felony carrying the exact same sentence as rape. His attorney told the prosecutor his client did not want to be labeled a rapist, neither in prison nor afterward.

It is not uncommon for clients to plea to prison when the state doesn't even seek it, or plea to more prison time than offered, just to avoid the label of being a sexual offender or predator, in exchange for the state amending the charge to an offense that does not require the label.[58]

Defense attorneys know in advance the likelihood of conviction at trial and the benefits of accommodating the prosecutor's and judge's busy schedule. As Albert W. Alschuler has written: "Virtually every aspect of today's system of criminal justice, in short, seems designed to influence defense attorneys to adopt the motto: when in doubt, cop him out."[59] So the defense attorney can accomplish through bargaining what would be unlikely to be accomplished at trial, that is, a favorable charge and sentence. For public defenders, the constraint of the large case load and crowded court calendar is similar to that of the judge, and the public defender is eager to resolve cases through bargains.

The added dimension of charging a fee for professional services rendered enters the picture for privately retained legal counsel. Charging the appropriate fee is always a hit or miss proposition for private criminal defense attorneys. Sometimes a really severe charge ends up being rather simple to handle compared to a minor felony or a misdemeanor. It's always important to learn as much about a case before entering it as legal counsel as possible. The client should be interviewed, the court file reviewed, and any information that law enforcement or the prosecution will share should be welcomed. Defense attorneys typically do not charge by the hour—the closest they might come to doing that is charging a "trial fee" for the time spent preparing for and being in trial.[60]

Defense attorneys often have two separate fee schedules for handling a case, one if the case is settled out of court and another if the case goes to trial. The negotiated plea provides a service for their clients and compensation, without the arduous work of preparing for trial. Their compensation may or may not increase with a trial, but with "deep-pocket," or wealthy defendants, where the pain of even a lenient bargained result is unappealing, the defense attorney may realize large fees for a contested trial.

Issues in Plea Bargaining

Many unresolved issues in our system of plea bargaining exist. The peculiar way plea bargaining is conducted raises several questions. Not only is the bargaining process informal and hard to see and evaluate, as already noted, but it is rarely litigated because most bargains are kept and both the state and the defendant benefit. Appellate courts only decide cases brought to them by parties directly interested in the outcome of a plea bargain and, if everyone directly involved profits from the bargain, there is no one to appeal. Thus the appellate courts, including the U.S. Supreme Court, have not shaped law and practice here as they have in more commonly litigated decision points in the criminal justice process. Legislation and court decisions are totally silent about plea bargaining in many jurisdictions. Court rules make the process more visible, but still many issues of controversy and uncertainty about bargaining continue. We describe some of them below.

Is Justice Achieved through Plea Bargaining?

The major issue is whether plea negotiation with some control is justified on the grounds of expediency or whether it is a distortion of our criminal justice ideology. Is plea bargaining a proper form of criminal justice in our society? Is an inducement-based system any more proper than one which rests on coercion? Coercion is clearly contrary to our system of government. Is a promise by a prosecutor to "recommend" probation really any different from a threat to "throw the book" at a defendant who pleads not guilty? Is the dropping of a charge in an indictment to a lesser charge a proper practice when the prosecutor, court, and defendant know that the defendant committed the more serious crime and that the evidence in fact supports conviction on the higher offense? This question has been raised by appellate courts and various commissions. Some observers of plea bargaining condemn it as intrinsically improper to our idea of justice. One appellate court judge stated: "Justice and liberty are not the subjects of bargaining and barter." However, on a rehearing this same judge found that "proper" bargaining is appropriate and may be a necessity.[61]

Although on the surface plea negotiations appear to be intrinsically improper and therefore dangerous and corrupting, the administrative realities of current adjudication practices make bargaining—expressed or implicit—normative. The fact is that criminal justice has become so dependent on plea bargaining to keep the court calendar from becoming hopelessly clogged that it could not be instantly eliminated. The abolition of plea bargaining would inundate our already overtaxed prosecutorial and judicial facilities,[62] creating an even larger backlog of cases.

Nevertheless, several efforts have been made to eliminate, or at least seriously limit, the scope of plea bargaining. Several jurisdictions to be discussed in Chapter 9 have severely restricted plea bargaining.[63] Furthermore, some fear that where bargaining has been reduced, sentence lengths will increase. This may be a popular sentiment in a law-and-order political atmosphere, but the added strain placed on most state's correctional facilities, which already face understaffing problems, merit further consideration.

While the controversy is still very strong, courts and commissions that condemn plea negotiation are in a minority today. The U.S. Supreme Court has generally supported the practice,[64] and former Chief Justice Burger has stated:

> [plea bargaining] is an essential component of the administration of justice. Properly administered, it is to be encouraged. If every criminal charge were subjected to a full-scale trial, the States and the Federal Government would need to multiply by many times the number of judges and court facilities.

The prompt handling of criminal cases through plea discussions is not only an essential part of the process but a highly desirable part for many reasons:

1. It leads to prompt and largely final disposition of most criminal cases;
2. it avoids much of the corrosive impact of enforced idleness during pretrial confinement for those who are denied release pending trial;
3. it protects the public from those accused persons who are prone to continue criminal conduct even while on pretrial release; and
4. by shortening the time between charge and disposition, it enhances whatever may be the rehabilitative prospects of the guilty when they are ultimately imprisoned.[65]

The American Bar Association, as well as the American Law Institute, have accepted plea agreement procedures.[66] Furthermore, a revision of Rule 11 of the Federal Rules of Criminal Procedure (a part of the Model Code of Pre-Arraignment Procedures approved by the U.S. Supreme Court) contains detailed provisions for plea agreement procedures.[67]

Who Is in Charge of Plea Bargaining?

All current suggestions for controlling bargaining practices require that an accurate record of any plea agreements be made and submitted to the appropriate court for approval. This raises the issue of whether the prosecutor or the judge is the final arbiter of the bargaining decision. Normally the prosecutor is understood to be in charge of the bargain. Only the prosecutor is in a position to know the work load of the office and the number of cases he or she is able to prosecute. But the issue goes beyond that. In their zeal to prosecute a particular defendant, the prosecutor and the police sometimes undermine their case against at least one other codefendant. To assure a conviction against one defendant, the cooperation of another is sometimes needed. Is this decision a prerogative of the prosecutor and police alone? Should the trial court serve merely as a rubber stamp for the prosecutor's and police department's decision?

The answer is no. As a result, courts are given an oversight function in plea bargaining causes: A judge may withhold approval of a plea bargain if the prosecutor has failed to give consideration to the public interest or to the deterrent aspects of the criminal law. Judges, for example, in Florida, can reject plea bargains and they needn't point to an abuse of prosecutorial discretion. Judges are the final arbiter over disposition; if they don't like the recommended disposition, they can say to the state that "if your case is that cruddy, you need to drop it, but I am not doing this deal." In other jurisdictions, the state even needs the court's approval to drop charges off an indictment.[68]

Of course, judicial interference in plea bargaining may be dictated by the type of crime. For example, no judge wants to be seen as being soft on sex crimes, anymore than a prosecutor does. In such situations, unless the Constitution or a statute provides an avenue of attack on the evidence, prosecutors' sentencing philosophies tend to prevail over those of defense attorneys.[69]

Must Promises Be Kept?

If the prosecutor and the accused make a bargain and the deal is kept, usually there is no aggrieved party and no appeal. If, however, a prosecutor offers some concession and a defendant, relying on this, pleads guilty—and then for some reason the state reneges on its part of the bargain—the defendant naturally feels cheated. If he or she can show an unkept promise, the defendant can win one of two remedies: (1) withdrawal of the guilty plea and a chance to go to trial on the original charge (which, since the defendant bargained, he or she probably does not want) or (2) an order by an appellate court that the bargain be kept. The latter is simple enough and is a more common practice than plea withdrawal. This works well if the bargain is within the traditional authority of the prosecutor or court. If, for example, a defendant was promised probation and instead was incarcerated, the appellate court, if convinced a worthwhile plea bargain agreement was not implemented, can simply order probation (see *Santobello v. New York* (1971)).[70]

Does Everyone Have an Equal Opportunity to Bargain?

The American Bar Association's Standards Relating to Pleas of Guilty ends its discussion with the following proviso: "Similarly situated defendants should be afforded equal plea-agreement opportunities."[71] Which defendants could be more similarly situated than persons with equivalent prior records who are "rap partners" (codefendants in the same crime)?

This situation arose in a case from the District of Columbia involving two burglars named Newman and Anderson who were partners in housebreaking. After arrest, they were both indicted for felonious burglary and larceny. Anderson, through counsel, negotiated with the prosecutor and obtained a bargain allowing him to plead guilty to the misdemeanors of attempted housebreaking and petty larceny. Newman requested the same bargain but the prosecutor declined to grant it.

Newman was convicted and appealed to the Federal Circuit Court (Washington, DC, is a federal jurisdiction) on the grounds that he was denied equal protection of the law (all persons must be treated equally under the Fourteenth Amendment). That is, he argued that he had been denied the plea bargain granted to his rap partner despite their similar backgrounds. The court, however, denied him relief, saying, in part, "Two persons may have committed what is precisely the same legal offense but the prosecutor is not compelled by law, duty or tradition to treat them the same as to charges."[72]

This whole problem of equal plea-bargaining opportunities is complicated by the fact that bargaining, as well as the types of bargains offered and accepted, is generally informal, off the record, and neither written in statute nor posted on bulletin boards as common practice. A defendant, a local resident familiar with the courts, and a criminal defense lawyer aware of the prosecutor's bargaining practices may indeed achieve the normal, routine leniency of the district attorney in exchange for a plea. But what of a stranger or a lawyer who is unfamiliar with the "going rates" of bargains in a particular court system? For equal opportunity in bargaining to be achieved, must local practices and local norms of deals be posted somewhere? The equal protection issue is also raised in cases in which one rap partner agrees to testify against the other in exchange for charging or sentencing leniency. However, showing that the prosecution is treating similarly situated defendants differently, without just cause, can allow a court to do things such as depart from the sentencing guidelines.[73]

Thus, equal protection is one of the major unresolved issues of plea bargaining as a major form of adjudication in our criminal justice process. We try to control this somewhat today by making bargains part of the record at arraignment, but this neither provides adequate information for strangers to the system nor compels prosecutors to offer similar bargains to comparable defendants.

Does Bargaining Convict the Innocent?

Can the guilty plea system be so seductive that innocent persons plead guilty? If a defendant, particularly one with prior convictions, is arrested for a crime he or she did not commit and, in spite of a prior record, is offered probation for a plea by the prosecutor, might the defendant plead guilty despite his or her innocence? The alternative is to face a jury at trial, always a problematic situation. Should the jury convict in spite of actual innocence, imprisonment could result. In these circumstances, probation no doubt looks good. In fact, in *North Carolina v. Alford* (1970),[74] the U.S. Supreme Court held that a guilty plea can still be accepted and is valid even if someone maintains their innocence for the crime that he or she has pled guilty to—all that is required for acceptance of the plea is that it is knowingly entered into; it does not have to be an admission of guilt. This is referred to as entering an *Alford* plea.

So the problem of the innocent pleading guilty remains, and no doubt will remain, with us. The fact is, myths notwithstanding, there is no firm assurance that even a full-scale jury trial will always accurately separate the guilty from the innocent. And there is evidence that innocent people have been convicted by trial after a full-scale adversary proceeding, although it is not common. Thus it is likely that some innocent offenders will continue to choose a lenient sentence rather than risk trial. On the other hand, it cannot be said that the bargaining process is any more likely to be inaccurate than the trial system—at least no compelling evidence has been shown to support such an assumption. Of course, one can go into almost any jail or prison in the country today and, whether inhabitants arrive there by plea or trial, be told by almost everyone there that they are innocent. Thus, it may well be that the careful and proper exercise of discretion by prosecutors in our bargaining system works to standardize the law and to fit punishments to the fine gradations that occur in the behavior and backgrounds of the thousands of defendants who are processed in this manner every day.

Does Bargaining Nullify Police Efforts and Ignore the Victim?

By and large the police who arrest a defendant are often not asked, indeed might not be informed or much less consulted, about leniency in exchange for a plea. However, "[m]ost states provide victims with some level of prosecutorial consultation about a negotiated plea agreement; however, the extent of their participation varies widely from state to state. In no state is the right to confer interpreted as the right to direct the prosecution of the case or to veto decisions of the prosecutor.... In at least 22 states, the victim's right to confer with the prosecutor requires a prosecutor to obtain the victim's views concerning the proposed plea.... A third of the states permit the victim to be heard, either orally or in writing, at plea entry proceedings."[75] Should a prosecutor's first responsibility be to honor the wishes of a victim, or should all crimes be viewed as crimes against "the people," not just a specific victim?

Does Plea Bargaining Circumvent Constitutional Protections?

A defendant who pleads guilty, with or without striking a bargain, waives the necessity for the state to provide evidentiary proof of guilt and, in an overwhelming number of jurisdictions, waives all rights to challenge police arrest or search behavior.[76] This means that not only is the test of the amount of evidence held by the state bypassed but so is the legality of the manner in which this evidence was obtained. All the important Supreme Court cases on the early stages of the criminal justice process—*Mapp*, *Miranda*, even *Gideon*—are irrelevant in the case of a defendant who pleads guilty. Thus a guilty plea, no matter how obtained, not only does not sharpen and hone the law in regard to search, interrogation, force, or other important law enforcement issues, it waives their examination altogether. The plea avoids many more legal issues than it answers.

Does Bargaining Lower Respect for Justice?

Plea bargaining is an unmistakable example of wheeling and dealing. Though it may be perfectly proper, it has the aura of a "fix" about it. For example, a person charged with one crime may bargain for conviction on a lesser one. Some observers argue that such arrangements breed disrespect for the law and our justice system. Indeed, the major lesson may be that everything can be "arranged" with the right lawyer and a willing prosecutor. Cynicism is the result—another crack in the foundation of justice in our society.

Only people sophisticated in the ways of the criminal justice system or a person caught in the web of arrest and prosecution can see the justice in a negotiation model. For most of us, something that is accepted practice in all sorts of civil legal disputes, from auto accident claims to labor relations, seems somehow inappropriate in criminal matters. How can a crime be negotiated or a compromise plea arranged? This, of course, is exactly what plea bargaining is. The settlement, negotiation, and compromise practices of civil disputes are carried over into the criminal sphere. But if settling "out of court" is desirable in most civil matters, somehow it is not quite as respectable in criminal cases.

Does Bargaining Conceal the Whole Truth?

When a defendant is publicly tried, all the minute details of his or her conduct are made public, not only in the courtroom but in the media as well. A guilty plea, bargained or not, is less than revealing. There is a conviction, yes, but what about motives and other details of the crime? They are buried in the plea. The plea is so cryptic, so unrevealing, that this very avoidance of publicity may be one of the major factors leading to the frequency of convictions in this manner. But to the public, hungry for news, the plea fails to reveal any of the gory details. In a routine case, this makes little difference except to those acquainted with the offender or the victim. But when the defendant is prominent or notorious, when a political figure, movie star, professional athlete, or other well-known person is involved, a simple plea of guilty to the charge does not satisfy the public's need (some say "right") to know all the facts. In short, should the newsworthy be allowed to hide their conduct while admitting their guilt? This, like many of the other issues surrounding plea bargaining, remains controversial and has by no means been resolved.

Summary

Convictions obtained by plea bargaining, however, stand just as a conviction won in the crucible of a jury trial. For cases that are plea bargained or not prosecuted at the discretion of the prosecutor, the criminal justice process stops. But if the case is not successfully negotiated and the prosecutor does not exercise the discretion of *nolle prosequi*, the next stage in the process is trial. It is here that constitutional rights for defendants can be found on full display and that is now where we turn to examine the splendor and majesty of the courtroom and the courtroom working group.

Chapter 9

Arraignment and Trial

Image by moodboard at fotolia.com.

"It is incumbent upon this Court that every citizen, whether a prince or a pauper, be treated equally."

—Judge Marc Lubet[1]

Seeking Justice: Prince or Pauper

The Trial of the Twentieth Century and the Factor of Celebrity on Fairness

Should it matter that one is a prince or a pauper upon becoming entangled in criminal justice? One's station in life may influence the response to such a question.

Some would argue that it does matter and a prime example cited is the acquittal (finding of not guilty) of O.J. Simpson at his murder trial for the deaths of Nicole Brown Simpson and Ronald Goldman. O.J. was able to pay for a "dream team" of defense attorneys: Johnnie Cochran, F. Lee Bailey, Robert Shapiro, Gerald Ulman, Barry Scheck, Peter Neufeld, etc.; a jury consultant by the name of Jo-Ellen Demitrius to administer a questionnaire to all prospective jurors in an attempt to identify jurors who would be most favorable to O.J.; and his own investigators and expert witnesses to counteract the "mountain of evidence" amassed by the state and pick apart every nuance of the investigation undertaken by the Los Angeles Police Department against O.J.

Nicole Brown Simpson in a 911 call can be heard pleading with a police dispatcher: "He's O.J. Simpson. I think you know his record." Indeed, his record was known. There had been too many films, commercials, football commentaries. There had been too many touchdowns. The stadiums had already been filled on too many occasions by O.J. Due to his celebrity status, the kind of justice meted out to him would not be the same as that for others. There would not be a level playing field this time. The blindfold on the goddess of justice had been knocked askew, and the scales were no longer balanced.[2]

Based on what you know about the matter, do you believe a pauper would have fared as well as O.J. Simpson in this case?

Do you believe O.J. was truly innocent, not guilty, or guilty? Why?

To assist you in identifying subjects for the following questions, you might check out the Smoking Gun, Arresting Images website: http://www.thesmokinggun.com/mugshots/index.html.

Can you think of examples where those with fame and fortune have benefited from their celebrity?

Can you think of examples where those with fame and fortune have been treated more harshly, so as to make an example of them, upon encountering the criminal justice system?

Are you aware of any examples where persons with fame and fortune have been treated relatively the same as everyone else?

Consider the former wide receiver for the Super Bowl Champion New York Giants—Plaxico Burress. Investigate the Plaxico Burress matter.[3] What dictated the outcome in the case? Do you think his punishment (two years in prison followed by two years of supervised release as part of a plea deal) for having a concealed weapon in a Manhattan nightclub, whereby he accidentally shot himself in the thigh, was fair? What if he had been in such an establishment in Tennessee, Virginia, Georgia, or Arizona as a resident with a concealed weapon?[4] What are means that can be used to attempt to ensure that princes and paupers are treated equally within the criminal justice system?

About This Chapter

A public and fair criminal trial is a hallmark of the American system of justice. The process by which persons are accused and convicted, the mechanism by which the state gains the right to intervene in a person's life by means of sanctions and punishments, is steeped in formality, ritual, and often drama. The courtroom scene in which a doggedly determined public-servant prosecutor engages a slick, professional defense attorney has long been a favorite subject of television (*Law and Order*, for instance) and movies (*A Time to Kill* and *Presumed Innocent*, for instance). Each of

Figure 9.1 The Adjudication Process

Arraignment	Pretrial Motions	Trial	Verdict	Sentencing
Enter a plea: • Guilty → sentence • Not guilty • *Nolo contendere*	Motion to dismiss Motion to determine competency to stand trial Motion to suppress evidence Motion to disclose and discovery Motion for change of venue Motion for continuance	Bench or jury trial Selection of jury Opening statements Case for the prosecution Cross-examination Motion for judgment of acquittal Case for the defense Cross-examination Rebuttal Closing arguments Instructions to the jury Jury deliberation and verdict	Guilty Not guilty "Hung jury"	

us is familiar with this contest, and we are equally familiar with the structure and arrangement of a courtroom. After the O.J. Simpson trial (considered to be the trial of the century) brought new and widespread attention to television coverage of the trial, many Americans have tuned in to what is now called tru TV, a cable television channel devoted to real-life trials.

This chapter details the procedures whereby a person progresses from being accused of a crime to being convicted of one. Each of the stopping-off places along the way to conviction or acquittal are examined (see **Figure 9.1** for a flow chart of these steps). As discussed in Chapter 8, despite the central importance of the right to a fair trial to our system, a very small percent of cases actually go all the way to trial.[5] But for those cases, several very important decisions must be made by prosecutors, accused, defense attorneys, judges, and juries. This chapter describes the practical and legal influences on those decisions. Consider **Critical Thinking 9.1** below.

Critical Thinking 9.1 What Were You and Your Attorney Conferring About?

As noted by Yale Kamisar, "the courtroom is a splendid place where defense attorneys bellow and strut and prosecuting attorneys are hemmed in at many turns. But what happens before an accused reaches the safety and enjoys the comfort of this veritable mansion? Ah, there's the rub. Typically, he must pass through a much less pretentious edifice, a police station with bare back rooms and locked doors.

In this gatehouse of American criminal procedure—through which most defendants journey and beyond which many never get—the enemy of the state is a depersonalized 'subject' to be 'sized up' and subjected to interrogation tactics and techniques 'most appropriate for the occasion'; he is 'game' to be stalked and cornered. Here ideals are checked at the door, 'realities' faced, and the prestige of law enforcement vindicated. Once he leaves the 'gatehouse' and enters the 'mansion'—if he ever gets there—the enemy of the state is repersonalized, even dignified, the public invited, and a stirring ceremony in honor of individual freedom from law enforcement celebrated.... I suspect that it is not so much that society knows and approves of the show in the gatehouse, but that society does not know or care."[6] Unfortunately for many it is what has taken place outside the splendor of a courtroom that will dictate their fate.

Sheriff Grady Judd of Polk County, Florida, capitalizing on a Florida Supreme Court opinion,[7] allows his employees to tape and review telephone conversations between jail inmates and their attorneys. Sheriff Judd maintains that this allows him to seize on yet another avenue to gather evidence to use against defendants, and he promises to send whatever he finds on to the prosecutor's office to prosecute offenders.

Sherriff Judd, in similar fashion to Sheriff Powell's rationale for enforcing blue laws discussed in Chapter 1, indicates he didn't make the law, he just enforces the law. Judd maintains that most inmates he has talked with about the new policy are all for it, as it assures their attorneys will come to the jail and talk with them where their conversations will not be recorded. Almost in concert with Kamisar's statement above, Sheriff Judd concluded, "I can tell you right now that the hard-working, God-fearing men and women of this community that obey the law are not concerned about whether or not an inmate in the county jail can talk on the telephone with his lawyer."[8]

Of course, most persons in jail, as we saw in Chapter 7, have not been convicted of the crime that has currently landed them in jail. What about the presumption of innocence? Would such a policy favor some detainees over others? How do you reconcile one's Sixth Amendment right to consult with legal counsel and one's Fifth Amendment right not to incriminate one's self with Sheriff Judd's policy?

The Courts

A courtroom working group consists of players who are regulars, who remain day after day as the parade of cases passes through. But actors or not, the people who appear in court, and those who play the leading court roles, are engaged in making decisions with enormous consequences, up to and including issues involving life and death. To better understand how these decisions are made, we first discuss the organization of the court system by jurisdiction: federal and state courts, both trial and appellate.

The federal court system is established under the authority of Congress, and includes both trial and appellate courts, as described in the U.S. Constitution:

> The judicial Power of the United States, shall be vested in one supreme Court, and in such inferior Courts as the Congress may from time to time ordain and establish. (U.S. Constitution, Art. III, Sec. 1)

In addition, each state has its own independent court system, all of which also include (with some variation in detail) appellate and trial courts and which handle the vast majority of criminal cases in the United States.

Federal Courts

Federal Trial Courts

The federal district courts are the trial courts for violations of federal law and crimes committed on federal property. Ninety-four federal district courts in the United States, Guam, Puerto Rico, the Virgin Islands, District of Columbia, and the Northern Mariana Islands are presided over by 678 United States district court judges. Like all federal judges, U.S. district court judges are appointed for life by the president of the United States with the advice and consent of the U.S. Senate. Customarily federal district court judicial vacancies are filled by a recommendation to the president from a state's senior U.S. senator who is a member of the president's political party.[9]

Because of the heavy caseload in federal district courts, federal district judges in turn sometimes appoint federal magistrates who hear some cases in magistrate courts. Federal magistrate judges do not have life tenure. Full-time magistrates serve for an eight-year term and part-time magistrates for a four-year term. They can be re-appointed at the end of their terms. Magistrates have limited power to hear pretrial motions, misdemeanor cases, and bail hearings. In addition, federal magistrates can issue warrants, review habeas corpus petitions, and hold pretrial conferences.[10]

Federal Appeals Courts

The U.S. Courts of Appeals, sometimes called the "Federal Circuit Courts of Appeals," are located in twelve geographic circuits, one of which covers exclusively the District of Columbia. There is also a 13th, the U.S. Court of Appeals for the Federal Circuit, which has nationwide jurisdiction over specialized matters dealing with patents, international trade, and appeals from the Court of Federal Claims. There are 179 judges in these thirteen circuits, all of whom, like U.S. district court judges, are appointed for life by the president. Each circuit has at least six judges, and circuits with larger caseloads have more judges. The federal appellate courts may hear cases as one body (en banc) or, unlike the U.S. Supreme Court, may hear cases in groups or divisions of three or five judges. The circuit courts hear appeals from the district courts and typically vote to affirm or reverse a lower-court decision.[11]

The U.S. Supreme Court is the highest court in the land. The Court has original jurisdiction in some matters, meaning that if the parties cannot resolve a particular matter no other court can intervene and the matter can come directly to the U.S. Supreme Court. These matters usually concern conflicts between states and, in recent years, only involve about one or two cases heard by the Court per year.[12] Thus, almost all the cases that come before the Court arrive via appeal from other courts (federal or state) or, more precisely, through petitions for a writ of certiorari. Certiorari is derived from Latin and means "to be fully informed." The U.S. Supreme Court, with discretionary review, via a writ of certiorari, orders a lower court to produce the record of a case so that it may be reviewed.

Approximately 80 or so cases of the thousands of cases referred to the Supreme Court are heard and considered by the Court each year.[13] The rest are dismissed *per curiam*, which means that the decision of the lower court is left alone.[14] At least four of the justices must vote affirmatively on a given case to allow it to be considered by the Court. This is known as the **rule of four.**[15] Thus, the Supreme Court has great leeway in shaping social change and is the last word in applying the U.S. Constitution to criminal justice practices.

The members of the United States Supreme Court have been educated in the nation's elite law schools: Harvard (Chief Justice John G. Roberts, Jr., Neil M. Gorsuch, Anthony M. Kennedy, Stephen G. Breyer and Elena Kagan), Yale (Clarence Thomas, Samuel A. Alito, Jr., and Sonia Sotomayor), and Columbia (Ruth Bader Ginsburg).[16] These individuals, appointed by the president, reach the Court via highly publicized and often contentious spectacles, as U.S. Senators on the judiciary committee engage in the practice of advice and consent. Throughout history, there have been those who could not muster enough votes to make it onto the Court.

The significance of these justices and other federal judges having life tenure should not be minimized. Such a status is thought to contribute to independence of thought by judges, for only by their own choice to retire or quit, their death, or impeachment can they be removed from office. Thus, it is not easy to get rid of them once they have been appointed. Fifteen federal judges have been impeached in our nation's history.[17] Harry Claiborne of Nevada was the first federal district court judge to be sent to prison and was removed from office while incarcerated, as the cumbersome impeachment process is not easily set into motion. Claiborne was released in 1987 after serving seventeen months for income tax evasion and ultimately committed suicide in 2004.[18] Alcee Hastings of Florida was removed from office in 1989 "on charges of perjury and conspiring to solicit a bribe."[19] Hastings was elected to the U.S. House of Representatives in 1992 and continues to serve as a congressman.[20]

State Courts

Each state has its own system of courts that handle the overwhelming majority of the criminal prosecutions in the United States. Each state system includes both trial and appellate courts.

State Trial Courts

Most states have minor trial courts with limited jurisdiction, which handle less serious criminal and civil matters, such as probate and small claims. Likewise, major trial courts, commonly referred to as circuit, district, or superior courts, where most jury trials take place and felonies are processed, can be found in most states. Some smaller states may have a single set of trial courts which can hear the entire spectrum of criminal and civil cases.[21] Judges preside over the state trial courts and conduct the day-to-day prosecutions of criminal defendants.

The judge in any given court is not the only individual involved in the courtroom processes. Several others are also major players: the defendant, the prosecutor, the defense lawyer, and perhaps a trial jury. Others involved include the bailiff, court clerks, court reporters, and witnesses for the defense and for the prosecution, who offer testimony about the facts in the case. In some cases, "expert" testimony is given by expert witnesses who have established expertise about a particular issue involved in the trial.[22] For instance, a ballistics expert can testify whether a bullet fragment was fired by a particular weapon, or fingerprint experts can testify as to the "match" between prints found at the crime scene and those of the defendant, or a DNA expert can testify that biological evidence does or does not match the defendant's.

Also, since pleadings and trials are public (unlike grand jury proceedings) citizens uninvolved in the case may be present in the courtroom as observers. And press reporters, who, with some exceptions, represent the print media, may be present. In recent years, a number of states have allowed television cameras in courtrooms as well. The emergence of Court TV (now known as tru TV) and the complete televising of O.J. Simpson's murder trial have heightened the debate as to whether trials should be televised.[23] A state-by-state guide is available that identifies state regulations on cameras in the courtroom, with states such as California, Florida, Nevada, and New Hampshire allowing broad discretion to the presiding judge in a case, and states such as Illinois, Louisiana, New York, and South Dakota not allowing cameras in any of their trial courts.[24] The U.S. Supreme Court in *Estes v. Texas* (1965) reversed the conviction of a defendant after his trial was televised over his objection. Possible interference to a defendant for a fair trial as the result of cameras in the courtroom identified by the Court included: interference with the judiciary, improper influence on jurors, and impairment of witness testimony.[25] The Court, however, in *Chandler v. Florida* (1981), even though concerns were reiterated about judges playing to the cameras, concluded that states may choose to allow cameras in courtrooms as long as one's right to a fair trial is not infringed upon.[26] While federal courts have traditionally been reluctant to allow cameras at the federal level, the U.S. Senate Judiciary Committee has approved a bill that would provide for televising public sessions of the U.S. Supreme Court and even lower federal court proceedings at a judge's discretion. However, even if the bill is ultimately passed, it is unclear whether the measure would be binding upon the federal courts.[27]

State Appeals Courts

Thirty-five states have intermediate appellate courts situated between the trial courts of general jurisdiction and the state supreme court. Parties are generally considered to have a right to appeal to these intermediate appellate courts. Therefore, the courts must hear the case, but the focus is on whether proper procedures were followed at the lower-court level or whether errors were made. Generally, no fact-finding is done by the court at this level, nor is additional evidence allowed. The judges usually sit in panels of two or three to hear appeals.

The highest appellate court in any state is usually referred to as the supreme court. In those states that have an intermediate court of appeals, the state supreme court generally has discretionary review and original jurisdiction in limited instances, meaning that the court does not have to hear most of the cases appealed to it. In similar fashion as the intermediate appellate courts, the state supreme courts process cases and generally sit in panels of three, five, seven, or nine judges/justices to hear appeals.[28]

Selection of State Court Judges

Across the states there are five methods in place for selecting judges. These five methods are **legislative appointment, gubernatorial appointment** (patterned after the federal model of judicial selection), **merit selection** (also known as **the Missouri Plan**), **nonpartisan election** (with no party affiliation listed on the ballot), and **partisan election** (whereby political party affiliation is listed by the name of the judicial candidate on the ballot).

Only two states employ **legislative appointment** for judges (South Carolina and Virginia). Today, only three states allow the **governor** to nominate judicial appointees who then must be confirmed by the state senate (Maine and New Jersey) or a commission on judicial appointments in California. It should be noted that in twenty-eight states that allow contested elections to select judges the governor is authorized to make interim appointments of judges to fill vacancies that may arise. This time on the bench and exposure can prove to be advantageous when such appointees come up for election. Similarly, nine states (Alabama, Georgia, Indiana, Kentucky, Minnesota, Montana, Nevada, North Dakota, and Wisconsin) use **the Missouri Plan** to appoint judges to interim vacancies. While there are variations on this method, the way the process typically works is that a nominating commission of some sort reviews applicants and then recommends the best qualified persons to an elected official (in most cases the governor) for selection. Fifteen states utilize **the Missouri Plan** as their sole means of selecting judges (AK, CO, CT, DE, HI, IA, MD, MA, NE, NH, NM, RI, UT, VT, and WY).

Fourteen states use **nonpartisan elections** as the primary means of selecting their judges (AR, GA, ID, KY, MI [while party affiliation is not listed for S. Ct. candidates on the general election ballot, they may be nominated at party conventions], MN, MS, MT, NV, NC, ND, OR, WA, and WV). Six states rely on **partisan elections** to select their judges (AL, IL, LA, OH [candidates are nominated in partisan primary elections, then no party affiliations are reflected on the general election ballot], PA, and TX). Nine states use **the Missouri Plan** in combination with other selection methods, typically with appellate court judges being chosen through merit selection and some or all lower-court judges either chosen through **partisan** or **nonpartisan election** (AZ, FL, IN, KS, MO, NY, OK, SD, and TN).

Retention elections are used in a number of states after a judge has served an initial term (terms of course vary across the states and by level of court) in office. The judge's name is placed on the ballot, and voters are simply asked the question as to whether or not they want to retain the judge in office. No other name is placed on the ballot to contest the incumbent judge. The judge is essentially running on his record. Usually, judges are retained in office in these types of election, unless something highly controversial has happened during their previous term. There have been occasions where interest groups have utilized high-priced ad campaigns to unseat judges who had rendered unpopular decisions for the group. For example, judges have been portrayed as soft on crime by overturning death sentences and dumped out of office. **Retention elections** are typically linked to judges who reached office via **the Missouri Plan.**

Politics are involved in all of the above methods of judicial selection. Some maintain that **the Missouri Plan** is less political.[29] However, generally to become a member of the nominating commission one must be somewhat of a political animal. Via exit polls, it has been determined that the vast majority of persons who just voted in elections are unable to name one judge that they voted for when judicial candidates were on the ballot. With partisan elections of judges, voters, typically not knowing the identity of judicial candidates, tend to rely on party affiliation to determine how they vote. In nonpartisan elections, with no party affiliation listed on the ballot for candidates, voters have been found to rely on the suspected ethnicity of surnames or gender to decide how to cast their vote.

Unlike the federal system, most states do not provide for life tenure for judges either on appellate or trial courts. As such, in 2008, candidates seeking election for vacancies on state supreme courts raised $34 million. From 2000 through 2009, with 39 states electing some of their judges, $206.4 million was raised by high court judicial candidates. Interest groups over the same time period have spent almost $40 million on judicial election ads. Both current U.S. Supreme Court Justice Ruth Bader Ginsburg and former Justice Sandra Day O'Connor have called for an end to judicial elections.[30] See **Critical Thinking 9.2** on judicial campaign financing.

Critical Thinking 9.2 About Judicial Campaign Financing

The Code of Conduct for United States Judges states: "A judge should avoid impropriety and the appearance of impropriety in all his activities ...; and a judge should perform the duties of his office impartially and diligently.... They must disqualify themselves whenever there is a question about their impartiality, such as when they are related, acquainted with, or have had business dealings with any of the participants."[31]

As discussed in Chapter 2, the founding fathers believed that factions (interest groups) would balance each other out within the marketplace of ideas. However, the founding fathers likely could not have envisioned what has become of the potential influence of campaign contributions upon judicial campaigns. Some lawyers and or law firms hedge their bets by contributing to the campaigns of all candidates within their jurisdiction running for judgeships. Others simply may wait until after the election to send a check to the winners among the judges running for office to cover expenses incurred during the course of the campaign.

What if you were a judge and you were sitting in judgment of a conflict between two parties and one of the parties had contributed $3 million to your judicial campaign? Could you decide the matter fairly? Is there any appearance of impropriety present? Should you disqualify (recuse) yourself from participation in the case?

This very matter made it before the United States Supreme Court in a case entitled: *Caperton v. A.T. Massey Coal Company* (2009).[32] The United States Supreme Court decided that West Virginia Supreme Court Justice Brent Benjamin, who refused to recuse himself in a matter before the West Virginia court, was in error. He had ruled in a case where a $50 million verdict against a company operated by a litigant who spent $3 million on Justice Benjamin's election was involved. The case was reversed and remanded to the West Virginia Supreme Court with the stipulation that Benjamin not participate in the proceedings.[33]

Which of the methods discussed for selecting judges do you prefer? Explain why.

The Courtroom Setting

Courtrooms provide the forum for the most formal stages in the criminal justice process. None of the informality of the police station exists. Court proceedings require decorum on the part of all the participants and observers. People who cause disruptions, including defendants, are forcefully and promptly removed from the courtroom and may be held in contempt of court, which frequently results in a fine, time in jail, or some other sanction. The judge wears a robe and is seated on an elevated bench. Everyone in the courtroom rises when the judge enters or exits the courtroom. The jury sits to one side in a jury box. Members of the press are seated at specially designated tables. Onlookers are placed behind a rail, or bar, in front of which sit the defendant and defense attorneys. The district attorney is seated at a separate table.

The setting no doubt embodies our concept of justice, just as police uniforms signify authority and force, and a walled prison represents punishment. Not only is the setting deliberately formal, but the procedures followed are rigidly circumscribed and controlled by law, tradition, and the gavel of the judge. Who may speak, when, and in what order are clearly predetermined and rigidly monitored by the judge. What can and cannot be said is also prescribed by the rules of evidence and by trial rules which are enforced by the court.

If one of the purposes of the pomp and circumstance surrounding court proceedings is to induce respect—perhaps even awe—for the law, the setting and the ritual used in arraignment and trial achieve that aim, except among the most cynical, radical, recalcitrant, or oblivious observers. It is through these proceedings that the criminal justice system separates the innocent from the guilty, releases the innocent, and prepares the guilty to move on to their just deserts. Defendants either become free citizens again or move on to the status of offender, of convicted criminal. All of the earlier decision steps in the criminal justice process—taking the suspect into custody, charging him or her with a crime—lead to these moments, these middle-stage decision points, where guilt is determined by full due process of law, and those found guilty enter into the final stages of the criminal justice process, sentence imposition, and sentence execution.

Arraignment: Entering a Plea

At some date after the filing of the indictment or information—ordinarily ranging from a few days to a few weeks, depending on the court calendar—the defendant is brought before a court of competent jurisdiction (a court empowered to conduct felony trials, misdemeanor trials, etc.) where he or she is once more notified of the constitutional right to trial, is presented with the formal charges, and is asked to plead to them. This is known as **arraignment.** In many instances, the judge will accept a guilty plea and schedule the case for sentencing immediately, thereby ending the proceedings just as though a full jury trial had resulted in a finding of guilty.

A guilty plea is to be *voluntarily*[34] and *knowingly*[35] entered into by defendants. In many instances defendants plead guilty without bargaining with the prosecutor, but plea bargains are to be voluntarily entered into by defendants.

Plea bargains typically involve defendants pleading guilty to one charge with the prosecution agreeing to drop or not to pursue other charges, an arrangement for the defendant to plead guilty straight up to the original charge(s) in exchange for assurance from the prosecutor for some sort of consideration regarding the sentence to be imposed, and/or an agreement where the defendant agrees to plead guilty to a less serious charge(s) than another charge(s) the prosecutor could pursue.[36] Judges tend to be very careful when accepting guilty pleas and are generally very thorough in advising defendants of what rights they are giving up. Consider **Field Practice 9.1** below on accepting a guilty plea at arraignment and **Field Practice 9.2**, which contains excerpts from Michael Vick's plea bargain with federal prosecutors.

Field Practice 9.1 Accepting a Guilty Plea at Arraignment

Speak Up!

Judge: You are Bernie Rogers?

Defendant: Yes sir.

Judge: Mr. Schuffstal, how does your client wish to plead?

Counsel: Guilty of burglary, Your Honor.

Judge: Mr. Rogers, you have just heard your attorney say you wish to plead guilty to burglary. Is that how you wish to plead?

Defendant: Yes sir.

Judge: Before I can accept your plea, I must ask you certain questions and tell you certain things. If you don't understand, stop me and I'll explain. If at any time you want to talk to your lawyer, let me know. I'll stop and you can talk with him privately for as long and as often as you want while we are doing this. You have been placed under oath and if you make any statements that are false, they can later be used against you in a prosecution for perjury. Do you understand what this means?

Defendant: Yes sir.

Judge: How old are you?

Defendant: 26.

Judge: Have you ever been treated for mental problems?

Defendant: No sir.

Judge: Are you now under the influence of any alcohol, drugs, or medication of any kind?

Defendant: No.

Judge: You do not have to plead guilty. You have the right to plead not guilty and have the following rights at trial: the rights to a jury, to see and hear witnesses testify and have your lawyer question them for you, to call witnesses and present evidence you want the jury to consider and to present any defense you might have to the jury; the right to testify yourself or not to testify; the right to require the prosecutor to prove your guilt by the evidence beyond a reasonable doubt before you can be found guilty. Do you understand these rights?

Defendant: Yes sir.

Judge: Do you understand that if I accept your plea, you give up each of these rights, that there will be no trial and all I have to do is sentence you, and that you give up your right to an appeal?

Defendant: Yes sir.

Judge: Mr. Schuffstal, have any agreements been made between the state and the defendant relative to any plea or any sentence?

Counsel: Yes, Your Honor. My client has agreed to plead guilty to a single charge of burglary in exchange for the prosecution's promise to drop additional charges and to recommend a guideline sentence.

Judge: Mrs. Prosecutor, is this correct?

Prosecutor: Yes, Your Honor.

Judge: Mr. Rogers, has anyone, including your lawyer, or the prosecuting attorney, or anyone else forced or pressured you into entering this plea?

Defendant: No sir.

Judge: Are you pleading guilty because you are guilty?

Defendant: Yes sir.

Judge: What actually did you do?

Defendant: Well, I took these tires from the gas station.

Judge: Did you use forcible entry to break into the gas station?

Defendant: Yes sir.

Judge: And how do you plead?

Defendant: Guilty.

Judge: Do you realize that by pleading guilty you could be sent to prison for three years?

Defendant: Yes sir.

Judge: And you still wish to so plead?

Defendant: Yes, I do.

Judge: Very well, I accept your plea of guilty. I am ordering a Presentence Investigation Report and set the date for sentencing three weeks hence, that is, at 10 a.m. on August 15.

Field Practice 9.2 Excerpts from Michael Vick's Plea Agreement[37]

Whereas a judge must verbally quiz the defendant as to whether or not he understands all the rights he was giving up by pleading guilty, in the plea agreement below between Michael Vick and the U.S. attorneys' office the rights are listed for him.

IN THE UNITED STATES DISTRICT COURT
FOR THE EASTERN DISTRICT OF VIRGINIA

Richmond Division

UNITED STATES OF AMERICA	)	
	)	
v.	)	CRIMINAL NO. 3:07CR274
	)	
MICHAEL VICK,	)	
a/k/a "Ookie,"	)	
	)	
Defendant.	)	

PLEA AGREEMENT

Chuck Rosenberg, United States Attorney for the Eastern District of Virginia, Michael R. Gill and Brian L. Whisler, Assistant United States Attorneys, the defendant, MICHAEL VICK, and the defendant's counsel have entered into an agreement pursuant to Rule 11 of the Federal Rules of Criminal Procedure. The terms of the agreement are as follows:

1. Offense and Maximum Penalties

The defendant agrees to plead guilty to Count 1 of the indictment charging the defendant with Conspiracy to Travel in Interstate Commerce in Aid of Unlawful Activities and to Sponsor a Dog in an Animal Fighting Venture, in violation of Title 18, United State Code, Section 371. The maximum penalties for the violation of this offense are a maximum term of 5 years of imprisonment, a fine of $250,000, full restitution, a special assessment, and 3 years of supervised release. The defendant understands that this supervised release term is in addition to any prison term the defendant may receive, and that a violation of a term of supervised release could result in the defendant being returned to prison for the full term of supervised release.

2. Factual Basis for the Plea

The defendant will plead guilty because the defendant is in fact guilty of the charged offense. The defendant admits the facts set forth in the statement of facts filed with this plea agreement and agrees that those facts establish guilt of the offense charged beyond a reasonable doubt. The statement of facts, which is hereby incorporated into this plea agreement, constitutes a stipulation of facts for purposes of Section 1B1.2(a) of the Sentencing Guidelines. Pursuant to USSG § 5K2.0 and 18 U.S.C. § 355(b)(1), the parties agree that the underlying facts relating to the victimization and killing of pit bull dogs as described in the Statement of Facts creates aggravating circumstances not adequately taken into account by the Sentencing Commission in formulating the guidelines and that, in order to advance the objectives set forth in 18 U.S.C. § 35552(a)(2), an upward departure is necessary in this case to achieve the statutory purposes and goals of sentencing in this case. Therefore, pursuant to Rule 11(c)(1)(B), the parties agree that an upward departure to a base offense level of 15 is warranted in this case, and, following Acceptance of Responsibility credit pursuant to USSG § 3E1.1, an adjusted offense level of 13. The parties agree that neither side will move for departure above or below that offense level, except as contemplated by paragraph 13 of this agreement. The government agrees to recommend sentencing at the low end of the applicable guideline range, provided that the defendant fulfills his obligations under this plea agreement. The defendant understands that this agreement is merely a recommendation and is not binding on the sentencing judge.

3. Assistance and Advice of Counsel

The defendant is satisfied that the defendant's attorney has rendered effective assistance. The defendant understands that by entering into this agreement, defendant surrenders certain rights as provided in this agreement. The defendant understands that the rights of criminal defendants include the following:

a. the right to plead not guilty and to persist in that plea;

b. the right to a jury trial;

c. the right to be represented by counsel—and if necessary have the court appoint counsel—at trial and at every other stage of the proceedings; and

d. the right at trial to confront and cross-examine adverse witnesses, to be protected from compelling self-incrimination, to testify and present evidence, and to compel the attendance of witnesses.

Also, note that in Michael Vick's plea agreement Vick accepted responsibility for his actions. He had an adjusted offense level of 13 under federal sentencing guidelines. Vick was sentenced to 23 months and actually served 18 months in prison for his role in the dog fighting ring.[38] Compare this sentence to where an offense level of 13 would place him on the sentencing Table 10.2 in Chapter 10. How does this stack up? Was the time Vick was sentenced to by the judge in line with the plea agreement with the prosecutors in the case? Why do you think it was or was not? Compare Michael Vick's plea agreement to that of Michael Flynn—Donald Trump's former National Security Adviser. Flynn was charged with making false statements to the FBI. Note that Flynn's agreement, unlike Vick's, is contingent upon his cooperation with the Special Counsel's office. Flynn's agreement can be found in Appendix A of the textbook and is known as a cooperating witness agreement.

Both sides hope to gain something from plea bargaining, defense a lighter sentence for their client and prosecution a conviction. However, "[t]he majority of research on race and sentencing outcomes shows that blacks are less likely than whites to receive reduced pleas."[39]

This also allows the prosecution to manage their resources and not spread them too thin. From time to time and place to place, plea bargains have been banned or restricted in the United States. For example, there was a ban on plea bargaining in Alaska, implemented by Attorney General Avrum Gross in 1975. But this ban had eroded by 1990 and plea bargaining was common. In 2013 a new policy issued by the Attorney General Michael Geraghty forbade prosecutors from making deals with defendants regarding sentencing in exchange for a plea deal. This applied to the most serious classes of felonies, and all cases involving a sexual assault, sexual abuse of a minor, or domestic violence. This policy was partly in response to the case of a male by the name of Jerry Active, who, just hours after being released from partially serving a seven-year sentence to community supervision, broke into an apartment, killed an elderly couple, and raped a 2-year-old girl. Active had been the beneficiary of an "inappropriately soft plea agreement" that was due to a failure on the part of prosecutors, the judge, and corrections to recognize that he had a previous record involving a similar felony conviction. Prosecutors are still permitted to use charge bargaining, although they cannot offer to reduce the length of a sentence.[40]

Some jurisdictions in Arizona, Iowa, Louisiana, Michigan, Oregon, and Texas have banned plea bargaining at various times. It is estimated that roughly 90 percent of cases that reach the courts ultimately result in guilty pleas. It is believed that even if that number of cases resolved by guilty pleas dropped down to 80 percent that court administrators would have to double the number of all judicial personnel (to include judges, clerks, bailiffs, jurors) and facilities. Thus, plea bargaining is considered to be beneficial not only to defendants and prosecutors but also to the functionality of the judicial system.[41]

Pleas available to a defendant at arraignment are (1) **not guilty**, (2) **guilty** and, in some places, (3) **guilty but insane or not guilty by reason of insanity**, and (4) **nolo contendere** (no contest). This latter plea, available at the discretion of the trial judge in most of the states and in the federal jurisdiction, has the same criminal effect as a guilty plea—the defendant receives a criminal record and can be sentenced. But, unlike the guilty plea, a no contest plea may not be used in any subsequent civil action as proof that the defendant committed the act. *Nolo contendere* pleas are commonly entered in white-collar cases in which a corporate defendant is likely to be sued for damages and occasionally in cases involving traditional charges, such as driving under the influence where a civil suit is likely to be brought.[42]

If a defendant stands mute (does not respond) or otherwise refuses to answer the charges, a not guilty plea is entered. If the defendant pleads not guilty, the arraignment ends by setting a date for the trial. Once again, release on bail or release on recognizance (ROR) is considered, with the judge having a choice to continue either, to raise or lower the amount of bail, or to deny release and send the defendant to jail to await trial.

Guilty Plea Procedures

Even if a defendant pleads guilty or *nolo contendere*, the judge need not accept the plea. If, from the behavior, appearance, or words of the defendant during the brief arraignment process, the judge is led to believe that a defendant is mentally incompetent, or somehow does not seem to understand what is happening, or that the plea may be involuntary or greatly inaccurate in terms of what actually happened, the court may delay arraignment. This is often done to allow for psychiatric diagnosis or to enable the defendant to confer with counsel. However, the judge may simply reject the guilty plea without giving reasons and set a trial date just as if the defendant had pleaded not guilty.

In deciding whether to accept a plea of guilty, all judges, both federal and state, are required to *personally address* the defendant and make inquiries to establish each of the following:

1. The defendant knows of his or her right to a trial and that a guilty plea is a waiver of this right.
2. The defendant is "voluntarily" pleading guilty (i.e., was not forced or threatened into the plea). As stated in *Boykin v. Alabama* (1969), guilty pleas are to be voluntary.[43]

3. The defendant understands the nature of the charges. As long as pleas of guilty are "intelligently" (knowingly) entered into, even if the rationale for the plea is to avoid the death penalty, such pleas are legally valid (*Brady v. United States* [1970]).[44]
4. The defendant is aware of the possible maximum sentence that can be imposed if he or she pleads guilty.

Judges, therefore, address the voluntariness of the plea, the defendant's understanding of the charge, and the defendant's awareness of the consequences of pleading guilty in light of judicial inquiry.

Withdrawal of a Guilty Plea

A defendant whose plea of guilty has been accepted by the court may later decide to withdraw the guilty plea in order to go to trial. This change of heart may occur at any time after arraignment, and may rest on a variety of factors, ranging from hiring a new lawyer who advises a not guilty plea, to dissatisfaction with the sentence, to a belief that the state has somehow reneged on some pre-plea promise.

To withdraw a guilty plea, the defendant must petition the court with a motion for withdrawal. In most jurisdictions, the trial judge has discretion as to whether such a motion should be granted, and jurisdictions vary as to particulars admitted to in a withdrawn guilty plea, which can be used against an individual in further court appearances.[45]

Presentence Investigations and Sentencing

If a defendant pleads guilty (or *nolo contendere*) and if, after examination in open court, the judge accepts the plea, the defendant stands convicted of a crime just as much as if he or she had been found guilty in a full-scale jury trial. After the plea is accepted by the court, the defendant is bound over for sentencing, that is, a date is set for the imposition of the sentence on the now convicted offender. Except in a few instances of very minor offenses (traffic violations where a fine is the maximum punishment) and more serious offenses that carry legislatively mandated prison terms (which give the judge no discretion as to sentence), the sentencing date is usually a few weeks or a month after the arraignment. This gives probation officers attached to the court time to conduct a presentence investigation, if one is to be conducted, into among other things the social and criminal background of the offender, his or her personal traits, employment, educational history, and the impact of the crime on the victim(s)—information for the judge to use in making the sentencing decision.

Presentence investigations (PSIs) are discussed in more detail in Chapter 11. Also, an example of a PSI is provided in Appendix B.

During the interval between conviction and sentencing, the offender may be referred to jail or sent to jail if he or she has been free on pretrial release. So, a bail or jail decision, just as described in Chapter 7, must be made again at this point.

Figure 9.2 Typical Outcome of Felony Defendants

Typical outcome of 100 felony defendants arraigned in state courts in the 75 largest counties, May 2006

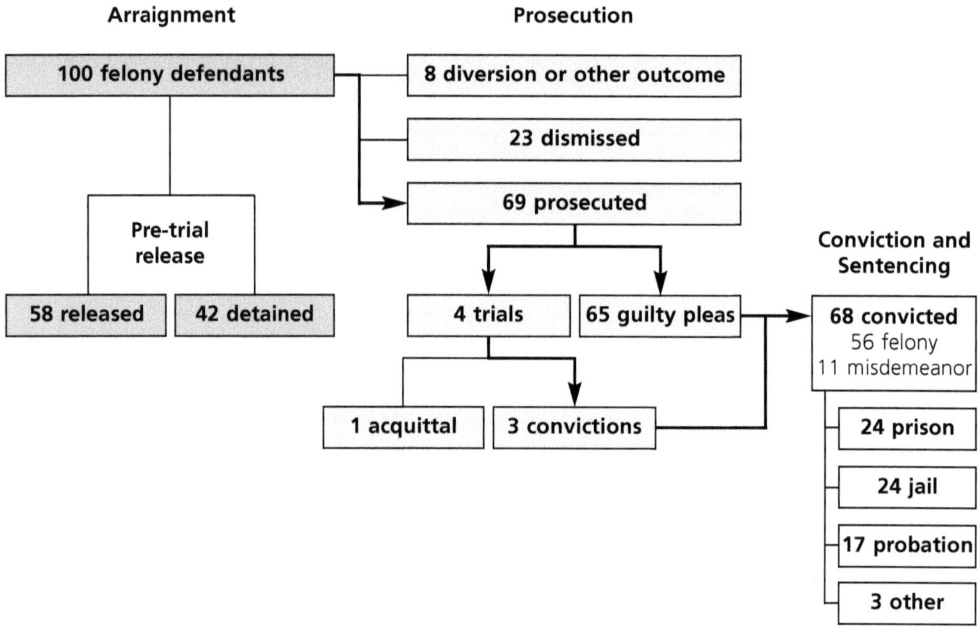

Note: Typical outcome based on the percentage reported for key measures. Numbers may not add to exact totals because of rounding.

Plea bargaining, which may begin very early—indeed, sometimes it starts before the defendant is in custody—may go on right through the trial if the judge chooses to allow it. Though it is not common, it is not altogether rare either for a defendant to move to withdraw a not guilty plea, changing it to guilty; this is often the result of a plea bargain negotiated right in the middle of the trial. The defense is allowed to negotiate for a reduction in the charge or leniency in a proposed sentence right up until a verdict is rendered by the jury or the judge accepts a plea, and this contributes to the fact that most prosecutions result in convictions. See **Figure 9.2** for example.[46]

Pretrial Motions

Before the trial is conducted, several important decisions are made by the judge in response to written requests, called pretrial motions, on behalf of the prosecution or defense. Several motions are available to each side, the most common being the following:

1. *Motion to dismiss.* A defendant may file a motion to dismiss the case based on the failure of the prosecution to allege a crime, or because the documents filed by the prosecution are inaccurate. Usually, if the court grants the motion to

dismiss, the prosecution is granted time to re-file the charges and correct the documents.

2. *Motion to determine the competency of the accused to stand trial.* Usually this motion is filed if the defense believes the defendant is mentally ill, or if a defense of insanity is planned.
3. *Motion to suppress evidence.* Three types of suppression motions are common. First, the defense can seek to exclude evidence obtained through search and seizure if it appears the search was carried out without a warrant or if the legality of the warrant was questionable. Second, the defense can move to exclude confessions, admissions, or other statements made to the police by the defendant if it appears they were not made voluntarily. Third, the defense may challenge the pretrial identification of the accused if it appears that police procedures violated due process standards.[47] See **Field Practice 9.3** below to see two types of suppression motions made in Astronaut Lisa Nowak's case. Excerpts from the judge's ruling on the suppression motions can be seen at the end of this chapter.

Field Practice 9.3 Houston There Is a Problem: This Woman Is a Rocket Scientist

Astronaut Lisa Nowak "put on a special NASA diaper (so she wouldn't have to stop), drove 900 miles, donned a wig and sunglasses and allegedly blasted [Colleen] Shipman with pepper spray and tried to kidnap her from the parking lot of Orlando International Airport. Police say she carried a 4-in. knife, large trash bags and a hammer."[48]

Though married, it seems Nowak had maintained a sexual relationship for over two years with fellow astronaut Bill Oefelein. However, Oefelein had recently declared his love for Air Force Captain Colleen Shipman to Nowak and expressed his desire to see Shipman exclusively. Nowak intercepted steamy emails between Oefelein and Shipman and even learned Shipman's flight itinerary and arrival information for Orlando.[49]

Nowak was charged with attempted kidnapping and potentially faced a life sentence. Her bail was set at $25,000, and she was allowed to return to her home in Houston subject to electronic monitoring while awaiting trial. At a suppression hearing, Nowak's attorney, Donald Lykkebak of Orlando, made motions to have admissions made by Nowak to the Orlando police and evidence obtained by the police from a search of her vehicle suppressed. Lykkebak argued that the admissions and the search of her automobile had been unlawful.[50]

Confessions/admissions and consents to search are to be knowingly and voluntarily entered into. In fact, the prosecutor in the case argued at the suppression hearing, which aired on Tru TV, that this woman was a "rocket scientist." How could she not know her rights? And, with her mental and physical toughness to be an astronaut, how could her interactions with the police have been less than voluntary?

The circuit court judge ruled that the admissions obtained from Nowak were involuntarily made and that in accordance with the fruit of the poisonous tree doctrine, discussed in Chapter 5, anything that followed from such illegalities on the part of the police (information leading to the search of her automobile) was also tainted and could not be used against her.[51] See excerpts from the judge's ruling on the suppression motions at the end of this chapter.

On appeal by the State, the Florida District Court of Appeal upheld the circuit court judge's ruling on the inadmissibility of statements made by Nowak. However, the appellate court ruled that the search was legally permissible. The appellate court stated that "the inevitable discovery" doctrine, discussed in Chapter 5, broke the nexus between Nowak's involuntary admissions and the search of the car. The police would have eventually located the car without Nowak telling them where it was located. Also, the appellate court reasoned that based on the victim's statement, instruments involved in the attempted abduction, and the likelihood that elements of Nowak's plan and planning would be in her vehicle, it was common sense that probable cause existed for a search of the vehicle irrespective of any illegal statements made by Nowak to the police.[52]

4. *Motion to require the prosecution to disclose the identity of a confidential informant.* Here the court must balance the individual right of the accused to prepare a defense against the public's interest in protecting the free flow of information to the police. Trial judges have a great deal of discretion in these matters, and if the informant was an "active participant" in the offense, the prosecution may have to disclose the informant's identity.
5. *Motion for a change of venue.* This is filed if the defense believes that pretrial publicity makes it impossible to seat an impartial jury and obtain a fair trial.
6. *Motion for a continuance.* This may be filed by either the prosecution or the defense to postpone a trial for any number of reasons, including illness or emergency situations involving the defendant, the prosecutor, the defense counsel, or important witnesses which make it impossible for them to appear in court in a timely manner. Sometimes the motion is made when one side or the other has not had adequate time to prepare for the trial.
7. *Motions for discovery.* This is a procedure used by either party to obtain information in the possession of the other side. Usually the scope of what can be properly discovered is limited by law or local procedures, and usually the defense is entitled to more discovery than the prosecution since the defense can invoke the privilege against self-incrimination to prevent revelations of certain types of evidence. Pretrial motions are often argued in open court hearings.
8. *Motions in limine.* This is a motion asking for a pre-trial ruling on the admissibility, or inadmissibility, of a particular piece of evidence or part of testimony. This can be on any potential objection which may be made at trial. Obtaining

Image by LeggNet at istockphoto.com.

pre-trial rulings on key pieces of evidence helps the attorneys focus their trial strategies and can facilitate plea negotiations.[53]

Often the decision of the judge about pretrial motions, especially regarding the suppression of evidence, can make or break the prosecution's case. These hearings determine to a great extent what evidence will be presented to the jury during the trial.

Attorneys for both prosecution and defense have an interest in each of the pretrial motions. And, owing to discovery motions, very little information relevant to the trial is unknown by each side by the time the trial begins. This is known as pretrial discovery.

Pretrial Discovery

Usually, the accused is entitled to know before the trial the names and addresses of witnesses the prosecution intends to call and any written statements they may have made. Likewise, the accused is entitled to all statements made by codefendants and the name of anyone who heard such statements; a transcript of grand jury minutes, reports, and statements by experts on issues relating to the case; the results of physical or mental tests; any physical evidence; and the results of scientific tests relevant to the case. In short, the accused must have access to anything the prosecutor intends to introduce as evidence, and any record of prior convictions of persons the prosecution intends to call as witnesses.[54]

The prosecution is usually entitled to require the accused to appear in a lineup;[55] to provide voice exemplars so witnesses may make an identification of voice; to be fingerprinted; to pose for photographs not involving reenactments of the crime; to try on articles of clothing relevant to the case (such as a bloody glove or red bandana); to submit specimens of body fluids, material under the fingernails or in the hair, or any other materials from his or her body relevant to the case; to provide samples of handwriting; and to undergo tests the court deems reasonable and necessary. The aforesaid matters concern physical evidence, and, as such, are not protected by one's

Fifth Amendment right not to incriminate one's self. Self-incrimination has to do with speaking/admitting one's guilt, not with physical specimens—including the sound of one's voice.[56]

Also, the prosecution is entitled to know the defenses the defense intends to use, such as alibi, insanity, etc., along with the names and addresses of defense witnesses, written statements or anything else the defense intends to submit as evidence. Any evidence in favor of the alibi to be used, and whatever other information the court in its discretion allows the prosecution to seek can be ascertained as well.

As you can see, pretrial discovery practically eliminates any surprises at trial. This simplifies things, and the balance of information contributes to the plea-bargaining process. Realistically though, the discovery process favors the defense, as prosecutors are supposed to turn any exculpatory evidence (evidence which points to the defendant's innocence) over to the defense, while defendants do have Fifth Amendment rights not to incriminate themselves—unless they choose to waive those rights.[57]

Reasonable Doubt and the Presumption of Innocence

The criminal trial, bench or jury, demands the highest level of evidence to convict; that is, conviction only if guilt has been proved "beyond a reasonable doubt"—not *any* doubt, but any "reasonable" doubt. This is a much higher standard than the "probable cause" needed to indict or the "preponderance of evidence" used in deciding civil lawsuits, or even the "clear and convincing" proof required in some civil proceedings. While legally these aforesaid concepts are not defined with precision, it has been suggested that various levels of certainty be attached to them and other standards we have discussed. For example, del Carmen has classified "reasonable suspicion" as 20 percent certainty; both "probable cause" and a "preponderance of the evidence" as requiring more than 50 percent certainty; "clear and convincing evidence" as constituting at least 80 percent certainty; and to find someone "guilty beyond a reasonable doubt" at least 95 percent certainty would be required.[58]

Moreover, at trial our belief in the "presumption of innocence" reaches full flower. Until the trial, from arrest through charging, the criminal justice process moves along on an increasing belief in the *guilt* of the suspect. Police do not arrest, nor do grand juries indict, on a presumption of innocence. True, we place great value on the presumption of innocence, but it does not really come into play until the trial stage of our justice system. For at trial the entire burden is on the state—the prosecutor—to demonstrate beyond a reasonable doubt all the elements required to prove the accused's guilt: the mental state (*mens rea*, guilty state of mind/intent), the act (*actus reus*, or act designed to be criminal, such as shooting to inflict death), and the consequences of the act (deprivation of property or life, for instance).

Defendants may do or say nothing at trial, but this is rare. At a minimum, through their attorneys, they usually challenge the state's evidence by cross-examining witnesses and questioning the reliability of physical evidence such as blood analysis or ballistics tests. Additionally, defendants may enter a defense, for instance, insanity, to negate the required mental state for the crime, or may plead entrapment or a number of other defenses to negate any or all the arguments of the prosecution. Witnesses for the defense, including expert witnesses, may take the stand and, under oath and subject to cross-examination by the prosecutor, rebut some or all of the evidence of the state. This defense or these rebuttal witnesses need not prove innocence; they need merely raise a reasonable doubt about the defendant's guilt.

The Criminal Trial

The Sixth Amendment to the Constitution:

> In all criminal prosecutions, the accused shall enjoy the right to a speedy and public trial, by an impartial jury of the State and district wherein the crime shall have been committed, which district shall have been previously ascertained by law, and to be informed of the *nature* and *cause* of the accusation; to be confronted with the witnesses against him; to have compulsory process for obtaining witnesses in his favor, and to have the assistance of counsel for his defense.

Each provision of this amendment, as with the provisions of most of the constitutional amendments, has been litigated, interpreted, and refined over the years. And yet each provision remains controversial: for example, courts are still coping with such matters as what "speedy trial" means in practice, when and under what conditions the public (and the press) can be excluded from a trial, whether and why venue (location of the trial) can be changed, how witnesses may be compelled to testify and whether they must confront the accused in all cases, and how impartial juries can be found, among other issues. As with all constitutional phraseology, the Sixth Amendment sounds simple, but the complexity of situations that arise to test the meaning of each word is staggering. And the changing members and changing philosophies of succeeding Supreme Courts have indeed made the Constitution a dynamic rather than a static document.

In most places, defendants who plead not guilty to felony charges can opt for either a jury or a bench trial, the latter meaning the judge acts alone as the fact finder. In general, jury trials in felony cases can be waived if both the defendant and the defense counsel agree. In some states, the prosecutor must consent to such a waiver.[59] In the federal system, with consent of the prosecution and the court, a defendant's request to waive a jury trial may be granted.[60]

Bench Trials

In *most* cases, a defendant can request to stand trial before a judge sitting alone. This is a bench trial for the word "bench" is commonly used as a synonym for "court" or "judge." Generally, jury trials are waived by defendants as a *tactical matter* in cases involving highly technical legal issues. The judge, being a lawyer, understands and is accustomed to considering fine and subtle points of law, whereas jurors are "civilians" and may not fully understand important legal matters in a technical defense. Bench trials tend to proceed much faster than jury trials.

Jury trials are eagerly sought in cases that have intense emotional overtones, where the outcome is more likely to rest on jury sympathies than on fine points of the law. For instance, a defendant accused of a complex fraud or charged with a conspiracy to commit a crime may choose a bench trial because of the legal complexities involved in proving such crimes. On the other hand, a defendant charged with the homicide of a fatally ill relative who wishes to enter a defense of "mercy killing" may perhaps prefer to be tried by a jury of peers who may be sympathetic to the personal overtones of the case.

Sometimes defense attorneys hope to have cases decided on the basis of factors outside the evidence or the law. This is referred to as "jury nullification"—whereby the defense may seek to put the police on trial or challenge the legitimacy of the law their client is accused of violating, for example, diverting attention from the defendant.[61] Waiver of jury trial is often believed to be advantageous to a defendant when (1) the case has been the subject of a great deal of adverse publicity, (2) a highly technical defense will be utilized, or (3) it is believed that jurors are likely to be unsympathetic to the defense.

Contrary to the specific language of the Sixth Amendment above, while the right to a jury trial in felony cases is absolute, in cases where a lesser offense is charged jury trials are not always available. The U.S. Supreme Court in *Baldwin v. New York* (1970) held that the right to a jury trial exists for those offenses in which greater than six months of incarceration is mandated by statute.[62] In 1989, in *Blanton v. North Las Vegas*, the Court reiterated that "petty offenses," those offenses that carried the potential for six months or less imprisonment, are not accompanied by the right to trial by jury.[63] In 1996, in *Lewis v. United States*, the Court ruled that if an individual was facing prosecution for more than one petty offense simultaneously, which when potential penalties were added would equal to more than six months imprisonment, defendants in such circumstances do not have the right to a jury trial.[64] Petty offenses include the least severely punished misdemeanors and ordinance violations. These offenses include such acts as public intoxication, disorderly conduct, other public-order crimes, and minor traffic violations. Of course, what falls under the specific designation of petty offense varies from one set of statutes and one jurisdiction to the next.

A defendant has no constitutional right to receive a bench trial from a judge.[65] Also, the U.S. Supreme Court has ruled that it is reasonable for decisions regarding defense waiver of jury trials to be conditioned on the approval of both the prosecutor and the judge.[66]

In some states, the trial judge is required to file a memorandum in support of the finding of guilt after a bench trial. In contrast, juries do *not* give reasons for their findings of guilt or innocence. A jury decision to convict, however, may be *set aside* by the trial judge if the judge believes trial evidence failed to meet the "beyond a reasonable doubt" test. Occasionally the judge may issue a judgment of acquittal, sometimes called a "JOA" or a "directed verdict," without waiting for a jury finding.[67] But it is more common for a judge who is convinced the evidence is insufficient to *convict* to wait for the jury decision and to overrule the conviction, if such is the decision, than to order an acquittal beforehand. After all, the jury might not convict, meaning no judicial action would be necessary. Both the directed verdict and the setting aside of a conviction put a judge at odds with the jury and, like the prosecution, judges are political figures who try to avoid conflict and criticism. Post-verdict motions are filed by the defense prior to sentencing and most commonly come in the form of motions for a new trial. They are rarely granted.[68]

The judge's power to overrule the jury is one-directional only. No matter how convinced the judge is that a defendant is guilty, the judge *cannot* order a jury to convict, nor can the judge set aside an acquittal. The presumption of innocence is no longer just a presumption if either the jury or the judge so finds. And a finding of innocence cannot be overturned; only a conviction can be reversed by judicial action. The fact remains, however, that most jury trials (3 out of 4) result in the conviction of the accused for some offense, even if not the one charged.[69]

Speedy Trial

The "time to trial" is the time that elapses between the arrest of a suspect and the commencement of the trial, which, in our system of justice, must be "speedy." The time does not begin to accrue until an arrest has been made. Thus a suspect who has fled and cannot be located can hardly claim denial of a speedy trial when caught later and eventually tried.

Speedy trial provisions generally do not apply to absconders but to defendants already under arrest. Today, with the courts in many jurisdictions crowded, the time between arrest and trial is often very long even when both sides, state and defense, wish to get on with the process. The court calendar problem is such that trial justice is routine but slow. This remains a major problem for our criminal justice system, particularly in crowded metropolitan court districts. Speedy trial provisions, found today in most state statutes, seek to prevent undue delay in bringing cases to court and to prevent persons from being held for extended periods of time in custody awaiting final judgment.

Delaying a trial has advantages and disadvantages for both sides in criminal litigation. The state can continue to accumulate evidence and, in cases in which the defendant is being held in jail, can in effect punish the accused before trial by extending pretrial custody. The defense, on the other hand, might want a delay so that publicity about the crime cools down and witnesses' memories fade. In general, the intensity of feeling a case generates diminishes by the time of sentencing. Indeed, defendants' requests for continuances pose a major problem not solved by speedy trial statutory provisions, which generally relate only to the state's readiness to proceed. But a clever defendant, reluctant to go to trial, and free on pretrial release, can extend the time to trial considerably by seeking adjournments, or by changing lawyers, or by introducing multiple pretrial motions to change venue, exclude evidence, and so on. Delay is often an important defense tactic and a difficult one to control, for the court faces problems if it forces to trial a defendant who claims not to be prepared to be tried for a serious crime. In such cases, justice delayed may be justice denied for the victim of the crime.

The various court decisions and statutory speedy trial acts are designed primarily to force the *state* not to delay trials without good reason. In *Barker v. Wingo* (1972),[70] the U.S. Supreme Court outlined a four-prong balancing test to determine if a delay is unwarranted. These factors include the length of the delay, the reasons for it, the amount of prejudice to the defendant created by the delay, and the defendant's request for a speedy trial. In this particular case, Barker's trial was delayed for five years on various governmental requests for continuances before he was eventually tried, convicted, and given a life sentence. Interestingly, the Court held that Barker was *not* deprived of a speedy trial, thereby rejecting the doctrine of a "fixed-time rule" (i.e., "Trial must occur within 60 days"), stating instead that the speedy trial issue must be decided on a case-by-case basis.

Doggett v. United States (1992)[71]

Doggett was indicted on federal drug charges in 1980, but he left the country before the DEA could arrest him. Two years later, he returned to the United States and lived a law-abiding life openly under his own name, got married, earned a college degree, and found steady employment. A routine credit check resulted in his discovery for an outstanding warrant, and he was arrested in 1988, eight and one-half years after his original indictment. He objected to his prosecution, saying his right to a speedy trial had been violated. The Supreme Court agreed, ruling that the government was to blame for the extraordinary lag of time between indictment and arrest. The Court concluded that the government had been negligent in pursuing Doggett and determined that he had not known about the 1980 indictment until his arrest. Similarly, some state statutory schemes, such as those seen in Florida, would wind up with the same result but would base it on a violation of the statute of limitations. See the next section of this chapter.

The federal judicial system requires an indictment or information within 30 days of arrest, arraignment within 10 days of formal charging, and trial within 60 days of arraignment. These strictures apply to government prosecutors, but the times can be extended, as mentioned, by defense requests for continuances and delays. All 50 state constitutions provide a right to a speedy trial separate from the Sixth Amendment.[72]

Statutes of Limitations

One factor not yet mentioned that affects whether or not a trial takes place at all is statutes of limitations on the time allowed for the prosecution of certain crimes. The purpose of such restrictions is to promote fairness and protect persons from having to defend themselves against charges when time may have eroded facts and evidence that might be of assistance in their defense. Secondly, such limitations promote efficiency by encouraging government agents to promptly investigate crimes.[73]

Statutes of limitations place limits on the length of time police have to arrest a suspect and prosecutors have to bring him or her to trial, and the time begins with the commission of the offense. The federal Congress announced the criminal statute of limitations in 1790. Initially, the rule required that an indictment had to be made within two years of the commission of most offenses. In 1876, the time frame was extended from two years to three, and in 1954 from three to five years, which is the current statute of limitations for most federal offenses.

For very serious felonies—murder, for instance—there are *no* statutory limits, so that a killer who escapes detection for decades can still be tried when caught, no matter how old the evidence or how forgetful the witnesses. The federal government has also lifted limits for various acts of terrorism and physical or sexual abuse or kidnapping of a child. All states, except for South Carolina and Wyoming, have statutes of limitations.[74] Limitations vary from state to state, but typically misdemeanors must be prosecuted within twelve months and, as noted earlier, murder can always be prosecuted.[75] See No Limits to Prosecuting Murder Box below.

No Limits to Prosecuting Murder

In 1963 Medgar Evers, a prominent African American civil rights leader and secretary to the National Association for the Advancement of Colored People (NAACP), was murdered in Mississippi. His murder galvanized support for the enactment of civil rights laws. Byron De La Beckwith was charged for the homicide, and two juries were unable to reach a verdict. Then, in February 1994, after extended litigation and a lapse of more than thirty years since the murder, a Mississippi jury found Beckwith guilty of the murder of Medgar Evers.[76]

Jury Selection

Historically, trial juries have been composed of 12 members, but this is not a constitutional requirement. In *Williams v. Florida* (1970) the U.S. Supreme Court held that it was proper for states to use juries of as few as six persons in felony cases except in cases involving the death penalty.[77] Six-member juries are common in misdemeanor trials, with just over ten states requiring 12-person juries at that level. The majority of states and the federal government require 12-person juries in felony cases. Arizona and Utah actually use 8-person juries, and Connecticut and Florida use 6-person juries in their trial courts for non-capital felonies.[78]

Jury members are ordinarily selected by lot or chance from a master list of persons in the community where the trial will take place. This master list is known as the *venire* and is gleaned from such sources as local voter registration rolls, driver's license registrations, telephone directories, taxpayer registries, lists of utility customers, and/or motor vehicle owners. Whether this really gives a representative cross section of the community is debatable. People are not required to register to vote for example and may not own a car or a telephone. Thus, it is hoped that by relying on more than one source for prospective juror names the chances of achieving representativeness will be enhanced.

Only American citizens are allowed to serve, particularly if the list is drawn from registered voters. The elderly may be excluded, minors are ineligible for jury service, and those with felony convictions (unless they have had their rights restored, as discussed in Chapter 11) may not serve.[79] For example, the state of Mississippi requires persons considered as a prospective juror to be at least 21 years old and a registered voter or to have owned land in the county for at least one year. An individual convicted of an "infamous crime" (felony) cannot serve on a jury there, nor can anyone convicted of bootlegging in the past five years. Furthermore, Mississippi forbids those who are illiterate, "habitual drunkards," and "common gamblers" from serving on juries.[80]

Opportunities for submitting requests to be excused from jury service are available. Such excuses may include those with signed doctors' statements regarding serious physical or mental illnesses, those who are unable to provide child care and those who may suffer economic hardship as the result of jury service. Also, those who are members of essential occupations who cannot take the time to serve, such as firefighters, police officers, physicians, nurses, legislators, clergymen, and in many places attorneys, teachers, and professors may be excused as well. In general, the assembler of the eligible jury list (clerk of the court or jury commissioner) is lenient in excusing jurors unless there is a compelling need for a large jury panel.

An historic concern of jury selection has been the systematic exclusion of African Americans and other minorities from jury duty. And in the civil rights efforts of recent decades, appellate courts have often attempted to eliminate patterned discrimination in jury composition. Indeed, one of the results of increased voter registration for African Americans and other minority citizens has been that these groups have gained increased representation on jury selection lists. This, of course, is not the major purpose of voter registration—which is to give minorities a political voice—but it is an important side product.

Voir Dire

Once a panel of potential jurors willing and able to serve has been selected, some may still be excused from a particular case upon the request of the prosecutor or the defense counsel. These exclusions can take one of two forms: peremptory challenge and challenge for cause. A peremptory challenge is the informal dismissal of a potential juror upon the whim or trial sense of the prosecutor or defense lawyer; no explanation need be given or any cause demonstrated. Statutes or court rules usually limit the number of **peremptory challenges** allowed. Typically, the more serious the offense the more peremptory challenges that are allowed, and, in some instances, states may authorize the defense to have more of these challenges at their disposal than the prosecution.[81] As for challenges for cause, the prosecutor or defense attorney must prove to the judge that there is some factor in the potential juror's background or attitudes likely to bias his or her decision in the case, upon which basis the judge then grants or denies a dismissal of that prospective juror.

Peremptory challenges and removals for cause are both normally based on potential jurors' responses to *voir dire* questioning. For example, a prospective juror who is an avowed member of the Ku Klux Klan would likely be stricken from sitting in judgment of an African American defendant upon a challenge for cause being entered by the defense.

The *voir dire* ("to speak the truth") examination allows attorneys for both sides to question each potential juror in order to decide whether that person is suitable for the case from a prosecution or defense point of view. In general, *voir dire* focuses on the juror's previous familiarity with the case; his or her association with anyone involved in the case; his or her attitudes toward certain types of crimes, people, and punishments; any preconceived ideas about the guilt or innocence of the defendant; and any similar matters likely to affect the juror's eventual decision in the case.

In theory, the purpose of *voir dire* is to ascertain if a potential juror can render a fair and impartial verdict. In practice, neither peremptory nor for-cause jury exclusions based on the *voir dire* examinations are really designed to obtain an impartial jury. Both sides use both forms of exclusion tactically in attempts to build a jury favorable to the sides of the case the attorneys represent. Attorneys may have their own idiosyncrasies about what types of jurors will best serve their respective sides in a particular trial. For example, while generalities, the very affluent, professors, and social workers have been categorized as pro-defense, and bankers, school teachers, and career military personnel have been classified as pro-prosecution.[82] Continuing legal education courses are offered on how to select the right jury.[83] Of course, many high-profile trials include the employ of jury consultants (much like the O.J. Simpson murder trial discussed at the beginning of this chapter) who possess scientific and psychological backgrounds and often administer questionnaires to prospective jurors in an attempt to analyze them and achieve the best outcome for their respective sides.[84] It is hoped within this competitive process to select the jury that the make-up of the jury will be balanced out.

Unlike peremptory challenges, there is no limit to removals for cause. This is why jury selection may take so long and involve such a large pool of potential jurors in cases that have received a great deal of local publicity. If a crime has been heinous and the defendant is notorious, finding twelve local citizens who can be truly impartial in hearing the case may be difficult.

It remains a question whether the use of peremptory and for-cause challenges negates the formation of representative juries. There have been several interesting decisions on this point from the U.S. Supreme Court. In *Swain v. Alabama* (1965)[85] the court *upheld* the practice of using peremptory challenges to exclude jurors for reasons of race. However, in *Batson v. Kentucky* (1986)[86] the Court held that African Americans may *not* be excluded from a jury because the prosecutor believes they *may* favor a defendant of their own race. The Court held in *Batson* that:

1. The equal protection clause forbids a prosecutor to peremptorily challenge potential jurors solely on account of their race or on the assumption that black jurors as a group will be unable to impartially consider the prosecution's case against a black defendant.
2. A criminal defendant may establish a *prima facie* (on its face, or at first glance) case of purposeful racial discrimination in the selection of the jury based solely on evidence concerning the prosecutor's exercise of peremptory challenges at the defendant's trial, without showing repeated instances of such discriminatory conduct over a number of cases.
3. Once a defendant makes such a *prima facie* showing, the burden shifts to the prosecution to come forward with a neutral explanation for challenging the jurors which relates to the particular case being tried.

Although this decision effectively overturned *Swain*, the Court did not hold that it should be applied retroactively. The Court also ruled in *Powers v. Ohio* (1991) that under the Equal Protection Clause, a criminal defendant may object to race-based exclusions of jurors through peremptory challenges whether or not the defendant and the excluded jurors share the same race.[87] Furthermore, in 1994, in *J.E.B. v. Alabama*, the U.S. Supreme Court held that females cannot be discriminated against in the jury selection process and cannot as a group be assumed to be biased in a particular case.[88]

Jury selection has always been a controversial problem. In the colonial period, for example, when the United States was a country of towns and villages, selecting a jury of peers, "equals" in the common meaning of this term, could not be achieved, for major segments of the population, including women and slaves, were excluded from jury duty.

Stages in the Criminal Trial

After a jury has been selected and seated, the trial begins with an opening statement by the prosecutor, which is an attempt to tell the jury what crime the defendant is charged with and how all the necessary elements proving guilt will be demonstrated. (In bench trials, judges may dispense of the use of opening arguments and even closing statements that may be geared to laypersons.[89]) The defense may then make its own opening statement and often does so if the defense attorney feels the opening statement of the prosecutor was particularly harmful to the defense case. However, the opening statement of the defense may be deferred until it presents its own evidence.

Upon completion of the opening statement, the prosecutor presents his or her evidence—physical evidence such as fingerprints; testimonial evidence of witnesses or experts as to how, when, and where the physical evidence was obtained; eyewitness evidence; and any *circumstantial* evidence (i.e., any evidence from which a fact can be reasonably inferred—the defendant being seen with a gun near the scene of a shooting, for example). This is done through direct examination or questioning of states' witnesses.

After each witness for the prosecution has testified, the defense counsel may carry out a cross-examination in an attempt to cast some reasonable doubt on the evidence by questioning the manner in which the evidence was obtained or analyzed, or by questioning a witness's memory, or by showing inconsistencies in testimony, or perhaps by challenging the credibility or expertise of the witness. Cross-examination can also be used to attempt to extract favorable information as well. The prosecution then is allowed to question the witness again on redirect examination in order to give the witness an opportunity to clarify any issues raised in the cross-examination. Then this may be followed by a *re-cross* examination, that is, the defense counsel may again put questions to the witness based on redirect testimony.

After all the prosecutor's witnesses have presented their evidence and been cross-examined, and after the prosecution has presented all its other evidence the state *rests its case.* At this point the defense almost always moves for a directed verdict of acquittal in order to give the trial judge an opportunity to dismiss the case for lack of sufficient evidence. The motion for judgment of acquittal must be done to preserve appellate rights. This is primarily a tactical move, however, and the motion to acquit is routinely denied.

The American system of justice requires that each defendant, despite the evidence indicating guilt, be given their day in court to confront accusers and put forth a strong defense. Our system does not require a defense, actually, but rather that the prosecution (the state) proves beyond a reasonable doubt in the eyes of a jury that the defendant is guilty. Typically though, if a trial is taking place, the defendant, through his or her attorney, then introduces witnesses or other evidence that favor the defendant's claim of being not guilty. The defense may begin with an opening statement by counsel but is not required to do so. Normally, defense witnesses are sworn in and subjected to direct examination by the defense lawyers, then cross-examination by the prosecutor. After all the defense witnesses have been examined, cross-examined, and examined again on redirect, the defense rests its case. There may be some further witnesses called by both sides, in order, and cross-examined in a process called rebuttal. Rebuttal witnesses dispute the testimony of the defendant's witnesses. Then the defendant's rebuttal witnesses may be called to dispute the testimony of the prosecution's rebuttal witnesses. After the final cross-examination, the evidence phase of the trial is finally concluded. At the close of the defendant's case, or even if the defense doesn't present one, the judgment of acquittal motion is usually renewed to preserve appellate rights.

Usually at this point a recess is taken in the proceedings to allow the judge to prepare instructions to the jury. A conference is often held in the judge's chambers, and the attorneys for each side submit proposed instructions for the jury. The judge decides what the instructions will be and informs the attorneys, after which the attorneys will make sure the evidence presented at trial conforms with what they expected.[90]

Following this, first the defense and then the prosecution sum up by making closing statements. The defense tries to cast doubt on the prosecutor's evidence, or some of it, and the prosecutor—allowed the last word because the entire burden of proof is on the state—tries to show how the evidence introduced proves the defendant guilty "beyond a reasonable doubt."

After the closing statements, the judge charges the jury,[91] instructing them in the applicable points of the law, in the nature and meaning of evidence they have seen or heard, and about the meaning of "reasonable doubt." The jury then retires to another location to deliberate the guilt or innocence of the accused. If agreement among jury members is reached, they return to the courtroom and notify the judge of their decision, the verdict. The defendant then is asked to stand to hear the verdict of the jury. If the verdict is guilty, the judge sets a time for sentencing, usually some date in the future, which may allow time for a presentence investigation if one is to be performed.

If unanimity is required for a verdict and, after an extended period of time for deliberation, jury members find they cannot achieve such a consensus, they report their dilemma to the court. The judge then may suggest strongly that the jury deliberate further or may instead conclude that they are a "hung jury," one that cannot reach a unanimous decision (or sufficient majority with those juries not requiring unanimity) about guilt or innocence. If the jury cannot reach a verdict, the judge declares a mistrial. If this happens, the defendant may be tried for the same crime again before a different jury without the Fifth Amendment prohibition against double jeopardy applying.

Normally, after the verdict is announced, the judge dismisses the jury. Judges often use this occasion as an opportunity to thank the jurors for the important service they have rendered and to make a brief speech about the American system of justice. Remember, most judges do not have life tenure and are concerned about remaining on the bench.

Appeals and Postconviction Remedies

The appeal of criminal convictions in U.S. jurisdictions must be requested by the convicted defendant (now an offender) and granted at the discretion of the higher court.[92] Exceptions include the military system of justice, which provides for automatic appeals, a few states where a first appeal is a matter of right, or death penalty verdicts, which automatically trigger appeals. Appeals by the defendant must be instituted within a specified time after conviction, although for good cause appellate courts in some jurisdictions may extend this period.

Generally, there are two classes of appellate review sought by defendants. The first involves *appeal of conviction* by trial, including appeal of denial of pretrial motions to suppress certain evidence. Usually appeals of guilty plea convictions are not permitted because a guilty plea waives this right.[93] The second class involves *challenge of the conditions of custody*; this follows conviction and is referred to as post-conviction relief.

Appeals of convictions proceed in various ways, with a few jurisdictions requiring approval by the trial court first. But more commonly they proceed by a writ of error (requiring the appellate court to review the trial court or arrest record for errors) or other writs submitted to the appropriate appellate court. Appeal of custody is commonly initiated by a writ of *habeas corpus* (literally "you have the body," that is, the person in custody must be presented by agents of the sheriff or warden to the court to demonstrate just cause for holding the person).[94]

Appeals and other post-conviction remedies are usually decided on the basis of relevant records and briefs, including written presentations of arguments. Frequently appellate arguments are presented orally before the appellate court by counsel with the petitioner not physically present. This is an expensive process beyond the means of most petitioners. However, a series of U.S. Supreme Court cases has substantially expanded the right of poor petitioners to obtain court transcripts and the assistance of counsel at state expense, at least on first appeal.[95] In effect, under these decisions, if the state allows an appeal, then an indigent defendant has the right to free counsel for this purpose, and the transcripts are provided without cost. (However, it should be noted that the Prisoner Litigation Reform Act was passed by Congress in an attempt to thwart the clogging of courts with frivolous lawsuits.[96]) In addition, public defenders frequently pursue appeals available to their clients as well. Should a defendant prevail on an appeal and have their conviction overturned that does not necessarily mean that they cannot be retried. Oftentimes a higher court will reverse a lower court's decision and remand the case to the lower court to proceed in a manner consistent with the higher court's interpretation of the case. When this happens, this does not constitute double jeopardy; the defendant can be retried.

Some states also allow appeals by the prosecution, under certain restricted conditions. The state cannot appeal a trial court finding of not guilty, because the defendant is protected from retrial by constitutional prohibitions against double jeopardy. But a few states allow rather broad but "moot" prosecution appeals. These have the possible effect of settling a legal controversy raised by the case but result in no consequences for the individual defendant.[97] Usually such appeals deal with (1) dismissal of charges, indictments, informations, or any count thereof; (2) suppression of evidence before trial, including confessions, admissions, and evidence obtained by search and seizure; (3) an award of a new trial by the court; (4) an illegal sentence; or (5) discharge of the defendant on speedy trial grounds.

Serving Justice: Prince or Pauper

Circuit Court Judge Marc L. Lubet's assessment of Lisa Marie Nowak's motions to suppress:

In this case, Detective Becton made numerous statements and employed various techniques in order to obtain Defendant's admissions and consent.

Many of these statements and techniques were legally impermissible. He made direct and implied promises of benefit: "What you say can change what you're charged with, okay?"; "I can step up to the plate and speak up for you"; "And if you need help, you know, why that? Let's face it ... everybody needs help at some point in their life and you can't always do everything by yourself"; "I'm trying to give you the ability to try and make some good out of what happened"; "We can minimize the impact of what occurred" but "it depends on how honest you're gonna' be with me and what you tell me"; "I cannot help you control damage unless I know what's going on"; "If you want to tell me what's going on I might be able to help you considerably"; "I'm trying to help you out"; "I might be able to help you control some of the damage that's been done"; "We need to get her (Defendant) some help, whether it be counseling, whether it be whatever"; "Lisa's a stone cold criminal ... nothing more than a street thug ... if you tell me what's going on for me to sit here and say, 'You know what, Lisa is not a street thug' "; "Let me paint this picture, you and I start talking, we start sharing information.... I'm able, you're gonna' go to jail, I can't prevent that ... could be anywhere from 72 hours to 8 hours ... ; if you tell me what I think is the problem, okay, we have some red flags here Lisa needs some help"; "Well, again it depends on what you tell me.... Best case scenario we get into some counseling"; "I've been lending a hand out to help you, but you don't want to take it"; ..."I see some issues with you personally that I think can be taken care of, that will help make things better for you. And I will be more than happy to recommend to the State Attorney's office.... I think that, that will make all the difference in the world, in a positive way"; and "I'm going to highly recommend you get counseling." He made threats and used coercive psychological techniques: "Well, what you say can change what you're charged with ... right not we're looking at possible life felony of carjacking"; "I can't make you any promises right now"; ..."if you're not gonna' tell me why you're here tonight, then you're kind of on your own"; "if your children needed you like my daughter needed me this morning, you're not gonna' be there for them"; "You're gonna' either tell me where your car is or I'm gonna' go call KSC security and I'll find out where your car is and I'll tell them why I'm looking for your car"; "You're wasting my time and you're insulting my intelligence"; "Right now, as far as I'm concerned, Lisa's a stone cold criminal, she could care less.... She's nothing more than a street thug"; "But without knowing what's going on, she'll get back to just being a regular street thug"; "Then I'll go get a search warrant for your car and I'll search your car anyways"; and "I'll find out where your car is, I'll get the search warrant and I'll tow it." Additionally, Defendant was subjected to a barrage of questions during predawn hours and not given an opportunity to sleep or use a telephone. Although she was given the opportunity to use the restroom and was asked if she would like something to eat, she was questioned for six hours with Detective Becton using the various techniques set forth above and the Defendant had not slept during the preceding 24 hours. Finally, the audio recording of the interview reveals that Detective Becton's tone at various times throughout the interview became aggressive. Thus, based on the totality of the circumstances, this Court concludes Defendant's admissions were involuntarily made.

Generally, the State had the burden to show that consent to search was voluntary by a preponderance of the evidence. *Reynolds v. State*, 592 So. 2nd 1082 (Fla. 1992). However, if the consent follows illegal police activity, such as prolonged detention, threats to obtain a warrant, or repeated requests for consent, the State's burden is elevated to a clear and convincing standard. *Id.*; *see also Gonterman v. State*, 358 So. 2nd 595, 596 (Fla. 1st DCA 1978) (listing "repeated request for the consent" as an example of inappropriate conduct by the police seeking consent to search).

Because the facts of this case clearly demonstrate that the Defendant's consent following illegal police activity, such as a prolonged detention, threats to obtain a warrant and repeated requests for consent, this Court finds the State's burden is a clear and convincing standard. However, even if the State's burden was a preponderance of the evidence, this Court still could not find that the Defendant's consent was voluntary based upon the totality of the circumstances.

As set forth above, Defendant did not knowingly and intelligently waive her *Miranda* rights and her statements were involuntarily made under the totality of the circumstances.

It is incumbent upon this Court that every citizen, whether a prince or pauper, be treated equally. In each and every case, this Court must ensure that the constitutional protections afforded by our forefathers are scrupulously honored. Unfortunately, in this case these protections were not followed as the law demands. Therefore, this Court having weighed the credibility of the witnesses and having considered the totality of the circumstances finds the Defendant's admissions obtained by Detective Becton and the evidence obtained from the search of her vehicle must be suppressed. The totality of the circumstances examined by this Court in reaching this decision include Detective Becton's failure to answer Defendant's questions concerning a lawyer in a simple and straightforward manner; Detective Becton's minimization of the *Miranda* warnings; Detective Becton's request that Defendant speak to him prior to advising her of her *Miranda* warnings; the location of the interrogation; no phone calls being permitted by Defendant; no written waiver of *Miranda* being obtained; no written consent to search being obtained; Defendant's emotional and physical condition; the length of time Defendant was detained and interrogated; the promises of benefit made to Defendant; and the threats utilized against Defendant.[98]

As part of a plea bargain Nowak pled guilty to felony burglary of an automobile and misdemeanor battery, avoiding prison. Her plea deal required

her to be under probation supervision for a year, complete an anger-management class, and 50 hours of community service. She also was ordered to write a sincere letter of apology to Ms. Shipman and to have no further contact with her. Nowak's attorney, Donald Lykkebak, maintained that his client was treated just like any other first offender.[99]

Check out defense attorney Lykkebak's website at http://donaldlykkebak.com. Do you think Mr. Lykkebak was right? Was she treated just like any other first offender? Would a pauper have fared as well as a prince or an astronaut in this case? Did the astronaut not understand her right not to talk to the police? Did she involuntarily make admissions? Do you believe the search of her vehicle was legally justified? Explain your answers.

Summary

If a trial results in a "not guilty" verdict, the defendant is released from custody and the case is over. But if the defendant is found guilty, the matter is far from over. A sentence must be imposed. Chapter 10 introduces and describes the process of imposing sentences. Various types of sentences, both custodial and non-custodial, are examined, as well as the multi-faceted, sometimes contradictory, goals of sentencing.

Chapter 10

Sentencing Criminals: Prison or Probation, Life or Death

Image by dcdebs at istockphoto.com.

"I sentence you to be a chicken."

—Judge Michael Cicconetti[1]

Seeking Justice

Political debates over sentencing policies are often more emotional than rational. After the court has determined that the accused has broken the law, a punishment must be meted out. Even when the guilt question is settled, the more difficult question to answer is "What should be done about it?"

Decisions regarding sentencing convicted offenders are perhaps the most difficult that judges face. Judges make other important decisions, but most of them are pretty well constrained by law. In the area of sentencing, though, judges may often, if not constrained by sentencing guidelines or other legislative mandates, exercise considerable discretion based on their own philosophy of sentencing and personal attitudes toward the offenders or the offenses. What are the myriad purposes, or goals, of sentencing? How is sentencing influenced by community attitudes, shifts in penal practice, formal recommendations by professional groups such as the American Bar Association, and the law? What information is available to a judge to assist in the sentencing decision?

If you were a judge, charged with the responsibility of regularly deciding which offenders go to prison and which go home, who gets 6 years and who gets 15, what information would you seek to guide you about whether to be lenient or harsh? On what basis would you select sentence options? How can consistency and uniformity in sentencing be realized? Criminal sentences can take a number of forms, including fines, probation, and incarceration in jail or prison. And, of course, the death penalty is available in most states. So for people who make the sentencing decisions, the manner in which sentences should be determined poses an important area of great interest. Again, the conflicting views of the conservative and liberal crime control models are evident.

About This Chapter

This chapter examines the goals of criminal sentences, how sentences are imposed, who really makes the sentencing decision, how sentencing guidelines influence sentences, the role of the presentence investigation, sentencing options, and the involvement of judges in sentencing. Included within this assessment is an examination of the ultimate punishment in America—death.

Goals of Criminal Sentences

All sentences from the smallest fine to the longest prison term have a number of goals.[2] The basis for these goals lies deep in the philosophy underlying our criminal justice network. We want our criminal justice process to accomplish something, to achieve some social utility beyond merely solving crimes and catching criminals. We want to reduce the crime rate by stopping the criminal activities of apprehended offenders and deterring others from committing crimes. Sentencing is designed to attempt to achieve a number of certain goals, some of which may not always be compatible.

To Control and Prevent Crime

Whether short-range or long-range, the overall objectives of criminal justice fall into two general sets of purposes: the **control of crime** by solving crimes, arresting suspects, and processing and imprisoning offenders, and the **prevention of crime** through this processing or by other means. The crime control objective deals with the immediate situation and rests on the discovery of *past* criminal behavior, whereas crime prevention is *forward-looking*, forecasting and forestalling future crimes by present interventions.

To Punish Criminals

The **punitive ideal**, though among the most ancient approaches to crime control, is still a force of major significance. To some punishment is an end in itself, consistent with our moral support for an eye-for-an-eye concept of justice. But the punishment aspects of our crime control efforts are also designed to compel conformity by hurting violators, using pain to teach them to be good. The application of punishment to law violators *in proportion to the seriousness of their offenses* is the cornerstone of criminal codes and sentencing structures.

To Deter Criminals

Punishment is also intended to *deter potential violators*, to frighten them off, by demonstrating that crime does not pay. It is widely believed that permanent prevention of crime, if attainable at all, will require a basic modification of cultural values, the revision of opportunity structures, the reorganization of social class structures, and the elimination of economic imbalance. Personnel in criminal justice agencies generally see their preventive task in more modest terms. For the most part, *prevention* in the crime control context means short-range **deterrence** of potential violators.

Whether deterrence is actually possible is debatable. How many people would commit crimes if they were not deterred is not known and is not easily measured. **Absolute deterrence** occurs when crime is prevented or suppressed simply because there is a law against a particular act.[3] The law prevents some people from smoking marijuana, for instance, and many would perhaps choose to smoke it if it were legalized.

Certain offenses may be deterred: those that are planned, rational offenses where the chances of getting caught are immediate and certain. For example, posting a police officer near an apple barrel is likely to reduce the number of apples stolen. However, some acts of murder, child molestation, or other crimes of passion are difficult, perhaps impossible, to deter.

Deterrence involves two major approaches. The first is based on creating a belief in the certainty of criminal justice processing and the hope that the severity of official reactions when offenders are caught will deter other people from initiating criminal activities. Punishing the specific individual offender to prevent that individual offender from committing crime in the future is known as **specific deterrence.**[4] The death penalty would be the best example of specific deterrence. Because we know if we execute someone that individual will not return to commit another crime. **General deterrence**, on the other hand, sends a message to the general public: if you do this crime, this punishment will happen to you. This involves making an example out of perpetrators by punishing them in an attempt to deter others.

Deterrence requires the criminal justice system to appear *omnipresent*, its agents *visible*, arrest *certain*, and justice *swift*. Courts should appear somber and dignified, with a raised bench and the judges robed in black, indicating seriousness of purpose in court proceedings. Prisons too should look like prisons to those on the outside as well as to those incarcerated. The wall and the gun turrets of the maximum-security prison have dual functions: to control the inmates within and to demonstrate the severe price of crime to potential offenders on the outside.

Whenever decisions about a suspect, defendant, or offender are partly based on considerations of the likely effects on others, including the "public," the general deterrent function is being served. To make examples of those caught and proven guilty is widely believed to be effective in deterring others from the commission of crime. This is the basic argument of those favoring severe sentences, including the death penalty.

A fourth type of deterrence is known as **informal deterrence**. This type of deterrence involves extra-legal variables, factors outside of the criminal justice system that operate to keep persons in line. The pioneering work of **Travis Hirschi** on his social control theory identifies these forces. The family, schools, neighborhoods, religion, extracurricular activities (athletics, scouting, band, etc.), and career aspirations can serve as a means outside the justice system to keep persons bonded to conventional society and deter them from committing crime.[5] Typically, by the time a matter reaches a judge for sentencing, informal deterrence has broken down.

To Protect the Community

The criminal justice process is expected to protect the community from continued depredations by criminals. To accomplish this, authorities are permitted to take physical custody of suspects and offenders and to restrain them, subject to legislative and court limitations and controls. The ultimate power of restraint is symbolized by incarceration of convicted felons, the **restraint** and **incapacitation** of offenders to protect the community, an objective that most prisons achieve very well indeed.

Restraint for community protection is an important function from the very outset of the process. High bail and preventive detention reflect the community protection function. It may also be seen at the charging decision. Certainly, community protection is a consideration in plea negotiation. Sentencing alternatives directly reflect this function, and it is a major factor in determining probation conditions, prison program and housing assignments, selection for parole, and parole revocation. The entire correctional process rests always on a balance between the needs and desires of the offender and concerns for community protection, even in systems giving high priority to rehabilitative programs.

To Correct or Rehabilitate Criminals

Many persons who are convicted and sentenced will eventually return to the community. Thus, offenders should learn to live law-abiding lives once they are discharged from correctional custody. Progressive agencies attempt to provide positive programs designed to rehabilitate prison inmates by changing their attitudes and teaching them new vocational skills. Upon the offender's release, they also work to reintegrate offenders by assisting them to adjust to normal community living.

The discretion of the prosecutor to charge a defendant in court or to divert and not charge at all may be exercised with corrective purposes in mind. A basic motivation in plea negotiation is to individualize the consequences of conviction. And a trial itself may have corrective relevance. An opportunity to be heard, a day in court, a fair hearing have purposes beyond fact finding, perhaps acting to dispel cynicism and the belief in "railroading" not uncommonly expressed by offenders hurried through a guilty plea at a brief arraignment. Sentencing discretion is often delegated to courts in the expectation that the judge's choice will not only satisfy the punitive ideal but serve a corrective function as well.

The corrective function ties together the discrete stages of the criminal justice process. From the perspective of this function, it can be seen that decisions made at one point have relevance elsewhere and that overall functions are ultimately served by the degree of congruence of all decisions.

Restoring Justice via the Principles of Therapeutic Jurisprudence

Criminal justice tends to look backward to the time of an act, finding fault, assessing blame, and punishing. Therapeutic jurisprudence takes a different tack and is forward looking. **Therapeutic Jurisprudence** is concerned with the consequences of the offender's encounter with the criminal justice system long after his or her contact with the justice system has ended.[6] Its goals can also be pursued in accordance with the principles of **restorative justice**, which focuses on the three-dimensional interaction of offender, victim, and community, with emphasis on repairing the harm caused and healing the victim and community.[7] Surely, part of that healing process is to place supports in the community so no harm is caused by that individual in the future. See **Critical Thinking 10.1** and the example of Henry Farrell.[8]

Critical Thinking 10.1 Implementing Therapeutic Jurisprudence in Sentencing

Henry Farrell of Boca Raton, Florida, was arrested for the 190th time; this time for carjacking.

Farrell, 46, allegedly asked a male driver for a ride outside a Starbucks. According to a police report, when the driver refused, Farrell became belligerent and eventually yelled, "I'll blow your brains out." When Farrell put a hand into his waistband the motorist drove off and called police.

His rap sheet included loitering and prowling, disorderly intoxication, shoplifting, drug possession, [and] criminal mischief. Rather than criminal offenses, these offenses appear to reflect a person with mental health problems. In fact, Farrell is bipolar, a mental illness that causes people to swing from severe depression to extreme highs. Once you understand Farrell's mental health history, his rap sheet [is viewed differently].

So, what began as simple and straightforward turns into an example of one of the toughest, most complex problems we face as a society: What do we do with the mentally unstable who repeatedly break minor laws?

You can't fault the police necessarily for making 190 arrests on Farrell.

"We have a job to do," said Sandra Boonenberg, public information officer for the Boca Raton Police. "If there's a crime committed, we investigate it and, if it's warranted, make arrests."

With the idea of looking to the future via the concept of therapeutic jurisprudence in mind, what might be done now or could have been done long ago to benefit Henry, society, and the criminal justice system and prevent Henry from being a "frequent flyer" in and out of the criminal justice system?

Creation of an Ordered Society

It has been said that if criminals did not exist, they would have to be created, for they provide a necessary common enemy, a group of scapegoats, against whom we can measure our own righteousness.[9] The efficiency and the vengeance elements of criminal justice are reinforced by other elements that are more symbolic and ceremonial.

All of these goals of criminal sentencing coexist in any single sentence. However, one or another may predominate, so that a prison sentence may be primarily for treatment or primarily for incapacitation even though other goals, say deterrence and just desserts, are also intended. Sentencing goals vary from case to case and from one time period to another. For instance, rehabilitation has been a prominent, though not exclusive, ideal of sentences during most of the twentieth century. But today rehabilitation, although still prominent in theory and practice among correctional professionals, has taken a back seat to an emphasis on punishment and deterrence.[10] See viewpoints on sentencing in **Critical Thinking 10.2.**

Critical Thinking 10.2 Viewpoint on Sentencing

One Viewpoint: Sentencing Should Reflect a "Get Tough" Attitude Emphasizing Punishment and Incapacitation[11]

The proponents of this viewpoint start with the premise that "bleeding-heart" liberal judges short-circuit the criminal justice ideals by handing down lenient sentences—that their decisions merely turn criminals loose on society again to commit more crimes. "Get tough" laws are seen as the answer to this problem, especially for crimes involving guns, drug dealing, and other illegal activities which are particularly "hot" in the public eye.

The "get tough" approach emphasizes punishment, incapacitation, and retribution and scoffs at the rehabilitation of criminals. It would require mandatory sentences to take the sentencing discretion away from judges, the elimination of probation and suspended sentences as sentencing options, and abolishing plea bargaining since that practice creates a loophole in the system.

Another Viewpoint: Sentencing Should Emphasize Rehabilitation and Effective Use of Probation

Proponents of this viewpoint argue that prison is a poor solution to crime, that the rehabilitation of offenders is unlikely to occur in a prison setting, and that the use of prison sentences to punish rarely makes people better, only worse. Also, to merely increase the amount of time offenders spend in prison is seen as unrealistic, unworkable, and counterproductive to an effective criminal justice system. Proponents of this view do not see the problem as weak judges, for serious offenders have always been sentenced harshly. They see the problem as the prison solution itself—that no evidence exists to demonstrate that any time spent in prison makes people turn away from criminal behaviors.

Rehabilitation is the cornerstone of this approach. Most criminals stop committing crimes sooner or later anyway, according to this view, and rehabilitation programs can help them stop sooner. And probation, properly administered, is the best correctional program to achieve this goal because it is the only one that seems to work. Probation serves desirable social goals, is much cheaper than prison, and offers a variety of rehabilitative services unavailable in prison. What is needed is for probation officers to have frequent face-to-face contact with offenders, regularly enforce drug and alcohol tests, provide jobs and educational programs, and offer counseling and therapy.

In this viewpoint, probation is the most common sentence handed down to offenders, and virtually every offender is sentenced to probation first and to prison only on subsequent offenses. Therefore, if we can utilize it properly, and improve on its effectiveness, the use of probation can help reduce the amount of crime.

Imposition of Sentence

Except when an offender is convicted of a crime involving a mandatory sentence, the judge has discretion, usually within established guidelines, to select the type, length, and sometimes certain other conditions of a sentence. Depending on the of-

Image by James Steidl at fotolia.com.

fense and the law, the judge may be able to choose a fine, probation, or incarceration in a jail or prison. The latter alternative (incarceration) ordinarily depends on whether the offense is a misdemeanor (jail) or felony (prison). Probation can be given in either category. Fines are more commonly imposed in misdemeanor cases, alone or combined with probation or incarceration, but they may also be imposed in some felony cases. Fines are commonly levied in white-collar violations such as embezzlement, income tax evasion, and corporate fraud. And, of course, the death penalty is available in most states today in certain circumstances.[12]

The *major* decision at sentencing involves the choice between probation (community supervision without going to jail or prison) and incarceration in jail or prison. Some states utilize **split sentences**, whereby an offender can be sentenced to prison for determinate periods of time to be followed by a term of probation or assignment to a specialized court program such as drug rehabilitation.[13] Usually, however, the basic concern to the offender at sentencing is whether he or she will remain in the community on probation or go to prison. If the decision is incarceration, there are the matters of where and how long. If the decision is probation, the issues are the rules and conditions of supervision. See **Table 10.1** for types of felony sentences typically imposed in state courts.[14]

Probation

A judge may sentence a person to probation in a number of ways:

1. By imposing a prison sentence (3 to 10 years, perhaps) but *suspending its execution* and placing the offender on probation;
2. By *suspending imposition* of any prison sentence and placing the offender on probation;

Table 10.1 Types of Felony Sentences Imposed in State Courts, by Offense

Most Serious Conviction Offense	Percent of Felons Sentenced to—						
		Incarceration			Nonincarceration		
	Total	Total	Prison	Jail	Total	Probation	Other
All offenses	100%	69	41	28	31	27	4
Violent offenses	100%	77	54	23	23	20	3
Murder/Nonnegligent manslaughter	100%	95	93	2	5	3	2
Sexual assault	100%	81	64	18	19	16	3
Rape	100%	86	72	15	14	10	4
Other sexual assault[a]	100%	77	58	20	23	20	2
Robbery	100%	85	71	14	15	13	2
Aggravated assault	100%	72	43	30	28	25	3
Other violent[b]	100%	70	39	30	30	26	4
Property offenses	100%	67	38	29	33	29	4
Burglary	100%	73	49	24	27	24	3
Larceny	100%	69	34	34	31	28	3
Motor vehicle theft	100%	83	42	41	17	15	2
Fraud/Forgery[c]	100%	59	32	27	41	35	6
Drug offenses	100%	65	38	28	35	30	4
Possession	100%	63	33	31	37	33	4
Trafficking	100%	67	41	26	33	29	4
Weapon offenses	100%	73	45	28	27	25	2
Other specified offenses[d]	100%	70	36	34	30	27	3

Note: For persons receiving a combination of sentences, the sentence designation came from the most severe penalty imposed, with prison being the most severe, followed by jail, probation, and then other sentences, such as a fine, community service, or house arrest. Prison includes death sentences. In this table "probation" is defined as straight probation. Detail may not sum to total because of rounding. Data on sentence type were reported for 98% of the estimated total of 1,132,290 convicted felons. Percentages are based on reported data.

[a] Includes offenses such as statutory rape and incest with a minor.
[b] Includes offenses such as negligent manslaughter and kidnapping.
[c] Includes embezzlement.
[d] Comprises nonviolent offenses such as vandalism and receiving stolen property.

3. By placing the offender *directly on a sentence of probation*;
4. By *deferring judgment* and placing the offender on probation; or

5. By *adjourning judgment in anticipation of dismissal* and requiring the defendant to abide by probation conditions for a period of time.

The length of probation can be set within whatever limits are allowed by statute, though this may not necessarily be equal to the length of imprisonment provided for the same crime. For instance, if a crime carries a possible sentence of 20 years in prison, the term of probation may be only five years. Conversely, if a one-year prison term is authorized, a longer probationary period may be set by the court. In a number of jurisdictions conditions of probation can also be changed from time to time by the court.

Incarceration of Misdemeanants

Misdemeanants are sentenced to local jails. Jail sentences are for specified times up to one year. Lesser sentences, up to a month, are commonly expressed in days—10 days, 30 days—and longer sentences in three-month intervals—three months, six months, nine months, or one year. Some jails have work-release programs in which low-risk inmates go to work during the day and report to lockup at nights and on weekends. In most cases jail time is "flat," that is, there is no minimum and maximum spread. Instead the inmate serves precisely the sentence imposed by the court.

Judicial Variations in Sentencing

Like all people, judges often have idiosyncrasies that may affect their sentencing practice. Certain judges may have reputations for either harsh or lenient sentencing in certain types of cases. One judge may abhor narcotics violations and impose long sentences in these cases. Another may view narcotics violations as minor, particularly if "soft" drugs are involved. There are "gun" judges who tend to impose long sentences on any offender who had a gun during the commission of a crime, whether or not the gun was used. But a gun judge may be lenient with sex offenders, believing they are sick rather than criminal. Defense lawyers who are aware of judicial likes and dislikes may spend considerable time "judge-shopping" to obtain sentencing hearings for their clients in a sympathetic or at least a less hostile court. Of course, the prosecutor may do the same for the opposite purposes.

A variety of factors beyond the nature of the offense itself may influence the judicial decision of long or short periods of imprisonment. Some judges may show more leniency to an offender who pleads guilty than to one who has had a full trial, or to an offender who is a police informer, or to one who has been a valuable state's witness, for example. Conversely, judges sometimes impose very long sentences, not to bury the offender in prison for many years, but to provide extended parole supervision in the belief that the offender will need intensive assistance upon his or her return to the community.[15]

Some judges have been shown to be biased against racial or ethnic groups. Others have been shown to prefer one race or ethnic group over another. And still other judges demonstrate no sentence disparity at all as regards to the convicted person's color.[16]

Research has shown that male judges tend to sentence female offenders more leniently than male offenders convicted of comparable crimes. Other studies have shown that judges affiliated with fundamentalist churches sentence black defendants more harshly than whites and that democratic judges are less discriminatory than others. Still other studies have investigated the factors involved in sentencing in rural courts, as well as various factors relating to the sex and race of both judges and offenders. The social background of judges has also been shown to affect sentencing behavior.[17]

Many judges try to "individualize" sentences as much as possible to fit the actual consequences of their sentences to the risk and reputation of both the offender and his or her family. It should be noted, however, that individualization is only one sentencing goal. Judges are lawyers, and in sentencing as in other matters they have strong allegiances to precedent. Over time it is not unusual for a judge to attempt to give comparable sentences for similar offenses and similar offenders.

Judges may also make sentencing decisions based on characteristics of the victim rather than the offender. Child victims, for instance, may lead a judge to hand down a harsher sentence. And, the race of the victim may matter sometimes, as when a white person is victimized by a black offender.[18]

But all the variations in sentencing are not attributable to the judge's personality or personal biases. Statistical data may raise questions regarding such judicial variation in sentencing, and when individual judges' decisions are analyzed a variety of factors appear to influence the decision.

Potential and Real Factors in Sentencing

Several factors have either been shown to influence the sentencing decision or have been suspected to do so. Age of the convicted person has been shown to act in the favor of the elderly and against the young. Judges may consider older offenders to be less of a threat to society, and they perhaps view younger offenders as a greater risk unless restrained.[19] Sentences for young first offenders are usually shorter and more clearly directed to rehabilitative programs in reformatories than sentences for "ordinary" adult criminals. Provisions often exist for expunging records if these young offenders show treatment progress. It is believed that there is more hope for successful rehabilitation with the young offenders. In many places, as will be discussed in Chapter 13, the most modern facilities and most of the professional rehabilitation staff are found in youth programs. In general, this is noncontroversial: a majority of all the participants in the criminal justice system give high priority to leniency and high-quality correctional programs for youthful offenders.

Sentencing elderly criminals to prison may be equivalent to a life sentence, and often the health problems of the aging offenders means that prison becomes a nursing home. Judges are often sympathetic to elderly offenders, suspecting they may be in need of nursing home care more than a punitive prison.

The gender of the convicted person has also been suspected of influencing the sentence. Generally, women and men receive similar sentences for similar crimes if the sentence is incarceration.[20] Judges have been found to be more favorable when sentencing women who are pregnant or who are needed to provide child care. Women often are granted pretrial release and lower bail than males, and that fact influences the sentence favorably rather than the gender specifically.[21] And, although women may be treated the same as men by police and prosecutors, judges are more likely to give more lenient sentences to women.[22]

The social or economic class of the convicted person may affect the sentencing decision, perhaps because of the poor person's inability to hire an expensive law firm or due to the person's appearance and demeanor in court.[23] Judges do tend to come from the middle class or above, and many defendants appearing before them are poor, leading some to suggest that "the rich get richer and the poor get prison."[24]

The race of the convicted person may also matter, as evidenced by the fact that proportionately more African Americans are in prison or on death row.[25] The race of the convicted person has long been pointed to as the determining factor in sentencing.[26] Several factors complicate this. First, sentencing varies from one jurisdiction to another, and while race may explain some of that variation, it does not explain all of it.[27] In fact, the race factor may balance out in certain jurisdictions where some judges sentence whites favorably and other judges sentence blacks favorably.[28] Additionally, misdemeanants and felons are treated differently sometimes according to race. In New York, for instance, one study showed that African Americans with the same prior record as a white person convicted of the same crime received harsher sentences. But, African Americans convicted of misdemeanors received more lenient sentences than their white counterparts, and if convicted of a crime without any prior record, they also received more lenient sentences than the white with no prior record.[29]

Extended-Term Sentences

Provisions exist for extended sentences for dangerous offenders, gangsters, and other persistent, professional criminals. Few would deny the existence of some very dangerous offenders—persons who have committed violent, atrocious crimes—who kill, maim, rape, and otherwise seriously jeopardize the safety of us all. The existence of career criminals—professionals who make crime their lifelong occupation—as well as of gangsters and racketeers who traffic in heroin, people, or arms and persons who extort, intimidate, and corrupt others, is an unpleasant reality. Distinguishing these offenders with accuracy and by acceptable means from ordinary, limited-threat offenders is not easy. And unfortunately, the problem of what to do with them once they have been identified remains.

In the past, the only provisions for extended periods of incarceration were for the "habitual criminal." In some places, an offender became automatically eligible for a long habitual offender sentence upon a third or fourth conviction; in others, "being a habitual offender" was a separate charge, with a trial, if any, devoted primarily to proof of the offender's prior record. The real consequence of habitual offender laws was that many minor but "persistent" violators who were not really dangerous were engulfed in the process and spent long stretches of time in prison.

Certain offenders can even be held *after* their criminal sentence has been completed by means of a **civil**, rather than criminal process. The U.S. Supreme Court on May 17, 2010, in *United States v. Comstock* upheld the Adam Walsh Child Protection and Safety Act. The Court ruled that Congress has legitimate authority to detain sex offenders past the expiration of their criminal sentences. If authorities can show "clear and convincing" evidence (a lesser standard than beyond a reasonable doubt) that an offender "currently 'suffers from a serious mental illness, abnormality, or disorder' and who 'as a result of that mental illness, abnormality, or disorder is 'sexually dangerous to others' in that 'he would have serious difficulty in refraining from sexually violent conduct or child molestation if released,' "[30] then the offender can be held even after completion of the criminal sentence.

Mandatory Sentences

The legislature may dominate the sentencing of certain offenders by fixing mandatory prison terms for conviction of a particular crime. The sentencing judge has no other option. In some jurisdictions, certain offenses such as those involving a firearm, drug trafficking, or some sex offenses are defined as nonprobationable, thus mandating a sentence of incarceration. In others, the probation alternative is left open, but if the judge imposes a prison sentence, the minimum or maximum length (or both) of incarceration is fixed by statute.

Mandatory sentencing also usually means that the sentence actually imposed mandates that each person convicted of the crime should receive the same mandatory sentence. The offender does precisely the amount of time ordered by the court without parole or other time off for good behavior.

Mandatory sentences are also called **determinate sentences**, to be contrasted with indeterminate sentences. Completely indeterminate sentences—one day to life—are much less common today than they were some years ago. These zero to life sentences still exist, however, in some places, usually for sex crimes in which the offender is also diagnosed as a "sex deviate" or "sex psychopath." In these cases, the actual sentence is left to the parole authorities to decide when, if ever, the offender will be released from prison.

The primary purpose of mandatory sentencing is to make sure the serious violent offenders are incarcerated for long periods of time without the possibility of early release. Two unanticipated effects of mandatory sentencing have lessened the desired effect. First, the number of people serving mandatory sentences has increased during the past 20 years, causing prison overcrowding in some places.[31] If mandatory sentences are handed down for low-level drug offenders (for instance as has happened in the federal jurisdiction), then space which may be needed in prison for more serious violent offenders may be taken.[32] Secondly, some police officers and prosecutors have actually elected in some cases to choose not to charge certain offenders with crimes which carry mandatory sentences, thereby shielding them from the harsh sentence.[33]

Who Really Makes the Sentencing Decision?

After conviction by trial or guilty plea, the defendant is brought to court for imposition of sentence. The hearing at which the sentence is imposed is considered a "critical stage" of the criminal justice process, and convicted offenders, including those who are poor, have a right to counsel at this time.[34]

Most sentences are imposed by a judge, but some variation exists depending on the law in different jurisdictions. Jury sentencing has existed since colonial times in some states. However, the practice has been questioned by those who have called for the abolition of jury sentencing because it is "nonprofessional and is more likely than judge sentencing to be arbitrary and based on emotions rather than the needs of the offender or society."[35]

The question of who *actually* makes the sentencing determination, and when, is complicated by prevalent plea-bargaining practices discussed earlier. In a plea agreement, the sentence is predetermined by the prosecutor. While the judge always has the option to reject such agreements, they seldom do.

The authority of the parole board comes into play between the minimum and maximum set either by statute or by the sentencing judge. The board has the authority to release any prisoner who has served the minimum sentence (or, in some places, after the minimum term minus time off for good behavior) and before the expiration of the maximum term.

Thus, the time served in prison for any crime may be a combined function of the three sources of authority. First, the outer limits are set by statute. Second, the judge may set a term less than the legislative limits. And third, actual time served may be a decision of the parole board within certain parameters set by the legislature and the court.

A Muddy Reality

Actually, the sentencing structure picture is even more complicated than outlined here. There are various combinations of these mandatory and discretionary terms across and within states. No uniform sentences are common to all jurisdictions. Sentencing provisions vary not only among the states and the federal jurisdiction but even within a single state for different kinds of crimes. Parsing this out across the country we can identify at least five major structures that have evolved for imposing prison sentences, each with some variations:

1. **Indeterminate sentencing:** Common in the early 1970s, parole boards had the authority to release offenders from prison at virtually any time.

2. **Determinate sentencing:** States introduced fixed prison terms, which could be reduced by good-time or earned-time credits.
3. **Mandatory minimum sentences:** States added statutes requiring offenders to be sentenced to a specified amount of prison time.
4. **Sentencing guidelines:** States established sentencing commissions and created ranges of sentences for given offenses and offender characteristics.
5. **Truth in sentencing:** First enacted in 1984, TIS laws require offenders to serve a substantial portion of their prison sentence (often 85 percent). Parole eligibility and good-time credits are restricted or eliminated.

This complex and somewhat confusing array of structures illustrates the conflicts between the major sources of authority in the criminal justice process. Mandatory sentences of any sort give sentencing power to the legislature and deny discretion to both judge and parole board. In systems where a judge can set a minimum sentence, this forecloses the possibility of parole until that minimum is served. On the other hand, systems that provide a large spread of time between minimum and maximum terms give to the parole board the power to determine the time that actually will be served.

Fair and Certain Punishment

For the most part, sentences stress *punitive* and *incapacitory* goals rather than treatment and rehabilitation of the offender. Death penalty provisions (hardly rehabilitative) have been adopted in most states, and the impetus for this extreme punishment reflects that emphasis. In the new capital punishment laws, as well as in other new sentencing proposals, fair and certain punishment is the major thrust of the change. The operational consequences of this are a move away from the indeterminate sentence—prison terms containing a spread of time between a minimum and a maximum period of incarceration—and the abolition of parole. It was argued, by prisoners as well as a number of others, that indeterminate sentencing and the use of parole gave too much discretion to state authorities.[36] The offender was always uncertain of his or her actual sentence, and the parole system allowed correctional authorities to increase or decrease the amount of punishment based on factors unrelated to the offender's criminal act.

Thus, though parole and indeterminate sentences were twentieth century reforms, in the twenty-first century we have emphasis on certain and definite punishments commensurate with the harm caused by the criminal acts. The focus is on how much punishment the offender deserves—"just deserts" directly related to conduct—rather than on treating the causes of the criminal behavior.[37]

Sentencing Guidelines

Several states, as well as the federal jurisdiction, have addressed the problem of **sentence disparity**: the situation in which judges' sentence decisions have too great a discrepancy and offenders convicted of the same crimes, and with equivalent background characteristics, have been sentenced to unreasonably disparate sentences. The purpose of guidelines is not to eliminate judges' discretion but to channel it as much as possible within acceptable limits. Another goal of guidelines is to make sentencing procedures neutral in terms of race, age, sex, and social and economic status.

Sentencing guidelines categorize crimes and then establish sentence score sheets, or matrices, within each category for determining sentence ranges. For instance, the Federal Sentencing Guidelines are accessible online, and the primary factors that guide sentencing are the severity of the current offense and the extensiveness of the prior criminal record of defendants. Factors are scored, a total score is tabulated, and the sentence range is computed by reference to the score sheet. The score sheet provides space for the "guideline sentence" and the "sentence imposed."[38]

If a judge wishes to give a sentence that exceeds the guideline, he or she may do so, but the sentence must survive appellate review, and an extraordinary reason must be shown to justify any sentence outside the guidelines. In such a way, the government can show an evenhanded sentencing procedure. Although sentencing guidelines have not been met with universal acceptance by judges and others, the appellate courts have generally upheld the constitutionality of their use.[39] Note the significant influence of criminal history and severity of current offense on sentencing decisions as reflected in the federal sentencing guidelines contained in **Table 10.2**.[40]

As indicated, most sentences are imposed by judges who, with the exception of those cases where conviction carries legislatively mandated sanctions, have a number of available alternatives. In the ordinary sentencing situation, however, the judge knows little about the defendant except for the formal conviction label. If a trial has been held, the judge may have formed some opinion about the character of the offender from testimony by witnesses or the defendant if he or she took the stand. But usually the judge faces a defendant who has pleaded guilty, which means contact between the two might have been limited to a few minutes and the exchange of only a few words.

To assist the court in imposing a fair and appropriate sentence, therefore, a **presentence investigation** (PSI) is sometimes conducted. Typically, PSI reports are conducted in all federal criminal cases; however, based on resources, custom, and legal mandates PSI reports may be severely limited and only performed in serious cases if at all; some defense attorneys may even pay for private PSI reports for their clients. PSIs are performed to gather relevant information about the offender to assist the judge in sentencing. The judge sets a date for sentencing, allowing time for the PSI report to be completed.

Actually, the PSI often serves broader purposes than the primary one of aiding the sentencing decision. For instance, probation/parole officers may use the PSI as a guide for establishing a casework plan. And prison intake officials often use it as a source of information to assist in classifying the newly arrived inmate. Later, the PSI surfaces again at the parole decision process. More than any other document, the PSI sticks with the offender on the journey through the correctional system.

Table 10.2 Federal Sentencing Guidelines

Sentencing Table (in Months of Imprisonment)

	Criminal History Category (Criminal History Points)						
	Offense Level	**I (0 or 1)**	**II (2 or 3)**	**III (4, 5, 6)**	**IV (7, 8, 9)**	**V (10, 11, 12)**	**VI (13 or more)**
Zone A	1	0–6	0–6	0–6	0–6	0–6	0–6
	2	0–6	0–6	0–6	0–6	0–6	1–7
	3	0–6	0–6	0–6	0–6	2–8	3–9
	4	0–6	0–6	0–6	2–8	4–10	6–12
	5	0–6	0–6	1–7	4–10	6–12	9–15
	6	0–6	1–7	2–8	6–12	9–15	12–18
	7	0–6	2–8	4–10	8–14	12–18	15–21
	8	0–6	4–10	6–12	10–16	15–21	18–24
Zone B	9	4–10	6–12	8–14	12–18	18–24	21–27
	10	6–12	8–14	10–16	15–21	21–27	24–30
Zone C	11	8–14	10–16	12–18	18–24	24–30	27–33
	12	10–16	12–18	15–21	21–27	27–33	30–37
Zone D	13	12–18	15–21	18–24	24–30	30–37	33–41
	14	15–21	18–24	21–27	27–33	33–41	37–46
	15	18–24	21–27	24–30	30–37	37–46	41–51
	16	21–27	24–30	27–33	33–41	41–51	46–57
	17	24–30	27–33	30–37	37–46	46–57	51–63
	18	27–33	30–37	33–41	41–51	51–63	57–71
	19	30–37	33–41	37–46	46–57	57–71	63–78
	20	33–41	37–46	41–51	51–63	63–78	70–87
	21	37–46	41–51	46–57	57–71	70–87	77–96
	22	41–51	46–57	51–63	63–78	77–96	84–105
	23	46–57	51–63	57–71	70–87	84–105	92–115
	24	51–63	57–71	63–78	77–96	92–115	100–125
	25	57–71	63–78	70–87	84–105	100–125	110–137
	26	63–78	70–87	78–97	92–115	110–137	120–150
	27	70–87	78–97	87–108	100–125	120–150	130–162
	28	78–97	87–108	97–121	110–137	130–162	140–175
	29	87–108	97–121	108–135	121–151	140–175	151–188
	30	97–121	108–135	121–151	135–168	151–188	168–210
	31	108–135	121–151	135–168	151–188	168–210	188–235
	32	121–151	135–168	151–188	168–210	188–235	210–262
	33	135–168	151–188	168–210	188–235	210–262	235–293
	34	151–188	168–210	188–235	210–262	235–293	262–327
	35	168–210	188–235	210–262	235–293	262–327	292–365
	36	188–235	210–262	235–293	262–327	292–365	324–405
	37	210–262	235–293	262–327	292–365	324–405	360–life
	38	235–293	262–327	292–365	324–405	360–life	360–life
	39	262–327	292–365	324–405	360–life	360–life	360–life
	40	292–365	324–405	360–life	360–life	360–life	360–life
	41	324–405	360–life	360–life	360–life	360–life	360–life

Generally, a probation officer is given the task of conducting the presentence investigation into the background of the person to be sentenced, bringing together facts and opinions about the offender that may inform and otherwise assist the judge in determining an appropriate sentence. Sometimes a clinical "diagnosis" of the offender is desired or mandated by law, and the offender may be sent to a clinic, hospital, or in some places to a prison for psychiatric and psychological assessment. In routine cases, however, the probation officer collects the available records (the offender's police record, commonly called a "rap sheet," employment history, school reports, and so on), interviews people who know the offender (family, friends, teachers, employers, sometimes the victim or witnesses, and so on), solicits the offender's own story of the crime, and may, if desired by the court, offer a personal "diagnosis" of the violator and make specific recommendations for sentencing. See Appendix B for an example of a PSI.

It is easy to see that the presentence report is an important aid to the sentencing judge. After all, he or she is dealing with years out of a person's free life and has the unwelcome task of balancing the effects of placing the offender in the brutal environment of a jail or prison against the prospect of that person continuing to be a threat to society. Most judges welcome all the information they can get about the past behavior, present circumstances, and mental condition of the offenders who come before them for sentencing. Offenders also have an interest in the content of the PSI because, if the information is false or misleading, the sentencing consequences may be devastating.

In some places the entire presentence report, including psychiatric diagnoses, is available to both the defense and the state's attorney. More commonly the disclosure issue has resulted in a compromise. In a number of places, a sentencing judge may reveal *part* of the report, withholding the identity of antagonistic informants but "summarizing" their adverse statements.[41] Some courts distinguish the factual contents of the report (police records and so on) from the opinions of respondents, allowing disclosure of the first part but not revealing sources of information in the second part.[42]

What is at stake in withholding some content from the offender is that erroneous information may influence a judge's sentencing decision. The general issue, clearly just emerging in the context of sentencing, is whether there are, should be, or will be, court-imposed limitations on the types of information included in presentence investigations. Probably there should be some restrictions. For instance, inaccurate or irrelevant information should not be allowed to serve as a basis for sentence determination.[43]

Victim Impact Statements

Victim Impact Statements have recently become a central part of the criminal justice process. Crime victims and their families have traditionally had little or no say in the criminal justice meted out to offenders. Police and prosecutors usually empathize with victims and their families, but defense attorneys have maintained that any input from them in the trial would prejudice an impartial jury. But in recent years a greater emphasis has been placed on taking into account the impact on and interest of the victims.[44] Victim impact statements can be ordered in all cases, including death penalty cases.[45] Victims' rights advocates argue that victims have a moral right to influence the sentence of their offender, critics argue that such statements prejudicially influence the sentencing decision too much, and still others believe that such statements bring the needed personal touch to an otherwise formal process.[46]

Many criminal court judges consider sentencing to be their most difficult task. As lawyers, they are professionally capable of conducting trials, ruling on the admissibility of evidence, and dealing with all the other matters that normally characterize the procedural and substantive issues of courtroom law. But sentencing is a different matter: it is not taught in law school courses and only rarely discussed in meetings or seminars of judges. Some sentencing situations that appear to be simple can raise very complex and controversial issues. Put yourself in the judge's robe for determination of sentence in **Critical Thinking 10.3.**

Critical Thinking 10.3 Thinking Critically about Sentences

You decide the most crucial components from a PSI for determining sentence.

Access the Federal Presentence Investigation Report at http://www.fd.org/pdf_lib/publication%20107.pdf (there is also an example PSI included in Appendix B of this textbook). How would you sentence the persons represented in the various reports? What factors were most important in arriving at your decision and why? Based just on the *facts* given, without full PSIs and assuming no limits on your sentencing discretion, what would be *your* sentences in the examples described at the link above and in the PSI in the Appendix? What goal(s) of criminal sentencing were you trying to achieve with your dispositions? Is it helpful to have guidelines to assist with your sentence or not?

Judges do not like to think of their sentencing patterns as disparate (different sentences for similar offenders convicted for the same offense), arbitrary, or capricious. Therefore, conscientious judges think a great deal about their own sentencing philosophies. In each case a judge must decide on priorities—whether sentencing should emphasize the deterrence of crime, restitution or victim compensation, the needs and feelings of the community at large, reducing the risk that the offender will commit further crimes, the impact of the sentence on the offender's family including, the effects of prison life on the physical or mental health of the convicted, the punishment or rehabilitation of the offender, or any other of the many possible goals the sentencing decision can have.

Sentencing is a serious matter, not only for the offender but for the judge who passes the sentence and the correctional authorities who must receive the offender. Indeed, sentencing affects the entire justice system. Is the sentence just? Is it fair? Does it accomplish what is intended? Is it fitting to our time and place in history? With these thoughts in mind, we now turn to the sentence of death.

The Ultimate Punishment: The Death Penalty

"Killing was wrong when I did it. It is wrong when you do it. How do you teach someone not to kill by killing?"

—Part of Joseph Carl Shaw's last statement before being executed in South Carolina's electric chair on January 11, 1985[47]

Few subjects arouse as much passion and interest as the death penalty. Execution is deeply ingrained in the minds of Americans as a historical reality and, according to many public opinion polls, most Americans believe that the execution of greater numbers of serious offenders would lead to less crime and violence in our society. On the other hand, many other people are opposed to capital punishment on moral, religious, or practical grounds. One is hard-pressed to find anyone not willing to express an opinion one way or the other about this subject.

However, in the criminal justice system, capital punishment is actually a minor contingency, an infrequent occurrence. Of the many hundreds of thousands of offenses committed, hundreds of thousands of offenders arrested, and tens of thousands of defendants tried and convicted, only a minuscule number of criminals are put to death. Although the subject is of critical importance to those affected by it, for most of us it is a distant issue.

Not only is capital punishment the ultimate sanction against crime, but it is irrevocable as well. Mistakes in this area, and there have been some, cannot be rectified. Although the death penalty serves some ends of justice—a life for a life, the ultimate incapacitation of the criminal—it apparently does not accomplish all that is hoped for it or all that it is believed to accomplish. Most advocates of the death sentence hope, and indeed believe, that its use in one case of murder will deter others inclined to homicide. But evidence does not bear this out. Executing death row prisoners has not stopped, or even lessened, the occurrence of capital crimes.

Executions in the United States

Earlier in our history, executions were public events and generated a great deal of interest. In the Massachusetts Bay Colony in the early 1600s, hundreds of people would travel at great inconvenience to observe a public hanging. In the nineteenth century, crowds gathered in Western towns to see outlaws executed, and photographs and historical records show that thousands of people have watched public executions in the twentieth century. The last legal, public execution in America took place on August 14, 1936, in Owensboro, Kentucky, where a black inmate by the name of Rainey Bethea was hanged. This is said to be the first execution in America overseen by a female, as Florence Thompson (who would pass the duty off to a drunken underling) was the sheriff of Daviess County. Reports are that a carnival like atmosphere existed, complete with souvenir hunters chipping away pieces of the gallows and as many as 20,000 persons in attendance.[48] Clearly, great interest—even fascination—in lawful death has existed throughout history.

The Puritan settlers in the Massachusetts Bay Colony brought to this continent an acceptance of the death penalty based on European practices, especially those of England, as well as their own understanding of Old Testament biblical teachings. The resulting code allowed the death penalty for persons convicted of a curious mixture of behaviors. Some of these offenses were considered to be sins (blasphemy, idolatry, witchcraft, or sodomy, for example), which were not included in the British law but were allowed under the Old Testament Law of Moses.[49] The oldest recorded execution of a juvenile on our soil took place in 1642 when one Thomas Granger, age 16, was hanged in Plymouth Colony for bestiality. He confessed to sexual encounters with a turkey, a cow, a horse, two calves, two goats, and five sheep. Each of the animals he had relations with was slaughtered in front of him before his execution.[50]

Other executions undertaken in the colonies were for traditional serious crimes (murder, for example), but their number did not approach the 350 or so capital offenses of English law. This mixture of Old Testament and English Common Law precursors resulted in a classification of crimes that were capital offenses in England but not in Massachusetts Bay (petty theft, for example), as well as crimes that were punished by death in Massachusetts but not in England (adultery, for example).

The number of offenses for which the death penalty applied in this country dwindled to 12 in the typical colony by the 1700s, but not before a large, but unknown, number of persons had been executed. In Boston alone there are records of executions by hanging condemned offenders on scaffolds erected in the city square, including men and women convicted of burglary, rape, murder, theft, and treason.[51] In each of the colonies, capital punishment was sufficiently accepted so that the authors of the U.S. Constitution and the Bill of Rights acknowledged it in the Fifth Amendment:

> No person shall be held to answer for a *capital*, or otherwise infamous crime, unless ... nor shall any person ... be twice put in *jeopardy of life* or limb ... nor shall he be ... *deprived of life* ... without due process of law (emphasis added).

Precise records do not exist regarding the imposition of death for crimes during the nineteenth century, but we are left to conclude, based on the records of plantation owners in the South prior to the Civil War, that a great number of blacks were executed. Many Southern states developed slave codes prior to the Civil War, that is, a set of codes applying only to blacks. In the 1830s, Virginia had seventy capital crimes for blacks and only five for whites. In 1848, Virginia enacted a law requiring death for blacks convicted of any crime punishable by three years or more in prison for whites. In 1816, Georgia required death for blacks who raped or attempted to rape whites but imposed a two-year sentence on whites convicted of rape.

During Reconstruction, despite the abolition of the slave codes, the race of the offender and that of the victim continued to be a major determinant of criminal penalties, including that of death. The law was a powerful tool of intimidation and was used to reinforce a caste system in which whites dominated and terrorized the black population with impunity. Support for this conclusion is offered by the following actual incident:

> On April 6, 1866, in Micanopy, Florida, a white man named John Denton shot and killed a black man for "insolence." Denton was arrested by U.S. Army troops, but a white mob met the soldiers in nearby Gainesville and freed the prisoner. Later, Denton was tried, convicted of manslaughter, ordered to pay court costs and to serve one minute in jail.[52]

Historians of the death penalty report that in addition to legal executions, a large number of lynchings, the process of "stringing up" a person by hanging him from a tree limb or other makeshift gallows, occurred. One study has claimed that over 5,000 persons were lynched in the United States between 1888 and 1918.[53] Between 1900 and 1962, according to another, 1,799 blacks and 196 whites were lynched, primarily in Southern and border states.[54] Many of these lynchings were hasty executions of people recently convicted. Some were expressions of mob anger after a black defendant was acquitted or his conviction was reversed. At times police participated in lynchings, and sometimes the pressure from vengeance-minded mobs forced immediate "trials" and executions referred to as "quick justice," so that the difference between a legal execution and a lynching was indistinguishable.

Fragmented records and tales from the West, like the stories about Judge Roy Bean, the "law west of the Pecos," lead us to conclude that hanging, lynching, and other forms of execution were not uncommon outside the South either. And racial discrimination in the imposition of the death penalty against Native Americans, Chinese, blacks, and other ethnic groups occurred throughout the United States.

From 1608 to 1976, there were a total of 14,489 documented executions in the United States. This is based on what is known as the Espy File and was compiled by M. Watt Espy and John Ortiz Smykla. The states leading the way in executions from 1608 to 1976, with over one thousand executions each, were Virginia (1,277), New York (1,130), and Pennsylvania (1,040).[55]

The Movement to Abolish the Death Penalty

After the end of World War II, the United States experienced a steady decline in the number of executions. By 1968 executions had ceased to occur altogether, although persons were still sentenced to death. The rate of sentences to death has far outdistanced the rate of executions.

The Legal Defense Fund staff of lawyers has spent a great amount of time investigating, defending, and appealing convictions in selected cases. Many of these cases involved African American defendants in the South accused of raping white women. Attorneys raised such civil rights issues as jury discrimination, forced or coerced confessions, and denial of the right to counsel.

Various approaches have been used by defense attorneys to challenge the legal use of the death penalty in the United States: the statistical argument,[56] the class action approach,[57] and challenges to due process based on jurors' preconceptions (the death-qualified jury).[58] Up until 2002, judges were the ultimate determinants of a death sentence or life in prison. After the Supreme Court decision in *Ring v. Arizona* (2002), juries, not the judge, would decide death sentencing.[59] With recent modifications to death penalty provisions in Florida and Delaware by state courts, the U.S. Supreme Court refused to hear a challenge to Alabama's death penalty system, which now leaves the state as the only one in the country that lets judges overrule juries and impose death sentences.[60]

Cruel and Unusual Punishment

The most tried avenue for overturning the death penalty has revolved around the cruel and unusual punishment clause of the Eighth Amendment. In 1972, the Supreme Court considered *Furman v. Georgia*, *Jackson v. Georgia*, and *Branch v. Texas* (heretofore referred to as *Furman*).[61]

Furman had been sentenced to death for murder and Jackson for rape, both in Georgia, while Branch was under a Texas death sentence for rape. All three men were black. In brief, the anti-capital punishment lawyers argued that the death penalty *as imposed* by the trial courts was *unusual* in that death was seldom carried out and, when it was, it was inflicted disproportionately against blacks, other minorities, and poor people. The lawyers further argued that the death penalty was *cruel* in that the intentional taking of a prisoner's life after a sometimes lengthy period of incarceration cannot reasonably be characterized as anything other than cruel. Thus the lawyers claimed that death sentences violated the Eighth Amendment by being both cruel *and* unusual punishment.

The Supreme Court decision, collectively known as *Furman v. Georgia*, ended capital punishment as it was then practiced in the United States. But the final document was long, complicated, and itself unusual in that each of the nine justices wrote separate opinions. Five of them held that the death penalty as applied in the cases before them was cruel and unusual; Justices Marshall and Brennan added that it was totally impermissible under any circumstances. The remaining four dissented. The Court did not say that the penalty of death itself constituted cruel and unusual punishment, only that as administered or applied in *Furman* there was a violation of the Eighth Amendment's prohibition against cruel and unusual punishment.

Four principles were stated by Justice Brennan. First, Justice Brennan wrote, a punishment was cruel and unusual if it did not "comport with human dignity," that is, if it was "so severe as to be degrading to the dignity of human beings." Physical pain was but one measure of this degradation. The more important element, according to Brennan, had to do with treating people as "non-humans, as objects to be toyed with and discarded." Such treatment was unacceptable. Justice Brennan's other three principles addressed the requirements that a severe punishment not be inflicted *arbitrarily*, *contemporary society find the penalty acceptable*, and such a penalty *not be excessive.* He found a punishment to be excessive if it was unnecessary, a "pointless infliction of suffering" where a less severe punishment would accomplish the same ends.

For the majority on the Court, the crux of the problem was perhaps best summed up by Justice Stewart. He objected to how the legal systems in the jurisdictions with capital punishment permitted "this unique penalty to be so *wantonly and so freakishly imposed.*" Justice Stewart likened it to the cruel and unusual process of being struck by lightning due to the capriciously random handful of persons on whom the ultimate penalty of death was brought to bear.

Capital Punishment after Furman

Immediately after the *Furman* decision, Florida led the movement to reinstate capital punishment by calling a special session of its legislature. Similar efforts were made in other states where the majority of voters apparently favored imposition of the death penalty for certain crimes.

The new Florida statute attempted to resolve the objections to capital punishment as "arbitrary and capricious" in the manner in which it is imposed by listing nine aggravating and seven mitigating circumstances to guide judges and juries in making their decisions. Georgia and Texas passed similar legislation.

Meanwhile, legislatures in Louisiana and North Carolina, responding to the objections expressed in *Furman* to the "arbitrary" use of the death sentence, enacted laws requiring the death penalty for certain crimes, that is, mandatory death sentences. They apparently misread *Furman*, for in 1976 the U.S. Supreme Court ruled those statutes unconstitutional.[62] At the same time the Court ruled against the Louisiana and North Carolina mandatory death sentences, it upheld capital punishment statutes in Georgia (*Gregg v. Georgia*), Florida (*Proffitt v. Florida*), and Texas (*Jurek v. Texas*), where aggravating and mitigating circumstances were allowed for examination and a bi-furcated trial process was established.[63] These new "approved" statutes were copied by several other states.

There was also another unresolved issue from *Furman*. Could a state impose a sentence of death for a crime in which no life was lost? In 1977, the Court in *Coker v. Georgia* declared Georgia's death penalty for rape unconstitutional, holding that the punishment of death was not proportionate to the crime of rape.[64]

A few states' legislatures sought mandatory death sentences for *some* murders, depending on the occupation of the victim or the prior conviction record of the perpetrator. New York, for example, enacted statutes providing capital punishment only for the intentional murder of an on-duty police officer or correctional officer or the murder of any person (usually a prison inmate) by a criminal already serving a life sentence for murder. However, in 1987 the Supreme Court, in a case of a lifer killing another inmate, ruled that there can be *no mandatory death sentence* even in such clearly difficult-to-control circumstances.[65]

The Two-Stage Trial

One way to satisfy the Supreme Court's requirement that the death sentence be fairly decided was to create a bifurcated trial, or two-stage trial, in capital cases. The first trial stage, adjudication, involves the determination of *guilt*, *innocence*, or *guilt to a lesser charge*. After the determination of guilt to a capital offense, the jury begins the second stage of the process, a hearing to decide if the death penalty should be imposed. The prosecution is allowed to "make a case" for execution; defense "makes a case" for leniency (i.e., life imprisonment). The prosecutor presents aggravating circumstances, which are argued to call for the sentence of death, and the defense presents mitigating circumstances, which are argued to justify a life sentence.

The jury then deliberates and makes a *recommendation* of life imprisonment or death to the trial judge, and the judge renders the final decision. In the majority of death penalty states, the trial judge does not have to follow the jury's recommendation (of either death or life in prison), but most judges do.

Aggravating and Mitigating Circumstances

The list of aggravating circumstances varies slightly from state to state, but Georgia's law that survived scrutiny in *Gregg* is representative. The death sentence can be imposed if any of the following conditions are involved. Those factors include the convicted person has been convicted previously of a *capital* felony; commission of another serious contemporaneous crime; the offender is a grave risk to others; monetary gain was the motivation for the crime; the victim was a police or judicial officer; the murder was a contract killing or it was a vile killing; the defendant was under sentence for another crime at the time of the act and/or sought to elude lawful arrest while committing the crime.[66] If any of these factors exist, then the prosecutor may seek the death penalty and normally argues before both judge and jury that they, too, should decide for death.

The statutes also describe a number of mitigating circumstances, the presence of which should normally guide the prosecutor to decide not to seek a death sentence, or should influence the judge or jury to decide that, even though guilt has been determined, death is not an appropriate sentence. The list of mitigating factors in the Georgia law is also representative of those found in other jurisdictions. These factors include the defendant killed under provocation, under the influence of drugs or alcohol, in self-defense and/or was interacting with an armed victim; the defendant cooperated with authorities or acted in good faith or with moral justification in committing the act, and/or the defendant does not appear to be a future threat to society; the strength of the evidence was questionable; the defendant had no significant prior criminal record, was underage, and/or suffered from a suspect emotional state at the time of the act.[67]

Post-*Furman* death penalty statutes, therefore, attempt to spell out the criteria and the process whereby persons are selected for capital punishment. As a final check on this process, the laws also require enhanced *oversight* (a speeded-up appeal) by the state supreme courts, often including *automatic appellate review*.[68]

Other significant death penalty decisions since *Furman* include *Atkins v. Virginia* (2002)[69] where it was determined that it constitutes cruel and unusual punishment to execute persons who are mentally retarded or mentally ill (*Ford v. Wainwright*, 1984).[70] Also, the procedures used for lethal injection in Kentucky, which uses the same combination of drugs as thirty other states, where determined not to constitute cruel and unusual punishment in *Baze v. Rees* (2008).[71] See **Field Practice 10.1** Reflections on the Death Penalty.

Field Practice 10.1 Reflections on the Death Penalty—Warden Chuck Cepak

In the spring of 1984, after completing a rewarding and challenging military career of some 26 years, I planned to pursue teaching at the high school level. Shortly after entering the university to pursue a second graduate degree, a staff training position at the South Carolina Department of Corrections (SCDC) caught my eye.

I applied and was hired to develop and implement a formal orientation and in-service training program at Central Correctional Institution (CCI), an 1860s vintage high-security prison housing violent offenders, Death Row inmates, and containing the old Death House. There, in one of the oldest operational prisons in America, began my correctional career. Over the next sixteen years, I worked for and with many fine dedicated professionals. In the midst of what was often a very negative and chaotic environment, we were all afforded countless opportunities to positively influence and better the lives of many.

My experience with prisons in the military had been limited to visiting soldiers in a stockade and seeing the United States Disciplinary Barracks at Fort Leavenworth, KS. Those facilities were disciplined, clean, and tightly controlled. What I saw my first day at work was very different.

The antiquated prison had a unique and colorful, yet dangerous inmate culture. Hundreds of inmates roamed the inner yard and the long hallway known as the tunnel. They wore a variety of street garb and had hair styles representing cultures of past decades. Some just hung out, while others sold individual cigarettes and handcraft items. Others were seeking or selling homemade alcohol, drugs, and sex. This negative snapshot of the criminal element, concentrated in one place, left me less than eager to return the next day. However, I was of the mind that if you accept a job you give it a fair shake, and so I did.

The same leadership, management, and people skills that were successful in the military were also applicable to prison operations. After 18 months, I advanced to Deputy Warden and then to Deputy Warden for Administration. In 1988, I moved to a prison that housed youthful offenders and back to CCI the next year, as the second in command. In 1991, Death Row was moved to Broad River Correctional Institution (BRCI), a modern high-security facility with a new Capital Punishment Facility (CPF).

In July 1992, I was appointed Warden of CCI with the specific mission of phasing down the staff and inmate populations and closing the old prison. Thanks to an excellent staff, prison operations at CCI were terminated in early 1994, and the facility was turned over to caretaker status.

In May 1994, I was appointed Warden of BRCI. The facility was challenged by a large-scale riot and hostage situation in April 1995. Although the hostage situation was resolved, several officers were seriously injured in the initial rioting.

In early June 1995, the South Carolina legislature amended the death penalty statute. Inmates sentenced prior to the new law had the option of electing electrocution or lethal injection. The first execution by lethal injection was scheduled for August 1995.

We had two months to get a lethal injection operation in place and begin rehearsals. I was given the opportunity to visit one state to examine their equipment and operational policies. The Construction and Maintenance Division constructed a prototype, and after minor modifications, a secure and simple gurney was operational. The institutional maintenance staff made the necessary modifications to the CPF and rehearsals began.

A team of screened volunteers was assembled, and after countless rehearsals, the first court ordered execution by lethal injection in South Carolina was carried out without incident on August 18, 1995. I had no idea that I would preside over twenty executions over a five-year period, one by electrocution and 19 by lethal injection.

Only one execution did not go as planned and that involved an inmate whose surface veins were collapsed, which prevented the routine placement of the IV. However, the medical team was absolutely outstanding. They took extreme care to locate a suitable vein and carefully insert the IV, and the execution, although delayed, was successfully carried out.

I will attempt to describe the mechanical process involved in both execution methods, but only in general terms. In electrocutions, the condemned inmate is strapped into a wooden chair and a conducting lubricant is applied to his shaved head. A copper headpiece containing a sponge liner soaked in a salt brine solution is fastened onto his head. A ground cable is fastened to his shaved leg. A positive electric cable is bolted to the headpiece. Lastly, a high-voltage current is cycled through the body for a brief time. Death is pronounced by a physician. There is a distinct and unpleasant odor in the chamber. This process is like something out of another time. It has often been described as barbaric.

Executions by lethal injection are much more humane. They are not prone to the horrific problems that have been reported with electrocutions in some states. Basically, the condemned inmate is secured to a specially designed gurney with outstretched arms strapped down to a specifically fabricated attachment. A heart monitor is attached. The IV needle is inserted and a saline drip is started. Then three chemicals are individually injected. The first induces unconsciousness, the second causes paralysis, and the third cardiac arrest.

We were required to attend post execution debriefings facilitated by a licensed and experienced psychologist. These provided an excellent forum for staff to express feelings and concerns and for necessary follow-up consultations or other appropriate action. In earlier years, it was commonplace to give the Warden a week or two of administrative leave after an execution. During my time in that capacity, it was practice to oversee an execution at midnight and to return to duty the next morning. This may have actually served me better by not providing the opportunity to dwell on each experience. I have the highest respect for my former and current colleagues and for all professionals who carryout this most difficult and stressful task.

I had held the opinion that a death penalty, equally and fairly applied, and serving as a meaningful deterrent, was appropriate for heinous crimes. Surely, the system was doing the very best it could to fulfill these requirements. My experiences with long delayed executions soon gave me serious doubt about their deterrent value. Equal application and fairness also became issues. The Illinois moratorium on executions in early 2000 affected my opinion significantly.

The majority in our society supports the death penalty, and politicians who are tough on crime are elected. How do we achieve equal application and true fairness when politics, socioeconomic standing, varying degrees of experience and competence amongst lawyers and judges, and the disparity of juries, as well as a host of other factors, all affect the outcome? Where is the deterrent value of an execution carried out over 20 or more years after the crime? Do folks really believe that such executions provide a deterrent and a safer society? Possibly, the only person actually deterred is the one who has been executed. (**What type of deterrence is Warden Cepak describing here?**) Society is safe from that person! There is probably more deterrent value in a life sentence served in a highly restricted environment. Should we examine why the murder rate in most countries that do not have the death penalty is much lower than in the U.S.? What are the chances that the systems involved will resolve these issues or will we continue to do the best we can?

Capital Punishment in the United States Today

As of October 6, 2017, a total of 1,461 inmates have been executed in the United States since the death penalty was re-instated in 1976. Thirty-one states, the federal government, and U.S. military allow the death penalty. However, neither New Hampshire nor Kansas has executed anyone since pre-*Furman* days. Nineteen states (Alaska, Connecticut, Delaware, Hawaii, Illinois, Iowa, Maine, Maryland, Massachusetts, Michigan, Minnesota, New Jersey, New Mexico ["[t]hough New Mexico has abolished the death penalty, its law was not retroactive, leaving 2 prisoners on its death row

Table 10.3 Total Number of Death Row Inmates as of April 1, 2017 = 2,843

State	# of Inmates	State	# of Inmates	State	# of Inmates
California	744	U.S. Government	62	Idaho	8
Florida	386	Mississippi	49	Washington	8
Texas	247	Oklahoma	47	Virginia	6
Alabama	193	S. Carolina	42	U.S. Military	5
Pennsylvania	169	Arkansas	36	Colorado	3
N. Carolina	154	Kentucky	33	South Dakota	3
Ohio	143	Oregon	33	Montana	2
Arizona	124	Missouri	25	New Mexico	2
Nevada	81	Indiana	12	New Hampshire	1
Louisiana	75	Kansas	10	Wyoming	1
Tennessee	62	Nebraska	10		
Georgia	62	Utah	9		

Source: Death Penalty Information Center.

and its lethal injection protocol intact"], New York, North Dakota, Rhode Island, Vermont, West Virginia, and Wisconsin), Puerto Rico, and the District of Columbia do not have "constitutional" capital punishment statutes in place.[72]

The most frequently used method of execution since 1976 is lethal injection (1,286), with some states allowing other options as backups. The second most common method of capital punishment in America since 1976 has been by electrocution (158). During this time period there have only been a few executions by lethal gas (11), hanging (3), and firing squad (3). Southern states have led the way by carrying out the majority of executions (1,184) as evidenced by the top ten jurisdictions and the number of executions (Texas, 543; Virginia, 113; Oklahoma, 112; Florida, 94; Missouri, 88; Georgia, 70; Alabama, 60; Ohio, 55; North Carolina, 43; South Carolina, 43). The majority of death row inmates are found in Southern states as well. See **Table 10.3.** Most of the executions occur in about one-third of the states, and since 1976 most of those have been in the South. See **Table 10.4.**[73]

As of April 1, 2017, death row inmates numbered 2,843 in the United States. From the time of Gary Gilmore's execution by rifle firing squad in Utah in 1977 through October 6, 2017, a total of 1,461 executions occurred. During 2016, 20 persons were executed in the United States all by lethal injection and, as of October 6, 19 persons have been executed in 2017, all by lethal injection. All of those executed in 2016 and so far in 2017 were male. From the beginning of 2016 until October 6, 2017, there have been 39 executions in the United States. Over half of those execu-

Table 10.4 Executions by Region since 1976 as of October 6, 2017

Region	Total
South	1191
Midwest	181
West	85
Northeast	4
Texas & Oklahoma Alone	654

Source: Death Penalty Information Center, https://deathpenaltyinfo.org/documents/FactSheet.pdf.

tions have taken place in Texas (12) and Georgia (10), with another 17 executions having been carried out in Alabama (4), Arkansas (4), Florida (3), Missouri (2), Ohio (2), and Virginia (2).[74]

As of October 6, 2017, **Table 10.5** below reflects the executions by race of inmates since 1976. Note blacks are almost three times more likely than their proportion in the overall U.S. population to be executed.[75]

Race of Offenders and Their Victims

Research has also shown that the chances of being executed increase drastically when the victim is white. See **Table 10.6.** Several studies have concluded that prosecutors are more likely to seek death sentences for minority racial offenders for crimes involving white victims and that sentences of capital punishment are handed down disproportionately for persons whose victims are white.[76]

As of October 6, 2017, the majority of persons on death row in America were nonwhite. African Americans totaled 42 percent of death row inmates, with Latinos comprising another 13 percent, and Asians and Native Americans, and other races comprised of about 3 percent of the death row inmate population. Whites accounted for approximately 42 percent of this population.[77]

Table 10.5 Race of Those Executed since 1976, as of October 6, 2017

Black	503	34.4%
Hispanic/Latino	120	8.2%
White	815	55.8%
Other	23	1.6%

Source: Death Penalty Information Center, https://deathpenaltyinfo.org/documents/FactSheet.pdf.

Table 10.6 Race of Victims in Death Penalty Cases since 1976, as of October 6, 2017

Black	15%
Hispanic/Latino	7%
White	76%
Other	2%

Source: Death Penalty Information Center, https://deathpenaltyinfo.org/documents/FactSheet.pdf.

Females under Sentence of Death

Women are rarely sentenced to death and account for less than 2% of inmates living on death row. As of April 1, 2017 53 women were living on death row in American prisons. Since 1976, sixteen women have been executed (as of October 6, 2017). Nine of those executions were carried out in Texas and Oklahoma. From January 1, 1973, through December 31, 2016, 181 death sentences have been imposed for women.[78]

Kelly Renee Gissendaner was executed in Georgia on September 30, 2015, for the murder of her husband, Doug Gissendaner. Gissendaner's case drew wide attention from the media and public for various reasons. Prior to her execution, Gissendaner was the only woman on Georgia's death row and the first woman executed by the state in 70 years (since 1945). Another reason for controversy was because she conspired with Gregory Owen, her lover at the time of the crime, to plot the murder of her husband. In 1997, Owen carried out the murder by stabbing Doug Gissendaner to death. In a plea agreement, Owen testified for the prosecution against Kelly Renee Gissendaner to escape the death penalty in exchange for a life sentence (but with a possibility of parole). Third, her execution had previously been set for two other dates. First, in February, but it was delayed due to inclement weather. Then, it was set again the following month. However, that execution date was also postponed due to reports from Department of Corrections' doctors that the lethal injection drugs on hand at that time were "cloudy." **Do you think that changing the date of an inmate's execution, on numerous occasions, violates the Eighth Amendment's clause on "cruel and unusual punishment?" Why or why not?**

During her incarceration Gissendaner completed a Certificate in Theology offered by the prison, and it had been noted by correctional staff that she counseled other troubled inmates. Reportedly, she sang "Amazing Grace" during her execution.[79] Among those who pleaded for the halt of her execution were Pope Francis, a former Georgia Supreme Court chief justice, and a former deputy director of the Georgia Corrections Department.[80]

The Demography of Death Row

First and last, the poor are much more likely to be executed in America than the wealthy. The chances of a rich person winding up on death row in this country are slim to none. "Almost all death row inmates could not [even] afford their own attorney at trial."[81]

At year-end 2013, almost half of the inmates on death row (48%) were known to have less than a high school education, with 13.3 percent having an eighth-grade education or less. Approximately 43 percent were known to have completed high school or a GED, with 9 percent having completed college.[82]

At year-end 2012, almost all death row prisoners were men. Two-thirds (67%) of death row prisoners had a history of felony convictions, and 8.6 percent had a previous conviction for homicide. Over half of death row inmates (50.2%) were age 40 to 54 years old. When the marital status of death row inmates was known, the following determinations were made year-end 2012. Over half of the death row inmates had never married, a little more than a fourth of the condemned were married when they were sentenced, and another fourth were divorced, separated, or widowed.

The Appeals Process

The average length of time spent on death row awaiting execution is about 11 years.[83] This delay is primarily the result of the time it takes to exhaust all legal appeals, including sentence review by the state's supreme court, as well as appeals on constitutional and procedural grounds. There is so much national interest in the death penalty that appellate courts allow the filing of ***amicus curiae*** briefs ("friend of the court" briefs filed by uninvolved third parties) in capital cases. The American Civil Liberties Union, which opposes the death penalty in all cases, is active in filing such briefs.

Moreover, after all appeals have been exhausted, it is common for those still to be executed to ask for executive clemency from the state governor (or, in federal cases, the president of the United States). All governors and the president have the power to pardon prisoners or commute (change) their sentences. In the case of a death row prisoner, attorneys may seek a reprieve (a delay in carrying out the execution) and a commutation to life imprisonment. Since 1976, there have been 246 grants of clemency (one at the federal level and three instances where governors did so for all death row inmates in their respective states—most notably Governor George Ryan in Illinois) for death row inmates in the United States.[84] And appeals do vacate (set aside) many death sentences.

At the same time, the lengthy appeals process takes money. Not only must lawyers and judges be paid, but the prisoner must be housed, fed, and protected. Combined legal and correctional costs of capital punishment cases can be very high indeed. Some unsophisticated observers might think imposition of the death penalty is a cheap solution to serious crime. "How much can the electricity cost? What's the price of a few cyanide tablets?" they might ask. But while the actual final surge of current or gurgle of gas or poison dispensed through a needle may be inexpensive, the overall costs are much higher. In California, a recent study concluded that the present costs of the death penalty in that state are $137 million for that system, whereas a system that would impose lifetime imprisonment instead of the death penalty would only cost $11.5 million. In Kansas, costs of death penalty cases have been found to be 70 percent more than non-capital cases. The primary costs for death penalty cases are said to emerge before and during trial, not in post-conviction proceedings. In Tennessee, death penalty trials are estimated on average to cost approximately 50 percent more than life imprisonment prosecutions, and in Maryland death penalty cases cost $3 million per case or three times that of non-capital prosecutions. Of course, money spent on carrying out the death penalty detracts from funds that could be spent on crime prevention and meaningful programmatic interventions.[85]

Public support for the death penalty seems to be waning, even within the nation's police. "In a national poll released in 2009, the nation's police chiefs ranked the death penalty last in their priorities for effective crime reduction. The chiefs did not believe the death penalty acted as a deterrent to murder, and they rated it as one of most inefficient uses of taxpayer dollars in fighting crime."[86] Practical reasons for releasing convicted murderers from prison many years after their conviction include the costs of incarceration. Many states face the high costs of maintaining aging prisoners, many of whom have developed chronic health problems in prison. Also, the aging process seems to diminish the antisocial impulses which initially led to the criminal violence of youthful convicted killers.[87]

Methods of Capital Punishment

All states have lethal injection as their primary method of execution. Thirty-six states (including New Mexico, which has abolished the death penalty for future cases but still has an inmate on death row), the United States government, and the U.S. military have lethal injection as their sole means of execution. Nine states (Alabama, Arkansas, Florida, Illinois, Kentucky, Oklahoma, South Carolina, Tennessee, and Virginia) have the electric chair as an optional, secondary method. Arizona, California, Maryland, Missouri, and Wyoming have the gas chamber as a secondary method. New Hampshire and Washington have hanging as a secondary method. For all intents and purposes, lethal injection is the sole method of execution in Utah and Oklahoma, as Utah no longer has this method as an option unless someone chose it prior to its elimination, and Oklahoma would only allow use of the firing squad if lethal injection and electrocution were found to be unconstitutional.[88]

The use of lethal injection—the newest method of execution—has become increasingly widespread. The major advantage of the method according to its proponents is that it is "painless." Federal offenders are executed by the method used in the state

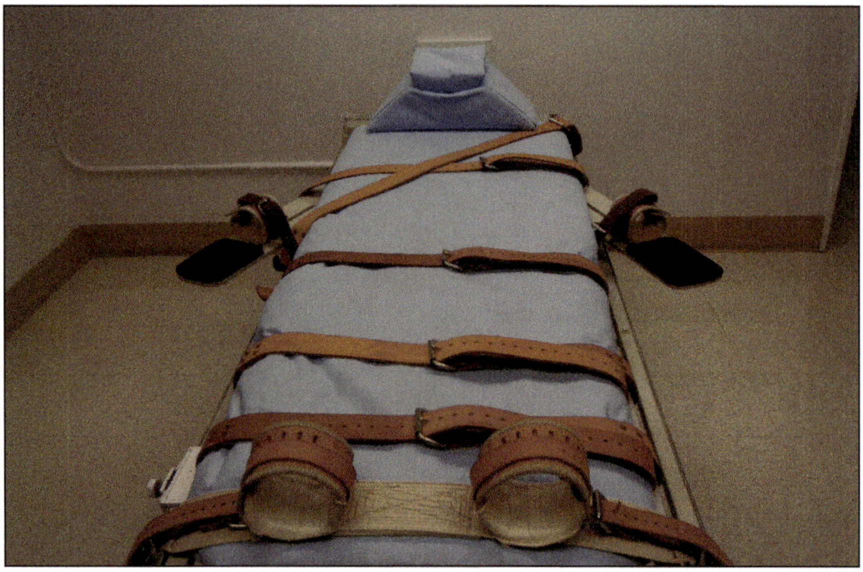

Gurney.

in which their execution takes place. As of May 4, 2010, the federal system had 59 (28 black, 23 white, 7 Latino, and 1 Native American) inmates on death row.[89] Most federal crimes that warrant the death penalty involve murder, but spying, treason, and illegal use of the mail service with intent to kill can conceivably bring about the penalty of death.[90] Federal death row is housed and executions take place at the United States Penitentiary in Terre Haute, Indiana.[91]

Continuing Controversies about the Death Penalty

The result of having a great number of people under the sentence of death is an overcrowded, expensive management problem for America's prison administrators. Many citizens express dissatisfaction with the slow rate of executions and the approximately 11-year gap between sentence and death. Letters to the editor in many local newspapers regularly express frustration regarding convicted offenders being held for so long on death row, the seemingly endless delays and appeals they are allowed, and the "lack of respect" for law and order perceived to result from this slow execution process. Meanwhile, highly motivated and industrious attorneys who work to put an end to capital punishment in this country continue to oppose executions.

The Case *for* Capital Punishment

Capital punishment is as controversial as any issue in criminal justice. In general, the proponents[92] of the death penalty argue that its use is justified in terms of just deserts—that taking the life of one who has taken another life is the only just retribution. This stance is supported by tradition going back to pre-biblical prescriptions found in the Code of Hammurabi of an eye for an eye and a tooth for a tooth.

Proponents also argue that the death penalty is necessary to deter others from committing murder and other atrocious crimes and that without it there would be little reason for criminals to refrain from killing even more frequently. They see, for example, a kidnapper having "nothing to lose" in killing rather than freeing a hostage without the death penalty to serve as a restraint.

They also argue that execution is the only assurance a criminal will never again commit a murder or any other crime (the ultimate assurance of specific deterrence). This is an assurance that does not hold for life-term prisoners who may, and indeed sometimes do, commit crimes while in prison or upon release.

Proponents also hold that the death penalty is an essential social symbol, expressing the boundaries of our cultural standards of decency and humanity. All societies must set outer limits beyond which deviant behavior cannot be tolerated; the death penalty, according to its proponents, is a clear and firm statement of our outrage at and revulsion for murderous acts.

Approximately two-thirds of Americans responding to Gallup polls at the end of the twentieth century indicated support for the death penalty for those convicted for murder, with almost half of those polled indicating that they do not believe the death penalty is used often enough.[93] Advocates maintain that death is generally seen as an appropriate societal response to certain crimes and criminals.

The Case *against* Capital Punishment

While the majority of Americans may favor the death penalty, one study found that white males, Republicans, and older persons are more likely to favor the death penalty, with most respondents concerned about the possible execution of innocent persons, limited access to the appellate process, and inadequate defense attorneys available for capital cases.[94] The most powerful argument against the death penalty is that mistakes can and have been made in its imposition. Innocent persons have been executed, and, of course, that there is no remedy for any such mistake. The research of Hugo Adam Bedau, a long-time opponent of capital punishment, and Professor Michael Radelet revealed that twenty-three persons died wrongfully at the hands of the state between 1900 and 1986, and another 300 persons were sentenced to death who were later either given new trials by higher courts or exonerated altogether. In 1987, Bedau and Radelet stated that in every year of the twentieth century one or more persons on death row have eventually been shown to be innocent.[95]

Support for the death penalty has declined dramatically over the past two decades. "A Pew Research Center poll in August and September 2016 found that 49% favor the death penalty for people convicted of murder, while 42% oppose it. But support is at its lowest level in more than 40 years. Democrats account for much of the decline in support over the past two decades. In 2016, just 34% of Democrats favored the death penalty, compared with 72% of Republicans."[96]

Recent Gallup polls reveal, as of 2016, 60% of the public support the death penalty, while about 37% are opposed to the sentence; 50% of respondents question whether the death penalty is administered fairly in America. Twelve states have abolished the punishment in the last decade.[97] In 1994, support for the death penalty peaked with 80% of Americans in favor of it. However, the most recent polls are more in line with the rate of support found in this country for the death penalty when *Furman v. Georgia* was decided in 1972—in two polls that year, one in March and one in November, 50% and 57% of respondents favored the death penalty.[98]

The number of death sentences delivered by the courts has declined every year from 2007 through 2016 (126 to 31), and the number of executions carried out have also dropped since 2009 (52 in 2009 to 20 in 2016).[99] Since 1973, there have been 159 people exonerated and released from death row in 27 different states in the U.S. The majority of the exonerations have taken place in five states, led by Florida (27), followed by Illinois (20), Texas (13), Louisiana (11), and Oklahoma (10).[100]

Furthermore, the Florida Innocence Project was founded in 2003. Since then the staff and lawyers have worked to exonerate 13 men, who collectively spent 259 years incarcerated for crimes they did not commit—including James Bain, who served longer than any exoneree in U.S. history, 35 years, based on inaccurate eyewitness identification. He was ultimately freed via DNA evidence.[101]

Opponents of capital punishment also maintain that the publicity surrounding an execution may attract unbalanced people to *commit* capital crimes rather than deter potential murderers, as they seek the attention given to the person being executed and therefore commit crimes in order to be on center stage themselves. Sometimes murder rates actually increase following executions, as individuals become desensitized to violence. This is referred to as **"the brutalization effect."**[102]

Moreover, opponents argue that even if you believe rational persons were likely to be deterred by the threat of capital punishment, the kinds of crimes for which we use capital punishment are essentially nondeterrable. In other words, as Judge Dennis Challeen argues, capital punishment laws are deterrents for those who are not the problem.[103] Murder, torture, mayhem, and the like originate in deep-seated psychological and psychiatric personality factors just as terrorism and espionage rest on "true-believer" political values. Neither twisted personalities nor political martyrs are amenable to change by making examples of others.

Opponents of capital punishment argue that people who have had practice at committing crime know that their chances of getting caught are diminished compared to someone who has never or rarely committed crime. So it is with the death penalty, if one doesn't think they are going to get caught or consider getting caught, the supposed general deterrent effect of the death penalty is severely compromised.

Also, though capital punishment is one of our oldest methods of dealing with offenders, the frequency of application seems to bear no relevance to the crime rate. If the general deterrence theory worked, theoretically there should be a decrease in serious crime where the death penalty is used and an increase where it is forbidden.

But in those states that had capital punishment and later abolished it, there was no increase in capital crimes. Conversely, in those states that did not have capital punishment but later adopted it, there was no decrease in capital crimes.

Opponents of capital punishment also point out that its use in the past clearly discriminated against the poor and against blacks and other minorities. They also feel that, given human nature and prejudice, no provisions in statutes or court rules can alter this in the future.

Finally, some opponents of capital punishment argue that the fact that it is in our codes even if not frequently used, is a *blight* on our claims to civility and humaneness. They see capital punishment as brutal and brutalizing and "deathwork" as not a proper occupation in a democratic society. The death penalty is not only a controversial political issue, but a controversial philosophic and moral issue as well.

The fact remains that we know little about the actual persons who kill. Neither our knowledge in that area nor our ability to predict who will kill has grown much since the time of the first murder of Abel by his brother Cain. Whatever the persuasiveness of the arguments and counter-arguments regarding the death penalty, it is clear that a majority of Americans wish to have it kept on the books and used for murder and perhaps for other atrocious crimes.

Summary

Sentences passed must be served, and the serving of sentences generally involves either community correction or incarceration. We now turn to the world of corrections, with its own series of decision points and issues. Most offenders will remain in the community to pay their debt to society. The history of community corrections will be considered, as will the various conditions those released into the community might be expected to abide by. Revocations for violations that may send a person on supervised release to incarceration will be addressed. Lastly, means for being discharged from supervision will be discussed.

Chapter 11

Community Corrections

Image by jeangill at istockphoto.com

"I have always endeavored to send these persons to school, or some place of employment, and but two, to my knowledge, have stolen since I bailed them, and this shows that nine out of ten have behaved well."

—John Augustus, Father of Probation, remarking on the success of the court releasing persons to his supervision in 1852[1]

Seeking Justice: Alternative Punishments in the Community

Shawn Gementera, a convicted mail thief, was ordered by a federal judge to stand outside a post office in San Francisco and hold a sign which read, "I stole mail. This is my punishment." Gementera appealed his sentence on the grounds that it constituted cruel and unusual punishment in violation of his Eighth Amendment rights.

The federal appellate court upheld the sentence. The Ninth Circuit Court of Appeals determined that "in comparison with the reality of the modern prison, we simply have no reason to conclude that the sanction ... exceeds the bounds of 'civilized standards' or other 'evolving standards of decency that mark the progress of a maturing society.'" The U.S. Supreme Court declined to hear the case, leaving the sentence in place.[2]

In Texas, Judge Buddie Hahn gave an abusive father a choice between spending 30 nights in jail or 30 nights sleeping in the doghouse where prosecutors alleged the man had forced his 11-year-old stepson to sleep.

In Georgia, Judge Sidney Nation suspended almost all of Brenton Jay Raffensperger's seven-year sentence for cocaine possession and driving under the influence in exchange for his promise to buy a casket and keep it in his home to remind him of the costs of drug addiction.

In Ohio, a municipal judge, Michael Cicconetti, cut a 120-day jail sentence down to 45 days for two teens who, on a Christmas Eve, had defaced a statue of Jesus they stole from a church's nativity scene. In exchange, the pair had to deliver a new statue to the church and march through town with a donkey and a sign reading "Sorry for the Jackass Offense."

In North Carolina, Judge James Honeycutt ordered four young offenders who broke into a school and did $60,000 in damage to wear signs around their necks in public that read "I AM A JUVENILE CRIMINAL." One, a 14-year-old girl, appealed the sentenced, and it was overturned.

One Texas state judge, Ted Poe, was known as "The King of Shame." His use of punishments included sentencing a person to shovel manure. Poe said that he liked to humiliate people because "[t]he people I see have too good a self-esteem." Poe was popular for what he called "Poe-tic Justice."

In Memphis, Judge Joe Brown became famous for allowing victims of burglaries to go to the homes of the thieves and take something of equal value. When asked about his authority to order judicially supervised burglaries, Brown explained with a hint of amazement that "under Tennessee law it appears to be legal." Brown eventually took his brand of justice to television as the host of his own syndicated court show.

North Carolina Judge Marcia Morey allowed speeders to send their fines to a charity for hurricane victims rather than to the state. Similarly, Wisconsin Judge Scott Woldt ordered Sharon Rosenthal, who stole money from the labor union where she was treasurer, to donate her family's Green Bay Packers seats to his preferred charity, the Make-A-Wish Foundation.[3]

In Muskogee, Oklahoma, 17-year-old Tyler Alred, who had been drinking alcohol underage before getting behind the wheel of his vehicle, which resulted in the death of his passenger/friend, pled guilty to manslaughter. By entering this plea, he was able to avoid prison; he received a deferred sentence from Judge Mike Norman—requiring him to submit to 10 years of probation supervision. One of the conditions of his release into the community was that he attend church on a regular basis during the duration of his conditional release.[4] **Do you think this is an appropriate sentence? What about the clause in the First Amendment of the U.S. Constitution pertaining to the principle that there should be separation of church and state? What if it were a hate crime, where a Muslim attacks a Christian? Would it be acceptable for a judge to order a Muslim to attend church on a regular basis or for a Christian to attend a mosque?**

What do you think of the types of community sentences that some call creative and innovative discussed above? Can you think of any kinds of these public punishments that would deter you from committing crime? What would Émile Durkheim, who was discussed in Chapter 2, say about such punishments? What would Cesare Beccaria say about such judicial discretion? In your opinion, should judges be allowed to craft such sentences or should this be a legislative function? Explain why or why not.

About This Chapter

Although many convicted criminals are removed from society to serve their sentences in jail or prison, the vast majority remain in the community, at home and at work, under the supervision of probation or parole agents. A number of community corrections approaches, including probation, are considered "front-end alternatives" to incarceration, as they occur prior to an offender going to prison. Probation is a sentence handed down by the judge to serve one's term entirely in the community without first going to jail or prison.[5] It is not total leniency. The sentence imposes rules and controls on the offender which are enforced by probation officers and can result in prison if not followed.

Parole, on the other hand, is the part of a sentence served in the community **after** the offender has spent another part of it in prison. A major distinction, then, between probation and parole is that probation is a sentence ordered by the judge after a person has been convicted of a crime. Parole is not a sentence from the court but a release decision made by a parole board after an offender has spent part of the sentence in an institution.

What's wrong with this statement? "The judge sentenced the convicted woman to serve four years on parole."

At year-end (2015), over 4.6 million adults were under federal and state **community supervision**, representing a 1.3% decrease from the year before (primarily due to a drop in people on probation). This equates to roughly 1 in every 51 adults in the country under some form of community supervision. Eighty-one percent of adults on community supervision are on probation (over 3.8 million, as of January 1, 2015). Numbers on parole increased, from 2014–2015, by 1.5%. Parolees increased for the first time in seven years from 450,800 (2014) to 463,700 (in 2015).[6]

The unpopularity of parole was fueled by a pervasive "get tough on crime" mentality and by sensationally broadcast horrific crimes perpetrated by released prisoners. See **Field Practice 11.1** below.

Field Practice 11.1 The Influence of the Media on Crime Policy

The release of Willie Horton on furlough from prison by then governor of Massachusetts Michael Dukakis is probably one of the biggest albatrosses placed around a politician's neck for a botched decision pertaining to a prisoner. It likely cost Dukakis the presidential election against George Herbert Bush. Horton was serving a life sentence for murder when he was allowed to have a weekend pass. He fled to Maryland, raped a woman, assaulted and bound her fiancé, and stole his car. He would be sentenced to two life terms plus 85 years for those crimes, and George Herbert Bush would become the 41st president of the United States after his campaign made the Willie Horton case a centerpiece of its advertisements.[7]

More recently, former Arkansas governor and Republican presidential candidate Mike Huckabee came under fire for having commuted a 95-year prison sentence of Maurice Clemmons. Clemmons allegedly shot and killed four Lakewood, Washington, police officers in November 2009.[8]

While reportedly in violation of his parole for assault with a deadly weapon, Lovelle Mixon shot and killed four Oakland, California, police officers in March of 2009. Mixon was ultimately shot and killed in a gunfight with SWAT officers.[9]

Other headlines include "Parolee Linked to Killing 5 Women in Michigan Capital"; "Paroled Rapist Charged with Killing 5 Women in New Jersey"; and "Man Charged with Killing 7 Chicago Women," and the police indicated these murders took place while the defendant was out on parole.[10]

How would you as a politician try to convince the public that parole and other types of release are needed for prisoners?

In an atmosphere of media and public scrutiny, fourteen states abolished discretionary parole board release by 2000. As noted by the American Probation and Parole Association, by 2009, 16 states' parole boards had either had the parole board abolished or had their parole power greatly diminished.[11] See **Table 11.1**.[12] "Truth in sentencing laws" (TIS laws) emerged in 1984. As seen in **Table 11.2**, 28 states, the District of Columbia, and the federal government enacted TIS laws, thereby requiring for all crimes, or at least for some crimes in some instances, as reflected in the table, that prisoners serve at least 85 percent of their sentence. The United States Congress even made federal grant money available for states to combat prison overcrowding via prison construction ironically by showing that inmates on average in their prison system were serving not less than 85 percent of their sentences.[13] As of 2015, thirty states reportedly met federal TIS requirements—mandating that prisoners serve 85% of their original sentence. Thus, TIS strictures have been blamed for contributing to the mass incarceration problem in America.[14]

Another by-product of the lack of early release is that many inmates are released into the community with *no* supervision or control. From 1990 through 2012, there was a 119% increase in the number of inmates who maxed out their sentence. More than 20 percent (22%) of those released from prison in 2012 were released by maxing out their sentence.[15] This means they maxed out or served their entire original sentence, entered the community with no correctional supervision, no conditions to comply with, and could not face revocation proceedings.[16] "Thirteen states released more than one-third of their inmates unconditionally in 2012, and max-outs accounted for more than 4 in 10 releases in nine states: Florida, Maine, Massachusetts, New Jersey, North Carolina, Ohio, Oklahoma, South Carolina, and Utah."

In fact, "Florida had the nation's highest max-out rate. The state abolished parole in 1983 and, like many states, adopted a determinate sentencing structure. It also was one of the first states to adopt a truth-in-sentencing measure, passing a law requiring all offenders who committed their crimes on or after Oct. 1, 1995, to serve at least 85 percent of their sentences. Since then, the number of inmates maxing out in Florida has risen steadily. In 1990, Florida released approximately 12,000 inmates, or 32 percent of offenders, without supervision. By 2012 the max-out rate had increased to 64 percent, resulting in more than 21,000 inmates leaving prison with no monitoring or support."[17]

At year-end 2015, over 6.7 million people in the U.S. were under some form of correctional supervision. One in 37 adults in America (2.7% of the population), the lowest rate since 1994, were under some type of correctional supervision. The majority of offenders were on probation (56.2%), with 22.6 percent in prison, only 11.3% on parole, and 10.6 percent in jail.[18] See **Table 11.3.**[19] With 69.1% of all persons under correctional supervision on probation or parole, community-based corrections is viewed as an alternative to incarceration. It is a less intrusive response to the criminal offense and is the means by which the majority of offenders in America are supervised.

This chapter traces the history of probation and parole, explains the advantages of community-based corrections over incarceration, and describes the world of supervised living while free from confinement. It deals with the conditions of community sentences, up to and including electronic monitoring and tracking. The rights of probationers and parolees are discussed, and a distinction is drawn between these two forms of community supervision in regard to permissible rules and conditions, the rights of authorities to search for and seize evidence, and the procedures and criteria for revocation. Modern techniques of community-based corrections are introduced in this chapter, techniques designed to rehabilitate rather than humiliate and to lessen the costs of imprisonment while attempting to provide an effective response to crime. The stressful nature of probation/parole officer jobs is examined in Chapter 14. The processes for revocation of probation and parole are explored in this chapter, and forms of executive clemency and types of discharge from sentences are also discussed.

Field Practice 11.2 In Their Own Words: Profile of Gina Enriquez, United States Probation Officer, District of Arizona

While enrolled at the University of Arizona, I found courses in the fields of psychology and sociology were ones which interested me most. I knew

Table 11.1 States That Have Abolished Discretionary Parole

All Offenders		Certain Violent Offenders
Arizona	Minnesota	Alaska
California[a]	Mississippi	Louisiana
Delaware	North Carolina	New York
Florida[b]	Ohio[d]	Tennessee
Illinois	Oregon	
Indiana	Virginia	
Kansas[c]	Washington	
Maine	Wisconsin	

[a] In 1976, the Uniform Determinate Sentencing Act abolished discretionary parole for all offenses except some violent crimes with a long sentence of a sentence to life.

[b] In 1995, parole eligibility was abolished for offenses with a life sentence and a 25-year mandatory term.

[c] Excludes a few offenses, primarily first-degree murder and intentional second-degree murder.

[d] Excludes murder and aggravated murder.

Source: Bureau of Justice Statistics, Reentry Trends in the U.S.[20]

Table 11.2 Truth-in-Sentencing Requirements, by State[21]

Meet Federal 85% Requirement		50% Requirement	100% of Minimum Requirement	Other Requirement
Arizona	Missouri	Indiana	Idaho	Alaska[c]
California	New Jersey	Maryland	Nevada	Arkansas[d]
Connecticut	New York	Nebraska	New Hampshire	Colorado[e]
Delaware	North Carolina	Texas		Kentucky[f]
District of Col.	North Dakota			Massachusetts[g]
Florida	Ohio			Wisconsin[h]
Georgia	Oklahoma[b]			
Illinois[a]	Oregon			
Iowa	Pennsylvania			
Kansas	South Carolina			
Louisiana	Tennessee			
Maine	Utah			
Michigan	Virginia			
Minnesota	Washington			
Mississippi				

[a] Qualified for federal funding in 1996 only.

[b] Effective July 1, 1999, offenders will be required to serve 85% of the sentence.

[c] Two-part sentence structure (2/3 in prison; 1/3 on parole); 100% of prison term required.

[d] Mandatory 70% of sentence for certain violent offenses and manufacture of methamphetamine.

[e] Violent offenders with two prior violent convictions serve 75%; one prior violent conviction, 56.25%.

[f] Effective July 15, 1998, offenders are required to serve 85% of the sentence.

[g] Requires 75% of a minimum prison sentence.

[h] Effective December 31, 1999, two-part sentence: offenders serve 100% of the prison term and a sentence of extended supervision at 25% of the prison sentence.

Table 11.3 Number of persons supervised by U.S. adult correctional systems, by correctional status, 2007 and 2015

	2007		2015	
Correctional populations	Population	Percent of total population	Population	Percent of total population
Total[a]	7,339,600	100%	6,741,400	100%
Probation[b]	4,293,000	58.5	3,789,800	56.2
Prison[b]	1,596,800	21.8	1,526,800	22.6
Parole[b]	826,100	11.3	870,500	12.9
Local jail[c]	780,200	10.6	728,200	10.8
Offenders with multiple correctional statuses[d]	156,400	:	174,000	:

Note: Counts were rounded to the nearest 100 and include estimates for nonresponding jurisdictions. Detail may not sum to total due to rounding and because offenders with multiple correctional statuses were excluded from the total correctional population. See Methodology.

: Not calculated.

[a] Total was adjusted to exclude offenders with multiple correctional statuses to avoid double counting. See Methodology.

[b] Population as of December 31.

[c] Population as of the last weekday in June.

[d] Some probationers and parolees on December 31 were held in a prison or jail but still remained under the jurisdiction of a probation or parole agency and some parolees were also on probation. In addition, some prisoners were being held in jail. They were excluded from the total correctional population to avoid double counting. See table 5 and Methodology.

Sources: Bureau of Justice Statistics, Annual Probation Survey, Annual Parole Survey, Annual Survey of Jails, and National Prisoner Statistics Program, 2007 and 2015.

these subjects would provide me with the opportunities to work with individuals of varying cultural, economic, and social backgrounds. After graduating from the University of Arizona with a Bachelor of Arts degree, I was employed by a mental health agency working with single head of household women and at-risk children. I developed interviewing skills for assessing individuals' needs and solicited the community for services such as food, shelter, and clothing for families in crisis.

Following my employment at the mental health agency, I began working with a local school district's Teenage Parent Program. Initially I served as the program's case manager, meeting with students who were pregnant and assessing their educational and healthcare needs. My responsibilities increased with the development of an intervention program, which consisted of providing teen pregnancy prevention presentations to middle and high school students while writing grant proposals for pregnancy prevention tools.

Prior to earning a master of social work degree from Arizona State University, I completed a practicum at a mental health center in Tucson. I worked with a mobile acute crisis response team in conjunction with law enforcement to conduct crisis interventions and develop treatment plans for individuals experiencing a mental health crisis. I also conducted mental status examinations and offered recommendations regarding client diagnosis and treatment.

In 1999, I began employment with the U.S. Probation Office in Tucson, as a probation officer assistant. I became familiar with conducting comprehensive criminal records investigations and learned to interpret and collect the data necessary to provide an accurate picture of a person's criminal and social history. Once I was promoted to a U.S. Probation Officer, I was responsible for interviewing case agents, victims, and other collateral resources to obtain information pertinent to sentencing issues. I also offered individualized sentencing recommendations to federal district court judges based on the defendant's current and previous criminal and social history.

I now supervise men and women released from federal prison or sentenced to probation to ensure compliance with court-imposed conditions, work to mitigate their risk to the community, improve their overall condition, and facilitate their reintegration into our communities. It is essential to establish a rapport with offenders and their families to ensure a successful reintegration while maintaining community safety. Maintaining positive working relationships with treatment providers and law enforcement agencies is critical for obtaining collateral information about offenders' conduct while on supervision. My current assignment also involves working with offenders who are identified as being high risk to recidivate due to their extensive criminal history and/or serious mental health and substance abuse issues. In this capacity, I often draw on the crisis management skills I developed with the mobile acute crisis response team and rely on my social work education when collaborating with treatment providers to develop treatment plans for offenders.

The educational decisions I made as an undergraduate set the course for my professional and personal growth. I am fortunate to have had the opportunity to work with people of different ages, cultures, and social backgrounds. Each professional career opportunity served as building blocks to my current career choice as a federal probation officer.

History of Probation

A cobbler from Boston named John Augustus is generally considered to be the "father of probation." In 1841, he provided bail and contributed to the reformation of a man accused of public drunkenness, an experience that began a lengthy period of similar efforts on the part of Augustus and that gave birth to the concept of probation. In his journal, Augustus wrote of that first encounter in the Boston City Court:

> In the month of August, 1841, I was in court one morning, when the door communicating with the lock-room was opened and an officer entered, followed by a ragged and wretched looking man, who took his seat upon the bench allotted to prisoners. I imagined from the man's appearance, that his offense was that of yielding to his appetite for intoxicating drinks.... The case was clearly made out, but before sentence had been passed out I conversed with him for a few moments, and found that *he was not yet past all hope of reformation*, although his appearance and his looks precluded a belief in the minds of others that he would ever become a man again. He told me that if he could be saved from the House of Correction, he never again would taste intoxicating liquors; there was such an earnestness in that tone, a look expressive of firm resolve, that I determined to aid him, I bailed him, by permission of the Court ... at the expiration of this period of probation, I accompanied him into the court room; his whole appearance was changed and no one, not even the scrutinizing officers, could have believed that he was the same person who less than a month before, had stood trembling on the prisoner's stand. The Judge expressed himself much pleased with the account we gave of the man, and instead of the usual penalty,—imprisonment in the House of Correction,—he fined him one cent and costs, amounting in all to $3.76, which was immediately paid. The man continued industrious and sober, and without doubt has been by this treatment, saved from a drunkard's grave.[22]

Augustus was so encouraged by this experience that he devoted much of the remainder of his life and his material resources to the aid of men, women, and children caught up in the criminal justice system. He opened his own house to offenders he "perceived to be not beyond all hope of reformation," provided clothing and food, and assisted in securing employment. In addition to helping several thousand people in need of charity, in the 18 years remaining before his death in 1859, Augustus "bailed" approximately 2,000 persons "on probation."[23] After his death the work continued under the direction of Rufus R. Cook, the chaplain of the county gaol (jail) and a representative of the Boston Children's Aid Society.[24]

In 1878, Massachusetts passed the first probation statute. By 1920, every state in the union had a legislatively created probation system in operation. The *concept* of probation resembled the Augustus model in terms of offender screening, assistance, reformation, and benevolence. Early legislative discussions focused on that model, emphasizing the need for probation officers to be recruited from the ranks of ministers, social workers, psychologists, and other like-minded professionals. However, when probation was *implemented* as an agency of the state the emphasis became *surveillance* and *enforcement of rules*. The first state probation officers tended to be retired sheriffs and others concerned primarily with the strict control of offenders.[25] Today every state's probation efforts revolve around a combination of rule enforcement and surveillance. They also incorporate such casework techniques as counseling, job placement, and similar forms of assistance.

Probation received great impetus as a correctional technique with the spread of the juvenile court movement after the turn of the century. And while the history of community sentences for felons is a stormy one, since both probation and parole were, and remain, controversial, they have in general proven effective and are now widely used in most states. (See **Table 11.4.**[26])

History of Parole

The word "parole" as we use it is derived from the French term for "word of honor."

The practice of allowing prisoners to leave confinement early upon giving their word that they will remain law-abiding had its early roots in Europe. About the middle of the nineteenth century, various forms of parole were developed almost simultaneously in Spain, Germany, and the British Isles. In these early systems, prisoners were allowed to return to their communities, not because early release was particularly rehabilitative, but simply because letting them go home helped alleviate prison overcrowding. At home, possessing a ticket-of-leave from the prison, they were placed under the supervision of local police officers. They were required to report monthly to the police, and the police helped them find jobs and otherwise offered oversight.[27]

Captain Alexander Maconochie pioneered the ticket-of-leave in the 1840s with European prisoners who had been sent to Australian penal colonies. He advocated moving prisoners through stages of regimentation. These stages were:

1. strict imprisonment, with virtually no freedom;
2. constricted labor on a chain gang performing hard labor to benefit the government;
3. supervised freedom within a confined area;
4. a ticket-of-leave, or conditional pardon to society;
5. full restoration of freedom without restraint or supervision.[28]

In Ireland, Sir Walter Crofton developed a similar system in the 1850s, although requiring stricter supervision while on ticket-of-leave.[29] In general the European "ticket-of-leave" system worked well—it did not seem to increase the danger to society in general and did, of course, lower "gaol" (jail) populations—and these positive effects were noticed in the United States. Since any parole system rests on an *indeterminate sentencing structure*, adapting parole to the United States required the introduction of a sentencing system with a time spread between the minimum and maximum term. The American tradition was *flat time*, determinate prison sentences like those currently imposed on misdemeanants and in several states for felonies as well.

Table 11.4 Characteristics of Adults on Probation, 2005, 2014, and 2015

Characteristic	2005	2014	2015
Sex	100%	100%	100%
Male	77	75	75
Female	23	25	25
Race/Hispanic origin*	100%	100%	100%
White	55	54	55
Black/African American	30	30	30
Hispanic/Latino	13	13	13
American Indian/Alaska Native	1	1	1
Asian/Native Hawaiian/Other Pacific Islander	1	1	1
Two or more races	--	--	--
Status of supervision	100%	100%	100%
Active	72	73	76
Residential/other treatment program	1	1	1
Financial conditions remaining	...	1	2
Inactive	9	5	4
Absconder	10	8	7
Supervised out of jurisdiction	2	6	2
Warrant status	6	2	5
Other	--	4	4
Type of offense	100%	100%	100%
Felony	50	56	57
Misdemeanor	49	42	41
Other infractions	1	2	2
Most serious offense	100%	100%	100%
Violent	18%	19%	20%
Domestic violence	6	4	4
Sex offense	3	3	4
Other violent offense	10	12	13
Property	23%	28%	28%
Drug	25%	25%	25%
Public order	19%	16%	15%
DWI/DUI	14	14	13
Other traffic offense	5	2	2
Other	14%	11%	12%

Note: Detail may not sum to total due to rounding. Estimates are based on most recent data and may differ from previously published statistics. See Methodology. Characteristics are based on probationers with a known type of status.

--Less than 0.05%.

...Not available.

*Excludes persons of Hispanic or Latino origin, unless specified.

Source: Bureau of Justice Statistics, Annual Probation Survey, 2005, 2014, and 2015.

An American prison reformer, Zebulon E. Brockway, was instrumental in establishing the first indeterminate sentencing law, in Michigan in 1869, where parole was first used with female convicts. However, shortly afterward the Michigan courts declared this law unconstitutional. Brockway later moved to New York, where he became superintendent of the newly constructed reformatory at Elmira. During the 1870s he succeeded in having an indeterminate sentence law adopted in New York. This became the basis for the first parole system for men in the United States when the Elmira Reformatory opened in 1876. Actually, the entire reformatory idea put into practice at Elmira, including the use of indeterminate sentences and parole, was considered more of an experiment than a trend. Parole did not generally become a feature of prison sentences for older, ordinary felons until after the turn of the century. By 1925, however, indeterminate sentences and parole were found in most jurisdictions in the United States, and by 1970 every state and the federal government used it in some form.[30]

In the 1970s, a number of states, under increasing pressure to "get tough on crime," adopted a presumptive system of flat-time (definite) sentences and abolished parole as unnecessary for *future* inmates, though parole boards were retained to decide cases already sentenced. However, even some of the states that abolished parole (Maine and California, among others) have reintroduced early release primarily because of prison overcrowding. It is not called "parole" of course, for this term is too "soft" in a "get-tough-on-crime" environment. Instead, parole boards are commonly called Boards of Prison Terms, which sounds tougher and more restraint-oriented. So in spite of the popularity of flat sentences, parole still is a significant way inmates are released from prison and is generally widely accepted as a viable and efficient correctional technique.[31]

Community Corrections: Offenders on Probation and Parole

The Case *for* Community-Based Corrections

Arguments in favor of community-based corrections usually rest on dissatisfaction with the state of affairs in prisons. Almost every argument *against* prisons can be restated as an argument *for* community-based programs.

Cost-Effectiveness

The total expenses of incarceration are difficult to assess. Prison building costs have escalated in recent years, and higher-security prisons tend to have greater annual costs per inmate than lower-security prisons. Of course, incarceration is costly; as noted in a study of the Vera Institute, of 40 state prison systems, "the total per-inmate cost averaged $31,286 and ranged from $14,603 in Kentucky to $60,076 in New York."[32] In fact, the total taxpayer cost in a 40-state analysis of prisons in a Vera Institute analysis was $38,903,304.[33] As noted by U.S. presidential candidate Bernie Sanders, "It costs a hell of a lot more money to put somebody in jail than send them to the University of Virginia.... If their incarceration surpasses four years, then it easily could surpass the cost of sending a student to the University of Virginia. Also, if that prisoner is held in a state such as New York, with high state prisoner incarceration costs of roughly $60,000 annually, it ... could outpace the cost of sending someone to [the University of Virginia.]"[34] For a similar comparison, the cost for attending Harvard University for the 2016–2017 academic year is listed as $43,280 for tuition alone, and $63,025 for tuition, room, board, and fees combined.[35] Furthermore, "Vera Institute researchers found that the total taxpayer cost of prisons [based on] 40 states that participated in [their] study was 13.9 percent higher than the cost reflected in those states' combined corrections budgets. The total price to taxpayers was $39 billion, $5.4 billion more than the $33.5 billion reflected in corrections budgets alone."[36]

As of 2016, the previously mentioned Vera Institute study was recognized as "the most recent authoritative source" for the costs of prisons in America. In their analysis, 25 states with the highest cost per prisoner are identified. The top five most costly states per prisoner were all Northern states: New York ($60,076), New Jersey ($54,865), Connecticut ($50,262), Vermont ($49,502), and Rhode Island ($49,133).[37] (Southern states tend to expend fewer dollars on average on inmates, while the Northeast spends the most.)[38]

Food, medical services, vocational and educational programming, 24-hour security year-round, and the other necessities of prison life are very expensive. Direct costs do not take into account the "invisible" costs of confinement—the loss of meaningful wages and of tax and social security revenues while an otherwise able-bodied person is confined, the social welfare costs of maintaining a prisoner's family, the loss of any major contribution to the overall economy.

Community-based programs, on the other hand, operate at a small fraction of the costs of incarceration. Daily costs of supervising an offender in the community versus in prison are said to be on average over 20 times less for community supervision. Estimates are that average costs for incarceration are around $79.00 a day for an offender, while supervision in the community is approximately $3.42 a day.[39] John DiIulio has offered the following caveat, "we spend next to nothing on community-based corrections. We get what we pay for."[40]

Of course, capital costs for community corrections programs are considerably lower, for there are no expensive security devices. Office space is all that is needed for non-residential programs. The expense of providing social services and other correctional programs is much less than in prison, because they are provided by social service agencies within the community on a referral basis. Moreover, since the offender usually maintains employment while under community supervision, the "invisible" costs do not accrue. Instead, the offender contributes to his or her own upkeep as well as the upkeep of others through taxes, social security, family support, and in some cases even restitution to victims. In short, prisons are financial liabilities, but community-based corrections can be assets.

Image by Zemdega at istockphoto.com.

Harmful Effects of Incarceration

Community-based programs help avoid the harmful effects incarceration can have on offenders. Disenchantment with imprisonment as a corrective measure has been widespread among criminologists for some time. Indeed, imprisonment has been found wanting as a rehabilitative device for inmates, a deterrent to other criminals, and a punitive response to criminal acts. And with the difficulties produced by the rapid increase of prison populations during the 1980s, the harmful effects of imprisonment have been further exacerbated.[41] Life in many institutions is at best barren and futile, at worst unspeakably brutal and degrading. Of course, prisoners in such institutions are unable to commit further crimes while serving their sentences, but the conditions in which they live are the poorest possible preparation for their successful re-entry into society, and often merely reinforce in them a pattern of manipulation or destructiveness.

As will be discussed in the next chapter, prison existence does not resemble life outside of prison, and to assume that people will learn to live law-abiding lives in the "real" world by spending a period of years in prison is untenable. In prisons, we house together, in intimate interaction, the worst among us. To think that such an institution will rehabilitate anyone is ridiculous. Probably the worst behavioral treatment setting in the nation is the maximum-security prison.

Prisoners have virtually every decision made for them every day, from when to get up in the morning to what to wear to what to eat. Every physical need may be met, but they are not taught how to meet those needs themselves in a responsible way. Therefore, even with the considerable advances made in penological practices one cannot avoid concluding that prisons often do the inmate more harm than good, and any benefit to society upon the prisoner's release is questionable. At the very least, such treatment is poor preparation for the demands of living outside.

Community-based programs, on the other hand, are not "total institutions."[42] They maintain some semblance of the social qualities of free life. They do not degrade offenders. They do allow sentenced offenders to have contact with the very type of law-abiding citizens society hopes they will become.

Community and Family Relationships

Community-based programs also help avoid social surgery, that is, the severing of a person's community and family relationships. Prison inmates are effectively cut off from spouses, children, employers, parents, friends, schools, churches, social service organizations, and fraternal and professional contacts. After release from prison, the re-establishment of any of these relationships is difficult. Prisons tend to be remote from the communities from which the prisoners come, making relationships with family and friends difficult to maintain. Community-based programs allow an offender to live with his or her family and to maintain other relationships including employment. And agencies within the community that may prove beneficial in rehabilitation, such as Alcoholics Anonymous, drug treatment programs, marital and vocational counseling centers, and religious organizations, can be utilized as well.

Success Rates

In terms of recidivism, community-based programs are no less successful than prison. Recidivism rates among offenders are relatively high for all post-conviction programs.[43] In fact, prison populations tend to be highly recidivist in nature since they are comprised of a sizeable number of persons who have previously been incarcerated or who were on probation earlier and sent to prison for committing additional crimes or breaking the rules of their probation.[44] Jessica Mitford has been criticized for likening the fairness of the parole board decision making process to that of rolling dice.[45] In actuality, we would probably do just as well by deciding who should be released from prison by flipping a coin. Even with our mass incarceration, according to the Vera Institute, 40 percent of "prisoners return to custody within three years of release."[46] In a Bureau of Justice Statistics study examining recidivism of federal and state prisoners who returned to the community under supervision over a five-year span of time, the following determinations were made. Forty-seven percent of the federal offenders were re-arrested, and 76.5% of the state prisoners were re-arrested. Of the federal offenders, 31.6% of them returned to prison, and 59.4% of the state offenders did so.[47]

Females released from prisons under state and federal community supervision were arrested and returned to prison much less often than their male counterparts.[48] At year-end in 2015, in a study of both state and federal agencies, females made up 25% of adults [including juveniles sentenced as adults] on probation (a 2% increase from 2005) and 13% of those on parole (1% increase from 2005).[49]

Women are less likely to be arrested for violent crimes than their male counterparts. According to the Federal Bureau of Investigation Uniform Crime Reports, women over the age of 18 accounted for roughly 20% of violent crimes and approximately 39% of property crimes in 2015.[50]

Most offenders put on probation do not go to prison. Almost two-thirds of probationers have been found to have successfully completed their probationary sentences.[51] Of course, this does not reflect what criminal justice system involvement these individuals may have after successfully completing probation. The type of offender (i.e., felon, sex offender, etc.), geographic location, and available programs/resources, among other things, may have an impact on whether a person who has been on probation re-offends and is incarcerated.[52]

Aside from recidivism rates, advocates of community-based programs point to other factors in favor of their approach: community-based programs provide about the same level of community protection as prisons. In addition, since community programs avoid the social surgery and harmful effects of imprisonment, offenders are usually not made worse by them. Scientific proof that incarceration of humans in prisons for any length of time has any beneficial effects is scarce. Yet the benefits of some community-based correctional programs have shown encouraging signs of success.[53] At the very least, advocates argue, community programs are no worse than prisons and are significantly cheaper with fewer damaging side effects.

The Case *against* Community-Based Corrections

The case against community-based correctional programs generally revolves around two themes:

1. Such programs are a form of "coddling" criminals; they are too lenient and do not serve as effective deterrents to crime for probationers themselves or for potential criminals in the general population.
2. Community-based corrections programs are usually unwelcome in most neighborhoods, especially when first proposed or instituted, because residents fear that unrestrained criminals will commit further crimes. As a result, they often are located in high-crime, lower-class areas, which by their nature are criminogenic.

Moreover, opposition to such programs also comes from some offenders who feel that the traditional use of probation, as well as the traditional methods of selecting for parole, gives too much discretion to judges and parole boards. This creates uncertainty over actual sentence lengths and results in supervision conditions based on factors not related to the criminal conduct of the offenders. Some offenders argue that selection for both probation and parole is racially biased so that minority offenders are disproportionately sentenced to prison.

The Future of Community-Based Corrections

Although cases of crimes committed by probationers and parolees can be found, as can illustrations of apparently unwarranted judicial or correctional leniency and abuses of discretion, most experienced observers of the criminal justice system support community sentences as safe and effective alternatives to incarceration.[54] Also, the records of probationers and parolees universally demonstrate a high success rate, in that they show the majority of probationers and parolees complete their sentences without committing further crimes.[55]

Faced with the current overcrowding in our prison systems, there is little doubt that probation will become even more widely used in the future due to the fact there simply is little room in prisons, and imprisonment is costly. The current emphasis on mandatory prison terms, coupled with prison overcrowding, means an increase in the number of early releases. If the prosecution and incarceration rates increase, or even if they continue at their present levels, correctional choices other than imprisonment will become even more important. From 2000 to 2008, the growth (an increase of 863,100 offenders) in the total correctional population in America was primarily reflected in the 58 percent of offenders under community supervision, with the remainder (42%) in jail or prison.[56] And for several years states have been encouraged to develop plans and time-tables for implementing a range of alternatives to institutionalization.[57] As such, by 2015, approximately 32% of offenders in America were incarcerated, and 68% were under some form of community supervision.[58]

Even critics of the early release of prisoners recognize the need for post-release supervision of offenders in the community. Likewise, few would deny the need for probation programs for those offenders who do not qualify for incarceration. Community supervision will continue to be valued as a means of helping offenders adjust to lawful living and of protecting the community. The emphases on work, restitution, and community service will continue to have an appeal as well. Probation will continue to be the most widely used criminal sanction because it is less costly, more humane, and no less effective for most offenders than incarceration.

Community-Based Correctional Programs

Although probation and parole have been used for a century or more, most of the techniques and programs found in most communities today were unheard of until the 1970s. The need for less costly alternatives to incarceration and the push for effective sanctions which benefit the offender while also protecting the community have led to the creation of innovative programs. The foundation for all community-based programs, however, continues to be probation and parole casework.

Probation and Parole Casework

Offenders on probation or parole are under the supervision of a field agent. College graduates in such areas as criminal justice, criminology, social work, and psychology customarily gravitate to positions as probation and parole officers. Optimal supervision of clients takes place in the community. Supervision in the office is artificial. Surely, an offender will be on their best behavior when visiting with an officer within the sterile atmosphere of his or her office.

In general, probation and parole supervision involves some surveillance—the probation officer must somehow keep track of the "clients." In routine cases this entails only regular office visits. In addition, the field agent is generally charged with helping offenders adjust, to become "reintegrated" into all aspects of a law-abiding life, including relationships with family, work, and the use of leisure time. The probation or parole officer may provide counseling when needed, or act as a kind of resource "broker," referring cases to the appropriate clinical resources in the community, helping offenders find jobs, enrolling them in educational programs, and otherwise guiding and assisting those who have any sort of adjustment problems.[59]

The task of supervising offenders involves both authority and helpfulness, a mixture that is not always easily reconciled. Probation and parole officers also have a duty to "protect the community" and inform the court of any deviation from rules and regulations. In fulfilling this responsibility, they have wide discretion to initiate revocation proceedings if offenders violate rules or conditions or otherwise fail to adjust satisfactorily to community living. This dual loyalty—to the interests of the community in general and to the offenders on their caseload—results in different "styles" of supervision. Some field agents use frequent threats of revocation to obtain conformity; others give priority to casework and counseling as a major supervisory style. There are disagreements among field agents over the importance of their law enforcement role in contrast to their social work functions. This dual loyalty may lead to conflict with other criminal justice agencies, primarily the police.

"A significant proportion of agencies have adopted classification and case management systems for their supervision operations. The Model System incorporates classification with a method of accounting for cases known as the 'workload' model. The workload model is based on differentiation among cases. Under the workload approach time factors into the weight that a case receives in assigning it to an officer and for accounting for its contribution to the officer's total responsibilities. For example, a case with a high priority would require 4 hours per month equaling 30 as a total caseload. Medium priority would require 2 hours per month equaling 60 as a total caseload. Low priority would require 1 hour per month equaling a total caseload of 120. This is based upon an officer having 120 hours per month to supervise offenders. The balance of the hours counting for leave, collateral duties,"[60] pre-sentence investigations and the like.

The Re-entry Policy Council of the Council of State Governments has made the following recommendations as seen below.[61]

Council of State Governments Recommendations Regarding Supervision of Probationers and Parolees

A. Focus supervision resources on the period directly following release.

B. Ensure contact between the supervision officer and probationer/parolee corresponds to level of risk presented.

C. Supervise probationers or parolees in the community where they live.

D. Coordinate the activities of local law enforcement and probation and parole agencies.

E. Leverage community-based networks to assist with the implementation of the supervision strategy, and consult family and community members regularly to determine their assessment of the person's adjustment to the home and/or neighborhood.

F. Assess periodically the extent to which the individual's transition into the community is proceeding successfully and modify the supervision plan accordingly.

G. Facilitate compliance by recognizing that people under supervision will require an adjustment period, and address the issues that this period poses.

Federal probation officers tend to have much smaller caseloads than state probation officers. Although it is common for offenders to be assigned at random to any probation or parole officer, some agencies experiment with caseloads of different sizes and matching specially trained officers with selected offenders. Examples of specialized caseloads include sex offenders, substance abusers, and persons with mental illnesses supervised by officers with special skills and training.[62] It has been recommended that some specialized caseloads should have no more than 35 persons to be supervised on them.[63] Many probationers and parolees present little risk of committing more crimes and have few adjustment needs, so their supervision need not be rigorous. In others, because they present higher risks or have complex adjustment problems, this calls for intensive supervision. In these cases, specially trained agents may be given reduced caseloads to permit very close surveillance and intensive counseling.[64]

Intensive Supervision Programs

Some offenders need more supervision, punishment, and control than standard casework provides but not to the extent that they must be incarcerated. A middle ground, or intermediate sanction, is the intensive supervision program (ISP). Intensive supervision caseloads have emerged in most states.[65] This allows offenders to be placed under supervision in the community who otherwise would likely have had to be incarcerated, potentially adding to a state's overcrowded prison problem.

Studies have shown that more, rather than fewer, rule violations are uncovered by probation officers, probably due to the closer contact they have with their cases. These detected rule violations led to a larger number of failures in the programs. Research has shown that while ISP improves participation in programs for participants it fails to lower recidivism and may even increase arrest rates and significantly escalates violation of supervision rates and returns to incarceration.[66] Of course, as noted by Byrne and Miofsky, a problem with the research in this area is that comparisons are made with others on routine probation; we do not know how those under intensive supervision stack up with those in jail or prison.[67]

Perhaps the higher rate of detected rule violations is due not only to the closer supervision imposed on the ISP caseload, but to the nature of the rules themselves. A typical ISP program has strict requirements:

1. Offenders must have five (5) face-to-face contacts per week with a field agent.
2. They must undertake 132 hours of mandatory community service.
3. They must observe a mandatory curfew.
4. They must be employed.
5. They are subject to a weekly check of local arrest records.
6. They are subject to automatic notification of arrest elsewhere via the state Crime Information Network Listing.
7. They must submit to routine and unannounced alcohol and drug testing.[68]

Most states have similar programs. They provide supervision that is more focused, more intensive, and more aggressive than standard casework. These programs also provide swift and certain penalties for violating probationary rules and conditions, such as curfews, drug and alcohol testing, and mandatory employment,[69] among others.

Intensive supervision programs only lessen prison crowding if persons placed in them would otherwise be prison-bound. If only offenders whose crimes would normally result in probation are placed in them, the program goals of saving money or reducing prison crowding are not achieved.

Community Residential Programs

Sentences served in the community and those served in correctional institutions are not necessarily distinct from each other. Many modern probation and parole services use a variety of community correctional centers, often called halfway houses and residential treatment centers, which provide a mixture of incarceration with community supervision. Offenders in community residential programs live in special facilities similar to dormitories or motels rather than in their own homes. Typically, they are confined to these quarters nights and weekends but are allowed to leave during weekdays to go to (or look for) work or school or counseling sessions (work release/study release). This type of program retains some of the security measures demanded of prisons while at the same time allowing selected offenders to retain some community ties, support their families, and gradually adjust to community living.[70]

Halfway houses imply that those living there are half free and half confined, as described above. But halfway houses serve various functions depending on the type of offenders targeted. Some halfway houses for offenders placed there in lieu of going to a prison or correctional institution are essentially halfway-*in* houses. In this setting, offenders have avoided the full weight of criminal sanction. They are given an opportunity to "pay their debt to society" as well as to maintain societal contacts and receive needed services available in the community. The idea is to divert offenders away from prison.

Halfway-out houses, on the other hand, serve to gradually integrate offenders back into society after their terms in prison. This is the more common type. Some inmates, especially those serving lengthy terms, have great difficulty adjusting to the free world, where they do not find the security and stability of the prison environment. Such institutionalized persons have historically had very high recidivism rates immediately after release and need a gradual release program.

The common practice before the implementation of gradual release programs was to provide an inmate whose term was completed with a new suit of prison-made clothes and a pair of shoes, a bus ticket to any city or town in the state, and $50 in cash. Often the newly released inmate, after years of separation from society, would arrive at a bus station alone, spend the $50, and soon be back to committing criminal acts. Gradual release through a halfway-out house usually places the offender in a job, and where that is the emphasis, the program is called work release. For others coming through the program they are placed in a vocational training school or college. Such programs are called study release. Work/study release allows an inmate to be eased back into society by spending the last three to six months of his or her sentence in a community-based halfway house where employment can be obtained, a bank account opened, one's driver's license renewed, and family and social relationships re-established—all with the support of correctional staff. Then, at the end of the sentence, the offender has a job, some savings, a place to live, and a chance to succeed on the outside as a law-abiding citizen.

Halfway-in house residents are typically under the supervision of probation officers or counselors. Halfway-out house residents are usually under the supervision of parole officers. In many jurisdictions probation and parole offices are combined so that a caseworker supervises a combination of persons on probation and parole. In such arrangements it is not uncommon for a counselor to supervise a person on parole who at an earlier time was on his or her probation caseload. In other jurisdictions the probation and parole functions are separated, often with probation operating as a county agency under the direction of the county judge and parole functioning as a state agency under the state's department of corrections or the governor's office.

House Arrest

House arrest requires a person to remain at home during specified hours of the day and night and may be coupled with electronic monitoring (next section). Permission to leave home is confined to emergencies and for necessary purposes such as employment and grocery shopping. Generally, house arrest is more stringent than intensive supervision programs, but the purposes are much the same: to lessen prison crowding and lessen the financial costs of criminal sanctions.

Several states have house arrest programs. Florida's Community Control Program (FCCP) was the first and largest. Thousands of offenders have been supervised in this way since Florida began the program in the early 1980s. Generally, persons in the program are more serious offenders than those on either standard probation or ISP, but somewhat less serious than those sent to prison. Some of the offenders may also be required to perform community service and to pay restitution.

House arrest programs are preferred by some judges and others because the offender is kept in the community, not sent away and forgotten. Also, house arrest is inexpensive, requiring only a field agent's time without the high costs of incarceration. Many offenders who would otherwise be housed in correctional institutions are maintained in their own houses.[71]

In some 20 years of operating the house arrest program in Florida, offenders under house arrest have murdered 234 people and sexually assaulted 538 persons. As of 2003, more than 10,000 offenders were under house arrest in Florida, and prison costs four times more than house arrest. Sixty percent of the offenders in Florida do not complete their time on house arrest, and most go to prison. The legislature has specified that agents should not have to monitor more than 25 persons on house arrest, but the Department of Corrections acknowledges that some caseloads are as high as 39 offenders.[72] Obviously, as seen with the Florida experience, house arrest is suspect as a program for reducing crime and recidivism.

Electronic Control of Probationers and Parolees

Relatively new and complex issues in probation and parole supervision involve the use of electronic surveillance and monitoring systems. Sophisticated electronic devices are used to track and otherwise monitor probationers and parolees. The offender is required to wear some form of electronic beeper, microphone, or distance-activated alarm. One of the simplest such devices is a wristband or anklet that sends a signal to a probation officer if the probationer strays more than a hundred yards or so from home. This form of house incarceration is an alternative to jail or prison for those offenders who are not good risks for full community freedom. Devices fixed to the offender's telephone, which is randomly called five or six times a day, alert the probation staff if the offender fails to answer in a given amount of time.

The first recorded use of electronic monitoring to supervise offenders took place in Boston, Massachusetts, in 1964. It became exceedingly popular with Judge Jack Love in New Mexico in 1984 when he put it to use after being inspired by the Spider Man comic book.[73] It is estimated that there are approximately 140,000 electronic monitoring devices in use in the United States.[74] Usually, offenders must pay the expenses of their own electronic monitoring according to a sliding scale based on the offender's ability to pay. The cost to individuals varies from $5–25 or more per day.[75]

Electronic monitoring has been a popular sanction for driving under the influence, drug related offenders, domestic batterers, sex offenders, petty thieves, and embezzlers.[76] For example, in 2006, 22 states passed legislation to implement global positioning systems (GPS) to monitor sex offenders. Legislation mandating lifetime monitoring of some sex offenders has been passed in six states (Colorado, Florida, Missouri, Ohio, Oklahoma, and Wisconsin).[77] Electronic surveillance used in Florida, Massachusetts, South Carolina, and Tennessee are accessible via Internet links.[78]

All 50 states and the District of Columbia use electronic monitoring for some of their offenders. Monitoring systems tend to operate on Radio-Frequency (RF) or on

Global Positioning Systems (GPS). Enhance GPS technology has driven the increase in use of electronic monitoring for offenders. According to research conducted in 2015 by The Pew Charitable Trusts, electronic tracking of convicted offenders increased by roughly 140 percent between the years 2005–2015. In 2015 alone, more than 125,000 people were placed under electronic supervision (Pew, 2016). However, this represents a very small portion of the nearly 4.6 million people under community supervision (probation or parole) for that year.[79]

The full use of electronic surveillance is still to be felt. Problems exist, of course, with the technology. For instance, locations close to radio stations, poor telephone wiring, and special features on telephones such as call-waiting, along with power surges and other computer complications interfere with consistent and accurate telephonic communications.[80] Also, family members may be inconvenienced in their use of the telephone. And what are the ramifications of probationer tracking on others who are not criminal offenders? If a probationer under surveillance visits a friend not on probation, the visit and the relationship are still known to the probation staff and perhaps the police. If the probationer gets in trouble, can the electronic record of the visit be used legally to indict the friend in a conspiracy? These and other sticky issues have not yet been resolved.[81]

Electronic devices cannot monitor some kinds of illegal activity. For example, offenders with beepers can still become intoxicated, sell drugs from their homes, or rob the pizza delivery person. Electronic monitoring has been considered a failure in terms of reducing recidivism by some researchers.[82]

Shock Incarceration and Boot Camp

One program which enjoyed public appeal combines a relatively short period of imprisonment in a strictly regulated environment followed by another period of intensive supervision in the community. Known as shock incarceration or boot camp, it typically consists of 90 to 180 days in a military-like atmosphere in which offenders are required to participate in close-order drill, spit and polish military dress and behavior, physical fitness programs, and other activities which closely resemble Marine boot camp. The idea is to "shock" participants within a short period of time through total immersion in the highly structured, disciplined, and regimented program to abandoning the behaviors that landed them in the program in the first place. In 1983, the first adult boot camps opened in the states of Oklahoma and Georgia.[83] See the discussion regarding juvenile boot camps in Chapter 13.

Restitution and Community Service

One of the failings of imprisonment is that the victims of crimes gain no benefit from the incarceration of those who perpetrated them other than being protected from further victimization during the period of incarceration. One solution to this problem is *restitution*, or requiring the criminal to repay the victim for his or her losses. The idea is to restore victims to the conditions they enjoyed prior to the crime by repairing the damage, replacing the stolen property, or in some other way "making it right." The amount of restitution is calculated based on the harm done, or the amount of money or property stolen or damaged. Also, the costs of medical treatment or the costs associated with lost time from employment can be calculated for restitution. Restitution can give the victim a sense that justice has been done, a feeling of equity which is not usually created by the traditional courtroom experience of trial and sentencing. Also, by making amends the offender enhances his or her own likelihood of rehabilitation.[84]

Similarly, when a person is locked up in a prison in order to pay his or her "debt to society," it is difficult to see how society is compensated. So, community service programs have been developed which require offenders to perform some work for, or make some definite contribution to, the community harmed by the criminal behavior. Usually the amount and type of community service is computed by the number of hours or days the offender is expected to perform some type of work in the community.[85]

Restitution and community service programs have a universal appeal. The payment and work is viewed as punishment for the offender, but the victim or the community also gains some tangible benefit, or payment, in compensation for the crime. And this is accomplished with much less cost to the public than incarceration. Also, the emphasis on work and employment for the offender contributes to a belief that something good can result from the crime experience.

Special Problems and Needs of Female Offenders

By year-end 2015, about 25 percent of all those on probation and 13 percent on parole were women.[86] Criminal justice scholars and professionals recognize that special problems and needs exist for female offenders. Over half of all female offenders have children. Many are divorced or single and carry the responsibility for the care and support of their children alone. Many of these women are poorly equipped to provide for the parenting needs of their children, either financially, physically, or emotionally. Many are poorly educated and have suffered abuse and trauma before coming into contact with the criminal justice system.[87]

Incarceration always disrupts family relationships, but the problems are especially acute for women sentenced to prison. Since female offenders are more likely to accept their family responsibilities than male offenders, the disruptions caused by women's arrest, prosecution, and incarceration are especially problematic for family life.

Many women are sentenced to community-based correctional programs. The majority of crimes that females were arrested for in 2008 were non-violent crimes.[88]

Community-based correctional programs allow female offenders the opportunity to maintain their family relationships. When the full resources of community programs are made available, women are often able to secure the necessary education and training to obtain stable employment. Economic independence and effective parenting skills are the focus of the community-based correctional approach for female offenders. Vocational training, job development and placement, and follow-up services are very helpful in the effort to divert female offenders away from prison.

Family services are made available to female offenders more commonly than to male offenders. Temporary release, or furlough, programs allow mothers to receive the emotional rewards of child care while remaining under correctional supervision. Group training and programs relating to spouse abuse and substance abuse are geared to address the special needs of female offenders. Aside from criminal entanglements, many women offenders must also deal with their own negative self-images, gender discrimination, and social disadvantages. These problems can be addressed in community-based programs better than by incarceration in a distant institution.

Female offenders have a high rate of substance abuse. About 36 percent of females arrested in 2010, according to the Bureau of Justice Statistics, were arrested for drug and alcohol related crimes.[89] These crimes included: drug abuse violation, drug sale/manufacturing, drug possession/use, driving under the influence, violation of liquor laws, and drunkenness. Even for those arrested for non-drug crimes, many are in need of substance abuse treatment.

Rules and Conditions of Probation and Parole

In addition to supervision, probationers are subject to rules and conditions fixed by the courts, while parolees must abide by similar rules fixed by parole boards. Usually standard rules apply to all probationers and parolees, but occasionally special rules or prohibitions are imposed if, in the opinion of a judge or a board, they are necessary to help a particular offender adjust and to prevent him or her from committing new crimes. For example, a sex offender may be required to participate in psychiatric counseling as a special condition of probation or parole.

Standard Rules and Conditions

The standard regulations for probation are virtually identical to those for parole. It is common to require probationers and parolees to refrain from associating with "known criminals," to abstain from liquor or to use it only in moderation, not to possess firearms, to remain in the community, not to change jobs, and not to marry or move without the permission of their field agents. In general, they must keep their activities and whereabouts known to the authorities and not change status in any way without the prior notification and consent of the probation or parole service. In addition, they may be required to maintain a "cooperative" posture with supervising officers. These rules and conditions, as well as any special conditions, are normally given to potential probationers and parolees in printed form with a requirement that they sign a document agreeing to abide by them if they wish community sentences.

Whatever the specific set of rules and conditions imposed in any jurisdiction, a person on probation or parole is held to a higher standard of morality and is more restricted in his or her movements than citizens not under such a sentence. Violation of any rule or condition is grounds for revocation with subsequent incarceration. A probationer is under the control of both the probation officer and the sentencing judge, and like the Sword of Damocles, imprisonment constantly hangs over his or her head. Parolees also face possible return to prison for any infraction of the rules or conditions imposed on them.

Special Rules and Conditions

Since parolees are convicted felons, some courts view parolees as merely "inmates outside the walls" and as such have lost many of the rights of free citizens and are subject to restraints and controls not applicable to law-abiding persons. Some experts argue that just about any rule is permissible, except those that violate the Eighth Amendment prohibition against cruel and unusual punishment, since both probationers and parolees are free to refuse community sentences and opt for prison if they object to the conditions. At best, this argument seems impractical and coercive. Initially, most probationers and parolees are willing to agree to almost any condition to escape confinement. See **Field Practice 11.3** on special conditions.

Challenges to conditions are not normally over the common requirements that the offender remain law-abiding, sober, and keep his or her whereabouts known. More often litigated are the special conditions attached to the sentencing of a particular offender or class of offenders. Unique or peculiar interpretations of essentially vague conditions, such as a requirement to "cooperate with your probation officer," can also become the basis of litigation when given as the reason for revocation.

Field Practice 11.3 Special Conditions

1. Essay

An offender convicted of assaulting a police officer was placed on probation for two years by the court. In addition to imposing the standard rules of supervision, the sentencing judge ordered the offender to pay the medical costs incurred by the victim and write an essay entitled "Why the Police Should Be Entitled to the Respect of the Citizenry," to be submitted to the court for approval.

2. Go to Church

A youthful offender convicted of robbery (purse snatching) was placed on probation for three years with a special condition that he "regularly attend a church of his choice" and present evidence to the court that he was complying with this condition.

3. Checks and Balances

A woman convicted for forgery, writing bad checks to a number of businesses in the community, was placed on two years' probation by a judge with a special condition that she refrain from having any checking accounts during that time.

4. Keep Clear

An unemployed janitor with multiple offenses of shoplifting from Wal-Mart was placed on probation for three years with a special condition that he was not to go on the premises of any Wal-Mart.

Generally, probation and parole rules are believed proper if the rule is related in some way to the crime for which the offender was convicted or if the required behavior is reasonably related to future criminality. Consider the conditions placed on 70-year-old O.J. Simpson, former Heisman Trophy winner and Pro Football Hall of Famer, upon being paroled after serving nine years of a thirty-three year sentence in Nevada for armed robbery and kidnapping in an attempt to get his sports memorabilia back. Of course, he is remembered by many for the controversial trial when he was acquitted for the murders of his ex-wife Nicole Brown Simpson and Ronald Goldman.[90]

Here are Simpson's conditions of parole upon walking out of a Nevada prison on October 1, 2017. While it is speculated that O.J. Simpson ultimately desires to relocate to Florida, he is restricted from leaving Nevada or changing his residence without prior approval from the Nevada Division of Parole and Probation (NDPP). He is required to submit a monthly report regarding his activities on a form supplied by NDPP. No association with felons or anyone involved in criminal activity is permitted. He is to have no possession, control, or access to weapons unless needed for employment and has prior authorization from NDPP. No use, purchase, or possession of drugs is allowed unless legally prescribed by a medical professional; no use of marijuana—even if it is legal in the jurisdiction—is acceptable. Alcohol may be consumed but not to excess; a .08 blood alcohol level is considered excessive. Testing for alcohol and or drugs is at the discretion of NDPP and can be required at any time.[91]

Searching Probationers and Parolees

An offender sentenced to prison is totally under the physical control of the state. Inmates retain many of the constitutional rights afforded to all citizens, but restrictions on search and seizure under the Fourth Amendment are not among them. Prison inmates can have their persons and cells searched at any time, randomly or at the whim of prison officials, without warrants and with no need on the part of the authorities to show probable cause. Whether the same broad right exists to search parolees and probationers under community sentence is not an easy question to answer because of different laws in different states and because the legal status of a parolee is not quite the same as that of a probationer.

A number of courts take the position that a parolee is an inmate serving part of his or her sentence on the street by the grace of the parole board. According to this view, parolees as "inmates outside the walls" can be searched in exactly the same way as prisoners still in confinement. Probationers, on the other hand, may have never been inmates. For this reason, some courts allow parolees to be searched without suspicion, along the inmate model, but require probationer searches to conform to Fourth Amendment restrictions the way they would for any law-abiding citizen.

The authority of parole officers to search is justified by the written agreement paroled inmates are required to sign, giving permission in advance for parole authorities to search their persons or premises. Under this agreement, it is assumed that the parolee has consented to any search, making a warrant or a valid arrest an unnecessary prerequisite.

The guiding cases on searches of probationers are *Griffin v. Wisconsin* (1987)[92] and *U.S. v. Knights* (2001).[93] *Griffin* held that warrantless searches of those on probation are allowed under the Fourth Amendment. Such searches, it was concluded, fall under the "special needs" exception and are reasonable. The U.S. Supreme Court further clarified in 2001 in *Knights* that mere reasonable suspicion is all that is required to search a probationer. The Court noted that those on probation are more prone than law-abiding citizens to break the law and have a greater inclination to conceal their wrongdoing. The Court did not address whether Knights' conditions of probation legally authorized and obligated a consent to search on his part. Neither of those cases says anything about how to address suspicionless searches that might be conducted.

That question would appear before the U.S. Supreme Court in a case involving a parolee in *Samson v. California* (2006).[94] It has been maintained that "[t]raditional notions of consent require a voluntary, intelligent, and knowing waiver of a known right." In *Samson*, the parolee accepted a search condition prior to being paroled. Thus, a question becomes how coercive is such an agreement for the parolee. In trying to balance the state's interests with those of parolees, the state authorities argued that there are "grave safety concerns about parolees and parolees have no Fourth Amendment rights"; therefore, the balance is in favor of the state. The lower California state court had relied upon a 1998 California Supreme Court decision, *People v. Reyes*, which held "that searching a parolee does not require individualized suspicion."

The Court in *Samson* held that "[t]hough most states have decided to increase the requirements for searches, this has no bearing upon the constitutional floor set by the Fourth Amendment. The Court also said that there is no merit to the argument that suspicionless searches give blanket discretion to law enforcement officials. The Court concluded that California's prohibition on arbitrary, capricious, or harassing searches provides sufficient protection for parolees' Fourth Amendment rights and, therefore, no additional procedural safeguards are necessary to protect the rights of parolees."[95] See **Criminal Justice 11.1** on polygraph surveillance of probationers.

Criminal Justice 11.1 Ethics: Polygraph Surveillance

A probation and parole officer with a large caseload of men convicted of sex crimes against children decided to give unannounced polygraph tests to selected offenders. He suspected that where the victim of the sexual abuse still lived in the same house as the offender the possibility of continued misconduct existed. None of his caseload admitted to any continued victimization, and he received no direct allegations, but he was convinced the probation or parole rules against the behavior were not always obeyed. Therefore, with the assistance of a friendly polygraph examiner, he began the practice. When one of his caseload came to the office for a scheduled appointment, the officer ushered him into another office where the polygraph equipment was set up. On several occasions when the offender saw the equipment he immediately confessed to wrongdoing. On other occasions, the offender was found to be telling the truth when he denied the activity, and sometimes the offender was caught in a lie.

The officer rejected arguments that such "lie detector" tests were not reliable, not accepted as trial evidence, and were perhaps a constitutional violation. He did not use the test results to revoke probation or parole and lock the offender up, but rather as a tool for counseling. He said, "All I know is that since I began the practice my caseload has been much more cooperative and honest with me. I think I have protected some kids, too."[96]

In *Minnesota v. Murphy*, 465 U.S. 420 (1984), the U.S. Supreme Court held that a probation officer was not required to advise a probationer of his or her *Miranda* warnings before asking him/her potentially incriminating questions. A condition of Murphy's probation in Minnesota was that he was "to be truthful with the officer in all matters." The Court concluded that Murphy indeed had the right not to incriminate himself regarding new charges, just as a suspect does before a grand jury, but, just like there, a probation officer is not required to advise the suspect of that right. As a condition of his probation though, not responding truthfully or evading questions could signal a problem and lead to revocation proceedings. It is upon this backdrop that polygraph surveillance of probationers operates. As a condition of probation, probationers agree to be polygraphed. According to probation officers, negative polygraph results send up red flags to step up surveillance. Polygraphs are not considered scientifically accurate enough to be admitted at the trial court level (see *Frye v. U.S.*, 293 F. 1013 (D.C. Cir. 1923). Since the results are being utilized as a tool to bring revocation proceedings and the probationer has consented to the condition of polygraph veracity, there is no violation of one's Fifth Amendment rights.[97]

1. Do you believe it is appropriate to use the polygraph test for this purpose when the test results are not admissible in court?

2. Which is more important to you, to protect society or to honor individual due process rights of offenders?
3. Do you see any differences between electronic surveillance and polygraph surveillance?

Model Conditions of Community Supervision

Because the conditions imposed on probationers and parolees vary so greatly from place to place, it is not possible to present a representative list of them. However, the drafters of the Model Penal Code prepared a set of "reasonable" conditions for probationers which courts might follow if they choose. (See "Conditions of ... Probation" below.) Most of them are not unusual, although they are by no means uniformly imposed by courts across the nation and, even though they were specifically designed for probationers, they apply to parolees as well. The most controversial condition is the final one, requiring any special condition to be related to rehabilitation and not unduly restrictive or "incompatible" with the probationer's "freedom of conscience."

Conditions of ... Probation

The Court, as a condition of its order, may require the defendant:

a. to meet his family responsibilities;
b. to devote himself to a specific employment or occupation;
c. to undergo available medical or psychiatric treatment and to enter and remain in a specified institution, when required for that purpose;
d. to pursue a prescribed secular course of study or vocational training;
e. to attend or reside in a facility established for the instruction, recreation or residence of persons on probation;
f. to refrain from frequenting unlawful or disreputable places or consorting with disreputable persons;
g. to have in his possession no firearm or other dangerous weapon unless granted written permission;
h. to make restitution of the fruits of his crime or to make reparation, in an amount he can afford to pay, for the loss or damage caused thereby;
i. to remain within the jurisdiction of the Court and to notify the Court or the probation officer of any change in his address or his employment;
j. to report as directed to the Court or the probation officer and to permit the officer to visit his home;

k. to post a bond, with or without surety, conditioned on the performance of any of the foregoing obligations;

l. to satisfy any other conditions reasonably related to the rehabilitation of the defendant and not unduly restrictive of his liberty or incompatible with his freedom of conscience.[98]

The drafters of the American Bar Association's Standards Relating to Probation similarly suggest that no condition be imposed that is incompatible with the probationer's "freedom of religion." The National Advisory Commission's standard, *Corrections*, requires only those conditions "necessary to provide a benefit to the offender and protection to the public safety." It also recommends that the conditions imposed in an individual case be tailored to meet the particular needs of that offender and his or her community and that the mechanical imposition of uniform conditions on all defendants be avoided.[99]

Revocation

Rules and Regulations of Parole and Supervised Release

Inmates released on parole or mandatory release are subject to supervision by field agents and must agree to abide by various rules and conditions. The rules and conditions of parole are drafted by the parole board, and the inmate must sign an agreement to follow those rules if he or she wishes to be released. There are two kinds of rules: *general*, which apply to all parolees, and *special*, which are set by the board in specific cases to assist the particular individuals in making it on the street. An example of a special rule might be to "receive regular outpatient psychiatric counseling" in a case where the board thinks the inmate is emotionally disturbed as well as criminal, or an inmate with a long history of alcoholism may be required to regularly attend Alcoholics Anonymous meetings.

Rules for compliance with parole are similar to those for compliance with probation. Obviously, individuals on probation or parole can be considered for revocation if they are arrested for committing new offenses. However, they can also be revoked for not complying with their conditions of probation or parole, such as not being home after curfew or drinking alcoholic beverages if those are conditions proscribed for them. These would not be violations for adults not on probation or parole, but are considered "technical violations" for those who are on probation or parole.[100]

General conditions of parole may vary somewhat from state to state, but they are all quite similar. Parolees must agree not to associate with "known criminals," to refrain from drinking to excess, not to use any mind-altering drugs, to keep a curfew (remain at home and be in bed by a certain time each night), not to change employment without prior approval by a parole officer, to support their families, not to leave the jurisdiction without prior permission from the parole authorities, not to possess firearms, and to "cooperate" with the parole officer, including reporting regularly and being willing to have the parole officer make "unannounced" visits to the place of employment or the home of the parolee. And, of course, the parolee must agree to remain law-abiding.

Violation of these rules or the commission of new crimes makes the offender subject to revocation with subsequent incarceration or re-incarceration. There is nothing automatic about revocation. It is a discretionary decision initiated by the supervising probation or parole officer.

Parole Revocation

In general, revocation of parole or mandatory release requires a more elaborate procedure than is necessary for initial sentence to community supervision. This is consistent with a general tradition in administrative law surrounding the removal of a privilege once granted and in which the holder is considered to have a vested interest in the privilege so that its removal is protected by more procedural safeguards than are required for its denial in the first place. In an analogous manner, a university may deny a student admission in a much more cursory fashion than it could later expel him or her.

Due Process at Revocation

Not every violation of parole conditions results in revocation. Usually, a parolee is counseled to abide by the conditions of parole by the parole officer, who then typically "works with" the parolee to help him or her adjust to lawful living. Therefore, the parole officer enjoys broad discretion, and that discretion has resulted in some vague rules and regulations, such as parolees being required to avoid associating with "undesirable" people.

The parole revocation process begins when a parole officer discovers, or has reason to believe, a parolee has violated a rule or condition or when the parolee is arrested for a new crime. The parole officer makes an initial determination of whether the infraction or arrest is serious enough to call for revocation. If so, the decision to seek revocation is usually referred to a supervising parole officer for ratification. Then, depending on the requirements in the particular jurisdiction, an administrative warrant sufficient to detain the parolee may be sought from a parole board member or, if this is not required, the supervising field agent may issue a hold order to detain the parolee until a revocation hearing can be held.

Until 1972, the common practice in many jurisdictions was for a parolee to be taken into custody and jailed when a revocation order was issued and then returned from the community to a prison where, at some later date—days, weeks, or even months later—a hearing into the appropriateness of the revocation was held. This worked an obvious hardship on any parolee if it turned out that revocation was inappropriate because the charges were unfounded or otherwise unjust. In many ways, it was comparable to denying bail to a person arrested for a crime, or refusing prehearing release to an alleged probation violator. But in the case of return to prison, the situation was more extreme. Removal from the community to the prison, even for a short duration, not only interrupted the parolee's family life and employment, but, since prisons are often distant from the scene of a violation, also created serious problems should witnesses, complainants, or others, including local counsel, be required or desirable at the hearing.

All this was changed by the Supreme Court in 1972 with the *Morrissey v. Brewer* decision. In that case, Morrissey admitted that he had violated his parole conditions by buying a car under an assumed name and operating it without permission, giving false statements to police concerning his address and insurance following a minor accident, obtaining credit under an assumed name, and failing to report his place of residence to his parole officer. The parole officer recommended that his parole be revoked for his continuing violation of parole rules. The Court established certain due process requirements for parole revocation, but stopped short of granting offenders the right to counsel.

Morrissey v. Brewer, 408 U.S. 471 (1972)[101]

Our task is limited to deciding the minimum requirements (for parole revocation) of due process. They include a) written notice of the claimed violations of parole; b) disclosure to the parolee of evidence against him; c) opportunity to be heard in person and to present witnesses and documentary evidence; d) the right to confront and cross-examine adverse witnesses (unless the hearing officer specifically finds good cause for not allowing confrontation); e) a "neutral and detached" hearing body such as a traditional parole board, members of which need not be judicial officers or lawyers; and f) a written statement by the fact-finders as to the evidence relied on and reasons for revoking parole. We emphasize there is no thought to equate this second stage of parole revocation to a criminal prosecution in any sense; it is a narrow inquiry; the process should be flexible enough to consider evidence including letters, affidavits, and other material that would not be admissible in an adversary criminal trial.

One problem with parole revocation that has been rarely addressed is the availability of sanctions short of revocation for infractions of rules. In general, revocation has been handled as an either-or proposition: The parole officer who discovers rule infractions either does nothing or commences full-scale revocation proceedings. The following alternatives have been suggested:

1. The parolee should receive a reprimand and warning from the board.
2. Parole supervision and reporting should be intensified.
3. Reductions for good behavior should be forfeited or withheld.

4. The parolee should be remanded, without revocation of parole, to a residence facility for such a period and under such supervision or treatment as the board may deem appropriate.
5. The parolee should be required to conform to one or more additional conditions of parole which may be imposed.
6. The parolee should be arrested and returned to prison to await a hearing to determine whether his parole should be revoked.[102]

Perhaps parolees should be able to earn "good time" off the remainder of their supervision, much as prisoners earn good time off their maximum sentences. And perhaps parolees who no longer require supervision and guidance should be granted early discharge from parole if no foreseeable risk to the community exists. (See **Field Practice 11.4.**)

Field Practice 11.4 Crisis Driving Policy

Serving Justice: Megan's Law

Megan's Law came about after the rape and murder of 7-year-old Megan Kanka by a previously registered sex offender—Jesse Timmendequas. The law requires registration of sex offenders and community notification on their whereabouts. The bill was signed into law by President Clinton in 1996.[103]

How would your community react to news about the past behaviors of a new resident? Should a person be forbidden to return to society, to live in peace, after they have paid their debt to society by serving the sentence imposed by a court of law?

Most people were angered by the fact that Timmendequas had been released early from a maximum sentence in prison. On the one hand, a person should have the opportunity to reclaim a meaningful life after paying one's debt to society through serving a prison sentence. But, on the other hand, citizens in a neighborhood such as Hamilton Township have rights too, don't they? Many of them believe they should have known, should have been informed of the child victimizing history of Timmendequas and his companions. But, even if they had known, how would their lives have been different? We hear about the horror stories of criminals committing crimes after serving time in prison, but what about those who are released from correctional caseloads and are rehabilitated, able to live law-abiding lives? Should they be punished because of the repeat offenses of others?

Does not justice require that a person have a second chance, an opportunity to change their lives for the better?

Why do you think Timmendequas was released after serving 6 years and 10 months of the 10-year sentence he received in New Jersey for offenses against children? This was one early release which had a very bad result. Of course, the plea agreement was the primary factor in the sentence of Timmendequas, but how do you think the parole authorities arrived at an opinion that he was ready for release?[104]

Is it possible that public policies made in the wake of sensational cases such as Megan's may be over-reactions by society, that cooler heads should prevail in the legislative process? If all offenders are labeled after they have served their sentences, and if society is informed of the whereabouts of every offender who has served their sentence, can anyone be truly rehabilitated and returned to society safely? The rights of victims, and potential victims, conflict sometimes with the rights of the accused.

Discharge from Sentence

The formal criminal process ends when an offender has successfully completed the sentence, whether in jail, on probation, in prison, or on parole or mandatory release. Normally the "ex-offender's" conviction record remains on file, as does all of the other material and information gathered about him or her by the court and correctional authorities. Many of the corollary effects of felony conviction, including loss of voting rights and inability to obtain certain licenses or franchises or to enter certain occupations or professions, may affect offenders for many years after they have served their sentences. And the status of "ex-con" may haunt someone for a lifetime.

Most jurisdictions have procedures for **restoration of rights** lost by conviction. In general, the ex-offender must apply to a court for restoration sometime after sentence completion (commonly five years) and cooperate in whatever investigation is ordered by the court.

Procedures for the restoration of rights or the expungement of records used today vary widely across the nation and are of limited success. Some damaging effects of conviction and serving a sentence may be diminished, but the negative status of having been convicted (or of having been a convict) tends to persist throughout the lifetime of the ex-offender. In Maine and Vermont, those convicted of felonies never lose their right to vote; inmates are even allowed to vote while incarcerated. Thirty-eight states and the District of Columbia allow for the automatic restoration of voting rights for felons upon their release from incarceration. In some states, ex-felons have to wait a specified amount of time before their voting rights can be restored. In some states, an ex-felon must submit an application for restoration of voting rights. However, in Alabama, Arizona, Florida, Iowa, Kentucky, Mississippi, Nevada, Virginia, and Wyoming rights are restored only upon court action or gubernatorial pardon. It has been argued that blocking a person's right to vote creates political disenfranchisement for a felon.[105]

Executive Clemency: Pardon, Commutation, and Reprieve

Executive clemency has long historical roots. Early records of pardoning power are found in the Mosaic and Vedic laws. In 1066 William the Conqueror brought to England the view that pardoning power is the exclusive prerogative of the king. Over the years this became a very powerful common law tradition and has played an important role in the development of the U.S. legal system. Today executive clemency takes three major forms: pardons, commutations, and reprieves. A pardon generally restores a person convicted of a crime to noncriminal status by an act of executive clemency. Full pardons with complete restoration of civil rights are typically granted in cases where it is shown after trial that the person was totally innocent of the crime for which he or she was convicted. However, pardons are granted not only to the innocent. They also serve as acts of mercy and as rewards for meritorious deeds performed while under sentence, among other exceptional circumstances. Pardons may even be granted posthumously.[106] In many jurisdictions pardons can be "conditional," that is, they can be used to restore only some of the rights lost by conviction.

Commutation of sentence is not a pardon but an executive order lowering an offender's minimum or maximum sentence to make the inmate eligible for parole. For example, a prisoner sentenced to life who has demonstrated an exceptional level of rehabilitation or performed some meritorious act may have his or her sentence commuted to a specific term of years less than life, which allows the parole board to consider an early release. The parole board, though appointed by the governor, does not necessarily grant parole every time the governor commutes a sentence.

Reprieve is a form of executive clemency allowing a chief executive to halt executions that have been ordered by a judge and jury. A governor's reprieve may merely delay the execution, or it may be accompanied by a commutation, reducing the sentence of the prisoner to life imprisonment. The reprieve power of governors has assumed new significance today in light of Supreme Court decisions affirming the constitutionality of death penalty provisions in a number of states. The number of prisoners on death row has become the largest in our history. Today, governors of states with large death house populations find themselves potentially confronting hundreds of reprieve decisions, a situation no governor faced for over a decade between 1972 and 1982 when the death penalty was temporarily not utilized following the U.S. Supreme Court decision *Furman v. Georgia.*

Sometimes pardon, commutation, or reprieve is granted on the executive's own motion, but more commonly a prisoner files a formal petition with the governor. If it seems warranted, the governor may order the parole board, correctional authorities, or in some instances a special pardon board to investigate the case and make recommendations.

Although executive clemency is a very important power, often dramatic when used, pardon and commutation are not major methods of prisoner release. In most states only a handful of inmates are granted any form of executive clemency in any year.

Also, pardons, commutations, and reprieves may have *conditions attached* by the executive, which generally cannot be effectively challenged by the recipient. Reprieves may be temporary—for example, granting a pregnant woman convicted of murder a stay of execution in order to have her child and then reinstituting the sentence.

It may be that pardons and other forms of executive clemency will assume greater significance if the trend to definite sentences continues. Any correctional system housing an inmate population with no possibility of parole faces a good deal of pressure, not only from overcrowding, but from humanitarian considerations, and a more liberal pardoning system could become increasingly attractive. Such pardon commissions would investigate eligible inmates year round. This would be a major change from the common practice of a few traditional "Christmas pardons" granted by the governor each year. We began our discussion considering alternative punishments, and we come back to that inquiry as we close this chapter. (See **Field Practice 11.5** below.)

Field Practice 11.5 Serving Justice: Alternative Punishments in the Community

Public humiliation is not universally accepted as effective and proper. Some believe teenagers may be harmed unnecessarily by the practice and point out that juvenile offenders often have experienced plenty of abuse and humiliation in their lives already. Critics say such practices sometimes ignore, or may even reinforce, the root causes of crime. A person with a poor self-image, or lack of esteem, may be pushed even further into a deviant lifestyle if subjected to public humiliation. Offenders with deep psychological problems may be damaged. And, in a perverse way, some offenders may even relish the public notoriety associated with such a public punishment.

Community-based correctional programs, on the other hand, attempt to modify behavior in more private ways; some say it is perhaps too private. When a serious offender such as a child killer or molester is placed in a community program, and local residents are not informed, some feel threatened unnecessarily. They want more publicity about who lives in their community and what behaviors they have been arrested for.

How do you assess the relative merits of public humiliation as a criminal sanction? Do you believe such a policy reflects the worst instincts of society, or does it provide a useful tool in rehabilitating an offender? Given the advantages of community-based correctional programs, what steps do you believe could be taken to "sell" the idea to the public, to convince citizens that it is in their own best interests to encourage good community programs?

Summary

Community-based corrections accounts for much of the correctional caseload. A prime motivation for keeping people in the community under supervision is to keep them acclimated to life in society. Unfortunately, as we have discussed, many of those persons under some form of community supervision go to prison or return to prison as the result of committing technical violations, not the commission of new crimes. There are some example programs that show promise, such as Hawaii's Project HOPE, which will be discussed in more detail in Chapter 14. The general concept is one of intervening quickly if infractions while under community supervision occur. However, the emphasis is on utilization of alternative sanctions, such as a short stint in jail to "shock" the offender's system. The goal is to avoid full-blown revocation and long-term incarceration. Also, states such as California, Illinois, and South Carolina are offering financial incentives to county probation agencies who lessen the amount of those under community supervision that are sent to prison, thereby saving the state money.[107] But a large number of convicted criminals serve their sentences as inmates in a large variety of prisons and correctional institutions. We examine those next.

Chapter 12

Punishments, Prisons, and Prisoners

Image by Jeffrey Zalesny at fotolia.com.

"It's odd what becomes of immense importance when one realizes one's freedom is about to be curtailed. It is frightening and difficult to grasp those realizations....

"The judges, the lawyers, the prosecutors do not really know what it's like to be incarcerated. They do not know that time passes slowly, there are no good educational opportunities, there is little of value with which to pass the time....

"I didn't miss the cappuccino. I missed the idea of cappuccino."

Reflecting on having crafted a manger scene, crocheted and started a yoga course while incarcerated, Martha Stewart remarked, "See what one can do with nothing?"

"[T]here is no place like home."

—Martha Stewart[1]

Seeking Justice: Two Opinions about Correctional Institutions

One Opinion: Since a large amount of crime is committed by a small number of chronic offenders, the amount of crime can be reduced by locking up those few chronic offenders. We should identify those chronic offenders and selectively incapacitate them in secure institutions, provide self-help programs for those who wish to take advantage of them, but maximize the deterrence benefits of "tough but fair" prison environments. Rehabilitation programs are largely ineffective for most criminals and a waste of taxpayers' money. Prisons have become too soft, too comfortable, and the prisoners' rights movement has given prisoners benefits which many poor, law-abiding citizens do not have. Since mandatory sentences began in the mid-1970s, crime rates have declined as the prison populations have increased.

Another Opinion: Crime rates have not come down as a result of the increased use of imprisonment. Rather, the decrease in crime is because of demographics, especially the recent decrease in the number of males in the 14- to 24-year age group. Society cannot accurately predict and identify chronic offenders. To make room for the high-risk offenders would mean a huge monetary cost to support the increased prison population. The political costs of reducing prison terms for low-risk offenders, which would be necessary to make room for high-risk offenders in the prison system, would be too high. Constitutional principles and protections for all citizens, even those in prison, are necessary in a democracy. We should develop and enhance vocational training and prison industries programs which will equip prisoners to find meaningful, well-paying employment after completion of their prison terms. Nothing should be done which would violate the basic constitutional rights and protections of prisoners.

About This Chapter

Not all stereotypes of prison are accurate. Not all correctional facilities are maximum-security jungles. Not all inmates are animals. Not all prisoners are dangerous. But the loss of freedom and loss of pleasures and privileges of normal life make the threat of prison an ominous specter for most of us, especially we who have had no personal experience as prisoners. Does the threat of imprisonment deter us from crime? Perhaps, for many, especially those who have been inside before, the incarceration experience is not so bad. For others who have had no privileges or pleasure on the outside, prison offers security, care, associations, and an escape from the responsibilities of freedom.

The History of Prisons and Correctional Institutions

Facilities for the detention and confinement of criminals have existed throughout recorded history. References to prisoners are found in some of the world's earliest literature and, in antiquity, various natural and human-constructed structures were utilized to house prisoners. Ancient Semitic nomads utilized dry wells or cisterns to confine persons who, in one way or another, had deviated seriously enough from social norms to incur punishment. The offender would be lowered into the pit with ropes and left until further steps could be decided or until the prisoner died from exposure or starvation or from attack by wild animals. The use of pits or dry wells for confinement was common in many ancient cities. Early Egyptians housed prisoners in a walled, fortress-like tower until the king decided how to dispose of them. Moreover, underground prisons, "courtyard" prisons, and "house arrest" were all utilized in cultures thousands of years before the Greek and Roman eras.[2]

Often, prisoners in antiquity were put to death or used as a slave labor force. But for most, a period of incarceration preceded either of these more drastic sanctions. In a sense, early prisons were like the death rows of modern societies rather than prisons where incarceration, in itself, is the punishment.

Early Egyptian art depicts the transportation of prisoners in single file, hands bound behind them, each prisoner connected to the next by a rope tied to hooks which ran through the cheek or lip. For many, being condemned to hard labor in salt mines or on construction projects, such as the pyramids, was a death sentence, for they would die on the job. Prisoners were often transported to distant places of labor. At night, or when the prisoners were not otherwise engaged in labor, they were confined, sometimes bound, and almost always held in remote, hostile surroundings, making escape virtually impossible.[3]

One of the earliest known penal codes dates back to 1750 B.C., the Code of Hammurabi. It predates the Bible and is based on the principle of *lex talionis*, which is simply the law of retaliation, mere vengeance, "an eye for an eye, and a tooth for a tooth." Liars might have their tongues ripped out, or rapists might be castrated.

Many early punishments were *apotropaic* in nature, actions aimed at warding off evil spirits. Collective punishments were often rendered whereby citizens would participate in lynchings, and the operation of the *Halifax gibbet* (a crude precursor to the guillotine). This allowed citizens to participate in executions while being able to avoid full responsibility for the death. Stoning to death is the oldest known form of collective execution.

The ancient Greeks engaged in stoning, crucifying, death by fire, *garroting* (choking with an iron collar), *gibbeting* (subjecting to public humiliation), branding, banishment, and originated the punishment of breaking persons on the wheel. The ancient Greeks tended to incarcerate individuals only long enough to figure out what their punishment would be; imprisonment in and of itself was not a punishment.

The ancient Romans used imprisonment *as* a punishment. However, they tended to use makeshift structures as prisons instead of erecting buildings specifically for the purpose of housing prisoners. For example, the Mamertine Prison, established around 640 to 616 B.C., notorious for its dungeons, had been part of the early Roman sewer system. With influence from the Romans the Burgundian Code (A.D. 500) was developed, whereby punishments for various acts were proscribed based on the class of those involved. The Justinian Code (A.D. 529) was instituted by the Roman emperor of the same name to try to establish consistency in making punishments fit crimes.

The Romans also developed a special type of punishment for those who committed *parricide* (the killing of a parent). They would place the culprit inside a sack with a rooster, snake, monkey, and canine and then throw the sack into a river or the sea.[4]

During the Middle Ages, the duty of clans and family members to defend their own and seek vengeance upon the perpetrator(s) when wronged was pronounced. However, this could prove costly as blood feuds developed and could literally deplete the work force. In place of such detrimental retaliation, the concept of *wergeld* and *friedensgeld* were used. Wergeld allowed the perpetrator or his kin to pay the victim or his family the determined worth of the person (i.e., a 1,500-shilling person) who had been wronged without further blood being shed.[5] Nobles were of course valued more than servants. Friedensgeld was a payment to the state for damage to the public peace.[6] Obviously, the wealthy were at an advantage in such matters. Even today, while crime is a personal matter, prosecutions are sought on behalf of the state (i.e., State v. _____ or United States v. _____).

The Middle Ages also saw the emergence of feudalism, as service was traded for "land, protection, and justice." Makeshift prisons, similar to those of early Rome, were prominent. The influence of the church in punishment is seen via use of the ordeal and the Inquisition. The ordeal consisted of arrangements whereby guilt or innocence would be determined by tests or ordeals. For example, an accused person, weighted down with a boulder, would be thrown into a river. If the person floated, the person was considered innocent. If the person sank, the person was considered guilty. This test could also be used to detect witches. The belief was that if someone were truly innocent God would intervene to save them. Ultimately, under feudalism corporal punishment and fines emerged as the primary forms of punishment, because the infliction of death and exile would deplete the labor force.

Galley slavery was popular and a good economical use of prisoners to pull the oars on ships as global exploration and expansion occurred. Seafaring advancements such as sails and steam led to the demise of galley slavery.[7]

Dungeons, gaols (the original spelling of jail), workhouses, and similar facilities for criminals in medieval Europe and Asia were generally short-term lockup arrangements to hold offenders only until they could be executed, pilloried, branded, or transported to overseas penal colonies. Some American settlements and Australia served as penal colonies early in their histories, receiving prisoners banished and transported by ship from European countries. The British abruptly stopped the practice of shipping inmates to America when the Revolutionary War broke out and started sending its exiles to Australia. The conditions on transport ships could be horrid, with persons often dying in transit to penal colonies. For the most part, such practices ended in the early 1800s, although there were a few exceptions such as Siberia, in the Soviet Union, and Devil's Island, owned by France and located off the coast of South America. Boatloads of offenders from other societies became increasingly unwelcome on foreign shores. Some countries, including the United States, even moored hulks (ships), also known as "floating hells," in harbors or on river banks to house prisoners in decrepit conditions.[8]

In colonial America, many of the early punishments were public in nature. In a rural, homogeneous society, public humiliation could be an effective punishment. Such punishments in early America included flogging (whipping), branding, and use of the *brank* for public gossips. This was a birdcage like device placed over the criminal's head with a gate placed over the mouth and a metal spike positioned on the culprit's throat to make it painful to talk. The ducking stool, stocks which held prisoners in a seated position, or the pillory which held them in a standing position, placed the offender in the town square. Citizens would hurl objects at prisoners and sometimes nail their earlobes to the pillory. The only way to extricate one's self after having been sufficiently humiliated would be to rip one's earlobe(s) or have the ear cut from the board. Either way, a mark would be left that would permanently identify one as a criminal.[9]

Among the reasons for the development and spread of imprisonment was the lack of suitable new locations for penal colonies. Prisons were developed as alternative, internal, penal colonies. They became state-run, closed, walled communities called penitentiaries. The historic method of removal by banishment to foreign lands was no longer available, so a new form of removal was needed.

In America, we still practice the historic method of "**outlawry**"[10] whereby criminals are simply driven out of organized society, placed outside the protection of the laws of civilized society, removed from the midst of honest citizens. Indeed, the removal of criminals from society and the placing of them in secure facilities simply to get them away from the company of the noncriminal population is a very popular way to deal with criminals. Political leaders and legal authorities have traditionally dealt with unwanted problem people by forcibly removing them from the community—sometimes by banishment or transportation, sometimes by incarceration. Contemporary judges have been heard to justify a sentence of imprisonment by saying, "I just wanted to get him off the streets for a while."

Here's what one of the inmates in the *Scared Straight* television depiction of hardened inmates said:

> What would your parents do with a dog that constantly pissed on the living room furniture? They'd get rid of it, that's what. Well, don't you know that every time you are brought into the court for a B & E, or mugging, or drugs that you are pissing on the judge's furniture and sooner or later the judge is going to get fed up and get rid of you? And then you go to prison!

Prisons in the United States

Maximum-security prisons and reformatories, as we know them, originated and developed in the United States.[11] Initially, in America, we too relied on makeshift structures to house inmates. In fact, Newgate Prison in Simsbury, Connecticut, was an abandoned copper mine that opened in 1773 to house inmates. A year later the nation's first prison riot would take place at this same establishment.[12]

Denial of freedom as punishment for crime had a particular attraction in the early years of our republic, for we had just emerged from a revolutionary struggle over freedom. What could be more punitive than taking freedom away from deviant citizens? But restraint and punishment were not the only reasons used to support the idea of imprisonment. In the years between 1820 and 1840, when the first prisons were built in the United States, prisons were justified and rationalized on philosophical and moral grounds. Though it may seem strange today, early prisons were designed to be utopian societies, not only models for control and treatment of criminals, but also examples of a social order that could be generalized. Historian David Rothman points out that the design of the prison originally attempted to eliminate the specific influences that were breeding crime in the community. As Rothman has written:

> Rather than stand as places of last resort, hidden and ignored, these institutions became the pride of the nation. A structure designed to join practicality to humanitarianism, reform the criminal, stabilize American society, and demonstrate how to improve the condition of mankind, deserved full publicity and close study.[13]

Two types of prisons were developed in the United States, and for a number of years advocates of one kind argued with advocates of the other over their relative merits. One type was developed in Pennsylvania and reflected a strong Quaker influence. The Walnut Street Jail (1790) in Philadelphia was the first public facility in America designed to use incarceration as the principal means to correct behavior and was used solely to house convicted felons. Initially, no work was performed by inmates at the Walnut Street Jail, but prisoners began to literally go insane and modifications were made over time. The Walnut Street Jail is considered to be the first penitentiary, having been constructed for that purpose, and would ultimately meet its demise due to overcrowding.[14]

The Quaker influence evolved into what would come to be known as the **Pennsylvania Prison System.** Its major characteristic was **solitary confinement** of prisoners; it is sometimes called the **segregate prison.** Inmates, held in solitary confinement, were isolated from the outside world and one another and were expected to remain in their cells, ultimately allowed to work in solitude, read the Bible, reflect on their crimes and "repent." Hence the term **penitentiary,**[15] again reflecting the influence of the church, evolved from Latin terms meaning "penitence" and "repentance," but also shares the same root with "revenge," "pain," and "punishment."[16]

A different kind of prison was built at Auburn, New York. Known as the **Auburn Prison System,** this institution held prison inmates in cells at night but released them in the daytime to work together at various forms of hard labor. This **congregate system** rested on the belief that the way to repentance and reform, and indeed the way to salvation, lies through hard work, in contrast to the Pennsylvania system where repentance itself was the "way." Both systems imposed total silence on prisoners, and in New York an elaborate form of marching—a shuffle called the **lock step**—was imposed on them as they moved, in silence, from their cells to their places of work.

As Rothman pointed out, both types of prisons became world-famous, were visited and evaluated, and had their merits debated by scholars, politicians, and reformers. In this battle over the "best" system, the Auburn plan generally prevailed. The extended solitary confinement of the Pennsylvania system tended to drive prisoners insane and was very costly, whereas the congregate, work prison could help support itself by the labor of inmates.

Auburn Prison, built between 1819 and 1823, was quickly followed by similar prisons at Ossining (Sing Sing) and Dannemora (Clinton Prison). Eventually the Auburn plan spread nationwide and indeed became an international prototype of a maximum-security prison.

The **National Prison Association** was created and met for the first time in Cincinnati in 1870 in a spirit of progressive reform. The prison practices which had been generally accepted up to that time—lockstep, fixed sentence, isolation, silence—were now criticized and rejected by the majority in attendance. The famous Declaration of Principles, enunciated in Cincinnati in 1870, called for major reforms, including use of the Irish mark system and rewards for good conduct. The goal of the prison should be to make industrious free citizens, not orderly and obedient prisoners. Religion and education became the two most important means to reform; prisons should be small and house prisoners by type. Prisoner discipline should be fair. Society must understand that it is responsible for the conditions that breed crime. Sentences should be fixed and disparities removed. Industrial training should be fully offered; and inmates should receive social training. Silence rules should be abolished,[17] and over time prisoners would be allowed to communicate with each other while working. These reforms also required improving prison productivity and profitability.

In the 1870s a **reformatory** for young adult felons was established at Elmira, New York. Structurally, it was maximum-security, built very much like Auburn Prison, but its program included educational and vocational training opportunities as well as work. As Auburn became the prototype prison, so **Elmira** became the prototype reformatory, copied throughout the nation and the world. Also, popular after the Civil War was the **state lease system**. With slavery abolished, there was a need for cheap labor. Farmers, particularly in the agrarian, rural South, leased inmates from prisons to work their fields. This practice ultimately subsided around the beginning of the twentieth century, as states began to capitalize on operating their own prison industries to occupy inmates and make a profit.

Much of that profit was coming at the expense of the private sector. Therefore, in 1929 the **Hawes-Cooper Act** was passed by Congress and required prison-made products to be subject to the laws of any state to which they were shipped. In other words, a massive state like Texas could put members of the private sector out of work in a small state like Maine by being able to ship cheaply made prison products there and undercut the private sector. This law meant that the receiving state could now outright ban or place restrictions on prison-made products from other states. A subsequent law, the **Ashurst-Sumners Act**, was amended in 1940 to completely outlaw the interstate shipment of prison-made products.

What has now emerged is what is referred to as the **state-use system.** Under this system, prison-made products can only be sold to and used by governmental agencies. Prisoners manufacture license plates, make desks for public schools, make mattresses for prisons, etc. The federal system established their own Federal Prison Industries, which was authorized by Congress in 1934, and it primarily supplies products to the military today.[18] Most people want inmates to work. But, what would you have them do? They are not to perform work that would undermine the private sector and are therefore somewhat limited in their job prospects.

Modern Correctional Institutions and Prisons

The newspaper headline screams "CONVICTED KILLER GETS 25 YEARS IN JAIL." No. Wrong. As we discussed in Chapter 7, **jails** are local institutions designed for short stays, less than one year for sentenced minor offenders. Most jail inmates are awaiting trial or sentence. No one is sentenced to jail for more than one year.

Correctional institutions are more commonly representative of what most people mean when they say "jail." Correctional institutions house prisoners who will be released and returned to society sooner or later. Emphasis is placed on a wide range of programs made available to inmates in the hopes of equipping them for their future life of freedom. Correctional institutions provide recreation, education, vocational training, libraries, leisure-time activities, religious services, and a great number of other elements of society in miniature.

Reformatories house youthful offenders. Commonly, a reformatory is thought to be a place of incarceration for juvenile delinquents. Juveniles are generally housed in training schools, whereas reformatories hold young felons, generally those in the 18- to 21-year age group.

Prisons are maximum-security, long-term institutions where prisoners serving the longest terms are housed. Prisons are complex social systems characterized by their own problems and heterogeneous populations. Prisons are more confining than correctional institutions. A number of inmates in prisons may be kept in their cells 23 hours each day, sometimes referred to as super-max. Release, if it will come at all, is generally a long time away in the future.

Prisoners are classified and transferred from one institution to another as a means of keeping them from preying on one another. Prison discipline is maintained—a tough but necessary part of prison life needed to prevent riots, killings, escapes, and the smuggling of contraband. Inmate rights are protected and prison actions are governed by leading court cases. The world of prison inmates is not pretty. It is the end of the line in our criminal justice process, and the maximum-security prison, historically as well as currently, is one of the harshest, most brutal, and most brutalizing structures created by human beings.

These distinctions in nomenclature emerged with the so-called professionalization of the field of corrections during recent decades and the desire to modify the harsh images elicited by the terms "prison" and "guard." To some extent these name changes reflect modification in correctional philosophy from punishment to rehabilitation, or correction. Unfortunately, perhaps, many prisons simply changed the sign on the gates, leaving the inside conditions the same as before.

Prisons and the Community

Confinement facilities exist in every state and federal jurisdiction of the United States, and in virtually every country in the world. Prisons and other correctional institutions are usually located in sparsely populated areas. Older prisons may exist in urban centers, but newly built and opened institutions generally are located far away from cities. This is because of the lower costs associated with buying undeveloped land and the relative absence of community opposition to constructing such facilities in less populated areas. Indeed, many prisons have proved to be the economic salvation of small towns. They become the major employer in the area, hiring their correctional officers and other staff from among the local residents. Prisons also contribute to local economies by purchasing many goods and services from nearby merchants, resulting in a business that is relatively unaffected by swings in the economy or seasonal changes. There are no off seasons or summer vacations among the criminal population.

A Growth Industry

"The American prison system is massive. So massive that its estimated turnover of **$74 billion** eclipses the GDP of **133 nations.**"[19] Many prisons and correctional institutions in the United States are filled to overcapacity. At the end of 2015, 18 states and the Federal Bureau of Prisons (BOP) were operating at or above 100 percent of their highest prison capacity. In Texas, for instance, federal authorities have housed excess inmates in tents. To further illustrate this problem, some jurisdictions operating over the capacity for which their facilities were designed, rated, or operationally intended included Illinois (145%), Nebraska (125%), Massachusetts (123%), the BOP (120%), Delaware (117%), and Hawaii (115%).[20] As we discussed in Chapter 1, America has the highest incarceration rate in the world.[21]

Very few observers would predict a substantial decline in rates of imprisonment, although the number of inmates may drop as the various "baby boomers" (and their children, the "echo boomers") grow older and move out of the typical inmate age group. Citizen-led initiatives to decriminalize or legalize substances such as marijuana may continue. However, even if prison-prone populations decline, we may still maintain a large prison population because states have an enormous financial and political investment in institutions of confinement.

Once a prison is constructed, it tends to be used, and it is very rare for a prison to ever be closed, no matter how old it is. As a matter of fact, no sooner is a prison constructed than it becomes full—even overcrowded. We are bound to a policy of imprisonment due to some extent to the fact that we have built more and more facilities for confinement, as additions to older prisons, not as replacements.[22]

Private Prisons

Publicly traded corporations like Corrections Corporation of America and GEO Group exists to make profits. Combined, both companies generated over **$2.53 billion**

Image by mukem at istockphoto.com.

in revenue in 2012, and represent more than half of the private prison business.[23] Private correctional facilities are mainly located in Western and Southern states. The U.S. leads the way in such institutions, followed by a few private facilities in Australia and the United Kingdom.[24] At year-end 2015, six states (Hawaii, Mississippi, Montana, New Mexico, North Dakota, and Oklahoma) housed roughly 20% of their inmate population in privately operated prisons.[25] In 2015, about 8% of state and federal prisoners (126,300 inmates) were incarcerated in private prison facilities. This number was down by 4% (5,500) from the year before.[26]

State, local and federal governments may contract the operation of some inmate services (such as construction, food, or medical) to private entities, or they may contract the total operation to a private corporation. Typically, bids are submitted, whereby the private company offers to enter a contract with a governmental entity at X amount of dollars per inmate. Due to overcrowding and potential cost savings, private prisons have become a growing response to handling prisoners in America. Private prisons can often undercut state and federal governments by offering lower wages to employees, particularly in rural areas, as individuals there, often in economic dire straits, are just pleased to have a job even if it is at less than state or federal wages.

Private prison operations have been touted by proponents for their ability to save money. One private prison director likened the monitoring of the cash flow for correctional purposes to the eye he keeps on his own personal check book. When operating as a private corporation, the dollars one saves can wind up as bonuses in your own pocket, he said. He maintained that when an item was needed for the facility, such as a lawnmower, he could shop around for the best deals as a private prison director, whereas state and federal prison administrators would be locked in by bids on where they must shop and may very well have to pay exorbitant prices. The director even added that when he worked previously as an administrator for the federal bureau of prisons, at the end of the fiscal year, with $10,000 left in his budget, he rushed out and bought $10,000 worth of marble trash cans for the grounds. He said he knew if he didn't spend the money, the money would go back to the federal government, and it would be extremely difficult for him to justify receiving as much money for the next fiscal year's budget.

It can indeed be profitable to lock individuals up, and it is even possible to invest in private prison corporations on Wall Street.[27] However, cost saving measures may undermine services, and if services to inmates are diminished this may prove costly in the long run in terms of their potential successful reintegration into society. Furthermore, concerns have also arisen about how deals are brokered with the private corrections entities and governmental agents.

Reportedly, Roger L. Green, a state legislator in New York, was provided roughly $2,000 a month in services, including a minivan, a driver, cell phone, free meals, and workers for his campaigns, by Correctional Services Corporation (CSC)—a private prison company. Seventeen of 22 of CSC's employees at one half-way house were purportedly found to have been out campaigning for various New York lawmakers. CSC gave tens of thousands of dollars in campaign contributions to democratic candidates in New York, and those connected with the company contributed more than $27,500 to Governor Pataki's re-election campaign. Over a nine-year period, the company earned in excess of $22 million in New York state contracts.[28]

Classification and Reception Centers

Prior to the 1970s, it was common for a sentencing judge to specify the prison or reformatory where an offender was to serve his or her sentence. Since then judges generally do not name a particular prison but instead transfer custody of the offender to the department of correctional services. The offender is then transported to a **reception center**, where he or she is classified and assigned to an available prison. The convicted offender is normally housed there for a period of weeks while undergoing observation and medical and psychological testing and evaluation. Then the inmate is placed in the correctional institution within the state which has the proper programs to meet his or her set of needs.

Prisons must take who they get. The police can make discretionary decisions as to what laws to enforce and which offenders to arrest. Prosecutors have considerable discretion regarding which offenders to prosecute and for which crimes, and the judge has discretion regarding which of several alternative sentences to impose. But the correctional system alone has absolutely no discretion as to which offenders enter its gates. Correctional institutions, particularly prisons, serve as the end of the line of the criminal justice process. The only discretionary decisions correctional institutions can make are where to place their prisoners and what privileges to allow them; those decisions are important for both prisoners and institutions.

Image by slobo at istockphoto.com.

Classification and Institutional Security

The first order of prisons is to have and to hold. The primary, foremost, and critical decision in classification is **security**. This has three dimensions: (1) the likelihood the inmate will escape or attempt to escape, (2) the likelihood the inmate will hurt correctional officers or other prisoners, and (3) the likelihood the prisoner will attempt to smuggle in contraband. Security considerations affect the types of jobs prisoners can be assigned to, where they are celled, and the amount of freedom they have to move around within the institution.

The federal and state correctional systems have diversified facilities so that some choice of correctional setting is available at the time of classification. Prisons and reformatories are generally distinguished by their degree of security, which relates not only to perimeter control and internal gates and bars, but also to the types of industrial and treatment programs offered by the institution. The majority of state correctional facilities in America are minimum security, followed by approximately 25 percent of institutions designated as medium security, and roughly 20 percent of prisons as maximum security.[29]

After classification, inmates must be transferred to a correctional institution and begin serving time in the general prison population. Some prisons may require further evaluation and classification once an inmate arrives at their assigned facility. The most frequently used internal classification schema was developed by Dr. Herbert Quay and is known as the Adult Inmate Management System (AIMS).[30] The AIMS allows prison administrators to evaluate inmates in an attempt to determine who among the inmate population is more likely to be aggressors and who is more likely to be preyed upon. Upon identification, administrators then strive to keep these groups separated. Prison classification caseworkers can assist with this assessment to determine where to house inmates within a prison. Caseworkers also advise inmates on projected release dates, possible transfers to other institutions, custody reductions, and what programs and privileges are available to them.

Maximum-security prisons are typically surrounded by high fences or walls, usually 18 to 25 feet tall, with gun towers placed at strategic intervals. Inmates are housed in individual cells that rise in tiers (called galleries) in cellblocks. Prisons commonly operate industries, or shops, which produce goods used by state agencies. Schools and other treatment programs are designed for inmate rehabilitation. Services operate for feeding and clothing and meeting the health needs of prisoners. Sections of maximum-security prisons are separated by gates, interior fences, and walls, and prison staff members are very concerned with preventing possible escapes, riots, and inmate possession of **contraband** (anything forbidden by prison rules), such as cell phones, money, weapons, or narcotics. Some proportion of the population in any maximum-security prison is "locked down," that is, they remain in their cells continually except for periodic showers and limited recreation, which may consist of pacing back and forth in isolation within a small caged area. Any movement of inmates within the institution is closely regulated and monitored.

Medium-security prisons are usually enclosed by chain-link fences topped with barbed wire. Inmates are much less regimented and relatively free to movement within the institution. Inmates are allowed to move about to recreation areas, the library, and other areas of the institution. Industries tend to be more modern and meaningful—computer programming, auto repair, or furniture construction—in contrast to the laundries and auto-tag shops often found in maximum-security prisons. Generally, medium-security institutions receive only prisoners who have been carefully screened for risk of escape or assault. Except in the federal system, these prisoners ordinarily do not come directly from the courts but are transferred from maximum-security prisons or reception centers.

Minimum-security prisons typically do not have fences, and the security around the perimeter is more relaxed. An escape from a minimum-security institution only requires a person to walk away. There are no armed guards, no gun towers, no barbed wire or electronic devices to make sure prisoners stay put. Generally, less dangerous prisoners are housed there—those with short sentences, those without lengthy criminal records, or those who are on their way out of the prison system after years served in more secure institutions without causing serious problems. The grounds resemble a school campus, and a nearly normal lifestyle is experienced by inmates and staff alike. Family visits are more leisurely and take place more often. Housing arrangements are usually dormitory-style, sometimes even private or semiprivate rooms with more privacy than in more secure institutions. A wide range of programs exist to help inmates prepare for life on the outside, including vocational training, academic education, psychiatric treatment, counseling, and drug and alcohol counseling. Work release and study release programs are encouraged, whereby trusted prisoners are allowed to travel away from the institution to attend school or to work during the day, only to return to the institution at night. See **Critical Thinking 12.1** regarding classification decisions.

Critical Thinking 12.1 What Classification Is Best? You Decide

1. Bank Robber

Price Gaudette, a 38-year-old man, arrived at the Classification and Reception Center facing a sentence of 30 years for the armed robbery of the

Household Finance Loan Company of Austin, Texas. The FBI suspected Gaudette of a series of armed bank robberies throughout the Southwest but were unable to make a positive identification due to his unique talent for disguise. Gaudette was charming, likable, had a very positive attitude, and expressed a desire to devote his time in incarceration to the "improvement of his fellow man" in any way possible. He had served two years of a five- to eight-year term for armed robbery when he was in his early twenties. No other arrest record was found.

1. Should he be confined in a maximum-security cellblock because of his lengthy sentence?
2. Is minimum security too risky for him because of his ability to disguise himself and perhaps escape easily?
3. Should the emphasis be on job training, peer counseling, and other efforts to rehabilitate him away from a life of crime?
4. Or, should he be placed in an environment in which he can quietly spend his time "improving his fellow man?"

2. Colombian Connection

George Engle, a 22-year-old man convicted of drug smuggling, was received by the department of corrections facing a five-year term. Engle had no prior arrest record as a juvenile or adult. He had been caught unloading a fishing boat filled with bales of marijuana in what was reported as a "major drug bust." Engle stated that he was unemployed, broke, and when a friend offered him $5,000 for one night's work he agreed—only to get caught in what he said was his first and only experience in crime.

1. Should classification focus on job training? Education? Improving his self-image?
2. Or, should the prison experience be used to teach him the lessons of crime, to reform him?
3. A community-based facility would enable him to find employment near his home, but would that be too much leniency or temptation?
4. Is George a "situational offender" who truly committed his first crime and was so unlucky as to get caught? Is he already rehabilitated?

3. Dirty Harry

Harry Phelps, a 19-year veteran police officer, was received on a sentence of 15 years for extortion in a much-publicized case in which Phelps had been involved in providing "protection" to an illegal gambling operation in Phoenix. Although he had no prior police record, his personnel record reflected a series of serious accusations ranging from alleged brutality to soliciting a bribe. Phelps was arrogant and hostile, and stated that he had been a scapegoat for corrupt politicians.

1. Should he be placed in a maximum-security cell for his own protection? If so, he will not be able to participate in work, educational, or other rehabilitation programs. And, he will be unable to participate in programs which would enhance his early release.
2. Should he be housed at another prison out of state?
3. Should he be placed in population in a medium-security prison and left to take care of himself?
4. What responsibility should the prison system have regarding the care of bad cops? Or, is he just another prisoner with no special rights or needs?

Inmates and Animal Training Programs

At Lowell Correctional Institution Work Camp, outside of Ocala, FL, female inmates housed in honors dorms have an opportunity to participate in the W.O.O.F. (Women Offering Obedience & Friendship) program. As a general rule, six dogs are placed with 12 inmate trainers for an eight-week session of behavioral training. The inmates teach the dogs basic obedience commands, crate training, and manners. The dogs and inmates live together in a separate housing unit, where the dogs get constant companionship, reinforcement, and attention.

The primary goal of the W.O.O.F program is to prepare participants, both the women and dogs, with the socialization and communication skills needed to succeed outside of institutional confinement. Participation in the program also encourages the women to further their educational and vocational training, and allows them to acknowledge their own personal goals. Participation in this program offers the inmates an opportunity to give back to the community by training shelter dogs the basic skills needed for socialization and obedience that allow them to become eligible for adoption as family pets. Once the dogs complete their training successfully they are available for adoption through the Marion County Humane Society.

Another example of correctional programming involving animal training is implemented at a minimum-security corrections facility for men located outside of Riverton, Wyoming. The inmates serving time here have earned a transfer as a result of good behavior at a previous institution. The men are primarily involved in the mustang program this is a part of the programming at the Wyoming Honor Farm.

The program is a result of a partnership between the Department of Corrections and the U.S. Bureau of Land Management (BLM) that established the country's second inmate mustang program. The program participants assist the BLM by caring for and training wild herds of mustangs so that they can become adoptable. In addition to training the horses, the men also work to manage cattle, bale hay, and farm a variety of crops. These agricultural tasks help the inmates to their build self-esteem, as well as, to learn important life skills such as arriving to work on time and taking directions from supervisors. In turn, the BLM is provided with a means and the labor to manage and control the wild mustang populations.[31]

The Number and Characteristics of Prisoners

At year-end in 2015, an estimated 1,526,800 inmates were under state and federal prison authorities' jurisdiction, down by 2% from the year before. This was the smallest number of prison inmates since 2005 (a population of 1,525,900 inmates).[32] The prison population had previously experienced a low upward trend for decades. When those incarcerated in the United States had reached 1 in 100 adults in 2006, it was the largest proportion ever in America. By 2012 that ratio had shifted to about 1 in 108 adults.[33]

One cause for the decline was that some states experienced large budget deficits, prompting them to rethink their sentencing and release practices, but declines in prison admissions and increases in releases reportedly began prior to the manifestation of the financial woes. States had begun to come to the realization that "they could effectively reduce their prison populations, and save public funds, without sacrificing public safety.... [States] enacted reforms designed to get taxpayers a better return on their public safety dollars."[34]

The 2015 *incarceration rate* for the U.S. decreased nearly 3% from 471 per 100,000 in 2014 to 458 per 100,000 in 2015.[35] Females comprised about 7% of the prison population nationally at year-end 2015. Males were imprisoned at a rate about thirteen times greater compared to females (863 compared to 64 per 100,000) (these rates include juveniles). At year-end 2015, females and males ages 30 to 34 had the highest imprisonment rates (2,050 per 100,000 for males and 184 per 100,000 for females), also reflecting the largest portion of both male and female inmates sentenced to prison (16.5% for males, 19% for females). In the 30–34 age group, imprisonment rates were 5,948 per 100,000 black males, 2,365 per 100,000 Hispanic males, and 1,101 per 100,000 white males. In the 30–34 age group for women, the imprisonment rates were 255 per 100,000 blacks, 175 per 100,000 Hispanics, and 164 per 100,000 whites.[36]

In fact, from 1977 to 2004 the numbers of women state prisoners increased by 757 percent, reflecting a rate almost double that of male prisoners during that time period (388%). When federal prisoner numbers were included with state prisoner counts for women, female prisoners increased from 11,212 to 96,125 from 1977 to 2004.[37]

Between 2012 and 2014 the total female inmate population increased again by another 4%. However, the total female prison population decreased by more than 1% between 2014 and 2015.[38] Females comprised 7% of the decline for federal prison inmates, and 2% of state prison populations; "[t]he male imprisonment rate declined by almost 3% from 2014 to 2015 (889 per 100,000 U.S. male residents) (863 per 100,000)."[39]

"The female imprisonment rate was down by almost 2% from 2014 (65 per 100,000 U.S. female residents) to 2015 (64 per 100,000). There were twice as many white females (52,700) as black females (21,700) in the sentenced prison population at year-end 2015, but the imprisonment rate for black females (103 per 100,000 U.S. female residents) was twice the rate for white females (52 per 100,000)."[40]

Violent offenders represented more than half (54%) of the sentenced male state prisoners. More than a third (36%) of female prisoners were violent offenders. Eighteen percent (223,700) of male state prisoners and 28% (26,000) of females were sentenced for property offenses. Twenty-five percent of female state prisoners (23,500 females) and 15% of male state prisoners (182,700 males) were sentenced for drug offenses.[41]

In 2014, more than half (53%) of state prisoners were serving sentences for violent offenses, compared to 19% for property offenses and less than 16% for drug crimes. About half of all federal inmates were serving sentences for drug offenses, and 7% were serving sentences for violent offenses.[42]

Over half (53%) of state prisoners sentenced to over a year in prison in 2014 were serving time for a violent offense; 19 percent of those sentenced prisoners were serving time for property crimes and about 16% for drug crimes. The most prolific violent crime committed by state prisoners was murder (13 percent), followed closely by robbery (12.8 percent) and rape/sexual assault (12.4 percent). Burglary was the most frequent property crime of those incarcerated in state prison. About half of federal inmates were serving sentences for drug offenses, and 7% were serving sentences for violent offenses.[43]

In 2015, according to the U.S. Census Bureau, the population in the United States consisted of 77.1 percent whites, 13.3 percent blacks, and 17.6 percent Hispanics (note, does not sum to 100 because Hispanics may also be counted as whites).[44]

As of 2015, roughly 35 percent of *all* sentenced prisoners were black, 34 percent were white, and 22 percent were Hispanic. While imprisonment rates had declined for all races and were the lowest since 2005, blacks were more likely to be imprisoned at a rate of about five and one-half times greater than white males, and more than two times greater than Hispanics.[45]

"A smaller percentage of whites were serving sentences of more than one year in state prison for violent offenses (47% or 210,400 prisoners) than blacks (58% or 263,800) or Hispanics (59% or 152,900).... Whites had a higher percentage of sentenced prisoners serving time in state facilities for rape or sexual assault (16%) than blacks (8%) or Hispanics (13%). Whites also had a higher percentage of offenders serving a sentence of more than one year in state prison for property crimes (25%) than blacks (16%) and Hispanics (14%) at year-end 2014. The proportion of prisoners sentenced to more than one year in state prison for drug offenses was roughly equal between whites, blacks, and Hispanics (15.0% or 67,800 white prisoners, 14.9% or 68,000 black prisoners, and 14.6% or 28,800 Hispanic prisoners).... Almost 50% (92,000 prisoners) of sentenced federal prisoners on September 30, 2015, were serving time for drug offenses."[46]

Among *female* prisoners incarcerated during this time period (year-end 2015), about 50 percent were white, 21 percent were black, and 17 percent were Hispanic. Among *male* prisoners incarcerated during this time period, about 33 percent were white, 37 percent were black, and 22 percent were Hispanic. Other races made up about .12 percent for females and .09 percent for males' populations.[47]

Most women inmates are convicted of nonviolent offenses, and many were drug and alcohol abusers at the time they committed their offenses. Roughly 25% of female state inmates, compared to 15% of males, were sentenced for drug charges. In federal prison about 59% of females and 49% of males were serving sentences for drug charges. The majority of female prisoners also report having suffered either physical or sexual abuse.[48]

Roughly 40% of state prisoners have been found not to have a high school diploma, while only 18% of the age-appropriate general population is lacking one. Lack of educational attainment and race have been found to be associated with incarceration and recidivism. High school dropouts and blacks are more likely to be imprisoned than others in America.[49]

While overall incarceration rates and correctional populations declined, 18 states increased their prison populations. The leading states were Oklahoma, with an increase of 900 prisoners, and Virginia, up 860 prisoners.[50]

At year-end 2015, one in 37 adults (2.7% of the adults in the U.S.) was under some form of correctional supervision, the lowest rate since 1994. About 7 in 10 persons were under community supervision, and 3 in 10 under institutional supervision in state and federal jurisdictions.[51]

See **Table 12.1**[52] for significant changes in state and federal prison counts from 2014–2015. Prisoner counts dropped in the federal system and in 29 states, with Vermont, Alaska, Utah, Massachusetts, and Indiana leading the way in the decline of prison populations. The federal prisoner population also experienced a decrease from 2014–2015 with a nearly 7% drop, the lowest since 2006.[53] This has led to a major decrease in the overall U.S. prison populations.

Table 12.1 Significant Changes in State and Federal Prison Counts from 2014–2015

Lowest Rates of Imprisonment 2015	Highest Rates of Imprisonment 2015
Maine 132 per 100,000	Louisiana 776 per 100,000
Massachusetts 179 per 100,000	Oklahoma 715 per 100,000
Minnesota 196 per 100,000	Alabama 611 per 100,000

Six other states had rates of more than 500 per 100,000. These included: Mississippi (609), Arizona (596), Arkansas (591), Texas (568), Missouri (530), and Georgia (503).[54]

In terms of recent figures, the highest incarceration rate by region of the country is found in the South, followed by the West, Midwest, and Northeast, with Louisiana leading the way, with an incarceration rate of 776 per 100,000 residents, followed by Oklahoma, Alabama, Mississippi, Arizona, and Arkansas. See **Table 12.2.**[55]

According to the Vera Institute, 40 percent of "prisoners return to custody within three years of release."[56] In a Bureau of Justice Statistics study examining recidivism of federal and state prisoners who returned to the community under supervision over a five-year span of time, the following determinations were made. Forty-seven percent of the federal offenders were re-arrested, and 76.5% of the state prisoners were re-arrested. Of the federal offenders, 31.6% of them returned to prison, and

Table 12.2 State Prison Rates per 100,000 Resident Population by Region, 2015

MIDWEST	387	NORTHEAST	302
Illinois	360	Connecticut	312
Indiana	412	Delaware	441
Iowa	281	Maine	132
Kansas	328	Massachusetts	179
Michigan	429	New Hampshire	217
Minnesota	196	New Jersey	228
Missouri	530	New York	260
Nebraska	279	Pennsylvania	387
North Dakota	233	Rhode Island	204
South Dakota	413	Vermont	206
Ohio	449	**SOUTH**	**551**
Wisconsin	377	Alabama	611
WEST	**429**	Arkansas	591
Alaska	306	Florida	496
Arizona	596	Georgia	503
California	329	Kentucky	489
Colorado	364	Louisiana	776
Hawaii	262	Mississippi	609
Idaho	436	Maryland	339
Montana	355	North Carolina	352
Nevada	444	Oklahoma	715
New Mexico	335	South Carolina	414
Oregon	376	Tennessee	425
Utah	215	Texas	568
Washington	252	Virginia	457
Wyoming	413	West Virginia	386

59.4% of the state offenders did so.[57] Recidivism rates (return to prison after release rates) have been found to be less for educated prisoners.[58]

Older inmates have increased in number due to mandatory sentencing laws, three-strikes and truth-in-sentencing laws, which require inmates to serve up to 85% of their sentences in confinement. Many older inmates suffer from HIV and tuberculosis, and many are former drug users, habitual smokers, and alcoholics. With the aging population of prisoners serving long-term mandatory sentences, and the inclination of judges to sentence youthful offenders to long terms, the prison population continues to age. Over 19% of the nation's prison population in 2015 was age 50 or over, with over 35,000 inmates age 65 or older.[59] According to the PEW Center, healthcare costs for aging prisoners are sizeable.

The American prison system is a massive expense to state governments, and in turn, the taxpayers. Estimates show that the cost of incarceration averages $80 billion annually.[60] Annually states spend anywhere from $14,780 (Alabama) to $69,355 (New York) to incarcerate the average inmate.[61] According to a 2012 study conducted by the Vera Institute of Justice, the 700% increase of incarceration (since the 1970s) has cost taxpayers $39 billion.[62] From 1980 to 2013, there was a 324% increase in correctional spending at the state and local level compared to a 107% increase in spending over this period of time on public kindergarten to 12th grade education. Twenty-three states doubled their correctional spending, and, actually, seven states (Idaho, Michigan, Montana, North Dakota, South Carolina, South Dakota, and West Virginia) increased their rate of spending on prisons five times that of education over this time period.[63]

Prisons are big business in America. In Australia, they call their wardens "general managers." Perhaps we should do so as well or call them chief executive officers (CEOs). The Pew Center emphatically stated that "[m]ore prison spending brings lower public safety returns."[64] The National Council on Crime and Delinquency (NCCD) in a special report has maintained that in the face of exorbitant correctional costs savings could be realized across the country if those serving time for non-serious and nonsexual offenses were released from confinement and placed on alternative sentences in the community. The NCCD researchers indicated that approximately 25 percent of those incarcerated in 2008 would meet such criteria for release and estimated that if 80 percent of those meeting these criteria for release were returned to the community it could result in a savings of almost 10 billion dollars nationwide.[65]

How many prisoners will we have by next year? What can be done to alleviate the crisis of prisoner growth? Does this system work? Also, see Critical Thinking 12.2.

Critical Thinking 12.2 Transgender Inmates

Think about the issue of gender as it relates to the placement of where an inmate will serve his or her time, or housing placement within that institution. Common practice is for an inmate to be incarcerated at an institution of their birth sex. However, when placing transgender inmates within a prison population based on this practice, chances of victimization of that inmate increases. If a transgender inmate is physically attacked, he or she may be placed in solitary confinement for their protection, and to reduce the instances of prison violence within the general population. Some may argue that this results in punishment for the victim rather than a means of offering protection since administrative segregation is often an isolating and thus psychologically damaging form of confinement. **What are suggestions to be made regarding the imprisonment of transgender inmates? Learn more at:** http://www.huffingtonpost.com/entry/sandy-brown-transgender-inmate-legal-victory_us_5603160be4b0fde8b0d12518.

Prison Subculture

Sociologists have conducted considerable research on the "prison community,"[66] often referred to as the **prison subculture.** Prisons, after all, are small, self-contained societies with rules, norms of behavior, ethical codes, formal and informal sanctions, and a whole range of complex relationships between keepers and inmates and inmates and other prisoners. Early studies of prison subculture concluded that the values were in direct opposition to those found in free society. Prison subculture was a result of the conditions of incarceration, an adaptation to the prison environment. In that environment a new language, specific group structure, and different sexual behavior emerge. Some characteristics of the subculture are imported from outside, especially gang and ethnic groupings. But other elements are indigenous to the prison environment, created by people who have spent a majority of their lives behind bars. See **Critical Thinking 12.3.**[67]

Critical Thinking 12.3 Entering the Society of Captives

What do Plaxico Burress, Michael Vick, Bernie Madoff, Mike Tyson, and Martha Stewart have in common? They all hired prison consultants to advise them on the nuances of serving time in prison. Who else knows how to do time better than someone who has done time? Larry Levine has a website entitled Wall Street Prison Consultants on which he displays his prison identification card, a list of prisons he has served time in, and responses to frequently asked questions. While Herbert J. Hoelter has not served time, he has served as a consultant to Martha Stewart, Bernie Madoff, and Michael Vick on sentencing and how to navigate the prison environment. Hoelter maintains, "knowledge is power."

Should everyone experience the same pains of imprisonment for like crimes? Should the wealthy be able to ameliorate the prison experience by hiring consultants to help them do their time? Is this equal justice?

Accommodations between correctional officers and prisoners are necessary to allow the total institution to function. Officers comprise about 60 percent of the prison staff, their pay is typically low, and they usually operate within a rank structure similar to policing, which often attracts former military personnel. Job entry requirements are generally lower than for anyone else employed in the criminal justice system, and turnover rates are generally high. Inmates, of course, do not usually enjoy being monitored. Officers are affected by the people they have to work with—both staff and convicted felons. Within the prison environment the subculture of prisoners also

Image by oneword at istockpoto.com.

involves the presence of a custodial staff, which is there to protect everyone, enforce rules, observe the inmates, and maintain order.

Inmate types—Gresham Sykes in *The Society of Captives* identified prison argot, a special language specific to a particular group. Sykes described the "inmate code" and identified various types of inmates including "rats" (snitches), the "gorilla" (preys on the weak by force or intimidation to acquire what he wants), "ball busters" (openly rebel against their captors even though they know it is a lost cause), and the "tough" (one quick to do battle with his fellow inmates).[68] The inmate code represents a survival response, not only to the rigors of prison life but to the label of "criminal" and the damage to one's self-image brought about by the fact of incarceration.

Prisoners who exploit fellow prisoners are playing a dangerous game since they cannot escape the company of their victims. Eventually, anyone who successfully exploits a weaker individual is certain to lose to a more powerful or more skillful exploiter. Thus, the main traits affirmed by the inmate code are dignity, composure, courage, and the ability to "take it" and "hand it out" when necessary.[69]

Prison Conditions

Prison conditions prior to the second half of the twentieth century were generally horrible everywhere in the world. Despite the United States Constitution's prohibition against "cruel and unusual" punishment, prisoners have endured unrelentingly harsh conditions throughout most of the history of the United States. Prisons have typically been dirty, crowded, dangerous, depressing institutions. The prison administrator's familiar adage, "This ain't no hotel we're runnin'!" which characterized responses to complaints about prison conditions in previous decades and centuries, today must be tempered by requirements of Supreme Court decisions and other constraints on prison conditions. American prisons were not designed to be places *for* punishment, but places to confine convicted criminals *as* punishment, the denial of freedom being the penalty for crime.

Although living in prison today is a far cry from earlier days, prison life has yet to meet the standards set for it by American society. It is drab and unpleasant at best, and degrading and brutal at worst. Many of the prototype prisons built in the 1800s still exist: Auburn, Sing Sing, and Dannemora (also known as Clinton and "Little Siberia") are still operating in New York, modernized, of course, and now called correctional facilities. The lock step and silence systems are gone and the ready use of whip and lash to force conformity is no longer allowed in the United States. Yet incarceration in maximum-security prisons is still a harsh existence. Modern medium- and minimum-security prisons have softened the architecture and reduced the drabness of steel bars and gray paint. Educational and training programs in many of these "pastel prisons" are better, more closely related to outside work opportunities than the original forms of hard labor. But they hold only a few selected prisoners. In the main, the walls, cellhouses, treeless yards, and regimented existence of early prisons remain the pattern in maximum-security institutions today.

Prisoner lifestyle is controlled by the **principle of least eligibility**. This principle limits the kinds of food, housing, care, and treatment afforded prisoners to levels common to the poorest, "least eligible" members of free society. In short, prison conditions were not permitted to exceed bare minimum necessities. This mentality led Congress to prohibit inmates from receiving Pell Grants for college courses, even though educated inmates are less likely to return to prison.[70] Consider in **Critical Thinking 12.4** such deprivations and more occurring to someone who spends 35 years in prison for a crime he did not commit.

Critical Thinking 12.4 Stuck in Time, or Out of Sight-Out of Mind

Measured against progress in society generally, changes in the conditions of imprisonment have been minimal. In the early days of Auburn even horses were a luxury in our society, and since then our technology has placed men on the moon. We have educated our population, invented the Internet, increased life expectancy, become a leading world power; confronted Freud, Marx, and Darwin; changed in size and perhaps in morality. Yet prisons remain very much what they have always been. Any changes made have been made slowly and reluctantly.

Why do you think this is true? Has society chosen to keep prisons and prisoners out of sight and out of mind, providing only television images and reading materials as links to the outside world? What implications does this separation from society have for those who are ultimately released back into the society from which they have been cut off?

Consider James Bain. In 1974, Bain was a 19-year-old boy with no prior criminal record who was convicted of kidnapping and raping a 9-year-old boy based largely on the boy's identification of him as the perpetrator. Eyewitness identification is often faulty. At the age of 54, Bain was released from prison when DNA evidence exonerated him. He spent 35 years in prison for a crime he did not commit, longer than any of the other 245 inmates that had been released before him in America via post-conviction DNA testing. Upon release, he used a cell phone for the first time ever to call his mother. He'd never used an automatic teller machine. Under Florida law, Bain is entitled to $50,000 for every year incarcerated, which adds up to $1.75 million.[71]

How can you give someone a year of their life back, 5 years, 20 years, 30 years? It was not until *Coker v. Georgia*, 433 U.S. 584 (1977), that executions for the crime of rape where a murder was not involved were halted by the U.S. Supreme Court. What if James Bain had been executed? What responsibility and accountability do criminal justice employees have to get it right?

Institutional Rules and Regulations

The life of an inmate today, while certainly better in many ways than that of his early Auburn counterpart, is still one of strict regimentation, rigid rules, and conditions (See **Critical Thinking 12.5** below). It is often asserted that **prison rules** are imposed with malevolent intent, as part of a "degradation ceremony" required to satisfy the punishment goal of the incarceration of felons.[72] And there is little doubt that many present-day prison rules and regulations can be traced directly to earlier antecedents in the prisons at Auburn and in Pennsylvania, reflecting the beliefs then held about the nature and reform of criminal behavior. But a number of regulations, though abrasive in their impact, are simply the results of bureaucracy, the occasionally mindless rules of processing thousands of men and women.

Critical Thinking 12.5 Prison for Dummies

Thomas Murton, on whom the movie *Brubaker* starring Robert Redford was based, has indicated that putting a person in prison to teach them how to live in society is like putting a person on the moon to teach them how to live on earth. The environments are extremely different. Murton describes the prison as "an autocratic, dictatorial system.... The man most likely to obtain parole is the man who adapts to the autocratic system of the prison, the one who adjusts and becomes a robot, the one who isn't bothered by somebody telling him when to get up, when to eat and everything else; he's the one most likely to regain his freedom. He's also the one most likely to fail outside, because in free-world society, decisions aren't made for him anymore."[73]

Judge Dennis Challeen[74] has characterized the imprisonment experience in the following terms:

We want them to be responsible ...

So we take away all responsibilities.

We want them to be trustworthy ...

So we put them where there is no trust.

We want them to be non-violent ...

So we put them where there is violence all around.

We want them to quit being the tough guy ...

So we put them where the tough guy is respected.

We want them to quit hanging around with losers ...

So we put all the losers in the state under one roof.

We want them to quit exploiting us ...

So we put them where they exploit each other.

We want them to take control of their lives, own their problems, and quit being a parasite ...

So we make them totally dependent on us.

Based on the comments of Warden Tom Murton and Judge Dennis Challeen, how would you run the correctional system? How would you sell your ideas on operating the correctional system to lawmakers and the public?

Maximum-security male prisons are usually designed to hold 1,000 to 5,000 inmates, with the average population being between 1,000 and 2,000 men. Women's prisons are smaller since fewer adult female inmates than their male counterparts require incarceration.

Prisons are "total institutions"[75] housing reluctant populations requiring intensive security as well as provisions for feeding, housing, work, recreation, and all other aspects of life in a single-sex community. Prison rules and regulations have tended to proliferate simply to meet the requirements of mass care, feeding, and custody. Usually there are fewer rules and a more relaxed, less regimented lifestyle in medium- and minimum-security institutions.

Nonetheless, prisoners are isolated from normal community contacts. Visits from approved family members are allowed but severely circumscribed. A few jurisdictions today permit some inmates to have conjugal visits with lawful wives.[76] Some prison systems allow selected prisoners to go home on short furloughs, with requirements to report and curfews. Prisoners may write and receive mail, though traditionally both outgoing and incoming mail is subject to being read by prison officials, as there is a legitimate security interest in doing so.[77] Conferences with attorneys are not limited, and some prisons permit phone calls to families at specified intervals.

Maximum-security inmates spend a good deal of time locked in their cells when they are not working in one of the prison industries. The locked cell is not only pun-

Image by Zemdega at istockphoto.com.

ishment, but protection, for it keeps other inmates out. Perhaps the worst and most dangerous aspect of imprisonment is forced association with other felons, for prisons hold some offenders who are aggressive and dangerous to other inmates within the prison as well as to people on the street.

Prisoners' Rights, Due Process, and Discipline

In a very real sense, prison inmates are "**outlaws.**" Their status places them outside many of the legal protections afforded ordinary citizens. In years past the outlaw status of prisoners was almost complete; they really were "outside the law." The Supreme Court of Virginia in *Ruffin v. Commonwealth* (1871)[78] declared that convicted, imprisoned felons were "slaves of the state" and that they were in fact civilly dead as far as their rights were concerned. It was as if a wife could consider herself a widow upon her husband hitting the prison gates. There was no way to protest a condition of imprisonment, for communication with the outside world was extremely curtailed, and, appellate courts, even if reached, would rarely respond to inmate petitions.[79]

Prisoners are subject to search without specific probable cause, as legitimate security interests within prison override any Fourth Amendment rights prisoners may have.[80] Remnants of civil death remain, as only two states, Maine and Vermont, allow incarcerated felons to vote. Virginia and Kentucky do not allow for the re-instatement of voting rights for convicted felons even after they have completed their sentences.[81] Inmates can also be forced to comply with a wide assortment of restrictions on personal freedom ranging from type of clothing worn to where and when they can physically move around the institution.

It was not until almost 100 years after *Ruffin* that appellate courts would abandon their **"hands-off" policy** and became willing to consider prisoner appeals, particularly where a constitutional infringement was alleged.[82] The pivotal case was *Cooper v. Pate* (1964), which involved a question of religious freedom for black Muslim inmates. The Court essentially opened the floodgates for more prisoner rights cases by indicating no clear and present danger was presented by the inmates to security and that the orderly running of the institution was not threatened by inmates practicing their religion.[83] See **Critical Thinking 12.6** below.[84]

Critical Thinking 12.6 The Case for Reform

Warden Thomas Murton encountered an Arkansas prison system in the late 1960s that had inmate trustees armed with guns to guard other prisoners. Some black inmates were required to clip the grass with their fingernails, and there was the "Tucker Telephone" at one prison used to force inmates to divulge secreted information or for disciplinary purposes. The old, rural crank telephone was wired via electrodes that were attached to the convict's big toe and penis. When the phone was cranked, six volts of electricity would be discharged into the inmate's body. This process was repeated until the inmate was believed to be properly punished, revealed the confidential information, or passed out—which was referred to as having received "a long-distance call." Murton was abruptly summarily dismissed by the governor from his job in Arkansas after he began digging on prison grounds at the behest of inmates and uncovered bodies believed to be inmates buried on the prison grounds. In fact, according to Murton, the grand jury even contemplated indicting him for grave robbing.

It is these types of abuses that led to courts considering prisoner rights cases and intervention into the operation of prisons. In *Holt v. Sarver* (1969),[85] U.S. District Court Judge J. Smith Henley declared several elements of the Arkansas prison system to be in violation of the Eighth Amendment's prohibition against cruel and unusual punishment, and he established a consent decree whereby the Arkansas prison system authorities were to respond within 30 days as to how they planned to address recommendations proffered by Judge Henley. In *Holt v. Sarver II* (1970),[86] Judge Henley held the entire Arkansas prison system to be unconstitutional and ordered the prison administration to develop a plan of action.

Should inmates have rights? Which ones? Why? Why not?

Just because there are prohibitions in place for preventing cruel and unusual punishment that does not mean prevention of abuse always occurs behind prison walls. Consider the case of Darren Rainey. He was an inmate with schizophrenia serving time in the Dade Correctional Institution in Florida. He was locked in a scalding shower for two hours, with flesh peeling off his body, before he died. Prosecutors concluded, "[p]lacing an inmate who has defecated upon himself in a shower to decontaminate himself is not conduct that is criminally reckless. There was no evidence of any intent to harm Rainey."[87] **Upon reflection, do you think criminal charges should have been brought against correctional personnel? Can you determine if there was a civil lawsuit?**

While still recognizing the necessity for administrative discretion in maintaining custody of inmates, appellate decisions during more recent years have tended to distinguish more sharply between the rights inmates lose through conviction and incarceration than those they retain. The scope of appellate court intervention has gone beyond curbing cruel and unusual punishment to such matters as censorship of mail, freedom of speech and religion, access to courts and counsel, the further deprivation of liberty resulting from placing unruly inmates in segregation, and a variety of other issues relating to internal prison control.[88] During what has been termed the "intervention" phase, beginning in the mid-1960s, the Court was more amenable to considering prisoners' rights claims.[89]

However, a partial return to the hands-off doctrine seems currently in evidence as the U.S. Supreme Court has refused to grant certiorari for a significant number of cases involving **prisoners' rights** issues. Since 1980 what has been referred to as the "nominal" or "'one-hand-on, one-hand-off'" phase has been in effect for the Court.[90] The current Supreme Court does not appear to be eager to address matters relating to the treatment of prisoners. But the prisoners' rights cases most recently decided by the Court have served to tighten the control of prison administrators and to make legal redress of grievances more difficult for inmates.[91] For example, in *Turner v. Safely* (1987), the U.S. Supreme Court carved out a "reasonableness test" for determining what legitimately constitutes a threat to institutional security.[92] The decision in this case exhibits a certain deference to the decision-making ability of prison administrators. See **Criminal Justice 12.1** below regarding security concerns within prison.

Furthermore, the Prison Litigation Reform Act passed by Congress in 1996 has proven prohibitive for the filing of lawsuits by inmates. In an effort to curb frivolous prison lawsuits, the act requires payment of a filing fee, with payment paid in full in advance if the inmate has had three previous strikes, i.e., three previous suits dismissed for not stating a proper claim or that were frivolous or malicious in nature. Prisoner initiated lawsuits have dropped from 41,000 in 1995 to less than 25,000 annually while there are one-half million more inmates today.[93]

Criminal Justice 12.1 Ethics: Security for Whom? From Whom?

The following two cases represent problems facing correctional officers. The first is typical, the second unusual. Is security the number one priority?

1. Look What I Found

The cell house captain of D block in a maximum-security prison ordered the inmates in the four companies under his command held in their cells while other blocks fell out for work assignment. After the other companies marched off, D block officers searched every cell and subjected each inmate to a strip search. Extensive contraband, including twenty-seven homemade knives (shanks) and sixteen blackjacks, was seized. Appropriate notations of contraband possession were written for inclusion in the inmates' files, but no disciplinary reports were filed.

<u>Discussion</u>: Contraband, including weapons, exists in every prison and correctional institution. Prisoners have unlimited time to plan and scheme

ways to circumvent rules prohibiting possession of contraband, while correctional officers are few in number and have other matters to occupy their time and attention. Unannounced cell searches are one way contraband is discovered. Here, officers found many weapons and notations were made on prisoners' files as appropriate. Yet, no effort was made to discipline the prisoners further.

1. What is the purpose of such searches and confiscations?
2. Is the intent to merely get as many weapons as possible out of prisoners' possession?
3. Do searches and confiscations heighten or lessen prisoner stress?

2. Watch This Guy!

An inmate with an extensive criminal history, including convictions for arson, bombing, and attempted escape, was classified as "Maximum Security" and placed in a "Restricted Company" by the classification committee of the prison. Whenever he leaves the vicinity of his cell block (to meet with his attorney, report on sick call, meet with his family in the visiting room, or otherwise), standard operating procedures require him to be shackled with leg irons and handcuffs attached to a belly chain and escorted through the institution, with the tunnel cleared of all inmate traffic, by two correctional officers.

Discussion: This case sounds a little like the character Hannibal the Cannibal from the novel and movie *The Silence of the Lambs*. Such special precautions are not widespread in prisons and correctional institutions. But, the control of very dangerous, violent inmates does impact prison routine.

1. What can be done for the very dangerous?
2. Can a person be locked up continuously?
3. Should the safety of staff and other inmates be the number one consideration?
4. Should we remember that although prisoners are human beings, some must be dealt with cautiously?

Disciplinary Hearings

The correctional officer's most used weapon is the ink pen. It is used to write inmates up for disciplinary violations and restrict or take away various privileges. While the full legal dimensions of the trend toward more comprehensive prisoners' rights have yet to be played out, it is clear that inmates today are afforded a greater measure of administrative due process in challenging decisions made about them while in prison. Hearings and/or appeals on such matters as segregation (solitary confinement), **loss of "good time"**[94] (i.e., time off for good behavior), and similar matters, are now permitted in many jurisdictions.

Of course, a concern in prisons is the potential for inmates harming themselves. Placing an inmate in solitary confinement can exacerbate the possibility of an inmate's suicide. In fact, thc number of inmate suicides in prisons is on the rise. The number of suicides increased 30% between 2013 and 2014 (from 192 to 249). In 2014, suicides accounted for roughly 7% of all deaths in state prisons. This is the largest amount since 2001.[95]

A federal district court addressed the issue of in-prison discipline in 1971 in ***Landman v. Royster.*** This decision was the result of a class-action suit brought by Virginia prison inmates against correctional officials. Among other things, the prisoners alleged extensive use of solitary confinement and of other punishments for prison rule infractions, including bread and water diets, placing inmates in chains, keeping prisoners nude in solitary confinement in unheated cells, and denial of medical treatment. The court declared that minimum due process standards are necessary when solitary confinement, transfer to maximum-security confinement, or loss of good time are imposed, or when a prisoner is held in padlock confinement for longer than 10 days. The prison also must write out the specific rules relating to such disciplinary measures and post them throughout the institution.[96] Many prisons today provide inmates with inmate guidebooks, which include a listing of prison rules and potential punishments. For example, the first offense for "refusing to obey a direct order" could range from no penalty up to three months of administration segregation and/or three months' loss of good time. The first offense for having been found responsible for sexual assault might range from 9 to 36 months loss of good time and/or administrative segregation. Penalties for second offenses would also be specified and more severe.

Many of the procedures implemented by the Virginia court would be put in place by the U.S. Supreme Court three years later. In 1974, the U.S. Supreme Court decided a prisoners' rights case originating in the state of Nebraska, ***Wolff v. McDonnell.***[97] The decision was sweeping and inclusive, dealing with such matters as due process requirements in loss-of-good-time proceedings and disciplinary procedures generally, including questions of an inmate's right to call and examine witnesses and to assistance of counsel. Other issues dealt with included mail censorship, the retroactivity of appellate court holdings in prisoners' rights cases, and various prison administration matters.[98]

Wolff v. McDonnell (1974)

Justice White delivered the opinion of the Court, and his position was definitely contrary to the "hands-off doctrine" when he said "a prisoner is not wholly stripped of constitutional protections when he is imprisoned for crime. There is no iron curtain drawn between the Constitution and the prisons of this country."

The Court stated that prisoners are entitled to the following due process rights in disciplinary cases:

1. Advance written notice of the charges must be given the inmate at least 24 hours prior to the disciplinary hearing.
2. The disciplinary board must give a written statement as to the evidence relied on in their decision.
3. The accused inmate can call witnesses or provide documents for his or her defense if doing so poses no undue hazard to institutional safety or correctional goals.
4. Either a staff member or a fellow inmate is to be provided as counsel for an illiterate inmate or in cases so complex the inmate may be unable to adequately comprehend or defend against the charge.
5. The prison disciplinary board must be impartial in its decisions. For example, the officer who reported the violation cannot sit on the tribunal.

Inmates do not, under *Wolff*, have the right to actual legal counsel or to confront and cross-examine accusers. Also, the rights specified in *Wolff* only apply to disciplinary cases which are serious, those that may result in confinement to solitary or the loss of good time.

After *Wolff*, other Supreme Court decisions addressed the issue of disciplinary hearings. ***Baxter v. Palmigiano***[99] affirmed *Wolff*'s decision that inmates charged in prison disciplinary hearings do not have the right to counsel or to confront and cross-examine witnesses. However, *Baxter* further held that an inmate's decision to remain silent and to invoke a Fifth Amendment right against self-incrimination could be used as an indication of the inmate's guilt in such proceedings, unlike in criminal cases in a court of law.

Then, in 1985 in ***Ponte v. Real***,[100] the U.S. Supreme Court ruled that if prison officials refuse an inmate's request to call witnesses on his or her behalf, and that refusal is challenged, the officials must explain their refusal either at the hearing or later in court if the inmate alleges the refusal resulted in a deprivation of liberty. Then, also in 1985, in ***Cleavinger v. Saxner***[101] the Court held that members of a disciplinary board only have qualified immunity, not absolute immunity like judges, and therefore may be held liable for what they do unless they can prove they acted in good faith.

The U.S. Supreme Court decided the case of ***Lee v. Washington* (1968)**. In that case, the Court held that prison officials may in "good faith" segregate inmates by race in an effort to "maintain security, discipline, and good order."[102]

Protective Custody

While administrative segregation (on lock down in your cell) is a potential penalty for many disciplinary infractions, inmates seeking protective custody can be locked down as well. Thus, those fearing for their safety can face the same consequence as those who have broken institutional rules. Consider Inmate Jones in **Field Practice 12.1**.

Field Practice 12.1 Inmate Jones

Inmate Jones puts a note in the deputy warden's mailbox in the tunnel. The deputy warden upon reading the note first thing Monday morning called Inmate Jones to his office for a meeting. Inmate Jones told the deputy warden that he had received a mysterious note slipped under his bunk saying that Inmate Jones is a dead man with a picture of a stick figure and a hangman's noose. Inmate Jones has just been denied a transfer to another institution. Is this a ploy to get to another more modern prison? You're the deputy warden, and you offer Inmate Jones protective custody, but he refuses. He says he has his reputation as a man to think about and that the inmate code will not allow him to behave as such a weakling. You ask him to sign a waiver showing that he refused protective custody. He refuses to do so, indicating that such paperwork in his file would threaten his masculinity. He turns to leave your office.

Do you lock him up anyway? What if you don't and he is shanked tonight?

Loss of Good Time

A significant form of discipline for prisoners is the loss of good time. Sentences are significantly reduced by good-time provisions, and when those days which have been deducted from the sentence a person is to serve are put back on for disciplinary reasons, the inmate's sentence is obviously lengthened. The potential threat of disciplinary hearings, administrative segregation, and the taking of good time are all part of the correctional officer's arsenal for maintaining security and control of prisoners. See **Critical Thinking 12.7** regarding disciplinary hearings.

Critical Thinking 12.7 Disciplinary Hearings

Supreme Court decisions have altered the manner in which prisoners may be disciplined, and the resulting procedural steps necessary in punishing prisoners make this a complex, although common, part of institutional life. Consider the following cases.

1. Heil Hitler

A 24-year-old white inmate appeared before a prison disciplinary board charged by his cellblock officer with "attempting to incite a riot." The inmate was reputed to be a leader of the Aryan Brotherhood, an inmate group devoted to white supremacy and support of a neo-Nazi ideology. After a fight between two other inmates, one white and the other black, this inmate agitated among his cellblock colleagues for a massive retaliatory raid on a black Muslim group, housed in a cellblock nearby, who shared yard recreation time with this inmate and his cohorts. This inmate continued to shout "Cut the black mothers! Tomorrow we'll cut the black mothers!" after he was ordered to be silent and even after lights out. The disciplinary board ordered the inmate to be placed in solitary confinement for 30 days and to forfeit any and all "good time" he had accumulated.

1. Racial tensions exist in many American prisons. Should correctional officers control racial animosities? How?
2. A correctional institution is an integrated, multi-racial total institution. Any overt racist behavior can result in serious trouble in the close contact environment. How do the racial biases of staff members contribute to the problem?
3. Do you agree that authorities must discipline the offender and restore order and confidence on the part of inmates that overt racial attacks will not be condoned?
4. Loss of *all* "good time" and 30 days in solitary is a major, severe punishment in prison. Is it justified in this case?

2. Pain in the Head

A 19-year-old inmate appeared at a prison disciplinary hearing charged with refusing to work in the laundry and talking back to a correctional officer. He explained he was sick at the time, plagued with a serious headache, although he had not reported for sick call. The board placed an official reprimand in his file and ordered loss of recreational privileges for three days.

1. Inmates have mood swings, physical ailments, and poor work habits, and sometimes these problems will result in confrontations with officers. Should this be considered in this case?
2. Correctional officers demand "respect" and obedience to orders, so when an inmate refuses to obey an order or otherwise violates a rule, no matter what the reason, some disciplinary action must be taken, they believe. Do you agree?
3. Loss of "good time" is not imposed here, as it could have been, and the loss of three days of recreational privileges is not severe. The official reprimand will be seen and considered when parole or other release decisions are considered. Is that punishment sufficient?

3. Making Her Mark

A 20-year-old female inmate appeared before a prison disciplinary court accused of tattooing (with a needle, cigarette ashes, and ink) the word "owned" on the thigh of her female lover and with fighting. She explained that the other girl wanted the tattoo and indeed had insisted on mutual "branding," a common practice in the prison. However, this inmate had refused reciprocal tattooing, and a fight ensued. Both "tattooing of self and others" and "fighting" violated prison rules. The disciplinary court ordered her held in "keeplock" (locked in her own room during the working day and during recreational periods as well as at night) for one week and the forfeiture of two months' good time.

1. Female inmates often scar or tattoo their bodies as part of the inmate society, even though this is against the rules. Should the correctional authorities bother with such behaviors as this?
2. Fighting is a possible problem in all institutions, male or female. Inmates' intimidation of other inmates must be curtailed as much as possible. Is confinement and loss of two months' "good time" a very severe response to the incident?

Overcrowding

The prison population has grown very rapidly since 1980, and many prisons are bulging at the seams. In order to house more inmates in existing facilities, cells have been modified to create "bunk beds" instead of single beds for inmates, a process called **double-bunking.** This means that two inmates can be placed in a single cell, or eight inmates in a four-person cell, and so forth. Is such **overcrowding** of prisoners a violation of the constitutional prohibition against cruel and unusual punishment?

In 1981, in ***Rhodes v. Chapman,***[103] the U.S. Supreme Court concluded that double-bunking as such is not unconstitutional, but that if the totality of conditions in the prison is bad, if the staff is inadequate, or cell space too limited, or work programs nonexistent, or if recreation, medical care, or diets are inadequate, or if inmates are required to stay in crowded cells for too long each day ... then, perhaps, the Constitution has been violated. In *Rhodes*, the Court concluded that the Southern Ohio Federal Correctional Facility, a medium-security prison built in the 1970s, was a quality institution with gymnasiums, workshops, school rooms, chapels, hospital ward, commissary, barber shop, library, visitation area, recreation field, and a garden. Each cell had approximately 63 square feet, hot and cold running water, a cabinet, a shelf, and a radio. The Court concluded that, although the inmates were double-bunked, the totality of conditions did not constitute cruel and unusual punishment. The Court stated that "the Constitution does not mandate comfortable prisons," and that harsh or restrictive conditions are "part of the penalty that criminal offenders pay for their offenses against society."[104] See **Criminal Justice 12.2** on double bunking below.

Criminal Justice 12.2 Ethics: How Much Personal Space Does a Person Need? Double-Bunking Crowded Prisons

For the prison administrator who faces the constant stream of buses hauling new prisoners to the institution, the new inmates must be housed within existing facilities. Without flexible release practices, every bit of space is used in the housing of prisoners. Double-bunking is an option.

Since inmates in such facilities typically only spend their sleeping hours confined in such a space, such crowding has not been considered "cruel and unusual punishment." But for inmates, crowding means less privacy, less security, and a strain on facilities and staff of the institution.[105] Disputes are inevitable over television viewing, noise, body hygiene, and other problems caused by living in close quarters. This places an added burden on the prison administration to maintain peace and order.

1. Should inmate concern for their own comfort, or health, or safety be considered in assigning them to double-bunked cells?
2. Do you agree that the relatively small amount of time actually spent in the cell should not make the double-bunked crowding a very important inconvenience?
3. What are your own personal space needs?

Perhaps the single largest problem to face the prison system in this country is the tremendous increase in the number of prisoners who must be housed in limited capacity institutions. In some states, there truly is no more room in the inn. During the 1990s and the beginning of this century, two factors have caused the serious overcrowding problems found in several states: tougher sentencing laws and high unemployment rates.

In many states, all repeat offenders are required to serve at least one half of their sentences before becoming eligible for parole. Some states, such as Florida, require such offenders to serve 85% of their sentences prior to eligibility for parole. The federal government requires the same before inmates can leave prison on supervised release. These policies are a result of mandatory sentencing laws enacted by "get tough" legislatures.

In California, under its three-strikes-and-you're-out law, a third-time convicted felon, on any felony, can receive 25 years to life. In fact, Gary Ewing was sentenced to 25 years to life in that state after being convicted for stealing three golf clubs from a pro shop. Ewing appealed the sentence, maintaining that it constituted cruel and unusual punishment in violation of his Eighth Amendment rights, as he argued that the sentence was grossly disproportionate to the crime committed. Interestingly, Justice Kennedy joined in the majority opinion that upheld Ewing's sentence.[106] However, Justice Kennedy has publicly criticized California's three strikes law stating, "The law's sponsor ... is the correctional officers' union, 'and that is sick.'" He also pointed to the costs of incarceration in America and noted that sentences in the United States are eight times longer than sentences in Europe.[107] With such sentencing schemas, the result is that a large percentage of prisoners now must be kept in prison longer than in previous years. And, if they are kept longer, fewer spaces are made available for new inmates. Simple mathematics tells us that if the rate in new inmate admissions exceeds the rate of existing inmate releases, the natural consequence is crowded prisons.

The unemployment rate also impacts state prisons. If a person cannot find employment outside the prison, he or she may not be released. Parole authorities typically want a "work plan" for those inmates who otherwise qualify for early release. As of March 2010, fifteen states reflected double digit unemployment rates, with Michigan at 14.1 percent unemployment and Nevada at 13.4 percent unemployment leading the way.[108] So, inmates who come from any of those areas find it very difficult to get jobs, especially with the added handicap of a prison record.

Medical Care for Prisoners

Since a prisoner cannot secure medical care for himself or herself as needed as one would in the outside world, institutions have a legal obligation to provide inmates with adequate medical services. The absence or inadequacy of medical care is considered by the courts to be cruel and unusual punishment.

The leading Supreme Court decision regarding prison medical care was the 1976 ***Estelle v. Gamble***[109] case, in which the Supreme Court held that "deliberate indifference" to the serious medical needs of inmates constitutes cruel and unusual punishment. By this the Court did not mean malpractice on the part of prison medical staff, but a deliberate indifference to the pain and suffering of inmates as demonstrated by (1) the failure of prison doctors to respond to a prisoner's needs, or by (2) correctional officers who delay or deny intentionally an inmate's access to medical care, or by (3) correctional officers who intentionally interfere with prescribed treatments of inmates. Medical care is defined as including mental health (*Bowring v. Godwin*, 1977)[110] and dental care, as well as other medical needs.

The Treatment Mandate of Some Prison Sentences

For the most part, prison sentences are used to punish offenders and incapacitate them, to hold them for long periods of time apart from society to protect the community from their predatory activities. Some call it warehousing or risk management.[111] See **Critical Thinking 12.7.** There is rarely any clear legislative intent that such sentences are for the purpose of treatment or rehabilitation. Yet, especially where drug abuse or addiction is evident, treatment may be mandated.

A prisoner who is found to be psychotic is commonly transferred to a **hospital for the criminally insane**, often a maximum-security institution, for whatever psychiatric treatments are offered there. But many inmates under sentences with a treatment mandate are neither insane by legal standards nor psychotic by psychiatric diagnostic criteria. They remain in prison and are presumed to be receiving treatment. Appellate courts have shown an increased willingness to intervene in cases where it is alleged that the requirements for treatment in mental hospitals are not being carried out, but rarely have they addressed the question of whether correctional services have fulfilled, or can fulfill, whatever "specialized treatment" has been demanded by legislation.

Sometimes prisons are faced with the problem of having to treat inmates who do not want treatment, especially those who are dangerous and need antipsychotic medication. In 1990, in ***Washington v. Harper***,[112] the Supreme Court concluded that forcing such treatment is acceptable when the inmate is dangerous either to self or others or is gravely disabled, the medication is administered for treatment under the supervision of a licensed psychiatrist, and the medication is in the best medical interests of the inmate. Under such conditions, a judicial hearing is not required to force treatment.

The status of in-prison therapy has changed little over the years, although some states have opened special "diagnostic and treatment" centers or "medical facilities" for inmates. However, courts are still coping with prisoner allegations that legislative treatment and rehabilitative mandates are not being carried out in traditional prison settings. Even when special treatment programs are available, the issue is further complicated by inmate insistence on a right to refuse treatment or rehabilitative efforts if they wish. Is it possible to "rehabilitate" someone who does not wish to be rehabilitated? Consider **Critical Thinking 12.7** below.

Critical Thinking 12.7 Should Medical or Psychological Treatment of Prisoners Be Forced or Voluntary?

Norval Morris advocated imprisonment only for repetitively violent criminals. He suggested that all treatment programs in these prisons be voluntary. He argued that the only required activities for inmates should be the assigned daily work stints and participation in a small "living group" in which treatment would be made available on a voluntary basis.[113] Likewise, the National Advisory Commission on Criminal Justice Standards and Goals suggested, "No offender should be required or coerced to participate in programs of rehabilitation or treatment nor should the failure or refusal to participate be used to penalize an inmate in any way."[114]

These suggestions were made almost forty years ago; do you agree or disagree with them? Why or why not? What if you were an inmate? What if you were a correctional officer?

Legal Trends

The field of administrative law dealing with prisoners' rights mushroomed during the 1970s and 1980s,[115] and as with many trends, the causes of this were varied but closely related. The increasing willingness of appellate courts to intervene at post-sentence stages of the criminal justice process occurred in a cultural context of expanded legal services for the poor. This, coupled with an increased concern for the civil rights of racial and ethnic minorities, who are disproportionately overrepresented in prison populations, came at a time of widespread cynicism about governmental claims of benevolence or effectiveness. Prison riots focused public and professional attention on prisons, and these riots were both cause and effect of an increasing political awareness among prisoners. One result of this was the creation of various commissions empowered not only to investigate prison conditions but to look at the whole concept of prisons and make suggestions for reform.[116]

Prisoners' rights decisions addressed a variety of failings in the prison system. Inmates were granted more access to lawyers and to legal documents and papers through prison law libraries.[117] Poor inmates were provided with writing materials to draft legal documents, with notary services, and with postage to mail documents to the courts. The limits on these resources are decided by the courts on a case-by-case basis.[118] Although prisons do not have to provide free lawyers to inmates filing appeals, prisoners cannot be denied access to the help of other inmates, known as "jailhouse lawyers," who are often quite knowledgeable about the law.[119]

Prisoners place a high value on visits by people from the outside. The courts have generally given a higher priority to the right of inmates to receive visits from attorneys, ministers, and court officials than to their right to receive visits from family members and friends. Courts allow prison authorities to limit visiting hours, in the interests of prison security and order. And they can deny "contact visits"—visits in which the inmate can be face to face with a visitor to the point of touching—if such visits would raise legitimate fears for institutional security.[120]

The First Amendment rights of inmates have been litigated a great deal. Freedom of religion is recognized for inmates to the extent that they must be allowed to follow the rules of their religion, within reason. Inmates cannot be required to attend religious services if they do not wish to do so. Freedom of the press is recognized for inmates in that they must be allowed access to news and to members of the press who themselves wish to have access to the institution, although face-to-face interviews with journalists may be denied.[121]

Inmates have the right to send and receive mail, but prison authorities have wide-ranging powers to decide whether to reject incoming publications if they feel such materials may create a clear and present danger detrimental to the prison's security.[122] After realizing prison officials' concerns about the introduction of contraband in the form of drugs and weapons concealed in publications, the court ruled that prison authorities might legitimately require that such mailings must originate from the publisher and cannot be brought into the prison any other way.[123] The authorities can, however, reject magazines for being obscene or pornographic, even if they come directly from the publisher. All mail may be screened for contraband, but legal mail is generally inspected by prison authorities in the inmate's presence. Prisoners have considerable rights to send mail outside the institution.

A number of prisons have introduced selected-inmate councils to funnel prisoner grievances to administrative officials. In some correctional systems there are ombudsmen, persons neutral to the correctional system who hear and attempt to negotiate inmate complaints or demands.[124]

Despite such developments, incarceration in prisons and reformatories remains—aside from the death penalty—the most extreme and socially degrading example of the full power of the state to punish and force compliance. It is a vortex in our criminal justice system, a controversial method of control that is undergoing change but currently used to punish, restrain, and perhaps rehabilitate 1.6 million offenders.

Prison Riots

American prisons have periodically experienced violent, damaging, and murderous inmate **riots.**[125] And the riots have often called forth violent and deadly reactions by prison officials, guards, police, and militia. In 1987, Cuban detainees in federal prisons near Atlanta and Baton Rouge took hostages and rioted when learning that Fidel Castro had agreed to their deportation back to Cuba. Most, if not all, of these detainees had been serving time in Cuban prisons before they came to the United States. Apparently, they preferred life in U.S. prisons to life in Cuban prisons.[126]

The Cuban detainee disturbances were not the worst. They did not result in loss of life. An extremely violent riot took place in the New Mexico State Prison in Santa Fe in 1980. Twelve correctional personnel were held hostage and some were beaten, stabbed, and/or sodomized. However, the inmates directed their worst violence toward themselves. Thirty-three inmates were killed by other prisoners, many by blowtorches. Inmates broke into the inmate records' section to identify snitches and pedophiles for maiming and torturing. Homosexual rapes were common. The prisoners also gained access to the prison pharmacy and many became high on drugs, with a number overdosing.[127] The riot was eventually put down, but inmate murders (and the murders of some correctional officers, too) continued in the New Mexico facility for some time.

In 1983, a riot occurred in Sing Sing Prison in New York. Hostages were taken, and for a while it looked like the situation could become as serious as what had happened at New York's Attica Prison 11 years earlier. At Attica, eleven correctional personnel and thirty-two inmates lost their lives, and a subsequent investigation determined that when the prison was stormed and overtaken by armed New York state troopers that they actually killed thirty-nine of those individuals; at Sing Sing, however, the disturbance eventually ended without any deaths.

In 1993 on Easter Sunday in Lucasville, Ohio, a riot broke out between some 500 prisoners. Thirteen correctional officers were taken hostage, and one officer and nine inmates were killed. This disturbance constituted the longest prison riot in American history in which lives were lost. It lasted eleven days.[128]

More than 300 prison riots have been documented in the United States since the first one in 1774, and over 90 percent of them have occurred since 1952.[129] Since the early fifties, major riots have occurred in over a dozen states, often at different prisons in the same state. In addition, many other prisons have had disturbances that did not result in full-out rioting, but which nevertheless caused loss of life and extensive property damage. And in-prison gang fighting and murders occur even today on a regular basis in many prisons across the country.

Much has been written about and elaborate theories developed as to why prison riots break out in some prisons and not in others, or why a riot occurs at one particular time and not another, or, for that matter, why riots occur at all. Prison overcrowding has been blamed. Various power groups in inmate subcultures, including gangs, have been blamed. Racial tensions, sexual deprivations, sudden get-tough rule enforcement, poor food, lack of recreation, different child-rearing patterns in various ethnic groups, and a myriad of other factors and conditions have been blamed. Various experiments in prison management, including inmate participation in developing prison rules and enforcing regulations, have been tried. Hundreds of post-riot reports have been written, wide-ranging recommendations have been made (see Field Practice 12.2), training in human relations has been given to correctional officers, theories of crime causation have been constructed, and race relations and cultural awareness seminars have been conducted to make officers more sensitive to the needs of and better able to communicate with inmates. But, this has been all to no, or little, avail.

One study of the governance of prisons showed a breakdown in warden and correctional officer controls of prison security to be the common thread in all riots. This imaginative, well-documented analysis carefully reviewed all the complex reasons put forward as causes of prison conflicts and disorders—from power groups in inmate subcultures to the politicization of racial and ethnic minorities—and tested them against simple violations of sound security measures.[130] The conclusion it reached, so much simpler and more direct than the prison subculture type of analysis, was that the root factor behind these problems is the loss of staff control. The study compared maximum-security prisons in three prison systems, Michigan, California, and Texas, each of which has its own different management style. And on almost every variable, including cost of confinement, it rated prisons high on control as much better. The study's author, John J. DiIulio, Jr., concluded that in running a prison, order is the first item of importance, and that without order and control the other two major aspects of prison life—amenities (i.e., good food, cleanliness, and so forth) and service (i.e., programs for improving the life chances of inmates, from remedial reading to vocational training)—are bound to be inferior. Inmates in a prison that is unsafe and filled with out-of-control predatory gangs can hardly engage in rehabilitative or remedial efforts. Moreover, correctional officers in prisons with a high level of control have much higher ***esprit de corps***, less stress, and much better job satisfaction (less turnover, etc.) than those in institutions with lax security. And riots almost always occur where there is sloppy, careless, and negligent security management.

Other models of prison riots exist. Martin and Zimmerman[131] suggest a **typology of prison riots**, which includes DiIulio's explanation, called (1) collective behavior and social control. The other prison riot types, or causative explanations, include (2) environmental conditions, including quality-of-life factors; (3) spontaneous outburst, such as in a pressure-packed situation where only a spark is needed to set off simmering hostilities; (4) conflict, in which the repressive power structure of the prison is directed against powerless inmates; (5) power vacuum, which may occur during abrupt changes in administration or power relationships; and (6) rising expectations, which occur when inmates expect more quality of life than the institution delivers.

Former warden, now professor, Rick Seiter maintains that most riots are not planned or precisely initiated by inmates. Instead, the interface of **environmental factors** and **a precipitating event** or spark[132] seems to bring seething passions to a boiling conflagration. Regardless of the type of riot or its cause, though, effective prison management seems to be the best prevention, or hope of prevention. See **Field Practice 12.2** regarding the impact of riots and lawsuits on correctional policy.

Field Practice 12.2 Crisis Driving Policy—Lawsuits and Riots

Unfortunately, while all else has failed, a collective action by inmates in the form of a class-action lawsuit or a prison riot may very well get the attention of prison administrators, the public, the courts, and/or lawmakers. Former commissioner of the South Carolina Department of Corrections (SCDC) Bill Leeke lamented that for seventeen years in a row he had gone to the legislature telling them that the SCDC system was overcrowded and understaffed; seventeen years in a row his requests for appropriate levels of funding were denied. It was not until a class action lawsuit by inmates that the court required the SCDC via a consent decree to come in to compliance with staffing and space requirements so as to be able to provide adequate security for inmates. Similarly, riots, with media exposure, can have the same effect on the improvement of prison conditions.

How would you as a corrections commissioner try to convince lawmakers and the public to increase prison funding?

How Prisoners Are Released from Prison

Across the nation inmates are released from prisons in a number of ways:

1. on parole;
2. at a mandatory release date, which is generally the maximum sentence less time off for good behavior;
3. upon completion of the maximum sentence;
4. and by pardon or commutation of sentence.

The frequency of use of these types of release varies considerably from jurisdiction to jurisdiction. This variation stems from differences in legal requirements from one state to the next; organization of correctional systems, including differences in the quality of parole services; local customs; and the characteristics of inmate populations held in prisons. In states with strong and frequently used probation services, prison populations may be largely composed of "residue" violators or "heavies," those who are dangerous or so persistent in their criminality that probation supervision would place the community at risk and likely be ineffective. Parole boards in jurisdictions where probation is frequently used see different types of offenders from those in

Image by Aaron Kohr at fotolia.com.

states where probation is less often used and where prisons hold more of a mix of less serious violators and "heavies."

Although many correctional facilities group various types of offenders together, every prison population is composed of a mixture of personalities, offense categories, age groupings, and lifestyles—a complexity regarding correctional populations not always recognized by the public. Individual offenders are diverse—they cannot be lumped together into one all-encompassing category. Some are disturbed and frustrated young adults, others are old and senile, while still others are alcoholics, drug addicts, or sex deviants. Some are committed to conventional values, others are not. Many prisoners come from urban slums and are members of minority groups that suffer economic and social discrimination.

Offenders also tend to lack education and vocational skills. Many have had failures in relationships with family and friends and exhibit a pattern of cumulative failure that prevents them from developing a sense of self-respect. All this complicates decisions about release and creates obstacles to rehabilitation for the offenders themselves.

Advocates of Early Release

Early release of inmates, and the subsequent supervision of them as they settle back into the free world, includes parole and supervised release after good time accumulations permit early release. Good reasons exist for making the early release decision.

In part parole and other forms of supervised early release became popular simply because it is more humanitarian than long prison sentences. As already noted, prison sentences in the United States are among the longest in the world. Legislatures often enact unusually severe sentences during times of high publicity about crime. Likewise, sentencing judges may be outraged and angry at the time of sentencing, when memory of the crime is still fresh. In such moments of anger or high publicity, judges have been known to impose extremely harsh prison terms. A system that permits parole allows tempers to cool and the actions of the offender to be viewed more dispassionately years later, thus offering an opportunity to mitigate sentences whose harshness appeared justified at the time they were handed down.

Early release also offers a chance to reduce the prison terms of offenders who, although guilty of serious crimes in the past, have aged and matured in prison and are no longer likely to violate the law again. It is also accepted as a way to control inmate behavior by offering the possibility of early release for those willing to participate in prison programs and cooperate with officials.

Early supervised release is also defended along economic lines since street supervision is much less costly than incarceration. In relatively uncrowded institutions with good educational and treatment programs, the costs are higher. Prisoners can be supervised on parole for only a small fraction of these amounts. And while on parole the offender can be gainfully employed, pay taxes, and support his or her family. Family welfare support is a significant cost to the community when a breadwinner is imprisoned.

Finally, advocates of early release point out its rehabilitative value, for supervised re-entry into the community is almost always safer and more effective than simply letting prisoners walk through the gates to freedom upon release. In general, according to parole advocates, giving due deference to critics of parole who see it as either too lenient or too harsh, years of experience with the practice have generally proved its effectiveness.

Critics of Early Release

The history of early release in the United States has been stormy. The idea of releasing convicts before their sentences expire has been vigorously opposed from its beginnings to the present day. When a well-publicized and horrible crime is committed by a person who has been released from prison prior to the completion of the sentence, many in the public become outraged. But institution authorities generally endorse good time provisions because inmates are rewarded for good behavior and penalized when they break rules. This gives correctional authorities some tools to use to control inmate behavior, something that is missing when inmates know they must serve a definite term no matter how they behave.

Objections have been raised about parole, however, for a variety of other reasons. For instance, the constitutionality of parole was challenged on a number of grounds, among them that it was an infringement on judicial sentencing authority, that it usurped the pardoning powers of the chief executive, and even that it was an unlawful delegation of the legislative function. Generally these arguments were rejected by the courts, and the legal foundation for parole became well established. Civil rights advocates have called for more due process at parole hearings, claiming that boards act arbitrarily and do not follow proper forms of due process and procedural regularity in their hearings. Some have sought to curb the discretion of parole boards, and legal challenges to denial of parole have raised a number of demands, such as permitting lawyers at parole hearings:[133] Appellate courts, including the U.S. Supreme Court, have been reluctant to interfere in parole *granting* procedures.[134]

Making the Parole Release Decision

The grant of parole at first was defined as an act of grace, of mercy, on the part of the state. It was a *privilege* afforded to a few but the right of none. The inmate's date for parole eligibility is made earlier than the sentence imposed by the judge, say a 10-year sentence to prison, with parole eligibility in not less than 5 years. In some places, inmates must apply for parole consideration. In others, consideration for parole is automatic as the eligibility date approaches. In general, the grant, deferral, or denial of parole is discretionary with a parole board, commonly a panel of officials appointed by the governor and independent of both prisons and courts.[135]

In most states, members of the parole board personally interview an inmate at, or shortly before, the time he or she becomes eligible for parole. This is not a universal practice, however. In some states, instead of interviews the board reviews case file materials, and personal hearings are conducted only in selected cases. In some jurisdictions, parole authorities employ a staff of "hearing officers" to conduct interviews and make recommendations to the board. Many parole boards are small, and in large states they must travel constantly, often making the parole hearing a hurried experience.

The procedures of the hearing itself are variable, ranging from a few short questions to, more rarely, full-scale proceedings involving witnesses, lawyers, and evidence for or against release, subject to adversary examination. Some boards may hear only a few inmate cases each day; others may handle 40 or more applications daily.

Careful and deliberate parole hearings can serve several important functions helpful to both the parole board and the prospective parolee. If the hearing has the appearance as well as the substance of fairness, it can enhance the prospects of successful completion of parole by promoting respect for the system of justice. Where the offender plays an active role in planning or deciding on his or her terms of parole, a greater commitment to the parole plan should follow. Conversely, where the person is dealt with abruptly, indirectly, or unfairly, or where arbitrary decisions are made without explanation, successful parole may be undermined. The hearing itself can provide an opportunity for both the inmate and the parole board to ascertain and discuss reliable information. Sometimes, however, inmates are encouraged to be truthful and frank in responding to questions at the parole interview, and then those statements are used to justify denial of parole. It has been suggested that certain due process protections, including *Miranda*-type warnings, should be extended to the parole interview.[136]

Criteria for Release on Parole

In deciding whether to grant or deny parole, the board does not rely solely on information from the interview, but has before it the complete correctional and police file on the prisoner (often including the presentence investigation) and some form of parole plan prepared by the prisoner with the assistance of the correctional staff. A typical parole plan contains information on where the parolee will be employed (or where he or she reasonably expects to obtain employment) and other intentions regarding lifestyle if returned to the community.

The traditional assumption has been that prisoners who are paroled are "good risks," that is, they have matured or have been rehabilitated and are not likely to commit any more crimes. However, the risk of recidivism must always be considered in any parole decision, and it is usually not all that easy to determine. An experienced parole board member once said to the authors:

> Everybody thinks a parole board's job is to let good-risk inmates out early. This is not the way it works. First, there are not any good-risk inmates. The way prisons are today all of them are lousy risks. The real function of the Board is to decide when, if ever, and under what conditions to let bad-risk inmates out. Remember, they are going to come out anyway. We prefer to have some of them leave under field supervision.

The factors parole boards must consider in their decisions in addition to the risk of recidivism can be summarized as follows:

1. The chances the inmate will conform to parole rules and regulations.
2. Whether release would be bad for overall prison morale, as in the case of an inmate who has been a serious disciplinary problem, where parole would appear to be a reward for such behavior.
3. The realistic chances of suitable employment and living conditions presented in the inmate's parole plan.
4. The community's willingness to have the parolee return.
5. Whether the release would promote disrespect for the law, as in the case of a serious offense or a notorious offender.
6. Whether the inmate has served about the average time for persons convicted for the same crime.
7. Whether the person could benefit from further involvement in prison training and educational or rehabilitative programs.[137] Additional factors could also be considered such as family life on the outside, occupational skills, past use of narcotics or alcohol, and a great deal more.[138]

In general, if an inmate meets the guideline criteria for release, he or she must be paroled unless the parole board can justify its denial in writing.[139] Parole, in short, is "presumptive" unless there are aggravating factors that the parole commissioners can identify and use to justify denial of release. Early release of inmates is also seen as necessary to accommodate the numbers of incoming inmates.

To ease the flood of incoming inmates, correctional authorities have tried to "cap" the prison population, that is, to refuse to accept any new prisoners from the courts. This is an approach advocated by some academicians.[140] But this can enrage judges, legislators, sheriffs, and police, who normally have the task of delivering new inmates to the correctional system, and in general, capping the prison population has not worked.

So the pressure has been placed on parole boards to control the flow of inmates through release. In effect, parole systems are being asked to relieve the overcrowding in prisons and to make room for those convicted offenders awaiting transfer to prison by letting more prisoners out, and letting them out earlier in their sentences. This relatively new pressure on parole boards adds a new dimension to the process of making release decisions, as each board grapples with the issues of recidivism risk, inmate and prison needs, and community safety in the face of intense prison space requirements.

Mandatory Release: Good Time Laws

Mandatory release before the maximum sentence is served is possible in most states. It differs from parole in that the decision does not rest with a parole board and future risk is not a concern. Mandatory release laws enacted by the legislature allow "time off for good behavior" in prison. Most states allow prison inmates to earn good time. Specific statutes give a formula by which a sentence is reduced by the number of days or weeks of good time a prisoner accumulates for each month served.[141]

The primary purpose of good time is prison control, for it gives inmates who conform with regulations hope of earlier release. Another purpose is to provide supervised re-entry into the community for offenders who, for whatever reasons, were not paroled. Thus mandatory release in some states requires the prisoner to agree to supervision until the court-imposed maximum sentence expires. However, in many jurisdictions the inmate on mandatory release walks free, without supervision, just as if he or she had served the maximum time.

Historically, good time was *given* by prison officials to particular inmates who demonstrated good behavior. These days, for the most part, good time is automatically calculated for all prisoners, though it can be *taken away*, in whole or in part, for misbehavior. Like parolees, supervised offenders on mandatory release *can* have their freedom *revoked and be returned to prison* to complete their full sentences.

Maxing Out

Some prisoners serve every day of the maximum sentence handed down by the judge. This is called "maxing out." People serving short-term misdemeanant sentences, felony inmates who have received very short maximum terms, a year or a year and a day, for example, max out. Also, longer-term inmates who are uncooperative, lose good time because of disciplinary reports, or otherwise fail to earn early release may serve their entire sentence. Persons incarcerated for the first time are almost invariably released prior to completion of maximum sentence, either on parole or on mandatory release.[142] The law requires inmates to be released on expiration of their maximum sentences, no matter what their attitude or likelihood of committing additional crimes, so long as they have not committed additional crimes while in prison.

Inmates in all jurisdictions can turn down the chance for parole, and in some places they can waive their good-time credits, thereby refusing mandatory release. This usually occurs in cases where the parole or mandatory release date is close to the sentence expiration date, and the inmate prefers to complete the time in prison to be totally clear, avoiding all community supervision upon release. Parole rules and conditions are often quite strict and act to curb parolees' freedom of movement and to cramp their lifestyles. Nevertheless, most prisoners welcome parole or mandatory release and have no wish to max out. However, some might prefer to max out their sentence over other methods of release.

Some Prefer to Max Out

Theodore Streleski was a Stanford University doctoral student in mathematics when he took a ball-peen hammer and bludgeoned to death one of his former professors. Streleski purportedly viewed his act as a form of protest after the university declined to grant him a Ph.D. after 16 years of study. Streleski received a seven-year prison sentence for the murder. He came up for parole three times, but he refused to accept parole—as one of the conditions was that he could not go onto the Stanford campus. Streleski opted to max-out his sentence, much to the chagrin of his remaining dissertation committee members, so that he would not be restrained by restrictions on his movement within the community.[143]

Summary

Many prisons are overcrowded. Many states have also been building new prisons. However, it is an extremely costly experiment to try to build our way out of this quagmire. In other states, earlier-than-usual release of more inmates on the back end makes room for entry of more prisoners on the front end. This seems to be the current trend. However, as political will and administrations change, the directions of corrections may experience upheaval. A lot hangs in the balance, and time will tell.

Dismal fiscal realities may continue to slow the growth of the prison empire in the United States, but, we do know that the multi-faceted purposes of punishment and prisons will continue to impact prisoners throughout the twenty-first century. The next chapter will focus on the juvenile justice system.

Chapter 13

Juvenile Justice

Betsy Matthews, PhD, Eastern Kentucky University

Image by ImagesbyTrista at istockphoto.com.

Adolescence is a developmental period characterized by suboptimal decisions and actions that are associated with an increased incidence of unintentional injuries, violence, substance abuse, unintended pregnancy, and sexually transmitted diseases.[1]

Seeking Justice: Restoring the Juvenile Justice System

The youth crime wave has reached horrific proportions from coast to coast. For example, in Philadelphia, more than half of the 433 people murdered in 1994 were males between the ages of 16 and 31. All but 5 of the 89 victims under 20 were non-white. In Los Angeles, there are now some 400 youth street gangs organized mainly along racial and ethnic lines: 200 Latino, 150 black, the rest

Image by shironosov at istockphto.com.

white or Asian. In 1994, their known members alone committed 370 murders and over 3,300 felony assaults.

But what is really frightening everyone from D.A.s to demographers, old cops to old convicts, is not what's happening now but what's just around the corner—namely, a sharp increase in the number of super crime-prone young males.

Nationally, there are now about 40 million children under the age of 10, the largest number in decades. By simple math, in a decade today's 4- to 7-year-

Image by manley099 at istockphoto.com.

olds will become 14- to 17-year-olds. By 2005, the number of males in this age group will have risen about 25 percent overall and 50 percent for blacks.

To some extent, it's just that simple: More boys begets more bad boys. But to really grasp why this spike in the young male population means big trouble ahead, you need to appreciate both the statistical evidence from a generation of birth-cohort studies and related findings from recent street-level studies and surveys.

The scientific kiddie-crime literature began with a study of all 10,000 boys born in 1945 who lived in Philadelphia between their tenth and eighteenth birthdays. Over one-third had at least one recorded arrest by the time they were 18. Most of the arrests occurred when the boys were ages 15 to 17. Half of the boys who were arrested were arrested more than once. Once a boy had been arrested three times, the chances that he would be arrested again were over 70 percent.

But the most famous finding of the study was that 6 percent of the boys committed five or more crimes before they were 18, accounting for over half of all the serious crimes, and about two-thirds of all the violent crimes, committed by the entire cohort.

This "6 percent do 50 percent" statistic has been replicated in a series of subsequent longitudinal studies of Philadelphia and many other cities. It is on this basis that James Q. Wilson and other leading crime doctors can predict with confidence that the additional 500,000 boys who will be 14 to 17 years old in the year 2000 will mean at least 30,000 more murderers, rapists, and muggers on the streets than we have today.

—Excerpted from J. DiIulio, "Here come the super-predators," *The Weekly Standard*, November 27, 1995

The above news story, and others like it, incited fear of the juvenile population, particularly of black boys, and contributed to the unraveling of a juvenile justice system as we knew it. Since its inception, the juvenile justice system has been rooted in a rehabilitative ideology and designed to serve the best interests of the child. The forecasts of DiIulio and others, however, created moral panic and led 47 states to enact punitive policies allowing for mandatory minimum sentences for juveniles or making it easier for youth to be tried as adults.[2] Some states went as far as building supermax facilities to house these dangerous young offenders. These changes reflected a "fundamental shift in juvenile justice philosophy" where "traditional notions of individualized dispositions based on the best interests of the juvenile were being diminished by interests in punishing criminal behavior."[3]

Fortunately, the frightening forecasts never came to fruition. Still, juvenile offenders were punished harshly through tough-on-crime policies akin to those driving the adult criminal justice system. Now, two decades later, we are still struggling to get back on track with a more benevolent, rehabilitation-oriented approach to juvenile justice that recognizes the vulnerabilities of adolescence and supports the goal of reformation.

About This Chapter

In this chapter we will examine the nature and extent of delinquency in the United States and shed some light on why some youth engage in delinquency and others don't. We will then trace the history of the juvenile justice system, beginning with the model of family government and ending with contemporary juvenile corrections programming. Pressing issues (e.g., disproportionate minority confinement, the school to prison pipeline, waivers to adult court) will be discussed along the way to a better understanding of how we respond to delinquency in the United States.

What Is Juvenile Delinquency?

Juvenile delinquency refers to "behaviors that are prohibited by the family or juvenile code of the state and that subject minors to the jurisdiction of the juvenile court."[4] This legal definition includes both status offenses and delinquent acts. **Status offenses** are behaviors that are considered illegal when committed by persons who have not yet reached the age of majority such as truancy, liquor law violations, ungovernability, runaway, and curfew violations. In contrast, **delinquent acts** are behaviors that would be considered a crime if committed by an adult such as theft, assault, or robbery.

Field Practice 13.1 Sexting—A New Type of Delinquency

Sexting "can apply to sexually explicit messages or images sent via text message, e-mail or Internet sites." A 2008 survey revealed that 20 percent of teens reported posting or sending nude or partially nude images of themselves.[5] Moreover, a 2014 study at Drexel University found that fifty-four percent of kids acknowledged that they had sexted under the age of 18.[6] Under current law, sending sexually explicit images via cell-phone or the Internet could result in felonies relating to child pornography. A law has been proposed via one state legislature to govern such photos or videos sent between minors. The law would seek to decriminalize such offenses between minors by setting up gradations of the severity of punishment, with the first offense being a nominal fine and completion of community service hours. Not until the fourth offense would a potential felony be considered.[7]

The definition of a **minor** varies across states, with each specifying in statute the upper age boundary of juvenile court jurisdiction.[8] The upper age limit is 17 in 40 states and the District of Columbia, 16 in eight states, and 15 in two states. Of the 18 states that have specified a lower age boundary for juvenile court jurisdiction, 11 have set it at age 10, one at age 8 (Arizona), four at age 7 (Connecticut, Maryland, Massachusetts, and New York) and one at age 6 (North Carolina). Lower limits are based on the concept of ***doli incapax***, which assumes that very young children are incapable of forming the intent to commit a crime.

Image by nito100 at istockphoto.com.

Elrod and Ryder point out two key problems with the legal definition of delinquency.[9] First, the definition is overly broad and fails to account for the frequency and seriousness of youths' conduct. The delinquent label is attached to a youth adjudicated for a first offense of running away just as it is to a youth adjudicated for a third violent offense. This is important to consider given that labeling a youth delinquent can lead to further problem behaviors (see **Critical Thinking 13.1**).

Critical Thinking 13.1 Labeling Theory

According to **Labeling Theory**, which was previously addressed in Chapter 2, there are negative consequences associated with labeling a youth as delinquent.[10] The key assumption of the theory is that a delinquent label, attached to youth through various status degradation ceremonies (e.g., arrest, court hearings, trials), contributes to strains on relationships and blocked social, educational, and work opportunities. The label, then, becomes a master status, taking precedence over all other characteristics of the individual. In turn, the youth begins to alter his/her behavior to conform to the master status of delinquency. It's a self-fulfilling prophecy, and what was at first experimental, normal behavior of an adolescent, or **primary deviance**, is now a stable pattern of behavior, or **secondary deviance.**

Do you think labeling theory provides a valid explanation for how youth become engaged in a pattern of delinquency? If yes, what can be done to avoid the labeling process?

Second, decisions about the point at which someone becomes a responsible adult seem arbitrary and in conflict with other laws that limit youth from engaging in adult behaviors. In New York, for example, you can be tried as an adult at age 16,[11] far before you can buy cigarettes or vote. Moreover, upper age boundaries for juvenile justice jurisdiction do not account for the fact that the rate of maturity varies drastically from youth to youth. There is no magical number that demarcates the transition to adulthood and ensures that one has the capabilities presumed to accompany that adult status.

Trends in Delinquency

The extent of delinquency in the United States varies according to how it is measured. There are two primary types of data that are used to measure delinquency. **Official data sources** are compiled by police and juvenile justice agencies and describe the extent and nature of delinquency that comes to the attention of the police, courts, or corrections agencies. Because official data are collected periodically, they are often used to examine delinquency trends and to evaluate juvenile justice policies. The most popular source of official data is the **Uniform Crime Reports** (which was discussed in Chapter 1) that reports on the number and type of offenses known to police.

Self-report data (also discussed in Chapter 1) are compiled from studies that ask people to report on their own behavior. Two of the most well-published self-report studies include the **National Youth Survey** and the **Monitoring the Future** project (both were discussed in Chapter 1).

Together, official and self-report data sources provide a fairly comprehensive picture of delinquency in the United States. Key findings from each regarding juveniles are reported below.

The Uniform Crime Reports (UCR)

UCR data allow us to examine patterns of crime over time. One of the most well-documented patterns of crime is the **age-crime curve** (**Figure 13.1**).[12] As can be seen, the rate of arrest increases dramatically and steadily from ages 10–18. In all three time frames presented, the rate of arrest peaks in the late teens and then steadily declines with older age groups.

Critical Thinking 13.2 Adolescent Development

What is it about the teen years that contributes to such high rates of delinquency? Adolescence is a distinct period of human growth and development. During early adolescence (ages 10–15) kids undergo more developmental change than any other time except birth to 2 years old, experiencing rapid and significant changes physically, intellectually, and socially.[13] Later adolescence is characterized by identity formation, with youth seeking their own

Figure 13.1 Age-Crime Curve

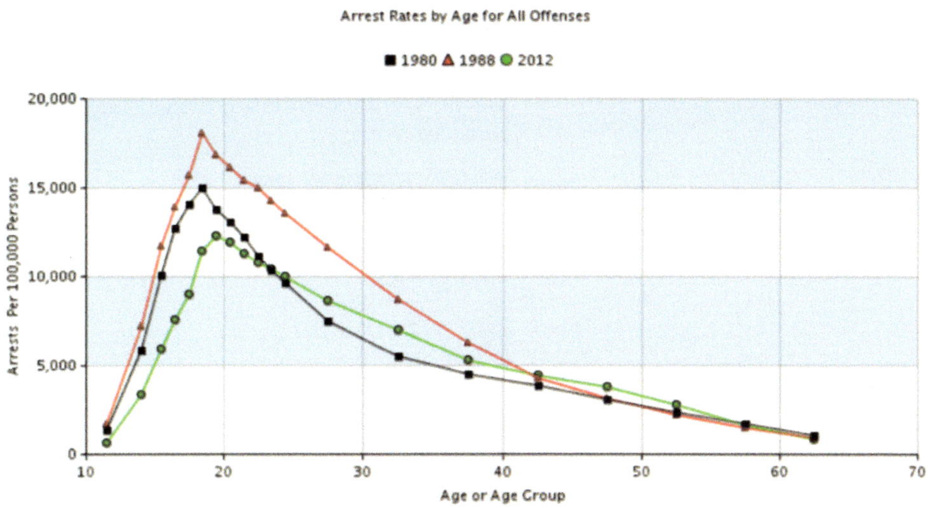

Howard N. Snyder and Joseph Mulako-Wangota. Bureau of Justice Statistics. (Arrests per 100,000 in age group.) Generated using the Arrest Data Analysis Tool at www.bjs.gov (January 10, 2017).

sense of individuality and independence. This quest for independence sometimes leads youth to engage in risky behaviors. For example, in a 2015 study of adolescent drug use, any lifetime use of illicit drugs was reported by 24 percent of twelfth graders,[14] and in 2014, there were 24.2 births for every 1,000 adolescent females ages 15–19.[15] Some attribute this risky behavior to the underdeveloped pre-frontal cortex in the brains of adolescents, which is responsible for planning, reasoning, and impulse control.[16] As the pre-frontal cortex develops, adolescents are capable of making better judgements. This development often coincides with legitimate opportunities for engaging in adult roles (e.g., work) and promotes more prosocial and responsible behaviors.

Given what we know about adolescent development, how can we best respond to risky and delinquent behavior of adolescents?

Despite the high rate of offending among teenagers, they actually account for a small proportion of crime in the United States. In 2014, juveniles accounted for 12 percent of the U.S. population and nine percent of all arrests (**Figure 13.2**).[17] They accounted for 11 percent of arrests for violent crimes and 15 percent of arrests for property crimes.

Juvenile arrest trends from 1980–2013 are illustrated in **Figure 13.3**.[18] The steep increase in juvenile crime from 1984–1996 prompted criminologists to predict the emergence of juvenile super-predators who would inflict unspeakable violence on U.S. citizens.[19] But the predictions were wrong; since the mid-1990s juvenile arrest rates have steadily declined, reaching an all-time low in 2013. What accounted for the decline in juvenile delinquency? No one can say for sure, but many believe that

Figure 13.2 Juvenile Proportion of Arrests

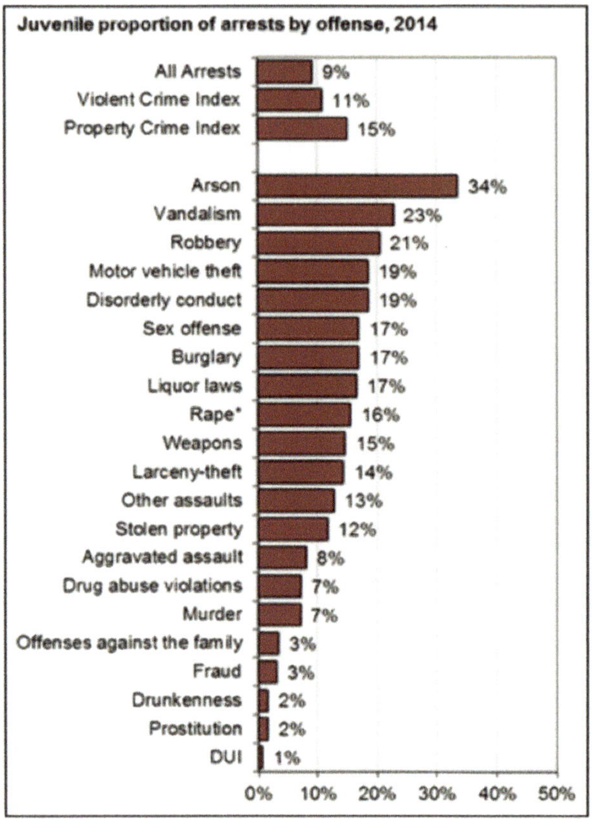

OJJDP Statistical Briefing Book. Online. Available: http://www.ojjdp.gov/ojstatbb/crime/qa05102.asp?qaDate=2014. Released on December 13, 2015.

improved policing practices, an improved economy, and a decreased demand for crack-cocaine have helped to lower rates of delinquency.[20]

In addition to collecting data on the number of crimes known to police, the UCR collects data on the demographic characteristics of offenders, allowing for the comparison of arrest rates by gender and race. **Figure 13.4** reveals a **gender gap in delinquency** with rates of arrest for males being up to four times higher than rates for females through the mid-1990s.[21] Since that time, the gender gap has closed, somewhat, due to steady decreases in arrest rates for males and relatively stable arrest rates for females.

There has been a lot of speculation about the closing gender gap. Why didn't arrest rates for girls decline in the same manner as boys' arrest rates? Some assert that cultural shifts in expectations for female behavior have made delinquency more acceptable among girls.[22] Others claim that chivalry is dead and that police are more likely to arrest girls than they were in the past.[23] The bulk of the evidence, however, points to changes in the way in-home, family conflicts were handled.[24] Once considered

Figure 13.3 Arrest Rates of Juveniles for All Offenses

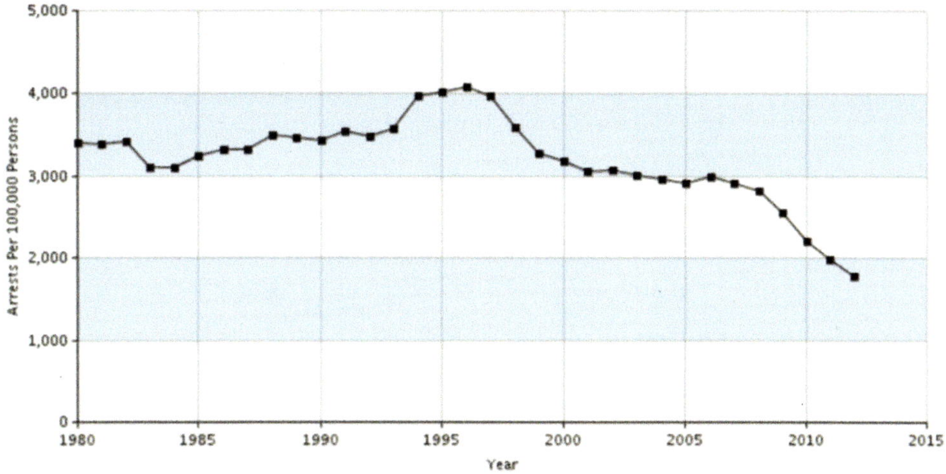

Howard N. Snyder & Joseph Mulako-Wangota. Bureau of Justice Statistics. (Arrests rates of juveniles for all offenses.) Generated using the Arrest Data Analysis Tool at www.bjs.gov (January 10, 2017).

private matters, or crimes of domestic violence, these incidents were now classified as simple assaults. Because girls' violence is more often aimed at family members, and boys' violence is more likely to occur outside of the home, this change had a larger effect on girls. Girls' increased rate of arrest for simple assaults contributed to

Figure 13.4 Arrest Rates by Gender

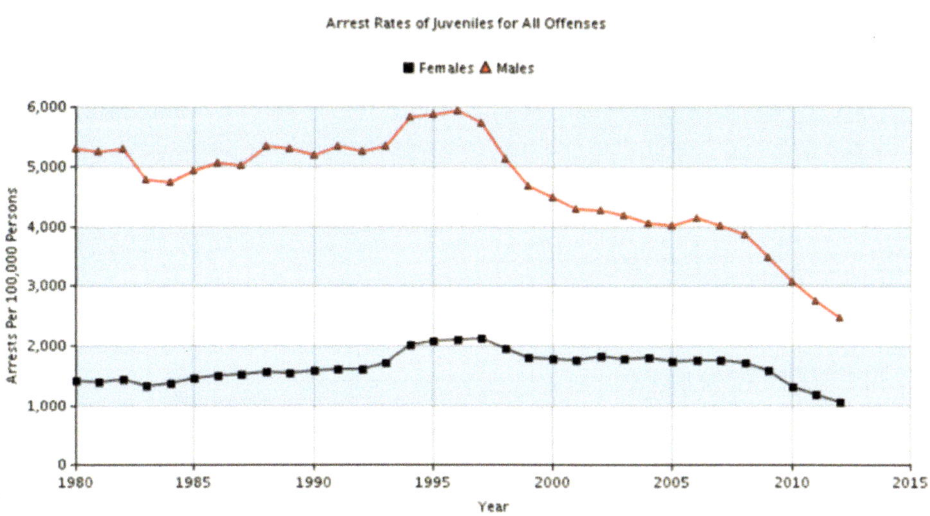

Howard N. Snyder & Joseph Mulako-Wangota. Bureau of Justice Statistics. (Arrest rates by gender.) Generated using the Arrest Data Analysis Tool at www.bjs.gov (January 10, 2017).

Figure 13.5 Arrest Rates by Race

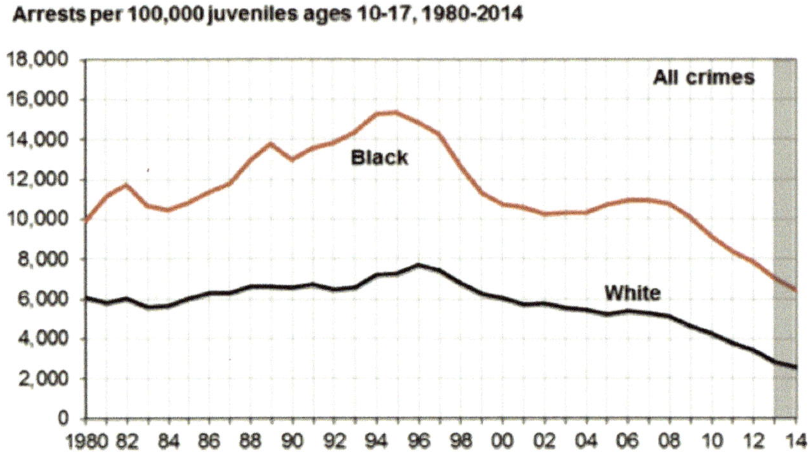

Howard N. Snyder & Joseph Mulako-Wangota. Bureau of Justice Statistics. (Arrests rates by race.) Generated using the Arrest Data Analysis Tool at www.bjs.gov (January 10, 2017).

inflated rates of arrest overall, giving the impression that the gender gap in delinquency was narrowing and girls were becoming more violent.

Black youth are arrested at much higher rates than their white peers for drug, property, and violent crimes (**Figure 13.5**).[25] This data reflects the first point at which **disproportionate minority contact (DMC)** occurs in the system (see **Field Practice 13.1**). What the data doesn't tell us is what accounts for the differences in the arrest rates of black and white youth. **Do minority youth commit more crime? Are their crimes more serious? Or do police respond differently to black and white youths?**

Field Practice 13.2 Disproportionate Minority Contact (DMC)

DMC in juvenile justice occurs when minority youth come into contact with the system at a higher rate than their representation in the general population.[26] Despite recent reductions in juvenile arrest rates, black youth continue to be arrested at twice the rate of white youth.[27] And it doesn't stop with arrest. Research suggests that, despite similar offense histories, minority youth receive harsher treatment than white youth at nearly every stage of the juvenile justice process.[28]

Although causes of DMC are hard to isolate, three factors have been implicated.[29] First, both official and self-report measures reveal minority youths' higher rate of engagement in serious and violent crimes. Second, black youth are more likely to be arrested due to heavier police involvement in poor, urban neighborhoods. Third, a significant body of research suggests that racial bias is associated with the overrepresentation of minority youth throughout the juvenile justice system.[30]

More punitive system responses lead to poor outcomes for black youth, including stigma, social isolation, and diminished educational performance due to school interruption.[31]

Moreover, racial and ethnic disparities are "driving deep distrust of the system and rightfully raising questions about fairness and equity."[32] When procedures are perceived to be unfairly applied, rules and laws, and the authorities who enforce them, lose their legitimacy.[33]

Since the 1988 reauthorization of the Juvenile Justice and Delinquency Prevention Act, states have been mandated to assess DMC and implement corrective strategies. In 1994, Congress strengthened the mandate by threatening states who fail to address DMC with the loss of formula grant funding.[34] In response, states have engaged in several strategies for reducing DMC, including the collection of data to raise awareness about the problem and to discover the points in the system where DMC is most likely to occur; the development of early intervention services and alternatives to incarceration for minority youth; and implicit bias and cultural competency training for juvenile justice professionals.[35] Unfortunately, studies designed to assess these and other initiatives have revealed no significant changes in the level of DMC.[36]

As previously discussed in Chapter 1, there are two primary weaknesses of the UCR.[37] First, the data may reflect enforcement practices rather than the true distribution of delinquency. That is, it may reflect changes in the allocation of police resources, changes in crime classifications, or changes in the manner in which police react to certain subgroups. Second, because the UCR only measures crimes known to police, the true distribution of delinquency is underestimated. Because of these shortcomings, other methods of measurement are essential for trying to determine the extent and nature of delinquency.

Self-Report Data

The National Youth Survey (NYS) was one the most comprehensive self-report studies of delinquency.[38] A national sample of 1,725 youth were interviewed at three different times over a five-year period. The NYS included 47 items measuring a range of delinquent behaviors and factors that are believed to be related to delinquent behavior. The results suggested that over 80 percent of youth surveyed admitted to committing at least one delinquent offense over their lifetime. On average, youths reported having committed between 36–53 delinquent acts over the five-year study period with the frequency escalating in the late teens. Most youth were involved in minor crimes with only a small percentage engaged in UCR Crime Index offenses.

Overall, levels of offending for black and white youth were similar; black youth were slightly more involved in serious crime. Similarly, the proportion of middle and lower-class youth who engaged in delinquency was comparable, with lower-class youth reporting slightly more involvement in more serious offenses. Finally, although the prevalence rates for males was higher than that for females, this gender gap was much smaller than that reported in the UCR.

Monitoring the Future (MTF) is a study of adolescent substance use that has been conducted annually since 1975.[39] About 44,900 eighth, tenth, and twelfth grade students in 382 schools nationwide participated in the 2015 MTF survey. The survey measured levels of drug and alcohol use, perceived risks associated with drug and alcohol use, attitudes toward drug and alcohol use, and perceived availability of drugs and alcohol. The 2015 survey results revealed a continued decline in the use of many types of illicit drugs. The annual prevalence rate for the use of *any* illicit drug was 14.8 percent for eighth graders, 27.9 percent for tenth graders, and 38.6 percent for twelfth graders. Alcohol was the most widely used substance by teenagers followed by marijuana and amphetamine use without a doctor's orders. Sixty-four percent of teenagers reported consuming alcohol by the end of high school, and 26 percent had done so by eighth grade. Finally, attitudes toward drug use remained unchanged from earlier years with the exception of attitudes toward marijuana, which moved toward greater acceptance of the drug.

Self-report measures provide a good alternative to the UCR because they uncover the **dark figure of crime**—discussed in Chapter 1, or the crimes not known to police and not sensitive to changing laws or biased enforcement practices. They suffer, however, from a different set of problems, including inaccurate recall and omission or embellishment by youth; lower-class and black youth being less likely to report involvement in crime; and blacks, females, and court identified delinquents being underrepresented in studies due to their common absence from school. Despite these problems, self-report studies are considered a valid measure of delinquency and are a standard method for examining patterns and causes of delinquent behavior.[40]

Risk and Protective Factors

Why do some youth engage in delinquency and others do not? The answers are quite obvious when these youth are raised in very different social environments. But, what about siblings or good friends that make different behavioral choices despite similar upbringings and experiences? And what about that kid that beat the odds and avoided delinquent behavior in the face of family problems and a violent social environment? The answer lies in the balance of risk and protective factors for delinquency that each youth has. **Risk factors** are biological, psychological, and social factors that increase one's likelihood of engaging in delinquency. **Protective factors** are those factors that decrease one's likelihood of engaging in delinquency. Protective factors promote **resiliency** by buffering the effects of risk factors and helping youth bounce back from adversity.[41]

For the past 30 years, researchers have been working to identify common risk and protective factors.[42] Risk factors include drug availability, family conflict, academic failure, and peers who engage in problematic behavior. Examples of protective factors include healthy beliefs and clear standards of behavior, attachment to family and schools, and individual factors such as intelligence and good interpersonal skills. The constellation of risk and protective factors is unique for every child. It is rare that a single risk factor leads to delinquency; rather it is the accumulation of factors that heightens the risk. The beauty of the risk-protection framework lies in the guidance it provides for individualized programming for youth. The best delinquency prevention/intervention programs work on reducing risk factors and building protective factors simultaneously.[43]

Field Practice 13.3 A Case Study

Sam, age 17, is a junior in high school. He is an athletic kid with a good sense of humor and kind personality. He lived with his parents in a nice, middle class neighborhood. He had a good relationship with both parents. His mother had a difficult time setting boundaries and holding him accountable, which sometimes created conflict in the home.

In middle school Sam began struggling in school. He found it difficult to focus and sit still and was always getting in trouble with his teachers. He was ultimately diagnosed with ADHD and prescribed Adderall. He also went to counseling. His behavior and performance in school improved. During his sophomore year, however, Sam's struggles with school escalated. He lost interest in school and went from an A/B to a D/F student. He began skipping school and dropped out of baseball, which he had played all his life. He also began hanging out with a new group of friends and began experimenting with drugs and alcohol.

Sam's problems at school and home created troubles with his parents. Nothing they did, in terms of punishment, seemed to work. Sam ran away from home on several occasions and refused to follow his parents' rules. At their wits' end, Sam's parents decided to file charges of beyond parental control with the local court.

Can you identify the risk and protective factors at play in Sam's life? What intervention strategies would you propose for addressing Sam's needs?

History of Juvenile Justice

Up to the sixteenth century, children were viewed as the property of adults, to be traded, abandoned, or killed as the parents saw fit.[44] Children were only useful if they could somehow contribute to the family. Girls were vulnerable to infanticide since it was believed that they didn't have the strength needed to be productive. Boys were often sent to an apprenticeship, where they would work for another family in exchange for property, or a farm animal. At very young ages, children were put to work on family farms, and often exploited. Children weren't viewed as having distinct developmental needs.[45] They were treated like little adults. Thus, when they broke the law, they received adult punishment—typically some type of corporal punishment or institutionalization.

Model of Family Government

In the early years of colonization (1600s–1700s), the **model of family government** was in full force.[46] The family was responsible for maintaining social control over children. The father had absolute authority over all family affairs; wives and children were expected to abide by the father's wishes. One early law prescribed the death penalty for children who disobeyed their father.[47]

At the end of the eighteenth century, this model of family government broke down.[48] The family-based production units were replaced with early factory systems. Children comprised about 50 percent of the labor force in the cotton mills. Increased child labor contributed to the weakening of family ties; long hours competed with family chores and general education and spiritual guidance. Conditions of poverty spread and the social control that was dependent on a strong family unit began to deteriorate. Fearing a new dangerous class of people, Americans began to develop new measures to control wayward youth who threatened social stability.

Houses of Refuge

The Society for the Prevention of Pauperism, comprised of wealthy established merchants or professionals, believed that institutionalized treatment was necessary for children subject to pauperism.[49] Opposing the practice of putting youth in adult jails, they worked to establish the New York **House of Refuge** in 1825, and by the 1840s, approximately 25 more facilities were established throughout the country. As preventive institutions, the early houses of refuge could accept not only delinquent children, but also dependent and neglected children.[50] Houses of refuge were meant to be schools of instruction characterized by education, labor, discipline, and a mental and moral regimen. Many historians, however, view the houses of refuge as a means of protecting class privileges and of controlling social unrest.[51]

Early state intervention in the lives of youth was based on the British common law doctrine of ***parens patriae*** or "state as the father."[52] Because children were not of full legal capacity, the state had the responsibility to protect children. In other words, seen as incapable of caring for themselves, the child was deemed to be in need of the state's benevolent intervention. This concept was given legal standing in ***Ex parte Crouse*** **(1838)**.[53]

Mary Ann Crouse was committed to Philadelphia House of Refuge by her mother, who claimed that she could no longer control Mary Ann's conduct. Her father argued, in *Ex parte Crouse* (1838), that she was being punished without having committed a criminal offense and without the benefit of a trial. Pennsylvania Supreme Court ruled that, based on the doctrine of *parens patriae*, the state was obligated to protect her since her parents were unable to control her behavior. The Court further ruled that, because her placement was for the purpose of reforming her rather than punishing her, formal due process protections were not necessary. Had the court examined the circumstances in the house of refuge, it would have discovered crowded and deteriorated conditions within which children were receiving harsh punishment and being exploited for their labor.[54] Despite this, the houses of refuge prevailed, having received judicial endorsement of the doctrine of *parens patriae.*

Placing Out

The Civil War and industrialization left thousands of misplaced children roaming the streets of New York looking for money, food, and shelter and banding together in gangs. Many of these vagrant children, some as young as five, were arrested by police and locked up with adult criminals, others were placed in the house of refuge, and some were left to fend for themselves on the streets. Concerned about the plight of these children, Charles Loring Brace, a member of a prominent family from Connecticut and a minister, founded the Children's Aid Society, whose mission was to relocate these children to the West, where they were needed as labor on the expanding farms.[55] Between 1854 and 1929, more than 100,000 children were sent, via orphan trains, to rural America through a system called "**placing out**." They would debark the train and stand in a line, as if up for auction. Men and women would look them over and pick the one that seemed best suited to their family and labor needs.

Once a child was selected, a contract of sorts would be signed between the people taking the children in and the organizations sponsoring the children.[56] The contract stated that the child "shall be indentured until the age of 21." In exchange, the families would send the child to school, feed and clothe them, and treat them as if they would their own children. Some children got lucky and fell into the hands of a caring family. Others, however, were treated as indentured servants.

Eventually, the receiving states began to complain about being a depository for young criminals.[57] In Illinois, the Juvenile Court Act of 1899 placed restrictions on the number of youth that could be imported. The idea, however, of placing youth with families, carried over into other juvenile justice practice and laid the foundation for modern-day foster care.

Reform Schools

Due to dissatisfaction with the houses of refuge, newer institutions called **reform schools** were introduced as a more compassionate form of intervention for criminal youth and "crime-prone" youth who had been left without the proper parental care.[58] By 1890, almost every state had a reform school. Reform schools were located in rural areas to remove youth from the influence of urban environments. Youth lived in small groups in cottages to simulate a family system. As the name implies, these institutions were designed to reform youth through a focus on education and hard work. To avoid idleness, youth engaged in military drills and physical exercise.

Like the houses of refuge before them, the reform schools became overcrowded and devoid of any type of treatment and education. This time, when a child's incarceration was challenged, the state didn't fare so well. In ***People v. Turner*** **(1870)** Daniel O'Conell was committed to Chicago Reform School against his parents' wishes because he was perceived to be in danger of becoming a pauper.[59] He had committed no crime. His parents challenged his incarceration. The Illinois Supreme Court found that the conditions of the school and the harsh treatment that occurred therein, represented imprisonment without the benefit of treatment and education as required by the *parens patriae* doctrine. Based on this, the Court ruled that only children who had committed a crime could be subjected to state intervention, and then, only after affording them due process. The Court also held that parental rights were to be upheld except upon proof of gross misconduct on the part of the parent.

Field Practice 13.4 The Child Savers

History is laced with references to groups of philanthropists and middle-class or well-to-do citizens who were instrumental in juvenile justice reforms from the mid-1800s through the turn of the century. These groups became known as the **Child Savers** and their work reflected a national child saving movement with far-reaching implications.[60] Groups like the Children's Protective Union in Memphis and the Children's Aid Society in New York, concerned about poor and transient children in the cities, used their influence and resources to pass laws and develop programs to "rescue, control, and regulate children and youths."[61] They were behind the development of reform schools and placing out programs. They also were successful in getting compulsory school laws passed and instituted a program called the friendly visitors program, which involved women visiting families to investigate possible cases of child neglect. One of the most notable programs was the playground movement. Nationwide, public playgrounds were developed to provide youth with a clean and safe place to engage in wholesome activities, all the while being supervised and taught good morals.[62] Perhaps their greatest accomplishment was the development of the juvenile court, a mechanism for intervening in the lives of neglected, dependent, and delinquent children without the constraints of the criminal courts' due process requirements.

Tony Platt, in his historical analyses of the child saving movement in Illinois, argued that "the benevolent rhetoric of progressive juvenile justice masked a class-based system of harsh punishment; the child savers created new categories of youthful crime (status offences), deprived urban youth of due process and increased the role of the state in the daily lives of the working class."[63] His work has been criticized for being a leftist and overly simplistic application of the conflict perspective.[64] Even Platt, himself, admitted to making a one-dimensional argument about the role of women reformers as a "moral enterprise" that "filled a void in their own lives."[65] A later analysis of the child saving movement in Memphis, however, supported Platt's original arguments. Sheldon and Osborne found that the juvenile justice reform increased social control over youth, particularly lower-class youth; those most actively involved in juvenile justice reform were wealthy and prominent people in Memphis; and the training youth received corresponded to "the kinds of occupations that would ensure, on release, continued dependent and lower-class status for these youths."[66]

Development of the Juvenile Court

In the late 1800s, juvenile cases were still tried along with adults in criminal courts. Juries, leery of sending youth to prison, would acquit youth rather than impose severe sanctions on them.[67] Reformers weren't happy with the courts' leniency, nor were they happy about youth being placed in adult jails or prisons, where they were abused, exploited, and corrupted. The reformers advocated for a separate legal mechanism for intervening with children.[68] Their wishes were granted with the passage of the Illinois Juvenile Court Act of 1899, which was "an act to regulate the treatment and control of dependent, neglected and delinquent children"[69] and authorized the first juvenile court in Cook County, Illinois.

The act mandated that a special courtroom in the county be designated as the juvenile court. It only applied to children under the age of 16. A very broad net was cast as to who was a dependent or neglected child, and any "reputable person" having knowledge of a neglected, dependent, or delinquent child was eligible to file a petition with the court. A child found to be dependent or neglected was committed to an institution or to the care of some reputable citizen or association. Delinquent children were committed to the guardianship of a probation officer or placed in an institution within the county. The youth could be discharged from custody whenever the court felt his or her reformation was complete. The act required separation of juveniles from adults when incarcerated and barred the detention of children under age 12 in jails. The new juvenile court operated under the *parens patriae* philosophy, focusing on rehabilitation rather than punishment.[70] The Court was characterized by informality; attorneys for the state or the youth were not considered essential to the operation of the system.

The philosophy of the court, or concept of *parens patriae*, was reaffirmed in 1905 by ***Commonwealth v. Fisher***.[71] A 14-year-old was indicted for larceny. The district attorney claimed that, under the Juvenile Court Act, formal prosecution was not required. The child was committed to the house of refuge for seven years. In an appeal, the defendant argued that an adult committing the same crime would have received a far lesser sentence. The Supreme Court of Pennsylvania upheld the sentence, stating:

> It [the Act] is to save, not to punish; it is to rescue, not to imprison; it is to subject to wise care, treatment and control rather than to incarcerate in penitentiaries and jails; it is to strengthen the better instincts and to check the

> tendencies which are evil; it aims, in the absence of proper parental care, or guardianship, to throw around a child, just starting in an evil course, the strong arm of the parens patriae.

The idea of the juvenile court spread rapidly. By 1925, a functioning juvenile court existed in all of the forty-eight states except Maine and Wyoming.[72]

Policing and Juveniles

The basic functions of policing include law enforcement, or the detection, apprehension, and prevention of illegal behavior; service, or efforts by the police to assist citizens; and order maintenance, or intervening in situations that threaten to disturb the peace. It is the order maintenance role that most often involves dealing with juvenile offenders (e.g., disbursing juveniles from public places; breaking up parties). Although seemingly benign incidents, these encounters shape the attitudes that police and youths have of one another. This is important to consider given that individuals who see the system as unfair and question its legitimacy are more likely to break the law.[73]

As gatekeepers, with broad discretionary powers, police determine which youth will be subjected to juvenile justice intervention. Police have several options available to them when dealing with juvenile offenders. They can warn and release, release the youth to his or her parents, refer the juvenile to a diversionary program operated by the police or a community agency, or detain the youth and refer him/her to the juvenile court.[74] The choice that police make can have significant impacts on a youth's behavioral trajectory. A recent study, for example, found that being stopped or arrested by police increased juveniles' likelihood of future delinquency.[75] The challenge for police is to ascertain what constitutes normal adolescent behavior that poses no real threat to the community and what reflects a pattern of behavior that may escalate to more serious offenses.

Critical Thinking 13.3 Moffitt's Taxonomy of Youthful Offenders[76]

Terrie Moffit followed a group of youth over time to examine changes in their offending pattern and factors that influence those changes. She found that there were two primary groups of youthful offenders. The first was called "**life course persistent offenders.**" The life course persistent group was a small group of offenders who began to engage in antisocial behavior at an early age and continued this behavior during their adolescent and adult years. Moffit found that these kids commonly suffered from neuropsychological problems and extreme family dysfunction. The behavior of this group escalated in severity over time and, although the rate of offending declined, it persisted into adulthood.

The second group, which included the majority of delinquents studied, was called "**adolescence-limited offenders.**" For this group, offending was of short duration and ceased as they left adolescence. Their delinquent behavior

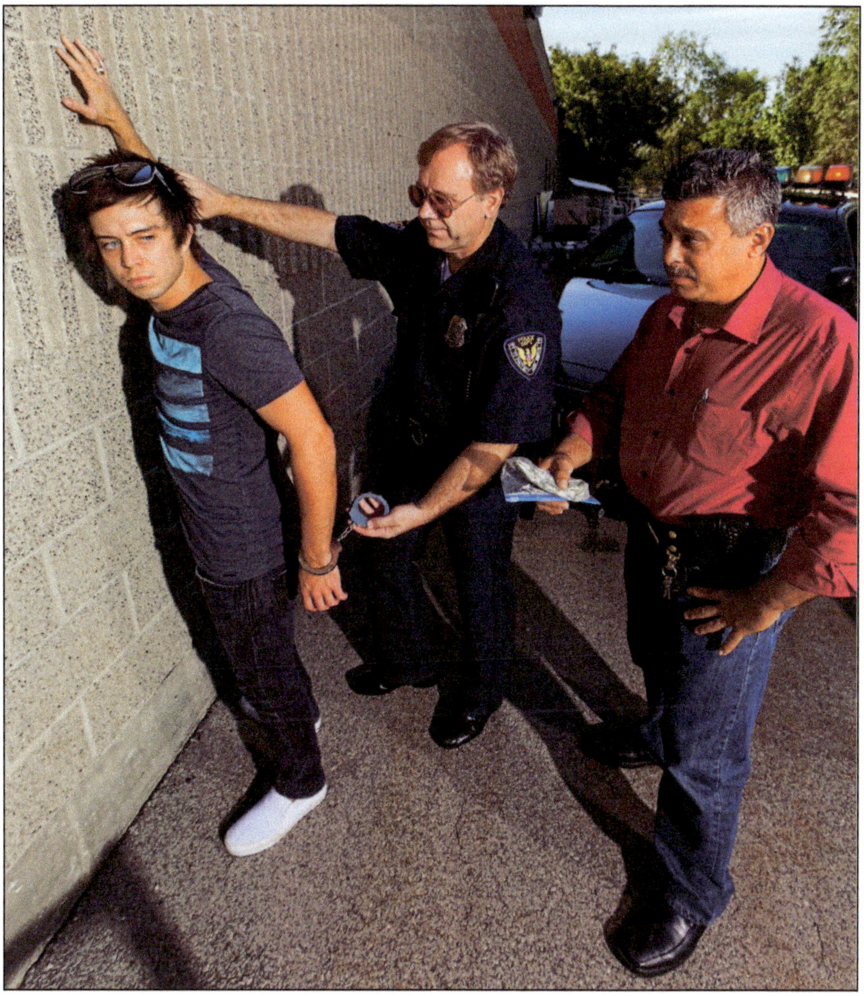

Image by TerryJ at istockphoto.com.

reflected social mimicry of the life course persistent offenders who appeared so mature and free of parental controls. As these youth aged and took on adult roles, their antisocial behavior usually ceased.

The obvious question is, how do we respond to the behavior of this adolescent-limited group of juvenile offenders? Some would argue for "radical nonintervention," or a "do nothing" approach that views experimental delinquent behavior as a normal response to adolescent development and experiences—behavior that will dissipate if left alone. Others assert, however, that juvenile courts have an obligation, under the principle of *parens patriae*, to intervene in the antisocial behavior of youthful offenders. What do you think?

Research reveals several factors that determine how police respond to youth, including:

- The seriousness of the offense;
- The presence of community programs for dealing with adolescent behaviors;
- Community attitudes toward the police and delinquency;
- The wishes of complainants;
- The demeanor of the youth; and
- The gender, race, and social class of the youth.[77]

The seriousness of the offense and the youth's demeanor are most influential in the decision to arrest.[78] Youth that are unusually antagonistic or disrespectful are more likely to be arrested. Minorities, males, and lower-class youth are more likely to be arrested even when controlling for type of offense.[79]

Police response to juveniles is complicated by the conflicting roles that officers are expected to play when it comes to youth.[80] In addition to enforcing the law and maintaining order, police are expected to protect juveniles from potentially abusive homes, and prevent future delinquency by referring them to community services. Some police agencies have specialized juvenile units or dedicated youth officers, the philosophy being that these units are more knowledgeable about youth crime and can assume a more preventive role by serving as a liaison with resources available in the community.[81] A study of specialized juvenile units in Canada revealed that when compared to general patrol officers, specialized officers were more likely to consider the youth's home and school situation in their decision-making process, more likely to refer youth to external agencies for services or to pre-charge diversion programs, and less likely to file formal charges against youth.[82]

Short of specialization, police agencies should receive training on how to intervene with youth. Developmental factors affect how youth respond to police and the degree to which they understand their rights and various police processes. In the remainder of this section, we discuss three salient issues in the policing of juveniles that have garnered attention from the media and courts.

Juvenile Interrogation

As in the case of adults, youth must be given a *Miranda* warning prior to any custodial interrogation. This safeguard against self-incrimination and potential police intimidation is especially important for youth given the significant power differentials between them and the police. A valid waiver of *Miranda* rights requires that youth understand their rights and the consequences of the waiver, and that the waiver is made free from police coercion, i.e., knowingly and voluntarily entered into. Research demonstrates that adolescents, as a group, do not have a sufficient understanding of the warning.[83] Some police agencies report modifying their *Miranda* warnings by using simpler language, but a review of recorded interrogations revealed that this type of modification was uncommon.[84]

The key issue in the U.S. Supreme Court case, ***Fare v. Michael C*** (1979) was whether a juvenile had knowingly, intelligently, and voluntarily waived his rights.[85] The juvenile,

Image by Rpsycho at istockphoto.com.

Michael C., had been brought to the Van Nuys, California, police station for questioning under suspicion of murder. Before the interrogation started, Michael requested to speak to his probation officer. His request was denied. Michael then agreed to speak with officers and waived his right to having counsel present. During the interrogation, Michael made incriminating statements and sketches. At his murder trial in juvenile court, Michael's attorney moved to suppress his statements and sketches, arguing that his request to speak to his probation officer constituted an invocation of his Fifth Amendment right to remain silent. The court ultimately decided that the admissibility of a waiver of one's right not to incriminate his or her self should be assessed within the **totality of circumstances**, mandating inquiry into all the factors surrounding the interrogation: including the juvenile's age, criminal justice experience, education, and intelligence and into whether the youth has the capacity to understand the warnings given.

Relying on this standard in this case and review of the transcript of a tape-recorded conversation between Michael C. and police in an interrogation room, the U.S. Supreme Court determined that Michael C. had legally waived his right to remain silent. The U.S. Supreme Court also concluded that his request to see a probation officer was by no means the equivalent of asking for an attorney. Probation officers and defense attorneys perform very different roles within the criminal justice process. Probation officers have a dual loyalty to society and public safety as well as the improvement or rehabilitative interests of those under their supervision. Defense attorneys are to zealously represent their clients' interests. A probation officer would have no legal obligation to protect one's right not to incriminate his or herself, while a lawyer would.

Field Practice 13.5 Helping Police Interrogate Juveniles Properly

Advisory from Steve Hurm, Regional Legal Advisor, Florida Department of Law Enforcement to police personnel regarding juveniles and *Miranda*:

NOTES: ... (F)irst, when you read *Miranda* to a juvenile, make sure you read the entire warning. The failure to include one part can doom an otherwise good confession. Second, you may interrogate a juvenile suspect without the presence or knowledge of his parents, unless the suspect asks to speak with them before answering questions. Courts will consider these factors in determining whether a juvenile confession is admissible: (1) the way *Miranda* warnings are given; (2) the age, experience, background and intelligence of the child; (3) whether the parents were contacted and whether the child had an opportunity to speak with them prior to giving the statement; (4) whether the questioning occurred in a police station; and (5) whether the child signed a written waiver of rights.

A more recent case, ***J. D. B. v. North Carolina*** (2011), examined the issue of what constituted "custodial" interrogation with a juvenile.[86] Prior Supreme Court cases called for a two-step analysis for determining whether a suspect was in custody.[87] The first step was to consider all of the "circumstances surrounding the interrogation." The second step was to inquire whether under the circumstances "a reasonable person would have felt he or she was at liberty to terminate the interrogation and leave." This case involved J.D.B., a thirteen-year-old boy in seventh grade who was pulled out of class by a uniformed police officer and brought to a "closed-door conference room" where he was questioned about break-ins in the area. Two police officers and two school administrators were present at the interrogation. J.D.B. was not informed of his *Miranda* rights, his freedom to leave the room, or given the opportunity to contact his parents. After being pressured by the officers and the administrators, and threatened with juvenile detention, he confessed to the break-ins. He was charged with larceny, and breaking and entering. The trial court judge denied his motion to suppress his confession after determining that he was not in custody during the police questioning and that his statements were voluntary. This finding was upheld by the North Carolina Court of Appeals and J.D.B. was found delinquent. The Supreme Court of the United States, however, ruled in favor of J.D.B., arguing that age must be considered in the custody determination for police questioning of children who are more likely to be intimidated by authority and feel obligated to submit to police when an adult in similar circumstances would feel free to leave.[88]

Another problematic aspect of juvenile interrogation is the interrogation technique itself. The most popular method of interrogation in the United States is the **Reid Method.**[89] The Reid Method is designed to produce a confession and is based on the assumption that there is already cause to believe that the suspect committed the offense. The method has been sanctioned by the Supreme Court. The technique involves three key processes. First, investigators isolate the suspect to establish dominance and authority over the suspect, emphasize the seriousness of the situation, and destabilize the suspect. Second, they minimize blameworthiness by expressing empathy and understanding. Third, investigators use tactics to break down denial; they interrupt the suspect, bring in another officer to play the bad guy, and lie about the strength of the evidence against them. Research suggests that these same techniques are used with adults and juveniles alike.[90]

The Reid Method has been criticized for its psychological manipulation and the potential for leading to false confessions.[91] This is especially concerning as it relates to juvenile interrogation. Youth's desire to please authority and pressure to provide the right answer may increase the chances of a false confession.[92] Moreover, due to immature thinking, youth cannot see the bigger picture; they think that the only way to get out of the interrogation is to sign a statement and make the assumption that they can take back what they said at a later time.

One of the best examples of an interrogation gone wrong for a juvenile is the Michael Crowe case.[93] Michael's sister, Stephanie, was murdered in her room at home while the rest of the family was sleeping. All of the family members were brought in for questioning later that day. Michael was the only one to be advised of his *Miranda* rights. That same day, officers interviewed a local transient, Mr. Tuite, who had been seen around the Crowe house earlier that week. Finding nothing alarming, he was released shortly thereafter. Michael and his younger sister Shannon were taken, by police, into protective custody. Unbeknownst to his parents, Michael was questioned at three different times while in protective custody, with the third session lasting over three hours. During this session, Michael was asked to take a "voice verification exam" and told that the results suggested some deception in his story. He was also told, erroneously, that the police found blood in his room. The investigator then introduced to Michael the idea that he killed Stephanie but did not remember doing it and ended the interrogation shortly thereafter. Michael was interviewed a fourth and final time the following day. Investigators pushed hard for a confession, convincing Michael that it would be the best thing for his family. They also indicated that, if he helped them out with the investigation, he could avoid jail time and get the treatment he needed. Succumbing to the pressure, Michael fabricated a story about how he and two of his friends killed Stephanie. Similar interrogation tactics were used with the other two teenagers who both ended up confessing to the crime. A grand jury issued indictments against all three boys for murder and conspiracy to commit a crime. About seven months later the court suppressed much of the evidence from the interrogations due to the coercion used by officers. Still, a trial date was set for the following month. In the meantime, one of the youth's defense attorneys and the prosecution requested that DNA testing be conducted on the clothing collected from Tuite early in the investigation. The DNA results revealed spots of Stephanie's blood on the clothing. The indictments against the boys were dismissed and five years later Tuite was convicted of voluntary manslaughter.

This is but one example of how coercion and deceptive interviewing tactics can be used to get a confession from a juvenile. Although there has been no move to invalidate the application of the Reid Method to juveniles, several recommendations have been made for protecting minors under interrogation, including videotaping the interrogation of all juveniles, limiting the length of interrogation, having a parent or interested adult present, and banning the use of deception.[94] Recent evidence, however, suggests that no major modifications have been made to the way that police interrogate juveniles.[95]

Curfew Laws

The majority of cities in the U.S. have passed **curfew laws** for teens that restrict youth from public places during specified times (e.g., 11:00 p.m. to 6:00 a.m.).[96] Curfews are designed to reduce opportunities for youth to engage in delinquency and to protect juveniles from victimization. They may also promote increased parental control and supervision over youth. The general public supports curfews as a common-sense approach to delinquency.[97]

Curfew laws give police the authority to stop juveniles out past curfew and to, potentially, detect additional delinquent behaviors. The threat of being stopped for a curfew violation is believed to act as a deterrent to delinquency, but many have questioned whether the *possibility* of catching youth is worth the intrusion on young people's privacy.[98] Challenges to curfew laws have been heard in the lower courts on the basis that the laws violated the civil rights of adolescents by restricting their freedom of movement and other liberties. Generally, the courts have upheld such laws as long as they are narrowly tailored and allow accommodations for reasonable activities such as work or after-hours school events.[99]

The logic of curfew laws has been challenged on the basis of two important findings. First, most juvenile crime is committed during the hours before and after school with a small proportion occurring during curfew hours.[100] Second, police enforcement of curfew laws is curtailed by a lack of resources allocated for the effort.[101] Perhaps the most damning evidence against curfew laws are the studies that question their effectiveness. Three comprehensive reviews of studies on curfew laws suggest that the laws have a negligible effect on juvenile delinquency and victimization.[102] This research may open the doors to more legal challenges against curfew laws.

Police in Schools

Law enforcement's first foray into schools was with the **Drug Abuse Resistance and Education Program (D.A.R.E.)**. According to the D.A.R.E. America website, D.A.R.E., founded in Los Angeles in 1983, now operates in 75 percent of U.S. school districts and 52 countries.[103] D.A.R.E. is described as "a police officer-led series of classroom lessons that teaches children from kindergarten through 12th grade how to resist peer pressure and live productive drug- and violence-free lives." The core curriculum for fifth and sixth graders is the only one that has been adopted widely and subjected to intense evaluation.[104]

Image by asiseeit at istockphoto.com.

Evaluations of D.A.R.E. reveal some benefits for students, including enhanced knowledge about drugs, improved social skills, and improved attitudes about drug use and the police.[105] Other results are not so favorable. A collection of over 30 studies reveals that any positive attitudes toward drug use and the police dissipate within one to two years and that the impacts of D.A.R.E. on student drug use are negligible.[106]

Despite evidence that D.A.R.E. is not effective at reducing drug use, key stakeholder groups show continued support for the program. For example, police officers view D.A.R.E. as a way to bridge cultural divides in minority communities;[107] educators support it for building good relationships between police and students;[108] and parents believe that participation in D.A.R.E. reduces children's likelihood of using substances and facilitates dialogue about drug use between them and their children.[109] It is this political support that keeps the funding for D.A.R.E. coming. Millions of dollars are spent each year on a program that has not been shown to achieve its primary goal.

In recent years, police have become a fixture in public schools across the United States as a reaction to high-profile incidents of school violence. According to the National Center for Education Statistics, 30 percent of U.S. public schools had a **School Resource Officer** (SRO) during the 2013–2014 school year.[110] SROs are sworn law enforcement officers who are employed by a law enforcement agency and funded through local law enforcement or education budgets.[111] The National Association of School Resource Officers refers to a triad model of SRO responsibility that includes roles as educator, informal counselor, and law enforcer.[112] SROs often engage in law-related education, which equips students with knowledge about the fundamental principles and values of laws, legal processes, and the legal system.[113] They also develop relationships with students whom they counsel and mentor on an informal basis. Most of a SRO's time, however, is spent on school safety and law enforcement activities.[114]

Supporters of SROs cite nationwide reductions in the number of school-based arrests and disciplinary infractions as evidence of SRO effectiveness.[115] The problem with using these statistics as an indicator of success is that they don't differentiate between schools with SROs and schools without SROs, nor do they account for other factors that may have contributed to this decline. Some studies use pre- and post-measures to examine the effectiveness of SROs. For example, a study of a high school in Ohio found that, compared to pre-SRO data, disruptive behavior, expulsions, suspensions, office referrals, and arrests decreased over the two-year study period.[116] A study of schools in the Southeastern United States compared rates of arrests in 13 schools with an SRO and 15 schools without an SRO, and found that schools with an SRO had lower rates of arrests for assault and weapons possession but higher rates of arrest for disorderly conduct charges.[117] Similar findings regarding increased arrests for minor offenses were found in Ohio and Miami-Dade County, Florida.[118]

It is these latter findings regarding the increased rates of arrest for minor charges that concern scholars and civil rights advocates.[119] Although few empirical studies can tie this pattern directly to the introduction of SROs in schools, there are several reasons to believe that SROs contribute to higher numbers of school-based arrests and to what some call the ***school to prison pipeline.***[120] First, as the result of their presence in schools, SROs may witness more crime. Second, having a SRO available facilitates the reporting of school crime that was historically not reported. Third, as SROs become more involved in school discipline, behaviors are relabeled as arrestable offenses that require law enforcement intervention (e.g., a school fight becomes an assault).

Two other concerns about SROs have to do with students' rights against unreasonable search and seizure and their rights when being questioned about misconduct.[121] Regarding the former, the same probable-cause standards outside of school apply to law enforcements' investigative work inside of school. This is true unless educators initiate an investigation and invite the SRO to assist. In that capacity, SROs operate under the educator's special constitutional standard of reasonable suspicion (*New Jersey v. T.L.O.*, 469 U.S. 325 (1985).[122] Similarly, by asking the principal to question a student, the SRO could circumvent having to advise students of their *Miranda* rights prior to questioning.

As can be seen, there is much controversy about the role of SROs. More research is needed to fully understand the effects that SROs have on students' arrests and rights.

The Contemporary Juvenile Court

Although the juvenile court continues to operate under the philosophy of *parens patriae*, much has changed over the years. The juvenile court, once characterized by informality, is now infused with due process requirements similar to those found in adult court, and what was once grounded in a rehabilitative ideology is now more reflective of a balanced approach that places an equal emphasis on youth accountability.[123] In this section of the chapter we will provide a generic description of the juvenile court process as it varies from court to court and even from case to case. We will then review court cases that have changed the operation of the juvenile court and provided more due process rights to juveniles. Finally, we will take a look at how the courts deal with two extreme subgroups of young offenders—status offenders and serious, violent offenders.

The Juvenile Court Process

The number of juvenile court cases in the United States increased steadily from 1960 to 1997 (from 400,000 to 1.8 million) largely due to a push for more youth accountability.[124] Between 1997 and 2013, in concert with a reduction in arrests for juveniles, the number of court cases declined 44 percent. An estimated 1,058,500 cases were processed through juvenile court in 2013. Most of the cases handled in juvenile court in 2013 involved property offenses (35%), followed by person and public order (26% each) and drug (13%) offenses. Of the cases processed in 2013, 53 percent involved youth 15 and under, 72 percent involved males, and 62 percent involved white youth.

The juvenile court process is triggered by a referral. In 2013, 82 percent of cases were referred by the police with the remaining referrals being made by parents, school officials, victims, or probation officers.[125] The first decision to be made is whether or not to detain the youth. An **intake officer** that works with the court generally makes this decision. A youth is more likely to be detained if there is probable cause that the youth committed a crime, the youth is at risk of harming himself or others, and if the youth is not likely to appear in court.[126]

Field Practice 13.6 Preventive Detention for Juveniles

In *Schall v. Martin* (1984), Gregory Martin, age 14, was arrested and charged with first-degree robbery, second-degree assault, and criminal possession of a weapon. Martin lied to police about his name and was detained overnight prior to his initial appearance the next day. Probable cause was found to substantiate all the charges, and Martin was held for a total of fifteen days until an adjudicatory (fact-finding) hearing was conducted. Prior to the hearing, a writ of habeas corpus (an argument that Martin was being unlawfully detained) was filed on his behalf. The U.S. Supreme Court held that the preventive detention of juveniles by states is constitutional if judges perceive these juveniles as posing a danger to the community if released short of an adjudicatory hearing. Such detention is not considered punitive in nature and serves a "legitimate and compelling state interest."[127]

If a youth is detained, a **detention hearing** in juvenile court must be held within a specified period of time, usually 24 hours, to revisit the question of detention.[128] In 2013, 21 percent of youth were detained while awaiting their adjudicatory hearing.[129] Black youth were significantly more likely to be detained than white youth.

The Annie E. Casey Foundation, Justice Policy Institute, and other advocacy groups have pushed for a decrease in the use of detention, citing studies that show a negative impact on the mental and physical well-being of youth in custody.[130] Studies reveal high rates of mental illness among youth upon their intake to detention, and an increased likelihood of suicide or self-harm. Evidence also suggests that detention pulls youth deeper into the juvenile and criminal justice system.[131] For example, a study in Florida found that when controlling for other factors, including severity of offense, detained youth were three times more likely to end up being committed to a juvenile facility than similar youth who were not detained.[132]

The second decision point in the juvenile court process involves **intake screening** to determine the most appropriate way to handle a case. The intake officer makes one of three basic decisions: (1) to dismiss the case for lack of evidence, (2) to resolve the matter informally (i.e., divert the youth from the juvenile justice system), or (3) to formally process the case in juvenile court.[133] Cases that are resolved informally, or diverted (45 percent), may involve a referral to counseling, the payment of restitution, unsupervised probation, or some other sanction. As long as the youth complies with the sanction and stays out of trouble, his/her case is dismissed and he/she avoids having a juvenile record. If, however, the youth doesn't comply with requirements of the sanction, he/she may be brought back in front of the court for formal processing.

Critical Thinking 13.4 Diversion from the Juvenile Justice System

Even after a youth has been referred to the juvenile justice system there are opportunities for diversion. **Diversion** refers to any action that minimizes further penetration into the system and can occur at any stage.[134] The primary objective of diversion is to avoid the consequences of labeling. It also enhances system flexibility and reduces the burden placed on juvenile courts.

There are many forms of diversion.[135] One option is to do nothing. That is, beyond a stern warning, the judge may decide that no further intervention is required. A more common form of juvenile diversion occurs when youth are referred to a community-based agency for case management and counseling services. These agencies typically include a range of services including individual, group, and family counseling for a range of problem areas. In this type of diversion, youth are typically released from any further direct contact with the juvenile court, and once they complete the recommended services their case is dismissed or terminated. A popular form of diversion is known as **Teen Court** or Youth Court.[136] Rather than participating in the formal juvenile court process, youth are referred to a teen court, where local youth assume the roles of attorneys, jurors, and judges who review the facts of the case and choose an appropriate sanction. Common teen court sanctions include a letter of apology, restitution, and community service.

Despite potential benefits of diversion, there are several criticisms. One criticism of diversion has to do with the juveniles' rights to due process.[137] Diversion programs, like Teen Court, are not held to the same due process standards of the formal juvenile court. In fact, most diversion programs require youth to admit their guilt prior to acceptance into the program. This becomes a problem when youth fail to follow through with the requirements of the diversion program and are referred back to the juvenile court to face formal charges and, possibly, a harsher penalty.

Other criticisms have to do with whether or not diversion programs are meeting their goals. One concern is that because of its coercive nature and net-widening, diversion programs may be just as stigmatizing and costly as formal juvenile court intervention.[138] **Net-widening** refers to the practice of placing offenders in diversion who would have gotten a lesser penalty (possibly an outright dismissal or a small fine) had diversion not been available. The true test, of course, is whether or not diversion programs are successful in reducing the subsequent delinquency of youth. A recent meta-analytic review of 45 studies of diversion found that diverting youth from formal court channels reduced their likelihood of delinquency.[139]

Is diversion from the juvenile justice system an appropriate response to delinquency? Under what circumstances?

After a decision has been made to formally process a case, the intake officer refers the case to the prosecutor for a second-level screening.[140] The prosecutor's role is to establish jurisdictional authority over the case (e.g., residence, age, location of offense) and to determine if there is probable cause and admissible evidence. Sometimes a prosecutor will reject the intake officer's recommendation and suggest that the case be dismissed. If the prosecutor agrees with the intake officer's decision, a petition is filed and the case is scheduled for a follow-up hearing. A **petition** is similar to a complaint in the adult system; it tells the court what the juvenile did wrong and asks the court to take jurisdiction over the child.[141] Fifty-five percent of the cases referred to juvenile court result in a petition.[142]

Once a petition is filed, the case is set for an adjudication hearing. **Adjudication hearings** are fact-finding hearings that can take two forms. Most commonly, they are plea-taking hearings during which youth admit committing the offense outlined in the petition. Alternatively, they are trials similar to those in adult court. Prosecutors present evidence and call witnesses to prove beyond a reasonable doubt that the youth has committed the offense, and defense attorneys try to establish reasonable doubt as to the allegations. The key difference between an adjudication hearing and a trial is that there is no jury; the judge hears the evidence and determines a youth's guilt or innocence.[143] Another difference is that many youth waive their right to an attorney.

There is controversy as to what the appropriate role for defense attorneys is in juvenile court.[144] In criminal court, the attorney is supposed to put on a zealous defense to establish reasonable doubt and get an acquittal for the client. The juvenile court is less adversarial. Getting a client off may mean that a youth doesn't get the help s/he needs. So, in the best interests of the child, defense attorneys often play the role of a concerned adult, encouraging youth to plead guilty rather than fight the case, even when there may be grounds to do so.

Moreover, several studies have found that youth with attorneys actually fare worse than youth who are not represented.[145] There are many speculations as to why this is — defense attorneys are overworked and underpaid, which may lead to poor quality of services. Additionally, working in juvenile court is not seen as very prestigious and that may further undermine the amount of time an attorney devotes to a case.[146]

Fifty-five percent of cases result in an **adjudication** of delinquency either through a plea or trial.[147] An adjudication is similar to a conviction in adult court in that it means that the judge has determined that the youth committed the act in question.[148] Different terminology is used to reflect the belief that youth are less culpable of criminal offenses due to their age and lack of maturity. The other 44 percent of the cases that are not adjudicated are either dismissed (59%), placed on informal probation (28%), or assigned to some other sanction (13%).[149] Even though many of the youth who are not adjudicated are subject to a sanction of some sort, they avoid having an official record of delinquency.

Once a youth is adjudicated delinquent, the case is set for a **disposition hearing.** The disposition hearing is the juvenile court equivalent to a sentencing hearing in criminal court. A juvenile probation officer prepares a **pre-dispositional report** that is similar to a pre-sentence investigation and report in adult court. The report includes information on the youth's past record of delinquency, school attendance and performance, family history, peer relationships, record of abuse or neglect, and physical and mental health. Based on this information, the probation officer makes a recommendation to the court regarding the youth's disposition.

Disposition options available to the court vary across jurisdictions. The main choices are community-based sanctions (e.g., fines, community service, probation, day treatment) or out-of-home placements (e.g., foster care, group homes, or secure care facilities). In 2013, the majority of adjudicated youth (64%) were placed on probation, 24 percent were placed outside the home, and 12 percent were given some other type of community-based sanction such as payment of restitution or fine, community service, or counseling.[150] The number of youth in out-of-home placements increased from 1985 to 2000; since that time we have seen a steady decline.[151] Youth ages 16 or older, males, and black youth were somewhat more likely to receive a disposition of an out-of-home placement.[152]

Field Practice 13.6 Justice for Sale

Two judges on the bench in Luzerne County, Pennsylvania, Mark A. Ciavarella Jr., 58, and Michael T. Conahan, 56, were charged with racketeering, conspiracy, and related charges for placing thousands of youth in private juvenile justice facilities in exchange for $2.6 million in kickbacks.[153] The kickbacks were discovered after an investigation by the Juvenile Law Center that uncovered several irregularities. The investigation revealed that during a five-year period of time over 50 percent of youth appearing before these judges lacked legal representation, and 60 percent of them were removed from their homes, many for first time, minor offenses.[154] Follow-up investigation revealed that decisions to place youth were made in minutes, with youth being shackled and taken into custody before bewildered kids and parents knew what was happening. Many of these youth spent multiple years in these facilities.

United States District Judge Edwin M. Kosik sentenced Ciavarella to 29 years in prison and Conahan to 17.5 years in prison. Robert Powell, the former owner of the private detention centers, was sentenced to 18 months in prison for his role in the scandal.[155]

In two rulings prior to the U.S. District Court's decision during the five-year span, the Pennsylvania Supreme Court ordered that all petitions of youth adjudicated by Ciaverella between 2003 and 2008 be dismissed and that their records be expunged. Additionally, a federal class action lawsuit seeking monetary damages was filed on behalf of the children and parents who suffered emotional trauma and financial loss as a consequence of the corruption scheme. The matter is still being litigated.[156]

Juveniles and Due Process

Between 1966 and 1971, the rulings in several landmark Supreme Court cases expanded the due process rights of juvenile offenders. Prior to this, the court had ruled in favor of fewer due process rights for juveniles based on the idea that youths were receiving a "compensating benefit" under the principle of *parens patriae*.[157] That is, because youth were being rehabilitated rather than punished, due process rights were deemed unnecessary. *Kent v. United States* (1966), *In re Gault* (1967), and *In re Winship* (1970) questioned the extent to which this compensating benefit existed; they rejected the argument that youths were being protected rather than punished and, accordingly, afforded juveniles many of the due process rights granted to adults.[158]

Kent v. the United States (1966) involved 16-year-old Morris Kent, who was arrested for rape and robbery.[159] Following his admission to the offenses, and in anticipation of a possible waiver to adult court, Kent's attorney filed a motion for a hearing on the issue of jurisdiction. The judge did not rule on the motion, and instead, waived the case to adult court without any hearing or written statement as to the grounds for the waiver. Kent was found guilty in criminal court and sentenced to 30 to 90 years in prison. His attorney appealed the case all the way to the U.S. Supreme Court, arguing that the judge had not made a full investigation as required by law and that Kent had been denied due process. The Supreme Court ruled the waiver invalid, concluding that Kent's due process rights were violated by denying his attorney access to all records involved in the waiver, and by the judge's failure to provide a written statement on the reason for the waiver.

In re Gault (1967) involved a 15-year-old boy, Gerald Gault, who was arrested for allegedly making obscene phone calls to an adult woman.[160] The complainant never appeared in court to testify and there were never any specific charges filed stating what Gault did. Moreover, Gault was not represented by an attorney, nor were any transcripts made of the hearings. Gault was adjudicated delinquent and sentenced to the state training school for a six-year sentence. The maximum penalty for an adult committing the exact same offense was a $50 fine and two months in jail. Gault's parents filed a petition for a writ of habeas corpus, which requires the government to produce the prisoner so that the court can determine the legality of his/her custody. The writ was dismissed by both the Superior Court of Arizona and the Arizona Supreme Court. The Gaults sought relief in the Supreme Court of the United States. The Court reversed the lower court's ruling and determined that juveniles facing the possibility of incarceration were entitled to certain procedural safeguards under the due process clause of the Fourteenth Amendment, including the rights to adequate notice of the charges against them, confront and cross-examine their accusers, the assistance of counsel, and the right against self-incrimination.

In re Winship (1970) involved a 12-year-old boy arrested for stealing $112 from a woman's purse, an act of larceny had it been committed by an adult.[161] A New York Family Court found Winship guilty based on a preponderance of the evidence, acknowledging that the evidence did not establish his guilt beyond a reasonable doubt, and sentenced him to a training school for one and a half years. Winship appealed the court's use of the lower burden of proof. The appeal was rejected in both the Appellate Division of the New York Supreme Court and in the New York Court of Appeals. The U.S. Supreme Court heard the case and ruled that the "beyond a reasonable doubt standard" was a fundamental constitutional safeguard that must be applied to adults and juveniles alike.

The next case to challenge juvenile court procedures was ***McKeiver vs. Pennsylvania*** (1971), which involved juveniles brought to trial without a jury.[162] Joseph McKeiver and Edward Terry, fifteen- and sixteen-year-old boys, were charged with robbery, theft, assault, and escape. At trial before the Juvenile Court of Philadelphia, each was denied a request for a jury trial. A Superior Court affirmed the decision, as did the Supreme Court of Pennsylvania. The case was appealed to the U.S. Supreme Court, which also declined to extend the adult right to a jury trial to juveniles. The Court reasoned that it did not want to turn the juvenile court into a fully adversarial process. To do so, Justice Blackmun reasoned this would establish so little differentiation between the juvenile and adult trial processes that it could appear there would be no need for separate juvenile and adult systems. Moreover, jury trials were not perceived to be an absolute necessity for accurate determinations of delinquency. In this case the Court drew a line in the sand arguing that jury trials would destroy the traditional character of juvenile proceedings.[163]

Confidentiality of Juvenile Proceedings

Early juvenile courts were open to the public and permitted publication of information about juvenile court proceedings.[164] By 1952, however, many states had statutes that excluded the general public from juvenile court proceedings. In some states, reporters were allowed to attend and report on the hearings but they were prohibited from disclosing the identity of the juvenile. Restrictions regarding the disclosure of the juvenile's name were deemed necessary to avoid stigmatizing the youth and to avoid giving the youth any recognition that might propel him/her toward further delinquency.[165] Advocates of confidentiality also argued that publicity would embarrass the family and result in public ridicule.

There are two basic arguments against confidentiality.[166] The first argument was put forth in the 1960s amid concerns about youths' due process rights. Opponents of confidential juvenile courts argued that public access to, and scrutiny of, the juvenile courtroom would provide a check on corrupt practices and improve the integrity of proceedings. The second argument came in the mid-1980s along with concerns about rising juvenile crime and the victim rights movement. Opponents argued that the citizens, neighbors, and schools had a right to "fair warning" about youth who pose a danger to others. They also argued that victims should have greater access to the juvenile court and input into case outcome.

In the mid-1980s, several states changed their statutes to permit the public to attend certain proceedings.[167] As of 2010, the courts in three states were open to the public with no restrictions; the courts in 15 states were open to the public but the judge had the discretion to close them at any time; the courts in 20 states were open with some restrictions, usually based on age and offense criteria; and the courts in 13 states were closed to the public but the judge had the discretion to open them at any time.[168] Additionally, in 46 states, school notification laws permitted courts to notify schools when students have committed delinquent acts. Some of these laws limit school notification to youth charged with serious or violent crimes.[169] There is no way to know about the effects of greater public access to juvenile courts. With advances in technology, however, we can be assured that the confidentiality of juvenile court will continue to erode.

Critical Thinking 13.5 Confidentiality of Juvenile Proceedings

With advancements in law enforcement technology, media/public access to information shared by the police over the airwaves became a concern. Consider ***Smith v. Daily Mail Publishing Co.*** **(1979)**.[170] A 15-year-old student was allegedly shot and killed by a 14-year-old student at a local school. Reporters from two Charleston, West Virginia, newspapers were monitoring the police band radio frequency, and upon learning of the incident they hurried to the school to gather information. Both newspapers published pieces on the shooting that included the name of the declared assailant in the case. Three radio stations also broadcasted the name across the airwaves.

At issue in this case is "whether a West Virginia statute violates the First and Fourteenth Amendments of the United States Constitution by making it a crime for a newspaper to publish, without the written approval of the juvenile court, the name of any youth charged as a juvenile offender." West Virginia was one of five states at the time that had blanket criminal sanctions for such violations. The Court reasoned that judges familiar with cases appearing before them could determine under what circumstances to release names of alleged juvenile offenders and when to withhold such information, and that those who violated such judicial orders could conceivably be held in contempt of court. Moreover, the Court held: "A state law making it a crime to publish the name of a student charged with a crime is unconstitutional."[171]

Do you think the names and identities of juveniles who commit delinquent acts should be made public? Would this deter or encourage crime?

The Courts and Status Offenders

Recall that status offenses, such as truancy, liquor law violations, ungovernability, runaway, and curfew violations, are those behaviors that are considered illegal when committed by persons who have not yet reached the age of majority. It has been argued that status offenses are often indicative of underlying problems in the youth's family, school, and community, and therefore, the state has an obligation to step in and help the youth.[172] In some states, status offenses have been decriminalized and are handled by child welfare agencies or family courts that are better suited for addressing the youths' needs.

Nationally, status offenders only comprise about 16 percent of the juvenile court caseload.[173] In 2013, juvenile courts formally processed 109,000 status offense cases.[174] Fifty-one percent of the status offense cases involved a truancy charge. The majority (58%) of status offense cases involved males. Females, however, accounted for 55 percent of runaway cases, the only status offense in which they represented a larger proportion of the caseload than males.

Juvenile court responses to status offenders have evolved over the years. Prior to the 1970s, many status offenders were institutionalized as a means of protection.[175] In 1974, the **Juvenile Justice and Delinquency Prevention Act** set forth a requirement regarding the deinstitutionalization of status offenders.[176] Youth who committed status offenses were not to be placed in secure detention or locked confinement. This core requirement of the act was designed to limit the extent to which youth who committed status offenses were exposed to youth engaged in delinquent acts, and to encourage their referral to services that could better address their needs. States followed suit and moved toward the deinstitutionalization of status offenders until the 1980s, when tough responses were encouraged for all youthful misbehavior.[177] A 1980 amendment to the act called the **Valid Court Order** (VCO) exception allowed judges to place adjudicated status offenders in locked facilities if they had violated a court order.[178] For example, a youth on probation for truancy who violates a condition of his/her probation by skipping school again could now be institutionalized. The VCO is used by 30 states. Although designed as an exception, the VCO was used fairly frequently and contributed to the increased incarceration of status offenders.[179]

With the reauthorization of the act in 2002, and research revealing the detrimental effects of incarceration on youthful status offenders, there was another push for deinstitutionalization. Recent statistics suggest that the use of detention for status offenders has decreased substantially since 2002.[180] In 2013, seven percent of petitioned status offense cases were detained. Truancy cases were the least likely to involve detention, and runaway cases were the most likely to involve detention. Among adjudicated status offenders, eight percent received out-of-home placement, a decrease from 11 percent in 2002.[181] Fifty-four percent were placed on probation, and 38 percent received some other sanction (e.g., community service, counseling).

Juvenile Waivers

As concerns about juvenile crime increased during the 1980s and 1990s, many states enacted laws making it easier to transfer youths to adult courts. These **juvenile waiver** laws were based on the belief that more punitive responses than those imposed in juvenile court were needed to deter the new breed of violent juvenile offenders.

Field Practice 13.7 Adult Crime, Adult Time?[182]

Lionel Tate, a 170-pound 12-year-old boy killed a little girl while imitating professional wrestling moves. Tate's mother, Kathleen Grosset-Tate, was babysitting the 48-pound, six-year-old girl named Tiffany. After serving Lionel and Tiffany dinner, Grosset-Tate went upstairs to sleep. At about 10:40 pm Lionel woke his mother saying that Tiffany wasn't breathing. Grosset-Tate called 911 and administered CPR. Tiffany was rushed to the hospital and pronounced dead. An autopsy showed she suffered a fractured skull, lacerated liver, broken rib, internal hemorrhaging, and numerous cuts and bruises. Lionel told police that he picked Tiffany up and accidentally hit her head against a table. In an interview with a psychologist, Lionel claimed to have accidentally thrown Tiffany into a stairwell's handrail and a wall while trying to throw her onto a sofa. A jury found him guilty of first-degree murder, and at age 14, he was sentenced to life in prison without parole.

Within two years, an appeals court threw out Tate's conviction on the basis that he wasn't given a mental competency hearing prior to his trial. Tate then pleaded guilty to second-degree murder, and was given credit for the three years that he already served in the juvenile facility, a year of house arrest, and 10 years of probation. A year later, Lionel was caught breaking house arrest and carrying an eight-inch knife. The judge added five years to his term of probation. Then, a little more than six months later, he was arrested again for robbing a pizza deliveryman at gunpoint. Tate was sentenced to 10 years for the robbery and 30 years for violating his probation. The sentences were to run concurrently.

Today, there are three types of juvenile waivers.[183] The first is a **judicial waiver** that occurs when a juvenile court judge, after considering the merits of the case, uses his discretionary authority to send the case to the criminal court. Juvenile court judges have always had this ability, but by the 1970s formal judicial waiver laws existed in nearly every jurisdiction. Since that time, changes to the laws governing judicial waivers have lowered the age of eligibility. The second type of juvenile waiver is a **legislative waiver** whereby certain classes of crime are statutorily excluded from juvenile court jurisdiction. Excluded crimes include violent crimes such as murder, rape, and aggravated assault. These statutes typically specify the age at which youth can be transferred to adult court. Between 1979 and 2003, 29 states enacted some form of legislative waiver. Since 2003, eight of these jurisdictions have modified their statutes, making more classes of crime eligible for waiver to adult court. The third type of juvenile waiver is a **prosecutorial waiver**. This type of waiver gives prosecutors the authority to file a case in criminal court based on the gravity of the offense. As of 2014, 15 states allow prosecutorial waivers.

The number of cases waived to adult court through prosecutorial and legislative waivers is unclear. The number of judicial waivers, however, doubled from 1985 to 1994 when it peaked at 13,600 cases.[184] Since 1994, the number of cases waived has decreased steadily, and in 2013, 3,980 cases were judicially waived to adult court.[185] This decline in judicial waivers is, at least partially, driven by the decline in violent juvenile crime; it may also be attributed to the increased use of other types of waivers.[186]

Available research challenges the wisdom of juvenile waivers in three key ways. First, transferring a youth to adult court does not guarantee more severe sanctioning. Some studies have found that juveniles sentenced to criminal court were more likely to receive probation sentences than if they had proceeded though the juvenile system.[187] Other studies found that when youth were sanctioned harshly in the adult system, parole authorities released them after serving less time than they would have served in the juvenile system.[188] Second, juveniles transferred to adult courts are more likely to reoffend when compared to youth retained in juvenile court.[189] Third, there is no evidence to suggest that waiver laws have any general deterrent effect on violent juvenile crime.[190]

These laws and other punitive measures reject the notions upon which the separate juvenile justice system was based—that youth are less mature and, therefore, less culpable than adults—and have eroded the concept of *parens patriae*. Recent rulings in court cases on the death penalty and sentences of life without parole, however, have somewhat reversed the trend toward harsh punishments for youth.

Juveniles and the Death Penalty

The United States has a long history of executing juveniles. The first documented execution of a juvenile was in 1642, when Thomas Granger, age 16, was hanged in Plymouth Colony, Massachusetts, after a conviction for bestiality.[191] Since that time, 361 individuals have been executed for crimes committed when they were juveniles.[192] Despite several requests, it wasn't until 1987, in ***Thompson v. Oklahoma*** (1988) that the Supreme Court would consider the constitutionality of the death penalty for juveniles.[193] Thompson, age 15, was found guilty of the brutal murder of his former brother-in-law and sentenced to death. Later, the U.S. Supreme Court vacated the judgment and "concluded that the 'cruel and unusual punishment' prohibition of the Eighth Amendment, made applicable to the States by the Fourteenth Amendment, prohibits the execution of a person who was under 16 years of age at the time of his or her offense."[194] The ruling was based on two key considerations. First, 18 states prohibited the execution of persons who committed the offense under the age of 16, and another 27 states prohibited the execution of any juvenile. Based on this, the Court perceived there to be a national consensus forbidding the imposition of capital punishment for crimes committed before the age of 16. Second, the fact that only five of the 1,393 persons sentenced to death by juries between 1982 and 1986 were less than 16 at the time of the offense, "leads to the unambiguous conclusion that the imposition of the death penalty on a 15-year-old offender is now generally abhorrent to the conscience of the community."[195]

Juveniles ages 16 and 17 at the time of the act were sentenced to death until 2005 when the Supreme Court struck down the death penalty for juveniles in ***Roper v. Simmons*** (2005).[196] At the age of 17, Christopher Simmons committed murder, and at the age of 18 he was convicted and sentenced to death. In *Roper v. Simmons* the U.S. Supreme Court found that "the rejection of the juvenile death penalty in the majority of States; the infrequency of its use even where it remains on the books; and the consistency in the trend toward abolition of the practice" combined with the fact that "the United States is the only country in the world that continues to give official sanction to the juvenile death penalty" reflected a national consensus against the practice of executing juveniles.[197] The majority opinion also cited medical and social-science evidence that teenagers are too immature to be held accountable for their crimes to the same extent as adults. The *Roper v. Simmons* ruling spared the lives of 72 juvenile offenders who were on death row at the time. These youth were resentenced to a life sentence with little or no possibility of parole.[198]

Juveniles and Life without Parole (LWOP)

With the ban on the death penalty, the harshest sentence available for juveniles is now life without parole (LWOP). Nineteen states, however, have banned life without parole sentences for juveniles, and three recent Supreme Court rulings have limited its use in the other states.[199] In ***Graham v. Florida*** (2010), the U.S. Supreme Court ruled that the use of juvenile LWOP be limited to homicide offenders.[200] The decision purportedly affected 129 juveniles, 77 of whom were serving life sentences in Florida.[201] In ***Miller v. Alabama and Jackson v. Hobbs*** (2012) the Supreme Court ruled that *mandatory* LWOP for juveniles violated the Constitution's ban on cruel and unusual punishment.[202] Although youth could still be sentenced to LWOP, such a sentence could not be imposed automatically and without considering the youth's age and other circumstances of the offense. Finally, in ***Montgomery v. Louisiana*** (2016) the Supreme Court applied the 2012 ruling retroactively, meaning that about 2,000 men and women serving mandatory LWOP sentences for murders they committed as juveniles may now have a chance for release.[203]

Like *Roper v. Simmons* before them, these three rulings were rooted in the idea that children are different. Because of their immaturity and failure to appreciate risks and consequences, youth cannot be held to the same standards as adults; to do so would result in disproportionate punishment. In the majority opinion for *Montgomery*, Justice Kennedy reiterated that life terms for juvenile offenders must be reserved for the "rare juvenile offender who exhibits such irretrievable depravity that rehabilitation is impossible."[204]

A national survey of 1,579 juvenile lifers revealed sobering details about the population of youth serving LWOP sentences.[205] For example:

- 79 percent of respondents reported witnessing violence in their homes;
- More than half (54.1%) witnessed weekly violence in their neighborhoods;
- 46.9 percent experienced physical abuse, including 79.5 percent of girls;
- 20.5 percent reported being victims of sexual abuse;
- A third (31.5%) were raised in public housing;
- Two in five respondents had been enrolled in special education classes; and
- Fewer than half (46.6%) of these individuals had been attending school at the time of their offense.

These are just a few of the statistics that highlight the extreme disadvantage these youth experienced prior to their incarceration. It has been argued that these statistics reflect the failing of other systems that are intended to protect youth.[206]

Juvenile Corrections

As previously indicated, the key decision a juvenile court judge has to make at the disposition hearing is whether to order the youth into out-of-home placement or place him/her in a community-based sanction. Although programmatic choices are limited in some jurisdictions, most judges have a variety of programming options available to them. In this section of the chapter, we will describe the nature and effectiveness of the most common correctional options.

Out-of-Home Placement

Although most juvenile courts try to minimize the number of out-of-home placements, there are times when removal from the home is in the best interest of the youth. Out-of-home placement is typically limited to those youth who are engaging in serious, repeated delinquency and/or have unsafe home environments and ranges from group homes to incarceration in adult prisons.

Group Homes

Group homes are small facilities designed for 8–12 medium- to high-risk youth who, due to troubles in the family, school, or community, may benefit from out-of-home placement. According to the Office of Juvenile Justice and Delinquency Prevention there were 360 group homes housing youth adjudicated for law violations in 2014.[207] Eighty-one percent of these group homes were privately operated. Most of these homes were staff secure, with only one in eight reporting any type of doors or gates for confining youth.

Although group home models are many and varied, there are two common models. The first is the Teaching Family Model (TFM) that emphasizes family-style living. This model incorporates structured behavioral modification systems and highly trained live-in house parents who engage in proactive teaching interactions with the youth that are focused on prevention and youth skill acquisition.[208] The second model incorporates more individual psychotherapy and uses rotating staff for resident supervision. Long-standing problems with this second model include inadequate pay and benefits and a lack of staff training and support.[209]

Findings from studies comparing the outcomes of youth in group homes and community-based programs have been mixed with two finding more favorable outcomes for the youth in community-based treatment,[210] two finding no differences in outcomes,[211] and one finding more favorable outcomes for youth in group care.[212] One longitudinal study of group homes in Los Angeles found that seven years after discharge 36 percent of participants had used hard drugs in the past year; 27 percent reported five or more symptoms of substance dependence; 66 percent reported doing something illegal in the previous year; 37 percent reported being arrested; and 25 percent reported serving the previous 90 days in jail or prison.[213]

Although these studies are not very encouraging, it is important to note that not all group homes are created equal. Group homes that involve youths' families in treatment, have shorter lengths of stay, and offer after-care services are associated with better outcomes.[214] The Teaching-Family Model (TFM), is also associated with better outcomes. Studies comparing the TFM model to other types of residential care found greater improvements in academic functioning and fewer offenses during treatment.[215]

State Training Schools

The most restrictive juvenile corrections options are secure care facilities, which are the option most similar to adult prisons. These institutions are commonly called "**training schools**," reflecting their emphasis on education and other types of rehabilitation. According to the most recent Juvenile Residential Facility Census, there are 176 of these facilities across the nation.[216] The type and level of security varies across facilities. Many are "staff secure" facilities in which security is accomplished by the staff through close monitoring of youth and visitors. Others have a variety of security options, including locked sleeping rooms for youth, locked doors or gates, and perimeter razor wire.

The more secure facilities are reserved for the most serious and chronic juvenile offenders. Approximately 38 percent of juveniles committed to secure facilities have been adjudicated for a person offense.[217] Most have a prior history of delinquency and have undergone various types of community-based intervention before being incarcerated. The median time spent by juveniles in state-level secure facilities is 106 days.[218]

Secure care facilities share many common features.[219] They are characterized by a high level of structure throughout the day. The typical schedule requires youth to participate in a variety of planned activities from 6:00 am until 9:00 pm. Youth enjoy about one hour of free time per day. Common activities include educational programming, individual and group counseling, and recreational activities. Although educational programs are more individualized in institutions, most of the youths' day is spent in a classroom setting. Additionally, a range of interventions is provided to youth in order to address their individual risks and needs. Most institutions have established mental health, substance abuse, and sex offender treatment programs. Some institutions specialize in one type of intervention.

Phase systems and **token economies** are common behavioral modification techniques used to encourage participation and compliance among the youth.[220] Youth typically enter into the facility on an orientation phase during which they learn the rules and get acclimated to the institution. Once they achieve the requirements of this phase they can progress through the next phases that involve more responsibility and more privileges. Youth who violate the rules can be moved back a phase as a consequence of their behavior. In token economies, youth earn "tokens" or points for accomplishing specific tasks (e.g., maintaining good hygiene, cleaning their room). These points can then be exchanged for some type of reward (e.g., an extra privilege, a snack). Although these types of behavioral modification systems are associated with increased compliance and lower rates of institutional misconduct, they do little to promote long-term behavioral change once a youth leaves the institution.[221]

Due to the variation in recidivism measures and follow-up periods, it is difficult to estimate a national rate of recidivism for youth released from correctional institutions. Three states using the measure "any new arrest" reported recidivism rates of 55 percent; 8 states using the measure "any new conviction/adjudication" reported rates of 33 percent.[222] Many juvenile justice professionals attribute high rates of recidivism to a lack of transitional or aftercare services for youth upon their release from the institution. Others suggest that the inmate subculture that emerges in these secure institutions undermines any rehabilitative potential.

Inmate subcultures develop as the result of common norms and values that youth bring with them into the facility and in response to the deprivations that youth experience while incarcerated.[223] The subculture is characterized by an inmate code of behavior. Youth learn very quickly that ratting on their peers will result in a physical beating and/or social ostracism, and that showing any emotion is viewed as a sign of weakness. Youth adapt to the inmate code as a means of survival. That is, in response to the real or perceived threat of violence within these institutions, many youth become involved with exploitation, violence, contraband, and a variety of other negative behaviors. For this reason, and the high recidivism rates associated with incarceration, secure care facilities for juveniles are viewed by many as criminogenic environments that solidify delinquent attitudes and behaviors.[224]

Field Practice 13.8 Trauma-Informed Care: An Emerging Practice

An emerging strategy for juvenile institutions is the development of "trauma-informed" or "trauma-sensitive" cultures of care. This strategy is rooted in research that has revealed a high prevalence of trauma among institutionalized youth. The manifestations of this trauma include mistrust, extreme emotionality, and aggression, all of which can be mistaken for defiance, which may lead to punishment or even physical restraint. In trauma-informed cultures of care staff receive intensive training on the symptoms of trauma, the effects it has on youth, and their role in preventing the re-enactment of trauma. The development of caring interpersonal relationships with youth is viewed as the cornerstone of trauma-informed treatment. Interventions within these trauma informed cultures of care are designed to address past victimization and equip youth with improved coping skills. Research is needed to examine their effects.

Boot Camps

Following the lead of the adult system, juvenile boot camps were developed as an alternative to more traditional secure care facilities. As with the adult models, **juvenile boot camps** were designed for first-time, nonviolent offenders and emphasized strict regimens, military drill, and hard labor. The programs sought to develop personal pride in the youth, emphasizing physical fitness and appearance.[225] Although secondary to the boot camp regimen, youth also were required to participate in group treatment programs, education programs, substance abuse education classes, and prerelease classes. The appeal of boot camps quickly spread and with the help of federal funding from the Juvenile Justice Delinquency and Prevention Act, seventy boot camps were in operation across the country by the year 2000.[226]

Despite the widespread appeal of boot camps, there was considerable debate about their merits.[227] Proponents of juvenile boot camps argued that the military model provided the structure and control needed for a safe environment, built camaraderie and discipline, and fostered respect for staff. Opponents argued that the military model undermined the type of therapeutic relationships and atmosphere needed for positive development, failed to address youths' individual needs, and created an environment that was antithetical to their home environment.

Research on boot camps is mixed. Surveys comparing staff and juveniles from 27 boot camps and 22 traditional residential facilities revealed that perceptions regarding boot camps were generally more favorable and that boot camp participants became less impulsive and less antisocial.[228] Despite these positive results, outcome studies have found no significant differences between the recidivism rates of boot camp participants and control groups of offenders in other types of correctional programs.[229]

These results may be due to a major difference between real boot camps and juvenile justice boot camps. Soldiers who experience military boot camp, leave there with a sense of esprit de corps, a common mission, and a job. Juvenile boot camp participants, however, disperse from boot camps and return to the same disjointed and dysfunctional environments that landed them in boot camp in the first place. Without proper aftercare they are likely to return to their old ways.

Field Practice 13.9 The Martin Lee Anderson Act

Fourteen-year-old Martin Lee Anderson died at a Pensacola, Florida, hospital after collapsing the previous day at the now-closed Bay County Sheriff's Office Boot Camp. Six months before his death, Martin Lee Anderson was arrested for stealing his grandmother's Jeep Cherokee. He was sent to boot camp after violating his probation for trespassing at school. He died during his first day at camp. Anderson collapsed while running laps. At least seven staff members responded by beating him for thirty minutes. Finally, to revive him they pushed ammonia capsules up his nose while holding his mouth shut. Instead, he suffocated to death. A security videotape caught eighty minutes of the incident, from the time the guards restrained him until medical personnel arrived to take him to the hospital.[230]

Two state medical examiners were split in their opinion about the cause of his death, with one saying it was from a sickle cell trait, a previously undiagnosed blood disorder, and the other saying the guards smothered him. Seven boot camp officers and a nurse were acquitted on state charges of aggravated manslaughter of a minor. After an investigation, federal authorities decided not to bring federal charges, as they did not believe that they could show that those officials involved acted "willfully."[231] With the passage of the Martin Lee Anderson Act, the Florida legislature closed all boot camps in the state.

By the year 2000, boot camps had begun to fall out of favor due to their ineffectiveness, and several states closed down all boot camp operations (Arizona, Colorado, Georgia, and North Dakota). In 2002, Congress began to pull funding for juvenile boot camps.[232] Jamie Muscar identifies the Detention Diversion Advocacy Program in San Francisco, California, and the Boatbuilding Apprenticeship Program in Alexandria, Virginia, as promising alternatives to boot camps.[233] These programs combine both discipline and rehabilitation, while removing the militaristic components of boot camps. Education, vocational training, counseling, positive interaction with role models, and aftercare are also emphasized.

Juveniles in Adult Prisons

As discussed previously, most states enacted laws in the mid-1990s making it easier to transfer serious juvenile offenders to adult courts for sentencing and disposition. In 1995, the number of juveniles sentenced to adult prisons reached its peak at about 6,500.[234] According to the most recent statistics available from the Bureau of Justice Statistics, 993 youth under the age of 18 entered the adult prison system in 2015.[235] These admissions represented one percent of all state prison admissions. Despite the significant decline, great concern has been expressed regarding the potential ramifications of placing youth in adult prisons.

Past research reports basic differences in the design and management of adult and juvenile facilities.[236] For example, juvenile facilities are generally smaller, have fewer security features, and report a lower staff to inmate ratio. As might be expected, studies have found that managers and staff in juvenile settings are more aligned with the rehabilitative philosophy than their adult counterparts. These design features and staff ideologies are important to the extent that they shape the operational realities of institutions, and in turn, create different experiences for youth. For example, most studies have found that youth in adult prisons are less likely to receive educational and counseling services. In contrast to these earlier studies, however, a more recent study found that youth in adult prisons reported greater access to counseling, case workers, and drug treatment.[237] It also found, however, that youth in juvenile facilities rated staff-inmate interactions as more positive. Unfortunately, this study did not include a comparison of outcomes to see which is more important, the provision of services or the relationships with correctional staff.

The outcomes for youth in adult facilities may speak for themselves. When compared to similar youth in juvenile facilities, they are more likely to be physically victimized,[238] more likely to become involved in disciplinary problems,[239] and more likely to recidivate upon release.[240] These findings have contributed to the decline in the use of adult prison for youth and led to the development of **blended sentencing**. Blended sentencing involves the use of the juvenile correctional system, the adult correctional system, or both.[241] For example, in some states, transferred youth who are sentenced to a period of incarceration are placed in a juvenile facility until age 18 at which time they are transferred to an adult facility.[242] This and other blended sentencing schemes are designed to ameliorate the negative effects of the harsh prison environment on developmentally unprepared youth.

Community-Based Programs

Generally speaking, research paints a gloomy picture of secure facilities for youth. Furthermore, there is evidence to suggest that intervention provided in the community is associated with greater reductions in recidivism.[243] Interventions delivered in a community context allow youth to maintain important social ties. They also provide youth with the opportunity to test new skills in their natural environment while still receiving support from corrections and treatment personnel. Although the types of community sanctions are many and varied, the discussion here will be limited to probation, select intermediate sanctions, and aftercare.

Probation

The most common community-based sanction is juvenile probation. Approximately 64 percent of adjudicated youth nationwide are placed on probation.[244] **Probation** is the conditional release of youth into the community where they are provided with supervision and treatment. Juvenile probation operates in much the same way as adult probation: youth are assigned to a probation officer who monitors their behavior and requires them to abide by certain conditions that are designed to control and treat their behavior. Key differences include smaller caseload sizes, a stronger focus on individualized treatment of youth, and greater collaboration with schools, families, and other community contexts in which the juvenile lives.

The probation experience can vary from youth to youth. Low-risk youth, or youth who present minimal safety concerns to the public, may be placed under a minimum level of supervision that requires only that they visit with a probation officer periodically to review behavior and progress. For example, a youth might be required to report to his probation officer once a month and submit to random drug testing as a means to monitor his drug use and evaluate his need for treatment. In contrast, higher risk youth, or youth with a high likelihood of recidivism, are required to meet more frequently with their probation officer and participate in various types of intervention programs. Youth who fail to comply with the rules and regulations of probation can be charged with technical violations and returned to juvenile court for contempt. If the youth is found to be in contempt, the judge can continue the youth on probation (perhaps with stricter conditions) or revoke the youth's probation and impose another, more severe sanction.

Because of the variation in probation, both within and across jurisdictions, it is difficult to gauge its effectiveness. Most research suggests that probation is at least as effective at reducing delinquency as is the institutional treatment of youth. Given this, and the lower costs of probation, it remains an appealing correctional option for juvenile courts.

Intermediate Sanctions

In addition to probation, most jurisdictions have a range of **intermediate sanctions** for youth who are high enough risk to require more than probation but not high enough to require out-of-home placement. Their development in juvenile corrections paralleled that which took place in adult corrections throughout the 80s and 90s when the "get tough" movement was at its peak. Common goals for intermediate sanctions in both juvenile and adult corrections include: diverting offenders from long-term institutional settings; saving money; providing judges with sanctioning options that are proportionate to the crime; and enhancing public safety through increased surveillance and control. For juvenile courts, intermediate sanctions are recognized as important sentencing options that enable judges to individualize dispositions to youths' situations. Common types of intermediate sanctions include intensive supervision probation, drug courts, and electronic monitoring, which operate similarly to their adult counterparts (see Chapter 11).

Intensive supervision probation (ISP) is the most common form of intermediate sanction for juveniles. Through intensive monitoring, ISPs are expected to restrain youths' movements within the community, and as a result, limit their opportunity to engage in delinquency. Some programs, like Boston's Operation Night Light and Kentucky's Juvenile Intensive Supervision Teams have developed a police-probation partnership to monitor youth in the community. A handful of studies, and only a few with sufficient methodological rigor, have compared the case outcomes of regular and intensive probation for juveniles; none have found significant differences in the rate of new arrests.[245]

An intermediate sanction that is unique to juvenile justice is the **day treatment center**. Centers vary greatly but most have four things in common: They provide a range of counseling services; focus on the educational needs of youth; are staffed by a combination of educational, counseling, and court personnel; and are designed to serve high-risk youth who struggle in the mainstream educational environment. Some day treatment centers operate as alternative schools where youth get counseling services during the school day. Others operate as a one-stop shop where youth, who attend a public school, come afterward for counseling and supplemental educational services. There is no research regarding the effectiveness of day treatment centers.

Aftercare

The period of transition from a highly structured institutional program back to the community is characterized as disorienting, alienating, and stressful. The process for youth is doubly challenging as they experience the dual transition from confinement to community and from adolescence to adulthood.[246] A period of incarceration often exacerbates existing structural disadvantages by straining social bonds to family members and interrupting the youths' educational trajectories. The high rate of recidivism following confinement has been explained by the system's failure to address these structural conditions.[247]

Aftercare is the juvenile justice version of parole. Effective aftercare begins as the youth enters the institution and involves formal (e.g., juvenile court; schools) and informal (e.g., family, neighbors) networks in pre-release planning and post-release supervision.[248] It stands in contrast to traditional practices that compartmentalize agencies' work with juvenile offenders, and, instead, promotes interagency collaboration among all of the agencies that work with youth. It also promotes continuity of care, building on behavioral and skill gains made in the institution. A case management approach is used to refer youth to a range of services in the community (e.g., substance abuse treatment, mental health counseling, family counseling) and to monitor youths' progress during the transition period. Research suggests that the provision of high-quality aftercare is associated with reduced rates of recidivism.[249]

What Works to Reduce Delinquency?

What types of interventions are most effective at curbing delinquency? There is no easy answer and no "magic bullet." Since the 1980s, however, a group of researchers has worked to identify programmatic factors associated with positive outcomes for youth. The remainder of this chapter provides an overview of key principles of effective intervention followed by a description of specific types of programs that are associated with lower rates of recidivism among delinquent youth.

Principles of Effective Intervention

Through the systematic review and synthesis of available studies, several principles of effective correctional intervention have been identified.[250] Programs that follow these principles have reduced recidivism by as much as 40 percent.

The **risk principle** instructs agencies to match youth to program intensity and duration based on their level of risk for recidivism.[251] This requires agencies to use a **risk assessment** system to sort youth into high-, medium-, or low-risk groups. The higher the risk, then, the more intensive treatment and sanctions a youth would receive. Research suggests that programs achieve better outcomes when they target high-risk youth for participation.[252] Moreover, there is evidence to suggest that over treating low-risk youth can actually increase their likelihood of recidivism by exposing them to higher risk youth and by interfering with any positive social bonds they may have.[253]

The **needs principle** suggests that programs should spend the bulk of their time on interventions that target specific criminogenic needs of youth. **Criminogenic needs** are dynamic factors associated with delinquent behavior. Criminogenic risk factors were discussed in Chapter 2 and are applicable to both adults and juveniles. The most common and strongest criminogenic needs are antisocial personality, antisocial peers, and antisocial attitudes.[254] Other criminogenic needs include substance abuse, low educational achievement, low family affection, and poor disciplinary practices. Given our knowledge about these risk factors, it makes sense to invest in services designed to enhance the supervision and discipline within a family, increase school performance, and teach the skills needed to deal with peer pressure. It is also important, however, that we use **needs assessments** to discover the factors that underlie each youth's behaviors, and develop individualized case plans for addressing those needs. Failing to match proper services with criminogenic needs impedes a program's ability to decrease recidivism.[255]

The **responsivity principle** refers to the way in which youth respond to various correctional staff and programs and includes two components. **General responsivity** suggests that youth involved in the juvenile justice system respond best to interventions that are based in cognitive-behavior/social learning theories.[256] These types of interventions help youth identify the thoughts, beliefs, and values that contribute to their antisocial behavior, and teach them how to replace them with more healthy, prosocial thoughts, beliefs, and values. They also teach youth interpersonal and coping skills that are needed to engage in prosocial behaviors (e.g., responding to peer pressure, anger management). Skill development is accomplished through the use of modeling techniques and positive reinforcement. **Modeling** involves skill demonstration by the treatment provider followed by role playing that provides the youth with a chance to practice the skill. **Positive reinforcement** is essential for encouraging youth to develop and maintain positive behaviors. A basic tenet of human behavior is that we behave in ways that bring us the most benefits. The difficulty in juvenile corrections is finding benefits for youth that outweigh the thrill of adventure and other benefits that risky behavior can sometimes provide. The types of reinforcements used in correctional programming may include verbal praise, an extra privilege, or some type of tangible reward like a snack or a new game.

Specific responsivity refers to the removal of barriers that may interfere with a youth's treatment.[257] This could be as simple as ensuring that the youth has transportation to treatment or as complex as addressing his/her mental health needs. Regarding the latter, for example, it may be necessary to address a youth's depression prior to expecting him/her to be successful in substance abuse counseling or educational programming. Specific responsivity also refers to matching youth to staff and programs based on their learning and communication styles. For example, shy youth may not respond well to a probation officer with a loud, confrontational approach, and youth with intellectual deficits may not respond well to a highly verbal probation officer.

Critical Thinking 13.6 Gender-Responsive Programming

The pathways to delinquency are different for boys and girls.[258] Male offending is more often associated with positively valued features of masculinity such as aggression, risk-taking, and economic independence. Female offending is frequently prompted by relational conflict with family and friends. Other differences include girls' higher rates of sexual abuse and mental health disorders, both of which lead to illicit drug use and delinquency. In recognition of these and other key differences, juvenile justice agencies are beginning to provide girls with **gender-responsive programming** that addresses their unique needs. For example, effective girls' programming is rooted in the **relational model** that focuses on helping girls heal damaged relationships and providing the opportunity to develop healthy relationships with prosocial others.

What are some other differences between boys and girls that might affect their responses to juvenile justice staff and programs?

Finally, the **fidelity principle** suggests that programs delivered with fidelity to the model, can significantly reduce recidivism rates.[259] For example, a program called

Aggression Replacement Training (ART) uses very specific content and processes to help youth manage their anger. Research revealed that when the model was closely followed, the results were a 24 percent decrease in the recidivism of participants. When the program wasn't implemented with fidelity, however, the results were a seven percent increase in recidivism. Promoting program fidelity involves intensive staff training and coaching along with quality assurance measures for holding staff accountable to the model.

These four principles apply to both institutional and community based programs. Adherence to the risk, need, and responsivity principles has been found to produce significant reductions in recidivism. One study found that programs that did not adhere to any of the principles actually produced a slight increase in recidivism.[260] Programs that adhered to all three principles produced, on average, recidivism reductions of 28 percent.

Evidence-Based Programs

Funding in the juvenile justice system is often tied to the use of **evidence-based programs**, or programs that have been shown, through repeated outcome evaluations, to effectively reduce recidivism. Systematic reviews of available outcome evaluations have identified a range of programs as evidence-based, including cognitive behavioral interventions previously described. Several others are described below.

Family-Based Interventions

Research demonstrates that programs are significantly more effective when they involve the family in the youth's intervention.[261] There are three types of family interventions, in particular, that have produced significant reductions in recidivism. The first of these is **multidimensional treatment foster care (MTFC)**.[262] MTFC is designed as an alternative to residential placement for youth ages 12–17 who have problems with chronic antisocial behavior, emotional disturbance, and delinquency. Youth are placed in a family setting with specially trained foster parents for six to nine months. The foster parents provide a closely supervised, structured, and supportive environment for the youth. They monitor and reinforce the youth's participation in skills training, school-based behavioral interventions, and psychiatric consultation for medication management when necessary.

The birth families of youth in MTFC receive parent training on how to provide consistent discipline, supervise and provide encouragement to youth, and use a behavior management system to encourage prosocial behaviors. Therapy provided to parents is designed to prepare parents for their child's return home, reduce conflict, and increase positive relationships in the family. All interventions are monitored through weekly meetings of a treatment team that includes a program supervisor, a family therapist, an individual therapist, a child skills trainer, and a daily telephone contact person. Post-treatment comparisons of youth in group care and youth in MTFC revealed that boys and girls in MTFC had lower rates of official delinquency and fewer days in a locked settings.[263] Additionally, boys in MTFC were more likely to complete the treatment program and less likely to run away from placement.

The second family-based intervention found to be effective in reducing delinquency is called **functional family therapy (FFT)**.[264] FFT is designed for high-risk youth ages 11–18 and aims to address familial risk and protective factors. FFT involves weekly one-hour sessions with clinically trained therapists in an outpatient setting over a three-month period. The therapy moves through four key phases. First, is the engagement phase which focuses on establishing rapport with the youth and his/her family. Second, is the motivational phase during which therapists focus on reducing the negativity and conflict within the family and analyzing family processes such as interaction patterns, sources of resistance, and resources. Third, is the behavioral change stage which involves skills training in family communication, parenting, problem-solving and conflict management. The fourth and final stage is the generalization stage that aims to provide families with the capacity to sustain changes made in therapy and to access community resources when needed to prevent relapse to earlier familial patterns. A large-scale evaluation demonstrated that when delivered with high adherence to the model FFT was associated with significant reductions in felony and violent crimes.[265] The evaluation also revealed that FFT was most effective with the highest risk youth.

The third type of family intervention is **multi-systemic therapy** (MST).[266] MST is designed for youth ages 12 to 17 who are presenting with serious antisocial behaviors, including delinquency. The primary goal of MST is to keep these youth at home and in school. MST accomplishes this through a home-based model of intensive intervention. Therapists have small caseloads of four to six families and are available 24 hours, seven days a week. They meet with families anywhere from once a day to once a week depending on the family's needs. MST therapists concentrate on improving parent effectiveness by identifying strengths and developing support systems in the community. They also focus on removing barriers to positive family functioning such as parental substance abuse and poor relationships between partners. Studies have found that youth in MST had significantly lower rates of recidivism than youth participating in individual treatment or no treatment, and that families in MST demonstrated greater family cohesion post-treatment.[267] Another study reported lower rates of arrest for youth in MST along with improvements in school and work, family relationships, and moods and emotions.[268]

Aggression Replacement Training

Aggression Replacement Training (ART) is a group-based therapy designed to reduce youths' aggressive and violent behavior by teaching them prosocial skills for managing their anger.[269] ART is a 10-week program delivered to 8–12 youth in one-hour sessions, three times per week. It includes three interrelated components, including structured learning training, anger control training, and moral reasoning. The structured learning training engages youth in direct instruction and role playing that teaches youth prosocial responses to difficult situations such as responding to failure, dealing with an accusation, and responding to the feelings of others. The anger control training focuses on helping youth identify triggers for their aggressive behavior and teaches them techniques for controlling their angry impulses. The moral reasoning component of ART exposes youth to moral dilemmas, giving them an opportunity to problem solve and gain a better understanding of how their behavior impacts others. One study found that when delivered with fidelity ART resulted in a 24 percent reduction in recidivism as compared to a control group of youth.[270] Another study found that ART participants had improved social skills and reduced rates of problem behaviors at school and home.[271]

Restorative Justice for Low-Risk Offenders

Restorative justice is more of a philosophy than a program. It differs from retributive justice in a few key ways. First, it focuses on the restoration of victims, offenders, and communities injured by crime rather than mere punishment of the offender. Second, it integrates victims, offenders, and communities more fully into the justice process. In retributive and utilitarian justice, the government takes responsibility for punishing an offender. This is done in isolation from the community. In restorative justice, community input and support is sought. It's more of a grassroots approach to resolving problems of crime.

Following is a brief description of specific programs and practices that support the restorative justice philosophy:

- **Victim restitution**: requires youth to pay victims for damages and other losses incurred as the result of the crime.
- **Community service**: youth are required to provide free labor to a public or nonprofit agency in the community as payback for the consequences of the crime committed.
- **Victim-offender mediation**: victims and offenders participate in a meeting, mediated by a trained facilitator, to discuss reasons for the crime, consequences of the crime, and possible avenues for restoring the victim to his/her pre-crime state.
- **Sentencing circles**: uses a traditional circle ritual and structure rooted in Native American tradition to involve interested community members in the resolution of the crime. Common participants include the victim and his/her supporters, the offender and his/her supporters, the judge and other court personnel, and police. Within the circle, people take turns sharing their feelings about the crime and work together to develop a plan for healing all affected parties and preventing future crimes.
- **Family group conferencing**: The victim and the offender, and the family, friends, and key supporters of both, are brought together with a trained facilitator to discuss how they have been harmed by the offense and how the harm might be repaired.[272]

Youth are sometimes referred to a restorative justice program as a stand-alone sanction or diversionary option. Other times, they are required to participate in the program as a condition of probation. Either way, program placement is contingent on the youth admitting their involvement in the offense and agreeing to participate. A review of 21 restorative justice programs, primarily victim-offender mediation and family group conferencing programs, demonstrated that they are effective in reducing the recidivism of low-risk offenders.[273] The programs have also been found to contribute to greater victim satisfaction. The effectiveness of restorative justice programs has not been tested on higher risk offenders.

Summary

The way we respond to delinquency in the United States has come a long way. What was once an informal, loosely defined system of privately run programs has grown into a large, formal, government-run operation. The juvenile court, the cornerstone of the juvenile justice system, has shifted from a purely rehabilitative focus to a more balanced emphasis on rehabilitation and accountability, and its processes have become more formal with the introduction of due process rights. Given these changes, that bring juvenile court more in line with adult court, some question whether we still need a separate juvenile court. The fact remains, however, that juveniles are different—they lack the maturity and culpability of adult offenders and should, therefore, be afforded the opportunity for reformation within a context that can better address their needs.

Recent decisions about the death penalty and life without parole, and policies regarding the deinstitutionalization of status offenders, are reversing the trend toward punitive policies observed in the 1980s and 90s. Professionals are working to bring juvenile justice back to what its founders intended—a system that acted in the best interests of youth. There is still plenty of work to be done. Police, corrections professionals, and judges need to recognize the vulnerability of adolescence and make decisions that provide youth with the best chance for transitioning to a safe and productive adult life.

The next chapter will focus on the future of the criminal justice system. Dismal fiscal realities may continue to slow the growth of the prison empire in the United States, but we do know that the multi-faceted purposes of punishment and prisons will continue to impact prisoners throughout the twenty-first century. Technological advances can be for good or ill. Terrorism will continue to be a primary concern of our country. Constructive ways of addressing immigration will still need to be explored. Innovative and evidence-based alternatives to incarceration are needed, especially for persons with mental illnesses who encounter the criminal justice system. To successfully navigate the future of the criminal justice system, the stress inducing aspects of criminal justice organizations and the stress levels of criminal justice professionals need to be kept in check.

Chapter 14

Future Issues and Trends in Criminal Justice

Image courtesy of the Library of Congress.

"Having information about the future can have disastrous consequences. Even if your intentions are good, it can backfire drastically."[1]

Seeking Justice

This experiment called America has lasted for well over two hundred years. Our history has been marred with wars, incivilities, and institutionalized racism. Yet, through all of it, our nation has endured. Military conflicts continue, and, while race relations have improved, there is still much work to be done. Ours is a legacy of periods of unrest coupled with great accomplishments. At times "political correctness" appears to rule the day, but this can be fleeting—changing seemingly as easily as one political administration transitions out and another in. While we cannot change our history, hopefully we can learn from it as we look to the future. However, just because we can see into the future, does not mean that our outcomes will be positive. We may be able to admire the problem, but will we be able to devise workable solutions or just make things worse?

Image by Tomasz Trojanowski at fotolia.com.

About This Chapter

Crises will likely continue to drive future policy in criminal justice. Whether crisis driven or not, there is a need for more collaboration and cooperation within and across organizations in combating crime and social problems for the future. Terrorism, immigration, the criminalization of mental illness, and the massive fiscal empire that is criminal justice will greatly influence the future.

Criminal justice does not operate within a vacuum. Our Founding Fathers could not have imagined the technologically advanced society we now live in with the Internet, personal computers, self-driving cars, cellular phones, DNA analysis, drones, Amazon's Echo/Alexa, and social media (Facebook, Twitter, Periscope). Of course, some of these innovations can be used for good or ill. Work within criminal justice, while often portrayed as action-packed and even glamorous in one-hour edited television dramas, is often monotonous, boring, and stressful. We constantly seek approaches to improve justice. The future presents new challenges to criminal justice. Some are not so much in the future as the present, such as terrorism, immigration, criminal justice practitioner stress, technological advances, the criminalization of mental illness, the use of evidence based practices, and fiscal constraints on the justice system.

Terrorism

Edith Flynn wrote, "The scourge of international and national terrorism will continue to challenge the United States well into the twenty-first century. It represents a unique, pervasive, and costly challenge to this country's ideals, principles and safety. The full dimensions of its threats have yet to be recognized by this nation."[2]

Image courtesy of the Library of Congress.

That statement, written by Flynn in 1996, proved to be quite prophetic on September 11, 2001. Just because we can predict the future, we cannot necessarily change it. As we discussed in Chapter 1, the tragic 9/11 attacks led to the establishment of the Department of Homeland Security. Several terrorists or enemy combatants[3] have been brought to justice. Included among them are John Walker Lindh (the so-called American Taliban, who received a 20-year sentence and asked for a reduced sentence),[4] Richard Reid (also known as the shoe bomber, who was sentenced to life),[5] and Zacarias Moussaoui (who received a life sentence and, although he was in jail at the time of the 9/11 attacks, he is reportedly the only person that has been charged in a U.S. courtroom for the attacks).[6] President Bush transferred Jose Padilla from military custody, and he was successfully prosecuted in civilian, criminal court. He received 17 years and 4 months in prison for being a member of a cell to support violent jihad campaigns in Afghanistan and elsewhere. Legal debates have focused on the significance of this designation in that an enemy combatant is not considered a lawful combatant and therefore does not have the full rights of a prisoner of war extended to him by the Geneva Convention.

Reactions by the United States to the events on 9/11 and terrorism have also led to several important U.S. Supreme Court cases. The Court held in *Rasul v. Bush* (2004) that the right to *habeas corpus* and access to relief in U.S. civil courts extends to "all ... dominions under the sovereign's control,"[7] including the foreign nationals at Guantanamo Bay, Cuba. Also, in *Hamdi v. Rumsfeld* (2004), the U.S. Supreme Court ruled that due process requires that a U.S. citizen who is detained in the United States as an enemy combatant should be allowed to have the factual basis for his detainment brought and considered before a neutral decision-maker.[8] More recently, the U.S. Supreme Court decided *Holder v. Humanitarian Law Project* (2010)[9] in which the Court determined that all types of aid, including advice and training on peaceful and legal activities, to designated terrorist groups may be denied by the government without violating free association and speech rights.[10]

Much of the War on Terror is being waged internationally. However, law enforcement officers in cities, towns, and hamlets throughout America are also affected. Many American police departments have sought and received money to "fight terrorism," although no apparent basis for believing terrorists will likely attack their jurisdictions exists. But federal money for any reason is not usually rejected by local criminal justice agencies.

In terms of terrorism on American soil, then "President Obama declared that '[n]o foreign terrorist organization has successfully planned and executed an attack on our homeland.... The attempt to disconnect 'lone wolf' terrorists from the terror organizations who often inspire them does nothing to alleviate the pain [caused by them;] the reality is that..., scores of innocent Americans have been murdered on U.S. soil by jihadists, most of whom were inspired by or acting under the direction of foreign terror groups, particularly the Islamic state." (A list of such acts since President Obama took office in 2009 includes the following).

> ***Little Rock**, Arkansas, June 1, 2009. Abdulhakim Mujahid Muhammad shot and murdered one soldier, Army Pvt. William Andrew Long, and injured another, Pvt. Quinton Ezeagwula, at a military recruiting station in Little Rock. Muhammad reportedly converted to Islam in college and was on the FBI's radar after being arrested in Yemen—a hotbed of radical Islamic terrorism—for using a Somali passport, even though he was a U.S. citizen. In a note to an Arkansas judge, Muhammad claimed to be a member of al-Qaeda in the Arab Peninsula, the terror group's Yemen chapter.*
>
> ***Fort Hood**, Texas, November 5, 2009. Major Nidal Malik Hasan shot up a military base in Fort Hood and murdered 14 people. Hasan was in contact with al-Qaeda terrorist Anwar al-Awlaki prior to the attack and shouted "Allahu Akbar!" as he fired upon the soldiers on the Fort Hood base. After being sentenced to death, Hasan requested to join ISIS while on death row. It took six years for President Obama to acknowledge the shooting as a terror attack instead of "workplace violence."*
>
> ***Boston**, Massachusetts, April 15, 2013. Tamerlan and Dzhokhar Tsarnaev set off two bombs at the 2013 Boston Marathon, killing three and injuring over 260 people. The Tsarnaev brothers later shot and murdered Massachusetts Institute of Technology police officer Sean Collier. The Tsarnaev brothers were self-radicalized through online jihadist propaganda and through a mosque with ties to al-Qaeda.*
>
> ***Moore**, Oklahoma, September 24, 2014. Alton Nolen beheaded a woman, Colleen Huff, at a Vaughan Foods plant and stabbed and injured another person. While Nolen's motives are unclear, he appears to have been another radicalized Muslim who was obsessed with beheadings.*
>
> ***Queens**, New York, October 23, 2014. Zale Thompson, another self-radicalized Muslim, injured two police officers with a hatchet before being shot dead by other cops. Thompson reportedly indoctrinated himself with ISIS, al-Qaeda, and al-Shabab—a Somali jihadist terror group—websites and was a lone wolf attacker.*
>
> ***Brooklyn**, New York, December 20, 2014. Ismaayil Brinsley shot and murdered two police officers execution-style and his Facebook page featured jihadist postings and had ties to a terror-linked mosque.*

***Garland**, Texas, May 3, 2015. Two gunmen shot up the Curtis Culwell Center in Garland, where a Mohammed cartoon contest was taking place, and were killed by a police officer. ISIS claimed responsibility for the attack.*

***Chattanooga**, Tennessee, July 16, 2015. Muhammad Youssef Abdulazeez shot and killed four Marines and a sailor at a military base in Chattanooga and was believed to have been inspired by ISIS.*

***San Bernardino**, California, December 14, 2015. Two radical Islamists, Syed Farook and Tashfeen Malik, shot and murdered 14 people and injured 22 others at an office holiday party.* (To be further discussed by Gary Cox in Field Practice 14.1.)

***Orlando**, Florida, June 12, 2016.* As discussed in Chapter 2, *Omar Mateen, 29, opened fire at a gay nightclub, killing 49 and injuring 53. The FBI investigated Mateen twice before his rampage, but did not take any substantive action. Officials believe Mateen was self-radicalized but he pledged fealty to ISIS leader Abu Bakr al-Baghdadi before his death. "The real muslims will never accept the filthy ways of the west," Mateen posted on his Facebook page after committing his heinous act at Pulse nightclub. "I pledge my alliance to (ISIS leader) Abu Bakr al Baghdadi ... may Allah accept me," he wrote.*

***St. Cloud**, Minnesota, September 17, 2016. Dahir Ahmed Adan, a 20-year-old Somali refugee, began hacking at people with a steak knife at a Minnesota mall, injuring nine people before he was shot dead by off-duty police officer Jason Falconer. The FBI said numerous witnesses heard Adan yelling "Allahu akbar!" and "Islam! Islam!" during the rampage. He also asked potential victims if they were Muslims before inflicting wounds in their heads, necks, and chests. The FBI believe he had recently become self-radicalized. (As the* Daily Wire *highlighted, the* Minneapolis Star Tribune *attempted to blame "anti-Muslim tensions" for his murderous actions.)*

***New York City/New Jersey**, September 17, 2016. Ahmad Khan Rahami, a 28-year-old naturalized citizen from Afghanistan, set off multiple bombs in New York and New Jersey. In Chelsea, his bomb resulted in the injury of over 30 people. Rahami wrote in his journal that he was connected to "terrorist leaders," and appears to have been heavily influenced by Sheikh Anwar, Anwar al-Awlaki, Nidal Hassan, and Osama bin Laden. "I pray to the beautiful wise ALLAH, [d]o not take JIHAD away from me," Rahami wrote. "You [USA Government] continue your [unintelligible] slaught[er]" against the holy warriors, "be it Afghanistan, Iraq, Sham [Syria], Palestine."*

***Columbus**, Ohio, November 28, 2016. Abdul Razak Ali Artan, an ISIS-inspired 20-year-old Somali refugee who had been granted permanent legal residence in 2014 after living in Pakistan for 7 years, attempted to run over his fellow Ohio State students on campus. After his car was stopped by a barrier, he got out of the vehicle and began hacking at people with a butcher knife before being shot dead by a campus police officer. He injured 11 people, one critically. ISIS took*

Image by Allkindza at istockphoto.com.

credit for the attack, describing Artan as their "soldier." Just three minutes before his rampage, Artan posted a warning to America on Facebook that the "lone wolf attacks" will continue until America "give[s] peace to the Muslims." He also praised deceased al-Qaeda cleric Anwar Al-Awlaki as a 'hero.'"[11]

Professor Gary Cox, formerly of the West Jordan Police Department in Utah, describes how interagency cooperation, communication, and lessening of "turf wars" have resulted from Homeland Security. He also acknowledges the difficulty for authorities to become aware of self-radicalized terrorists. See **Field Practice 14.1.**

Field Practice 14.1 Impact of Terrorism on Local Law Enforcement

Prior to the terrorist events of September 11, 2001, the levels of law enforcement in the United States were, for the most part, very separate and distinct in their missions and activities. A few multi-agency task forces were the exception—i.e., DEA/Metro Narcotics Task Forces blending local, state, and federal law enforcement officers in an effort to combat illegal drug trafficking. More typical, however, were the "turf wars" between the government levels.

The attacks on the World Trade Center and the Pentagon brought to light the need for intergovernmental/inter-agency planning, collaboration, cooperation, and communication. While the statutory responsibility of investigating terrorist events falls squarely on the shoulders of the FBI, we learned the hard way that local law enforcement is still the first to respond, remains throughout the investigation, and is left to clean up when everyone else has gone home.

Significant changes made at the federal level had a direct and immediate impact on local and state police. The U.S. Department of Homeland Security (DHS) brought a wide variety of federal agencies under one umbrella of leadership. DHS also provided training and grant funding to state and local police to help them identify critical infrastructure sites in their jurisdictions, conduct threat assessments on those assets, and protect them. Community-Oriented Policing strategies of some departments were improved since a significant number of the critical infrastructure sites are privately owned, such as, oil refineries, major food suppliers, and communications company facilities/equipment. Local police were required to get out of their patrol cars and develop working relationships with those business owners. They identified potential weaknesses of important facilities and improved disaster response training along with emergency services.

Federal agencies made significant changes in how they work with local police—not taking over or controlling, but providing support and resources to programs and investigations that would otherwise struggle. The FBI's cooperation with and support of regional child abduction response teams (CART) and gang enforcement efforts have significantly enhanced those efforts. The U.S. Marshal's Office helps coordinate with local officers in Joint Criminal Apprehension Teams (JCAT) to multiply the labors of locating and bringing to justice those who have fled to avoid prosecution. The vast resources of the federal agencies have become more accessible to local officers, enhancing their ability to successfully fulfill their responsibilities without having the case "pulled out from under them" by the feds.

Regional Joint Terrorism Task Forces (JTTF) and "fusion centers," much like multi-agency task forces, caused federal agencies to find ways to open files to local police without compromising security. Local police began sharing the information they got from the cop on the beat with the state and federal agencies.

Local law enforcement found itself spending more time and resources on homeland security tasks—like preventative patrols, security for special events and dignitaries, and critical infrastructures. All of this has resulted in a very effective prevention of terrorist events within the borders of the United States of America.

The Al Qaeda attacks on September 11, 2001, did create some additional and continuing problems for American police. The backlash of assaults and other hate crimes against people of Middle Eastern descent has put law enforcement in a challenging position. They have to both protect the victims and investigate/prosecute people who see themselves as patriots acting in the interest of our country. A significant spike in these kinds of hate crimes occurred during the last year of the 2016 presidential election campaign.

During the years since the 9/11 attacks, the USA Patriot Act allowed federal agencies, particularly the FBI, to develop robust capabilities to intercept communications between terrorist organizations and potential recruits or between the members of these organizations as they planned attacks. There is a long list of successful law enforcement interventions that foiled or prevented attacks from being carried out. This interference caused the enemy to change their strategies. The Islamic State began calling on its supporters located throughout the world to take the initiative to carry out their own attacks. Walter Purdy, president of the Terrorism Research Center, testified in a congressional hearing that, "anybody with a smart phone or a computer can become radicalized online."[12] As the technology changes, intelligence-gathering agencies also try to adjust in order to keep up, but these efforts are often hampered by civil liberties concerns.

The internet and social media have played a significant role in the recruiting and radicalization of Americans and legal residents in the country.[13] This technology has allowed vulnerable or like-minded people to make easier connections to recruiters, here and abroad, who can lavish attention on potential recruits and nurture the radicalization process. This applies not only to foreign terrorist organizations like ISIS/ISIL, but to anti-government extremists, neo-Nazi/white supremacists, Black Lives Matter, eco-terrorists, animal rights, Pro-life (anti-abortion), and other groups willing to encourage or conduct illegal, violent acts in an attempt to further their cause. Most of these groups are active on Facebook, Twitter, Instagram, YouTube, and other Internet communication platforms, which local police simply do not have the resources (or legal authorization) to monitor. Such use of social media was, for example, utilized to promote and gather participants for protests concerning the removal of a Confederate monument in Charlottesville, Virginia recently.[14]

Some individuals, like the couple in San Bernardino, California (Syed Rizwan Farook and his wife, Tashfeen Malik), stay undetected because they don't use the regular communication systems at all. While Malik and Farook had no collaboration with a larger terrorist organization via the internet (emails, Skype, etc.) or telephone conversations (including text messaging) for the intelligence agencies to intercept, they were radicalized after "consuming poison on the Internet," according to the director of the FBI, James B. Comey.[15] In planning their attack, they only spoke face-to-face with Enrique Marquez Jr., who supplied them with two rifles.[16] Similar examples are found with the Orlando nightclub mass shooting and other lone wolf attacks in the U.S. and around the world.

The transition from planning and perpetrating major events like the attack on the World Trade Center to smaller, more local attacks done by self-radicalized individuals, has created a challenge for law enforcement at all levels. The need to work together, across federal, state, and local lines, has never been greater. Police must focus their attentions now on not only the threatening terrorist organizations, but also on the radicalization of individuals who, in many cases, have been "model citizens" and do not fit the mold of the "typical" terrorist.

Recent research results from the University of Maryland has offered what they call "the ingredients of the universal process that governs radicalization." The process of radicalization, according to Professor Arie Kruglanski, who directed the research, includes three identifiable components, which he calls "the three Ns of radicalization."

> The first N is the individuals' need; this is the motivation that propels them in the direction of extremism. That need is the quest for personal significance, the overpowering desire to matter, to have respect in one's own eyes and those of others. The second N is the ideological narrative that identifies the road to significance; in the case of violent extremism that road, promised to bring individuals significance and glory, is violence against an enemy said to perpetrate crimes against one's group (ethnicity, religion, nationality). The third N is the social network that validates the ideological narrative and rewards individuals (by status and esteem) for implementing the ideological injunctions.[17]

Identifying these new threats before they commit a violent act is still difficult, at best,[18] and local law enforcement is in the better position to find these people—but only with the combined resources that can only come from redeveloping and nurturing close relationships with the communities they serve and the support of the federal intelligence-gathering agencies. The renewal of the "If You See Something, Say Something" campaign is an example of police agencies' efforts to encourage the necessary communication between observant citizens and their law enforcement partners. This relationship requires trust—the kind of trust Community-Oriented Policing efforts developed between police officers and the businesses, communities, and individuals they serve. Sharing the gleaned information through the fusion centers and federal agencies ensures the disbursement of intelligence to a broader audience of "boots on the ground" who can use it in their local prevention efforts.[19]

All of these changes have added to the growing burdens of local law enforcement administrators who are already overwhelmed with meeting the expectations of their communities through increased calls for service. Fortunately, violent crime rates have been on the decline in most parts of the country. However, the work to prevent terrorist attacks is more than making up for the crime reduction. Prevention necessarily requires proactive efforts which identify predictable patterns of behavior. Police are generally able to gather that kind of intelligence only through the confidential, informal sharing of information from people who trust that the agency will do something about it. And law enforcement needs to reinforce that trust by taking action that will either support the suspicion or find that it was a "false alarm." That all takes time and resources, but most of all, it takes commitment and communication between all levels of the law enforcement community.[20] **What information is contained within Fusion Centers? Should there be a distinction between terrorist acts perpetrated by those who are self-radicalized and those acts undertaken by foreign terrorist groups on American soil?**

Throughout the book we discuss the importance of maintaining a crucial balance between protecting public safety and respecting civil liberties. A pivotal issue in law enforcement today is, how much regulation does law enforcement need? Protections of civil liberties sometimes decrease as crime rates increase, and the U.S. Supreme Court seems to be in the middle of a post-9/11 easing of constitutional protections. This can be seen, for example, with the issue of police use of force discussed in Chapter 6,[21] enhanced interrogation techniques, potential erosion of *Miranda* with terrorist suspects,[22] and search and seizure practices.

Some believe Americans are less free. Country music legend Merle Haggard, who served time in San Quentin Prison at the age of 21, has observed,[23] "In 1960, when I came out of prison as an ex-convict, I had more freedom under parolee supervision than there's available ... in America right now."[24] These competing interests of public safety and individual freedoms which are ingrained in the American way of life will continue to vie for recognition in the future.

Immigration Law Enforcement

"Give me your tired, your poor,
Your huddled masses yearning to breathe free,
The wretched refuse of your teeming shore.
Send these, the homeless, tempest-tost to me,
I lift my lamp beside the golden door!"[25]

—Statue of Liberty inscription

As U.S. Senator Barbara Mikulski has said, "America is not a melting pot, it is a sizzling cauldron."[26]

Immigration

It is estimated that there are at least 11.1 million unauthorized immigrants in the United States, which constitutes approximately 3.5% of the nation's population. It is estimated that Mexicans comprise 52% of these unauthorized immigrants. Fifty-nine percent of all these unauthorized immigrants are said to reside in six states—

Image by Graffix at istockphoto.com.

California, Texas, Florida, New York, New Jersey, and Illinois; about 66% of all unauthorized immigrants in America have resided here for at least a decade.[27] Immigration policy and enforcement is the responsibility of the federal government. But some jurisdictions, such as the state of Arizona, have sought to bring local agencies into immigration enforcement. Many criminal justice agencies prefer not to have immigration enforcement added to their responsibilities. As we have previously indicated, communities typically get the type of law enforcement that they want. Many rural and agrarian counties need and capitalize on cheap migrant labor to harvest their crops and make a profit. Some of those workers may be undocumented, either living temporarily in America to earn money to send to their impoverished families abroad or as long-term residents who have families and a deeper stake in the American culture. Frankly, without these workers, there might not be enough laborers, and if citizens could be found to do the work, they would demand to be paid a higher wage than illegal immigrants, which could undermine business profits. Even so, "[i]n the 105 years between 1892 and 1997, the U.S. deported 2.1 million people—meaning that under presidents [George W.] Bush and [Barack] Obama, the number of people deported by the U.S. in the course of a century was more than doubled [over 4.5 million] in just 16 years of consecutive presidencies."[28]

Immigration arrests spiked in the first few months of President Trump's administration. *The Washington Post* reported ... that U.S. Immigration and Customs Enforcement (ICE) officials arrested 21,362 immigrants from January to mid-March, up 32.6 percent from the same time last year. In 2016, ICE arrested 16,104 immigrants. The *Post* reported that 29,238 immigrants were arrested in the same time period in 2014, and 18,031 were arrested in 2015. Nearly three-quarters of the arrested immigrants had criminal convictions, according to the report. But the biggest increase was in arrests of immigrants without criminal records. While President Trump mentioned in his first address to Congress the establishment of an office of Victims of Immigration Crime Enforcement (VOICE), ICE arrests of immigrants with no criminal records more than doubled at the start of Trump's term to 5,441.[29] Twenty-seven victim assistance specialists and 21 community relations officers are slated to be assigned to VOICE to keep victims in the U.S. harmed by undocumented immigrants apprised of their criminal processing and potential deportation. Critics maintain that

Image by chapin31 of istockphoto.com.

there are lower levels of crime among immigrants in this country than native-born Americans.[30]

Meanwhile, Texas saw the largest increase in the number of immigrants detained in the month of February recently on record. A 57% increase in jailed inmates from 2,989 to 4,684 occurred; more are expected based on campaign promises from President Trump.[31] ICE is said to be reopening private prisons (an industry supportive of Donald Trump's election) and adding beds at county jails to expand deportation machinery.[32]

Attorney General Jeff Sessions has announced that more immigration judges will be hired to combat backlogs in immigration courts. Twenty-five judges were put in place at border detention centers, and the plan is to place 50 more judges by the end of the year and 75 more the following year to expedite the deportation process.[33]

Sheriffs, who are typically responsible for enforcing the law in the rural, agrarian parts of counties, are elected. They must strive to accommodate their constituents, particularly the ones who may be major campaign contributors. Large-scale farmers in citrus, fruit, vegetables, and the like operate in a time-sensitive industry. When the crops are ready for harvest, they must be harvested lest they rot in the fields. Laborers are needed without a lot of employment screening or interviews. Farmers do not wish to have their work force tampered with, and they do not covet the responsibility of investigating the immigration status of workers. Costs go up and profit goes down. This loss would impact the overall economy of the county and limit their ability to do good works in the community. The understaffed federal law enforcement agencies are unable to totally stem the tide of undocumented workers, so if a more robust enforcement is sought, pressure falls to local sheriffs.

Image by vichinterlang at istockphoto.com.

Immigration law violations are either civil or criminal in nature. Examples of civil violations include being illegally present in America or failing to depart the country when their visa expires or student status changes. They are subject to civil deportation proceedings. Criminal immigrants would include those entering the United States illegally, coming back into the U.S. after deportation, or purposefully refusing to leave the U.S. after a deportation order. Local police and sheriffs' agencies, already under pressure to provide traditional law enforcement services, usually are not eager to add the investigation, arrest, and incarceration of immigration law violators, either civil or criminal, to their workload. But pressure from some state governors or legislatures, such as Arizona's, or from federal Department of Homeland Security sources, is felt.

Another area of concern under the Trump administration concerns the Deferred Action for Childhood Arrivals (DACA), also known as Dreamers. This involves undocumented immigrants brought to this country as children. There are an estimated 800,000 of these individuals. At present, the Trump Administration has deferred to the Congress to resolve this issue.[34] Surely, whatever decision is reached, it is liable to be litigated in the courts.

Some jurisdictions have established **sanctuary cities**, where state and/or local law enforcement officials are not required to check the immigration status of people they arrest. In some instances, they wait until a person is convicted of a crime before notifying U.S. Immigration and Customs Enforcement (ICE) agents, part of the Department of Homeland Security. This has been described as a "don't ask, don't tell" stance toward the immigration status of residents.[35] Sanctuary cities have been described as a misnomer, because it is maintained that in many instances it would be more appropriate to refer to sanctuary counties, as it is estimated that there are approximately 600 sanctuary counties in America that don't fully cooperate with federal immigration officials—often ignoring immigration detainers.[36] President Trump has threatened to withhold federal funding from those jurisdictions that operate as sanctuaries for unauthorized immigrants. Estimates are that the 10 largest jurisdictions face up to $2.27 billion in cuts. The mayor of Newark, New Jersey, has condemned such a threat from President Trump and said it would equate to a form of making sanctuary cities into "fugitive slave catchers."[37]

Of course, any such attempts would likely end up in a prolonged court battle.[38] In fact, in the first court engagement, a U.S. district judge in San Francisco held that Trump had exceeded his presidential authority by signing an executive order threatening to withhold federal funding from local jurisdictions identified as sanctuary jurisdictions, which could impact up to 300 locales. The judge ruled that Congress had the power of the purse and the authority to enact such legislation—not the president.[39] Most recently, the governor of Texas, Greg Abbott, signed an order via Facebook Live banning sanctuary cities beginning September 1, 2017, in the state of Texas. It is likely headed for a protracted legal battle.[40]

The 2015 death of Kate Steinle in San Francisco, reportedly shot to death by an undocumented immigrant from Mexico who had been deported five times, became a rallying cry for the Trump presidential campaign to curtail the protections offered by sanctuary jurisdictions. Even though Immigration and Customs Enforcement (ICE) authorities were not notified when the undocumented immigrant was released from the jail in San Francisco prior to Ms. Steinle's death, Magistrate Judge Joseph C. Spero dismissed the suit brought by the family of Kate Steinle by stating, "No law required the Sheriff's Department to share [the undocumented immigrant's] release date with ICE, nor did any law forbid [the sheriff] establishing a policy against such cooperation."[41] Furthermore, the immigrant charged with Kate Steinle's murder was acquitted; however, it is anticipated that he will be deported for being a felon with a firearm.[42]

Case law is contradictory on the issue of immigration enforcement, as are messages from the U.S. Department of Justice. Congress has added to the confusion as well. In some jurisdictions, memoranda of understanding are chiseled out between federal and state and/or local law enforcement agencies to designate who is responsible for what.[43] The Major Cities Chiefs of Police, which consists of police chiefs from the sixty-four largest police departments in the country, passed a resolution stating " 'the decision to enter this area of enforcement should be left to the local government and not mandated or forced upon them by the federal government through the threat of sanctions or the withholding of existing police assistance funding.' "[44]

The issue, therefore, is who sets the priorities for local criminal justice agencies, the state or federal government or local governments? In many respects, this is a battle between the rights of states and locales and the power of the federal government. It will be interesting to see how this issue is resolved, as the Trump administration seems to favor state and local concerns over federal government intervention on some matters—like in Chapter 6 regarding the discussion of consent decrees being used to monitor local criminal justice agencies. However, on the issue of "sanctuary cities," the administration wants federal interests to trump those of local jurisdictions. **Can you also think of another criminal justice related area that we have discussed in the text where the Trump administration has indicated that they prefer federal intervention over laws passed, often initiated by voters, within sates and locales?**

Arizona has been a recent battleground between the federal and state and local governments over enforcement of immigration laws. On the one hand, some believe states can better identify the needs and wants of their citizenry free of any federal influence. Perhaps states and localities can experiment on whether crime rates drop, more crime goes unreported, or whether illegal immigration harms the local economy. On the other hand, the state or local government may find that its community benefits by designating itself a sanctuary city.[45] **Can you think of examples of how a local jurisdiction might be benefited by invoking a "sanctuary status"?**

In one sense, this issue is a conflict between federal and local law enforcement priorities. Some criminologists contend that unequipped police, with insufficient tools and knowledge to act as federal immigration officers, will violate civil rights and could make costly mistakes, which will lead to lawsuits. They believe local agencies would be forced to deviate from their crime-fighting mission and place the funding burden on local governments for what is a federal responsibility. Also, enforcement measures have been unsuccessful at controlling who enters and remains in the United States. Furthermore, rounding-up and deporting undocumented immigrants, guilty of nothing more than being present in our country, is neither practical nor realistic.[46] (For example, see a presentence report concerning an immigration case in Appendix B of this textbook.)

The United States Congress, sensing the growing dissatisfaction in some states and among some of the public, attempted to craft new legislation to address the areas of greatest reform. But when those efforts stalled and ultimately failed, some private citizens even via the Internet have recruited and formed coalitions of "minutemen" to patrol the border,[47] and some city and state governments decided to make their own laws.[48] Perhaps this issue presents an opportunity for enhanced cooperation among the various levels of government in the United States and international cooperation between this country and those from which illegal immigrants come to the United States.[49]

If such cooperation does not occur, the prognosis is not good—nor is the impact on local police. Racial profiling would be the only way a police officer would know who should be required to carry papers proving that they have a right to be in the United States. That would put more strain on police-community relations, cause people of color to avoid contact with the police, and make it more difficult for local police to investigate crimes and track down fugitive offenders.[50] Adding to the confusion, the Trump administration has expressed a desire to end the Deferred Action for Childhood Arrivals (DACA) program. This is an initiative that has provided legal protections for dreamers—individuals brought to this country as children. Unfortunately, Congress has yet to act on this issue.[51] **If you were a member of the U.S. Congress, what legislation would you craft to deal with America's immigration situation?**

Stress: Criminal Justice Practitioner Participation in Decision-Making

Police Officers

Policing has traditionally been considered a high-stress occupation. Police suffer from maladies such as heart disease, cancer, alcoholism, drug abuse, divorce, and suicide. In a recent study of police officers, females were found to report significantly more symptoms of physical stress than males. This may be due to the fact that males have been found to be less likely to self-reveal physical problems, tending to exhibit a stiff upper lip, playing things close to the vest, and following the Tough Guy Syndrome. Those police officers who desire to participate in workplace decision-making but were not able to do so were found to be most likely to be physically stressed.[52]

Correctional Officers

Prisons are stressful environments, not just for those confined but also for those who work there. Frontline correctional personnel, correctional officers, have been found to be particularly susceptible to stress related problems. High rates of suicide, divorce, alcoholism, heart attacks, ulcers, and elevated blood pressure have been associated with prison work. These problems prove costly for correctional institutions and can translate into excessive employee absenteeism and turnover. As with police officers, a key variable linked to thoughts of quitting, job stress, and physical stress for correctional officers is the atmosphere for participating in decisions that affect one in the workplace. Correctional personnel who are satisfied with their input in decisions that affect them in the workplace are significantly less stressed and less likely to think about quitting their jobs than those who were not satisfied with their participation in workplace decision-making.

Probation Officers

Probation and parole officers also experience high rates of stress. The same symptoms of stress that police and correctional personnel experience are found in probation and parole officers. Federal probation and pretrial services officers have been found to be less stressed than state probation officers. The smaller caseloads of federal probation officers may certainly be a factor in this difference. Even though a low salary is not said to be a satisfier, it can be a cause of dissatisfaction if the amount paid is too deficient. The number one stressor for state probation officers when compared to federal probation and pretrial services officers is inadequate salaries.[53] But just as the ability to participate in decisions that affect one in the workplace was seen as a pivotal variable in impacting stress levels of police and correctional officers, it was also determined to be a crucial variable in probation/parole officer stress.[54] State probation officers were less likely than federal probation officers to perceive the atmosphere for participation in workplace decision making as a positive one. Those employed as state probation officers experienced significant amounts of organizational stress when compared to federal probation officers.[55]

Potential Solution to Criminal Justice Practitioner Stress

A challenge for criminal justice agencies in the future is to make the workplace less stressful. Although the removal of the causes of stress, such as the restricted ability to participate in decisions that affect one in the workplace, is believed to be the most effective way to reduce stress, it has been the least utilized means. Instead, institutions typically try to change people to fit institutions instead of adapting organizations to accommodate people.[56] "[F]ocusing on the individual is analogous to examining the personality of cucumbers to discover why they turned into sour pickles without analyzing the vinegar barrels in which they had been submerged."[57] Lastly, while females working in the criminal justice system may be more likely to report physical symptoms of stress, they are also more likely than their male counterparts to seek and receive professional help. Women clearly seem to exhibit more openness in confronting the causes of stress in their professions. This bodes well for the future, especially with the increased number of women in leadership positions in criminal justice. Women have helped to humanize criminal justice in many ways and de-escalate potentially flammable situations encountered in the field and in institutions. But gender aside, future criminal justice agencies will need to respond to the needs, both physical and mental, of the increasingly educated workforce entering the profession.

Technological Advancement

Technological advancements are likely to continue at a rapid pace throughout the twenty-first century. Such progress will have a significant impact on criminal justice. The twentieth century saw enormous changes in criminal justice practice. One senior deputy, Brian Garrett of the Polk County Sheriff's Office, describes changes he has seen in jails and law enforcement in a career that spans over thirty years in **Field Practice 14.2.**

Field Practice 14.2 Changes in Law Enforcement Technology During My Career

I started my law enforcement career with the county sheriff's office in 1977 as a "jailer," not a deputy, not a corrections officer, not a detention deputy, a jailer. The detention facilities at the time were the main jail downtown, holding about 300 inmates, and the stockade facility—a medium-security inmate work camp located just southeast of town.

The technology of detention at the time was primitive. The location and movement of inmates was tracked by individual name tags on a large board representing all of the cellblocks and cell beds in the jail. When an inmate was moved the jailer called the book-in sergeant who in turn made the physical change by moving the name tag on the big board. Book-in records were cards typed and filed alphabetically in file drawers. Fingerprints were taken manually by rolling fingers in ink and applying them to cards to be filed, with a copy forwarded to the FBI. Sometimes months later we would learn a fugitive had been booked into the jail and released under an alias without ever knowing he or she had an outstanding warrant.

Now the book-in process is highly computerized. Fingerprints are electronically scanned and researched through a national database that will return fugitive warrant matches in minutes or hours. Regardless of the alias the person used when booked in, the person can lie but the fingerprints never do.

Inmates now are swabbed for DNA samples when arrested for certain offenses. Those samples go into a national database, which has resulted in the arrests of persons for unsolved felonies decades old. Inmates are now fitted with an identification bracelet with their photograph on it to prevent the release of a prisoner attempting to use an outgoing prisoner's identification.

The jail itself was a mixture of the old and the new when I started. Half of it was relatively modern for the times, with cell blocks containing a dayroom with adjoining sleeping cells, these had electric locks and doors but were routinely overcrowded, making it difficult to use the "new technology" to keep officers safe. The other half of the jail was old, very old, and not much different than the jails in old Hollywood Westerns. It was dimly lit with manually operated doors with large keys opening into narrow halls. One section was called the "hole," not because it was punishment but because it was physically isolated from the other cells due to the layout of the old jail. Smoking was allowed in the jail. It was a filthy, unhealthy environment for officers and inmates alike, not to mention the thriving trade in cigarettes for favors within the jail.

Televisions came into use during my time in the jail, and they were very useful tools for managing inmate behavior. For example, bad behavior on Super Bowl Sunday meant no Super Bowl on television. You would be amazed at how well inmates got along on special television event days.

As a rule, officers did not carry any sort of weapon in the jail, no mace, no baton, no shield, and certainly no firearms. As a result, any violent behavior by an inmate had to be met with violence by the officers. Injuries to officers were common. Detention officers are now equipped with chemical agents, restraint chairs, and electric shields that make dealing with an unruly inmate safer for both the officers and inmates, and escape attempts by force are extremely rare.

The women's section of the jail 30 years ago consisted of one "matron" female officer on duty at any given time and she might have 30 female inmates total to watch over. Today there are hundreds of female inmates in the system at any given time.

The jail I worked in was closed several years ago. The new facility makes use of electronic security doors, large expanses of shatterproof glass and video monitoring of inmates and the facility. It is scheduled for a major expansion this year using even newer confinement technology. Closed circuit television first appearance court hearings are the norm now, requiring fewer movements of inmates and resulting in a safer work environment and decreased costs.

On the Road as a Deputy Sheriff

When I graduated the academy in 1978, I was assigned to one of the most rural portions of a 2,000-square-mile county. My field training consisted of riding with the veteran sergeant for most of one night and an experienced deputy another night. Sixteen hours of field training, and I was released to duty in a single deputy patrol car carrying a gun I could not legally purchase because I was too young to do so, 20.

The issued equipment consisted of a uniform, a 12-gauge shotgun, a straight baton, handcuffs, and a used patrol car with a radio that was then 20 years old. Deputies were not issued portable radios (walkie talkies) because administrators believed they would allow deputies to "goof off." As a result, if you were the only officer out on a dangerous or in-progress call, once you left your car you had no means of communicating that you needed help or, worse yet, that you were injured. It was not unusual to hear a civilian voice on the radio stating that the deputy was getting beat up by a suspect and needed help right away. Since the patrol district was several hundred square miles in size and often manned by just two or three deputies, help could be a long time getting to you. The in-car radios were interesting in that they were tube type, which means that when you keyed the microphone to speak you had to wait until the light on the radio turned from red to green in order for your words to be transmitted.

As odd as it sounds, even though you worked the night shift, you were not issued a flashlight. You bought your own, and it did not pay to be cheap when doing so. When suddenly confronted by a violent suspect you protected yourself with what you had in hand. If you were working at night, it was most often a flashlight. I recall driving up on a highway patrol trooper fighting with a large male suspect in the middle of the road, and the trooper struck the subject with a six "D" cell Rayovac flashlight. The blow stopped the subject, but the flashlight came apart and slung batteries for 50 feet down the road. I spent a lot of money at the time and bought a "streamlight" that was made of aircraft aluminum. It would not come apart if you ran over it with a car. That was a wise investment, and I still have that flashlight.

Personal body armor was just becoming available for law enforcement officers at the time, but the agency did not provide it. I bought two or three different vests before the agency started issuing them. The first models were extremely hot, bulky, and uncomfortable, but I wore them religiously. I don't know if it was because I realized the importance of the vest or if it was because I had spent a half month's salary on it and was determined to get my money's worth out of it. I am now issued the newest version of body armor. It is still uncomfortable, but it is lighter and provides better protection than ever. For those who wonder why all officers don't wear body armor; put on a tee shirt, a sweatshirt, a pair of heavy jeans, and your heaviest winter jacket, then go jog around the block in mid-August. That should give you an idea of what it is like to wear body armor. Body armor on duty is now mandatory with our agency.

My first patrol car was a hand-me-down 1976 Chevrolet Nova, no AM/FM radio, no power locks, no power windows. I was told I was lucky it had air-conditioning. It was not unusual to drive a car with over 100,000 miles on it. The newest cars for law enforcement are built strictly for police use, and many functions such as computers and radar are built into the car from the factory. Many cities are also equipping emergency vehicles with transponders that are capable of triggering traffic signals to allow emergency vehicles to always have the right-of-way when responding to emergency calls.

I am issued a "taser," an electronic muscular disruption device, and the closest thing to a *Star Trek* phaser yet. I am also issued an aerosol chemical spray (tear gas) that is hard for violent subjects to ignore. A collapsible metal baton is also issued, giving deputies a selection of tools to deal with combative subjects short of lethal force. I have no doubt that the use of tasers has saved far more combative subjects from death than have died inadvertently from their use.

In 1977 all reports were handwritten and it was not unusual to have 8–10 reports a shift. The time needed to write the reports impacted the time spent in proactive patrol. The current report writing system in each officer's computer has a spell and grammar check and eliminates illegible handwriting altogether.

Deputies are now issued a laptop computer with cellular internet access allowing them instant access to hundreds of different databases while in the field. They can not only pull up the status of a driver's license, but the picture as well, making it difficult to use another person's identity. All reports are also generated on these computers, and the reports can be electronically submitted to and reviewed by a supervisor with the capability of dumping them into the master report system without ever printing them on paper. Even traffic citations can be written by swiping the license in a reader similar to a credit card processor that automatically prints the citation with the charge you entered from a drop-down list. The capability exists now for a fingerprint to be scanned in the field, processed via internet connection, and matched to the national database within minutes.

The use of laptop computers also allows access to databases like Google earth that will display an aerial view of the area you are working to individual houses. This is particularly useful in emergency and tactical responses to seal off escape routes or locate water and other dangers to lost children or wandering Alzheimer's patients.

Local agencies are now using an automated license plate reader that uses a high-speed camera to read license plates and submit them via computer to the national database. The system alerts the operator to stolen vehicles or vehicles wanted in connection with a crime. The system can process thousands of plates in an hour, whereas a human operator might be able to do a few dozen manually. Officers can drive through congested mall and hotel parking lots, for example, scanning for suspended licenses and stolen vehicles.

When I started here the person answering the complaint line would write the information about the call on a paper card that would be placed on a conveyor belt and sent into the radio dispatch room that was physically isolated from the call takers to cut down on noise. The dispatcher read the information, dispatched the call, and eventually cleared it using a manual time stamp machine.

Now my agency uses a system that computerizes calls for service from the time they are received until the time the deputy arrives on scene. Global positioning systems in each patrol car allow the dispatch computer to instantly see who the closest unit to a pending call is and the approximate response time to the call. The dispatcher has access to the information as soon as the call taker enters the first bit of information. This allows for a quicker response since the deputy can be en-route to the call while the caller is still providing additional information.

Cellular telephones have had a huge impact on police services. It is common for deputies en-route to emergency calls to contact the complainant directly by phone, getting constant updates on what is occurring at the scene. As a result, the deputies are better prepared to safely handle the call once they arrive. Law enforcement agencies work with cell phone providers to trace cell phones to determine what area that phone is in. Phones equipped with Global Positioning System (GPS) can be tracked within feet by the companies' equipment. Many alibis have been broken by tracking when and where a cell phone was used. We have used a cell phone to communicate directly with a murder suspect and convince him to give up without resistance. Even sent text messages can be remotely retrieved upon service of a search warrant.

The cell phone technology also extends to cell based surveillance equipment, for both still and video camera systems that can provide real time monitoring of remote locations. The cameras are equipped with motion sensors and infra-red capabilities that allow pictures even on a dark night.

Surveillance cameras in general are becoming much more prevalent in banks, shopping centers, public gathering spots, and even private residences. Dashboard mounted cameras in patrol vehicles are common, and several recent shooting deaths of police officers have been caught on tape.

The downside of much of this technology is that when it fails, and it does, and that is the only way deputies have been trained to do something, operations can suffer significantly.[58]

Technological innovations can obviously bring about improvements to law enforcement. However, they can also be used to bring about serious negative consequences—even death. Consider the following examples.

Tysen Benz, an 11-year-old from Michigan, killed himself after reading texts and other messages on social media indicating his 13-year-old girlfriend had killed herself. He was unknowingly pranked. No one bothered to intervene when he posted on social media that he was going to commit suicide because of this matter. The juvenile considered responsible for this tragedy was charged with use of a computer to commit a crime and malicious use of telecommunication services.[59]

> Massachusetts teen Michelle Carter was charged with involuntary manslaughter for reportedly encouraging her boyfriend, Conrad Roy, through text messages to kill himself via carbon monoxide poisoning in his truck. He got out of the vehicle at one point, and she directed him to get back in. Although her attorneys have tried to quash the texts, the messages reveal that she "warn[ed] her suicidal boyfriend that 'it's now or never' and to 'just do it.' In one message the then-17-year-old [Carter], who claimed to Conrad that she would look after his family, texts: 'People who commit suicide don't think this much. They just could do it.'"[60] More of the text messages between Carter and Roy can be viewed at http://metro.co.uk/2016/08/01/in-full-chilling-texts-from-girl-who-encouraged-boyfriend-to-kill-himself-6042041/.

Whitney Beall, a 23-year-old female, used a live streaming app on her cellular phone called Periscope to boast of her drunk driving exploits while driving. Calls began to come into the local police department about her actions. A police officer downloaded the app and was able to follow her live streaming of the event. The police recognized landmarks in her live video streaming and were able to close in on her and make an arrest as she hit the curb when they stopped her.[61] Footage of the video is available on YouTube at https://www.youtube.com/watch?v=kHR-PKfPg0c.

The Periscope app was also reportedly used by Marina Lonina, 18, of Ohio to live stream the rape of her 17-year-old friend by Raymond Gates, 29. Gates and Lonina face a host of charges including "kidnapping, rape, sexual battery and pandering sexual matter involving a minor."[62]

In video streaming on Facebook Live a 15-year-old girl was shown being raped in Chicago. As many as six individuals violated her. Two boys, ages 14 and 15, were arrested for their part in the attack. About forty individuals watched the gang rape of the young girl on Facebook. Some individuals have since even been bullying the victim on social media. There are those that contend that those who view such crimes occurring have a legal obligation to report such acts to the police. However, "[l]egal experts say it would be very difficult to prove criminal charges against someone who views a crime on a live stream and doesn't report it. 'Generally, ordinary citizens are not legally required to report a crime or to do anything to stop it,'... There is no general duty to be a good Samaritan."[63] **What are your thoughts? Should there be penalties for those who observe criminal activity and do not report it to the police? What about possible retaliation to the viewer if they report such crimes?**

In another Facebook Live streamed attack, in Chicago, 4 blacks, 2 males and 2 females, "accused of torturing a mentally disabled man were charged with a hate crime and aggravated kidnapping among other charges.... The ... 30-minute video shows a man tied up and his mouth covered, cowering in the corner of [a] room. His attackers laugh and shout 'f*ck Donald Trump' and 'f*ck white people' as they kick and punch him and cut into his forehead with a knife."[64]

Steve Stephens, 37, reportedly shot and killed at random Robert Godwin, Sr., 74, in Cleveland. He then uploaded the video of the encounter and shooting to Facebook, claiming that he had killed 13 people and was on his way to kill number 14.[65] **Do you think mediums such as Facebook encourage some to commit heinous acts? Should users be prohibited from uploading videos or live streaming in such venues? Do you think there should be penalties for those who violate rules of etiquette?**

A man in Arkansas had some guys over to watch a football game, and the next morning one of the men was found dead in a hot tub in the backyard. The homeowner, James Bates, was charged with murder. Police in Arkansas served a search warrant to ascertain information from Amazon Echo, which usually is triggered by the key word Alexa, for the two days surrounding the death. However, this device has been known to record information even when not triggered. While the recordings are rather brief, the police are interested in any information contained therein. Of course, search warrants should be specific in their scope and should not allow for fishing expeditions. Amazon confirmed that Bates was the owner of the device and produced some of his purchase history. However, Amazon issued the following statement: "Amazon will not release customer information without a valid and binding legal demand properly served on us. Amazon objects to overbroad or otherwise inappropriate demands as a matter of course."[66]

Two video gamers reportedly got into an argument while playing Call of Duty online. One of them allegedly dared the other one to "swat" him. "Swatting" refers to someone reporting a fictitious crime to the police with the desire to get a SWAT team deployed. A call was placed to a 911 dispatcher in Wichita, Kansas, where the police expected to find a man holding his mother and brother at gunpoint after having shot

Image by agnormark at istockphoto.com.

his father in the head. All of this was not true, but the police arrived and shot and killed the unknowing and innocent homeowner. The caller was later arrested in Los Angeles. The particular charges are uncertain as this book goes to press. Pertinent legislation often lags behind such crimes.[67]

Another example of misuse of technology can be found with "Fantasy Rape" postings on Craigslst. Angela Maria Diaz was sentenced to five years in prison for kidnapping, false improsonment, and falsely reporting a crime to a police officer. Diaz indicated on Craigslist that she wanted to live out a rape-fantasy. However, she falsely accused her husband's ex-fiancee, who spent approximately 90 days in jail, of wanting to have her raped.[68] In Wyoming, an ex-boyfriend reportedly posed on Craiglist as his former girlfriend requesting a violent rape fantasy. A man responded, believing he was communicating with the female, but he was actually interacting online with the ex-boyfriend. The man ultimately went to the female's residence and allegedly bound, blindfolded, gagged, and raped the 25-year-old woman with a knife pressed against her throat. Both the assailant and the ex-boyfriend were arrested. The ex-boyfriend was charged with conspiracy to commit first-degree sexual assault.[69]

See **Critical Thinking 14.1** on how advances in technology are sometimes like a two-edged sword; they can aid criminal justice professionals, but they can also expose them as well.[70]

Future Trends

Advances in technology lead to headlines like: "California First Time DUI Offenders Get Interlock Devices,"[71] "OnStar Technology Leads to Accused Murderer's Arrest,"[72] "Police in Finland believe they have caught a car thief thanks to a DNA sample taken from a sample of his blood found inside a mosquito,"[73] "A Different Kind of Bling: Bracelet Tracks Alcohol Consumption, Monitoring Device Like Lohan's Samples Sweat, Records Ethanol Levels."[74] Several trends seem to have potential to either enhance criminal justice, or complicate it.

Image by AzmanL at istockphoto.com.

DNA[75] testing is projected to identify more criminals in the future and to set more persons wrongly convicted free.[76] Consider the matter of Andrew David Jensen, 42, who allegedly broke into house in Ventura, California, in October of 2016. While there, he made a deposit in the toilet and did not flush. Police, through DNA testing, traced the fecal matter back to Mr. Jensen; he was arrested for burglary in July of 2017.[77]

In the future, in the face of severe economic woes, prison populations may level off or even decline. The continued legalization of marijuana within the states is likely to continue, and it will be interesting to see how the federal government responds. Furthermore, an opioid epidemic has been identified in America, with 64,000 drug overdose deaths reported in 2016. This crisis exceeds the number of U.S. soldiers that died in Vietnam and those that died at the peak of automobile crashes, the HIV/AIDS epidemic, and gun deaths in America.[78] See also the Netflix documentary—*Heroin(e)*.

Likewise, citizens will continue to look to the appellate courts to clarify criminal justice practices, and the question will remain to what extent the U.S. Supreme Court will get involved. For example, the U.S. Supreme Court agreed to intervene in a case from California on prison overcrowding, *Schwarzenegger v. Plata* (09-1233). In this and related cases, the Court determined that the California Department of Corrections fell short of delivering minimal care to prisoners with serious medical and mental health issues resulting in needless suffering and death. The Court ordered the release in excess of 30,000 inmates.[79]

Financially strapped units of government will attempt, in tight fiscal times, to generate revenue through traffic enforcement. Some counties and towns receive a large portion of their budgets through traffic fines. "Speed cameras" have been tried in Arizona and abandoned.[80] Red-light cameras are being tried and generating contentious resistance in communities and the courts, and proceeds from them are even being used to assist in the funding of educational institutions.[81]

Critical Thinking 14.1 Are "Wii" Having Fun Yet?

While we know that video surveillance can be an aid to the police in capturing criminals, it can also prove to be to the detriment of criminal justice practitioners as aberrant acts are caught on tape. Sheriff deputies, accompanied by officers from other agencies, served a search warrant at a suspected drug dealer's house. Reportedly, within 20 minutes of entering the suspect's home, while some of the drug task force members were searching for drugs, other officers had turned on the big screen television and commenced to engage in Wii bowling. There were spares and strikes and high fives among the participants all caught on videotape. The officers did not realize, until it hit the press, that their actions were being recorded via a computer with a wireless security camera attached. Posturing is taking place as to whether the actions by the bowlers will invalidate the search. A defense attorney says yes, and the sheriff says no.[82]

The Wii bowling incident made it to the pages of *Playboy Magazine*, where the sheriff is quoted saying, "[t]hat's a wii bit more media coverage than we intended." However, the county sheriff says he "has always wanted to be on the cover of the *Rolling Stone*."

What do you think? Considering our discussion of search and seizure in Chapter 5, is the search valid? Can the evidence seized be used against the suspect? Should anything happen to the bowling officers? Should the alleged drug dealer be allowed to videotape persons in his home without their knowledge?

Cybercrime over the Internet, identity theft, and digital child pornography violations are likely to increase over time, as will the electronic sophistication in apprehending such offenders.[83] Camera surveillance should be expanded within prisons to better ensure safety for all. GPS tracking of probationers and parolees, to include sex offenders, will expand. Intelligence gathering and sharing of information between correctional and law enforcement officials will increase, especially concerning gang affiliations inside and outside of prison.[84] Also, technology used to combat terrorism abroad will increasingly be used to protect our borders. The U.S. is currently using predator drones four miles up into the sky to patrol the Mexican and Canadian borders, as well as the Caribbean. Forty thousand pounds of drugs and some 7,000 illegal immigrants have been intercepted in the past five years. While no persons are aboard the drones, their high-powered cameras can direct enforcement personnel to locations on the ground for penetration.[85]

Drones can aid law enforcement by locating suspects or reconstructing crime scenes or vehicle crash scenes.[86] Drones also can be armed. In fact, when Dallas police officers were being picked off by a sniper, the chief of police ordered an armed land-based drone—a robot—to be sent in to eliminate the perpetrator.[87] Law enforcement agencies in 13 states (Alabama, Arizona, Arkansas, California, Florida, Georgia, Idaho, Minnesota, North Dakota, Ohio, Oklahoma, Texas, and Washington) have either borrowed Customs and Border Patrol drones or have applied for their own authorization to utilize drones.[88] In fact, over a two-year span of time it is estimated that Customs and Border Patrol drones were used in almost 700 missions by other federal, state, and local agencies. Their surveillance has included non-border patrol activities such as looking for marijuana plants and meth labs. Civil libertarians have raised concerns about privacy issues for the general public with drones circling overhead.[89]

While the police are finding use for drones, criminals and terrorists are also doing so. A drone has crashed onto the White House lawn. Drones have been used to smuggle drugs across the border and even onto prison yards in the United States.[90] A teenager in Connecticut mounted a handgun to a drone with firing capability, and, on another occasion, he attached a flamethrower to a drone—posting his handy work in YouTube videos.[91]

Some prisons have begun to engage in video medicine. For example, in Pennsylvania "some prisoners [are] monitored and treated for chronic diseases at in-house prison medical units using video teleconferencing for pre- and post-operative consultations."[92] This of course cuts down on medical and transportation costs. It also lessens security concerns in the community and reduces the concerns of medical personnel for their own safety. Use of video teleconferencing for arraignments and/or in-custody visitation is not uncommon in various jails and correctional facilities and will likely increase in use in the future.[93] Such methods reduce the possibility of the transfer of contraband from visitors to inmates, cut down on transportation costs, and limit risks to security. One man reportedly used a drone to catch his wife of 18 years having an extra-marital affair (see the video at http://www.insideedition.com/headlines/19908-high-infidelity-man-uses-drone-to-catch-wife-of-18-years-who-he-says-is).[94]

Video cameras and what they capture can also create problems for the general public. Consider the case of Tyler Clementi in **Critical Thinking 14.2.**

Critical Thinking 14.2 Anti-Bullying Legislation

Tyler Clementi, a Rutgers University freshman, jumped to his death from the George Washington Bridge after his intimate contact with another male was streamed live online. The legislature at both the state and federal level sprang into action, introducing anti-bullying legislation, with the act at the federal level bearing Clementi's name.

As noted by one state lawmaker, "We in the legislature have a habit when there is a tragedy to decide to do something when there may be a law [addressing the circumstance already]. Videoing someone in an intimate act is already a crime."[95] Thus, this is another example of crisis driving policy.

What is bullying? If you were a legislator, what would you do?

Attitudes about Criminal Justice

Public attitudes appear to be less hardened regarding criminal justice than in the past. There is strong support among Americans for expanding addiction treatment. In fact, 63% of citizens surveyed contend that "we put too many non-violent drug offenders in prison instead of treating their addiction[;] 78% believe we need to treat drug and alcohol addiction more as a health problem and less as a criminal problem." Eighty-six percent of citizens favor allowing additional gain-time for federal prisoners who participate in programs to reduce re-offending, such as drug treatment and job training initiatives. In excess of 60% of voters think that federal prisons house too many non-violent offenders; almost 75% of voters favor sentencing reform.[96] The latest Gallup Poll reveals that only 50% of Americans surveyed believe that the death penalty is applied fairly.[97] Media scrutiny focusing on use of legal injection to carry out the death penalty in Arkansas is likely to add to concerns about the use of executions. The state of Arkansas wanted to speed up the clock by executing eight inmates in 11 days via lethal injection before one of the drugs to be used in the execution exceeded its expiration date. However, a federal judge intervened by staying the executions. However, the Attorney General of Arkansas has appealed the judge's ruling.[98] **What ultimately happened in this matter? Do you agree or disagree with the ultimate decision? Why or why not?**

Slate, Johnson, and Colbert in a study of police officers found that overall their number one stressor was negative media reports about the police, even more so than fear of killing someone in the line of duty or being killed themselves.[99] With that in mind, consider the following sex scandal that played out in newspapers and on television involving the police department in Lakeland, Florida.

An investigation of the Lakeland Police Department (LPD) by the State Attorney's Office determined the following.

> "1. As many as ten sworn LPD officers have engaged in sex acts and sexually suggestive behavior while on duty over the past seven years with an LPD civilian employee. The sex acts occurred, among other places, at the Lakeland Police Department, other City of Lakeland Municipal Buildings, in Lakeland Police Department patrol cars, in city parks and on private property.
>
> 2. While there were also allegations of LPD officers engaging in sex acts with the LPD civilian employee off duty and in other jurisdictions, the focus of this investigation was for on duty actions of the officers.
>
> 3. Of the ten current or former officers who engaged in sex acts or sexually suggestive behavior, five are supervisors and ranked members of LPD.
>
> 4. Seven sworn current or former officers admitted, under oath, to the allegations of the LPD civilian employee. Two sworn officers partially admitted

and partially denied, under oath, the allegations of the LPD civilian employee. One sworn officer denied, under oath, the allegations of the LPD civilian employee.

5. We question the credibility of three LPD sergeants, Bryan McNabb, Rusty Longaberger and David Woolverton. I will not use their testimony pending the outcome of the internal affairs investigation. We will, in light of your determination and fact finding, make a final decision.

6. Not only are the officers directly involved in this matter at fault. There were other LPD employees who knew about what was going on during this time period, but declined to get involved and stop it."

The investigation revealed that the crime analyst, who was married, had sex with an officer more than once at church, at work, and in the parking lot after the funeral of an officer who had been killed in the line of duty. She and a captain were involved in sexting, and he took a picture of his penis on her cell phone to pass along to another woman he was interested in dating; he did go on to have sexual activity with this woman. The crime analyst reported having sex in a closet at the police station with a sworn officer, who was a police recruiter. However, the recruiter reported that he became woozy and was unable to perform a sexual act because of his erectile dysfunction.

Three officers were issued what are known as "death letters" by the State Attorney's Office for perceived deception during the investigation and refusal to take a polygraph. In other words, the State Attorney was indicating that there would be no reliance on the testimony of these officers in any future matters considered for prosecution.[100]

The crime analyst was ultimately terminated, as were two officers. Six other officers either resigned or retired. However, police officers in Florida have a strong Bill of Rights, and, with help from the Union, one of the sergeants who admitted having sex with the crime analyst off duty—although believed to be deceptive—was re-instated at the rank of officer with the State Attorney's Office still refusing to accept testimony from him.[101] **Should police officers, who can't perform full duties, i.e., arresting individuals and testifying in court, be allowed to stay on the police force?**

Lakeland Police Department is not the only agency to be rocked by sex scandals exposed by the media. For example, law enforcement agencies in San Francisco, Oakland, and Louisville have been disgraced for the sexual proclivities of some of their officers.[102]

Alternatives to Incarceration

Some believe that much of the hope for the future success of criminal justice hinges on successful re-entry of persons into the community after their encounters with criminal justice.[103] Former U.S. Attorney General Janet Reno has been touted as one of the first to bring experts together to consider the implications and ramifications of successful offender re-entry. The average drug dealer has been said to barely make minimum wage, but society has paid dearly to thwart his efforts with burgeoning jail and prison populations. The National Drug Czar no longer talks about a "drug war." Mass incarceration has succeeded in reducing crime, but the strategy has diminishing returns. The offense rate of the top 20 percent of offenders is more than 10 times that of the average prisoner—a few very active criminals commit most of the crime. But under the current system, offenders who could be more cheaply deterred or rehabilitated instead incur the most expensive—and, from the perspective of its effect on the community, damaging—form of punishment possible. This is why, even as the number of incarcerated people has increased exponentially, crime hasn't decreased at the same rate.[104]

Some states have implemented "graduated sanctions." For example, most persons who have parole violations, in one study 81 percent, as the result of a technical violation, do so most frequently for failure to report as required and for failure to get authorization to change addresses. They did *not* commit new crimes. Probation officers maintain there should be less harsh options available than being forced to lock someone up, options such as residential assessment centers.

Hawaii's Opportunity Probation with Enforcement (HOPE) is a promising program with graduated sanctions, emphasizing the swiftness of punishment more than the severity of punishment. A select group of frequent violators were placed in this streamlined program so that when violations occurred, such as a negative urinalysis or curfew violation, paperwork was kept at a minimum, and an expedited hearing transpired. The hearing would take place within 48 hours of the violation, instead of weeks or months later, and would generally lead to a brief jail term. Less severe punishments (short jail stays) cost less, and deliver the certainty of punishment over the severity of the punishment. This HOPE pilot project resulted in an 80% drop in the overall rate of missed and failed drug tests, and the missed-appointment rate fell from 13.3% to 2.6%. Despite the fact that offenders admitted to the program were more prone to violating, the trend continued as the program expanded. The optimism surrounding HOPE is also about the program's bipartisan appeal. HOPE retains the use of punishment as a deterrent, meaning it is "tough" enough for conservatives, while at the same time reducing the prison population, which is what liberals want.

Democratic Congressman Adam Schiff and Republican Congressman Ted Poe, both former federal prosecutors, have joined together in the House of Representatives to initiate a grant program for states to implement versions of HOPE. Some criminologists believe such reforms would cut the crime rate and the prison population could be cut in half in 10 years. As stated by Congressman Schiff, " 'We don't have to be tough on crime; we have to be smart on crime ... or, we'll be bankrupt on crime.' "[105]

Such a transition won't come easy. There are those who are benefitting from business as usual in the lock-'em-up-and-throw-away-the-key empire that has become the correctional system in America. These groups can make campaign contributions in an attempt to see that their interests are represented. Pockets of resistance may also come from correctional officer unions, private prison corporations, and bail bondsmen.[106]

The Criminalization of Mental Illness

Throughout this book we have discussed how crisis tends to drive policy in criminal justice. Although more reasoned solutions would be preferable, we believe that crises will continue to influence policy in the future. No place is this more evident than in the interface of criminal justice and mental health, where sometimes tragic consequences have resulted from inadequate preparation for the authority of criminal justice to meet the uncertainties of mental imbalance. Some criminologists believe that the police officer of the future will adopt an increased role of caregiver to the public.[107] We believe that all of criminal justice, not just the police, will assume a more pronounced interface with mental health issues, or crises.

Criminal justice has become the *de facto* mental health system. There are more persons with mental illnesses in jails and prisons in this country than in state or private hospitals. In fact, the three largest inpatient psychiatric facilities in the United States today are jails—the Los Angeles County Jail, Rikers Island in New York City, and Cook County Jail in Chicago. There are more persons with mental illnesses in each of those jails than in any public or private hospital in America. Very likely in whatever current state you are residing, a jail or a prison is housing more persons with mental illnesses than any hospital in your state.

While mental health treatment services are often either essentially non-existent, inadequate, or selectively offered in the community, criminal justice has been identified as "the system that can't say no"—particularly jails. Jails are open 24/7, 365 days a year, and when there is often nowhere else to turn for law enforcement as part of their "social concern" role, there is always jail.

This is not an altogether new situation. In 1988, a Memphis Police Department officer tragically shot a man with mental illness. The Memphis Police Department met with a local community group affiliated with the National Alliance on Mental Illness (NAMI) to better understand the issues surrounding persons with mental illnesses. NAMI's membership is comprised of family members who have loved ones with a mental illness, consumers of mental health services, professional members, such as psychiatrists, and advocates.

From that meeting a prototypical Memphis Model of Crisis Intervention Team (CIT) training was created that is the most replicated police training method for achieving successful resolutions with persons with mental illnesses in crises. Within the model, select officers receive 40 hours of training on, among other things, the signs and symptoms of mental illnesses, psychotropic medications, and de-escalation skills. Role playing can be used, and eight hours of the training involves police interacting with persons with mental illnesses who are not in crisis. CIT has been found to reduce injuries to both officers and persons with mental illnesses and to link persons to treatment in the community and divert them from criminal justice.[108] CIT training is now being expanded into jails and prisons in an attempt to de-escalate incidents in those settings as well.[109]

Specialty courts have also begun to spring up around the country. There are now drug courts,[110] homeless courts,[111] veterans courts,[112] and mental health courts, for example. The first mental health court in America began operation in Broward County, Florida, in 1997. It also emerged as a result of a tragedy. See **Field Practice 14.3.**

Field Practice 14.3 Crisis Driving Policy

A man, who had previously suffered a traumatic head injury, began to hear voices in a grocery store. He ran outside and knocked an elderly lady down. Her bag of groceries spilled to the ground. Witnesses observed the man trying to put her groceries back into the bag, but they believed he was trying to rob her. The lady ultimately died from injuries sustained in the fall, and the fellow with the head injury was indicted for manslaughter.

The man's defense attorney got word to the grand jury that his client had sought and been refused treatment for his condition, and that if they were going to indict his client that they should indict the mental health and criminal justice systems for failing his client time and again and putting him in the position for this to happen. The grand jury launched an investigation that resulted in a 153-page report critical of both the mental health and criminal justice systems in the handling of persons with mental conditions. The grand jury's recommendations provided the impetus for establishment of Broward County's mental health court.[113]

How many jurisdictions in America today could withstand such grand jury investigations?

A number of other agencies have visited and replicated various aspects of the Broward County mental health court. Mental health courts tend to rely on the principle of therapeutic jurisprudence that we discussed in Chapter 10. Some mental health courts accept only misdemeanants, others accept felons. Some have probation officers assigned to monitor clients. Some have a finding of guilt, with some of these jurisdictions allowing for expungement of the conviction upon successful completion of the program, but all strive to link persons with mental illnesses to treatment in the community to stop them from being "frequent fliers," recycling time and again, through the criminal justice system.[114] See **Field Practice 14.4.**

Field Practice 14.4 Crisis Driving Policy

Four mornings a week, between 2 and 6 a.m., New York City Department of Correction's buses would drop off persons with mental illnesses, who had received psychiatric care while in jail, at Queens Plaza with $1.50 in cash and a two-fare Metrocard. Why between 2 and 6 a.m. for drop offs? New Yorkers would be much less likely to become aware of such a practice. This practice ultimately led to what is known as the *Brad H.* lawsuit. At the time the suit was filed, Brad H. was actually a 44-year-old homeless man with schizophrenia who had been treated 26 times in jail for mental illness but never received any treatment in the community or assistance with accessing Medicaid benefits,

Social Security disability payments, or shelter upon any of his releases back into the community. The *Brad H.* complaint addressed a practice in which at least 25,000 jail inmates a year were receiving mental health treatment in jail, but almost no one received discharge planning for release, which set individuals up to fail and return to the criminal justice system. Mental health treatment in jails and prisons has been mandated by the U.S. Supreme Court in *Estelle v. Gamble*, 1976; however, discharge planning has largely been ignored by such institutions and the *Brad H.* attorneys pursued the Department of Correction on the prohibition against cruel and unusual punishment and a New York State law, entitled the Mental Hygiene Law, that dictates that providers of inpatient mental health treatment services must provide discharge planning.

The policy changes sought in the *Brad H.* class-action suit asked for each of the following upon release from jail for persons with mental illnesses: an adequate supply of medication, at least a shelter with a bed, access to mental health services, and assurance of immediate benefits like Medicaid and food stamps without a 45-day waiting period. Without intervention, New York City contributed to the failure of individuals at great costs in terms of needless human suffering, both for persons with mental illnesses and other members of society with whom untreated persons with mental illnesses may interact. The suit is still being monitored/renegotiated as this text goes to press.[115] See **Field Practice 14.5**.

Field Practice 14.5 Crisis Driving Policy

On January 3, 1999, Andrew Goldstein pushed Kendra Webdale, a 32-year-old woman, to her death in a New York subway station. A month and a half earlier Goldstein entered the emergency room at Jamaica Hospital in Queens requesting hospitalization. He reported he was hearing voices, his brain had been removed, and he had been inhabited by people. He said the voices were warning him that something would happen. He was unable to cope. He had a history of psychosis when off his medication. At various times, he had told psychiatrists that he was turning purple, that he had shrunk six to eight inches, that he had lost his neck, had developed an oversize penis because of contaminated food, and that a homosexual man named Larry was stealing his excrement from the toilet "through interpolation," then eating it with a knife and fork.

The voices seemed so real and relentless, that on November 24 a psychiatrist wrote, "He requested eyeglasses so that he will find the people talking to him." He was hospitalized from November 24 to December 15. Under the intense financial pressure of managed care to discharge psychiatric patients within three weeks, Goldstein was released with a seven days' supply of medication and a piece of paper informing him to seek counseling at Bleuler Psychotherapy Center. In a few days he stopped taking his medication. It was not anyone's job to follow up with him. Instead, on December 26, a Bleuler worker mailed a form letter requesting that Goldstein phone the clinic by January 6, or else his case would be closed. On January 3, at 5:06 p.m., the N train pulled into the station at 23rd Street and Broadway and Kendra Webdale was pushed underneath and died. She was a stranger to Goldstein. He never saw her face. As he later wrote in his confession: "I felt a sensation, like something was entering me ... I got the urge to push, shove or sidekick. As the train was coming, the feeling disappeared and came back.... I pushed the woman who had blond hair."

In October of 2006, after several attempts at justice, Andrew Goldstein entered into a plea bargain that would send him to prison for 23 years to be followed by five years of supervised release.[116]

Discussions of outpatient treatment often focus on tragic incidents carried out by individuals such as Andrew Goldstein. There were numerous missed opportunities to provide him treatment. Kim Webdale, the sister of Kendra Webdale, testified before Congress to say that the more she and her family delved into Kendra's tragic death, the more Kim found her sister to have been the "unsuspecting victim of a sick man and an equally sick system."

Policy changes were sought by the Treatment Advocacy Center (TAC) in Arlington, Virginia, which has used the tragic death of Kendra Webdale and the denial of treatment to Andrew Goldstein as a rallying cry to modify civil commitment laws. The laws would encourage states to adopt "assisted outpatient treatment laws" to make it easier to link persons to treatment in the community and hopefully thereby divert them from criminal justice. Largely due to the efforts of TAC, 44 states now have assisted outpatient treatment laws on the books.[117] TAC also continues a list of preventable tragedies on their website.[118] However, the usage of these laws varies from state to state and jurisdiction to jurisdiction. See **Field Practice 14.6.**

Field Practice 14.6 Crisis Driving Policy

Almost two weeks after Seung-Hui Cho's rampage, police remained at a loss as to why Cho shot and killed thirty-two fellow college students and professors at Virginia Tech University. The problem may very well be trying to apply rationality to irrational behavior. The reason for Cho's killing spree, which was characterized at the time as "the deadliest shooting rampage in American history," may be as simple as the mantra he went into on his televised videotaped manifesto shown on NBC television. Cho compared his suffering with Christ's and disdainfully assails those who have everything, saying, "You had everything you wanted. Your Mercedes wasn't enough, you brats. Your golden necklaces weren't enough, you snobs. Your trust fund wasn't enough. Your vodka and Cognac weren't enough. All your debaucheries weren't enough. Those weren't enough to fulfill your hedonistic needs. You had everything."

In terms of rationality, it did not matter that most students at Virginia Tech are not very wealthy. What mattered was that Cho in his own mind did not measure up and felt persecuted.

In the aftermath of the Cho massacre at Virginia Tech, a commission put in place to review the incident issued an almost 250-page report with recommendations for legal and policy changes. The commission hopes an incident like this will never occur again.[119] Of course, had signs been appropriately noticed and law already in place followed, this may have never happened in the first place.

Most persons with mental illnesses are not violent. However, when their access to treatment is inadequate or blocked, problems can emerge and tragedies occur. Criminal justice is the arena where many mentally ill persons surface in need of treatment. Although the root problem is not crime, criminal justice is the first responder to any disturbance or misbehavior, no matter how later diagnosed. See **Field Practice 14.7.**

Field Practice 14.7 Crisis Driving Policy: Crisis Intervention Training

Sgt. Jack Richards of the Ventura Police Department in California fully understands the importance of CIT training and its emphasis on de-escalation techniques. He was involved in a fatal shooting of a person with mental illness earlier in his police career. He had received no training to provide adequate response to mental health symptoms and behavior, and he believes that was a significant contributing factor to creating unnecessary situations that led to hostile confrontations like the one he encountered.[120]

One study found that two-thirds of U.S. hospitals dump patients with mental illnesses who are unable to pay. Markowitz (2006) found a predominance of private psychiatric hospital beds in cities to be significantly associated with increases in both arrest and crime rates. This suggests that when the mental health system is privatized, police have fewer referral options to mental health treatment and are more likely to make an arrest. The result is the criminalization of persons with mental illnesses.

Criminal justice, although not originally designed to solve mental health problems, is responsible for decisions regarding persons with mental illnesses coming into contact with criminal justice. Most of the research regarding the interface of the mental health and criminal justice systems has been published in psychiatric journals. Perhaps there is promise in the criminal justice system working collaboratively with the mental health system. Mental health systems lack the clout and leverage with policymakers and the community that criminal justice has.

Currently, most funding efforts aimed at stopping persons with mental illnesses from recycling through the criminal justice system are spearheaded by criminal justice personnel. Sheriffs, police chiefs, judges, and the associations they belong to have been quite influential in bringing about meaningful change and influencing lawmakers. At least some of the criminal justice agencies which have long been the dumping ground for society's ills have begun to stand up collectively, and sometimes in multi-system collaborations, to stop the revolving door of criminal justice for persons with mental illnesses.

It seems that what has worked best in fighting against the criminalization of persons with mental illnesses is collaboration: bringing together law enforcement, judges, prosecutors, public defenders, corrections officials, mental health clinicians, mental health advocates, consumers of mental health services, family members with loved ones with mental illnesses, and victims' advocates to craft workable, meaningful solutions. If additional mental health treatment services are needed, then such multi-system collaborations can be quite formidable in lobbying lawmakers to address needs.

In a civilized society, we are morally responsible for catching those persons with mental illness that we can and saving them from going over the edge of the cliff into the abyss of the criminal justice system. Criminal justice practitioners are logically positioned, whether they want to be or not, as the gatekeepers for salvaging persons with mental illnesses.

There is no shame in being mentally ill. A person should not have to commit a crime to have a chance at some semblance of treatment in America. The shame is in not receiving adequate treatment, and any entity that obfuscates that treatment should be considered criminal.

You have just been appointed by the governor of your state to come up with reasoned solutions to the broken interface of the mental health and criminal justice systems in your state that has caused the criminal justice system to become the de facto mental health system. What key players would you call to the table to collaborate with you on stopping the recycling of non-violent persons with mental illnesses through the criminal justice system? What recommendations would you make?

Evidence-Based Practices

> *Most of us have thought of the statistician's work as that of measuring and predicting ... but few of us have thought it the statistician's duty to try to bring about changes in the things that he [or she] measures.*
>
> —W. Edwards Deming[121]

The buzzword for the future seems to be to embrace "evidence-based practices."[122] We will see more intelligence-led policing in the future. Just as there has been a movement toward evidence-based medicine, there will be more emphasis on data-driven decision-making in professional policing. We will search for evidence of what works and when it works.[123]

This approach also meshes nicely with the Compstat (Computer Statistics) meetings model associated with former Chief William Bratton of the New York and Los Angeles Police Departments.[124] "[P]olicymakers need to be provided not only with the reasons for implementing policies but also the numbers to justify their existence. The exceptional high-profile event, while often a catalyst for political action, usually posits the wrong premise to build effective policy and practice. The more informed approach … is to look at history and recent data to move towards the thoughtful resolution of competing ideas. [T]he cost to 'do it right' will be enormous, but the cost of not doing so, both in terms of human suffering and financially, is even greater."[125]

Oftentimes the movies and television shows portray misleading examples of justice in America. Consider **Critical Thinking 14.3** below.

Critical Thinking 14.3 Hollywood and Comparative Criminal Justice

"With its tremendous influence on attitudes about justice, Hollywood also stands to influence the development of criminal justice systems throughout the world. The television program *Law and Order* is currently viewed in more than 40 countries, and *CSI* in more than 22. Although entertainment, such programs affect people's expectations of the justice system. For example, most countries do not try criminal cases in front of juries, yet American films and television create expectations that justice includes jury trials, perhaps lending support to the introduction of jury trials in Russia."

Of course, the irony of this is, as we have discussed, most cases never go to trial in the U.S., so no jury is involved in dispensing most of the justice in America.

Motivations for committing crime vary from person to person and situation to situation. What would it take for you to commit a crime? Take a look at the following examples in **Critical Thinking 14.4.**

Critical Thinking 14.4 Food for Thought

What would need to happen for you to go rob at gunpoint a convenience store clerk tonight? What would it take for you to dress up like Santa Claus, go to your ex's parents' home, first shoot the little girl who came to the door, and then slaughter eight others with guns? Bruce Jeffrey Pardo did it in Covina, California, on a Christmas Eve. He then set the house on fire and shot and killed himself. This all happened purportedly because he had recently lost his wife, his job as an aerospace engineer, and even his dog.[126]

What would it take for you to strap explosives to your body, walk into a busy shopping mall, and detonate them, killing yourself and others? Could some promise of the afterlife convince you to do it? How could such disdain for certain elements of society fester to such a boiling point? Is there anything that could influence you to do such a thing? How can we convince others not to act so horrifically?

Image by stevecoleimages at istockphoto.com.

Conclusion

Sadly, the massacre at Virginia Tech discussed earlier in this chapter, was surpassed by the Pulse nightclub shooting in terms of the number killed. Even worse, as this book goes to press, the shooting from the Mandalay Bay Hotel in Las Vegas, Nevada, directed at a country music concert crowd constitutes the largest mass shooting in modern American history—at least 59 dead, including the shooter, and around 500 wounded or injured.[127] Criminologist Grant Duwe explains why the qualifier "modern" American history is used to refer to the Vegas shooting. He indicates how other atrocities in America in the late 19th century and early 20th century inflicted on Native Americans and African Americans exceed the recent carnage, but he maintains when it is the "haves" killing the "have nots" criminal charges are rare as is public acknowledgement.[128]

As noted by Joseph Gusfield, we as a society have a tendency to push the actions of individuals who commit such unconventional acts as mass murder into the sick deviant category because law-abiding citizens cannot fathom the possibility of a rational person engaging in such reprehensible behavior, and it helps conventional society to better cope with such atrocities.[129] Thus, the search for a motive in the Vegas shooting will continue, and the gun control debate will ensue once again. Of course, America's fascination with guns remains, and the prominence of the Second Amendment's right to bear arms is evident in U.S. Supreme Court cases *District of Columbia v. Heller* (2008) and *McDonald v. Chicago* (2010).[130] In Chapter 2, we discussed frontier justice; today, some states allow conceal-carry permits and others even open carry for citizens to possess guns in public places. In Polk County, Florida, the sheriff's office has established a sentinel program whereby the department trains volunteer administrators and faculty at a local Christian college to carry concealed weapons to be able to intervene should an active shooter situation emerge.[131] **Would you volunteer to participate in such a program? Would you want your faculty member to do so? Do you see any potential problems with such a program?**

Another mass shooting has occurred in America, this time on Valentine's Day 2018 at Marjory Stoneman Douglas High School in Parkland, Florida, resulting in 17 deaths. Since 2000, there have been in excess of 40 active shooter incidents at schools across America. In retrospect, warning signs were apparently present.[132] On at least four occasions local or federal law enforcement authorities were warned that the shooter would possibly unload on a school, and even the FBI acknowledged failing to follow through. If only, for example, the perpetrator could have been civilly committed or brought under the jurisdiction of a mental health court to control his conduct, this horrific event may not have ever happened.[133] Perhaps the impact of this shooting will be different. Potential responses have ranged from arming teachers, tightening background checks for firearm purchases, increasing the age limit for purchasing assault weapons, disallowing the sale of such guns altogether, limiting the amount of ammunition that can be held in gun magazines, and focusing on mental illness. While it is unclear what actions will be taken, especially with many politicians having received money from the National Rifle Association, it is believed some changes will be made. The remaining students at Stoneman Douglas have found their voice, they come from an affluent area (with census data revealing a median annual income of over $130,000 for Parkland residents compared to the state of Florida's $50,000 median income) with the ability to be heard. **What changes, if any, have been made to gun laws and/or treatment of persons with mental illnesses after the Parkland shooting?**

Sensationalized stories and Hollywood dramas will continue to grab the headlines, along with serial killers. Stories magnify celebrities and athletes in trouble with the law, such as Chis Soules of *Bachelor* fame and Tiger Woods.[134] Likewise, in 2017, the primary reasons for arrest of NFL football players have centered around assault, drugs, and disorderly conduct.[135]

Bruce J. "Vila says [crime fighting] will continue to fall into three categories: reducing the opportunity for crime, changing the motivation of people who commit crimes, and altering people's fundamental values—including nurturing positive values in young children—to minimize the likelihood of future criminal behavior."[136] First of all, highly sophisticated technological means are utilized to detect and curb crime and will continue to be developed into the future.

Secondly, motivations for committing crime vary and are not always readily understood. However, a prediction for the future is that a lack of homogeneity in the United States and globally will increase, and diversity will become even greater in the makeup of populations. This has the potential for disharmony.[137] Those individuals within society with a lack of connectedness, those who feel marginalized and alienated, are more likely to engage in aberrant behavior and fall prey to inappropriate associations where they can gain "status."

While exceptional cases and dramatic portrayals may drive policy, most of the day-to-day business of criminal justice takes place with what Attorney Johnnie Cochran said, after he won the acquittal for his multi-million dollar client O.J. Simpson in what has been termed the "Trial of the Century," "not with the O.J.s, but with the No J.s."[138] Some of those in the headlines may or may not be salvageable, but we must not let them distract us, because many of those falling through the cracks are looking for a reason to conform. Most of us at one point or another wanted to be accepted. It is incumbent upon our society to foster and offer opportunities for inclusiveness and look for common ground as diversity increases in America and throughout the world.

In terms of Vila's third point, "to alter people's fundamental values ... to minimize the likelihood of future criminal behavior," the author Stephen Covey once said that we should "seek first to understand, then to be understood."[139] In this increasingly diverse world we need to come to comprehend the meaning of John Stuart Mill's words below.

Walk a Mile in My Moccasins before You Judge Me

"[T]he world, to each individual, means the part of it with which he comes in contact; his party, his sect, his church, his class of society[.] ... [I]t never troubles him that mere accident has decided which of these numerous worlds is the object of his reliance, and that the same causes which make him a Churchman in London, would have made him a Buddhist or a Confucian in Pekin."

—John Stuart Mill[140]

Cooperation could alleviate much of the injustice seen in American society and in the world in general and in criminal justice in particular. No doubt a cooperative approach between agencies of criminal justice, as well as related agencies in mental health and other social providers, will increase in the future as shrinking resources demand less extravagance and more production and service.[141] Had there been more cooperation among the various entities, many of the crises discussed throughout the book would not have occurred. Cooperation can lead to agreements specified in writing via memorandums of understanding so that all concerned will know whose job it is and so that accountability can be better ensured.

In the future, we believe cooperation between the various components of the criminal justice system across levels of government will improve. We also believe more opportunities for citizen interaction with criminal justice professionals will occur. While we believe there must be increased efforts to include the disenfranchised within mainstream society and give them a reason to conform, we are less sanguine. As Victor Hugo once said, "[h]e who opens a school door, closes a prison."[142] We should strive to expect more out of our criminal justice professionals, and all of the others who tangentially keep the system afloat, as well as to increase our positive expectations for the least among us.

Appendix A

Michael Flynn Plea Agreement

U.S. Department of Justice

The Special Counsel's Office

Washington, D.C. 20530

November 30, 2017

Robert K. Kelner
Stephen P. Anthony
Covington & Burling LLP
One CityCenter, 850 Tenth Street, NW
Washington, DC 20001-4956

FILED
DEC 01 2017
Clerk, U.S. District and Bankruptcy Courts

Re: United States v. Michael T. Flynn

Dear Counsel:

This letter sets forth the full and complete plea offer to your client, Lieutenant General Michael T. Flynn (Ret.) (hereinafter referred to as "your client" or "defendant"), from the Special Counsel's Office (hereinafter also referred to as "the Government" or "this Office"). If your client accepts the terms and conditions of this offer, please have your client execute this document in the space provided below. Upon receipt of the executed document, this letter will become the Plea Agreement (hereinafter referred to as "this Agreement"). The terms of the offer are as follows:

1. Charges and Statutory Penalties

Your client agrees to plead guilty to the Criminal Information, a copy of which is attached, charging your client with making false statements to the Federal Bureau of Investigation in violation of 18 U.S.C. § 1001.

Your client understands that a violation of 18 U.S.C. § 1001 carries a maximum sentence of 5 years' imprisonment; a fine of $250,000, pursuant to 18 U.S.C. § 3571(b)(3); a term of supervised release of not more than 3 years, pursuant to 18 U.S.C. § 3583(b)(2); and an obligation to pay any applicable interest or penalties on fines and restitution not timely made.

In addition, your client agrees to pay a special assessment of $100 per felony conviction to the Clerk of the United States District Court for the District of Columbia. Your client also understands that, pursuant to 18 U.S.C. § 3572 and § 5E1.2 of the United States Sentencing Guidelines, *Guidelines Manual* (2016) (hereinafter "Sentencing Guidelines," "Guidelines," or "U.S.S.G."), the Court may also impose a fine that is sufficient to pay the federal government the costs of any imprisonment, term of supervised release, and period of probation.

2. Factual Stipulations

Your client agrees that the attached "Statement of the Offense" fairly and accurately describes your client's actions and involvement in the offense to which your client is pleading guilty. Please have your client sign and return the Statement of the Offense as a written proffer of evidence, along with this Agreement.

3. Additional Charges

In consideration of your client's guilty plea to the above offense, your client will not be further prosecuted criminally by this Office for the conduct set forth in the attached Statement of the Offense.

4. Sentencing Guidelines Analysis

Your client understands that the sentence in this case will be determined by the Court, pursuant to the factors set forth in 18 U.S.C. § 3553(a), including a consideration of the applicable guidelines and policies set forth in the Sentencing Guidelines. Pursuant to Federal Rule of Criminal Procedure 11(c)(1)(B), and to assist the Court in determining the appropriate sentence, the parties agree to the following:

A. Estimated Offense Level Under the Guidelines

The parties agree that the following Sentencing Guidelines sections apply:

U.S.S.G. §2B1.1(a)(2)	Base Offense Level:	6
	Total:	6

B. Acceptance of Responsibility

The Government agrees that a 2-level reduction will be appropriate, pursuant to U.S.S.G. § 3E1.1, provided that your client clearly demonstrates acceptance of responsibility, to the satisfaction of the Government, through your client's allocution, adherence to every provision of this Agreement, and conduct between entry of the plea and imposition of sentence.

Nothing in this Agreement limits the right of the Government to seek denial of the adjustment for acceptance of responsibility, pursuant to U.S.S.G. § 3E1.1, and/or imposition of an adjustment for obstruction of justice, pursuant to U.S.S.G. § 3C1.1, regardless of any agreement set forth above, should your client move to withdraw your client's guilty plea after it is entered, or should it be determined by the Government that your client has either (a) engaged in conduct, unknown to the Government at the time of the signing of this Agreement, that constitutes obstruction of justice, or (b) engaged in additional criminal conduct after signing this Agreement.

In accordance with the above, the applicable Guidelines Offense Level will be at least 4.

C. Estimated Criminal History Category

Based upon the information now available to this Office, your client has no criminal convictions.

Accordingly, your client is estimated to have zero criminal history points and your client's Criminal History Category is estimated to be I. Your client acknowledges that if additional convictions are discovered during the pre-sentence investigation by the United States Probation Office, your client's criminal history points may increase.

D. Estimated Applicable Guidelines Range

Based upon the agreed total offense level and the estimated criminal history category set forth above, your client's estimated Sentencing Guidelines range is zero months to six months' imprisonment (the "Estimated Guidelines Range"). In addition, the parties agree that, pursuant to U.S.S.G. § 5E1.2, should the Court impose a fine, at Guidelines level 4, the estimated applicable fine range is $500 to $9,500. Your client reserves the right to ask the Court not to impose any applicable fine.

The parties agree that, solely for the purposes of calculating the applicable range under the Sentencing Guidelines, neither a downward nor upward departure from the Estimated Guidelines Range set forth above is warranted, subject to the paragraphs regarding cooperation below. Accordingly, neither party will seek any departure or adjustment to the Estimated Guidelines Range, nor will either party suggest that the Court consider such a departure or adjustment, except as provided in the preceding sentence. Moreover, your client understands and acknowledges that the Estimated Guidelines Range agreed to by the parties is not binding on the Probation Office or the Court. Should the Court determine that a different guidelines range is applicable, your client will not be permitted to withdraw his guilty plea on that basis, and the Government and your client will still be bound by this Agreement.

Your client understands and acknowledges that the terms of this section apply only to conduct that occurred before the execution of this Agreement. Should your client commit any conduct after the execution of this Agreement that would form the basis for an increase in your client's base offense level or justify an upward departure (examples of which include, but are not limited to, obstruction of justice, failure to appear for a court proceeding, criminal conduct while pending sentencing, and false statements to law enforcement agents, the probation officer, or the Court), the Government is free under this Agreement to seek an increase in the base offense level based on that post-agreement conduct.

5. Agreement as to Sentencing Allocution

Based upon the information known to the Government at the time of the signing of this Agreement, the parties further agree that a sentence within the Estimated Guidelines Range would constitute a reasonable sentence in light of all of the factors set forth in 18 U.S.C. § 3553(a), should such a sentence be subject to appellate review notwithstanding the appeal waiver provided below.

6. Reservation of Allocution

The Government and your client reserve the right to describe fully, both orally and in writing, to the sentencing judge, the nature and seriousness of your client's misconduct, including any misconduct not described in the charges to which your client is pleading guilty.

The parties also reserve the right to inform the presentence report writer and the Court of any relevant facts, to dispute any factual inaccuracies in the presentence report, and to contest any matters not provided for in this Agreement. In the event that the Court considers any Sentencing Guidelines adjustments, departures, or calculations different from any agreements contained in this Agreement, or contemplates a sentence outside the Guidelines range based upon the general sentencing factors listed in 18 U.S.C. § 3553(a), the parties reserve the right to answer any related inquiries from the Court. In addition, if in this Agreement the parties have agreed to recommend or refrain from recommending to the Court a particular resolution of any sentencing issue, the parties reserve the right to full allocution in any post-sentence litigation. The parties retain the full right of allocution in connection with any post-sentence motion which may be filed in this matter and/or any proceeding(s) before the Bureau of Prisons. In addition, your client acknowledges that the Government is not obligated and currently does not intend to file any post-sentence downward departure motion in this case pursuant to Rule 35(b) of the Federal Rules of Criminal Procedure.

7. Court Not Bound by this Agreement or the Sentencing Guidelines

Your client understands that the sentence in this case will be imposed in accordance with 18 U.S.C. § 3553(a), upon consideration of the Sentencing Guidelines. Your client further understands that the sentence to be imposed is a matter solely within the discretion of the Court. Your client acknowledges that the Court is not obligated to follow any recommendation of the Government at the time of sentencing or to grant a downward departure based on your client's substantial assistance to the Government, even if the Government files a motion pursuant to Section 5K1.1 of the Sentencing Guidelines. Your client understands that neither the Government's recommendation nor the Sentencing Guidelines are binding on the Court.

Your client acknowledges that your client's entry of a guilty plea to the charged offense authorizes the Court to impose any sentence, up to and including the statutory maximum sentence, which may be greater than the applicable Guidelines range. The Government cannot, and does not, make any promise or representation as to what sentence your client will receive. Moreover, it is understood that your client will have no right to withdraw your client's plea of guilty should the Court impose a sentence that is outside the Guidelines range or if the Court does not follow the Government's sentencing recommendation. The Government and your client will be bound by this Agreement, regardless of the sentence imposed by the Court. Any effort by your client to withdraw the guilty plea because of the length of the sentence shall constitute a breach of this Agreement.

8. Cooperation

Your client agrees to cooperate with this Office on the following terms and conditions:

(a) Your client shall cooperate fully, truthfully, completely, and forthrightly with this Office and other Federal, state, and local law enforcement authorities identified by this Office in any and all matters as to which this Office deems the cooperation relevant. Your client acknowledges that your client's cooperation may include, but will not necessarily be limited to: answering questions; providing sworn written statements; taking government-administered polygraph examination(s); and participating in covert law enforcement activities. Any refusal by your client to cooperate fully, truthfully, completely, and forthrightly as directed by this Office and other Federal, state, and local law enforcement authorities identified by this Office in any and all matters in which this Office deems your client's assistance relevant will constitute a breach of this Agreement by your client, and will relieve this Office of its obligations under this Agreement, including, but not limited to, its obligation to inform this Court of any assistance your client has provided. Your client agrees, however, that such breach by your client will not constitute a basis for withdrawal of your client's plea of guilty or otherwise relieve your client of your client's obligations under this Agreement.

(b) Your client shall promptly turn over to this Office, or other law enforcement authorities, or direct such law enforcement authorities to, any and all evidence of crimes about which your client is aware; all contraband and proceeds of such crimes; and all assets traceable to the proceeds of such crimes. Your client agrees to the forfeiture of all assets which are proceeds of crimes or traceable to such proceeds of crimes.

(c) Your client shall submit a full and complete accounting of all your client's financial assets, whether such assets are in your client's name or in the name of a third party.

(d) Your client acknowledges and understands that, during the course of the cooperation outlined in this Agreement, your client will be interviewed by law enforcement agents and/or Government attorneys. Your client waives any right to have counsel present during these interviews and agrees to meet with law enforcement agents and Government attorneys outside of the presence of counsel. If, at some future point, you or your client desire to have counsel present during interviews by law enforcement agents and/or Government attorneys, and you communicate this decision in writing to this Office, this Office will honor this request, and this change will have no effect on any other terms and conditions of this Agreement.

(e) Your client shall testify fully, completely and truthfully before any and all Grand Juries in the District of Columbia and elsewhere, and at any and all trials of cases or other court proceedings in the District of Columbia and elsewhere, at which your client's testimony may be deemed relevant by the Government.

(f) Your client understands and acknowledges that nothing in this Agreement allows your client to commit any criminal violation of local, state or federal law during the period of your client's cooperation with law enforcement authorities or at any time prior to the sentencing in this case. The commission of a criminal offense during the period of your client's cooperation or at any time prior to sentencing will constitute a breach of this Agreement and will relieve the Government of all of its obligations under this Agreement, including, but not limited to, its obligation to inform this Court of any assistance your client has provided. However, your client ~~acknowledges and agrees that such a breach of this Agreement will not entitle your client to~~ withdraw your client's plea of guilty or relieve your client of the obligations under this Agreement.

(g) Your client agrees that the sentencing in this case may be delayed until your client's efforts to cooperate have been completed, as determined by the Government, so that the Court will have the benefit of all relevant information before a sentence is imposed.

9. <u>Waivers</u>

A. Venue

Your client waives any challenge to venue in the District of Columbia.

B. Statute of Limitations

Your client agrees that, should the conviction following your client's plea of guilty pursuant to this Agreement be vacated for any reason, any prosecution, based on the conduct set forth in the attached Statement of the Offense, that is not time-barred by the applicable statute of limitations on the date of the signing of this Agreement (including any counts that the Government has agreed not to prosecute or to dismiss at sentencing pursuant to this Agreement) may be commenced or reinstated against your client, notwithstanding the expiration of the statute of limitations between the signing of this Agreement and the commencement or reinstatement of such prosecution. It is the intent of this Agreement to waive all defenses based on the statute of limitations with respect to any prosecution of conduct set forth in the attached Statement of the Offense that is not time-barred on the date that this Agreement is signed.

C. Trial Rights

Your client understands that by pleading guilty in this case your client agrees to waive certain rights afforded by the Constitution of the United States and/or by statute or rule. Your client agrees to forgo the right to any further discovery or disclosures of information not already provided at the time of the entry of your client's guilty plea. Your client also agrees to waive, among other rights, the right to be indicted by a Grand Jury, the right to plead not guilty, and the right to a jury trial. If there were a jury trial, your client would have the right to be represented by counsel, to confront and cross-examine witnesses against your client, to challenge the admissibility of evidence offered against your client, to compel witnesses to appear for the purpose of testifying and presenting other evidence on your client's behalf, and to choose whether to testify. If there were a jury trial and your client chose not to testify at that trial, your client would have the right to have the jury instructed that your client's failure to testify could not be held against your client. Your client would further have the right to have the jury instructed that your client is presumed innocent until proven guilty, and that the burden would be on the United States to prove your client's guilt beyond a reasonable doubt. If your client were found guilty after a trial, your client would have the right to appeal your client's conviction. Your client understands that the Fifth Amendment to the Constitution of the United States protects your client from the use of compelled self-incriminating statements in a criminal prosecution. By entering a plea of guilty, your client knowingly and voluntarily waives or gives up your client's right against compelled self-incrimination.

Your client acknowledges discussing with you Rule 11(f) of the Federal Rules of Criminal Procedure and Rule 410 of the Federal Rules of Evidence, which ordinarily limit the admissibility of statements made by a defendant in the course of plea discussions or plea proceedings if a guilty plea is later withdrawn. Your client knowingly and voluntarily waives the rights that arise under these rules in the event your client withdraws your client's guilty plea or withdraws from this Agreement after signing it.

Your client also agrees to waive all constitutional and statutory rights to a speedy sentence and agrees that the plea of guilty pursuant to this Agreement will be entered at a time decided upon by the parties with the concurrence of the Court. Your client understands that the date for sentencing will be set by the Court.

D. Appeal Rights

Your client understands that federal law, specifically 18 U.S.C. § 3742, affords defendants the right to appeal their sentences in certain circumstances. Your client agrees to waive the right to appeal the sentence in this case, including but not limited to any term of imprisonment, fine, forfeiture, award of restitution, term or condition of supervised release, authority of the Court to set conditions of release, and the manner in which the sentence was determined, except to the extent the Court sentences your client above the statutory maximum or guidelines range determined by the Court or your client claims that your client received ineffective assistance of counsel, in which case your client would have the right to appeal the illegal sentence or above-guidelines sentence or raise on appeal a claim of ineffective assistance of counsel, but not to raise on appeal other issues regarding the sentencing. In agreeing to this waiver, your client is aware that your client's sentence has yet to be determined by the Court. Realizing the uncertainty in estimating what sentence the Court ultimately will impose, your client knowingly and willingly waives your client's right to appeal the sentence, to the extent noted above, in exchange for the concessions made by the Government in this Agreement.

E. Collateral Attack

Your client also waives any right to challenge the conviction entered or sentence imposed under this Agreement or otherwise attempt to modify or change the sentence or the manner in which it was determined in any collateral attack, including, but not limited to, a motion brought under 28 U.S.C. § 2255 or Federal Rule of Civil Procedure 60(b), except to the extent such a motion is based on newly discovered evidence or on a claim that your client received ineffective assistance of counsel. Your client reserves the right to file a motion brought under 18 U.S.C. § 3582(c)(2), but agrees to waive the right to appeal the denial of such a motion.

F. Privacy Act and FOIA Rights

Your client also agrees to waive all rights, whether asserted directly or by a representative, to request or receive from any department or agency of the United States any records pertaining to the investigation or prosecution of this case, including and without limitation any records that may be sought under the Freedom of Information Act, 5 U.S.C. § 552, or the Privacy Act, 5 U.S.C. § 552a, for the duration of the Special Counsel's investigation.

10. Restitution

Your client understands that the Court has an obligation to determine whether, and in what amount, mandatory restitution applies in this case under 18 U.S.C. § 3663A. The Government and your client agree that mandatory restitution does not apply in this case.

11. Breach of Agreement

Your client understands and agrees that, if after entering this Agreement, your client fails specifically to perform or to fulfill completely each and every one of your client's obligations under this Agreement, or engages in any criminal activity prior to sentencing, your client will have breached this Agreement. In the event of such a breach: (a) the Government will be free from its obligations under this Agreement; (b) your client will not have the right to withdraw the guilty plea; (c) your client will be fully subject to criminal prosecution for any other crimes, including perjury and obstruction of justice; and (d) the Government will be free to use against your client, directly and indirectly, in any criminal or civil proceeding, all statements made by your client and any of the information or materials provided by your client, including such statements, information, and materials provided pursuant to this Agreement or during the course of any debriefings conducted in anticipation of, or after entry of, this Agreement, whether or not the debriefings were previously characterized as "off-the-record" debriefings, and including your client's statements made during proceedings before the Court pursuant to Rule 11 of the Federal Rules of Criminal Procedure.

Your client understands and agrees that the Government shall be required to prove a breach of this Agreement only by a preponderance of the evidence, except where such breach is based on a violation of federal, state, or local criminal law, which the Government need prove only by probable cause in order to establish a breach of this Agreement.

Nothing in this Agreement shall be construed to permit your client to commit perjury, to make false statements or declarations, to obstruct justice, or to protect your client from prosecution for any crimes not included within this Agreement or committed by your client after the execution of this Agreement. Your client understands and agrees that the Government reserves the right to prosecute your client for any such offenses. Your client further understands that any perjury, false statements or declarations, or obstruction of justice relating to your client's obligations under this Agreement shall constitute a breach of this Agreement. In the event of such a breach, your client will not be allowed to withdraw your client's guilty plea.

12. Government's Obligations

The Government will bring to the Court's attention at the time of sentencing the nature and extent of your client's cooperation or lack of cooperation. The Government will evaluate the full nature and extent of your client's cooperation to determine whether your client has provided substantial assistance in the investigation or prosecution of another person who has committed an offense. If the Government determines that your client has provided such substantial assistance, this Office shall file a departure motion pursuant to Section 5K1.1 of the Sentencing Guidelines, which would afford your client an opportunity to persuade the Court that your client should be sentenced to a lesser period of incarceration and/or fine than indicated by the Sentencing Guidelines. The determination of whether your client has provided substantial assistance warranting the filing of a motion pursuant to Section 5K1.1 of the Sentencing Guidelines is within the sole discretion of the Government and is not reviewable by the Court. In the event your client should fail to perform specifically and fulfill completely each and every one of your client's obligations under this Agreement, the Government will be free from its obligations under this Agreement, and will have no obligation to present your client's case to the Departure Guideline Committee or file a departure motion pursuant to Section 5K1.1 of the Sentencing Guidelines.

13. Complete Agreement

No agreements, promises, understandings, or representations have been made by the parties or their counsel other than those contained in writing herein, nor will any such agreements, promises, understandings, or representations be made unless committed to writing and signed by your client, defense counsel, and the Special Counsel's Office.

Your client further understands that this Agreement is binding only upon the Special Counsel's Office. This Agreement does not bind any other United States Attorney's Office, nor does it bind any other state, local, or federal prosecutor. It also does not bar or compromise any civil, tax, or administrative claim pending or that may be made against your client.

If the foregoing terms and conditions are satisfactory, your client may so indicate by signing this Agreement and the Statement of the Offense, and returning both to me no later than November 30, 2017.

Sincerely yours,

ROBERT S. MUELLER, III
Special Counsel

By: ______________________
Brandon L. Van Grack
Zainab N. Ahmad
Senior Assistant Special Counsels
The Special Counsel's Office

DEFENDANT'S ACCEPTANCE

I have read every page of this Agreement and have discussed it with my attorneys, Robert K. Kelner and Stephen P. Anthony. I fully understand this Agreement and agree to it without reservation. I do this voluntarily and of my own free will, intending to be legally bound. No threats have been made to me nor am I under the influence of anything that could impede my ability to understand this Agreement fully. I am pleading guilty because I am in fact guilty of the offense identified in this Agreement.

I reaffirm that absolutely no promises, agreements, understandings, or conditions have been made or entered into in connection with my decision to plead guilty except those set forth in this Agreement. I am satisfied with the legal services provided by my attorneys in connection with this Agreement and matters related to it.

Date: 11/30/17

Lieutenant General Michael T. Flynn (Ret.)
Defendant

ATTORNEYS' ACKNOWLEDGMENT

I have read every page of this Agreement, reviewed this Agreement with my client, Lieutenant General Michael T. Flynn (Ret.), and fully discussed the provisions of this Agreement with my client. These pages accurately and completely set forth the entire Agreement. I concur in my client's desire to plead guilty as set forth in this Agreement.

Date: 11/30/17

Robert K. Kelner
Attorney for Defendant

Stephen P. Anthony
Attorney for Defendant

Appendix B

The Presentence Investigation

UNITED STATES DISTRICT COURT
FOR THE WESTERN DISTRICT OF ATLANTIS
UNITED STATES OF AMERICA vs. Christian Sanchez Docket: 05-CR-00211-001-KGG

Prepared For: The Honorable Kelly G. Green
U.S. District Judge
Prepared By: Craig T. Doe
U.S. Probation Officer
(123) 111-1111
Assistant U.S. Attorney
Mr. Robert Prosecutor
United States Courthouse
Breaker Bay, Atlantis 00000-0000
(123) 111-1212
Defense Counsel
Mr. Arthur Defender (Appointed)
P.O. Box 1000
Breaker Bay, Atlantis 00000-1000
(123) 111-1313
Sentence Date: April 29, 2005
Offense: Re-entry After Deportation, 8 USC § 1326(a), a Class E felony. Up to two years imprisonment/$250,000 fine.
Release Status: Detained without bail since January 14, 2005.
Detainers: Immigration
Co-defendants: None
Related Cases: None
Date Report Completed: April 4, 2005

Restrictions on Use and Redisclosure of Presentence Investigation Report. Disclosure of this presentence investigation report to the Federal Bureau of Prisons and redisclosure by the Bureau of Prisons is authorized by the United States District Court solely to assist administering the offender's prison sentence (i.e., classification, designation, programming, sentence calculation, pre-release planning, escape apprehension, prison disturbance response, sentence commutation, or pardon) and other limited purposes, including deportation proceedings and federal investigations directly related to terrorists activities. If this presentence investigation report is redisclosed by the Federal Bureau of Prisons upon completion of its sentence administration function, the report must be returned to the Federal Bureau of Prisons or destroyed. It is the policy of the federal judiciary and the Department of Justice that further redisclosure of the presentence investigation report is prohibited without the consent of the sentencing judge.

Presentence Report
SANCHEZ, Cristian

Place of Birth: Guaymas, Sonora, Mexico
Date of Birth: January 10, 1982
Race: White, Hispanic
Sex: Male
SSN: None
FBI: 1112233A
USM: Unknown
SID: Arizona: AZ12345678
Other ID No.: Alien Registration: A090 000 900
PACTS: 08888
Education: 13 years
Dependents: Two (girlfriend and child)
Citizenship: Mexico
Last Address:
Colonia Indeus
Citahuis, No. 31
Navojoa, Sonora, Mexico
Names on Record: Sanchez, Christian; BORRON, Cristian Lugo; BURBON-LUGO, Cristian; LUGO, Cristian; LUGO, Cristian Canek; BORBON, Cristian Canek

PART A—THE OFFENSE
Charge(s) and Conviction(s)
1. On February 18, 2005, the defendant pleaded guilty to a single-count indictment charging that on or about January 14, 2005, the defendant entered and was found in the United States after having been deported, a violation of 8 U.S.C. § 1326(a).

2. Pursuant to Rule 11(c)(1)(C) and § 5K3.1, the parties stipulate to a sentencing range of zero to six months based on a Criminal History Category I. The government may withdraw from the agreement if it is discovered the defendant has a prior felony or aggravated felony conviction. The defendant waives rights to appeal the judgment and sentence if sentenced in accordance with the agreement.

The Offense Conduct
3. On January 14, 2005, a Border Patrol agent detected foot sign of several individuals near Naco, Arizona. After following the tracks, the agent encountered approximately 26 individuals, who were attempting to conceal themselves behind some brush. The individuals, including the defendant, admitted being citizens of Mexico and being in the United States illegally.

4. Further investigation revealed the defendant had five prior removals from the United States in 2004. A formal order of removal or deportation was signed by an immigration judge on December 17, 2004, and the defendant was removed to Mexico.

Offense Level Computations
5. The guidelines in effect at the time of sentencing are applied pursuant to 18 USC § 3553(a)(4) and § 1B1.11.
6. **Base Offense Level:** The guideline for a violation of 8 USC § 1326 is § 2L1.2(a). The Base Offense Level is 8. 8
7. **Specific Offense Characteristic:** None 0
8. **Victim-Related Adjustments:** None 0
9. **Adjustments for Role in the Offense:** None 0
10. **Adjustment for Obstruction of Justice:** None 0
11. **Adjusted Offense Level (Subtotal)** 8

12. **Adjustment for Acceptance of Responsibility:** Two levels are subtracted as the defendant clearly demonstrates acceptance of responsibility. § 3E1.1(a). -2
13. **Total Offense Level:** 6

PART B—DEFENDANT'S CRIMINAL HISTORY
Juvenile Adjudications
14. None

Adult Convictions
Date of Arrest Conviction/Court Date/Sentence Guideline/Points
15. 12/12/2004
(Age 22) Illegal Entry (misdemeanor)
8 U.S.C. § 1325; U.S. District Court, Tucson, Arizona, Docket 04-6185M-P 12/15/2004:
Time served § 4A1.1(c)

The defendant was represented by an attorney. According to immigration records and the defendant's automated criminal record, an immigration judge ordered the defendant removed from the country on December 17, 2004.

Criminal History Computation
16. The defendant's criminal history points total one, establishing a Criminal History Category

Other Criminal Conduct
17. According to immigration records, the defendant had four additional removals from the United States during 2004. Immigration records also noted that on August 9, 2004, the defendant was the driver of a vehicle seized for transporting 11 undocumented illegal aliens.

PART C—OFFENDER PERSONAL HISTORY

Personal and Family Data

18. The defendant is one of three children born to Jesus Sanchez, 44, a teacher, and Irma Lugo-Ramos, 42, a housewife. The defendant's parents and siblings, Solaya, 22, a student, and Jesus, 16, a student, reside in Navojoa, Sonora. The defendant has been involved in a relationship with Mariella Lopez, 22, for three years. They have a son, Cristian. His girlfriend and child reside with his parents in Navojoa.

19. The defendant reported he has lived in Navojoa for most of his life. He stated he had previously traveled to Phoenix on seven occasions and that he stayed there for no more than one month each time. Upon release, the defendant intends to return to his family in Navojoa.

According to immigration records, an immigration judge ordered the defendant removed from the United States on December 17, 2004.

PART D—SENTENCING OPTIONS

Custody

20. **Statutory Provisions:** The maximum term of imprisonment is 2 years. 8 U.S.C. § 1326(a).

21. **Guideline Provisions:** Based on a Total Offense Level of 6 and Criminal History Category of I, the guideline range for imprisonment is 0 to 6 months.

Supervised Release

22. **Statutory Provisions:** The court may impose a term of supervised release of not more than 1 year. 18 U.S.C. § 3583(b)(3).

23. **Guideline Provisions:** The authorized term of supervised release is one year. U.S.S.G. § 5D1.2(a)(3). If a term of imprisonment of more than one year is imposed, the court must impose a term of supervised release. U.S.S.G. § 5D1.1(a).

Probation

24. **Statutory Provisions:** The authorized term of probation is not less than one nor more than five years. 18 U.S.C. § 3561(c)(1).

25. **Guideline Provisions:** The authorized term of probation is at least one but no more than five years. U.S.S.G. § 5B1.2(a)(1).

Fines

26. **Statutory Provisions:** The maximum fine is $250,000. 18 U.S.C. § 3571.

27. **Guideline Provisions:** The fine range is $500 to $5,000. U.S.S.G. § 5E1.2(c)(3).

28. Subject to the defendant's ability to pay, the Court shall consider costs of imprisonment, probation, or supervised release. U.S.S.G. § 5E1.2(d).

Prison Halfway House Supervision

Costs Per Month: $1,931.97 $1,590.66 $292.21

Special Assessments

29. **Statutory Provisions:** A special assessment of $100 is mandatory. 18 U.S.C. § 3013(a).

Restitution

30. Restitution is not an issue.

PART E—CIRCUMSTANCES THAT MAY WARRANT DEPARTURE FROM USSC GUIDELINES

31. Presentation of information in this section does not necessarily constitute a recommendation for a departure from the advisory guideline range.

32. Pursuant to § 5K3.1, upon motion of the government, the Court may depart downward not more than four levels pursuant to an early disposition program authorized by the Attorney General of the United States and the United States Attorney for the District of Arizona.

UNITED STATES v. Christian Sanchez, DOCKET 05-CR-00211-001-KGG
TOTAL OFFENSE LEVEL: 6
CRIMINAL HISTORY CATEGORY: I
Statutory
Provisions Guideline
Provisions Plea Agreement
Provisions Recommended
Sentence
CUSTODY: Up to 2 years 0 to 6 months 0 to 6 months 6 months
SUPERVISED
RELEASE: Up to 1 year 1 year 1 year
PROBATION: 1 to 5 years 1 to 5 years
FINE: Up to $250,000 $500 to $5,000 Waive
RESTITUTION: Not an issue Not an issue Not an issue
SPECIAL
ASSESSMENT: $100 $100 $100
Justification

The defendant pleaded guilty to re-entry after deportation. The guideline calculations reflect the defendant's acceptance of responsibility and his placement in Criminal History Category I.

Unaccounted-for aggravating factors include the defendant's five prior removals from the country.

Although no charges were filed, immigration records reflected the defendant was a driver of a vehicle seized for transporting 11 illegal aliens. No unaccounted-for mitigating factors have been identified.

Considering all factors, an imprisonment sentence of six months, followed by one year of supervised release, is warranted to provide just punishment for the offense and to afford adequate deterrence to further criminal conduct.

In light of his pending removal from the United States, a special condition of supervised release is recommended ordering the defendant not to re-enter the United States without legal authorization.

Because the defendant does not have the means to pay a fine, it is recommended the fine be waived.

The special assessment is mandatory pursuant to 18 U.S.C. § 3013(a). Pursuant to 18 U.S.C. § 3583(d) the court shall order as an explicit condition of supervised release, that the defendant shall cooperate in the collection of a DNA sample from the defendant.

Voluntary Surrender
The defendant has been detained without bail since arrest and is not a candidate for voluntary surrender.
18 U.S.C. § 3143(a)(2).

Recommendation
It is respectfully recommended that sentence in this case be imposed as follows:
Pursuant to the Sentencing Reform Act of 1984, it is the judgment of the Court that Cristian Sanchez is hereby committed to the Bureau of Prisons for six months.
The defendant shall pay a special assessment of $100, which shall be due immediately. If incarcerated, payment shall begin under the Bureau of Prisons Inmate Financial Responsibility Program. Payments shall be made to the Clerk, U.S. District Court. The Court finds the defendant does not have the ability to pay and orders the fine waived.

Upon release from imprisonment, the defendant shall be placed on supervised release for one year.

While on supervised release, the defendant shall comply with the standard conditions of supervision.

The defendant shall comply with the following additional conditions:

You shall not re-enter the United States without legal authorization.

UNITED STATES PROBATION OFFICE
WESTERN DISTRICT OF ATLANTIS
Memorandum
DATE: April 28, 2005
FROM: Craig T. Doe, U.S. Probation Officer
THRU: Mary T. Clark, Supervising U.S. Probation Officer
SUBJECT: U.S. v Donald Reese, 05-CR-1000-KGG
TO: Honorable Kelly G. Green, U.S. District Judge

April 15, the defendant appeared before Magistrate Judge Mark Lerner and pleaded guilty to a single-count information charging the defendant with theft of mail, in violation of 18 U.S.C. § 1708. Following the entry of the plea, Magistrate Judge Lerner ordered the probation office to prepare a modified presentence investigation report.

A search through local criminal court records has revealed several prior arrests that the court was not previously made aware of. Among the defendant's prior arrests is a conviction for assault for which he was sentenced to two years of probation. As a special condition, the defendant was ordered to participate in an anger-management program.

According to local probation officials, due to the defendant's erratic behavior during these sessions, he was referred for a mental health assessment. The defendant has since been diagnosed with antisocial personality disorder and is under the care of a mental health professional. It appears that neither this conviction nor the defendant's mental health condition were known to the court when the defendant pleaded guilty.

Because a modified presentence investigation report was ordered, the probation officer has not yet fully investigated these issues. Based on these developments, we are requesting guidance from the court on how to proceed. Please feel free to contact us if you have any questions.[1]

1. The Presentence Investigation Report (March 2006, Rev.) Publication 107, Office of Probation and Pretrial Services, Administration Office of the United States Courts. Accessed July 22, 2010: http://www.fd.org/pdf_lib/publication%20107.pdf.

Notes

Chapter 1

1. Kathryn A. Power, "Transformation: Moving from Goals to Action." Joint National Conference on Mental Health Block Grants and National Conference on Mental Health Statistics, Arlington, Virginia, June 1, 2005, accessed March 23, 2010, http://mentalhealth.samhsa.gov/newsroom/speeches/060105.asp.

2. *Citizens United v. Federal Election Commission*, 558 U.S. 310 (2010).

3. CNN. "Obama Criticizes Campaign Finance Ruling," CNN Political Ticker, Turner Broadcasting System, Inc., January 20, 2010, accessed March 3, 2010, http://politicalticker.blogs.cnn.com/2010/01/21/obama-criticizes-campaign-finance-ruling.

4. Barack Obama, Address Before a Joint Session of the Congress on the State of the Union, January 27, 2010, accessed March 3, 2010, http://www.presidency.ucsb.edu/ws/index.php?pid=87433.

5. Jon Schuppe, "NRA Sticking With Trump, Breaks Own Record for Campaign Spending," *NBC News*, October 12, 2016, accessed January 22, 2018, https://www.nbcnews.com/news/us-news/nra-sticking-trump-breaks-own-record-campaign-spending-n665056

6. John Marshall had served as secretary of state in the presidential administration of John Adams and was appointed in the latter days of that administration to the U.S. Supreme Court. Another appointment to a midnight judgeship (it is referred to this because outgoing administrations often try to leave a mark on future governance with last-minute appointments) by Adams was that of a William Marbury. However, though Marbury's commission to a judgeship was signed and sealed, it was never delivered—likely due to an error by outgoing Secretary of State Marshall. With the new presidential administration of Thomas Jefferson the last-minute partisan appointments of the Adams administration were targeted, and incoming Secretary of State James Madison refused to deliver Marbury's judicial commission. Some felt that Marshall should recuse himself from the case since his involvement had likely had a hand in the commission and it not having been delivered under the Adams administration; instead, Marshall wound up writing the opinion for the United States, an opinion considered by many to be the most important opinion ever decided by the Court. Ironically, Marshall did not allow Marbury to be appointed to the judiciary but found that the legislation passed by Congress to allow Marbury to be appointed to the court was unconstitutional.

7. *Marbury v. Madison*, 5 U.S. (1 Cranch) 137 (1803).

8. Robert Wayne Pelton, *Loony Laws that You Never Knew You Were Breaking* (Markham, Ontario: Thomas Allen & Son, 1990).

9. Paul Larkin and John-Michael Seibler, "Time to Prune the Tree: The Need to Repeal Unnecessary Criminal Laws," Legal Memorandum 173, Heritage Organization, February 25, 2016, accessed January 21, 2017, http://www.heritage.org/research/reports/2016/02/time-to-prune-the-tree-the-need-to-repeal-unnecessary-criminal-laws.

10. The Free Dictionary by Farlex, "Blue Laws," accessed March 18, 2010, http://legal-dictionary.thefreedictionary.com/Blue+Laws.

11. Erin Delmore, "Behind Bergen County's Blue Laws," NJTV News, November 26, 2015, accessed January 21, 2017, http://www.njtvonline.org/news/video/behind-bergen-countys-blue-laws/.

12. Ibid.; J. B. Mackinnon, "America's Last Ban on Sunday Shopping," *The New Yorker*, February 7, 2015, accessed January 21, 2017, http://www.newyorker.com/business/currency/americas-last-ban-sunday-shopping; New York State Government, "Governor Cuomo and Legislative Leaders Announce Agreement to Modernize New York's Alcoholic Beverage Control Law," June 14, 2016, accessed January 21, 2017, https://www.governor.ny.gov/news/governor-cuomo-and-legislative-leaders-announce-agreement-modernize-new-yorks-alcoholic.

13. See "Richland Sheriff Responds to Blue Law Complaints," *Spartanburg Herald-Journal*, July 20, 1983, B7, accessed March 11, 2010, http://news.google.com/newspapers?nid=1876&dat=19830720&id=RVksAAAAIBAJ&sjid=Rc4EAAAAIBAJ&pg=6642,4790918.

14. Howard Becker, *Outsiders* (New York: The Free Press, 1963).

15. Mike Leco, "Sex in Las Vegas," accessed March 14, 2010, http://www.usatourist.com/english/places/lasvegas/sex.html.

16. Cherry Patch Ranch, The Best Little Whore Houses in Nevada, accessed March 14, 2010, http://cherrypatchwhorehouse.com; The Resort and Spa Sheri's Ranch, accessed March 14, 2010, http://www.sherisranch.com; The World Famous Historic Chicken Ranch, accessed March 14, 2010, http://www.chickenranchbrothel.com.

17. David Emery, U.S. Gov't Tried (and Failed) to Run Mustang Ranch, About.com: Urban Legends, December 17, 2008, accessed March 14, 2010, http://urbanlegends.about.com/od/government/a/mustang_ranch.htm.

18. Mike Gray, *Drug Crazy* (New York: Random House, 1998).

19. Carolyn Gallaher, *On the Fault Line: Race, Class, and the American Patriot Movement* (Lanham, MD: Rowman and Littlefield Publishers, Inc., 2002).

20. Mick Winter, *Peak Oil Prep* (Napa, CA: Westsong Publishing, 2006); see also Carolyn Gallaher, ibid.

21. Stan Medley Presents: Reefer Madness 1938, accessed March 21, 2010, http://stanmedley.org/blog/2008/11/25/stan-medley-presents-reefer-madness-1938.

22. James Q. Wilson, *Varieties of Police Behavior* (Cambridge, MA: Harvard University Press, 1978).

23. Art Swift, "Support for Legal Marijuana Use Up to 60% in U.S.," Gallup: Social Issues, October 19, 2016, accessed January 22, 2017, http://www.gallup.com/poll/196550/support-legal-marijuana.aspx; Kevin Hechtkopf, "Poll: 44 Percent Support Marijuana Legalization," Political Hotsheet, CBS News, October 20, 2009, accessed March 21, 2010, http://www.cbsnews.com/8301-503544_162-5403028-503544.html; see also Andrew Cohen, "Time for Marijuana Legalization? Opinion," CBS News, February 25, 2009, accessed March 21, 2010, http://www.cbsnews.com/stories/2009/02/25/opinion/courtwatch/main4828659.shtml?source=search_story.

24. Patrick O'Driscoll, "Denver Votes to Legalize Marijuana Possession," *USA Today*, November 3, 2005, accessed March 21, 2010, http://www.usatoday.com/news/nation/2005-11-03-pot_x.htm.

25. Governing: The States and Localities, "Governing Data: State Marijuana Laws in 2016 Map," 2016, accessed January 22, 2017, http://www.governing.com/gov-data/state-marijuana-laws-map-medical-recreational.html; Kate Abbey-Lambatz, "Maine's Recreational Marijuana Law Takes Effect This Month: A Total of Eight States Have Now Legalized Pot Use," *The Huffington Post*, January 3, 2017, accessed January 22, 2017, http://www.huffingtonpost.com/entry/maine-recreational-marijuana-law_us_586bac85e4b0d9a5945c5a0c.

26. Matt Laslo, "American High: State-by-State Guide to Legal Pot," *Rolling Stone*, April 19, 2017, accessed September 29, 2017, http://www.rollingstone.com/culture/lists/how-to-smoke-legal-pot-in-america-a-state-by-state-guide-w477307.

27. Storefront Political Media, "What Is the Difference between a Proposition, an Initiative and a Referendum on the Ballot?" *I Agree to See*, 2016, accessed January 23, 2017, http://www.iagreetosee.com/faq/difference-between-a-proposition-an-initiative-and-a-referendum/.

28. ProCon.org, "29 Legal Medical Marijuana States and DC." June 26, 2017, accessed September 29, 2017, https://medicalmarijuana.procon.org/view.resource.php?resourceID=000881.

29. The Week, "The Rise of Legal Weed in America," November 26, 2016, accessed January 23, 2017, http://theweek.com/articles/662621/rise-legal-weed-america.

30. Ryan J. Reilly, "Jeff Sessions Was Deemed Too Racist to Be a Federal Judge. He'll Now Be Trump's Attorney General," *The Huffington Post*, November 17, 2016, accessed January 23, 2017, http://www.huffingtonpost.com/entry/trump-attorney-general-jeff-sessions-racist-remarks_us_582cd73ae4b099512f80c0c2.

31. Jeremy Berke, "Here's Where President-elect Donald Trump Stands on Marijuana Legalization," *Business Insider*, November 9, 2016, accessed February 28, 2017, http://www.businessinsider.com/where-donald-trump-stands-on-weed-legalization-2016-11.

32. Sadie Gurman, "White House Expects Justice Department to Crack Down on Legalized Marijuana," Associated Press, February 24, 2017, accessed February 28, 2017, http://abc30.com/politics/white-house-expects-justice-department-to-crack-down-on-legalized-marijuana/1770816/.

33. Christopher Ingraham, "Virginia Republican Introduces Bill to End Federal Marijuana Prohibition," *The Washington Post*, March 2, 2017, accessed March 5, 2017, https://www.washingtonpost.com/news/wonk/wp/2017/03/02/an-unlikely-champion-introduces-bill-to-end-the-federal-war-on-marijuana/?utm_term=.119c597a77ae.

34. Ibid.

35. Christopher Ingraham, "Senator Cory Booker Puts Marijuana Legislation at the Center of His New Racial Justice Bill," *The Washington Post*, August 1, 2017, accessed September 29, 2017, https://www.washingtonpost.com/news/wonk/wp/2017/08/01/cory-booker-puts-marijuana-legalization-at-the-center-of-his-new-racial-justice-bil/?utm_term=.4550f330722b.

36. Paul Waldman, "Why Jeff Sessions's Marijuana Crackdown is Going to Make Legalization More Likely," The Washington Post, January 5, 2018, accessed January 11, 2018, https://www.washingtonpost.com/blogs/plum-line/wp/2018/01/05/why-jeff-sessions-marijuana-crackdown-is-going-to-make-legalization-more-likely/?utm_term=.479e7443028a.

37. Free Thought Project, "Jesse Ventura Ceases Trump Support, Publicly Blasts Hypocrisy Over Crackdown on Pot," *SteemNews*, February 27, 2017, accessed February 28, 2017, https://steemit.com/news/@tftproject/jesse-ventura-ceases-trump-support-publicly-blasts-hypocrisy-over-crackdown-on-pot.

38. Fredreka Schouten, "Private Prisons Back Trump and Could See Big Payoffs with New Policies," *USA Today*, February 23, 2017, accessed February 28, 2017, http://www.usatoday.com/story/news/politics/2017/02/23/private-prisons-back-trump-and-could-see-big-payoffs-new-policies/98300394/.

39. John H. Richardson, "Why Obama Really Might Decriminalize Marijuana," *Esquire*, December 23, 2008, accessed March 21, 2010, http://www.esquire.com/the-side/richardson-report/ obama-marijuana-legalization-122308.

40. Jonathan Burr, "How Profitable Are Pot shops? You'd Be Surprised," Moneywatch, CBS News, June 29, 2016, accessed January 29, 2017, http://www.cbsnews.com/news/how-profitable-are-pot-shops-youd-be-surprised/.

41. Janice Williams, "Marijuana in Colorado: Homelessness Will Be Fought with $13M from Tax Revenue, Governor Says," *International Business Times*, November 28, 2016, accessed January 29, 2017, http://www.ibtimes.com/marijuana-colorado-homelessness-will-be-fought-13m-tax-revenue-governor-says-2451728; Joel Warner, "Marijuana Legalization in Colorado: How Recreational Weed Is Attracting People, But Spiking the State's Homeless Rate," *International Business Times*, June 20, 2016, accessed January 29, 2017, http://www.ibtimes.com/marijuana-legalization-colorado-how-recreational-weed-attracting-people-spiking-2374204.

42. Tyler Koslow, "Cannabis by the Numbers: How Much Money Will States Bring in from Marijuana in 2016?" *Merry Jane*, May 17, 2016, accessed January 29, 2017, https://www.merryjane.com/news/cannabis-by-the-numbers-how-much-money-will-states-bring-in-from-marijuana-in-2016.

43. Erik Brady, "Celebrities High on Marijuana Businesses," *USA Today*, September 12, 2016, accessed January 29, 2017, http://www.usatoday.com/story/sports/2016/09/12/marijuana-business-whoopi-goldberg-willie-nelson-snoop-dogg/90125540/.

44. Ashley Halsey III, "Drugged Driving Eclipses Drunken Driving in Tests of Motorists Killed in Crashes," *Washington Post*, April 26, 2017, accessed April 26, 2017, https://www.washingtonpost.com/local/trafficandcommuting/drugged-driving-eclipses-drunken-driving-in-tests-of-motorists-killed-in-crashes/2017/04/25/38c01b4c-291a-11e7-a616-d7c8a68c1a66_story.html?utm_term=.454a761f204a.

45. Thomas J. Moran, "Just a Little Bit of History Repeating: The California Model of Marijuana Legalization and How It Might Affect Racial and Ethnic Minorities," *Washington and Lee Journal of Civil Rights and Social Justice* 17 (Spring 2011): 557–590; 573.

46. Richardson, op. cit. note 34.

47. Human Rights Watch, "Every 25 Seconds: The Human Toll of Criminalizing Drug Use in the United States," Human Rights Watch, October 12, 2016, accessed January 29, 2017, https://www.hrw.org/report/2016/10/12/every-25-seconds/human-toll-criminalizing-drug-use-united-states.

48. David Scharfenberg, "Blacks Are Still More Likely than Whites to Be Arrested for Marijuana," *Boston Globe*, October 6, 2016, accessed January 29, 2017, https://www.bostonglobe.com/metro/2016/10/06/report-finds-sharp-racial-disparities-marijuana-arrests/VKB2BB3Oqn1Rd0MHiXhFRN/story.html.

49. D. W. Neubauer, *America's Courts and the Criminal Justice System* (Pacific Grove, California: Brooks/Cole Publishing Company, 1992).

50. Steven F. Messner and Richard Rosenfeld, *Crime and the American Dream*, 4th ed. (Belmont, California: Wadsworth, 2007).

51. Samuel Walker, *Sense and Nonsense about Crime and Drugs: A Policy Guide* (Belmont, California: Thomson Wadsworth, 2006).

52. Ronald D. Hunter and Thomas Barker, *Police-Community Relations and the Administration of Justice*, 8th ed., (Upper Saddle River, NJ: Prentice Hall, 2011).

53. U.S. Department of Homeland Security, About DHS, June 29, 2016, accessed February 6, 2017, https://www.dhs.gov/about-dhs.

54. U.S. Department of Homeland Security, Fact Sheet: Department of Homeland Security Fiscal Year 2016 Budget, February 2, 2015, accessed February 6, 2017, https://www.dhs.gov/news/2015/02/02/fact-sheet-dhs-fy-2016-budget.

55. U.S. Department of Homeland Security, Budget-in-Brief Fiscal Year 2017, Homeland Security, 2017, accessed February 6, 2017, https://www.dhs.gov/sites/default/files/publications/FY2017BIB.pdf.

56. See Ross Douthat, "Prisons of Our Own Making," *New York Times*, January 13, 2009, accessed January 18, 2010, http://www.nytimes.com/2009/12/14/opinion/14douthat.html?_r=1; Ben Adler, "The Myth that Democrats Are Soft on Crime," *Newsweek*, January 15, 2009, accessed January 18, 2010, http://blog.newsweek.com/ blogs/thegaggle/archive/2009/12/15/the-democratic-crime-myth.aspx.

57. Ibid.

58. Leonard A. Sipes, Jr., "Is Crime Increasing in America?" 2017, accessed February 6, 2017, http://www.crimeinamerica.net/crime-rates-united-states/.

59. Danielle Kaeble and Lauren Glaze, *Correctional Populations in the United States, 2015*, U.S. Department of Justice, Office of Justice Programs, Bureau of Justice Statistics, December 2016, accessed February 11, 2017, https://www.bjs.gov/content/pub/pdf/cpus15.pdf.

60. Ibid.

61. The Sentencing Project, "Fact Sheet: Trends in U.S. Corrections," December 2015, accessed February 11, 2017, http://sentencingproject.org/wp-content/uploads/2016/01/Trends-in-US-Corrections.pdf.

62. Peter Wagner and Alison Walsh, "States of Incarceration: The Global Context 2016," Prison Policy Initiative, June 16, 2016, accessed February 11, 2017, https://www.prisonpolicy.org/global/2016.html.

63. Peter Wagner and Bernadette Rabuy, "Mass Incarceration: The Whole Pie 2016," Prison Policy Initiative, March 14, 2016, accessed February 12, 2017, https://www.prisonpolicy.org/reports/pie2016.html.

64. The Sentencing Project, op. cit.

65. Peter Wagner and Bernadette Rabuy, op. cit.

66. The Sentencing Project, op. cit.

67. Ibid.

68. Ibid.

69. U.S. Department of Education, "Report: Increases in Spending on Corrections Far Outpace Education," July 7, 2016, accessed February 12, 2017, https://www.ed.gov/news/press-releases/report-increases-spending-corrections-far-outpace-education.

70. Ibid.

71. Ibid.

72. The Sentencing Project, op. cit.

73. Louis Jacobson, "Donald Trump Wrong that the Murder Rate Is Highest in 47 Years," *Politifact*, February 8, 2017, accessed February 12, 2017, http://www.politifact.com/truth-o-meter/statements/2017/feb/08/donald-trump/donald-trump-wrong-murder-rate-highest-47-years/.

74. Ibid.

75. Erica L. Smith and Alexia D. Cooper, *Homicide in the U.S. Known to Law Enforcement*, Bureau of Justice Statistics, Washington, DC, December 30, 2013, accessed February 16, 2017, https://www.bjs.gov/index.cfm?ty=pbdetail&iid=4863; Ryan McMaken, "FBI: U.S. Homicide Rate at 51 Year Low," *MISES WIRE*, June 15, 2016, accessed February 16, 2017, https://mises.org/blog/fbi-us-homicide-rate-51-year-low.

76. Federal Bureau of Investigation, *Crime in the United States by Volume and Rate per 100,000 Occupants 1996–2015*, Table 1, Department of Justice, 2015, accessed February 16, 2017, https://ucr.fbi.gov/crime-in-the-u.s/2015/crime-in-the-u.s.-2015/tables/table-1.

77. Justin McCarthy, "Americans' Views Shift on Toughness of Justice System," *Gallup*, October 20, 2016, accessed February 12, 2017, http://www.gallup.com/poll/196568/americans-views-shift-toughness-justice-system.aspx.

78. John M. Scheb and John M. Scheb, II, *American Criminal Law* (St. Paul, MN: West, 1996).

79. *State Court Cases and Defendants*, Bureau of Justice Statistics, Washington, DC, accessed February 18, 2010, http://bjs.ojp.usdoj.gov/index.cfm?ty=tp&tid=22.

80. Peter Wagner and Bernadette Rabuy, op. cit.

81. Lindsey Devers, *Plea and Charge Bargaining: Research Summary*, Bureau of Justice Assistance, U.S. Department of Justice, January 24, 2011, accessed February 12, 2017, https://www.bja.gov/Publications/PleaBargainingResearchSummary.pdf.

82. Glenn R. Schmitt and Jennifer Dukes, *Overview of Federal Criminal Cases: Fiscal Year 2012*, United States Sentencing Commission, 2012, accessed February 13, 2017, http://www.ussc.gov/sites/default/files/pdf/research-and-publications/research-publications/2013/FY12_Overview_Federal_Criminal_Cases.pdf.

83. United States Attorneys, FY 2017 Performance Budget Congressional Submission, U.S. Department of Justice, 2017, accessed February 13, 2017, https://www.justice.gov/jmd/file/821011/download.

84. Glenn R. Schmitt and Jennifer Dukes, op. cit.

85. Ibid.

86. Eric Westervelt, "Measuring the Power of a Prison Education," NPR, July 31, 2015, accessed February 13, 2017, http://www.npr.org/sections/ed/2015/07/31/427741914/measuring-the-power-of-a-prison-education.

87. Federal Bureau of Investigation, *Crime in the United States, (2015) Table 29, Estimated Number of Arrests*, U.S. Department of Justice, Washington, DC, accessed February 13, 2017, https://ucr.fbi.gov/crime-in-the-u.s/2015/crime-in-the-u.s.-2015/tables/table-29.

88. John M. Scheb and John M. Scheb, II, *Criminal Law and Procedure* (St. Paul, MN: West, 1989), 6–7.

89. Federal Bureau of Investigation, *Uniform Crime Reports*, U.S. Department of Justice, Washington, DC, accessed February 20, 2010, http://www.fbi.gov/ucr/ucr.htm.

90. *National Crime Victimization Survey Resource Guide*, U.S. Department of Justice, Bureau of Justice Statistics, Washington, DC, accessed February 20, 2010, http://www.icpsr.umich.edu/ NACJD/NCVS.

91. Federal Bureau of Investigation, *Crime in the United States 2002* (Department of Justice, Washington, DC), accessed February 20, 2010, http://www.fbi.gov/ucr/cius_02/html/web/appendices/07-append02.html.

92. Federal Bureau of Investigation, Crime in the United States by Volume and Rate per 100,000, 2015, op. cit.

93. Ibid.

94. Ibid.

95. An excellent critical analysis of the limitations and use of the FBI index is available. See Robert M. O'Brien, *Crime and Victimization Data* (Beverly Hills, CA: Sage, 1986); see also Michael J. Hindelang, "The Uniform Crime Reports Revisited," *Journal of Criminal Justice* 2, no. 1 (Spring 1974): 1.

96. Uniform Crime Reporting (UCR) 2004 Summary Reporting, Frequently Asked Questions, Department of Justice, Federal Bureau of Investigation, accessed February 24, 2010, http://www.fbi.gov/ucr/ucrquest.htm.

97. Federal Bureau of Investigation, "About the Uniform Crime Reporting Program," U.S. Department of Justice, January 26, 2017, accessed April 23, 2017, https://www.bjs.gov/ucrdata/abouttheucr.cfm; also see property crime, https://ucr.fbi.gov/crime-in-the-u.s/2015/crime-in-the-u.s.-2015/offenses-known-to-law-enforcement/property-crime/propertycrimemain_final; violent crime, https://ucr.fbi.gov/crime-in-the-u.s/2015/crime-in-the-u.s.-2015/offenses-known-to-law-enforcement/violent-crime/violentcrimemain_final; arrests, https://ucr.fbi.gov/crime-in-the-u.s/2015/crime-in-the-u.s.-2015/tables/table-29.

98. Table 25, op. cit.

99. John T. Whitehead and Steven P. Lab, *Juvenile Justice: An Introduction*, 6th ed. (Cincinnati, OH: Anderson Publishing Company, 2008).

100. Bureau of Justice Statistics, National Crime Victimization Survey, Technical Documentation, September 2014, accessed February 17, 2017, https://www.bjs.gov/content/pub/pdf/ncvstd13.pdf; Michael R. Rand, "The National Crime Victimization Survey: 32 Years of Measuring Crime in the United States," U.S. Bureau of Justice Statistics, Siena Group on Social Statistics, Helsinski, Finland, February 2005, accessed February 17, 2017, http://www.stat.fi/sienagroup2005/sienarand.pdf.

101. Jennifer L. Truman and Rachel E. Morgan, *Criminal Victimization, 2015*, Publication and Product Detail, Bureau of Justice Statistics, Office of Justice Programs, October 20, 2016, accessed February 17, 2017, https://www.bjs.gov/index.cfm?ty=pbdetail&iid=5804.

102. Jennifer L. Truman and Rachel E. Morgan, *Criminal Victimization, 2015*, Bureau of Justice Statistics, Office of Justice Programs, U.S. Department of Justice, October 2016, accessed February 17, 2017, https://www.bjs.gov/content/pub/pdf/cv15.pdf.

103. Kara McCarthy, *Violent Crime Rate Remained Unchanged While Theft Rate Declined in 2008*, Bureau of Justice Statistics, Department of Justice, September 9, 2009, accessed February 20, 2010, http://bjs.ojp.usdoj.gov/content/pub/press/cv08pr.cfm.

104. U.S. Department of Justice, Bureau of Justice Statistics, *Criminal Victimization in the United States, 2006 Statistical Tables*, NCJ 223436, Table 101, Sept. 17, 2008, accessed February 27, 2010, http://www.ojp.usdoj.gov/bjs/ pub/pdf/cvus06.pdf.

105. U.S. Department of Justice, Bureau of Justice Statistics, *Criminal Victimization in the United States, 2006 Statistical Tables*, NCJ 223436, Table 102, Sept. 17, 2008, accessed February 27, 2010, http://www.ojp.usdoj.gov/bjs/pub/pdf/cvus06.pdf.

106. Reporting Crime, Southern Poverty Law Center, April 2009, accessed February 27, 2010, http://www.splcenter.org/publications/under-siege-life-low-income-latinos-south/reporting-crime.

107. McCarthy, op. cit.

108. Rana Sampson, *Acquaintance Rape of College Students*, U.S. Department of Justice, Office of Community Oriented Policing Services, March 2002, accessed February 27, 2010, www.cops.us doj.gov/pdf/e03021472.pdf; *Reporting Rape*, Rape Abuse & Incest National Network (RAINN), accessed February 20, 2010, http://www.rainn.org/get-information/legal-information/reporting-rape.

109. Rand, op. cit.

110. *Criminal Victimization in the United States*, Table 102, op. cit.

111. Golub, A., Johnson, B., Taylor, A. & Liberty, H. "The Validity of Arrestee's Self-Reports," *Justice Quarterly* 19, no. 3 (2002): 477–502.

112. Jon Greenberg, "Watch Out, 70% of Us Have Done Something that could put us in jail," *PUNDITFACT*, December 8, 2014, accessed February 17, 2017, http://www.politifact.com/punditfact/statements/2014/dec/08/stephen-carter/watch-out-70-us-have-done-something-could-put-us-j/.

113. The most common categories of known or suspected criminals compiled by the police include the names of alleged gamblers, prostitutes, narcotics pushers, and sex deviates, particularly rapists and child molesters. Specialized police units also frequently maintain lists of reputed organized crime members and alleged political extremists. See Suzanne Smalley, "Police Seek to Track Violent Offenders," *The Boston Globe*, February 15, 2006, accessed February 25, 2010,http://www.boston.com/news/local/massachusetts/articles/2006/02/15/police_seek_to_track_violent_offenders; Michael Gresham, "Area Police to Keep Tabs on Repeat Offenders," *Terrell Tribune*, July 22, 2009, accessed February 25, 2010, http://www.terrelltribune.com/articles/2009/07/22/news/doc4a6768 bb0ff69984125722.txt.

114. See Marvin E. Wolfgang, Robert M. Figlio, and Thorsten Sellin, *Delinquency in a Birth Cohort* (Chicago: University of Chicago Press, 1972), where those boys who were born in Philadelphia in 1945 and who resided there from their tenth to their fourteenth birthdays were defined as the cohort; for a more recent publication see Marvin E. Wolfgang, Terence P. Thornberry, and Robert M. Figlio, *From Boy to Man—Delinquency to Crime* (Chicago: University of Chicago Press, 1987).

115. Op. cit., 93; Elise Hansell, Charlotte Bailey, Nina Kamath, and Joseph M. Bessette, *The Crime Funnel*, Claremont McKenna College, April 2016, accessed May 10, 2017, http://10294-presscdn-0-68.pagely.netdna-cdn.com/wp-content/uploads/2016/05/28-April-Crime-Funnel-Natl-Report.pdf.

116. Carl E. Pope, *Offender-Based Transaction Statistics: New Directions in Data Collection and Reporting*, U.S. Department of Justice, Law Enforcement Assistance Administration (Washington, DC: U.S. Department of Justice, 1975). See also, generally, R. McCleary, B. C. Nienstedt, and J. M. Erven, "Uniform Crime Reports on Organizational Outcomes: Three Time Series Quasi-Experiments," *Social Problems* 29 (1982): 361.

117. William K. Rashbaum, "Retired Officers Raise Questions on Crime Data," *New York Times*, February 6, 2010, accessed March 23, 2010, http://www.nytimes.com/2010/02/07/nyregion/ 07crime.html?pagewanted=all; Michael Matza, Craig R. McCoy, and Mark Fazlollah, "Pressure Builds on City for Police Accuracy," *Philadelphia Inquirer*, November 15, 1998, accessed March 23, 2010, http://inquirer.philly.com/packages/crime/html/111598.asp.

118. Avery Appelman, "The True Cost of Crime in America," Appelman Law Firm, September 26, 2016, accessed April 23, 2017, https://aacriminallaw.com/true-cost-crime-america/.

119. Anne Fisher, "Employee Theft: U.S. Retail Workers Are Number 1 in Employee Theft," *Forbes*, January 26, 2015, accessed February 18, 2017, http://fortune.com/2015/01/26/us-retail-worker-theft/.

120. Ibid.

121. U.S. Department of Justice, Bureau of Justice Statistics, *2006 Justice Expenditure and Employment Extracts*, NCJ 224394, Table 1, accessed March 3, 2010, http://www.ojp. usdoj.gov/bjs/pub/sheets/cjee06.zip, file cjee0601.csv.

122. Paul Heaton, "Hidden in Plain Sight: What Cost-of-Crime Research Can Tell Us about Investing in Police," *Issues in Policing*, Rand Corporation, 2010, accessed February 18, 2017, http://www.rand.org/content/dam/rand/pubs/occasional_papers/2010/RAND_OP279.pdf.

123. Tracey Kyckelhahn, *Justice Expenditure and Employment Extracts—Preliminary, Table 1*, Bureau of Justice Statistics, February 26, 2015, accessed February 18, 2017, https://www.bjs.gov/index.cfm?ty=pbdetail&iid=5239.

124. Christian Henrichson and Ruth Delaney, *The Price of Prisons: What Incarceration Costs Taxpayers*, The Vera Institute, July 20, 2012, accessed February 18, 2017, http://archive.vera.org/sites/default/files/resources/downloads/price-of-prisons-updated-version-021914.pdf.

125. Ibid.

126. U.S. Department of Justice, *FY 2015 Budget Request: Prisons and Detention*, 2015, accessed February 18, 2017, https://www.justice.gov/sites/default/files/jmd/legacy/2013/09/07/prisons-detention.pdf.

127. Christian Henrichson and Ruth Delaney, op. cit.

128. Centers for Disease Control and Prevention, "Impaired Driving: Get the Facts," January 26, 2017, accessed February 18, 2017, https://www.cdc.gov/motorvehiclesafety/impaired_driving/impaired-drv_factsheet.html.

129. Barbara Marquand, "How Much Does a DUI Cost?" *Nerdwallet*, February 3, 2016, accessed February 18, 2017, https://www.nerdwallet.com/blog/insurance/cost-of-a-dui/; Craig Guilot, "The True Cost of a DUI," Esurance, 2017, accessed February 18, 2017, https://www.esurance.com/info/car/the-true-cost-of-a-dui.

130. Steven F. Messner and Richard Rosenfeld, 2007, op. cit.; Russell Mokhiber, "Twenty Things You Should Know about Corporate Crime," AlterNet, June 16, 2007, accessed March 7, 2010, http://www.alternet.org/story/54093; V. Kappeler, M. Blumberg, and G. Potter, *The Mythology of Crime and Criminal Justice*, 3rd ed. (Prospect Heights, IL: Waveland Press, 2000).

131. J. C. Helmkamp, K. J. Townsend, and J. A. Sundra, *How Much Does White Collar Crime Cost?* National Criminal Justice Reference Service, 2017, accessed February 18, 2017, https://www.ncjrs.gov/App/Publications/abstract.aspx?ID=167026.

132. Matthew B. Robinson and Kevin M. Beaver, *Why Crime?: An Interdisciplinary Approach to Explaining Criminal Behavior* (Durham, NC: Carolina Academic Press, 2009).

133. Aaron Chalfin, "Economic Costs of Crime," *The Encyclopedia of Crime and Punishment*, Wiley, October 2, 2015, accessed February 18, 2017, http://onlinelibrary.wiley.com/doi/10.1002/978 1118519639.wbecpx193/pdf.

134. Ibid.

135. Peggy M. Tobolowsky, Mario T. Gaboury, Arrick L. Jackson, and Ashley G. Blackburn, *Crime Victim Rights and Remedies*, 2nd ed., Durham, NC: Carolina Academic Press, 2010.

136. Chris Isidore, Shimon Prokupecz, and David Shortell, "Protecting Donald Trump Costs New York City More than $1 Million a Day," *CNN Money*, November 21, 2016, accessed February 22, 2017, http://money.cnn.com/2016/11/21/news/protecting-donald-trump/.

137. Drew Harwell, Amy Brittain, and Jonathan O'Connell, "Trump Family's Elaborate Lifestyle a 'Logistical Nightmare'—at Taxpayers' Expense," *Washington Post* (February 16, 2017). Accessed February 22, 2017: https://www.washingtonpost.com/business/economy/trump-familys-elaborate-lifestyle-a-logistical-nightmare—at-taxpayer-expense/2017/02/16/763cce8e-f2ce-11e6-a9b0-ecee7ce475fc_story.html?postshare=3851487333451275&tid=ss_tw&utm_term=.665df55f370d; Aaron Rupar, "Trump's First Month of Travel Expenses Costs Taxpayers Just Less Than What Obama Spent in a Year," *ThinkProgress*, February 20, 2017, accessed February 22, 2017, https://thinkprogress.org/trump-first-month-travel-expenses-11-million-a1feb6cd829b#.rqzvacqm1.

138. Ian Salisbury, "The Insane Numbers behind Trump's Deportation Plan," *Money*, November 14, 2016, accessed February 23, 2017, http://time.com/money/4566401/trumps-deportation-immigration-plan-numbers/.

139. Ibid.

140. Yvonne Wenger, "Unrest Will Cost City $20 Million, Officials Estimate," *The Baltimore Sun*, May 26, 2015, accessed February 23, 2017, http://www.baltimoresun.com/news/maryland/baltimore-city/; Spencer Irvine, "Remember This? Previous Black Lives Matter Riots Costs Baltimore Up to $20 Million, Ferguson $5.7 million," *Accuracy in Media*, September 23, 2016, accessed February 23, 2017, http://www.aim.org/on-target-blog/remember-this-previous-black-lives-matter-riots-cost-baltimore-up-to-20-million-ferguson-5-7-million/.

141. Chicago Tribune, "Dakota Access Protest Policing Costs Exceed $22M," January 10, 2017, accessed February 23, 2017, http://www.chicagotribune.com/news/nationworld/ct-dakota-access-protest-policing-costs-20170110-story.html; Forum News Service, "ND National Guard Costs Near $9M for Dakota Access Pipeline Response," *Inforum*, February 22, 2017, accessed February 23, 2017, http://www.inforum.com/news/4222807-nd-national-guard-costs-near-9-million-dakota-access-pipeline-response.

142. Alyssa Davis, "In U.S., Concerns about Crime Climbs to 15-Year High," *Gallup*, April 6, 2016, accessed February 18, 2017, http://www.gallup.com/poll/190475/americans-concern-crime-climbs-year-high.aspx.

143. Gallup, "Crime, Historical Trends," October 2016, accessed February 18, 2017, http://www.gallup.com/poll/1603/crime.aspx.

144. Justin McCarthy, "Americans' Worries about Most Crimes Similar to 2015," *Gallup*, November 14, 2016, accessed February 18, 2017, http://www.gallup.com/poll/197444/americans-worries-crimes-similar-2015.aspx.

145. M. D. Lieberman, A. Hariri, J. M. Jarcho, N. I. Eisenberger, and S. Y. Bookheimer, "An fMRI Investigation of Race-Related Amygdala Activity in African-American and Caucasian-American Individuals," *Nature Neuroscience* 8, no. 6 (May 8, 2005): 720–2, accessed March 9, 2010, http://www.ncbi.nlm.nih.gov/pubmed/15880106; Jill Mizell, "An Overview of Public Opinion and Discourse on Criminal Justice Issues," The Opportunity Agenda, August 2014, accessed February 18, 2017, https://opportunityagenda.org/files/field_file/2014.08.23-CriminalJusticeReport-FINAL_0.pdf.

146. Bureau of Justice Statistics. *Homicide Trends in the U.S., Trends by Race, (1976–2005)*. Office of Justice Programs, accessed March 9, 2010. http://bjs.ojp.usdoj.gov/content/homicide/race.cfm.

147. L. L. Brasier, "Man Faces Trial for Reading Wife's E-Mail," *The Ledger*, December 28, 2010, A1, A7.

Chapter 2

1. From Clarence Darrow, *Crime: Its Cause and Treatment*, Notable Quotes, Crime Quotes, accessed August 1, 2010, http://www.notable-quotes.com/c/crime_quotes.html.

2. *The Ledger*, January 19, 2017, Lakeland, Florida.

3. Broxterman received a five-year prison sentence and 20 years' probation for faking his credentials: see http://www.theledger.com/news/20170316/former-polk-state-professor-david-broxterman-gets-5-years-for-faking-credentials.

4. *The Ledger,* op cit.

5. FBI. *Crime in the United States, Table 23, Offense Analysis,* 2015, accessed February 19, 2017, https://ucr.fbi.gov/crime-in-the-u.s/2015/crime-in-the-u.s.-2015/tables/table-23.

6. Joseph Petrocelli, "Departments Patrol Response to Convenience Store Robberies," *Police: The Law Enforcement Magazine,* August 1, 2008, accessed April 12, 2010, http://www.policemag.com/Channel/Patrol/Articles/2008/08/Convenience-Store-Robberies.aspx.

7. *Rochin v. California,* 342 U.S. 165 (1952).

8. "When society acts to deprive one of its members of life, liberty, or property," wrote former Chief Justice Earl Warren, "it takes its most awesome steps. No general respect for, nor adherence to, the law as a whole can well be expected without judicial recognition of the paramount need for prompt, eminently fair, and sober criminal law procedures. The methods we employ in the enforcement of our criminal law have aptly been called the measures by which the quality of our civilization may be judged." *Coppedge v. United States,* 369 U.S. 438, 449 (1962).

9. Jordan Rudner, "Dallas Police Protestors Were United Before Sniper Attack," *The Texas Tribune,* July 8, 2016, accessed October 6, 2017, https://www.texastribune.org/2016/07/08/dallas-police-protesters-were-united-sniper-attack/.

10. *Miranda v. Arizona,* 384 U.S. 436 (1966).

11. *Gideon v. Wainwright,* 372 U.S. 335 (1963), held that the states have a duty in all serious criminal cases to provide counsel for those indigent defendants who have not knowingly and intelligently waived their right to counsel. The Court extended the duty to indigent defendants accused of minor crimes in *Argersinger v. Hamlin,* 407 U.S. 25 (1972).

12. *Wolff v. McDonnell,* 94 S.Ct. 2963 (1974).

13. In 1914, the Supreme Court held in *Weeks v. United States,* 232 U.S. 383 (1914), that the Fourth Amendment required the application of the exclusionary rule in federal prosecutions. In *Wolf v. Colorado,* 338 U.S. 25 (1949), however, the Court was divided on the issue of whether the rule had to be used in state courts where evidence had been obtained by unconstitutional search and seizure methods. The exclusionary rule was finally extended to state courts in *Mapp v. Ohio,* 367 U.S. 643 (1961), holding that evidence leading to the conviction of a defendant charged with possession of lewd and obscene material had been obtained illegally, and thus that it must be excluded as evidence. In 1984, the Supreme Court allowed a limited "good faith" exception to the exclusionary rule.

14. *Furman v. Georgia,* 408 U.S. 238 (1972).

15. An excellent treatise on the operation of this recurrent discretionary power is found in Kenneth C. Davis, *Discretionary Justice: A Preliminary Inquiry* (Baton Rouge: Louisiana State University Press, 1969).

16. Charles D. Breitel, "Controls in Criminal Law Enforcement," *University of Chicago Law Review* 27 (Spring 1960): 427.

17. Herbert L. Packer, *The Limits of the Criminal Sanction* (Palo Alto, Ca: Stanford University Press, 1968), esp. 160–161.

18. Ibid.

19. Samuel Walker, *Sense and Nonsense about Crime: A Policy Guide,* 2nd ed. (Pacific Grove, CA: Brooks/Cole, 1989), 10–11.

20. Packer, op cit., warns: "There is a risk in an enterprise of this sort that is latent in any attempt to polarize. It is, simply, that values are too various to be pinned down to yes-or-no answers. The models are distortions of reality. And, since they are normative in character, there is a danger of seeing one or the other as Good or Bad.... The attempt ... is primarily to clarify the terms of discussion

by isolating the assumptions that underlie competing policy claims and examining the conclusions that those claims, if fully accepted, would lead to demand consistently polarized answers to the range of questions posed in the criminal process. The weighty questions of public policy that inhere in any attempt to discern where on the spectrum of normative choice the 'right' answer lies are beyond the scope of the present inquiry. The attempt here is primarily to clarify the terms of discussion by isolating the assumptions that underlie competing policy claims and examining the conclusions that those claims, if fully accepted, would lead to" (154–155).

21. Walker, op. cit., 13.

22. Ibid., 13.

23. Packer, op. cit., 159–160.

24. Ibid., 160–162.

25. Ibid., 164–165.

26. Walker, op. cit., 16.

27. Ibid., 199–234.

28. Packer, op. cit., 164–165.

29. Ibid., 163–164.

30. See Benjamin Franklin in Alexander Volokh, "*n* Guilty Men," *University of Pennsylvania Law Review* 146, no. 2 (1997): 173.

31. Packer, op. cit., 166.

32. Jim Webb, *A Time to Fight: Reclaiming a Fair and Just America* (New York: Broadway Books, 2008), 229.

33. William Mathias, Richard C. Rescorla, and Eugene Stephens, *Foundations of Criminal Justice* (Englewood Cliffs, NJ: Prentice-Hall, Inc., 1980).

34. Cesare Beccaria, *On Crimes and Punishments*, trans. Henry Paolucci (Indianapolis: Bobbs-Merrill, 1963).

35. For a summary of Beccaria's writings as well as a description of the influence of the social contract writers, see George B. Vold, *Theoretical Criminology* (New York: Oxford University Press, 1958), 14–26. Also see George B. Vold and Thomas J. Bernard, *Theoretical Criminology*, 3rd ed. (New York: Oxford University Press, 1986), 18–35.

36. Liam Stack, "A Brief History of Deadly Attacks on Abortion Providers," *New York Times*, November 29, 2015, accessed February 19, 2017, https://www.nytimes.com/interactive/2015/11/29/us/30abortion-clinic-violence.html?_r=1; Crimesider, CBS News, "Poll: George Tiller's Murderer Life in Prison; What Do You Think?" April 2, 2010, accessed April 12, 2010, http://www.cbsnews.com/8300-504083_162-504083.html?keyword=poll&tag=contentMain;contentBody.

37. John J. Donohue and Steven D. Levitt, "The Impact of Legalized Abortion on Crime," Berkeley Program in Law and Economics, Working Paper Series, UC Berkeley, March 1, 2000, accessed April 12, 2010, http://escholarship.org/uc/item/00p599hk.

38. George B. Vold, Thomas J. Bernard, and Jeffrey B. Snipes, *Theoretical Criminology*, 4th ed. (New York: Oxford University Press, 1998).

39. Samuel Walker, *Sense and Nonsense about Crime: A Policy Guide*, 2nd ed. (Pacific Grove, CA: Brooks/Cole, 1989), 27–40; also see John Lewis Gillin, *Criminology and Phrenology* (New York: Appleton-Century, 1935), 195–241.

40. Quoted in Harry Elmer Barnes and Negley K. Teeters, *New Horizons in Criminology* (New York: Prentice-Hall, 1943), 159.

41. Ibid., 161.

42. William H. Sheldon, *Varieties of Delinquent Youth: An Introduction to Constitutional Psychiatry* (New York: Harper and Row, 1949).

43. See, for example, J. B. Cortes and F. M. Gatti, *Delinquency and Crime: A Biopsychological Approach* (New York: Seminar Press, 1972); also see Sheldon Glueck and Eleanor T. Glueck, *Physique and Delinquency* (New York: Harper, 1956).

44. Herman A. Witkin, et al., "Criminality in XYY and XXY Men," *Science* 193 (August 13, 1976): 547. See also Jan Volavka, et al., "EEGs of XYY and XXY Men Found in a Large Birth Cohort," in *Biosocial Bases of Criminal Behavior*, eds. Sarnoff A. Mednick and Karl O. Christiansen (New York: Fardner Press, 1977), 189–198.

45. C. Ray Jeffery, *Biology and Crime* (Beverly Hills, CA: Sage, 1979), 184. See also C. Ray Jeffery, *Criminology: An Interdisciplinary Approach* (Englewood Cliffs, NJ: Prentice-Hall, 1990), 166–210.

46. H. H. Goddard, *Feeblemindedness: Its Causes and Consequences* (New York: Macmillan, 1914); also see H. H. Goddard, "Feeblemindedness and Delinquency," *Journal of Psycho-Asthenics* 25 (1921): 168.

47. Vold and Bernard, op. cit., 73.

48. Travis Hirschi and Michael Hindelang, "Intelligence and Delinquency: A Revisionist Review," *American Sociological Review* 42 (August 1977): 571.

49. American Psychiatric Association, *Diagnostic and Statistical Manual of Mental Disorders*, 4th ed. (Washington, DC: American Psychiatric Association, 1994); Hervey Cleckley, *The Mask of Sanity* (St. Louis: C.V. Mosby, 1980).

50. L. C. Sobell, C. Breslin, and M. B. Sobell, "Substance-Related Disorders (Alcohol)" in *Adult Psychopathology and Diagnosis*, 3rd ed., eds., M. Hersen and S. M. Turner (New York: John Wiley & Sons, 1996).

51. Clifford R. Shaw and Henry D. McKay, *Social Factors in Juvenile Delinquency* (Washington, DC: Government Printing Office, 1931). Others identified with the Chicago School include Robert E. Parks and Ernest Burgess, *Introduction to the Scientific Study of Sociology* (Chicago: University of Chicago Press, 1924); also, William F. Whyte, *Street Corner Society: The Social Structure of the Italian Slum* (Chicago: University of Chicago Press, 1943).

52. For the answer to that question, after you have answered, you may go to: http://www.theledger.com/article/20090305/NEWS/903055031/1374?Title=Jermaine-Julian-Gets-Life-in-Fatal-Robbery.

53. Edwin H. Sutherland, *Principles of Criminology* (Philadelphia: Lippincott, 1922).

54. Edwin H. Sutherland, *The Professional Thief: By a Professional Thief* (Chicago: University of Chicago Press, 1937).

55. Ibid., 197.

56. Edwin H. Sutherland, *Criminology* (Philadelphia: Lippincott, 1939).

57. Robert L. Burgess and Ronald L. Akers, "A Differential Association-Reinforcement Theory of Criminal Behavior," *Social Problems* 14 (Fall 1966): 128. Also see Ronald L. Akers, *Deviant Behavior: A Social Learning Approach*, 3rd ed. (Belmont, CA: Wadsworth, 1985).

58. Albert K. Cohen, *Delinquent Boys* (New York: Free Press, 1955).

59. Walter B. Miller, *Juvenile Gangs in Context* (Englewood Cliffs, NJ: Prentice-Hall, 1967).

60. Émile Durkheim, *Suicide: A Study in Sociology* (1897), trans. George Simpson (New York: Free Press, 1951); *The Division of Labor in Society* (1893), trans. G. Simpson (New York: Free Press, 1933).

61. Ladybugblue. Days of Our Lives Newsroom, February 22, 2010, accessed April 9, 2010, http://soaps.sheknows.com/daysofourlives/news/id/6957/Days_Of_Our_Lives_Video_Clip_Philips_Rage.

62. Robert K. Merton, "Social Structure and Anomie," *American Sociological Review* 3 (1938): 672.

63. Nancy Gibbs, "Tracking Down the Unabomber," *Time*, April 15, 1996, 38–46.

64. Frances Robles, "Dylann Roof Photos and a Manifesto Are Posted on Website," *New York Times*, June 20, 2015, accessed February 22, 2017, https://www.nytimes.com/2015/06/21/us/dylann-storm-roof-photos-website-charleston-church-shooting.html?_r=1; Chris Weller, "A Former FBI Profiler Reveals the 2 Personality Traits that Helped Turn Dylann Roof into a Murderer," *Business Insider*, June 22, 2015, accessed February 22, 2017, http://www.businessinsider.com/dylann-roof-was-a-paranoid-narcissist-says-fbi-profiler-joe-navarro-2015-6; Ray Sanchez and Ed Payne, "Charleston Church Shooting: Who Is Dylann Roof?" CNN, December 16, 2016, http://www.cnn.com/2015/06/19/us/charleston-church-shooting-suspect/.

65. Aaron Katersky, James Gordon Meek, Josh Margolin, and Michael Edison Hayden, "What We Know About Omar Mateen, Suspected Orlando Nightclub Shooter," ABC News, June 12, 2016, accessed February 21, 2017, http://abcnews.go.com/US/omar-mateen-suspected-orlando-night-club-shooter/story?id=39790797; Ralph Ellis, Ashley Fantz, Faith Karimi, and Eliott C. McLaughlin, "Orlando Shooting: 49 Killed, Shooter Pledged ISIS Allegiance," CNN, June 13, 2016, accessed February 21, 2017, http://www.cnn.com/2016/06/12/us/orlando-nightclub-shooting/; Kyra Gurney, Julie K. Brown, Lance Dixon, and Nicholas Nehamas, "Omar Mateen's Immigrant Family Lived the American Dream—Or So It Seemed," *Miami Herald*, June 18, 2016, accessed February 21, 2017, http://www.miamiherald.com/news/nation-world/national/article84370692.html; CBS News, "Man Who Says He Was Omar Mateen's Gay Lover Speaks Out," June 21, 2016, accessed February 21, 2017, http://www.cbsnews.com/news/orlando-shooting-man-who-says-he-was-omar-mateen-gay-lover-speaks-out-univision/; Ralph Ellis, Ashley Fantz, Eliott C. McLaughlin, and Tim Hume, "Orlando Shooting: What Motivated a Killer?" CNN, June 14, 2016, accessed February 21, 2017, http://www.cnn.com/2016/06/13/us/orlando-nightclub-shooting/; Molly Hennessy-Fiske, Jenny Jarvie, and Del Quentin Wilber, "Orlando Gunman Had Used Gay Dating App and Visited LGBT Nightclub on Other Occasions, Witnesses Say," *Los Angeles Times*, June 13, 2016, accessed February 21, 2017, http://www.latimes.com/nation/la-na-orlando-nightclub-shooting-20160613-snap-story.html; WITW Staff, "Ex-wife of Orlando Omar Mateen Suggests He Was Gay," *New York Times*, June 14, 2016, accessed February 21, 2017, http://nytlive.nytimes.com/womenintheworld/2016/06/14/ex-wife-of-orlando-gunman-omar-mateen-suggests-he-was-gay/; Molly Hennessy-Fiske, "FBI Investigators Say They Have Found No Evidence that Orlando Shooter had Gay Lovers," *Los Angeles Times*, June 23, 2016, accessed February 21, 2017, http://www.latimes.com/nation/la-na-orlando-gay-fbi-20160623-snap-story.html.

66. Michael McGlaughlin, "'That's What Triggered It': Orlando Nightclub Shooter Revealed Motive to Police Negotiator," *Huffington Post*, September 23, 2016, accessed February 21, 2017, http://www.huffingtonpost.com/entry/omar-mateen-orlando-police-negotiator_us_57e5b13ae4b08d73b831834a.

67. Gillian Mohney, "What Is Ethan Couch's 'Affluenza': An Explainer," ABC News, December 30, 2015, accessed February 20, 2017, http://abcnews.go.com/Health/ethan-couchs-affluenza-explainer/story?id=36011293; Calia Klass and Alexa Valiente, "'Affluenza' DUI Case: What Happened Night of the Accident That Left 4 People Dead," ABC News, December 31, 2015, accessed February 20, 2017, http://abcnews.go.com/US/affluenza-dui-case-happened-night-accident-left-people/story?id=34481444; Kelly Stevenson and Meghan Keneally, "'Affluenza' Mom Tonya Couch Arrested on Felony Charge," ABC News, December 31, 2015, accessed February 20, 2017, http://abcnews.go.com/US/affluenza-mom-tonya-couch-held-felony-charge/story?id=36024813; Ken Molestina, "Attorneys for 'Affluenza' Teen Ethan Couch Ask to Have Him Released," *The Huffington Post*, September 1, 2016, accessed February 20, 2017, http://www.huffingtonpost.com/entry/ethan-couch-seeks-release_us_57c818fde4b078581f1128f5.

68. Richard A. Cloward and Lloyd E. Ohlin, *Delinquency and Opportunity* (New York: Free Press, 1960).

69. Travis Hirschi, *Causes of Delinquency* (Berkeley: University of California Press, 1969).

70. Vold, Bernard, and Snipes, op. cit., 202–203.

71. Gresham Sykes and David Matza, "Techniques of Neutralization: A Theory of Delinquency," *American Sociological Review* 22 (1957): 664–670.

72. Edwin M. Lemert, *Human Deviance, Social Problems, and Social Control* (Englewood Cliffs, NJ: Prentice-Hall, 1967).

73. Howard S. Becker, *Outsiders—Studies in the Sociology of Deviance* (New York: Free Press, 1963); John Kitsuse, "Societal Reaction to Deviance: Problems of Theory and Method," *Social Problems* 11 (Winter 1962): 131. See also Kai T. Erikson, "Notes on the Sociology of Deviance," *Social Problems* 9 (1962): 307.

74. Austin T. Turk, "Conflict and Criminality," *American Sociological Review* 31 (1966): 338; also see Austin T. Turk, *Criminality and the Legal Order* (Chicago: Rand-McNally, 1969).

75. William B. Chambliss, "Toward a Political Economy of Crime," *Theory and Society* 2, no. 2 (Summer 1975): 152; also see William B. Chambliss and Robert B. Seidman, *Law, Order, and Power* (Reading, MA: Addison-Wesley, 1971).

76. Richard Quinney, *Critique of Legal Order* (Boston: Little, Brown, 1973).

77. Anatole France, *The Red Lily* (1894), accessed on April 10, 2010, http://www.quotationspage.com/quote/805.html.

78. Mark Dowie, "Pinto Madness," *Mother Jones*, September/October 1977, accessed on April 10, 2010, http://www.autosafety.org/pinto-madness.

79. Statista, "Number of Active Registered Lobbyists in the United States 1998-2016," The Statistics Portal, 2016, accessed February 19, 2017, https://www.statista.com/statistics/257340/number-of-lobbyists-in-the-us/; Statista, "Total Lobbying Spending in the United States 1998–2016," Statistics Portal, 2016, accessed February 19, 2017, https://www.statista.com/statistics/257337/total-lobbying-spending-in-the-us/.

80. Allan Cigler, quoted in Jeffrey H. Bimbaum, "The Road to Riches Is Called K Street," *Washington Post*, June 22, 2005, accessed on April 12, 2010, http://www.washingtonpost.com/wp-dyn/content/article/2005/06/21/AR2005062101632.html.

81. Thomas Catan and Guy Chazan, "Soill Draws Criminal Probe," *The Wall Street Journal*, June 2, 2010, accessed July 30, 2010, http://online.wsj.com/article/NA_WSJ_PUB:SB100014240527 487 04875604575280983140254458.html.

82. William Chambliss, "State-Organized Crime," *Criminology* 27 (1989): 183–208.

83. George Lerner, "Ambassador: U.S. Moving to Support International Court," CNN, March 24, 2010, accessed on April 10, 2010, http://www.cnn.com/2010/US/03/24/us.global.justice/index.html.

84. Peter B. Kraska, "Criminal Justice Theory: Toward Legitimacy and an Infrastructure," *Justice Quarterly* 23, no. 2 (2006): 167–185. doi: 10.1080/07418820600688735.

85. J. J. Willis, "Bridging the Normative Gap in Graduate Criminal Justice Curricula: Teaching Theories of Justice," *Journal of Criminal Justice Education* 23, no. 1 (2012): 81–102. doi: 10.1080/105 11253.2011.630675.

86. Kraska, 2006, op. cit.

87. Peter B. Kraska and John J. Brent, *Theorizing Criminal Justice: Eight Essential Orientations* (Long Grove, IL: Waveland Press, 2011).

88. Ibid.

89. Ibid.

90. Ibid.

91. Ibid.

92. Michelle Alexander, *The New Jim Crow* (New York, NY: New Press, 2011).

93. Kraska and Brent, 2011, op. cit.

94. Stuart A. Scheingold, *The Politics of Street Crime: Criminal Process and Cultural Obsession* (Philadelphia, PA: Temple University Press, 1991).

95. Kraska and Brent, 2011, op. cit.

96. Marc Mauer & Sentencing Project (U.S.), *Race to Incarcerate* (New York: New Press, 1999).

97. Kraska and Brent, 2011, op. cit.

98. Ibid.

99. Steve Martinot, "On the Epidemic of Police Killings," *Social Justice* 39, no. 4 (2013): 52–75.

100. Kraska and Brent, 2011, op. cit.

101. David Garland, *The Culture of Control: Crime and Social Order in Contemporary Society* (University of Chicago Press, 2001).

102. See Risdon N. Slate, Jacqueline K. Buffington-Vollum, and W. Wesley Johnson, *The Criminalization of Mental Illness: Crisis and Opportunity for the Justice System*, 2nd ed., (Durham, NC: Carolina Academic Press, 2013).

103. Frank P. Williams III and Marilyn D. McShane, *Criminological Theory*, 5th ed. (Upper Saddle River, NJ: Prentice Hall, 2010).

104. Matt DeLisi and Kevin M. Beaver, *Criminological Theory: A Life-Course Approach* (Sudbury, MA: Jones and Bartlett, 2011); Stacey J. Bosick, "Operationalizing Crime over the Life Course," *Crime & Delinquency* 55, no. 3 (2009): 472–496.

105. Freda Adler, *Sisters in Crime: The Rise of the New Female Criminal* (New York: McGraw Hill, 1975).

106. Susan F. Sharp, *Mean Lives, Mean Laws: Oklahoma's Women Prisoners.* (New Brunswick, NJ: Rutgers University Press, 2014).

107. Ibid.; Joanne Belknap, *The Invisible Woman: Gender, Crime, and Justice*, 4th ed. (Stamford, CT: Cengage Learning, 2015).

108. Ibid., Sharp and Belknap.

109. Ibid., Sharp.

110. Williams and McShane, op cit., 180.

111. ABC7NY, "Sick of Living with Wife, Kansas Man Robs Bank to Go to Jail," WABC Eyewitness News, January 25, 2017, accessed March 21, 2017, http://abc7ny.com/news/sick-of-living-with-wife-man-robs-bank-to-go-to-jail/1719172/.

Chapter 3

1. Lenny Bruce, Quoteland, accessed August 1, 2010, http://www.quoteland.com/topic.asp?CATEGORY_ID=88.

2. The initial determination by a magistrate of probable cause to detain someone has been interpreted by the U.S. Supreme Court to not exceed 48 hours. Most jurisdictions try to expedite this process, getting an accused before a judicial authority within a few hours. Anything in excess of 48 hours for accomplishing this presentment of the accused before the court will become incumbent upon the police to explain why the delay was reasonable. See *County of Riverside v. McGlaughlin*, 500 U.S. 44 (1991).

3. *Kirby v. Illinois*, 406 U.S. 682 (1972).

4. See, for example, Lifers' Group Inc., *A Study of Parole Decisions for Lifers 2008* (Centerdale, RI: Phantom Prisoner, LTD., 2009), accessed April 21, 2010, http://www.cjpc.org/2008StudyofParoleBoardDecisionsforLifers.pdf.

5. Amy L. Solomon, Vera Kachnowski, and Avinash Bhati, *Does Parole Work?* (Washington, DC: Urban Institute, 2005), accessed April 21, 2010, http://www.urban.org/UploadedPDF/311156_Does_Parole_Work.pdf.

6. See Joseph A. Colquitt, "Alabama Legal Issues: Can Alabama Handle the Truth (in Sentencing)?" *Alabama Law Review* 60 (2009): 425; Miriam A. Cavanaugh, "If You Do the Crime, You Will Do the Time: A Look at the New 'Truth In Sentencing' Law in Michigan," *University of Detroit Mercy Law Review* 77 (2000): 375.

7. Jame J. Stephan. *Census of State and Federal Correctional Facilities, 2005*, Bureau of Justice Statistics, October 2008, accessed April 21, 2010, http://bjs.ojp.usdoj.gov/content/pub/pdf/ csfcf05.pdf.

8. Solomon, op. cit.

9. James Hirby, "What Rights Do Convicted Felons Lose?" *The Law Dictionary*, accessed September 30, 2017, http://thelawdictionary.org/article/what-rights-do-convicted-felons-lose/.

10. While such councils may not establish misdemeanors or felonies, they may enact ordinances that determine a state law is not applicable in their jurisdiction. Such conflicts are likely to be played out in the courts. See, for example, legalization of marijuana in Denver, Colorado: Patrick O'Driscoll, "Denver Votes to Legalize Marijuana Possession," *USA Today*, November 3, 2005, accessed April 20, 2010, http://www.usatoday.com/news/nation/2005-11-03-pot_x.htm.

11. Associated Press, "Court Upholds Conviction of Carlie Brucia's Killer," *Sarasota Herald Tribune*, December 17, 2009, accessed on March 18, 2010, http://www.heraldtribune.com/article/20091217/breaking/912179987?Title=Court-upholds-conviction-of-Carlie-Brucia-s-killer&tc=ar; Curtis Krueger, Richard Raeke, and Dong-Phuong Nguyen, "The Problem with Probation," *Saint Petersburg Times*, June 13, 2004, accessed on March 18, 2010, http://www.sptimes.com/2004/06/13/State/The_problem_with_prob.shtml; Jeremy Wallace, "It May Be a Law, But It Isn't Carlie's," *Sarasota Herald Tribune*, September 17, 2005, accessed on March 18, 2010, http://www.heraldtribune.com/apps/pbcs.dll/article?AID=/20050917/NEWS/509170645/-1/CARLIE&tc=ar; Mike Schneider, "Jurors Convict Mechanic of Abducting, Killing Carlie Brucia," *San Diego/Riverside North County Times*, November 18, 2005, accessed March 18, 2010, http://www.nctimes.com/news/national/back page/article_c783022b-25eb-5f1a-a301-adf622763ab0.html; Susan Candiotti, Allison Flexner, Patrick Oppmann, Kris Osborn, Rich Philips, and John Zarrella, "Key Evidence Missing in Carlie's Killing," CNN, February 6, 2004, accessed on March 18, 2010, http://www.cnn.com/2004/US/South/02/06/missing.girl.

12. John Frank, "Seeking Justice for Jessica," *St. Petersburg Times*, July 9, 2006, accessed March 18, 2010, http://www.sptimes.com/2006/07/09/Citrus/Seeking_justice_for_J.shtml.

13. Terry Aguayo, "Sex Offender Guilty of Rape and Murder of Florida Girl," *New York Times*, March 8, 2007, accessed March 18, 2010, http://www.nytimes.com/2007/03/08/us/08verdict.html; Keith Morelli, "Jessica Lunsford's Killer, John Couey, Dies of Cancer," *The Tampa Tribune*, September 30, 2009, accessed March 18, 2010, http://www2.tbo.com/content/2009/sep/30/010250/john-couey-dies-cancer-prison.

14. Raghuram Vadarevu, "Couey Told Police He Had a 'Problem,'" *St. Petersburg Times*, March 23, 2005, accessed March 18, 2010, http://www.sptimes.com/2005/03/23/Citrus/Couey_told_police_he_.shtml; Collins Conner and Barbara Behrendt, "Couey's Life Path Mostly a Dead End," *St. Petersburg Times*, March 27, 2005, accessed March 18, 2010, http://www.sptimes.com/2005/03/27/Citrus/Couey_s_life_path_mos.shtml.

15. The Jessica Lunsford Act (2005), Florida House of Representatives HB 1877, accessed March 18, 2010, http://www.flsenate.gov/data/session/2005/House/bills/billtext/pdf/h187705er.pdf.

16. Julia Crouse, "Complaints Follow Lunsford Act," *The Ledger* (Lakeland, Florida), November 7, 2005, B1.

17. The 2009 Florida Statutes, Title XLVIII, Chapter 1012, accessed March 18, 2010, http://www.leg.state.fl.us/Statutes/index.cfm?App_mode=Display_Statute&Search_String=&URL=Ch1012/Sec315.HTM; "Jessica Lunsford Act: Frequently Asked Questions," Leon County Schools, Tallahassee, Florida, accessed March 18, 2010, http://www.leon.k12.fl.us/public/business/purchasing/jessicalunsfordfaq.html.

18. Julia Crouse, op. cit.

19. John Frank, "5 Years after Jessica Lunsford's Death, Florida Revisits Sex-Offender Laws," *The Miami Herald*, February 24, 2010, accessed March 18, 2010, http://www.miamiherald.com/2010/02/24/1496561/floridas-tougher-sex-offender.html.

20. "State Supreme Court Upholds Part of Jessica's Law: Constitutionality of Jessica's Law Left for Lower Courts to Decide" San Diego 10 News, February 1, 2010, accessed March 18, 2010, http://www.10news.com/news/22406072/detail.html.

21. Paul Kane, "Randy Neugebauer Says He Called Out 'Baby-Killer' as Stupak Spoke on House Floor," *Washington Post*, March 22, 2010, accessed April 20, 2010, http://voices.washingtonpost.com/44/2010/03/stupak-called-baby-killer-on-h.html?wprss=44.

22. Thurman W. Arnold, "Law Enforcement: An Attempt at Social Dissection," *Yale Law Journal* 42 (1932): 1 (esp. 17–18).

23. The Capone theory is discussed in Monroe Freedman, "The Professional Responsibility of the Prosecuting Attorney," *Georgetown Law Journal* 55 (1967): 1030. It should also be noted, however, that this approach is by no means limited to the prosecution of notorious gangsters. In 1972, for example, the IRS acknowledged that it had created special investigative units with the aim of building tax evasion cases against alleged political extremists and drug pushers.

24. In 1988, the Iran-Contra Hearings before the U.S. Senate Judiciary Committee examined whether, and the extent to which, actions taken by officials in President Reagan's administration constituted violations of law. Much discussion throughout the country revolved around whether Oliver North was a criminal or a hero.

25. "Legislative Election of Judges," Judgepedia, July 24, 2009, accessed April 20, 2010, http://judgepedia.org/index.php/Legislative_election_of_judges.

26. Under fire, President George W. Bush accepted Harriet Miers' withdrawal of her name as a United States Supreme Court nominee after she had participated in Senate Judiciary Confirmation Hearings. President Reagan withdrew his nomination of Douglas Ginsburg to the Supreme Court when it became obvious that the Senate Judiciary Committee would reject his nomination. Later, the Senate rejected Robert Bork as well, another Reagan nominee. On many occasions presidential appointments of agency administrators have been rejected, as in the case of President Carter's nomination of Norval Morris to the Law Enforcement Assistance Administration.

27. Governors often make interim appointments of prosecutors when vacancies emerge, as seen in the following examples: Governor Ted Kulongoski, "Governor Appoints District Attorney for Morrow County," press release, August 31, 2006, accessed April 21, 2010, http://governor.oregon.gov/Gov/p2006/press_083106.shtml; Governor Phil Bredesen, "Bredesen Appoints Helper District Attorney General," press release, April 7, 2008, accessed April 21, 2010, http://www.tennesseeanytime.org/governor/viewArticleContent.do?id=1210&page=0.

28. See Governor Jim Gibbons, "Governor Appoints Public Defender," press release, September 18, 2008, accessed April 21, 2010, http://gov.state.nv.us/PressReleases/2008/2008-09-18PublicDefender.htm; Governor Arnold Schwarzenegger, "Governor Schwarzenegger Appoints Michael Hersek State Public Defender," press release, January 3, 2008, accessed April 21, 2010, http://gov.ca.gov/press-release/8404.

29. An example of this is the attempts made by Los Angeles Mayor Thomas Bradley to unseat Police Chief Gates after an incriminating video tape depicting Los Angeles police officers brutally beating a traffic violator who had led police on a chase was widely shown. Chief Gates, with civil service, refused to resign and could not be fired.

30. Presidential pardons sometimes occur. President Ford not only pardoned his predecessor but as one of his last acts in office also pardoned "Tokyo Rose" of World War II notoriety. One of the first acts of President Carter was the pardoning of draft evaders from the Vietnam War. Controversial pardons by President Clinton included Marc Rich and Susan McDougal; while President George W. Bush commuted Scooter Libby's sentence to spare him prison, his criminal record was not pardoned—see Michael Isikoff, "No Pardon for Libby," *Newsweek*, January 19, 2009, accessed

April 21, 2010, http://www.newsweek.com/id/180448. During his two terms in office, President Obama pardoned 212 individuals and commuted the federal sentences of 1,715 persons who had primarily been convicted of nonviolent drug offenses—see John Gramlich and Kristen Bialik, "Obama Used Clemency Power More that Any President Since Truman," *Pew Research Center*, January 20, 2017, accessed October 6, 2017, http://www.pewresearch.org/fact-tank/2017/01/20/obama-used-more-clemency-power/. Most grants of clemency come in a president's final days in office. However, President Trump in August of his first term pardoned former Arizona Sheriff Joe Arpaio who was convicted but not yet sentenced for defying a federal court order to stop racially profiling Latinos on suspicion of being in the country illegally.The eighty-five year old Arpaio had been on the presidential campaign trail with candidate Trump. Ryan Struyk, "This Chart Shows Why Trump's Pardon of Arpaio Was So Unusual," *CNN*, August 30, 2017, accessed October 6, 2017, http://www.cnn.com/2017/08/29/politics/trump-pardon-arpaio-chart-unusual/index.html; Suzanne Gamboa, "Former Arizona Sheriff Joe Arpaio Convicted of Crime for Ignoring Judge's Order," *NBC News*, July 31, 2017, accessed October 6, 2017, https://www.nbcnews.com/politics/politics-news/former-arizona-sheriff-joe-arpaio-convicted-crime-ignoring-judge-s-n788251. For general discussions of executive clemency, see Mark Strasser, "Forgiveness & the Law: Executive Clemency and the American System of Justice: Some Reflections on the President's Pardon Power," *Capital University Law Review* 31 (2003): 143; Jonathan Harris and Lothlorien Redmond, "Executive Clemency: The Lethal Absence of Hope," *American University Washington College of Law, Criminal Law Brief* 3 (2007): 2; Winthrop Rockefeller, "Executive Clemency and the Death Penalty," *Catholic University Law Review* 21 (1971): 94; Note, "Governor Reagan and Executive Clemency," *California Law Review* 55 (1967): 407.

31. U.S. Constitution, Art. V, sec. 2. See also Robert A. Friedlander, "Judicial Supremacy: Some Bicentennial Reflections," *Rutgers Camden Law Journal* 8 (1976): 24.

32. *Marbury v. Madison*, 1803.

33. The title of the highest state court is not always "supreme court." In New York, for instance, a supreme court is a trial court, with the highest appellate body known as the Court of Appeals.

34. See Lawrence Baum, *American Courts: Process and Policy*, 6th ed. (Belmont, CA: Wadsworth, 2008).

35. For a description of this intricate appellate process, with special emphasis on a landmark U.S. Supreme Court decision, see Anthony Lewis, *Gideon's Trumpet* (New York: Random House, 1964).

36. Jeff Bleich, Michelle Friedland, David Han, and Aimee Feinberg, "Supreme Court Watch: Very Special Masters—Handling the Supreme Court's Original Jurisdiction Cases," *San Francisco Attorney* (Winter, 2009) 45.

37. Typically, cases arrive at the U.S. Supreme Court via the Rule of 4 (4 Justices must agree to hear a case) to be discussed in a later chapter. See Rolando V. del Carmen, *Criminal Procedure: Law and Practice*, 8th ed. (Belmont, CA: Wadsworth, 2010).

38. Joseph Goldstein, "Police Discretion Not to Invoke the Criminal Process: Low Visibility Decisions in the Administration of Justice," *Yale Law Journal* 69 (1960): 543.

39. Historically, in England, a crime was considered a private matter, and, therefore, a criminal prosecution could be commenced by a private citizen. See David Hirschel, William Wakefield, and Scott Sasse, *Criminal Justice in England and the United States*, 2nd ed. (Sudbury, MA: Jones and Bartlett Publishers, 2008); Harry R. Dammer and Erika Fairchild, *Comparative Criminal Justice Systems*, 3rd ed. (Belmont, CA: Wadsworth, 2006).

40. OLR Research Report, "Florida's '10-20-Life' Law," January 23, 2013, accessed May 2, 2017, https://www.cga.ct.gov/2013/rpt/2013-R-0067.htm.

41. Sheila Dewan, "Duke Prosecutor Jailed; Students Seek Settlement," *New York Times*, September 8, 2007, accessed May 2, 2017, http://www.nytimes.com/2007/09/08/us/08duke.html; Lara Setrakian and Chris Francescani, "Former Prosecutor Nifong Disbarred," ABC News, June 16, 2007, accessed May 2, 2017, http://abcnews.go.com/TheLaw/story?id=3285862&page=1.

42. Ann Blythe, "City of Durham Settles Long-Running Lawsuit with Former Duke Lacrosse Players," *The Charlotte Observer*, May 16, 2014, accessed May 2, 2017, http://www.charlotteobserver.com/news/local/crime/article9122669.html.

43. Ben Trachtenberg, "No, You 'Stand Up': Why Prosecutors Should Stop Hiding behind Grand Juries," *Missouri Law Review* 80, no. 4 (Fall 2015), accessed May 2, 2017, http://law.missouri.edu/lawreview/files/2016/04/12.-Trachtenberg.pdf; Wesley Lowery, "Ferguson Protest Tries to Shut Down I-70, as Calls Continue for McCulloch to Step Down," *Washington Post*, September 10, 2014, accessed May 2, 2017, https://www.washingtonpost.com/politics/ferguson-protest-tries-to-shut-down-i-70-as-calls-continue-for-prosecutor-to-step-down/2014/09/10/2cb3a97c-37b4-11e4-8601-97ba88884ffd_story.html?utm_term=.09539c4dbae7.

44. Dara Kam, "Orlando-Area Prosecutor Sues Governor Rick Scott Over Removal," *The Daytona Beach News-Journal*, April 11, 2017, accessed May 2, 2017, http://www.news-journalonline.com/news/20170411/orlando-area-prosecutor-sues-gov-rick-scott-over-removal; Gai Tziperman Lotan, "State Attorney Ayala Files Lawsuit against Governor Scott in Death Penalty Cases," *Orlando Sentinel*, April 11, 2017, accessed May 2, 2017, http://www.orlandosentinel.com/news/breaking-news/.

45. Kristen M. Clark (August 31, 2017) "Florida Supreme Court Backs Gov. Scott in Orlando Death-Penalty Dispute," *Miami Herald*, accessed October 3, 2017, http://www.miamiherald.com/news/politics-government/state-politics/article170451127.html.

Chapter 4

1. As quoted from Carl McGowan in Kami Chavis Simmons, "New Governance and the 'New Paradigm' of Police Accountability: A Democratic Approach to Police Reform," *Cath. U.L. Rev*. 59 (Winter 2010): 373.

2. B. T. Hodges, personal communication, February 20, 2017.

3. Kelly McLaughlin, "Chicago's Former Top Cop Claims Black Lives Matter Is Leading to More Black Deaths and Preventing Police from Doing Their Jobs," *Daily Mail*, January 2, 2017, accessed March 5, 2017, http://www.dailymail.co.uk/news/article-4081796/Chicago-s-former-cop-claims-Black-Lives-Matter-leading-black-deaths-preventing-police-doing-jobs.html.

4. John Nolte, "Black Lives Matter? 2016 Chicago Homicides Surge 57% to 762," *The Daily Wire*, January 2, 2017, accessed March 5, 2017, http://www.dailywire.com/news/12065/black-lives-matter-2016-chicago-homicides-surge-57-john-nolte.

5. Sean Higgins, "Former Chicago Top Cop: Black Lives Matter Killing Blacks," *Washington Examiner*, January 1, 2017, accessed March 5, 2017, http://www.washingtonexaminer.com/former-chicago-top-cop-black-lives-matter-killing-blacks/article/2610687.

6. Black Lives Matter website, 2017, accessed March 5, 2017, http://blacklivesmatter.com/.

7. Melissa Chan, "Number of U.S. Police Officers Killed on Duty Rises to 5-Year High in 2016," *Time*, December 29, 2016, http://time.com/4619689/police-officers-killed-2016/; See Associated Press, "2016 Saw Increase in Number of Police Killed in Line of Duty," *CBS News*, December 29, 2016, accessed March 5, 2017, http://www.cbsnews.com/news/police-killed-line-of-duty-increase-2016/.

8. Officer Down Memorial Page, "Honoring Officers Killed in 2016," accessed March 5, 2017, https://www.odmp.org/search/year/2016.

9. Josh Feldman, "Black Lives Matter Releases Statement on Dallas Shooting," *Mediaite*, July 8, 2016, accessed March 5, 2017, http://www.mediaite.com/online/black-lives-matter-releases-a-statement-on-dallas-shooting/.

10. United States Census Bureau, "Quick Facts: United States," 2017, accessed March 5, 2017, https://www.census.gov/quickfacts/table/PST045216/00.

11. Note percentages do not add up to 100, as the race of some persons was unknown. *Washington Post*, "991 People Shot Dead by Police in 2015," *Washington Post*, 2016, accessed March 5, 2017, https://www.washingtonpost.com/graphics/national/police-shootings/; *Washington Post*, "Fatal Force: 963 People Have Been Shot and Killed by the Police in 2016," *Washington Post*, 2017, accessed March 5, 2017, https://www.washingtonpost.com/graphics/national/police-shootings-2016/.

12. Ashley May, "#AllLivesMatter Hashtag Is Racist, Critics Say," *USA Today*, July 13, 2016, accessed March 5, 2017, http://www.usatoday.com/story/news/nation-now/2016/07/13/why-saying-all-lives-matter-opposite-black-lives-matter/87025190/.

13. Bill Chappell, "Police and Black Lives Matter Hold a Cookout, and Praise Rolls In," *NPR*, July 19, 2016, http://www.npr.org/sections/thetwo-way/2016/07/19/486581466/police-and-black-lives-matter-hold-a-cookout-and-praise-rolls-in.

14. Thomas A. Critchley, *A History of Police in England and Wales*, 2nd ed. (Montclair, NJ: Patterson Smith, 1985); Samuel Walker, *A Critical History of Police Reform: The Emergence of Professionalism* (Lexington, MA: Lexington Books, 1977).

15. See Samuel Walker, *Popular Justice* (New York: Oxford University Press, 1980), and Daniel Devlin, *Police Procedure, Administration and Organization* (London: Butterworth, 1966).

16. See Patrick Pringle, *The Thief-Takers* (London: Museum Press, 1958), and Bruce Smith, *Rural Crime Control* (New York: Columbia University Institute of Public Administration, 1933). Also, see Critchley, op. cit.

17. John S. Dempsey and Linda S. Forst, *An Introduction to Policing*, 5th ed. (Clifton Park, NY: Delmar Cengage Learning, 2010).

18. See Patrick Pringle, *Hue and Cry* (New York: William Morrow, 1965).

19. Samuel Walker, *The Police in America: An Introduction*, 2nd ed. (New York, NY: McGraw-Hill Publishing Co., 1992); also see Samuel Walker, *A Critical History of Police Reform: The Emergence of Professionalism* (Lexington, MA: Lexington Books, 1977).

20. See for example Francis X. Hartmann (ed.), *Debating the Evolution of American Policing* (Washington, DC: National Institute of Justice, 1988).

21. George L. Kelling and Mark H. Moore, *The Evolving Strategy of Policing* (Washington, DC: National Institute of Justice, 1988) name three stages; See also, Dan Fleissner and Fred Heinzelmann *Crime Prevention through Environmental Design and Community Policing*, NIJ Research in Action, The National Institute of Justice, Office of Justice Programs, U.S. Department of Justice, Washington, DC., August 1996, accessed June 14, 2010, http://www.ncjrs.gov/pdffiles/crimepre.pdf; Michael J. Palmiotto, *Community Policing: A Police Strategy for the 21st Century* (Gaithersburg, MD: An Aspen Publication, 2000).

22. Hubert Williams and Patrick V. Murphy, *The Evolving Strategy of Police: A Minority View* (Washington, DC: National Institute of Justice, 1990).

23. Williams and Murphy criticize Kelling and Moore for not giving due attention to racism and slavery in their history of American policing. Where possible, we have included both perspectives.

24. Kelling and Moore, op. cit., 2–4.

25. See Robert Fogelson, *Big City Police* (Cambridge, MA: Harvard University Press, 1977); Roger Lane, *Policing the City: Boston 1822–1885* (Cambridge, MA: Harvard University Press, 1967); and Thomas A. Reppetto, *The Blue Parade* (New York: Free Press, 1978). For an analysis of innovative police techniques, see Jerome H. Skolnick and David H. Bagley, *This New Blue Line: Police Innovation in Six American Cities* (New York: Free Press, 1986).

26. U.S. Marshals Service, "Fugitive Task Forces: Local Fugitive Task Forces," U.S. Department of Justice, accessed June 14, 2010, http://www.justice.gov/marshals/investigations/taskfrcs/taskforces.htm.

27. Risdon N. Slate, "The Federal Witness Protection Program," *Criminal Justice Ethics* 16, no. 2 (Summer/Fall 1997): 20–34; Risdon Slate, "Silent Witness?" *Intersec: The Journal of International Security* 16, no. 3 (June 2006): 23–26.

28. See Bruce Smith, *Police Systems in the United States* (New York: Harper and Bros., 1949).

29. Erica Virtue, "US $1-million Bounty Placed on NARCO Chief's Head," *Jamaica Observer*, February 29, 2004, accessed August 1, 2010, http://www.jamaicaobserver.com/news/56402_US-1-million-bounty-placed-on-narco-chief-s-head.

30. Ibid. Williams and Murphy cite P. L. Reichel, "Southern Slave Patrols as a Transitional Police Type," *American Journal of Policing* 7, no. 2 (1988): 51–77, and T. Cooper (ed.), *Statutes at Large of South Carolina*, vol. 3, part 3 (Columbia, SC: A. S. Johnston, 1838), 568.

31. Williams and Murphy, op. cit., 4–5.

32. Williams and Murphy, op. cit., 5. Also cited therein, Roger Lane, *Policing the City: Boston: 1822–1885* (Cambridge, MA: Harvard University Press, 1967), and E. A. Savage, *A Chronological History of the Boston Watch and Police, from 1631–1865*, available on Library of American Civilization microfiche 13523 (Originally published in 1865.).

33. See P. S. Foner, *History of Black Americans: From Africa to the Emergence of the Cotton Kingdom* (Westport, CT: Greenwood, 1975), 206; also see I. Berlin, *Slaves without Masters: The Free Negro in the Antebellum South* (New York: Pantheon Books, 1974), 316–317. Both are cited by Williams and Murphy.

34. Ibid., 7. Also see M. Delaney, *Colored Brigades, 'Negro Specials' and Colored Policemen: A History of Blacks in American Police Departments* (unpublished manuscript, no date), 12, and J. W. Blassingame, *Black New Orleans, 1860–1880* (Chicago, IL: University of Chicago Press, 1973), 244.

35. Ibid., 8. Also, Walker, op. cit., Note 19; Delaney, op. cit., 20; and R. Lane, *Roots of Violence in Black Philadelphia: 1860–1900* (Cambridge, MA: Harvard University Press, 1986), 60–67.

36. Ibid., 8.

37. Ibid. Also see Foner, op. cit., 342.

38. Jerome H. Skolnick and James J. Fyfe, *Above the Law: Police and the Excessive Use of Force* (New York: Free Press, 1993), 1.

39. Stetson Kennedy, *The Klan Unmasked* (Gainesville, FL: University Press of Florida, 1990); Stetson Kennedy, "Secret Klan Documents Exposed!" 2010, accessed June 14, 2010, http://www.stetsonkennedy.com/klandocs.html.

40. David K. Shipler, "Khaki, Blue and Blacks," *New York Times*, May 26, 1992, accessed June 14, 2010, http://www.nytimes.com/1992/05/26/opinion/khaki-blue-and-blacks.html; For an assessment of the Rodney King matter see Jerome H. Skolnick and James J. Fyfe, op. cit.; Roland V. del Carmen, *Criminal Procedure: Law and Practice*, 3rd ed. (Belmont, CA: Wadsworth, 1995)—as noted by del Carmen the initial suit by King asked for $56 million, one million dollars for each of the 56 blows that King was struck by a police baton, primarily from Los Angeles Police Officer Lawrence Powell. Three officers were initially acquitted in the state trial, and a hung jury emerged in regards to Powell's involvement in the matter. Following riots in Los Angeles, the four officers were tried on federal charges (this did not constitute double jeopardy, as two separate jurisdictions were involved, i.e., state and federal). This time, Sergeant Stacy Koon and Officer Powell were convicted and received 30-month prison sentences. King would ultimately receive a jury award of $3.8 million in his civil lawsuit.

41. The Smoking Gun, "Mug Shots, Martin Luther King, Jr.," accessed June 14, 2010, http://www.thesmokinggun.com/mugshots/mlkingmug1.html.

42. Brian J. Foley, "Policing from the Gut: Anti-Intellectualism in American Criminal Procedure," *Md. L. Rev.* 69 (2010): 261, 266.

43. Adam Benforado, "The Geography of Criminal Law," *Cardozo L. Rev.* 31 (January 2010): 823.

44. National Organization of Black Law Enforcement Executives, "In the Age of Barack Obama, Is Race Still Relevant?" accessed June 15, 2010, http://www.noblenatl.org/index.php?option=com_poll&id=15:race-relevance.

45. Clifford D. Shearing and Philip C. Stenning, *Private Policing* (Beverly Hills, CA: Sage, 1987).

46. William C. Cunningham and Todd H. Taylor, *The Growing Role of Private Security* (Washington, DC: National Institute of Justice, May 1985).

47. Matt West and Paul Miller, The Railroad Police, Railroad Police Authority, accessed June 15, 2010, http://www.therailroadpolice.com/history.htm#Railroad Police Authority.

48. Cunningham and Taylor, op. cit.; Mike Zielinski, "Armed and Dangerous: Private Police on the March," *Covert Action Quarterly*, accessed June 15, 2010, http://mediafilter.org/caq/CAQ54p.police.html.

49. Bobby White, "Cash-Strapped Cities Try Private Guards over Police," *The Wall Street Journal*, April 21, 2009, accessed June 15, 2010: http://online.wsj.com/article/SB124027127337237011.html; See Jody Bennett, "Police: Going Private, International Relations and Security Network," ISN Security Watch, May 18, 2009, accessed June 15, 2010, http://www.isn.ethz.ch/isn/Current-Affairs/Security-Watch/Detail/?ots591=4888 CAA0-B3DB-1461-98B9-E20E7B9C13D4&lng=en&id=100297; See also Adam Mueller's argument on May 7, 2010, as to why private police are more economical and efficient than public police in "Public vs. Private Police; Which Would You Choose?," Cop Block, accessed June 15, 2010, http://www.cop block.org/130/public-vs-private-police-which-would-you-choose-2.

50. Amy Goldstein, "The Private Arm of the Law: Some Question the Granting of Police Power to Security Firms," *Washington Post*, January 2, 2007, accessed June 15, 2010, http://www.washington post.com/wp-dyn/content/article/2007/01/01/AR2007010100665.html.

51. Ibid., 17–18; Also see Albert J. Reiss, Jr., *Policing a City's Central District—The Oakland Story* (Washington, DC: National Institute of Justice, 1985).

52. John E. Eck and William Spelman, *Problem-Solving: Problem-Oriented Policing in Newport News* (Washington, DC: National Institute of Justice, 1987), 11. Also cited, Eric Monkonnen, *Police in Urban America, 1860–1920* (Cambridge, England: Cambridge University Press, 1981); and see Walker, op. cit.

53. Hartmann, op. cit., 4; Kelling and Moore, op. cit., 4–5. See also Richard G. Powers, *Secrecy and Power: The Life of J. Edgar Hoover* (New York: Free Press, 1987).

54. National Commission on Law Observance and Enforcement, *Report on Lawlessness in Law Enforcement, no. 11* (Washington, DC: U.S. Government Printing Office, 1931).

55. August Vollmer, *The Police and Modern Society* (Berkeley: University of California Press, 1936). Also see O. W. Wilson and Roy C. McLaren, *Police Administration*, 3rd ed. (New York: McGraw-Hill, 1972), and Gene E. Carte, *Police Reform in the United States: The Era of August Vollmer, 1905–1932* (Berkeley: University of California Press, 1986).

56. Williams and Murphy, op. cit., 10.

57. *Report of the National Advisory Commission on Civil Disorders* (New York: Bantam, 1968), 321, 304–305.

58. Ibid., 1, 2, 299.

59. See Eck and Spelman for an analysis of the effects of the reform era.

60. Eck and Spelman, op. cit., 1.

61. Ibid., 2.

62. See also Robert C. Trajanowicz and Denis W. Banas, *Perceptions of Safety: A Comparison of Foot Patrol versus Motor Patrol Officers* (East Lansing: National Neighborhood Foot Patrol Center, School of Criminal Justice, Michigan State University, 1985); Stephen Meagher, "Police Patrol Styles: How Pervasive Is Community Variations?" *Journal of Police Science and Administration* 13 (1985): 36–45; Margaret J. Levine, *Patrol Deployment* (Washington, DC: U.S. Department of Justice, 1985); Richard C. Larson, *Synthesizing and Extending the Results of Police Patrol Studies* (Washington, DC: U.S. Department of Justice, 1985).

63. See Timothy J. Flanagan, "Consumer Perspectives on Police Operational Strategy," *Journal of Police Science and Administration* 13, no. 1 (1985): 10–21.

64. George M. Pugh, "The Good Police Officer: Qualities, Roles and Concepts," *Journal of Police Science and Administration* 14, no. 1 (1986): 49–61; Herman Goldstein, *Policing a Free Society* (Cambridge, MA: Ballinger, 1976), 111–112. See also William K. Muir, *Police: Streetcorner Politicians* (Chicago: University of Chicago Press, 1977).

65. *Report of the National Advisory Commission on Civil Disorders*, 304–305.

66. Trajanowicz and Banas, op. cit.

67. John C. Fine, "Police on Horseback: A New Concept for an Old Idea," *The FBI Law Enforcement Bulletin*, July 2001, accessed June 15, 2010, http://findarticles.com/p/articles/mi_m2194/is_7_70/ai_77417455.

68. Segway, Case Study, Community Policing, Bridgeport, Connecticut, Police Department, "Segway PTS Give a Boost to Community-Based Policing," accessed June 15, 2010, http://www.segway.com/downloads/pdfs/Bridgeport_Police_Case_Study.pdf.

69. Carl Ent, "Bicycle Patrol: A Community Policing Alternative," *The Police Chief* 58 (1991).

70. Goldstein, op. cit., 49.

71. Albert J. Reiss, Jr., *The Police and the Public* (New Haven, CT: Yale University Press, 1971), 10–11.

72. Goldstein, op. cit., 49.

73. George L. Kelling, Tony Pate, D. Dieckman, and Charles E. Brown, *The Kansas City Preventive Patrol Experiment and Summary Report* (Washington, DC: Police Foundation, 1974). See also Carl Klockars (ed.), *Thinking about Police* (New York: McGraw-Hill Publishing Co., 1983) 130; Jerome Skolnick and David Bayley, *The New Blue Line* (New York: The Free Press, 1986), 4; Michael Gottfredson and Travis Hirschi, *A General Theory of Crime* (Stanford: Stanford University Press, 1990), 270; Michael Felson, *Crime and Everyday Life* (Thousand Oaks, California: Pine Forge Press, 1994) 10–11.

74. Quotation is from Klockars, 130.

75. Lawrence W. Sherman and David Weisburd, "General Deterrent Effects of Police Patrol in Crime 'Hot Spots': A Randomized, Controlled Trial," *Justice Quarterly* 12, no. 4 (1995): 625–645.

76. Ibid., 629, and this refers to "routine activities theory," which was discussed in Chapter 2.

77. Ibid.

78. Christopher S. Koper, "Just Enough Police Presence: Reducing Crime and Disorderly Behavior by Optimizing Patrol Time in Crime Hot Spots," *Justice Quarterly* 42, no. 4 (1995): 649–672.

79. Clark Howard, *The Zebra Killings* (London: New English Library, 1980).

80. President's Commission on Law Enforcement and Administration of Justice, *Task Force Report: The Police* (Washington, DC: U.S. Government Printing Office, 1967), 184–185.

81. Consider the concept of an "occupying army" from the Christopher Commission, which investigated the culture of the Los Angeles Police Department following the Rodney King incident.

82. John Eck, *Solving Crimes* (Washington, DC: Police Executive Research Forum, 1983), 69–93; Greenwood and Petersilia, *The Criminal Investigation Process*, vol. I.

83. Peter B. Bloch and Donald R. Weidman, *Managing Criminal Investigations* (Washington, DC: U.S. Department of Justice, 1975), 17.

84. Gary Cox, personal communication, June 7, 2010.

85. Goldstein, op. cit., 55. Goldstein writes: "Many of the techniques employed by detectives today are more heavily influenced by a desire to imitate stereotypes than by a rational plan for solving crimes. The myths and fantasies that pervade detective operations deter the police and the public from examining the utility of what it is that detectives in fact do."

86. Peter W. Greenwood and Joan Petersilia, *The Criminal Investigation Process*, vol. I; Jan M. Chaiken, *The Criminal Investigation Process*, vol. II; and Peter W. Greenwood, Jan M. Chaiken, Joan Petersilia, and Linda Prusoff, *The Criminal Investigation Process*, vol. III (Santa Monica, CA: Rand Corporation, 1975).

87. Gary Cox, personal communication, June 7, 2010.

88. Greenwood and Petersilia, op. cit.; Daryl F. Gates and Lyle Knowles, "An Examination of the Rand Corporation's Analysis of the Criminal Investigation Process," *Police Chief* 43 (July 1976): 20.

89. Klockars, op. cit., 130.

90. Bloch and Weidman, op. cit. The Rand report is not the only research on investigatory functions, nor is it the first call for the improvement of detective services. During the early 1970s, for example, the Police Foundation held a series of conferences on improving investigatory procedures through better management. And today there are various studies and reports outlining strategic and tactical alternatives that can be followed to make detective work more effective in solving crimes and apprehending suspects.

91. M. A. Farber, "Big Push on Crime Merely Pushes It Elsewhere, Many Officers Feel," *New York Times*, June 1, 1982, B1, B6, cited in John E. Conklin, *Criminology* (New York: Macmillan, 1989), 441.

92. Lorraine Green, "Cleaning Up Drug Hot Spots in Oakland, California: The Displacement and Diffusion Effects," *Justice Quarterly* 42, no. 4 (1995) 737–754; R. Barr and K. Pease, "Crime Placement, Displacement, and Deflection," in M. Tonry and N. Morris (eds.) *Crime and Justice*, Vol. 12 (Chicago: University of Chicago Press, 1990), 227–318.

93. Task Force Report, op. cit. 184–185.

94. *Report of the National Advisory Commission on Civil Disorders* (see note 57 above), 14. See also Raymond I. Parnas, "The Police Response to the Domestic Disturbance," *Wisconsin Law Review* (Fall 1967): 914–960.

95. William R. LePere, personal communication, May 28, 2010.

96. Tabatha R. Johnson, "The Public and the Police in the City of Chicago," The Chicago Community Policing Evaluation Consortium, Institute for Policy Research, Northwestern University, August 1993, accessed June 16, 2010, http://www.northwestern.edu/ipr/publications/policing_papers/ caps1.pdf.

97. Herman Goldstein, *Policing in a Free Society* (Cambridge, MA: Ballinger, 1977), 35.

98. Valerie Bauerlein, "Cops With a Twist: A New Tactic in Police, Community Relations," *The Wall Street Journal*, August 4, 2017, accessed December 16, 2017, https://www.wsj.com/articles/police-try-rebuilding-community-trust-with-ice-cream-1501872770.

99. George L. Kelling and William J. Bratton, *Implementing Community Policing: The Administration Problem* (Washington, DC: U.S. Department of Justice, July 1993).

100. Lawrence W. Sherman, Catherine H. Milton, and Thomas O. Kelly, *Team Policing: Seven Case Studies* (Washington, DC: The Police Foundation, 1973).

101. Ibid.

102. Eck and Spelman, op. cit., 18–19.

103. Robert Trajanowicz and Paul R. Smyth, *A Manual for the Establishment and Operation of a Foot Patrol Program* (East Lansing: National Neighborhood Foot Patrol Center, School of Criminal Justice, Michigan State University, 1985).

104. Kenneth J. Peak and Ronald W. Glensor, *Community Policing and Problem Solving: Strategies and Practices* (Upper Saddle River, NJ: Prentice Hall, 1996), 68–105. See also Richard Lacayo, "Back to the Beat," *Time*, April 1, 1991, 22–224; and Gordon Witkin and Dan McGraw, "Beyond 'Just the facts, ma'am,'" *U.S. News and World Report*, August 2, 1993, 28.

105. James Q. Wilson and George L. Kelling, "Making Neighborhoods Safe," *The Atlantic*, February 1989, 46–52. Also see New York City Police Commissioner Lee P. Brown's article "Community Policing:

A Practical Guide for Police Officials," in *Annual Editions: Criminal Justice 91/92*, (Guilford, CT: The Dushkin Publishing Group, 1991), 89–98, reprinted from *Perspectives on Policing* (Washington, DC: U.S. Department of Justice, September 1989), 1–11; George L. Kelling, *Police and Communities: The Quiet Revolution* (Washington, DC: The U.S. Department of Justice, 1988); and George L. Kelling, *Neighborhoods and Police: The Maintenance of Civil Authority*, (Washington, DC: U.S. Department of Justice, 1989).

106. Herman Goldstein, *Problem-Oriented Policing* (New York: McGraw-Hill, 1990).

Chapter 5

1. *Escobedo v. Illinois*, 378 U.S. 478, 490 (1964).

2. Ray Surrette, *Media, Crime and Criminal Justice: Images, Realities, and Policies* (Belmont, CA: Thomason/Wadsworth, 2007); and Frank Leishman and Paul Mason, *Policing and the Media: Facts, Fictions and Factions* (Devon, UK: Willan, 2003).

3. Preston Elrod and R. Scott Ryder, *Juvenile Justice: A Social, Legal and Historical Perspective* (Jones &Bartlett Learning, 2005) (police as gatekeepers); and Rutter, Michael, Henri Giller, and Ann Hagell, *Antisocial Behavior by Young People* (New York: Cambridge University Press, 1998).

4. See C. N. Famega, "Proactive Policing by Post and Community Officers." *Crime & Delinquency* 55, no. 1 (2009): 78–104; C. Clarke, "Proactive Policing: Standing on the Shoulders of Community-Based Policing," *Police Practice & Research: An International Journal* 7, no. 1 (2006): 3–17; A. L. Jackson and J. E. Wade, "Police Perceptions of Social Capital and Sense of Responsibility: An Explanation of Proactive Policing," *Policing: An International Journal of Police Strategies and Management* 28, no. 1 (2005): 49–68; Steward Field and Caroline Pelser (Eds.), *Invading the Private: State Accountability and New Investigative Methods in Europe* (Brookfield, VT: Ashgate-Dartmouth, 1998); and Donald Black, *The Manners and Customs of Police* (New York: Academic, 1980).

5. J. P. Blair, "What Do We Know about Interrogation in the United States?" *Journal of Police and Criminal Psychology* 20, no. 2 (2005): 44–57; and J. Kleinig, *The Ethics of Policing* (Cambridge: Cambridge University Press, 1996).

6. R. A. Leo, *Police Interrogation and American Justice* (Cambridge, MA: Harvard University Press, 2008).

7. D. O. Friedrichs, M. Schwartz, and P. Hillyard, "Social Harm and a Twenty-First Century Criminology," *Crime, Law and Social Change: An Interdisciplinary Journal* 48, no. 1–2 (2007): 1–72; and Wesley G. Skogan and Tracey L. Meares, "Lawful Policing," *The Annals of the American Academy of Political and Social Science* 593, no. 1 (May 2004): 66–83.

8. Rolando V. del Carmen, *Criminal Procedure: Law and Practice*, 8th ed. (Belmont, CA: Wadsworth, 2010).

9. *Illinois v. Wardlow*, 528 U.S. 119 (2000).

10. *U.S. v. Sokolow*, 490 U.S. 1 (1989).

11. See *U.S. v. Hensley*, 469 U.S. 221 (1985) concerning use of a wanted flier.

12. *Miranda v. Arizona*, 348 U.S. 436 (1966), 478–479.

13. *Kolender v. Lawson*, 103 S. Ct. 1855 (1983).

14. Hiibel v. Sixth Judicial District Court of Nevada, et al., 542 U.S. 177 (2004).

15. *Terry v. Ohio*, 392 U.S. 1 (1968).

16. Ibid.

17. *Minnesota v. Dickerson*, 508 U.S. 366, 375 (1993); see del Carmen, *Criminal Procedure*, 2010.

18. Lauren-Brooke Eisen, "*Kaley v. U.S.*: A Frightening Ruling," Brennan Center for Justice, New York University School of Law, March 4, 2014, accessed March 6, 2017, https://www.brennancenter.org/blog/kaley-v-united-states.

19. *Kaley v. U.S.*, 134 S. Ct. 1070 (2014).

20. *U.S. v. Robinson*, 414 U.S. 218 (1973).

21. See del Carmen, *Criminal Procedure*, 2010.

22. *United States v. McConney*, 728 F.2d 1195, 1199 (9th Cir.), cert. denied, 469 U.S. 824 (1984).

23. See del Carmen, *Criminal Procedure*, 2010.

24. *Weeks v. United States,* 232 U.S. 383 (1914); and ibid.

25. *Wolf v. Colorado*, 338 U.S. 25 (1949).

26. *Elkins v. U.S.*, 364 U.S. 206 (1960); and see del Carmen, *Criminal Procedure*, 2010.

27. See *Illinois v. Gates*, 462 U.S. 213 (1983).

28. D. S. Mann, Review of *Injustice for All:* Mapp vs. Ohio *and the Fourth Amendment*, by Priscilla H. Machado Zotti, in *Law & Politics Book Review* 15 no. 5 (May 2005): 382–385.

29. *Mapp v. Ohio*, 367 U.S. 643, 659 (1961).

30. James R. Acker and David C. Brody, *Criminal Procedure: A Contemporary Perspective*, 2nd ed. (Sudbury, MA: Jones & Bartlett Publishers, Inc., 2004).

31. Stephen Powers and Stanley Rothman, *The Least Dangerous Branch: Consequences of Judicial Activism* (Westport, CT: Greenwood Publishing Group, 2002).

32. *United States v. Leon*, 468 U.S. 897 (1984); *Massachusetts v. Sheppard*, 468 U.S. 981 (1984) (if the magistrate errs and the police are acting in good faith regarding the issuance of a search warrant), *Maryland v. Garrison*, 480 U.S. 79 (1987) (a court employee errs), and *Arizona v. Evans*, 514 U.S. 1 (1995) (if the police accidentally err); see also *Wong Sung et al. v. U.S.*, 371 U.S.471 (1963) (regarding the "purged taint exception" to the exclusionary rule); see *U.S. v. Crews*, 445 U.S. 463 (1980) and *Segura v. U.S.*, 468 U.S. 796 (1984) (regarding the "independent source exception" to the exclusionary rule); see *Nix v. Williams* 467 U.S. 431 (1984) discussed later in the chapter in Box regarding "inevitable discovery"; and see Otis H. Stephens and Richard A. Glenn, *Unreasonable Searches and Seizures: Rights and Liberties under the Law* (Santa Barbara, CA: ABC-CLIO Publishing, 2006). It should also be noted that, while liability may be limited, law enforcement officers and prosecutors can be sued for acting in bad faith—see Kathryn Wexler "Aisenberg Suit Alleges Bad Faith," *St. Petersburg Times*, September 9, 2003, accessed July 13, 2009, http://www.sptimes.com/2003/09/09/Tampabay/Aisenberg_suit_allege.shtml.

33. *Stoner v. California*, 376 U.S. 483 (1964).

34. *U.S. v. Matlock*, 415 U.S. 164 (1974).

35. *Georgia v. Randolph*, 547 U.S. 103 (2006).

36. *Illinois v. Rodriquez*, 497 U.S. 177 (1990).

37. Melinda Miller (director of community living), and William Carew (campus safety director), personal communication, June 30, 2009, Florida Southern College, Lakeland, Florida; Florida Southern Campus Housing Agreement, accessed July 1, 2009, http://www.flsouthern.edu/student_life/student handbook/pdf/Housing.pdf; see del Carmen, *Criminal Procedure*, 2010.

38. *Chimel v. California*, 395 U.S. 752 (1969).

39. *Carroll v. U.S.*, 267 U.S. 132 (1925).

40. *California v. Carney*, 471 U.S. 386 (1985).

41. *New York v. Belton*, 453 U.S. 454 (1981), addressed warrantless searches in the absence of consent or exigent circumstances of the passenger compartment of an automobile incident to a lawful arrest, and, as is often the case when the Court does not go beyond the factual circumstances before

it, questions remained; the following year, in *U.S. v. Ross*, 456 U.S. 798 (1982), the Court expanded the scope of warrantless searches beyond *Belton* to include searches of the trunk of an automobile when probable cause is present.

42. In *Arizona v. Gant*, 556 U.S. ___ (2009), the U.S. Supreme Court applied the *Chimel* (footnote 38 above) criteria (area immediately within one's reach) as an evidentiary basis for searches of vehicles on public thoroughfares.

43. *Florida v. Bostick*, 501 U.S. 429 (1991).

44. *California v. Acevedo*, 500 U.S. 565 (1991).

45. *Delaware v. Prouse*, 440 U.S. 647 (1979).

46. *Michigan Department of State Police v. Sitz*, 496 U.S. 444 (1990), which governs DUI checkpoints; see also *Indianapolis v. Edmond*, 531 U.S. 32 (2000), which held roadblocks assembled for general crime fighting purposes without reasonable suspicion, such as the flow of drugs, are not allowable.

47. *U.S. v. Martinez-Fuerte*, 428 U.S. 543 (1976).

48. *Illinois v. Lidster*, 540 U.S. 419 (2004).

49. See del Carmen, *Criminal Procedure*, 2010.

50. *South Dakota v. Opperman*, 428 U.S. 364 (1976).

51. *Illinois v. Caballes*, 543 U.S. 405 (2005).

52. *U.S. v. Place*, 462 U.S. 696 (1983).

53. *Florida v. Harris*, 133 S. Ct. 1050 (2013).

54. *Florida v. Jardines*, 133 S. Ct. 1409 (2012).

55. See del Carmen, *Criminal Procedure*, 2010.

56. For the "plain-view" doctrine see *Coolidge v. New Hampshire*, 403 U.S. 443 (1971). See also *Texas v. Brown*, 103 S. Ct. 1535 (1983); see del Carmen, *Criminal Procedure*, 2010.

57. *Chimel v. California*, 395 U.S. 752 (1969).

58. See del Carmen, *Criminal Procedure*, 2010.

59. *Warshak v. U.S.*, File Name: 07a0225p.06 (6th Cir. [2007]); ibid.

60. See del Carmen, *Criminal Procedure*, 2010.

61. R. E. Foster, *Police Technology* (Upper Saddle River, NJ: Prentice-Hall,2005); L. Moriarty, *Criminal Justice Technology in the 21st Century* (Springfield, IL: Charles C. Thomas, 2005).

62. See del Carmen, *Criminal Procedure*, 2010.

63. Paul Elias, "Federal Judge Tosses Warrantless Wiretap Cases." ABC News, June 3, 2009, accessed June 28, 2009, http://abcnews.go.com/Technology/WireStory?id=7749362&page=1.

64. Orin Kerr, "Supreme Court Agrees to hear 'Carpenter v. United States,' the Fourth Amendment Historical Cell-Site Case," *The Washington Post*, June 5, 2017, accessed October 6, 2017, https://www.washingtonpost.com/news/volokh-conspiracy/wp/2017/06/05/supreme-court-agrees-to-hear-carpenter-v-united-states-the-fourth-amendment-historical-cell-site-case/?utm_term=.5840af8a5b8d.

65. Samuel Nunn, "Measuring Criminal Justice Technology Outputs: The Case of Title III Wiretap Productivity, 1987–2005," *Journal of Criminal Justice* 36, no. 4 (2008): 344–353.

66. *Olmstead v. U.S.*, 277 U.S. 438 (1928).

67. See *Katz v. U.S.*, 389 U.S. 347 (1967); of course, words uttered into a public phone not in an enclosed phone booth, such as seen at airports, would not carry with them a reasonable expectation of privacy, as someone standing nearby could reasonably overhear such a conversation.

68. *U.S. v. White*, 401 U.S. 745 (1971).

69. *Lee v. U.S.*, 343 U.S. 747 (1952).

70. Video available at http://www.youtube.com/watch?v=tJoID7VwRtM.

71. Video available at http://www.youtube.com/watch?v=JpV83U0UI9U; Abby Goodnough, "Medical Student Is Indicted in Craigslist Killing," *New York Times*, June 21, 2009, accessed June 29, 2009, http://www.nytimes.com/2009/06/22/us/22indict.html.

72. Pete Fussey, "Observing Potentiality in the Global City: Surveillance and Counterterrorism in London," *International Criminal Justice Review* 17, no. 3 (2007): 171–192.

73. Jason Geary, "Robert Farley Pleads Guilty to Killing Father," *The Ledger*, May 22, 2009, accessed June 30, 2009, http://www.theledger.com/article/20090522/NEWS/905225070?Title=Robert-Farley-Pleads-Guilty-to-Killing-Father.

74. See *Orlando Sentinel*, "Pictures: Photos Entered as Possible Evidence in Casey Anthony Trial," accessed June 29, 2009, http://www.orlandosentinel.com/news/local/caylee-anthony/orl-casey-anthony-trial-case-photos,0,2398805.photogallery?track=orl-mark-promo-local-photobucket.

75. Ledger Staff Report, "Polk Deputies Rounding Up Child Pornography Suspects," *The Ledger*, May 28, 2009, accessed June 29, 2009, http://www.theledger.com/article/20090528/NEWS/ 905289961?Title=Polk-Deputies-Rounding-Up-Child-Pornography-Suspects.

76. Yahoo Answers, "How Do Police Catch People that Watch Either Child Pornography or Minors Watching It?" accessed June 30, 2009, http://answers.yahoo.com/question/index?qid=20090131170550AAC6KhD; "WWW FAQs: What Is an IP Address?" accessed June 30, 2009, http://www.boutell.com/newfaq/definitions/ipaddress. html.

77. See *Katz v. United States*, 389 U.S. 347 (1967).

78. *Oliver v. United States*, 466 U.S. 170 (1984).

79. *Kyllo v. U.S.*, 533 U.S. 27 (2001), 33.

80. Charlotte Twight, "Sovereign Impunity," *The Independent Review* 12, no. 4 (Spring 2008): 485–517.

81. Those acts include Title III of the 1968 Omnibus Crime Control and Safe Streets Act (also known as the Federal Wiretap Act—governs court processes for authorizing electronic surveillance of communications, to include Internet, facsimile, voice and e-mail), the 1978 Foreign Intelligence Surveillance (FISA) Act, the 1986 Electronic Communications and Privacy Act (ECPA), and the 1994 Communications Assistance for Law Enforcement Act (CALEA). Both Title III and FISA allow governmental wiretaps without court orders under exigent circumstances—when national security is endangered or to intercede when the chance of serious bodily injury or death is heightened, see del Carmen, 2010; Government Surveillance, "The Nature and Scope of Governmental Electronic Surveillance Activity," July 2006, accessed June 28, 2009, http://www.cdt.org/wiretap/wiretap_overview.html.

82. Gary T. Marx and Glenn W. Muschert, "Personal Information, Borders, and the New Surveillance Studies," *Annual Review of Law and Social Science* 3,(2007): 375–395.

83. See Susan N. Herman, "The USA PATRIOT Act and the Submajoritarian Fourth Amendment," *Harvard Civil Rights—Civil Liberties Law Review* 41(2006): 67–132; Controversial components associated with the PATRIOT Act include "sneak and peak" warrants (whereby unknowingly an individual's communications may be monitored or premises entered by government agents) and roving wiretaps that allow for tapping into any communication devices used by a suspect as they roam from place to place without further consultation with judicial authorities—see Government Surveillance, 2006; Alexander Diaz Morgan, "A Broadened View of Privacy as a Check against Government Access to E-Mail in the United States and the United Kingdom," *New York University Journal of International Law and Politics* (Spring, 2008); see Robert S. Mueller, III, Congressional Testimony: Sunset Provisions of the USA Patriot Act before the United States Senate Committee on the Judiciary, April 5, 2005, accessed June 29, 2009, http://www.fbi.gov/congress/congress05/mueller 040505.htm.

84. Conor Clarke, "Is the Foreign Intelligence Surveillance Court Really a Rubber Stamp?" *Stanford Law Review*, February 2014, accessed March 8, 2017, https://www.stanfordlawreview.org/online/is-the-foreign-intelligence-surveillance-court-really-a-rubber-stamp/.

85. Zack Whittaker, "Here's How Many US Surveillance Requests Were Rejected in 2015," *Zero Day*, April 30, 2016, accessed March 8, 2017, http://www.zdnet.com/article/us-spy-court-didnt-reject-a-single-secret-government-demand-for-data/.

86. *Riley v. California*, 134 S. Ct. 2473 (2014).

87. Associated Press, "FBI Sued over Hack into San Bernardino Terrorist's iPhone," *CBS* News, September 16, 2016, accessed March 9, 2017, http://www.cbsnews.com/news/fbi-sued-over-hack-into-san-bernardino-terrorists-iphone/; Adam Nagourney, Salman Masood, and Michael S. Schmidt, "Killers were Long Radicalized, F.B.I. Investigators Say," *New York Times*, December 7, 2015, accessed March 9, 2017, https://www.nytimes.com/2015/12/08/us/fbi-says-san-bernardino-assailants-were-radicalized.html; Melissa Chan and Matthew Katz, "2 Suspects Dead in San Bernardino Disability Center Shooting," *Time*, December 3, 2015, accessed March 9, 2017, http://time.com/4133250/shooter-san-bernardino-california/; Daily Mail Online Reporter, "Israeli Firm 'Helped FBI Crack San Bernardino Gunman's Cell Phone without Apple's Help,'" *Daily Mail*, March 29, 2016, accessed March 9, 2017, http://www.dailymail.co.uk/news/article-3514875/Israeli-firm-helped-FBI-crack-San-Bernardino-gunman-s-cellphone-without-Apple-s-help.html.

88. Philip Segal, "Cell Phone Pinging and Probable Cause," *The Ethical Investigator*, June 13, 2014, accessed March 9, 2017, http://www.ethicalinvestigator.com/cell-phone-pinging-and-probable-cause/; *U.S. v. Davis*, 754 F. 3d 1205 (11th Cir. 2014).

89. G. Wagner, "United States' Policy Analysis on Undercover Operations," *International Journal of Police Science & Management* 9, no. 4 (Winter 2007): 371–379, accessed May 1, 2009, doi:10.1350/ijps.2007.9.4.371\; See Gary T. Marx, "Thoughts on a Neglected Category of Social Movement Participant: The Agent Provocateur and the Informant," *American Journal of Sociology* 80 (1974): 402–442; and George E. Dix, "Undercover Investigations and Police Rulemaking," *Texas Law Review* 53 (1975): 294.

90. CBS News Los Angeles, "San Bernardino Police Pose as Homeless to Nab Drivers on Their Phones," April 3, 2015, accessed March 9, 2017, http://losangeles.cbslocal.com/2015/08/03/driving-message-home-san-bernardino-police-pose-as-homeless-to-nab-distracted-motorists/.

91. Associated Press, "Undercover New Hampshire Police Nab Cellphone Ban Violators," *Fox News*, October 1, 2015, accessed May 4, 2017, http://www.foxnews.com/us/2015/10/01/undercover-new-hampshire-police-nab-cellphone-ban-violators.html.

92. Matt Knox and Amy Robach, "NY Launches Specialized Vehicles to Nab Texting Drivers," *ABC News Good Morning America*, July 10, 2013, accessed March 9, 2017, http://abcnews.go.com/blogs/politics/2013/07/ny-launches-specialized-vehicles-to-nab-texting-drivers/.

93. Chris Matyszczyk, "Police Using Big Rigs to Catch Texting Drivers," *CNET*, October 31, 2013, accessed March 9, 2017, https://www.cnet.com/news/police-using-big-rigs-to-catch-texting-drivers/.

94. KEYE TV, "APD Using Buses to Catch Drivers on Their Phones," *CBS Austin*, February 10, 2016, accessed March 9, 2017, https://www.cnet.com/news/police-using-big-rigs-to-catch-texting-drivers/.

95. See William Queen's book *Under and Alone*, (New York: Random House, 2006), which chronicles his undercover law enforcement infiltration of the Mongols motorcycle gang. Queen discusses his involvement in drug and gun running with the gang and circumstances under which federal agents may be allowed to use illegal drugs.

96. Wagner, 2007.

97. Joseph A. Colquitt, "Rethinking Entrapment," *The American Criminal Law Review* (2004), accessed June 30, 2009, http://www.allbusiness.com/legal/laws/885814-1.html; Erik Luna, "Overextending the Criminal Law" in *Go Directly to Jail: The Criminalization of Almost Everything* by Gene Healey

(ed.) (Washington, DC: The Cato Institute, 2004); See Lawrence P. Tiffany, Donald M McIntyre, Jr., and Daniel Rotenberg, *Detection of Crime: Stopping and Questioning, Search and Seizure, Encouragement and Entrapment* (Boston: Little, Brown, 1967), Chap. 1.

98. Jerold H. Israel, Yale Kamisar, Wayne R. LaFave, and Nancy J. King, *Criminal Procedure and the Constitution* (West Publishing Co., 2008); See Tiffany, McIntyre, and Rotenberg, op. cit., 308–311.

99. Ibid.; see also *Sherman v. United States*, 356 U.S. 369 (1958). Jerold H. Israel, Yale Kamisar, Wayne R. LaFave, and Nancy J. King, *Criminal Procedure and the Constitution*, (West Publishing Co., 2008); Wayne R. LaFave, Jerold H. Israel, and Nancy J. King, *Principles of Criminal Procedure: Investigation* (West Publishing Co., 2004); Paul Finkelman, *Encyclopedia of American Civil Liberties* (Boca Raton, FL: CRC Press, 2006); Richard C. Donnelly, "Judicial Control of Informants, Spies, Stool Pigeons and Agent Provocateurs," *Yale Law Journal* 60 (1951): 1091; and Roger Park, "The Entrapment Controversy," *Minnesota Law Review* 60 (1976): 163–274.

100. See *State v. Long*, 216 N.J. Super. 269, 523 A.2d 672 (1987).

101. Colquitt, *Rethinking Entrapment*, 2004; the initial case decided by the U.S. Supreme Court concerning entrapment was *Sorrells v. U.S.*, 287 U.S. 435 (1932), a case concerning Prohibition.

102. Colquitt, *Rethinking Entrapment*, 2004.

103. Jenifer B. McKim, "Police Sting Leaves Dozens of Fugitives Reeling," *Boston Globe*, June 9, 1997, accessed July 13, 2009, http://www.encyclopedia.com/doc/1P2-8420545.html.

104. Brian Stelter, "'To Catch a Predator' Is Falling Prey to Advertisers' Sensibilities," *New York Times*, August 27, 2007, accessed July 13, 2009, http://www.nytimes.com/2007/08/27/business/media/27predator.html?pagewanted=all.

105. Chris Hansen, Correspondent, Dateline, NBC, August 7, 2007, accessed June 30, 2009, http://www.msnbc.msn.com/id/3949042.

106. Perverted Justice Foundation Incorporated, "How to Help," 2009, accessed June 30, 2009, http://www.pjfi.org/?pg=howtohelp; Perverted Justice, 2009, accessed June 30, 2009, http://www.perverted-justice.com.

107. Rational Wiki, Perverted Justice, December 27, 2016, accessed March 9, 2017, http://rationalwiki.org/wiki/Perverted_Justice.

108. Chris Hansen, "Hansen vs. Predator: Chris Hansen Catches a Plumber on the Prowl," *Crime Watch Daily*, September 20, 2016, accessed March 9, 2017, https://crimewatchdaily.com/2016/09/20/hansen-vs-predator-host-chris-hansen-catches-a-plumber-on-the-prowl/.

109. *Sorrells v. U.S.*, 287 U.S. 435, 446 (1932), a case concerning Prohibition.

110. Colquitt, *Rethinking Entrapment*, 2004.

111. *State v. Powell*, 68 Hawaii 635, 726 p. 2d 266 (1986); Dru Stevenson, "Entrapment and the Problem of Deterring Police Misconduct," 2004, accessed June 30, 2009, http://works.bepress.com/dru_stevenson/10.

112. *U.S. v. Russell*, 411 U.S. 423 (1973); *Jacobson v. U.S.*, 503 U.S. 540 (1992).

113. Thinkexist.com, Keith Richards Quotes, accessed December 12, 2010, http://thinkexist.com/quotation/i-ve_never_had_a_problem_with_drugs-i-ve_had/212949.html.

114. Ken Wallentine, *Street Legal: A Guide to Pre-trial Criminal Procedure for Police, Prosecutors, and Defenders* (Chicago, IL: American Bar Association, 2007); Floyd R. Finch, Jr., "Comment—Deadly Force to Arrest: Triggering Constitutional Review," *Harvard Civil Rights—Civil Liberties Law Review* 11 (1976): 361.

115. *Wallace v. Kato*, 549 U.S. 1362 (2007); Citizens may sue police officers for damages if they are improperly arrested. In common parlance, the citizen's claim is called "false arrest," but technically suit is brought under the tort of "false imprisonment," meaning that the person's freedom of movement was wrongfully curtailed, even for a brief period of time. The police officer's defense against an al-

legation of false imprisonment is that the arrest was lawful. Whether in fact the officer had "probable cause" to arrest is determined by the civil jury. In general, civil actions by citizens against police are not an effective means of curbing abuses of police power. See Herman Goldstein, "Administrative Problems in Controlling the Exercise of Police Authority," *Journal of Criminal Law, Criminology and Political Science* 58 (1967): 160.

116. See Michael R. Gottfredson and Don M. Gottfredson, Decision Making in Criminal Justice: Toward the Rational Exercise of Discretion, 2nd ed. (New York: Springer, 1987); Wayne R. LaFave, Arrest: The Decision to Take a Suspect into Custody (Boston: Little, Brown, 1965), 437–489.

117. *Michigan v. Mosley*, 423 U.S. 96 (1975).

118. A suspect in custody upon invoking the right to remain silent by requesting a lawyer can be questioned again without a lawyer present as long as the suspect initiates the subsequent conversation with the police (*Edwards v. Arizona*, 451 U.S. 477 [1981]).

119. *Maryland v. Shatzer*, 130 S.Ct. 1213 (2010).

120. See *Montejo v. Louisiana*, 556 U.S. ___ (2009).

121. *Miranda v. Arizona*, 384 U.S. 436 (1966).

122. Ibid.

123. *Duckworth v. Eagan*, 492 U.S. 195 (1989); del Carmen, op. cit., 345.

124. Carl Stern, "Death of Ernesto Miranda," NBC Nightly News, January 31, 1976, accessed June 30, 2009, http://icue.nbcunifiles.com/icue/files/icue/site/pdf/5210.pdf.

125. "Whether these restrictions on traditional police practices have actually reduced police effectiveness is a matter of some controversy, even among police and prosecutors; but a significant consensus among police officers of all ranks in every part of the country interprets these decisions as favoring the criminal and as deliberately and perversely hampering, indeed punishing, the police." David P. Stang, "The Police and Their Problems," in James T. Curran, Austin Fowler, and Richard H. Ward (eds.), *Police and Law Enforcement 1972* (New York: AMS Press, 1973), 36. Also see, for a related discussion of Supreme Court restraints on the police, "A Symposium on the Supreme Court and the Police: 1966," *Journal of Criminal Law, Criminology and Political Science* 57 (1966); and Fred E. Inbau, "Playing God: 5 to 4," *Journal of Criminal Law, Criminology and Political Science* 57 (1966): 377.

126. James W. Witt, "Non-Coercive Interrogation and the Administration of Criminal Justice: The Impact of *Miranda* on Police Effectuality," *Journal of Criminal Law, Criminology and Political Science* 64 (1973): 320–332. Also, according to Kamisar, a number of studies have established that a waiver of *Miranda* rights occurs with most suspects; thus, *Miranda* has had little effect on the amount of confessions—Yale Kamisar, "On the Fortieth Anniversary of *Miranda*: Why We Needed It, How We Got It—and What Happened to It," *Ohio State Journal of Criminal Law*, 2007; San Diego Legal Studies Paper No. 07-76, accessed June 28, 2009, at SSRN: http://ssrn.com/abstract=944546.

127. For example, if public safety is threatened the reading of the *Miranda* warnings can be dispensed with (*New York v. Quarles*, 467 U.S. 649 [1984]); roadside questioning of a driver as the result of a routine traffic stop does not require the *Miranda* warnings (*Berkemer v. McCarty*, 468 U.S. 420 [1984]); *Miranda* warnings are not required when a confession is the result of a suspect following advice from God (*Colorado v. Connelly*, 479 U.S. 157 [1986]), a law enforcement officer is posing as an inmate (*Illinois v. Perkins*, 496 U.S. 292 [1990]), or routine questions are being asked and videotaping of a drunk driving suspect are taking place (*Pennsylvania v. Muniz*, 496 U.S. 582 [1990]). Furthermore, if a confession is viewed as involuntary on appeal a conviction can still be upheld if the allowance of the confession at trial is viewed as a harmless error (*Arizona v. Fulminante*, 499 U.S. 279 [1991]).

128. *Brewer v. Williams*, 430 U.S. 387 (1977); *Nix v. Williams*, 467 U.S. 431 (1984).

129. *Rhode Island v. Innis*, 446 U.S. 291 (1980).

130. National Registry of Exonerations, "Currently 2,000 Exonerations," University of California Irvine, University of Michigan Law School, Michigan State University College of Law, 2017, accessed March 9, 2017, http://www.law.umich.edu/special/exoneration/Pages/browse.aspx.

131. Innocence Project, "DNA Exonerations in the United States," 2016, accessed March 9, 2017, https://www.innocenceproject.org/dna-exonerations-in-the-united-states/.

132. Innocence Project, 2016 accessed March 9, 2017, https://www.innocenceproject.org/.

133. Richard A. Leo and Kimberly D. Richman, "Mandate the Electronic Recording of Police Interrogations," *Criminology & Public Policy* 6, no. 4 (November 2007): 791–798, accessed May 1, 2009, doi:10.1111/j.1745-9133.2007.00467.

134. Thomas P. Sullivan, *Police Experiences with Recording Custodial Interrogations*, Center on Wrongful Convictions, Chicago, IL: Northwestern University School of Law, Summer 2004; International Association of Chiefs of Police, "Videotaping Interrogations and Confessions," *Policy Review* 10 (1998): 1–4.

135. Innocence Project, "False Confessions or Admissions," 2016, accessed March 9, 2017, https://www.innocenceproject.org/causes/false-confessions-admissions/.

136. See *Dickerson v. U.S.*, 530 U.S. 428 (2000).

137. County of Riverside v. McLaughlin, 500 U.S. 44 (1991).

138. David Hirschel, William Wakefield, and Scott Sasse, *Criminal Justice in England and the United States*, 2nd ed. (Sudbury, MA: Jones & Bartlett, 2008); Jerry Markon, "U.S. Can Confine Citizens without Charges: Court Rules," *Washington Post*, September 10, 2005, accessed August 13, 2009; Warren Richey, "Obama: Bring Guantanamo Detainees to US, Detain Some Indefinitely," *Christian Science Monitor*, May 21, 2009, accessed August 13, 2009; Del Quentin Wilber and Peter Finn, "U.S. Retires 'Enemy Combatant,' Keeps Broad Right to Detain," *Washington Post*, March 14, 2009, accessed November 15, 2010, http://www.washingtonpost.com/wp-dyn/content/article/2009/03/13/AR200903130 2371.html.

Chapter 6

1. George Santayana, *Reason in Common Sense: Volume One of "The Life of Reason"* (New York: Dover Publications, 1980).

2. Victor E. Kappeler, Richard D. Sluder, and Geoffrey P. Alpert, *Forces of Deviance: Understanding the Dark Side of Policing* (Prospect Heights, IL: Waveland Press, 1994), 176; 183.

3. Ibid.

4. D. Gelman, P. Rogers, K. Springen, F. Chideya, and M. Miller, "The Secrets of Apt. 213," *Newsweek*, August 5, 1991; Annetta Miller with Patrick Rogers and Lynn Haessly, "Serial-Murder Aftershocks," *Newsweek*, August 12, 1991.

5. William LePere, personal communication, May 28, 2010.

6. William LePere, personal communication, May 28, 2010.

7. As discussed in Chapter 2, the FBI acknowledges that such transiency can contribute to neighborhood deterioration and constitute a variable associated with crime—see Federal Bureau of Investigation, *Uniform Crime Reparting Statistics*, Uniform Crime Reports, U.S. Department of Justice, January 26, 2017, accessed October 6, 2017, https://www.ucrdatatool.gov/ranking.cfm.

8. James Q. Wilson and George L. Kelling, "Broken Windows," *The Atlantic* 249 (March 1982): 29–38.

9. William J. Bratton, James Q. Wilson, George L. Kelling, Eugene Rivers, and Peter Cove, "This Works: Crime Prevention and the Future of Broken Windows Policing," *Civic Bulletin* 36 (April 2004): 1–15, accessed April 3, 2017, https://www.manhattan-institute.org/sites/default/files/cb_36.pdf.

10. Robert C. Tranjonowicz and Denis W. Banas, *Perceptions of Safety: A Comparison of Foot Patrol versus Motor Patrol Officers* (East Lansing, MI: National Neighborhood Foot Patrol Center,

School of Criminal Justice, Michigan State University, 1985). See also Lawrence W. Sherman, "Patrol Strategies for Police," in *Crime and Public Policy,* ed. James Q. Wilson (San Francisco: ICS Press, 1983), and M. Hough, "Thinking about Effectiveness," *British Journal of Criminology* 27 (1987): 1.

11. See Jerome S. Skolnick, *Justice without Trial: Law Enforcement in Democratic Society*, 3rd ed. (New York: Macmillan, 1994). See also William A. Westley, *Violence and the Police* (Cambridge, MA: M.I.T. Press, 1970).

12. President's Commission on Law Enforcement and the Administration of Justice, *Task Force Report: Police* (Washington, DC: U.S. Government Printing Office, 1967), 145–156. See also Geoffrey P. Alpert, *Policing Multi-ethnic Neighborhoods: The Miami Study and Findings for Law Enforcement in the United States* (New York: Greenwood Press, 1988).

13. Ronald Weitzer and Steven A. Tuch, *Race and Policing in America: Conflict and Reform* (Cambridge, MA: Cambridge University Press, 2006).

14. For an excellent analysis of police-citizen encounters and the perceptions of the police regarding danger, real or imagined, see David H. Bayley and James Garofalo, "The Management of Violence by Police Patrol Officers," *Criminology* 27 (1989): 1–25.

15. James Q. Wilson, *Varieties of Police Behavior* (Cambridge, MA: Harvard University Press, 1968), 25–26. Also see Jeffrey S. Slovak, *Styles of Urban Policing* (New York: New York University Press, 1986). Such seeming indifference and even callousness may be symptomatic of underlying problems such as Post-Traumatic Stress Disorder experienced by police officers—see Anand Pandya, Richard Lamb, and Suzanne Vogel-Scibilia, "Psychological Profiles of Criminal Justice Practitioners: How Experiences and Attitudes Shape the Treatment of Those with Mental Illnesses," in *Criminalization of Mental Illness: Crisis and Opportunity for the Justice System*, eds. Risdon N. Slate and W. Wesley Johnson (Durham, NC: Carolina Academic Press, 2008), 301–320.

16. James Q. Wilson, op. cit.; Gene Stephens, *The Criminal Justice Reader* (Lexington, MA: Ginn Custom Publishing, 1982).

17. *Terry v. Ohio*, 392 U.S. 1 (1968).

18. Wayne R. LaFave, *Arrest: The Decision to Take a Suspect into Custody* (Boston: Little Brown, 1965), 61–226.

19. Ibid., 83–101.

20. Ibid., 102–124.

21. Ibid., 125–143.

22. Joseph Goldstein, "Police Discretion Not to Invoke the Criminal Process: Low-Visibility Decisions in the Administration of Justice," *Yale Law Journal* 69 (1960): 143.

23. Herman Goldstein, *Problem-Oriented Policing* (New York: McGraw-Hill, 1990). See also Malcolm K. Sparrow, Mark H. Moore, and David M. Kennedy, *Beyond 911: A New Era for Policing* (New York: Basic Books, 1990); Kenneth J. Matulia, *A Balance of Forces*, 2nd ed. (Gaithersburg, MD: International Association of Chiefs of Police, 1982); Gary Cordner, "Open and Closed Models of Police Organizations: Traditions, Dilemmas, and Practical Considerations," *Journal of Police Science and Administration* 6 (1978): 22–34; Robert Langworthy, *The Structure of Police Organizations* (New York: Praeger, 1986).

24. Gary Cox, personal communication, July 5, 2010.

25. See Westley, op. cit., 118–119. Also see Herman Goldstein, "Toward Community-Oriented Policing: Potential, Basic Requirements, and Threshold Questions," *Crime and Delinquency* 33 (1987): 6–30; S. L. Johnson, "Race and the Decision to Detain a Suspect," *Yale Law Journal* 93 (1983): 214–258; Donald Black, *The Manners and Customs of the Police* (New York: Academic Press, 1980); and D. Smith, "The Neighborhood Context of Police Behavior," in *Communities and Crime*, eds. Albert Reiss and M. Tonry (Chicago: University of Chicago Press, 1986), 351–387.

26. Herman Goldstein, *Policing a Free Society* (Cambridge, MA: Ballinger, 1976), 111–112. See also William K. Muir, *Police: Streetcorner Politicians* (Chicago: University of Chicago Press, 1977).

27. Booker T. Hodges (deputy sheriff in Minnesota), personal communication, August 1, 2010.

28. *Rochin v. California*, 342 U.S. 165 (1952).

29. Joel Marino and Barbara Hijek, "Police Sting Uses Cash to Entice 82 Suspects," *Sun Sentinel*, August 28, 2009, accessed July 8, 2010, http://articles.sun-sentinel.com/2009-08-28/news/0908270417_1_undercover-officers-stimulus-money-child-support.

30. Eric Pera, "Polk County Sheriff's Office: Operation March Sadness Nets 104 Suspects," *The Ledger*, March 21, 2017, accessed April 2, 2017, http://www.theledger.com/news/20170321/polk-county-sheriffs-office-operation-march-sadness-nets-104-suspects.

31. Sherri Lonon, "2 Pasco Strip Clubs Face Multiple Citations, Fines," *Patch*, January 11, 2017, accessed April 2, 2017, https://patch.com/florida/newportrichey/2-pasco-strip-clubs-face-multiple-citations-fines.

32. National Human Trafficking Hotline (U.S. Department of Health and Human Services), accessed April 2, 2017: https://humantraffickinghotline.org/sex-trafficking-venuesindustries/hostessstrip-club-based.

33. Jessie Degollado, "Super Bowl Known as 'Largest Human Trafficking Event,'" *Houston KSAT12 ABC*, February 2, 2017, accessed April 2, 2017: http://www.ksat.com/news/super-bowl-known-as-largest-human-trafficking-event.

34. Graeme R. Newman and Kelly Socia, "Sting Operations, Problem-Oriented Guides for Police Response Guide Series, Guide No. 6," U.S. Department of Justice, Office of Community Oriented Policing Services, October 2007, accessed July 8, 2010, http://www.cops.usdoj.gov/files/RIC/Publications/e10079110.txt.

35. Ibid.

36. Newman and Socia, op. cit.

37. Bait Car, truTV, *CBS*, 2017, accessed April 2, 2017, http://www.tv.com/shows/bait-car/episodes/.

38. For example, a $100,000 reward was offered by several entities for information leading to the arrest of the killer of two Tampa Police Officers. However, each organization had their own requirements for under what conditions the money could be dispensed, and it remains unclear if and when all the money will be distributed to a confidential informant in the case. See Jessica Vander Velde, "Chief Says Reward Will Be Paid—But When and How Much?" *St. Petersburg Times*, July 8, 2010, accessed July 8, 2010, http://www.tampabay.com/news/publicsafety/article1107597.ece.

39. Gary Cox, personal communication, July 5, 2010.

40. John Frank, "Jury Delays Decision in Rachel Hoffman Murder Case," *St. Petersburg Times*, December 16, 2009, accessed July 8, 2010, http://www.tampabay.com/news/courts/criminal/jury-delays-decision-in-rachel-hoffman-murder-case/1058932; Josh Poltilove, "Rachel's Law on Confidential Informants Takes Effect Wednesday," *The Tampa Tribune*, June 30, 2009, accessed July 8, 2010, http://www2.tbo.com/content/2009/jun/30/301308/rachels-law-confidential-informants-takes-effect-w/news-breaking.

41. Geoffrey P. Alpert and Patrick R. Anderson, "The Most Deadly Force: Police Pursuits," *Justice Quarterly* 3 (March 1986): 1–14.

42. Patrick T. O'Connor and William L. Norse, Jr., "Police Pursuits: A Comprehensive Look at the Broad Spectrum of Police Pursuit Liability and Law," *Mercer L. Rev.* 57 (Winter 2006): 511.

43. Matthew R. Durose, Erica L. Smith, and Patrick A. Langan, *Contacts Between Police and the Public 2005*, Bureau of Justice Statistics, Office of Justice Programs, U.S. Department of Justice, April 29, 2007, accessed July 9, 2010, http://bjs.ojp.usdoj.gov/content/pub/press/cpp05pr.cfm; Ian Tuttle, "The DOJ's Policing Statistics Don't Lie," *National Review*, December 9, 2014, accessed May 9, 2017, http://www.nationalreview.com/article/394249/dojs-policing-statistics-dont-lie-ian-tuttle.

44. Ibid., 512.

45. Ibid.; Geoffrey Alpert quoted in Larry Copeland, "Deaths Lead Police to Question High-Speed Chase Policies," *USA Today*, April 23, 2010, accessed July 8, 2010, http://www.usatoday.com/news/nation/2010-04-22-police-chase-deaths_N.htm.

46. O'Connor, op. cit., 512.

47. Copeland, op. cit.

48. Thomas Frank, "Black people are three times likelier to be killed in police chases," *USA TODAY*, December 1, 2016, accessed April 3, 2017, https://www.usatoday.com/pages/interactives/blacks-killed-police-chases-higher-rate/.

49. O'Connor, op. cit., 517.

50. Robert Homant and Daniel Kennedy, "The Effects of High-Speed Pursuit Policies on Officers' Tendency to Pursue," *American Journal of Police* 13 (1994): 91–111. See also Daniel Kennedy, Robert Homant, and John Kennedy, "A Comparative Analysis of Police Vehicle Pursuit Policies," *Justice Quarterly* 9 (1992): 227–246. On the Chicago program, Daniel Borsky, "Driver's Ed for Police Puts Stress on Safety," *Chicago Tribune*, September 11, 1996.

51. Gary Cox, personal communication, July 5, 2010.

52. Copeland, op. cit.—Milwaukee PD changed their policy on pursuits after four people were killed by drivers fleeing police in three separate incidents in a two-month period.

53. *Scott v. Harris*, 550 U.S. 772, 374–375 (2007).

54. *Scott*, op. cit., 383; 385–386.

55. O'Connor, op. cit., 515.

56. Thomas Barker, "Rookie Police Officers' Perceptions of Police Occupational Deviance," *Police Studies* 6 (1983): 30–38.

57. Kami Chavis Simmons, "New Governance and the 'New Paradigm' of Police Accountability: A Democratic Approach to Police Reform," *Cath. U.L. Rev.* 59 (Winter 2010): 373.

58. See the Christopher Commission's discussion of this code of police silence phenomena at Warren Christopher, *Report of the Independent Commission on the Los Angeles Police Department* (Los Angeles: City of Los Angeles, 1991).

59. Simmons, op. cit.

60. Harvard Law Review, "The Supreme Court and the New Police," *Harv. L. Rev.* 122 (April 2009): 1706, 1710.

61. Simmons, op. cit.

62. Bayley and Garofalo, op. cit.; John Dugan and Daniel Breda, "Complaints about Police Officers: A Comparison among Types and Agencies," *Journal of Criminal Justice* 19 (1991): 165–171.

63. See Pandya et al., op. cit.

64. See, for example, Thomas Barker and David L. Carter, *Police Deviance* (Cincinnati: Anderson, 1986), and Michael Brown, *Working the Street: Police Discretion and the Dilemmas of Reform* (New York: Russell Sage Foundation, 1981).

65. Campbell Robertson, "5 Officers Indicted in Katrina Killing," *New York Times*, June 11, 2010, accessed July 7, 2010, http://www.nytimes.com/2010/06/12/us/12orleans.html?_r=1&ref=police_brutality_and_misconduct.

66. Campbell Robertson, "Jury Convicts 3 Officers Over a Killing in New Orleans," *New York Times*, December 10, 2010, accessed April 3, 2017, http://query.nytimes.com/gst/fullpage.html?res=9501E4DD123BF933A25751C1A9669D8B63; Times Picayune Staff, "Henry Glover Jury Finds 3 Officers Guilty in Death Burning of Algiers Man," December 9, 2010, accessed April 3, 2017, http://www.nola.com/crime/index.ssf/2010/12/henry_glover_verdict_form.html; Associated Press, "Five Years Trimmed from Sentence of Ex-New Orleans Cop Who Burned Body of Man Shot Dead by his

Colleague during Katrina Aftermath," *Daily Mail*, February 4, 2016, accessed April 3, 2017, http://www.dailymail.co.uk/news/article-3432425/5-years-trimmed-ex-cops-sentence-Katrina-body-case.html; John Simerman, "Now 10 Years Later, Anniversary of Henry Glover's Shooting Death by New Orleans Police Haunts Family," *The New Orleans Advocate*, September 7, 2015, accessed April 3, 2017, http://www.theadvocate.com/new_orleans/news/article_74933e7a-140c-5083-8e0a-dd3eba0eb363.html.

67. Monica Davey and Emma Graves Fitzsimmons, "Officer Accused of Torture Is Guilty of Perjury," *New York Times*, June 28, 2010, accessed July 7, 2010, http://www.nytimes.com/2010/06/29/us/29burge.html?ref=police_brutality_and_misconduct.

68. Lisa Fielding, "Protestors Call for Further Investigation into CPD Torture," *Chicago CBS 2 News*, January 13, 2017, accessed April 3, 2017: http://chicago.cbslocal.com/2017/01/13/protestors-call-for-futher-investigation-into-cpd-torture/.

69. Sarasota County Sheriff's Office, "News Release #: 07-017, Sheriff's Office Employee Arrested on Felony Charges," January 23, 2017, accessed April 3, 2017, http://www.sarasotasheriff.org/news/news-releases/item/sheriff%E2%80%99s-office-employee-arrested-on-felony-charges.html; see also Eric Levenson and Dakin Andone, "Police: Florida Deputy Tried to Kill Elderly Woman, Frame It as Suicide," *CNN*, January 24, 2017, accessed April 3, 2017, http://www.cnn.com/2017/01/24/us/florida-arrest-elderly/; Bybee was Sentenced to 15 years in Prison. See Carlos R. Munoz, "Judge Sentences former Deputy Frank Bybee to 15 years in Prison," *Herald-Tribune*, Sarasota, FL, (November 10, 2017), accessed December 12, 2017, http://www.heraldtribune.com/news/20171109/judge-sentences-former-deputy-frank-bybee-to-15-years-in-prison.

70. Rolando del Carmen, "Civil Liability in Law Enforcement," *American Journal of Police* 12 (1993): 87–99.

71. The Knapp Commission Report on Police Corruption (New York: Braziller, 1972).

72. Ellwyn Stoddard, "Organizational Norms and Police Discretion," *Criminology* 17 (1979): 159–171. See also Ellwyn Stoddard, "Blue Coat Crime," in *Thinking About Police*, ed. Carl Klockars (New York: McGraw-Hill, 1983), 338–347.

73. Lawrence W. Sherman, *Police Corruption: A Sociological Perspective* (Garden City, NY: Doubleday, 1974).

74. See Barker, op. cit.

75. Kevin Johnson, "For Cops, Citizen Videos Bring Increased Scrutiny," *USA Today*, October 18, 2010, accessed November 15, 2010, http://www.usatoday.com/cleanprint/?1289852508245.

76. Gary Cox, personal communication, July 5, 2010.

77. Kevin Sack, "Door-Busting Drug Raids Leave a Trail of Blood," *New York Times*, March 18, 2017, accessed April 3, 2017, https://www.nytimes.com/interactive/2017/03/18/us/forced-entry-warrant-drug-raid.html.

78. Durose, op. cit.

79. John Wihbey and Leighton Walter Kille, "Deaths in Police Custody in the United States: Research Review," *Journalist's Resource*, July 2, 2016, accessed May 9, 2017, https://journalistsresource.org/studies/government/criminal-justice/deaths-police-custody-united-states.

80. 2,002 persons died according to Christopher J. Mumola, *Arrest-related deaths in the United States: 2003–2005*. U.S. Department of Justice, Bureau of Justice Statistics, Washington, DC (2007); CBS News "Study Examines Police Use of Deadly Force," October 11, 2007, accessed July 9, 2010, http://www.cbsnews.com/stories/2007/10/11/national/main3359288.shtml?source=RSSattr=U.S._3359288; Data is much more consistently and meticulously maintained on law enforcement officers killed and assaulted in the line of duty as opposed to persons killed or injured by law enforcement personnel. Based on the latest statistics available for the year 2008, 41 officers (32 of whom were wearing body armor at the time of the attack) were feloniously killed in the line of duty, and 58,792 officers were assaulted in the line of duty. In addition, 2 federal law enforcement officers were killed and 1,347 assaulted in the line of duty. Law enforcement officers were more likely to be killed in the South, in

January, on a Friday, and between the hours of 12:01 a.m. to 4 a.m.—see Uniform Crime Reports, *Law Enforcement Officers Killed and Assaulted 2008*, Federal Bureau of Investigation, U.S. Department of Justice, accessed July 9, 2010, http://www.fbi.gov/ucr/killed/2008.

81. See for example, Geoffrey P. Alpert and Roger G. Dunham, *Understanding Police Use of Force: Officers, Suspects, and Reciprocity* (New York: Cambridge University Press, 2004); David A. May and James E. Headley, *Reasonable Use of Force by the Police* (New York: Peter Lang Publishing, 2008); James Fyfe, "Police Use of Deadly force: Research and Reform," *Justice Quarterly* 5 (1988): 165–205; Jerome Skolnick and James Fyfe, *Above the Law: Police and the Excessive Use of Force* (New York: Free Press, 1993); Dale Cloninger, "Lethal Police Response as a Crime Deterrent," *American Journal of Economics and Society* 50 (1991): 50–60.

82. Skolnick and Fyfe, ibid., 20.

83. Vivian B. Lord, *Suicide by Cop: Inducing Officers to Shoot.* (Flushing, New York: Looseleaf Law Publications, 2004).

84. Lorie Fridell, "Justifiable Use of Measures in Research on Deadly Force," *Journal of Criminal Justice* 17 (1989): 157–165.

85. CBS News, op. cit.; The officer, Justin Volpe, was sentenced to 30 years in prison, and Louima received more than $8 million dollars in legal settlements with the city and the police union—see Abner Louima, *New York Times*, July 9, 2010, accessed July 9, 2010, http://topics.nytimes.com/top/reference/timestopics/people/l/abner_louima/index.html.

86. Mumola, op. cit.

87. James J. Fyfe, "Who Shoots? A Look at Officer Race and Police Shootings," *Journal of Police Science and Administration* 9 (1981): 367–382. See also Mark Blumberg, "Race and Police Shootings: An Analysis of Two Cities," *Contemporary Issues in Law Enforcement*, ed. James Fyfe (Beverly Hills: Sage, 1981), 152–166.

88. See David Lester, "Predicting the Rate of Justifiable Homicide by Police Officers," *Police Studies* 16 (1993): 43.

89. This positioning of the police as judge and executioner made sense under English common law, where over 200 crimes were punishable by death. However, with the death penalty essentially limited to murder in 1985, the fleeing felon rule no longer served its intended purpose.

90. See James J. Fyfe, "Fleeing Felons and the Fourth Amendment," *Criminal Law Bulletin* 19 (1983): 525–528.

91. *Tennessee v. Garner*, 471 U.S. 1, 11 (1985).

92. *Harvard Law Review*, op. cit., 1722.

93. Abraham Tennenbaum, "The Influence of the *Garner* Decision on Police Use of Deadly Force," *Journal of Law and Criminology* 85 (1994): 241–260.

94. Risdon N. Slate in John S. Kiernan "Should Police Wear Body Cameras? Experts Pick Sides," *WalletHub*, October 5, 2016, accessed May 9, 2017, https://wallethub.com/blog/should-police-wear-body-cameras/25343/#risdon-n-slate.

95. Larry Buchanan, Ford Fessenden, K. K. Rebecca Lai, Haeyoun Park, Alicia Parlapiano, Archie Tse, Tim Wallace, Derek Watkins, and Karen Yourish, "Q & A: What Happened in Ferguson?" *New York Times*, August 10, 2015, updated, accessed April 10, 2017, https://www.nytimes.com/interactive/2014/08/13/us/ferguson-missouri-town-under-siege-after-police-shooting.html.

96. Erik Echolm, "Witnesses Told Grand Jury that Michael Brown Charged at Officer Darren Wilson, Prosecutors Say," *New York Times*, November 24, 2015, accessed April 10, 2017, https://www.nytimes.com/2014/11/25/us/witnesses-told-grand-jury-that-michael-brown-charged-at-darren-wilson-prosecutor-says.html?action=click&contentCollection=U.S.&region=Footer&module=WhatsNext&version=WhatsNext&contentID=WhatsNext&moduleDetail=undefined&pgtype=Multimedia.

97. Buchanan, op. cit.

98. Alan Blinder, "Mistrial for Officer Who Shot Walter Scott," *New York Times*, December 5, 2016, accessed April 10, 2017, https://www.nytimes.com/2016/12/05/us/walter-scott-michael-slager-north-charleston.html.

99. Alan Blinder, "Ex-Officer Who Shot Walter Scott Pleads Guilty in Charleston," *New York Times*, May 2, 2017, accessed May 4, 2017, https://www.nytimes.com/2017/05/02/us/michael-slager-walter-scott-north-charleston-shooting.html?_r=0; Alan Blinder, "Michael Slager, Officer in Walter Scott Shooting Gets 20-Year Sentence," *New York Times*, December 7, 2017, accessed December 12, 2017, https://www.nytimes.com/2017/12/07/us/michael-slager-sentence-walter-scott.html.

100. Ana Cabrera and Catherine E. Shoichet, "Tulsa Officer Betty Shelby Booked, Released on Bond," *CNN*, February 23, 2016, accessed April 10, 2017, http://www.cnn.com/2016/09/23/us/tulsa-officer-booked-released-on-bond/.

101. Bill Whitaker, "Officer Betty Shelby Breaks Silence on Terence Crutcher Shooting," *60 Minutes*, April 2, 2017, accessed April 10, 2017, http://www.cbsnews.com/news/terence-crutcher-unarmed-black-man-shooting-60-minutes/; Bill Chappell, "Tulsa Police Officer is Found Not Guilty in Death of Terence Crutcher," *NPR*, May 18, 2017, accessed October 6, 2017, http://www.npr.org/sections/the two-way/2017/05/18/528915380/tulsa-police-officer-is-found-not-guilty-in-death-of-terence-crutcher.

102. Associated Press, "Louisiana Officer Convicted in Shooting Death of 6-year-old Boy," *Chicago Tribune*, March 24, 2017, accessed April 10, 2017, http://www.chicagotribune.com/news/nationworld/ct-louisiana-police-shooting-guilty-verdict-20170324-story.html.

103. Associated Press, "Louisiana Officer Sentenced to 40 Years in Prison in Shooting Death of Autistic Boy," *Time*, March 31, 2017, accessed April 10, 2017, http://time.com/4721188/louisiana-officer-prison-sentence-killing-autistic-boy/. Greenhouse to plead guilty. Associated Press, "Marksville Moonlighting Marshal to Get 7½ years in Prison for Killing Autistic Boy," *Baton Rouge Patch*, September 30, 2017, accessed December 12, 2007, https://patch.com/louisiana/baton-rouge/louisiana-moonlighting-marshal-get-7-1-2-years-prison-killing-autistic-boy.

104. Claudia Lauer and Nomaan Merchant, "Family Wants Officer Who Shot Black Teen Charged with Crime," *The Ledger*, May 4, 2017, A12.

105. Claudia Lauer and Will Weissert, "Former Texas Cop Who Faces Murder Charge in Shooting of Black Teen Released on Bail," *Time*, May 6, 2017, accessed May 9, 2017, http://time.com/4769717/jordan-edwards-roy-oliver-balch-springs/.

106. Laura Jarrett, "Jeff Sessions Ushers in 'Trump Era' at the Justice Department," *CNN*, April 13, 2017, accessed May 4, 2017, http://www.cnn.com/2017/04/13/politics/jeff-sessions-new-era-for-doj/; Juliet Linderman (April 8, 2017) Baltimore: Police Overhaul Approved Over Trump Objections, *Lakeland Ledger*, A7.

107. Simmons, op. cit.

108. Tennenbaum, op. cit.

109. *Graham v. Connor*, 490 U.S. 386, 388–390 (1989).

110. Ibid., 396–397; 399.

111. Simmons, op. cit.

112. Harvard Law Review, op. cit.

113. Bureau of Justice Statistics, "Percentage of Local Police Officers Who Are Racial or Ethnic Minorities Nearly Doubled Between 1987 and 2013, U.S. Department of Justice, July 21, 2015, accessed October 6, 2017, https://www.justice.gov/tribal/pr/percentage-local-police-officers-who-were-racial-or-ethnic-minorities-nearly-doubled.

114. Kathie Warco, "Number of Female Police Officers on the Rise, *U.S. News & World Report*, March 25, 2017, accessed October 6, 2017, https://www.usnews.com/news/best-states/washington/articles/2017-03-25/number-of-female-police-officers-on-the-rise.

115. William T. Jordan, Lorie Fridell, Daniel Faggiani, and Bruce Kubu, "Attracting Females and Racial/Ethnic Minorities to Law Enforcement," *Journal of Criminal Justice* 37, no. 4 (2009): 333–341; See also Lynn Langton, *Women in Law Enforcement, 1987–2008*, Bureau of Justice Statistics, U.S. Department of Justice, Washington, DC, June 2010.

116. Warren Christopher, Report of the Independent Commission on the Los Angeles Police Department. Los Angeles: City of Los Angeles, 1991.

117. Ibid., 88.

118. Ibid., 89.

119. Ibid.

120. Robin A. Buhrke, A Matter of Justice: Lesbians and Gay Men in Law Enforcement. New York: Routledge, 1996.

121. Buhrke, op. cit.

122. Warren Christopher, op. cit.

123. Warren Christopher, Status Report of the Independent Commission on the Los Angeles Police Department. Los Angeles: City of Los Angeles, 1992.

124. Kappeler et al., op. cit.

125. See, for example, GOAL New York, accessed July 10, 2010, http://www.goalny.org/ Home.html; GOAL Chicago, accessed July 10, 2010, http://www.goalchicago.info/?page_id=8; Washington, DC—see Will O'Bryan, "Gay Cop Conclave Hits D.C.," *Metro Weekly*, May 8, 2008, accessed July 10, 2010, http://www.metroweekly.com/news/?ak=3429.

Chapter 7

1. American Bar Association, *Model Rules of Professional Conduct*, Client-Lawyer Relationship, Rule 1.6 Confidentiality of Information, Center for Professional Responsibility, accessed April 29, 2010, http://www.abanet.org/cpr/mrpc/rule_1_6.html.

2. Gerry Spence, "America's Courts Do Not Provide Social Justice" in *Social Justice: Opposing Viewpoints*, ed. Carol Wekesser (San Diego, CA: Greenhaven Press, Inc., 1990), 41.

3. NPR Books—Fresh Air (October 20, 2014) "One Lawyer's Fight for Young Blacks and 'Just Mercy,'" accessed October 3, 2017, http://www.npr.org/2014/10/20/356964925/one-lawyers-fight-for-young-blacks-and-just-mercy.

4. Peter Wagner and Bernadette Rabuy, "Mass Incarceration: The Whole Pie 2017," *Prison Policy Initiative*, March 14, 2017, accessed April 29, 2017, https://www.prisonpolicy.org/reports/pie2017.html.

5. Daniel W. E. Holt, "Heat in US Prisons and Jails," Sabin Center for Climate Change Law, Columbia Law School, New York, 2015, accessed April 29, 2017: https://web.law.columbia.edu/sites/default/files/microsites/climate-change/holt_-_heat_in_us_prisons_and_jails.pdf; Emily Files, "Corrections Chief Sees Structural Change Coming for Alaska's Community Jails," KHNS News, November 3, 2016, accessed April 29, 2017, http://khns.org/corrections-chief-sees-structural-change-coming-for-alaskas-community-jails; Leanne F. Alarid and Philip L. Reichel, *Corrections: A Contemporary Introduction* (Boston, MA: Pearson, 2008).

6. See Federal Bureau of Prisons, "Prison Types and General Information," U.S. Department of Justice, accessed April 23, 2010, http://www.bop.gov/locations/institutions/index.jsp.

7. Todd D. Minton and Zhen Zeng, *Inmates at Midyear 2014*, Bureau of Justice Statistics, 2015, accessed April 29, 2017, https://www.bjs.gov/content/pub/pdf/jim14.pdf.

8. Todd D. Minton and Zhen Zeng, *Jail Inmates in 2015*, Bureau of Justice Statistics, 2016, accessed April 29, 2017, https://www.bjs.gov/content/pub/pdf/ji15.pdf.

9. Ibid.

10. Breeanna Hare and Lisa Rose, "Pop. 17,049: Welcome to America's Largest Jail," CNN, September 26, 2016, accessed April 29, 2017, http://www.cnn.com/2016/09/22/us/lisa-ling-this-is-life-la-county-jail-by-the-numbers/index.html.

11. Bill Quigley, "Louisiana Number One in Incarceration," *The Huffington Post*, May 10, 2016, accessed April 29, 2017, http://www.huffingtonpost.com/bill-quigley/louisiana-number-one-in-i_b_9888636.html; See Louisiana State Penitentiary, General Information, accessed April 24, 2010, http://www.corrections.state.la.us/LSP/.

12. Minton and Zeng, 2016, op. cit.

13. Minton and Zeng, 2015, op. cit.

14. Wagner and Rabuy, op. cit.

15. Minton and Zeng, 2016, op. cit.

16. Wagner and Rabuy, op. cit.

17. Minton and Zeng, 2016, op. cit.

18. Ibid.

19. Danielle Kaeble and Lauren Glaze, *Correctional Populations in the United States, 2015*, Bureau of Justice Statistics, 2016, accessed April 30, 2017, https://www.bjs.gov/content/pub/pdf/cpus15.pdf.

20. Minton and Zeng, 2016, op. cit.

21. Ibid.

22. Ram Subramanian, Ruth Delaney, Stephen Roberts, Nancy Fishman, and Peggy McGarry, "Incarceration's Front Door: The Misuse of Jails in America," The Vera Institute, February 2015, accessed April 30, 2017, http://archive.vera.org/sites/default/files/resources/downloads/incarcerations-front-door-report.pdf.

23. Wagner and Rabuy, op. cit.

24. John Irwin, *The Jail: Managing the Underclass in American Society* (Berkeley, CA: University of California Press, 1985).

25. Patrick R. Anderson and Donald J. Newman, *Introduction to Criminal Justice*, 5th ed. (New York: McGraw-Hill Inc., 1993).

26. Larinda Slater, personal communication, August 1, 2010. Larinda Slater at the time of this submission was a jail program coordinator in Minnesota. She has a bachelor's degree in psychology and a master's degree in counseling and psychological services.

27. J. F. Fishman, Crucibles of Crime: The Shocking Story of the American Jail (New York: Cosmopolis Press, 1923).

28. As of 2007, according to the National Institute of Corrections, 18 states did not have statewide jail standards in place. See Mark D. Martin, *Jail Standards and Inspection Programs: Resource and Implementation Guide*, National Institute of Corrections (April 2007).

29. Margaret E. Noonan and E. Ann Carson, *Prison and Jail Deaths in Custody, 2000–2009*, Bureau of Justice Statistics, 2011, accessed April 29, 2017, https://www.bjs.gov/content/pub/pdf/pjdc0009st.pdf.

30. Margaret E. Noonan, *Mortality in Local Jails, 2000–2014—Statistical Tables*, Bureau of Justice Statistics, 2016, accessed April 29, 2017, https://www.bjs.gov/content/pub/pdf/mlj0014st.pdf.

31. Ibid.

32. James M. Byrne, Arthur J. Lurigio, and Roger Pimentel, "New Defendants, New Responsibilities: Preventing Suicide among Alleged Sex Offenders in the Federal Pretrial System," *Federal Probation* 73, no. 2 (September 2009), accessed April 25, 2010, http://bjs.ojp.usdoj.gov/content/pub/pdf/shsplj.pdf.

33. Noonan, 2016, op. cit.

34. Christopher J. Mumola, *Suicide and Homicide in State Prisons and Local Jails*, Bureau of Justice Statistics Special Report, U.S. Department of Justice, Office of Justice Programs, August 2005, accessed April 25, 2010, http://bjs.ojp.usdoj.gov/content/pub/pdf/shsplj.pdf.

35. See Byrne et al., op. cit.; World Health Organization, *Preventing Suicide in Jails and Prisons.* Geneva, Switzerland: World Health Organization Document Production Services, 2007, accessed April 25, 2010, http://www.who.int/mental_health/prevention/suicide/resource_jails_prisons.pdf; L. Thomas Winfree, "Toward Understanding State-Level Jail Mortality: Correlates of Death by Suicide and by Natural Causes, 1977 and 1982," *Justice Quarterly* 4, no. 1 (1987): 51–71.

36. World Health Organization, op. cit.

37. See World Health Organization, op. cit.; Daniel B. Kennedy and Robert J. Homant, "Predicting Custodial Suicide: Problems with the Use of Profiles," *Justice Quarterly* 5, no. 3 (1988).

38. See American Correctional Association, *Performance-Based Standards for Adult Local Detention Facilities*, 4th ed., Alexandria, VA: ACA, 2004; American Correctional Association, *Core Jail Standards*, Alexandria, VA: ACA, 2010.

39. Julia Zorthian, "Inmate Died After 7 Days Without Water in Milwaukee Jail, Prosecutors Say," *Time*, April 24, 2017, accessed May 10, 2017, http://time.com/4753586/miluakee-inmate-died-jail-dehydration-terrill-thomas/; Dave Umhoefer, "Inquest Jury into Inmate's Dehydration Death Recommends Charges Against 7 Employees," *Milwaukee Wisconsin Journal Sentinel*, May 1, 2017, accessed May 10, 2017, http://www.jsonline.com/story/news/investigations/2017/05/01/2-more-inmates-had-water-cut-off-after-dehydration-death-milwaukee-county-jail/101163514/.

40. County of Riverside v. McGlaughlin, 500 U.S. 44 (1991).

41. Pretrial Service Officers, *The Pretrial Services Officer's Role*, Probation and Pretrial Services Directory, U.S. Courts. Accessed April 25, 2010: http://www.uscourts.gov/fedprob/system/ pretrial.html.

42. John Clark and D. Alan Henry, *Pretrial Services Programming at the Start of the 21st Century: A Survey of Pretrial Services Programs*, Washington, DC: Bureau of Justice Assistance, July 2003 (NCJ 199773), accessed April 27, 2010, http://www.ncjrs.gov/pdffiles1/bja/199773.pdf.

43. Thomas H. Cohen, *Pretrial Release and Misconduct in Federal District Courts, 2008–2010*, Bureau of Justice Statistics, November 2012, accessed April 30, 2017, https://www.bjs.gov/content/pub/pdf/prmfdc0810.pdf.

44. Thomas H. Cohen, *Commercial Surety Bail and the Problem of Missed Court Appearances and Pretrial Detention*, 3rd Annual Conference on Empirical Legal Studies Papers, June 2, 2008, accessed April 26, 2010, http://papers.ssrn.com/sol3/papers.cfm?abstract_id=1130964##.

45. Brian R. Johnson and Greg L. Warchol, "Bail Agents and Bounty Hunters: Adversaries or Allies of the Justice System?" *American Journal of Criminal Justice* 27, no. 2 (2003), 145–165.

46. Samuel R. Wiseman (March 2014) "Pretrial Detention and the Right to Be Monitored, *The Yale Law Journal 123*(5), accessed October 3, 2017, https://www.yalelawjournal.org/article/pretrial-detention-and-the-right-to-be-monitored.

47. Thomas H. Cohen and Brian A. Reaves (November 2007) Pretrial Release of Felony Defendants in State Courts: State Court Processing Statistics 1990–2004, Bureau of Justice Statistics Special Report, U.S. Department of Justice, Office of Justice Programs. Accessed April 26, 2010: http://bjs.ojp.usdoj.gov/content/pub/pdf/prfdsc.pdf.

48. Johnson and Warchol, op. cit.

49. Adam Liptak, "Illegal Globally, Bail for Profit Remains in U.S.," *New York Times*, January 29, 2008, accessed April 27, 2010, http://www.nytimes.com/2008/01/29/us/29bail.html?ex= 1359349200&en=aff53e775b99c710&ei=5124&exprod=permalink.

50. Johnson and Warchol, op. cit.

51. *Taylor v. Taintor*, 83 U.S. 366, 371–372, (1872).

52. Jeanette Batz, "The Bailout Artist," *RiverFront Times* (St. Louis), June 26, 2002, 8, accessed April 26, 2010, http://www.riverfronttimes.com/2002-06-26/news/the-bailout-artist/8; Ronald Goldfarb, *Ransom: A Critique of the American Bail System* (New York: Harper & Row, 1965), ix.

53. Shannon M. Baker, Michael S. Vaughn, and Volkan Topalli, "A Review of the Powers of Bail Bond Agents and Bounty Hunters: Exploring Legalities and Illegalities of Quasi-Criminal Justice Officials," *Aggression & Violent Behavior* 13, no. 2 (March 2008).

54. Liptak, op. cit.

55. Lisa Foderaro, "New Jersey Alters Its Bail System and Upends Legal Landscape," *New York Times* February 6, 2017, accessed May 4, 2017, https://www.nytimes.com/2017/02/06/nyregion/new-jersey-bail-system.html?_r=1.

56. Eli Rosenberg, "Judge in Houston Strikes Down Harris County's Bail System," *New York Times*, April 29, 2017, accessed May 9, 2017, https://www.nytimes.com/2017/04/29/us/judge-strikes-down-harris-county-bail-system.html.

57. *Stack v. Boyle*, 342 U.S. 1 (1951).

58. Cohen and Reaves, op. cit.

59. Ibid.

60. Laura and John Arnold Foundation, Research Summary: Pretrial Criminal Justice Research, November 2013, accessed May 4, 2017, http://www.arnoldfoundation.org/wp-content/uploads/2014/02/LJAF-Pretrial-CJ-Research-brief_FNL.pdf.

61. Cherise Fanno Burdeen, *Jail Population Management: Elected County Officials' Guide to Pretrial Services*, National Association of Counties, Pretrial Justice Institute, Bureau of Justice Assistance, U.S. Department of Justice, September 2009, accessed April 28, 2010, http://www.pretrial.org/Docs/Documents/Jail%20Mgmt%20NACo%20PJI.pdf.

62. *Bandy v. U.S.*, 81 S.Ct. 197 (1960).

63. Cohen and Reaves, op. cit.

64. Vera Institute of Justice, *Programs in Criminal Justice Reform, Ten-Year Report, 1961–1971* (New York: Vera Institute of Justice, 1972).

65. U.S. Department of Justice, Bureau of Justice Statistics, *Pretrial Release and Misconduct* (Washington, DC: U.S. Government Printing Office, 1985).

66. Again, we acknowledge our indebtedness to Samuel Walker, *Sense and Nonsense about Crime*, 2nd ed. (Pacific Grove, CA: Brooks/Cole, 1989), 63–68, and to Herbert L. Packer, *The Limits of the Criminal Sanction* (Stanford, CA: Stanford University Press, 1968), 210–221.

67. Cohen and Reaves, op. cit.

68. Ibid.

69. Irving J. Klein, *Constitutional Law for Criminal Justice Professionals* (Miami: Coral Gables Publishing Co., 1986), 442.

70. Carol M. Miyashiro, "Research 2 Results (R2R)—The Pretrial Services Experience," *Federal Probation* 72, no. 2 (2008).

71. *Stack v. Boyle*, op. cit.

72. *United States v. Salerno*, 481 U.S. 739 (1987).

73. Bail Reform Act of 1984, PL98-473, Title II; see *United States v. Miller*, 753 F. 2d 19 (3d Cir. 1985).

74. United States v. Salerno, op. cit.

75. Ibid.

76. Ibid.

77. John M. Scheb and John M. Scheb, III, *Criminal Law and Procedure* (St. Paul, MN: West, 1989).

78. *Bandy v. U.S.*, op. cit.

79. *Powell v. Alabama*, 287 U.S. 45 (1932).

80. Ibid., 69.

81. *Betts v. Brady*, 316 U.S. 455 (1942). While the Sixth Amendment right to counsel was applicable to federal cases, it was left up to the states to determine its applicability in state cases. Justice Owen Roberts, who wrote the majority opinion, reasoned that most states did not require appointment of an attorney to ensure a fair trial and that the circumstances (Betts was not facing the death penalty) in this case did not warrant such an appointment.

82. *Gideon v. Wainwright*, 372 U.S. 335 (1963). The reason for the decision in Gideon's favor is summed up by the Court: "Lawyers to prosecute are everywhere deemed essential to protect the public's interest in an orderly society. Similarly, there are few defendants charged with crime, few indeed, who fail to hire the best lawyers they can get to prepare and present their defenses. That government hires lawyers to prosecute and defendants who have the money hire lawyers to defend are the strongest indications of the widespread belief that lawyers in criminal courts are necessities, not luxuries. The right of one charged with crime to counsel may not be deemed fundamental and essential to fair trials in some countries, but it is in ours. From the very beginning, our state and national constitutions and laws have laid great emphasis on procedural and substantive safeguards designed to assure fair trials before impartial tribunals in which every defendant stands equal before the law. This noble ideal cannot be realized if the poor man charged with crime has to face his accusers without a lawyer to assist him."

83. See *Strickland v. Washington*, 466 U.S. 688 (1984); *United States v. Cronic*, 466 U.S. 648 (1984); *Lockhart v. Fretwell*, 506 U.S. 364 (1993); *Wiggins v. Smith*, 539 U.S. 510 (2003); *Yarborough v. Gentry*, 540 U.S. 1 (2003); *Bell v. Cone*, 505 U.S. 685 (2002); *Mickens v. Taylor*, 535 U.S. 162 (2002).

84. Rolando V. del Carmen, *Criminal Procedure: Law and Practice*, 8th ed. (Belmont, CA: Wadsworth, 2010).

85. *Argersinger v. Hamlin*, 407 U.S. 25 (1972). The *Gideon* decision, while a landmark case on the right to counsel, left unsettled the question of whether states must provide lawyers for indigent defendants charged with any crime. *Powell* limited the right to capital cases; *Gideon* involved a felony conviction. What about defendants charged with misdemeanors? Nine years after *Gideon* and 40 years after *Powell*, the Supreme Court again considered the right to counsel at trial, this time in a case in which the defendant, convicted of carrying a concealed weapon, a misdemeanor, was sentenced to 90 days in jail. In *Argersinger v. Hamlin* the Court held that states must provide counsel at trial for poor defendants charged with any crime, whether it is called a petty offense, a violation, a misdemeanor, or a felony, if the offense involves a possible sentence of incarceration in a jail or prison. In effect, Argersinger expanded the right to a trial lawyer to all criminal cases where the real possibility of incarceration exists. Sometimes indigent defendants are required to reimburse the state for the costs of appointed counsel under the "Standards of Indigency."

86. Ibid., 37.

87. *Scott v. Illinois*, 440 U.S. 367 (1979), 367.

88. Kevin Sack, "Dylann Roof to Represent Himself at Trial in Charleston Church Shootings," *New York Times*, November 28, 2016, accessed May 1, 2017, https://www.nytimes.com/2016/11/28/us/dylann-roof-charleston-massacre.html?_r=0.

89. *Faretta v. California*, 422 U.S. 806 (1975); Kimberly A. C. Wilson, "A Tragedy for the Justice System," *Baltimore Sun*, October 21, 2003, accessed April 29, 2010, http://www.baltimoresun.com/news/maryland/bal-te.md.counsel21oct21,0,2576851.story.

90. See *Mayberry v. Pennsylvania*, 400 U.S. 455 (1971); also see *Illinois v. Allen*, 397 U.S. 337 (1970).

91. Katherine Ramsland, "Working the System: Famous Cases of Self-Representation," TruTV, accessed April 29, 2010, http://www.trutv.com/library/crime/criminal_mind/psychology/defending_oneself/13.html; New York Times News Service, "Victims' Families Cheer as Killer of N.Y. Commuters Get 200-Year Sentence," *Baltimore Sun*, March 23, 1995, accessed April 29, 2010, http://articles.baltimoresun.com/1995-03-23/news/1995082128_1_colin-ferguson-belfi-sentence.

92. Ralph Blumenthal, "Insanity Issue Lingers as Texas Execution is Set," *New York Times*, February 4, 2004, accessed April 29, 2010, http://www.nytimes.com/2004/02/04/us/insanity-issue-lingers-as-texas-execution-is-set.html; Ron Honberg, "The Intersection of Mental Illness and Criminal Law" in Risdon N. Slate and W. Wesley Johnson, *Criminalization of Mental Illness: Crisis and Opportunity for the Justice System* (Durham, NC: Carolina Academic Press, 2008), 324; *Panetti v. Dretke*, No. A-04-CA-042-SS (W.D. Tex. Sept. 29, 2004); *Panetti v. Quarterman*, 551 U.S. 930 (2007).

93. For a discussion of these methods of indigent defense, see Robert L. Spangenberg et al., *National Criminal Defense Systems Study* (Washington, DC: Bureau of Justice Statistics, 1986), updated by the Spangenberg Group in March 1987. See also Bureau of Justice Statistics (March 1988) *Report to the Nation on Crime and Justice*, 2nd ed., United States Department of Justice, accessed October 3, 2017, https://www.ncjrs.gov/pdffiles1/nij/105506.pdf.

94. James S. Kunen, *"How Can You Defend Those People?" The Making of a Criminal Lawyer* (New York: McGraw Hill, 1983). James Kunen wrote a book in which he asked the question in the title "How can you defend those people?" He then proceeds to explain in the remainder of the book how it can be done.

95. James Mills, "I Have Nothing to do with Justice," in John J. Bonsignore et al., *Before the Law: An Introduction to the Legal Process*, 2nd ed. (Boston, MA: Houghton Mifflin Company, 1979), 239; 247.

96. Jocelyn M. Pollock, *Ethics in Crime and Justice: Dilemmas & Decisions*, 2nd ed. (Belmont, CA: Wadsworth, 1994), 146; 147.

Chapter 8

1. Jeffrey C. Billman, "Did Lamar Spike It?" *Orlando Weekly*, November, 27, 2008, accessed July 26, 2010, http://www.orlandoweekly.com/news/story.asp?id=12783.

2. Will Jay, personal communication, June 15, 2010.

3. Steve Weinberg, "Covering Crime and Justice: How Prosecutors Work," *Criminal Justice Journalists*, accessed July 20, 2010, http://www.justicejournalism.org/crimeguide/chapter10/chapter10.html.

4. Doug Johnson, County Attorney's Office, Washington County Attorney, Minnesota, 2008, accessed July 20, 2010, http://www.co.washington.mn.us/info_for_residents/county_attorneys_office.

5. Weinberg, op. cit.

6. American Bar Association (ABA), *Standards Relating to the Prosecution Function and Defense Function* (Washington, DC: American Bar Association, 1993).

7. Weinberg, op. cit.

8. ABA, Standards Relating to the Prosecution Function and Defense Function.

9. Ibid.

10. Will Jay, personal communication, June 15, 2010.

11. Thomas H. Cohen and Tracey Kyckelhahn, *Felony Defendants in Large Urban Counties, 2006*, Bureau of Justice Statistics, U.S. Department of Justice, Office of Justice Programs, May 2010, accessed July 18, 2010, http://bjs.ojp.usdoj.gov/content/pub/pdf/fdluc06.pdf.

12. Ibid.

13. See Samuel Walker, *Sense and Nonsense about Crime: A Policy Guide* (Pacific Grove, CA: Brooks/Cole, 1989), and Herbert L. Packer, *The Limits of the Criminal Sanction* (Stanford, CA: Stanford University Press, 1968).

14. Joseph Sanborn, Jr., "A Historical Sketch of Plea Bargaining," *Justice Quarterly* 3 (1986): 113–116. See also Joan E. Jacoby, *The Prosecutor's Charging Decision: A Policy Perspective* (Washington, DC: U.S. Department of Justice, 1977), 1; also, see John Dawson, Steven Smith, and Carol DeFrances, *Prosecution in the State Courts* (Washington, DC: Bureau of Justice Statistics, 1992), 1–15.

15. Bureau of Justice Statistics, *Prosecution of Felony Arrests, 1988* (Washington, DC: U.S. Department of Justice, 1992).

16. These reasons for case dismissal are found in Barbara Boland and Ronald Sones, INSLAW, Inc., *Prosecution of Felony Arrests, 1981*, (Washington, DC: Bureau of Justice Statistics, 1986). See also K. M. Williams, *The Role of the Victim in the Prosecution of Violent Crimes* (Washington, DC: Institute for Law and Social Research, 1978).

17. Will Jay, personal communication, June 15, 2010.

18. Shannon Covalecchio-Van Sickler and Abbie Vansickle, "Lafave 'Over for Good,'" *St. Petersburg Times*, March 22, 2006, accessed July 18, 2010, http://www.sptimes.com/2006/03/22/news_pf/Hillsborough/Lafave_case__over_for.shtml.

19. Fox Tampa Bay, "Lafave Allowed Unsupervised Contact with Kids," October 29, 2009, accessed July 18, 2010, http://www.myfoxtampabay.com/dpp/news/local/hillsborough/judge_allows_lafave_supervised_contact_with_kids_102909.

20. Associated Press, "Teacher-Sex Offender Debra Lafave Free from House Arrest," *Sun Sentinel*, July 11, 2008, accessed July 18, 2010, http://www.sun-sentinel.com/news/florida/sfl-0711lafave teacher,0,6325083.story.

21. Will Jay, personal communication, June 15, 2010.

22. Will Jay, personal communication, June 15, 2010.

23. *Crawford v. Washington*, 541 U.S. 36, (2004).

24. Frank W. Miller, Prosecution: The Decision to Charge a Suspect with a Crime (Boston: Little, Brown, 1970), 11.

25. Thurman W. Arnold, "Law Enforcement—An Attempt at Social Dissection," *Yale Law Journal* 42, no. 1 (1932): 7.

26. Kenneth Culp Davis, *Discretionary Justice* (Baton Rouge: Louisiana State University Press, 1969), 170.

27. Will Jay, personal communication, June 15, 2010.

28. *United States v. Cowen*, 524 F.2d 785 (1975).

29. For instance, see *Brady v. United States*, 397 U.S.742 (1970); *Boykin v. Alabama*, 395 U.S. 238 (1969).

30. American Bar Association (ABA), *Standards Relating to the Prosecution Function and the Defense Function* (Washington, DC: American Bar Association, 1993).

31. Sarah Tanford, Steven Penrod, and Rebecca Collins, "Decision Making in Joined Criminal Trials: The Influence of Charge Similarity, Evidence Similarity, and Limiting Instructions," *Law and Human Behavior* 9 (1985): 319–337; and see Kenneth S. Bordens and Irvin A. Horowitz, "Joinder of Criminal Offenses," *Law and Human Behavior* 9 (1985): 339–353.

32. Wayne R. LaFave, *Arrest: The Decision to Take a Suspect into Custody* (Boston: Little, Brown, 1965), 595; see also Wayne R. LaFave and Frank J. Remington, "Controlling the Police: The Judge's Role in Making and Reviewing Law Enforcement Decisions," *Michigan Law Review* 63 (1965): 987.

33. Will Jay, personal communication, July 14, 2010; A "death qualified juror" is one who would neither ignore the law and sentence every person guilty of first-degree murder to death regardless of the aggravating and mitigating circumstances, nor one who could never apply the death penalty even if the aggravating circumstances outweighed the mitigating circumstances. This leads to a more conservative and politically homogenous group of jurors more likely to convict and more likely to agree with one another—according to some research.

34. Robert A. Carp and Ronald Stidham, *Judicial Process in America*, 4th ed. (Washington, DC: Congressional Quarterly, Inc., 1998), 150; Andrew D. Leipold, "Preliminary Hearing: A Procedural Overview, the Defendant's Right to a Preliminary Hearing, Other Functions of a Preliminary Hearing," 2010, accessed July 19, 2010: http://law.jrank.org/pages/1721/Preliminary-Hearing.html.

35. Rolando V. Del Carmen, *Criminal Procedure: Law and Practice*, 8th ed. (Belmont, CA: Wadsworth, 2010), 41.

36. Ibid.; Joshua S. Davidson, "What Is the Difference between a Grand Jury and a Preliminary Hearing?" Phoenix Criminal Defense Blog, April 2010, accessed November 22, 2010, http://www.jdavidsonlaw.com/Phoenix_Criminal_Defense_Blog/2010/April_.aspx.

37. See *United States v. Mandujano*, 425 U.S. 564, (1976).

38. *Coleman v. Alabama*, 399 U.S. 1 (1970).

39. Robert A. Weninger, "Criminal Discovery and Omnibus Procedure in a Federal Court: A Defense View," *Southern California Law Review* 49 (1976): 514. See also Note, *Georgia Law Journal* 56 (1967): 193; also see John M. Scheb and John M. Scheb II, *Criminal Law and Procedure, 8th ed*, (Independence, Kentucky: Cengage, 2014).

40. David B. Rottman and Shauna M. Strickland, *State Court Organization 2004*, Bureau of Justice Statistics, Office of Justice Programs, U.S. Department of Justice, August 2006, accessed July 19, 2010, http://bjs.ojp.usdoj.gov/content/pub/pdf/sco04.pdf.

41. *Coleman v. Alabama*, 399 U.S. 1, (1970).

42. *Hurtado v. California*, 110 U.S. 516 (1884).

43. Rottman and Strickland, op. cit.; del Carmen, op. cit.

44. United States v. Mandujano, op. cit.

45. Carp and Stidham, op. cit.

46. Rottman and Strickland, op. cit.

47. del Carmen, op. cit.

48. Will Jay, personal communication, June 15, 2010.

49. N. Gary Holton and Lawson L. Lamar, *The Criminal Courts: Structures, Personnel, Processes* (New York: McGraw-Hill, 1991).

50. Alissa Pollitz Worden, "Policymaking by Prosecutors: The Uses of Discretion in Regulating Plea Bargaining," *Judicature* 73, no. 6 (April–May 1990): 335–340; also see Malvina Halberstam, "Toward Neutral Principles in the Administration of Criminal Justice: A Critique of Decisions Sanctioning the Plea Bargaining Process," *Journal of Criminal Law and Criminology* 73, no. 1 (1982): 1–49.

51. Will Jay, personal communication, June 15, 2010.

52. Anthony Walsh, "Standing Trial Versus Copping a Plea: Is There a Penalty?" *Journal of Contemporary Criminal Justice* 6 (1990): 226–236.

53. Will Jay, personal communication, June 15, 2010.

54. Ibid.

55. See, for example, Hugo Bedau and Michael L. Radelet, "Miscarriages of Justice in Potentially Capital Cases," *Stanford Law Review* 37 (1987): 27–153.

56. Walsh, op. cit.

57. Will Jay, personal communication, June 15, 2010.

58. Will Jay, personal communication, June 15, 2010.

59. Albert W. Alschuler, "The Defense Attorney's Role in Plea Bargaining," *Yale Law Journal* 84 (1975): 1206. See also Arthur Rosett and Donald R. Cressey, *Justice by Consent* (Philadelphia: Lippincott, 1976), quote taken from p. 3. Also, for more on the culture of plea bargaining between prosecutors and defense attorneys, see Lisa McIntyre, *The Public Defender: The Practice of Law in the Shadows of Repute* (Chicago: University of Chicago Press, 1987).

60. Will Jay, personal communication, June 15, 2010.

61. *Sheldon v. United States*, 246 F.2d 571 (5th Cir. 1957). Reversed on confession of error of Solicitor General, 356 U.S. 26 (1958).

62. del Carmen, op. cit.

63. T. Church, "Plea Bargains, Concessions, and the Courts: Analysis of a Quasi-Experiment," *Law and Society Review* 10 (Spring 1976): 377–401.

64. See, for example, *Brady v. United States*, 397 U.S. 742; 90 S. Ct. 1463, 25 L. Ed. 2d 747 (1970); *Parker v. North Carolina*, 397 U.S. 790, 90 S. Ct. 1458, 25 L. Ed. 2d 785 (1970); *North Carolina v. Alford*, 400 U.S. 25 (1970). For a critique of Supreme Court decisions sanctioning the plea-bargaining process, see Malvina Halberstam, "Toward Neutral Principles in the Administration of Criminal Justice: A Critique of Supreme Court Decisions Sanctioning the Plea Bargaining Process," *Journal of Criminal Law and Criminology* 73, no. 1 (1982): 1–49.

65. *Santobello v. New York*, 404 U.S. 257 (1971).

66. American Bar Association, *Standards Related to Pleas of Guilty* (New York: Institute of Judicial Administration, 1968), Sec. 3.1, 60; American Law Institute, *Model Code of Pre-Arraignment Procedures* (Philadelphia: American Law Institute, 1972), Art. 350.

67. Federal Rules of Criminal Procedure, Rule 11, Pleas, Sec. (e). Amended 1 July 1975.

68. Will Jay, personal communication, June 15, 2010.

69. Ibid.

70. See Santobello v. New York, op. cit.

71. American Bar Association, *Standards Relating to Pleas of Guilty*, Sec. 3.1(c), 60.

72. See *Newman v. United States*, 382 F. 2d (D.C. Cir. 1967).

73. Will Jay, personal communication, June 15, 2010.

74. North Carolina v. Alford, op. cit.

75. "Victim Input into Plea Agreements," Legal Series Bulletin #7, Office of Justice Programs, U.S. Department of Justice, November 2002, accessed July 20, 2010, http://www.ojp.usdoj.gov/ovc/publications/bulletins/legalseries/bulletin7/2.html.

76. See Box 9.2 and excerpts from Michael Vick's plea agreement in Box 9.3 in Chapter 9.

Chapter 9

1. *State of Florida v. Lisa Marie Nowak*, Orders granting motions to suppress admissions illegally obtained and evidence from unlawful search by Circuit Judge Marc L. Lubet, November 2, 2007, accessed June 20, 2010, http://www.clickorlando.com/download/2007/1102/14499043.pdf.

2. Risdon N. Slate, "The Matter of O.J. Simpson in Black and White and Green," in *Representing O.J.: Murder, Criminal Justice and Mass Culture*, ed. Gregg Barak (Guilderland, NY: Harrow and Heston, 1996).

3. Hannah Storm, "Burress Gets Sentence in Gun Case," ESPN, accessed June 20, 2010, http://sports.espn.go.com/nfl/news/story?id=4493887.

4. Tennessee, Virginia, Georgia, and Arizona have recently passed laws allowing loaded guns in bars. See Malcolm Gay, "More States Allowing Guns in Bars," *New York Times*, October 3, 2010, accessed December 12, 2010, http://www.nytimes.com/2010/10/04/US/04guns.html.

5. It has been reported that roughly ninety-seven percent of cases in the federal court system are plea bargained—see Adam K. Miller, "Issues in the Third Circuit: A New System of Federal Sentencing: The Impact on Third Circuit Sentencing Procedure in the Wake of the Supreme Court's Landmark Decision in *United States v. Booker*," *Vill L. Rev.* 51 (2006): 1107; approximately 95 percent of defendants facing felony charges forego their right to a trial by jury in state proceedings and plead guilty—see Bruce P. Smith, "Plea Bargaining and the Eclipse of the Jury," *Annual Review of Law and Social Science* 1 (June 28, 2005), accessed July 13, 2010, http://arjournals.annualreviews.org/doi/abs/ 10.1146/annurev.lawsocsci.1.041604.115948?cookieSet=1&journalCode=lawsocsci.

6. Yale Kamisar, Wayne R. LaFave, and Jerold H. Israel, *Basic Criminal Procedure*, 6th ed. (St. Paul, MN: West Publishing Co., 1986), 512–513.

7. *Eugene W. McWatters v. State of Florida*, Supreme Court of Florida, 2010 Fla. LEXIS 406; *Fla. L. Weekly* S 35 (March 18, 2010): 169.

8. Tammie Fields, "Polk Inmates' Conversations to Be Recorded," WTSP 10 News, June 23, 2010, accessed July 15, 2010, http://www.wtsp.com/news/local/story.aspx?storyid=134678&catid=8; Jason Geary, "Sheriff Says He Will Record Inmate Calls to Lawyers and Use Them as Evidence," *The Ledger*, June 21, 2010, accessed July 15, 2010, http://www.theledger.com/article/20100621/NEWS/6215064.

9. "Federal Judgeships," Judges and Judgeships, United States Courts, accessed June 19, 2010, http://www.uscourts.gov/JudgesAndJudgeships/FederalJudgeships.aspx; "District Courts," Federal Courts, United States Courts, accessed June 19, 2010, http://www.uscourts.gov/FederalCourts/UnderstandingtheFederalCourts/DistrictCourts.aspx; Rolando V. del Carmen, *Criminal Procedure: Law and Practice*, 8th ed. (Belmont, CA: Wadsworth, 2010).

10. Ira P. Robbins, "Magistrate Judges, Article III, and the Power to Preside over Federal Prisoner Section 2255 Proceedings," *Fed. Cts. L. Rev.* 2 (2002): 1–36.

11. Del Carmen, op. cit., 7; "Courts of Appeals," United States Courts, Federal Courts, accessed June 19, 2010, http://www.uscourts.gov/FederalCourts/UnderstandingtheFederalCourts/CourtofAppeals.aspx; Federal Judgeships, op. cit.

12. "Original Jurisdiction," Legal Information Institute, Cornell University Law School, accessed June 19, 2010, http://topics.law.cornell.edu/wex/original_jurisdiction.

13. "How the Court Works/The Court's Workload and Staff," The Supreme Court Historical Society, accessed June 19, 2010, http://www.supremecourthistory.org/works/supremecourthistory_works_howthecourtworks_03.htm.

14. "Certiorari," Legal Information Institute, Cornell University Law School, accessed June 19, 2010, http://topics.law.cornell.edu/wex/certiorari.

15. del Carmen, op. cit., 6.

16. United States Supreme Court, "Biographies of Current Justices of the Supreme Court," April 11, 2017, accessed May 4, 2017, https://www.supremecourt.gov/about/biographies.aspx#NGorsuch.

17. "Federal Judges Who Have Been Impeached," Judgepedia, March 11, 2010, accessed June 19, 2010, http://judgepedia.org/index.php/Federal_judges_who_have_been_impeached.

18. *New York Times*, "Harry Claiborne, 86, is Dead; Was Removed as U.S. Judge," January 22, 2004, accessed June 19, 2010, http://www.nytimes.com/2004/01/22/us/harry-claiborne-86-is-dead-was-removed-as-us-judge.html.

19. "Federal Judges Who Have Been Impeached," op. cit.

20. Alcee L. Hastings, "Biography," (U.S. Congressman, Florida's 23rd District), accessed June 19, 2010, http://www.alceehastings.house.gov/index.php?option=com_content&view=article&id=60&Itemid=90.

21. Lawrence Baum, *American Courts: Process and Policy*, 6th ed. (Boston, MA: Houghton Mifflin, 2008).

22. See Patrick R. Anderson and L. Thomas Winfree, *Expert Witnesses: Criminologists in the Courtroom* (Albany: State University of New York Press, 1986).

23. For a discussion of cameras in the courtroom, see C-SPAN, "Cameras in the Court: Learn about the Justice's Views on the Issue of Opening the Court to Cameras, Based on Their Public Statements," accessed July 12, 2010, http://www.c-span.org/CamerasInCourt/default.aspx; John M. Scheb and John M. Scheb II, *Criminal Law and Procedure*, 2nd ed. (St. Paul, MN: West, 1996), 486; and S. L. Alexander, "Cameras in the Courtroom: A Case Study," *Judicature* 74, no. 6 (April–May 1991): 307–313.

24. Kathleen Kirby and Matthew Gibson, "Freedom of Information Cameras in the Court: A State-By-State Guide," Radio Television Digital New Association, May 25, 2007, accessed July 12, 2010, http://www.rtdna.org/pages/media_items/cameras-in-the-court-a-state-by-state-guide55.php?g=45%3fid=55.

25. *Estes v. Texas*, 301 U.S. 532, (1965).

26. *Chandler v. Florida*, 449 U.S. 560, (1981).

27. The Huffington Post, "Supreme Court Cameras: Senate Judiciary Committee OKs Bills to Allow Broadcast from Courts," April 29, 2010, accessed July 12, 2010, http://www.huffingtonpost.com/2010/04/29/supreme-court-cameras-sen_n_557704.html?ref=twitter.

28. "Understanding Federal and State Courts," Educational Resources, United States Courts, accessed June 19, 2010, http://www.uscourts.gov/EducationalResources/FederalCourtBasics/CourtStructure/UnderstandingFederalAndStateCourts.aspx; Baum, op. cit.

29. Malia Reddick, "Judicial Selection: The Process of Choosing Judges," American Bar Association, June 2008, accessed June 19, 2010, http://www.abanet.org/justice/pdf/judicial_selection_roadmap.pdf; American Judicature Society, "Methods of Judicial Selection," accessed June 19, 2010, http://www.judicialselection.us/judicial_selection/methods/selection_of_judges.cfm?state=; American Bar Association, "Fact Sheet on Judicial Selection Methods in the States," accessed June 19, 2010, http://www.abanet.org/leadership/fact_sheet.pdf.

30. Fredreka Schouten, "Fundraising for States' High-Court Races," *USA Today*, March 31, 2010, accessed June 19, 2010, http://www.usatoday.com/news/politics/2010-03-30-judges_N.htm.

31. Joccelyn M. Pollock-Byrne, *Ethics in Crime and Justice: Dilemmas and Decisions* (Pacific Grove, CA: Brooks/Cole Publishing Company, 1989).

32. Caperton v. A.T. Massey Coal Co., 556 U.S. ___ (2009).

33. Robert Barnes, "Court Ties Campaign Largess to Judicial Bias," *Washington Post*, June 9, 2009, accessed June 20, 2010, http://www.washingtonpost.com/wp-dyn/content/article/2009/06/08/AR2009060801366.html.

34. *Boykin v. Alabama*, 395 U.S. 238 (1969).

35. *North Carolina v. Alford*, 400 U.S. 25 (1970).

36. del Carmen, op. cit., 45.

37. *United States of America v. Michael Vick*, Plea Agreement, 2007, accessed June 20, 2010, http://assets.espn.go.com/media/pdf/070824/vickplea.pdf.

38. Times Topics, "Michael Vick," *New York Times*, August 14, 2009, accessed: June 20, 2010, http://topics.nytimes.com/top/reference/timestopics/people/v/michael_vick/index.html.

39. Lindsey Devers, *Research Summary: Plea and Charge Bargaining*, Bureau of Justice Assistance, January 24, 2011, accessed May 4, 2017, https://www.bja.gov/Publications/PleaBargainingResearchSummary.pdf.

40. Sharon Chamard, personal communication, January 17, 2017; Leon Watson and Sara Malm, "Pedophile Who 'Killed Elderly Couple and Raped Two-Year-Old' Had Been Released from Prison for Almost Identical Attack Just HOURS Earlier," *Daily Mail*, May 29, 2013, accessed May 4, 2017, http://www.dailymail.co.uk/news/article-2332555/Jerry-Active-killed-elderly-couple-raped-2-year-old-just-HOURS-released-prison.html.

41. del Carmen, op. cit.; FindLaw, "Plea Bargain Pros and Cons," 2017, accessed May 4, 2017, http://criminal.findlaw.com/criminal-procedure/plea-bargain-pros-and-cons.html.

42. Stephanos Bibas, "Harmonizing Substantive Criminal Law Values and Criminal Procedure: The Case of *Alford* and Nolo Contendere Pleas," *Cornell Law Review* 8, no. 6 (July 2003); Also see *Federal Rules of Criminal Procedure for the United States District Courts*, Rule 11, accessed July 12, 2010, http://www.almd.uscourts.gov/rulesproc/docs/Guilty_Plea_Colloquy.pdf.

43. *Boykin v. Alabama*, 395 U.S. 238, (1969).

44. *Brady v. United States*, 397 U.S. 742, (1970).

45. American Bar Association, *Standards Relating to Pleas of Guilty, Part II* (New York: Institute of Judicial Administration, 1968), Sec. 2.1(4).

46. Thomas H. Cohen and Tracey Kyckelhahn, *Felony Defendants in Large Urban Counties, 2006*, Bureau of Justice Statistics, Office of Justice Programs, U.S. Department of Justice, May 2010, accessed July 12, 2010, http://bjs.ojp.usdoj.gov/content/pub/pdf/fdluc06.pdf.

47. See John M. Scheb and John M. Scheb II, 504–507.

48. Bob Meadows, "Astronaut Update: A Surprising Police Report Casts Lisa Nowak's Bizarre Attack in a New Light," *People*, March 19, 2007, accessed July 12, 2010, http://www.people.com/people/archive/article/0,,20061542,00.html.

49. Ibid.

50. John Schwartz, "From Spaceflight to Attempted Murder Charge," *New York Times*, February 7, 2007, accessed July 12, 2010, http://www.nytimes.com/2007/02/07/us/07astronaut.html.

51. *State of Florida v. Lisa Marie Nowak*, Case No: 48-2007-CF-001796-0, Order Granting Motion to Suppress Admissions Illegally Obtained and Motion to Suppress Evidence from Unlawful Search, accessed July 13, 2010, http://www.wesh.com/download/2007/1102/14499284.pdf.

52. *State of Florida v. Lisa Marie Nowak*, In the District Court of Appeal of the State of Florida, 5th District, Case No: 5D07-3833 (2008), accessed July 13, 2010, http://www.5dca.org/Opinions/Opin2008/120108/5D07-3833.pdf.

53. Will Jay, personal communication, July 20, 2010.

54. Scheb and Scheb, op. cit.

55. The U.S. Supreme Court has held that a suspect does not have the right to an attorney for a line-up that is conducted prior to formal charges having been filed—see *Kirby v. Illinois*, 406 U.S. 682, (1972); Likewise, suspects do not have the right to an attorney at show-ups, whereby a suspect is shown to a witness or victim typically at the scene of the crime contemporaneous to the time the suspect is apprehended and before formal charges have been filed—see del Carmen, op. cit., 314; the U.S. Supreme Court has held that the right to counsel for defendants exists at line-ups after formal charges have been filed—see *United States v. Wade*, 388 U.S. 218, (1967). The purpose of counsel is not to prevent self-incrimination but to ensure that procedures employed by the police are fair—del Carmen, op. cit. 309; Photographs can be used in place of lineups, and lawyers are not required to be present to ensure fairness—regardless of whether formal charges have been filed—see *United States v. Ash*, 413 U.S. 300, (1973).

56. del Carmen, op. cit., 313.

57. Ibid.

58. Roland V. del Carmen, *Criminal Procedure: Law and Practice*, 2nd ed. (Pacific Grove, CA: Brooks/Cole Publishing Company, 1991); Will Jay, personal communication, July 20, 2010, cautions "I'd never

say probable cause is the equivalent of preponderance of evidence. Preponderance is 50.0000001%, but probable cause is simply whether a crime was probably committed and the defendant is probably the one who did it. Probable isn't equal to more than likely." Jay also adds, "A reasonable doubt is not a mere possible doubt, a speculative, imaginary or forced doubt. Such a doubt must not influence you to return a verdict of not guilty if you have an abiding conviction of guilt. On the other hand, if, after carefully considering, comparing and weighing all the evidence, there is not an abiding conviction of guilt, or, if, having a conviction, it is one which is not stable but one which wavers and vacillates, then the charge is not proved beyond every reasonable doubt and you must find the defendant not guilty because the doubt is reasonable.... A reasonable doubt as to the guilt of the defendant may arise from the evidence, conflict in the evidence or the lack of evidence." Florida Criminal Jury Instruction 3.7.

59. Article 3, Sec. 2, of the Constitution provides that "trial of all crimes ... shall be by jury" but by and large court decisions have allowed waiver. See *Patton v. United States*, 281 U.S. 276 (1930).

60. Rule 23, Federal Rules of Criminal Procedure, Legal Information Institute, Cornell University Law School, accessed July 13, 2010, http://www.law.cornell.edu/rules/frcrmp/Rule23.htm.

61. See Radley Balko, "Justice Often Served by Jury Nullification," Fox News, August 1, 2005, accessed July 13, 2010, http://www.foxnews.com/story/0,2933,163877,00.html.

62. *Baldwin v. New York*, 399 U.S. 66 (1970).

63. *Blanton v. North Las Vegas*, 489 U.S. 538 (1989).

64. *Lewis v. United States*, 518 U.S. 322 (1996).

65. "Prosecution of Process Crimes: Thoughts and Trends," *The Georgetown Law Journal Annual Review of Criminal Procedure* 37 (2008): 477.

66. *Singer v. United States*, 380 U.S. 24, 36 (1965).

67. This has long been permitted, see *France v. United States*, 164 U.S. 676, 17 S.Ct. 219, 41 L.Ed. 595 (1897). Also, see Federal Rules of Criminal Procedure, Rule 33, New Trial; Richard H. Winningham, "The Dilemma of the Directed Acquittal," *Vanderbilt Law Review* 15 (1962): 699; and American Bar Association, *Standards Relating to Trial by Jury*, Sec. 4.5(a).61. In deciding the case of *In Re Winship*, 397 U.S. 358 (1970), the Supreme Court stated that the government must prove all elements of the offense beyond a reasonable doubt. This has created a great controversy as it could mean that certain legal presumptions, such as the presumption of sanity, are unconstitutional. See Ronald J. Allen, "*Mullaney v. Wilbur*, the Supreme Court, and the Substantive Criminal Law—An Examination of the Limits of Legitimate Intervention," *Texas Law Review* 55 (1977): 269–301; and Anthony M. Doniger, "Case Comment—Unburdening the Criminal Defendant: *Mullaney v. Wilbur* and the Reasonable Doubt Standard," *Harvard Civil Rights—Civil Liberties Law Review* 11 (1976): 390.

68. David W. Neubauer, *America's Courts and the Criminal Justice System*, 9th ed. (Belmont, CA: Thomson Wadsworth, 2008).

69. Ibid., 300.

70. *Barker v. Wingo*, 407 U.S. 514 (1972).

71. *Doggett v. United States*, 505 U.S. 647 (1992).

72. Myles Braccio and Jessie Lundberg, "'The Mother of All Balancing Tests': *State v. Ariegwe* and Montana's Revised Speedy Trial Analysis," *Mont. L. Rev.* 69 (Summer 2008): 463.

73. Lindsey Powell, "Unraveling Criminal Statutes of Limitations," *Am. Crim. L. Rev.* 45 (Winter 2008): 115.

74. Ibid.

75. "State Criminal Statute of Limitations Laws," FindLaw, 2009, accessed July 14, 2010, http://law.findlaw.com/state-laws/criminal-statute-of-limitations.

76. David Stout, "Byron De La Beckwith Dies; Killer of Medgar Evers Was 80," *New York Times*, January 23, 2001, accessed July 14, 2010, http://www.nytimes.com/2001/01/23/us/byron-de-la-beckwith-dies-killer-of-medgar-evers-was-80.html.

77. *Williams v. Florida*, 399 U.S. 78, (1970).

78. David B. Rottman and Shauna M. Strickland, *State Court Organization 2004*, Bureau of Justice Statistics, Office of Justice Programs, U.S. Department of Justice, August 2006, accessed July 15, 2010, http://bjs.ojp.usdoj.gov/content/pub/pdf/sco04.pdf.

79. Rottman, op. cit.

80. John Helmert, "Going to Trial (Now What Do I Do?): Jury Selection in Mississippi Trial Courts," *Miss. C. L. Rev.* 28 (2009): 231.

81. Rottman, op. cit.

82. David Cromwell Johnson, "Voir Dire in the Criminal Case: A Primer," *Trial* 19 (October 1983): 62.

83. Eileen A. Scallen, "Evidence Law as Pragmatic Legal Rhetoric: Reconnecting Legal Scholarship, Teaching and Ethics," *Quinnipiac L. Rev.* 21 (2003): 813.

84. Debra Sahler, "Scientifically Selecting Jurors While Maintaining Professional Responsibility: A Proposed Model Rule," *Alb. L. J. Sci. & Tech.* 6 (1996): 383.

85. *Swain v. Alabama*, 380 U.S. 202 (1965).

86. *Batson v. Kentucky*, 476 U.S. 79 (1986).

87. *Powers v. Ohio*, 499 U.S. 400 (1991).

88. *J.E.B. v. Alabama*, 511 U.S. 127 (1994).

89. Will Jay, personal communication, July 14, 2010.

90. Ibid.

91. Ibid., some jurisdictions may do jury instructions before closing arguments.

92. According to Will Jay, personal communication, July 20, 2010, to get to federal court with a federal writ of habeas corpus, direct appeals in the state system must be exhausted. This usually is when the supreme court of the state, or whatever the court of last resort in a state is called, rules. If it is a federal question, then one can file a petition for a writ of certiorari to the U.S. Supreme Court on direct review. For a better understanding of petitions for writs of habeas corpus in state vs. federal courts, see http://www.supremecourt.gov/opinions/09pdf/09-5327.pdf; The basics of state appeals (at least in Florida) is that the state can appeal final pre-trial orders, such as motions to dismiss and suppress. The state can also cross-appeal errors during the trial if the defense appeals the conviction. And the state can petition for a writ of certiorari on non-final pre-trial orders (like motions in limine to exclude state evidence) but the standard is higher than mere error ... it's like *big* error, miscarriage of justice, disastrous to the state's case.

93. Exceptions to this are seen with *Santobello v. New York*, 404 U.S. 257 (1971), where the U.S. Supreme Court ruled that the prosecution must honor what it has agreed to in a plea agreement—this case dealt with a prosecutor who had assured the defendant he would not comment to the court at sentencing on what type of sentence the defendant should receive. However, when the sentencing date came around, a new prosecutor was in place and recommended a sentence to the court. The matter was vacated and remanded to the lower court to determine whether the plea bargain should be kept or the defendant should withdraw the plea. In *North Carolina v. Alford*, 400 U.S. 25 (1970), the U.S. Supreme Court held that a guilty plea can still be accepted and is valid even if someone maintains their innocence for the crime that he or she has pled guilty to—all that is required for acceptance of the plea is that it is knowingly entered into; it does not have to be an admission of guilt.

94. See American Bar Association, *Standards Relating to Criminal Appeals* (approved draft) (New York: Institute of Judicial Administration, 1970); and American Bar Association, *Standards Relating to Post-Conviction Remedies* (approved draft) (New York: Institute of Judicial Administration, 1967).

95. See *Griffin v. Illinois*, 351 U.S. 12 (1956), and *Douglas v. California*, 372 U.S. 353 (1963).

96. See Danielle M. McGill, "To Exhaust or Not to Exhaust: The Prisoner Litigation Reform Act Requires Prisoners to Exhaust All Administrative Remedies before Filing Excessive Force Claims in Federal Court," *Clev St. L. Rev.* 50 (2002–2003): 129.

97. See American Bar Association, *Standards Relating to Criminal Appeals*, Sec. 1.4.

98. *Florida v. Nowak*, Order Granting Motion to Suppress, op. cit.

99. John Schwartz, "Former Astronaut Makes Plea Deal," *New York Times*, November 11, 2009, accessed July 13, 2010, http://www.nytimes.com/2009/11/11/us/11astronaut.html?_r=1; CNN, "Ex-Astronaut in Love Triangle Case Avoids Prison with Plea Deal," November 10, 2009, accessed May 9, 2017, http://www.cnn.com/2009/CRIME/11/10/florida.astronaut.trial/; Fox News, "Ex-Astronaut Lisa Nowak Pleads Guilty to Burglary, Battery but Gets Light Sentence," November 11, 2009, accessed May 9, 2017, http://www.foxnews.com/story/2009/11/11/ex-astronaut-lisa-nowak-pleads-guilty-to-burglary-battery-but-gets-light.html.

Chapter 10

1. Judge Michael Cicconetti, "Judge: I Sentence You to Be a Chicken," July 28, 2007, accessed August 1, 2010, http://www.shortnews.com/start.cfm?id=63865—"Judge Michael Cicconetti has offered suspended sentences to Daniel Chapdelaine, Fabian Rodriguez-Ramirez, and Martin Soto for soliciting sex if they will take turns wearing a brightly coloured chicken suit while standing outside the courthouse. The men will have to hold a sign saying, 'No Chicken Ranch in Painesville' (a reference to the well-known Nevada Chicken Ranch where prostitution is carried out legally). The trio was caught after soliciting an undercover police officer. This isn't Judge Cicconetti's first sentence of this nature. Previously he ordered a couple to dress as Joseph and Mary and walk down the street with a donkey. Another man had to stand with a pig and a sign saying, 'This Is Not a Police Officer.'"

2. See John M. Scheb and John M. Scheb II, *Criminal Law and Procedure*, 2nd ed. (Minneapolis: West 1994), 590–594.

3. Ronald Akers, *Criminological Theories: Introduction and Evaluation* (Los Angeles, CA: Roxbury Publishing, 1994).

4. Ibid., 51.

5. Ibid., 56; Travis Hirschi, *Causes of Delinquency* (Berkley, CA: University of California Press, 1969).

6. Risdon N. Slate and W. Wesley Johnson, *Criminalization of Mental Illness: Crisis and Opportunity for the Justice System* (Durham, NC: Carolina Academic Press, 2008).

7. Leena Kurki, "Incorporating Restorative and Community Justice into American Sentencing and Corrections," *Sentencing and Corrections: Issues for the 21st Century*, U.S. Department of Justice, Office of Justice Programs, National Institute of Justice, September 1999, accessed March 22, 2010, http://www.ncjrs.gov/pdffiles1/nij/175723.pdf.

8. Ralph De La Cruz, "No Treatment after 190 Arrests? That's Insanity," *Sun Sentinel*, January 27, 2009, accessed May 23, 2010, http://articles.sun-sentinel.com/2009-01-27/news/0901260707_1_baker-act-mental-health-arrests.

9. The great sociologist Émile Durkheim once offered this example: "Imagine a society of saints, a perfect cloister of exemplary individuals. Crimes properly so called, will there be unknown; but faults which appear venal to the layman will create there the same scandal that the ordinary offense does in ordinary consciousness. If, then, this society has the power to judge and punish, it will define these acts as criminal and will treat them as such." From Durkheim's *The Rules of the Sociological Method* (New York: Free Press, 1956), 68–69.

10. D.A. Andrews, Ivan Zinger, Robert Hoge, James Bonta, Paul Gendreau, and Francis Cullen, "Does Correctional Treatment Work? A Clinically Relevant and Psychologically Informed Meta-Analy-

sis," *Criminology* 28 (1990): 369–404. See also Andrew von Hirsch, *Doing Justice: The Choice of Punishments* (New York: Hill & Wang, 1976), esp. 45–55.

11. We are again indebted to Samuel Walker, *Sense and Nonsense about Crime: A Policy Guide* (Pacific Grove, CA: Brooks/Cole, 1989), and Herbert L. Packer, *The Limits of the Criminal Sanction* (Stanford, CA: Stanford University Press, 1968).

12. See Scheb and Scheb, 590–595.

13. Jeffrey Tauber, "State Prison Based Models," May 19, 2008, accessed May 23, 2010, http://www.reentrycourtsolutions.com/wp-content/uploads/2009/11/STATE-PRISON-BASED-MODELS.pdf.

14. Sean Rosenmerkel, Matthew Durose, and Donald Farole, Jr., *Felony Sentences in State Courts, 2006—Statistical Tables*, Bureau of Justice Statistics, U.S. Department of Justice, Office of Justice Programs, December 2009, accessed May 23, 2010, http://bjs.ojp.usdoj.gov/content/pub/pdf/fssc06st.pdf.

15. See Robert O. Dawson, *Sentencing: The Decision as to Type, Length and Conditions of Sentence* (Boston: Little, Brown, 1969), 79–80, 173–202.

16. See Cassia Spohn, "The Sentencing Decisions of Black and White Judges: Expected and Unexpected Similarities," *Law and Society Review* 24 (1990): 1197–1216; James Gibson, "Race as a Determinant of Criminal Sentences: A Methodological Critique and a Case Study," *Law and Society Review* 12 (1978): 455–478; and Stephen Klein, Joan Petersilia, and Susan Turner, "Race and Imprisonment Decisions in California," *Science* 147 (1990): 812–816. John Gruhl, Cassia Spohn, and Susan Welch, "Women as Policymakers: The Case of Trial Judges," *American Journal of Political Science* 25 (1981): 308–322.

17. See generally Thomas L. Austin, *The Influence of Legal and Extra-legal Factors on Sentencing Dispositions in Rural, Semi-rural and Urban Counties* (Ann Arbor, MI: University Microfilms International, 1980); Cassia Spohn, John Gruhl, and Susan Welch, "The Effect of Race on Sentencing: A Re-examination of an Unsettled Question," *Law and Society Review* 16, no. 1 (1981–1982): 71–88; Darrell Steffensmeier and John H. Kramer, "Sex-based Differences in the Sentencing of Adult Criminal Defendants: An Empirical Test and Theoretical Overview," *Sociology and Social Research: An International Journal* 66, no. 3 (1982): 289–304; Martha A. Myers, "Social Background and the Sentence Behavior of Judges," *Criminology* 26, no. 4 (1988): 649–675.

18. See *McCleskey v. Kemp*, 478 U.S. 1019 (1987).

19. Dean Champion, "Elderly Felons and Sentencing Severity: Interregional Variations in Leniency and Sentencing Trends," *Criminal Justice Review* 12 (1987): 7–15.

20. Darrell Steffensmeier, John Kramer, and Cathy Streifel, "Gender and Imprisonment Decisions," *Criminology* 31 (1993): 411–446.

21. Ellen Hochstedler Steury and Nancy Frank, "Gender Bias and Pretrial Release: More Pieces of the Puzzle," *Journal of Criminal Justice* 18 (1990): 417–432.

22. Janet Johnson, Thomas Kennedy, and I. Gayle Shuman, "Gender Differences in the Sentencing of Felony Offenders," *Federal Probation* 87 (1987): 49–56.

23. David Willison, "The Effects of Counsel on the Severity of Criminal Sentences: A Statistical Approach," *Justice System Journal* 9 (1984): 87–101.

24. See generally Jeffrey Reiman, *The Rich Get Richer and the Poor Get Prison* (Boston: Allyn & Bacon, 1990).

25. See Cassia Spohn and Jerry Cederblom, "Race and Disparities in Sentencing: A Test of the Liberation Hypothesis," *Justice Quarterly* 8 (1991): 305–327; Darnell Hawkins, "Race, Crime Type and Imprisonment," *Justice Quarterly* 3 (1986): 251–269; and, James Unnever and Larry Hembroff, "The Prediction of Racial/Ethnic Sentencing Disparities: An Expectation States Approach," *Journal of Research in Crime and Delinquency* 25 (1988): 53–82.

26. See Alfred Blumstein, "On the Racial Disproportionality of the United States Prison Population," *Journal of Criminal Law and Criminology* 73 (1982): 1259–1281.

27. Robert Crutchfield, George Bridges, and Susan Pitchford, "Analytical and Aggregation Biases in Analyses of Imprisonment: Reconciling Discrepancies in Studies of Racial Disparity," *Journal of Research in Crime and Delinquency* 31 (1994): 166–182.

28. George Bridges, Robert Crutchfield, and Edith Simpson, "Crime, Social Structure and Criminal Punishment: White and Nonwhite Rates of Imprisonment," *Social Problems* 34 (1987): 345–361.

29. See Hawkins, op. cit., 267.

30. Sarah Miley, "Supreme Court Upholds Indefinite Detention of Mentally Ill Sex Offenders," *Jurist Legal News and Research*, May 17, 2010, accessed May 23, 2010, http://jurist.org/paper chase/2010/05/supreme-court-upholds-law-allowing-mentally-ill-prisoners-to-be-committed-longer-than-their-sentence.php; Andrew Cohen, "'Dangerous' Sex Offenders Can Be Imprisoned Indefinitely, Supreme Court Rules," *Politics Daily*, May 17, 2010, accessed May 23 2010, http://www.politicsdaily.com/2010/05/17/supreme-court-changes-the-rules-on-sentencing-juveniles-sex-off.

31. James Austin, *The Consequences of Escalating the Use of Imprisonment: The Case Study of Florida* (San Francisco: National Council on Crime and Delinquency, 1991).

32. National Institute of Justice, "21% of Federal Prisoners Found to Be Low-Level Drug Offenders," *Criminal Justice Newsletter*, February 1994.

33. Henry Scott Wallace, "Mandatory Minimums and Betrayal of Sentencing Reform: A Legislative Dr. Jekyll and Mr. Hyde," *Federal Probation* 57 (1993): 9–16.

34. See *Mempa v. Rhay*, 88 S. Ct. 254, 389 U.S. 128, 19 L. Ed. 2d 2 (1967); Fred Cohen, "Sentencing Probation and the Rehabilitative Ideal: The View from *Mempa v. Rhay*," *Texas Law Review* 47 (1968): 1.

35. National Advisory Commission on Criminal Justice Standards and Goals, *Courts* (Washington, DC: U.S. Department of Justice, 1973), Standard 5.1 and Commentary, 110.

36. American Friends Service Committee, *Struggle for Justice: A Report on Crime and Punishment in America* (New York: Hill and Wang, 1971), 84. Twentieth Century Fund, Task Force on Criminal Sentencing, *Fair and Certain Punishment* (New York: McGraw-Hill, 1976), 96–100.

37. Von Hirsch, 127–128.

38. United States Sentencing Commission, Guidelines Manual, § 3E1.1, Nov. 2008, accessed May 23, 2010, http://www.ussc.gov/2008guid/GL2008.pdf.

39. *U.S. v. Brady*, CA 9, No. 89-50079, 1/30/90. Although the Court for example in *Kimbrough v. U.S.*, 552 U.S. ___ (2007), indicated that trial judges more familiar with the nuances of a case may more liberally consider sentences alongside the sentencing guidelines.

40. Amendments to the Sentencing Guidelines, United States Sentencing Commission, May 3, 2010, accessed July 5, 2010, http://www.ussc.gov/2010guid/20100503_Reader_Friendly_Proposed_Amendments.pdf, 6.

41. See 18 U.S.C. Sec. 3552[d], 1995. Also, see 18 U.S.C., Fed.R.Cr.Proc. 32(c)(B)(1995).

42. For a discussion of presentence confidentiality see, for example, the Presentence Investigation Report, Administrative Office of the United States Courts, March 2006, accessed May 20, 2010, http://www.fd.org/pdf_lib/publication%20107.pdf.

43. For a general discussion of the PSI, see Arthur R. Spica, Jr., "Presentence Reports: The Key to Probation Strategy," *Corrections Today* 49 (1987): 192–196.

44. In 1983, Chief Justice Warren Burger criticized a lower court for "failing to take into account the interest of the victim." See *Morris v. Slappy*, 461 U.S. 1 (1983).

45. For the legal history of victim impact statements, see *Booth v. Maryland*, 482 U.S. 496 (1987); *South Carolina v. Gaithers*, 490 U.S. 805 (1989); and *Payne v. Tennessee*, 498 U.S. 1076 (1991).

46. Edna Erez and Pamela Tontodonato, "The Effect of Victim Participation in Sentencing on Sentence Outcome," *Criminology* 28 (1990): 451–474.

47. David Bruck, "The Death Penalty," *The New Republic*, 1985, accessed May 23, 2010, http://www.faulkner.edu/admin/websites/cwarmack/bruck.pdf.

48. Renee Montagne, "The Last Public Execution in America," NPR, May 1, 2001, accessed May 21, 2010, http://www.npr.org/programs/morning/features/2001/apr/010430.execution.html; Josh Katz, "On This Day Kentucky Holds Final Public Execution in the US," Dulcinea, August 14, 2009, accessed May 21, 2010, http://www.findingdulcinea.com/news/on-this-day/July-August-08/On-this-Day-Kentucky-Holds-Final-Public-Execution-in-the-U-S-.html.

49. See Chapin Bradley, *Criminal Justice in Colonial America, 1606–1660* (Athens: University of Georgia Press, 1982).

50. Charles L. Scott, "*Roper v. Simmons*: Can Juvenile Offenders Be Executed?" *J Am Acad Psychiatry Law* 33 (2005): 547–52, accessed May 21, 2010, http://www.jaapl.org/cgi/reprint/33/4/547.pdf.

51. See Bradley, op. cit.

52. Michael L. Radelet and Margaret Vandiver, "Race and Capital Punishment: An Overview of the Issues," *Crime and Social Justice* 25 (1986): 94–113. The incident cited by Radelet and Vandiver is taken from Jerrell H. Shofner, *Nor Is It Over Yet* (Gainesville: The University Presses of Florida, 1974).

53. Walter White, *A Man Called White* (New York: Viking Press, 1948), cited in Radelet and Vandiver, op. cit.

54. See Radelet and Vandiver, op. cit.

55. "Executions in the U.S., 1608–1976: The Espy File," Death Penalty Information Center, accessed May 21, 2010, http://www.deathpenaltyinfo.org/executions-united-states-1608-1976-state.

56. Wolfgang relates his experiences during *Maxwell* and other cases, and describes the difficulty in gaining acceptance for his testimony before the Arkansas Supreme Court. See Marvin E. Wolfgang, "The Social Scientist in Court," in *Expert Witnesses: Criminologists in the Courtroom,* eds. Patrick R. Anderson and L. Thomas Winfree (Albany: State University of New York Press, 1987), 20–35; indeed, 405 of the 455 men executed for rape between 1930 and 1967 were black, and no white man had ever been executed for the rape of a black woman; the drive to abolish the death penalty was therefore based on arguments about racial discrimination, which in turn were based on statistics gathered in Southern states. See also Bureau of Justice Statistics, *National Prisoner Statistics: Executions 1930–67*, No. 42 (Washington, DC: U.S. Department of Justice, June 1968), 10–11.

57. Jack Greenberg and J. Himmelstein, "Varieties of Attack on the Death Penalty," *Crime and Delinquency* 15 (1969): 112–120.

58. In *Witherspoon v. Illinois* (1968), the Court rejected the argument that a preselected pro-death penalty jury would be biased toward conviction, leading to death-qualified juries. However, the Court found that such a jury would be "uncommonly willing to condemn a man to die"; in *Lockhart v. McCree* (1986), the Court ruled that a person may not be excluded from a capital case jury for his or her opposition to the death penalty, but only if they told the court during *voir dire* that they would never vote for capital punishment regardless of the facts in a case. The Court also decided that two separate juries may be needed in capital cases, one to decide guilt or innocence and another to decide life or death; *Morgan v. Illinois* (1992), put the prosecution and defense on a level playing field by allowing both sides to ask a prospective juror during *voir dire* whether they would respectively vote **against** the death penalty or **for** the death penalty, regardless of the facts.

59. *Ring v. Arizona*, 536 U.S. 584 (2002).

60. Richard Wolf, "Supreme Court Lets Alabama Judges Impose Death Penalty," *USA Today*, January 23, 2017, accessed May 1, 2017, https://www.usatoday.com/story/news/politics/2017/01/23/supreme-court-alabama-florida-death-penalty-judge-jury/96947280/.

61. *Furman v. Georgia*, 408 U.S. 238 (1972); *Jackson v. Georgia*, 408 U.S. 238 (1972); and *Branch v. Texas*, 408 U.S. 238 (1972).

62. *Roberts v. Louisiana*, 428 U.S. 325 (1976); *Woodson v. North Carolina*, 428 U.S. 280 (1976).

63. *Proffitt v. Florida*, 428 U.S. 242 (1976); *Gregg v. Georgia*, 428 U.S. 153 (1976); *Jurek v. Texas*, 428 U.S. 262 (1976).

64. *Coker v. Georgia*, 433 U.S. 584 (1977). This decision was reaffirmed in *Kennedy v. Louisiana*, 128 S. Ct. 2641 (2008), in which a Louisiana statute that allowed for the execution of the perpetrator of the rape of a child where the victim did not die was declared unconstitutional.

65. *Sumner v. Schuman*, 107 U.S. 2716 (1987).

66. *Georgia Code* 27-2534.1(b) (1978).

67. Ibid.

68. Ibid. In this review, the state supreme court determines the following: Whether any *legal error* occurred; whether the death sentence is excessive or *disproportionate* when compared to other similar cases; whether its imposition was the product of *passion* or *prejudice*.

69. *Atkins v. Virginia*, 536 U.S. 304 (2002).

70. *Ford v. Wainwright*, 467 U.S. 122 (1984).

71. *Baze v. Rees*, 533 U.S. 35 (2008); There were concerns as to whether or not lethal injection was a form of cruel and unusual punishment. There were reported instances where executioners were unable to find a suitable vein, possibly causing the prisoner pain. Also there were reported instances where prisoners had violent reactions to the drugs and even prolonged amounts of time before death actually occurred.

72. Death Penalty Information Center, "States with and without the Death Penalty," November 9, 2016, accessed May 9, 2017, https://deathpenaltyinfo.org/states-and-without-death-penalty.

73. Death Penalty Information Center, "Facts about the Death Penalty," October 6, 2017, accessed October 8, 2017 https://deathpenaltyinfo.org/documents/FactSheet.pdf.

74. Death Penalty Information Center, "Facts about the Death Penalty," October 6, 2017 op. cit.

75. Ibid.

76. Ibid.

77. Ibid; See, for example, "Race and the Death Penalty," Death Penalty Information Center, accessed May 22, 2010, http://www.deathpenaltyinfo.org/race-and-death-penalty#rpts; Samuel Gross and Robert Mauro, *Death and Discrimination: Racial Disparities in Capital Sentencing* (Boston: Northeastern University Press, 1989).

78. Death Penalty Information Center, "Women and the Death Penalty," 2017, accessed October 8, 2017 from https://deathpenaltyinfo.org/women-and-death-penalty.

79. Tracy Connor, Dan Shepherd, and Gabe Gutierrez, "Georgia Woman Kelly Gissendaner Sings 'Amazing Grace' during Execution," NBC News, September 30, 2015, accessed May 9, 2017, http://www.nbcnews.com/storyline/lethal-injection/pope-urges-halt-execution-georgia-woman-kelly-gissendaner-n435566.

80. Death Penalty Information Center, "Women and the Death Penalty," 2017, op. cit.

81. Amnesty International, "Death Penalty and Arbitrariness," 2017, accessed May 3, 2017, http://www.amnestyusa.org/our-work/issues/death-penalty/us-death-penalty-facts/death-penalty-and-arbitrariness.

82. Tracy L. Snell, *Capital Punishment, 2013—Statistical Tables*, Bureau of Justice Statistics, December 19, 2014, accessed May 9, 2017, https://www.bjs.gov/content/pub/pdf/cp13st.pdf.

83. "Average Number of Months from Imposition of Death Sentence to Execution, United States, 1977–2008," Sourcebook of Criminal Justice Statistics, accessed May 22, 2010, http://www.albany.edu/sourcebook/pdf/t600242008.pdf.

84. "Clemency," Death Penalty Information Center, accessed May 23, 2010, http://www.deathpenaltyinfo.org/clemency.

85. "Death Penalty Cost," Amnesty International USA, accessed May 23, 2010, http://www.amnestyusa.org/death-penalty/death-penalty-facts/death-penalty-cost/page.do?id=1101084.

86. *The Death Penalty in 2009: Year End Report*, Death Penalty Information Center, December 2009, accessed May 23, 2010, http://www.deathpenaltyinfo.org/documents/2009YearEndReport.pdf.

87. Sources: David A. Kaplan, "New Rules on Death Row," *Newsweek*, April 29, 1991, 68; "Senate Sides with Bush in Passing Curbs on Death Row Inmate Appeals," *The Star-Ledger*, June 27, 1991, 10; Ginny Carroll, "Staying Clean: Life after Death Row," *Newsweek*, May 6, 1991, 56–57.

88. "Methods of Execution," Death Penalty Information Center, accessed May 23, 2010, http://www.deathpenaltyinfo.org/methods-execution.

89. "Federal Death Row Prisoners," Death Penalty Information Center, May 4, 2010, accessed May 23, 2010, http://www.deathpenaltyinfo.org/federal-death-row-prisoners.

90. "Federal Laws Providing for the Death Penalty," Death Penalty Information Center, accessed May 23, 2010, http://www.deathpenaltyinfo.org/federal-laws-providing-death-penalty.

91. "USP Terre Haute," Federal Bureau of Prisons, U.S. Department of Justice, accessed May 23, 2010, http://www.bop.gov/locations/institutions/thp/index.jsp.

92. See for example, Ernest van den Haag, "A Defense of the Death Penalty: A Legal-Practical-Moral Analysis," *Criminal Law Bulletin* 14 (January–February 1978): 51–68. Also, for views on the subject over the centuries, see Opposing Viewpoints Series, *The Death Penalty: Opposing Viewpoints* (San Diego: Greenhaven Press, 1991).

93. Lydia Saad, "Americans Hold Firm to Support for Death Penalty," Gallup, November 17, 2008, accessed May 21, 2010, http://www.gallup.com/poll/111931/Americans-Hold-Firm-Support-Death-Penalty.aspx.

94. Scott Vollum, Dennis R. Longmire, and Jacqueline Buffington-Vollum, "Confidence in the Death Penalty and Support for Its Use: Exploring the Value-Expressive Dimension of Death Penalty Attitudes," *Justice Quarterly* 21, no. 3 (2004): 521–546.

95. Hugo Bedau and Michael L. Radelet, "Miscarriages of Justice in Potentially Capital Cases," *Stanford Law Review* 37 (1987): 27–153.

96. David Masci, "5 Facts about the Death Penalty," Pew Research Center, April 24, 2017, accessed May 9, 2017, http://www.pewresearch.org/fact-tank/2017/04/24/5-facts-about-the-death-penalty/.

97. Jeffrey M. Jones, "U.S. Death Penalty Support at 60%," Gallup, October 25, 2016, accessed May 9, 2017, http://www.gallup.com/poll/196676/death-penalty-support.aspx.

98. Gallup, "Death Penalty," 2016, accessed May 9, 2017, http://www.gallup.com/poll/1606/death-penalty.aspx.

99. Death Penalty Information Center, "Facts about the Death Penalty," October 6, 2017, op. cit.

100. Ibid.

101. Innocence Project of Florida, "About the Innocence Project of Florida," 2017, accessed May 9, 2017, http://floridainnocence.org/content/?page_id=9966; Innocence Project of Florida, "James Bain," 2017, accessed May 9, 2017, http://floridainnocence.org/content/?page_id=1697.

102. Joanna Shepherd, "Why Not All Executions Deter Murder," *The Christian Science Monitor*, December 14, 2005, accessed May 23, 2010, http://www.csmonitor.com/2005/1214/p09s01-coop.html.

103. Dennis A. Challeen, *The NORP Think Factor*, 2nd ed. (Winona, MN: Staige Productions, 1994).

Chapter 11

1. John Augustus, *A Report of the Labors of John Augustus* (Boston: Wright & Hasty, Printers, 1852). (Lexington, KY: American Probation and Parole Association, Republished in 1984), 96–97.

2. Associated Press, "Supreme Court: High Court Backs Mail Theft Punishment," *USA Today*, November 28, 2005, accessed May 12, 2010, http://www.usatoday.com/news/washington/judicial/supremecourtopinions/2005-11-28-stolen-mail_x.htm; See also Bob Egelko, ("San Francisco / Shaming OKd as Part of Sentence / Court Upholds Thief's Wearing 'I Stole Mail' Sign," *San Francisco Chronicle*, August 10, 2004, accessed May 12, 2010, http://articles.sfgate.com/2004-08-10/bay-area/17437881_1_sentence-appeals-court-shawn-gementera.

3. Jonathan Turley, "Shame on You: Enough with the Humiliating Punishments, Judges," *Washington Post*, September 18, 2005, accessed May 12, 2010, http://www.washingtonpost.com/wp-dyn/content/article/2005/09/17/AR2005091700064.html.

4. Hillary Hanson, "Tyler Alred Sentenced to Go to Church after Manslaughter Conviction," *Weird News*, November 16, 2012, accessed May 3, 2017, http://www.huffingtonpost.com/2012/11/18/tyler-alred-church-manslaughter_n_2146619.html; Kimberly Hulsey, "Oklahoma Teen Sentenced to Church for Manslaughter," ABC News Channel 8 Tulsa, 2012, accessed May 3, 2017, http://abcnews.go.com/US/video/oklahoma-teen-sentenced-church-manslaughter-17738747.

5. The rare exception to this is something called shock probation that originated over 40 years ago in Ohio and has been implemented at various times by at least thirteen states. With shock probation, a convicted person would be placed in a penal institution for a brief period (30 days to 120 days) before being released on probation with the hope that it would "shock" them into comporting their behavior accordingly. Shock probation is not widely used and results on its effectiveness are inconclusive at best. See Edward J. Latessa and Paula Smith, *Corrections in the Community*, 4th ed. (Cincinnati, OH: Anderson Publishing, 2007), 76, 77.

6. Danielle Kaeble and Thomas P. Bonczar, *Probation and Parole in the United States, 2015*, Bureau of Justice Statistics, December 2016, accessed May 3, 2017, https://www.bjs.gov/content/pub/pdf/ppus15.pdf.

7. Steve Takesian, *Willie Horton: True Crime and Its Influence on a Presidential Election* (Lawrence, MA: Horton Book, 1989). See also an ad used against Dukakis during the presidential campaign, accessed May 13, 2010, http://www.bing.com/videos/watch/video/willie-horton-1988/17wtoya40.

8. Manuel Valdes, "Huckabee Commuted Sentence of Seattle Suspect," *Washington Times*, November 30, 2009, accessed May 13, 2010, http://www.washingtontimes.com/news/2009/nov/30/4-police-officers-killed-in-coffee-shop-ambush.

9. CNN, "Fourth Oakland Police Officer Dies after Weekend Shooting," CNN.com/Crime, March 24, 2009, accessed May 13, 2010, http://www.cnn.com/2009/CRIME/03/24/oakland.police.shooting.

10. See "Serial Murders," *New York Times*, May 13, 2010, accessed May 13, 2010, http://topics.nytimes.com/topics/reference/timestopics/subjects/s/serial_murders/index.html?query=PROBATION%20AND%20PAROLE&field=des&match=exact.

11. American Probation and Parole Association, "Probation and Parole Frequently Asked Questions," *APPA* (2009), accessed May 3, 2017, https://www.appa-net.org/eweb/DynamicPage.aspx?WebCode=VB_FAQ.

12. Paula M. Ditton and Doris James Wilson, *Truth in Sentencing in State Prisons*, Bureau of Justice Statistics Special Report, U.S. Department of Justice, Office of Justice Programs, January 1999, accessed May 12, 2010, http://bjs.ojp.usdoj.gov/content/pub/pdf/tssp.pdf.

13. Ibid.

14. Caitlin Curley, "Truth in Sentencing: Why America Locks People Up and Throws Away the Key," *GenFKD*, December 17, 2015, accessed May 3, 2017, http://www.genfkd.org/truth-in-sentencing-america-america-locks-people-up-throws-away-key-16856-2.

15. Adam Gelb, Karla Dhungana, Benjamin Adams, Ellen McCann, and Kathryn Zafft, *Max Out: The Rise in Prison Inmates Released without Supervision*, The Pew Charitable Trusts, June 2014, accessed May 3, 2017, http://www.pewtrusts.org/~/media/assets/2014/06/04/maxout_report.pdf.

16. Amy L. Solomon, Vera Kachnowski, and Avinash Bhati (March 31, 2005) Does Parole Work? Washington, DC: Urban Institute. Accessed May 12, 2010: http://www.urban.org/UploadedPDF/311156_Does_Parole_Work.pdf.

17. Gelb, et al., op cit.

18. Danielle Kaeble and Lauren Glaze, *Correctional Populations in the United States, 2015*, Bureau of Justice Statistics, 2016, accessed May 3, 2017, https://www.bjs.gov/content/pub/pdf/cpus15.pdf.

19. Ibid.

20. "Reentry Trends in the U.S.: Releases from State Prisons," Bureau of Justice Statistics, May 3, 2017, accessed May 3, 2017, https://www.bjs.gov/content/reentry/releases.cfm.

21. Ditton and Wilson, op. cit., 2.

22. John Augustus, *A Report of the Labors of John Augustus, for the Last Ten Years, in the Aid of the Unfortunate* (Boston: Wright & Hasty, Printers, 1852), 4–5. Reprinted as *John Augustus, First Probation Officer* (New York: National Probation Association, 1939).

23. Augustus, *First Probation Officer*, 40–41.

24. Clemens Bartollas, *Introduction to Corrections* (New York: Harper & Row, 1981), 148.

25. David J. Rothman, *Conscience and Convenience: The Asylum and Its Alternatives in Progressive America* (Boston: Little, Brown, 1980), 85.

26. Danielle Kaeble and Thomas P. Bonczar, *Probation and Parole in the United States, 2015*, Bureau of Justice Statistics, December 2016, accessed May 3, 2017, https://www.bjs.gov/content/pub/pdf/ppus15.pdf.

27. For historical developments of parole see Harry Elmer Barnes and Negley Teeters, *New Horizons in Criminology*, 2nd ed. (New York: Probation-Hall, 1951); Frederick Moran, "The Origins of Parole," *NPPA Yearbook* (1954): 71–98; Charles Newman, *Sourcebook on Probation, Parole and Pardons*, 2nd ed. (Springfield, IL: Charles C. Thomas, 1964); Sol Rubin, Henry Weihofen, George Edwards, and Simon Rosenzweig, *The Law of Criminal Corrections* (St. Paul, MN: West, 1963), Chap. 11.

28. Barnes and Teeters, op. cit., 351.

29. Ibid., 549ff.

30. Patrick R. Anderson, "Zebulon Brockway (1827–1920)" in *Encyclopedia of American Prisons*, eds. Marilyn D. McShane and Frank P. Williams III (New York: Garland, 1996), 65–66.

31. Richard P. Seiter, *Corrections: An Introduction*, 3rd ed. (Upper Saddle River, NJ: Prentice Hall, 2011).

32. Christian Henrichson and Ruth Delaney, "The Price of Prisons: What Incarceration Cost Taxpayers," The Vera Institute, July 20, 2012, accessed May 3, 2017, http://archive.vera.org/sites/default/files/resources/downloads/price-of-prisons-updated-version-021914.pdf.

33. Ibid.

34. Sean Gorman, "Sanders Says It Costs More to Go to Prison than to the University of Virginia," *Politifact Virginia*, November 23, 2015, accessed May 4, 2017, http://www.politifact.com/virginia/statements/2015/nov/23/bernie-s/sanders-says-it-costs-more-send-person-prison-univ/.

35. "Harvard at a Glance," Harvard University, 2017, accessed May 4, 2017, http://www.harvard.edu/about-harvard/harvard-glance.

36. Henrichson and Delaney, op. cit.

37. Kelsey Warner, "These States Have Highest Cost Per Prisoner," InsideGov, April 28, 2016, accessed May 4, 2017, http://political-issues.insidegov.com/stories/13011/states-highest-cost-per-prisoner.

38. James Austin, Wendy Naro, and Tony Fabelo, *Public Safety, Public Spending: Forecasting America's Prison Population 2007–2011*, Public Safety Performance, A Project of the PEW Charitable

Trusts, revised June 2007, 22, accessed May 14, 2010, http://www.pewtrusts.org/uploadedFiles/www pewtrustsorg/Reports/State-based_policy/PSPP_prison_projections_0207.pdf.

39. Sadhbh Walshe, "Probation and Parole: A Study in Criminal Justice Dysfunction," *The Guardian*, April 26, 2010, accessed May 4, 2017, https://www.theguardian.com/commentisfree/cifamerica/2012/apr/26/probation-parole-study-dysfunction.

40. Susan Urahn, et al., *One in 31: The Long Reach of Corrections*, The PEW Center on the States, March 2009, accessed May 15, 2010, http://www.pewcenteronthestates.org/uploadedFiles/PSPP_1in31_report_FINAL_WEB_3-26-09.pdf.

41. James Bonta and Paul Gendreau, "Re-examining the Cruel and Unusual Punishment of Prison Life," *Law and Human Behavior* 14 (1990): 347–372.

42. Erving Goffman, *Asylums* (Garden City: Anchor, 1961).

43. See Bureau of Justice Statistics, *Examining Recidivism*, Special Report NC5-96501 (Washington, DC: U.S. Department of Justice, 1985).

44. U.S. Department of Justice, Bureau of Justice Statistics, *Special Report* (Washington, DC: U.S. Government Printing Office, 1993), 3.

45. Jessica Mitford, "Mitford's Quibbles," *Time*, October 15, 1973, accessed May 10, 2010, http://www.time.com/time/magazine/article/0,9171,910775-2,00.html.

46. Henrichson and Delaney, op. cit.

47. Joshua A. Markman, Matthew R. Durose, Ramona R. Rantala, and Andrew D. Tiedt, *Recidivism of Offenders Placed on Federal Community Supervision in 2005: Patterns from 2005 to 2010*, Bureau of Justice Statistics, 2016, accessed May 4, 2017, https://www.bjs.gov/content/pub/pdf/ropfcs05p0510.pdf.

48. Ibid.

49. Kaeble and Bonczar, op. cit.

50. *Crime in the United States Table 33: Ten-Year Arrest Trends*, FBI: UCR, 2015, accessed May 4, 2017, https://ucr.fbi.gov/crime-in-the-u.s/2015/crime-in-the-u.s.-2015/tables/table-33.

51. Lauren E. Glaze and Thomas P. Bonczar (November 2011) Probation and Parole in the. United States, 2010, Bureau of Justice Statistics, accessed January 22, 2018, https://www.bjs.gov/content/pub/pdf/ppus10.pdf

52. Latessa, op. cit.

53. See Mark Cuniff and Mary K. Shilton, *Variations on Felony Probation: Persons under Supervision in Thirty-Two Urban and Suburban Counties* (Washington, DC: Criminal Justice Planners Association, 1991). Also see D. Wayne Osgood and Ineke Haen Marshall, "Criminal Careers in the Short-Term: Intra-individual Variability in Crime and Its Relation to Local Life Circumstances," *American Sociological Review* (October 1995).

54. Joan Petersilia, Susan Turner, James Kahan, and Joyce Peterson, *Granting Felons Probation* (Santa Monica, CA: Rand Corporation, 1985).

55. Bureau of Justice Statistics, *Examining Recidivism.*

56. Glaze, op. cit., 3.

57. Jackie Rothenberg, ("For State Prisons, West Isn't Best," *ABA Journal* (December 1, 2009), accessed May 16, 2010, http://www.abajournal.com/magazine/article/for_state_prisons_west_isnt_best/; See also "Alternatives to Incarceration Fact Sheet," Families Against Mandatory Minimums (FAMM), July 30, 2009, accessed May 16, 2010, http://www.famm.org/Repository/Files/Alternatives%20in%20a%20Nutshell%207.30.09%5B1%5DFINAL.pdf; John Gramlich, "States Seek Alternatives to More Prisons," State Policy and Politics, June 18, 2007, accessed May 16, 2010, http://www.stateline.org/live/details/story?contentId=217204.

58. Kaeble and Glaze, op. cit.

59. Risdon N. Slate, Erik Roskes, Richard Feldman, and Migdalia Baerga, "Doing Justice for Mental Illness and Society: Federal Probation and Pretrial Services Officers as Mental Health Specialists," *Federal Probation* 67 no. 3 (December 2003): 13–19.

60. American Probation and Parole Association, op. cit.

61. *Report of the Re-Entry Policy Council: Charting the Safe and Successful Return of Prisoners to the Community*, Council of State Governments, Reentry Policy Council, (New York: Council of State Governments, January 2005), accessed May 15, 2010, http://reentrypolicy.org/Report/PartII/Chapter II-E/PolicyStatement26/ResearchHighlight26-2.

62. Slate, et al., *Doing Justice*, op. cit.

63. Risdon N. Slate, Richard Feldman, Erik Roskes, and Migdalia Baerga, "Training Federal Probation Officers as Mental Health Specialists," *Federal Probation* 68, no. 3 (December 2004): 9–15.

64. Matthew G. Yeager, "Client-Specific Planning: A Status Report," *Criminal Justice Abstracts* (Washington, DC: National Criminal Justice Reference Service, 1992), 537–549.

65. Belinda R. McCarthy and Bernard J. McCarthy, "Contemporary Trends in Community Corrections: The Re-examination of Community Based Corrections," (New York: John Jay College of Criminal Justice, August 23, 1996, on-line); Billie S. Erwin, "Tools for the Modern Probation Officer," *Crime and Delinquency* 36 (1990): 87–111. See also, generally, Belinda Rogers McCarthy and Bernard J. McCarthy, *Community-Based Corrections* (Pacific Grove, CA: Brooks/Cole, 1991).

66. Travis, op. cit., 110; See also Doris L. MacKenzie,. *What Works in Corrections: Reducing the Criminal Activities of Offenders and Delinquents* (Cambridge: Cambridge University Press, 2006).

67. James M. Byrne and Karin Tusinski Miofsky, "From Preentry to Reentry: An Examination of the Effectiveness of Institutional and Community-Based Sanctions," *Victims & Offenders: Journal of Evidenced Based Policies and Practices* 4, no. 4 (2009), 348–356.

68. Erwin, op. cit., 2.

69. James M. Byrne, Arthur J. Lurigio, and Christopher Baird, "The Effectiveness of the New Intensive Supervision Program," *Research in Corrections* 2 (1989): 11.

70. See David E. Duffee and Edmund F. McGarrell, eds., *Community Corrections: A Community Field Approach* (Washington, DC: Bureau of Justice Statistics, 1990).

71. Marc Renzema, "Home Confinement Programs, Development, Implementation, and Impact," in *Smart Sentencing: The Emergence of Intermediate Sanctions*, eds. James M. Byrne, Arthur J. Lurigio, and Joan Petersilia (Newbury Park, CA: Sage, 1992), 42.

72. "House Arrest System Misfires," *The Ledger*, January 4, 2003, accessed May 15, 2010, http://www.theledger.com/article/20030104/NEWS/301040441?p=1&tc=pg.

73. Scott Vollum, "Electronic Monitoring: A Research Review," *Corrections Compendium* July 1, 2002, accessed May 16, 2010, http://www.allbusiness.com/public-administration/justice-public-order/906228-1.html.

74. Latessa, op. cit., 283.

75. Justin W. Patchin and Gary N. Keveles, Northwest Wisconsin Criminal Justice Management Conference, November 12, 2004, accessed May 16, 2010, http://www.uwex.edu/ces/flp/families/alternativestojailsresearchreview.pdf.

76. Ann H. Crowe, Linda Sydney, Pat Bancroft, and Beverly Lawrence, *Offender's Supervision with Electronic Technology: A User's Guide*, American Probation and Parole Association, October 29, 2002, accessed May 16, 2010, http://www.ncjrs.gov/pdffiles1/nij/grants/197102.pdf.

77. International Association of Chiefs of Police and the American Probation and Parole Association, Bureau of Justice Assistance, August 2008, accessed: May 16, 2010, http://www.ojp.usdoj.gov/BJA/pdf/IACPSexOffenderElecMonitoring.pdf.

78. "Global Positioning and Radio Frequency," Florida Department of Corrections, May 2006, accessed May 15, 2010, http://www.dc.state.fl.us/pub/gpsrf/2005/progtypes.html; Elise Castelli, "Global Positioning to Track Sex Offenders," *The Boston Globe*, September 21, 2004, accessed May 15, 2010, http://www.boston.com/news/local/articles/2004/09/21/global_positioning_to_track_sex_offenders; "Global Positioning Satellite (GPS) Monitoring," State of South Carolina Department of Probation, Parole, and Pardon Services, accessed May 15, 2010, http://www.dppps.sc.gov/ GPSMonitoring.html; *Monitoring Tennessee's Sex Offenders Using Global Positioning Systems: A Project Evaluation*, Tennessee Board of Probation and Parole in Conjunction with Middle Tennessee State University Department of Criminal Justice Administration, April 2007, accessed May 15, 2010, http://www.tn.gov/bopp/Press%20Releases/BOPP%20GPS%20Program%20Evaluation,% 20April%202007.pdf.

79. The Pew Charitable Trusts, "Use of Electronic Offender-Tracking Devices Expands Sharply," September 30, 2016, accessed May 4, 2017, http://www.pewtrusts.org/~/media/assets/2016/10/use_of_electronic_offender_tracking_devices_expands_sharply.pdf.

80. McCarthy and McCarthy, *Community-Based Corrections*, 126–127.

81. See Terry L. Baumer and Robert I. Mendelsohn, *The Electronic Monitoring of Non-Violent Convicted Felons: An Experiment in Home Detention* (Indianapolis: Indiana University School of Public and Environmental Affairs, 1990).

82. MacKenzie, op. cit.

83. Jaime E. Muscar, "Advocating the End of Juvenile Boot Camps: Why the Military Model Does Not Belong in the Juvenile Justice System," *UC Davis Journal of Juvenile Law and Policy* 12, no. 1 (Winter, 2008).

84. Douglas C. McDonald, *Restitution and Community Service* (Washington, DC: U.S. Government Printing Office, 1988).

85. James M. Byrne, Arthur J. Lurigio, and Joan M. Petersilia, eds., *Smart Sentencing: The Emergence of Intermediate Sanctions* (Newbury Park, CA: Sage, 1992).

86. Kaeble and Bonczar, op. cit.

87. Laura E. Bedard, "Making a Difference: Managing the Female Offender Population," CorrectionsOne, July 1, 2008, accessed May 17, 2010, http://www.correctionsone.com/corrections/articles/1842846-Making-a-difference-Managing-the-female-offender-population.

88. Uniform Crime Reports, *Crime in the United States, Table 33*, U.S. Department of Justice, Federal Bureau of Investigation, Washington, DC, 2008, accessed on May 17, 2010, http://www.fbi.gov/ucr/cius2008/data/table_33.html.

89. Howard N. Snyder, *Arrest in the United States, 1990–2010*, Bureau of Justice Statistics, 2012, accessed May 4, 2017, https://www.bjs.gov/content/pub/pdf/aus9010.pdf.

90. Paul Vercammen and Faith Karimi, O.J. Simpson Out of Nevada Prison After 9 Years, Plans to Stay in Vegas, *CNN*, October 2, 2017, accessed October 4, 2017, http://www.cnn.com/2017/10/01/us/oj-simpson-released-from-prison/index.html.

91. Associated Press, "Nevada's Conditions for O.J. Simpson's Life Outside Prison, *Chicago Tribune*, October 1, 2017, accessed October 4, 2017, http://www.chicagotribune.com/news/sns-bc-us-oj-simpson-release-conditions-glance-20171001-story.html.

92. *Griffin v. Wisconsin*, 483 U.S. 868 (1987).

93. *U.S. v. Knights*, 534 U.S. 12 (2001).

94. *Samson v. California*, 547 U.S. 843 (2006).

95. Rachael A. Lynch, "Two Wrongs Don't Make a Fourth Amendment Right: *Samson* Court Errs in Choosing Proper Analytical Framework, Errs in Result, Parolees Lose Fourth Amendment Protection," *Akron L. Rev.* 41 (July 2015): 651, 2008.

96. Risdon N. Slate and Patrick R. Anderson (September 1996) Lying Probationers and Parolees: The Issue of Polygraph Surveillance, Federal Probation, Vol. 60(3), 54–59.

97. Ibid.

98. American Law Institute, Model Penal Code, proposed official draft (Philadelphia: American Law Institute, 1962), Sec. 305.16.

99. National Advisory Commission, *Corrections*, Standard 5.4, 158.

100. Madeline M. Carter, *Responding to Parole and Probation Violations: A Handbook to Guide Local Policy Development*, U.S. Department of Justice, National Institute of Corrections, April 2001, accessed July 22, 2010, http://nicic.gov/pubs/2001/016858.pdf.

101. *Morrissey v. Brewer*, 408 U.S. 471 (1972).

102. American Law Institute, op. cit., Sec. 305.16.

103. Megan's Law, Sex Offenders Nationwide, Registered Sex Offenders Resources, accessed July 22, 2010, http://megans-law.net.

104. See William Glaberson, "Man at Heart of Megan's Law Convicted of Her Grisly Murder," *New York Times*, May 31, 1997, accessed July 22, 2010, http://www.nytimes.com/1997/05/31/nyregion/man-at-heart-of-megan-s-law-convicted-of-her-grisly-murder.html.

105. National Conference of State Legislatures, "Felon Voting Rights," September 29, 2016, accessed May 4, 2017, http://www.ncsl.org/research/elections-and-campaigns/felon-voting-rights.aspx.

106. Robert Farley, "Gov. Charlie Christ Will Pursue Pardon for Jim Morrison," *St. Petersburg Times*, November 16, 2010, accessed November 23, 2010, http://www.tampabay.com/features/music/article1134661.ece; Brendan Farrington and Suzette Laboy, "Fla. Pardons Morrison for Indecent Exposure," *The Ledger*, December 10, 2010, A1; A10.

107. Henrichson and Delaney, op. cit.

Chapter 12

1. Bill Adler, *The World According to Martha* (New York: McGraw Hill, 2006), 141, 148, 150, 151, 152.

2. Hans Jochen Boecker, *Law and the Administration of Justice in the Old Testament and Ancient East*, trans. Jeremy Moiser (Minneapolis, MN: Augsburg, 1980).

3. John H. Langbein, "The Historical Origins of the Sanction of Imprisonment for Serious Crime," *Journal of Legal Studies* 5 (1976): 35–60; Graeme R. Newman, "Theories of Punishment Reconsidered: Rationalizations for Removal," *International Journal of Criminology and Penology* 3 (1975): 180.

4. Edward Gibbon, Ancient History Sourcebook, "The Idea of Roman Jurisprudence," accessed May 8, 2010, http://www.fordham.edu/halsall/ancient/gibbon-chap44.html; Bryan Hill (July 19, 2015) "The Infamous Mamertine Prison and the Supposed Incarceration of Saint Peter," accessed October 2, 2017, http://www.ancient-origins.net/ancient-places-europe/infamous-mamertine-prison-and-supposed-incarceration-saint-peter-003447.

5. Daniel R. Coquillette, "The Lessons of Anglo-Saxon 'Justice,'" *The Green Bag: An Entertaining Journal of Law* 2 (Spring, 1991): 251; Katherine Fischer Drew, "The Development of Law in Classical and Early Medieval Europe: Public vs. Private Enforcement of the Law in the Early Middle Ages: Fifth to Twelfth Centuries," *Chicago-Kent Law Review* 70 (1995): 1583.

6. Victor Duruy, *The History of the Middle Ages*, 12th ed., trans. E. H. and M. D. Whitney (New York: Henry Holt and Co., 1891).

7. Michael Welch, *Corrections: A Critical Approach*, 2nd ed. (New York: McGraw Hill, 1993).

8. See Langbein op. cit.; Welch, op. cit.

9. Welch, op. cit., 42, 43.

10. Brian C. Kalt, "The Exclusion of Felons from Jury Service," *American University Law Review* 53, no. 1 (October 2003): 171.

11. David J. Rothman, *The Discovery of the Asylum* (Boston: Little, Brown, 1971), 79, 81.

12. Welch, op. cit., 45.

13. Ibid.

14. See Welch, op. cit.; Ruth E. Masters, *CJ: Realities and Challenges* (New York: McGraw-Hill, 2011).

15. See E. C. Hines (ed.), Transactions of the National Congress on Penitentiary and Reformatory Discipline (Albany, NY: Argus, 1871); Welch, op. cit., 49, 50.

16. Welch, op. cit., 26.

17. See Donald J. Newman, "Critique of Prison Building," *New England Journal on Prison Law* 8, no. 1 (1982): 121–139.

18. Richard P. Seiter, *Corrections: An Introduction*, 3rd ed. (Upper Saddle, NJ: Prentice-Hall, 2011).

19. Brian Kincade, "The Economics of the American Prison System," SmartAsset, February 3, 2017, accessed May 5, 2017, https://smartasset.com/mortgage/the-economics-of-the-american-prison-system.

20. E. Ann Carson and Elizabeth Anderson, *Prisoners in 2015*, Bureau of Justice Statistics, 2016, accessed May 5, 2017, https://www.bjs.gov/content/pub/pdf/p15.pdf.

21. The Sentencing Project, "Fact Sheet: Trends in U.S. Corrections," December 2015, accessed February 11, 2017, http://sentencingproject.org/wp-content/uploads/2016/01/Trends-in-US-Corrections.pdf.

22. Bureau of Justice Statistics, *Correctional Populations in the United States, 1988* (Washington, DC: U.S. Department of Justice, March 1991).

23. Kincade, op. cit.

24. James Austin and Garry Coventry, *Emerging Issues in Privatized Prisons*, National Council on Crime and Delinquency, U.S. Department of Justice, Office of Justice Programs, Bureau of Justice Assistance, February 2001, accessed May 5, 2010, http://www.ncjrs.gov/pdffiles1/bja/181249.pdf.

25. Bureau of Justice Statistics, "Summary: Prisoners in 2015," December 2016, accessed May 5, 2017, https://www.bjs.gov/content/pub/pdf/p15_sum.pdf.

26. Carson and Anderson, op. cit.

27. CCA (Corrections Corporation of America), "Investor Relations, Corporate Profile," accessed May 5, 2010, http://ir.correctionscorp.com/phoenix.zhtml?c=117983&p=irol-irhome.

28. Clifford J. Levy, "Prison Company's Courtship Provokes New York's Scrutiny," *New York Times*, February 17, 2003, accessed May 5, 2010, http://www.nytimes.com/2003/02/17/nyregion/17PRIS.html?pagewanted=1.

29. Ibid., 159.

30. Seiter, op. cit., 337.

31. Schmelzer, E. (Sept. 27, 2017). Wyoming inmates train mustangs, learn life lessons. *Capital Press*. Retrieved from http://www.capitalpress.com/Horses/20170927/wyoming-inmates-train-mustangs-learn-life-lessons.

32. Carson and Anderson, op. cit.

33. Lauren E. Glaze and Erinn J. Herberman, *Correctional Populations in the United States, 2012*, Bureau of Justice Statistics, December 2013, accessed May 5, 2017, https://www.bjs.gov/content/pub/pdf/cpus12.pdf.

34. The PEW Center on the States, "Prison Count 2010: State Population Declines for the First Time in 38 Years," revised April 2010, accessed May 5, 2017, http://www.pewtrusts.org/~/media/legacy/uploadedfiles/wwwpewtrustsorg/reports/sentencing_and_corrections/prisoncount2010pdf.pdf.

35. Carson and Anderson, op. cit.

36. Bureau of Justice Statistics (December 2016) "Prisoners in 2015," accessed October 3, 2017, https://www.bjs.gov/content/pub/pdf/p15_sum.pdf.

37. Judith Greene, Kevin Pranis, and Natasha A. Frost (2006) "Hard Hit: The Growth in the Imprisonment of Women, National Criminal Justice Reference Service, accessed October 3, 2017, https://www.ncjrs.gov/App/publications/abstract.aspx?ID=238811.

38. Carson and Anderson, op. cit.

39. Bureau of Justice Statistics (December 2016) op. cit.

40. Ibid.

41. Carson and Anderson, op. cit.

42. Bureau of Justice Statistics (December 2016) op. cit.

43. Carson and Anderson, op. cit.

44. U.S. Census Bureau, "Quick Facts United States," 2015, accessed May 4, 2017, https://www.census.gov/quickfacts/table/PST045216/00.

45. Carson and Anderson, op. cit.

46. Ibid.

47. Ibid.

48. Ibid.

49. Lois M. Davis, Jennifer L. Steele, Robert Bozick, Malcolm V. Williams, Susan Turner, Jeremy N. V. Miles, Jessica Saunders, and Paul S. Steinberg, "How Effective Is Correctional Education, and Where Do We Go from Here?" Rand Corporation, 2014, accessed May 7, 2017, http://www.rand.org/content/dam/rand/pubs/research_reports/RR500/RR564/RAND_RR564.pdf; Christopher Zoukis, "Inmate Education Levels," Prison Education.com, June 30, 2015, http://www.prisoneducation.com/prison-research-papers/inmate-education-levels/; Evan Horowitz, "What Are Your Chances of Going to Prison?" *Boston Globe*, March 19, 2015, accessed May 7, 2017, https://www.bostonglobe.com/metro/2015/03/19/what-are-chances-going-prison/n3g84nR4kJriEwM8nbT6ML/story.html.

50. Carson and Anderson, op. cit.

51. Danielle Kaeble and Lauren Glaze, (December 2016) "Correctional Populations in the United States 2015," Bureau of Justice Statistics, accessed October 3, 2017, https://www.bjs.gov/content/pub/pdf/cpus15.pdf.

52. Carson and Anderson, op. cit.

53. Ibid.

54. Ibid.

55. Carson and Anderson, op. cit.; Sourcebook of Criminal Justice Statistics Online, "Rate (per 100,000 Resident Population) of Sentenced Prisoners under Jurisdiction of State and Federal Correctional Authorities on December 31, by Region and Jurisdiction 1980, 1984–2012," accessed May 5, 2017, http://www.albany.edu/sourcebook/pdf/t6292012.pdf.

56. Christian Henrichson and Ruth Delaney, *The Price of Prisons: What Incarceration Cost Taxpayers*, The Vera Institute, July 20, 2012, accessed May 3, 2017, http://archive.vera.org/sites/default/files/resources/downloads/price-of-prisons-updated-version-021914.pdf.

57. Joshua A. Markman, Matthew R. Durose, Ramona R. Rantala, and Andrew D. Tiedt, *Recidivism of Offenders Placed on Federal Community Supervision in 2005: Patterns from 2005 to 2010*, Bureau of Justice Statistics, 2016, accessed May 4, 2017, https://www.bjs.gov/content/pub/pdf/ropfcs05p0510.pdf.

58. James S. Vacca, "Educated Prisoners Are Less Likely to Return to Prison," *Journal of Correctional Education,* December 2004, accessed May 6, 2010, http://findarticles.com/p/articles/mi_qa4111/is_200412/ai_n9466371.

59. Carson and Anderson, op. cit.

60. Aimee Picchi, "The High Price of Incarceration in America," CBS News, 2014, accessed May 4, 2017, http://www.cbsnews.com/news/the-high-price-of-americas-incarceration-80-billion/.

61. Vera Institute of Justice, *The Price of Prisons: Examining State Spending Trends 2010–2015,* accessed October 3, 2017, https://www.vera.org/publications/price-of-prisons-2015-state-spending-trends/price-of-prisons-2015-state-spending-trends/price-of-prisons-2015-state-spending-trends-from-the-director.

62. Vera Institute of Justice, *The Price of Prisons: What Incarceration Costs Taxpayers,* Center on Sentencing and Corrections, 2012, accessed April 4, 2017, https://storage.googleapis.com/vera-web-assets/downloads/Publications/the-price-of-prisons-what-incarceration-costs-taxpayers/legacy_downloads/price-of-prisons-updated-version-021914.pdf.

63. Danielle DeCourcey, ("The U.S. Values Prison More Than Education," *attn.com,* August 31, 2016, accessed May 7, 2017; Vera Institute of Justice, *The Price of Prisons: What Incarceration Costs Taxpayers,* Center on Sentencing and Corrections, 2012, assessed April 4, 2017, from https://storage.googleapis.com/vera-web-assets/downloads/Publications/the-price-of-prisons-what-incarceration-costs-taxpayers/legacy_downloads/price-of-prisons-updated-version-021914.pdf.

64. Susan Urahn, et al., *One in 31: The Long Reach of Corrections,* The PEW Center on the States, March 2009, accessed May 7, 2010, http://www.pewcenteronthestates.org/uploadedFiles/PSPP_1in31_report_FINAL_WEB_3-26-09.pdf.

65. Linh Vuong, Christopher Hartney, Barry Krisberg, and Susan Marchionna, *The Extravagance of Imprisonment Revisited, Special Report: Views from the National Council on Delinquency,* January 2010, accessed May 7, 2010, http://www.nccd-crc.org/nccd/dnld/Home/focus0110%20.pdf.

66. Gresham Sykes, *Society of Captives* (Princeton, NJ: Princeton University Press, 1958). Also see Edward Zamble and Frank J. Porporino, *Coping, Behavior, and Adaptation in Prison Inmates* (Secaucus, NJ: Springer-Verlag, 1988).

67. Jonathan Abrams, "Consultants Are Providing High-Profile Inmates a Game Plan for Coping," *New York Times,* October 10, 2009, accessed May 8, 2010, http://www.nytimes.com/2009/10/11/sports/11consultants.html?_r=1; Larry Levine, Wall Street Prison Consultants, accessed May 8, 2010, http://wallstreetprisonconsultants.com.

68. Sykes, op. cit.; See also, for example, John Irwin, *The Felon* (Englewood Cliffs, NJ: Prentice-Hall, 1970).

69. Gresham Sykes and Sheldon L. Messinger, "Inmate Social System," in *Theoretical Studies in the Social Organization of the Prison* (New York: Social Science Research Council Pamphlet 15, 1960), 14–15.

70. Todd R. Clear and George F. Cole, *American Corrections,* 6th ed. (Belmont, CA: Wadsworth/Thomson, 2003), 347, 348—the authors do note that "the Higher Education Act's 'Grants Program' for Youthful Offenders" with less than five years to serve does allow educational grants for inmates under age 25.

71. Shoshana Walter, "James Bain Freed after DNA Evidence Clears Him," *The Ledger,* December 17, 2009, accessed May 11, 2010, http://www.theledger.com/article/20091217/NEWS/912175058/1410?Title=James-Bain-Freed-After-DNA-Evidence-Clears-Him.

72. See, especially, Donald Clemmer, *The Prison Community,* rev. ed. (New York: Holt, Rinehart and Winston, 1958); Gresham Sykes, op. cit.; Donald R. Cressey (ed.), *The Prison: Studies in Institutional Organization and Change* (New York: Holt, Rinehart and Winston, 1961); and John Irwin and Donald R. Cressey, "Thieves, Convicts and the Inmate Culture," *Social Problems* 10 (1962): 143–155.

73. Tom Murton, "Playboy Interview," in John J. Bonsignore, et al., *Before the Law: An Introduction to the Legal Process*, 2nd ed. (Boston: Houghton Mifflin, 1979), 382.

74. Dennis A. Challeen, *Making It Right: A Common Sense Approach to Criminal Justice* (Aberdeen, SD: Melius and Peterson Publishing Corporation, 1986), 38, 39.

75. Erving Goffman, *Asylums* (Garden City, NY: Anchor Press, 1961).

76. Seiter, op. cit., 366, reports that six states, Washington, New York, New Mexico, Mississippi, Connecticut, and California, allow conjugal visits whereby married couples may engage in sexual relations.

77. *Procunier v. Martinez*, 416 U.S. 396 (1974).

78. *Ruffin v. Commonwealth of Virginia*, 62 Va. 790; 1871 Va. LEXIS 89; 21 Gratt. 790 (1871).

79. See Rolando del Carmen, *Briefs of Leading Cases in Corrections* (Cincinnati: Anderson Publishing, 1993). Also see, generally, Note, "Beyond the Ken of the Courts: A Critique of Judicial Refusal to Review the Complaints of Convicts," *Yale Law Journal* 72 (1963): 506; and Note, "Constitutional Rights of Prisoners: The Developing Law," *University of Pennsylvania Law Review* 110 (1962): 985.

80. *Hudson v. Palmer*, 468 U.S. 517 (1984).

81. The Sentencing Project, *Felony Disenfranchisement Laws in the United States*, September 2008, accessed May 9, 2010, http://www.sentencingproject.org/doc/publications/fd_bs_fdlawsinusMarch2010.pdf; they estimate that 5.3 million adults "have currently or permanently lost their voting rights as the result of a felony conviction."

82. See Note, "Judicial Intervention in Corrections: The California Experience—An Empirical Study," *U.C.L.A. Law Review* 20 (1973): 452. See also Fred Cohen, *Legal Norms in Corrections* (Consultant Paper, President's Task Force on Corrections, 1967), and Edward L. Kimball and Donald J. Newman, "Judicial Intervention in Correctional Decisions: Threat and Response," *Journal of Research on Crime and Delinquency* 14 (1968): 1.

83. *Cooper v. Pate*, 378 U.S. 546 (1964); Seiter, op. cit., 459. It should be noted that the practice of Satanism could conceivably be allowed in prison under the First Amendment's free exercise of religion clause as long as no legitimate penological interests are infringed upon—see *Howard v. United States*, 864 F.Supp. 1019 (1994); *McCorkle v. Johnson*, 881 F.2d 993 (1989).

84. Murton, op. cit., 382.

85. *Holt v. Sarver*, 300 F. Supp. 825 (1969).

86. *Holt v. Sarver II*, 309 F. Supp. 362 (1970).

87. Derek Hawkins, "An Inmate Died after Being Locked in a Scalding Shower for Two Hours. His Guards Won't Be Charged," *Washington Post*, March 20, 2017, accessed May 10, 2017, https://www.washingtonpost.com/news/morning-mix/wp/2017/03/20/an-inmate-died-after-being-locked-in-a-scalding-shower-for-two-hours-his-guards-wont-be-charged/?utm_term=.5d2001b4c109.

88. See Fred Cohen, "The Law of Prisoners' Rights: An Overview," *Criminal Law Bulletin* 24, no. 4 (July–August 1988): 321–349. Also see South Carolina Department of Corrections, *The Emerging Rights of the Confined* (Columbia: South Carolina Department of Corrections, 1972). See also Richard G. Singer, *Prisoners' Legal Rights: A Bibliography of Cases and Articles* (Boston: Warren, Gorham and Lamont, 1971).

89. Leanne F. Alarid and Philip L. Reichel, *Corrections: A Contemporary Introduction* (Boston, MA: Pearson, 2008), 400.

90. Ibid., 401.

91. Rolando del Carmen, *Briefs of Leading Cases in Corrections* (Cincinnati: Anderson Publishing, 1993). See also Rolando V. del Carmen, *Civil Liabilities in American Policing: A Text for Law Enforcement Personnel* (Englewood Cliffs, NJ: Brady/Prentice-Hall, 1991), 177–206. But for a recent exception see *Hudson v. McMillian* 60 *U.S. Law Week* 4151 (1992): 177–206.

92. *Turner v. Safely*, 482 U.S. 78 (1987).

93. The Prison Litigation Reform Act (PLRA) (1996), accessed May 9, 2010, http://www.aclu.org/images/asset_upload_file79_25805.pdf; David Crary, "Law Curbing Inmates' Lawsuits Questioned," *USA Today*, February 13, 2008, accessed May 9, 2010, http://www.usatoday.com/news/nation/2008-02-13-3685431048_x.htm.

94. Edward J. Latessa and Paula Smith, *Corrections in the Community*, 4th ed. (Cincinnati, OH: Anderson Publishing, 2007), 154—Legislatures in just about every state make some provisions for good-time reductions in sentences based on good behavior while incarcerated, or for participation in and completion of specified treatment or educational programs.

95. Margaret E. Noonan, *Mortality in State Prisons, 2001–2014-Statistical Tables*, Bureau of Justice Statistics, 2016, accessed May 5, 2017, https://www.bjs.gov/content/pub/pdf/msp0114st.pdf.

96. *Landman v. Royster*, 333 F. Supp. 1104 (E.D. Pa. 1974).

97. *Wolff v. McDonnell*, 418 U.S. 539 (1974).

98. Ibid., 555, 556.

99. *Baxter v. Palmigiano*, 425 U.S. 308 (1976).

100. *Ponte v. Real*, 37 CrL 3051 (1985).

101. *Cleavinger v. Saxner*, 106 S.Ct. 496 (1985).

102. *Lee v. Washington*, 390 U.S. 333 (1968), 334; Risdon N. Slate, W. Wesley Johnson, and Craig Hemmens, "Racial Segregation as a Correctional Management Tool: Beyond *Lee v. Washington*," *Corrections Management Quarterly* 3, no. 3 (Summer 1999): 66–75, 66.

103. *Rhodes v. Chapman*, 452 U.S. 337 (1981).

104. Ibid.

105. See Patrick R. Anderson and C. Gary Pettigrew, "Effects of Doublebunking on Adult Male State Prisoners," *Corrective and Social Psychiatry* 32, no. 2 (April 1985): 46–54; and Selwyn Raab, "New York to Install 3,000 More Prison Beds," *New York Times*, December 8, 1991, 52.

106. *Ewing v. California*, 538 U.S. 11 (2003).

107. Editorial, "Justice Kennedy on Prisons," *New York Times*, February 15, 2010, accessed May 9, 2010, http://www.nytimes.com/2010/02/16/opinion/16tue3.html.

108. Bureau of Labor Statistics, "Local Area Unemployment Statistics," United States Department of Labor, March 2010, accessed May 9, 2010, http://www.bls.gov/lau/; Bureau of Labor Statistics, "News Release Regional and State Employment and Unemployment—March 2010," United States Department of Labor, April 16, 2010, accessed May 9, 2010, http://www.bls.gov/news.release/pdf/laus.pdf. Note, unemployment rates presented are seasonally adjusted rates. Puerto Rico reflected the highest unemployment rate at 16.2 and the District of Columbia had an unemployment rate of 11.6 percent. The other states with double-digit unemployment rates were California, Rhode Island, Florida, South Carolina, Alabama, Georgia, Illinois, Kentucky, Mississippi, North Carolina, Ohio, Oregon, and Tennessee.

109. *Estelle v. Gamble*, 97 S. Ct. 285 (1976).

110. *Bowring v. Godwin*, 351 F.2d 44 (4th Cir. 1977).

111. Steven F. Messner and Richard Rosenfeld, *Crime and the American Dream*, 4th ed. (Belmont, CA: Wadsworth, 2007), 106.

112. *Washington v. Harper*, 110 S. Ct. 1028 (1990).

113. Norval Morris, *The Future of Imprisonment* (Chicago: University of Chicago Press, 1974), 112.

114. National Advisory Commission on Criminal Justice Standards and Goals, *Corrections* (Washington, DC: U.S. Department of Justice, 1973), Standard 2.9(6), 45.

115. Rolando del Carmen, *Civil Liabilities in American Policing: A Text for Law Enforcement Personnel* (Englewood Cliffs: Brady/Prentice-Hall, 1991), 177–206. But for an exception, see *Hudson v. McMillian*, 60 *U.S. Law Week* 4151 (1992).

116. Attica: The Official Report of the New York Special Commission on Attica (New York: Bantam, 1972); See also Tom Wicker, A Time to Die (New York: Ballantine, 1975).

117. *Bounds v. Smith*, 430 U.S. 817 (1977).

118. *Gaines v. Lane*, 790 F. 2d. 1299 (7th Cir. 1986).

119. *Hooks v. Wainwright*, 775 F. 2d. 2433 (11th Cir. 1985), and *Johnson v. Avery*, 393 U.S. 483 (1969).

120. *Block v. Rutherford*, 104 S. Ct. 3227 (1984).

121. *Pell v. Procunier*, 417 U.S. 817 (1974), and *Houchins v. KQED*, 438 U.S. 1 (1978).

122. *Sostre v. Otis*, 330 F. Supp. 941 (1971); *Thornburg v. Abbott*, 109 S. Ct. 1874 (1989).

123. *Guajardo v. Estelle*, 580 F.2d 748 (1978).

124. See Virginia McArthur, "Inmate Grievance Mechanisms: A Survey of 209 American Prisons," *Federal Probation* 38 (1974): 41; Timothy L. Fitzharris, *The Desirability of a Correctional Ombudsman* (Berkeley: University of California, Institute of Governmental Studies, 1973); and David D. Dillingham and Linda R. Singer, *Complaint Procedures in Prisons and Jails: An Examination of Recent Experience* (Washington, DC: U.S. National Institute of Corrections, 1980).

125. Randy Martin and Sherwood Zimmerman, "A Typology of the Causes of Prison Riots and an Analytical Extension to the 1986 West Virginia Riot," *Justice Quarterly* 7, no. 4 (December 1990): 711–737.

126. Ronald Smothers, "1987 Cuban Riots Taught Both Sides," *New York Times*, August 27, 1991, accessed May 10, 2010, http://www.nytimes.com/1991/08/27/us/1987-cuban-riots-taught-both-sides.html.

127. Mike Rolland, Descent into Madness: An Inmate's Experience of the New Mexico State Prison Riot (Cincinnati, OH: Anderson Publishing Co., 1997).

128. Seiter, op. cit., 427.

129. Martin and Zimmerman, op. cit.

130. John J. DiIulio, Jr., Governing Prisons: A Comparative Study of Correctional Management (New York: The Free Press, 1987).

131. Martin and Zimmerman, op. cit.

132. Seiter, op. cit., 428.

133. See Rolando del Carmen, *Briefs of Leading Cases in Corrections* (Cincinnati: Anderson Publishing, 1993).

134. Ibid. See especially *Greenholtz v. Nebraska Penal Inmates*, 442 U.S. 1 (1979); *Jago v. Van Curen*, 454 U.S. 14 (1981); *Board of Pardons v. Allen*, 482 U.S. 369 (1987).

135. A&E has a number of videos, whereby actual parole hearings can be viewed. Actual parole board decisions in Kentucky, Nevada, Louisiana, Montana, and Missouri are available. See for example, store.aetv.com/detail.php?p=67174&emailForm=true; store.aetv.com/detail.php?p=67190 &email Form=true; shop.history.com/detail.php?p=67173&v=aetv_show_investigative-reports& pagemax=all; shop.aetv.com/detail.php?p=67197&v=aetv_show_crime-and-investigation&pagemax=all; www.biography.com/listings/episode_details.do?episodeid=271804&airingid=413442; and www.cduniverse.com/productinfo.asp?pid=8149578.

136. Cloud H. Miller and Patrick R. Anderson, "Postsentence Defense: The Presentence and Parole Hearing Interview and Implications of *Estelle v. Smith* in Postconviction Due Process," *The Champion: Journal of the National Association of Criminal Defense Lawyers* 8, no. 6 (1984): 18–22.

137. See Belinda R. McCarthy and Bernard McCarthy, *Community-Based Corrections* (Pacific Grove, CA: Brooks/Cole, 1990).

138. These criteria are listed in the *Model Penal Code* at Section 305.9.

139. See P. B. Hoffman and S. Adelberg, "The Salient Factor-Score: A Non-technical Overview," *Federal Probation* 44 (1980).

140. Steven F. Messner and Richard Rosenfeld, *Crime and the American Dream*, 4th ed. (Belmont, CA: Thomson/Wadsworth, 2007).

141. See Bureau of Justice Statistics, *Correctional Population in the United States, 1985* (Washington, DC: U.S. Department of Justice, 1987), for a survey of good-time practices in state correctional systems.

142. Bureau of Justice Statistics, *Probation and Parole 1994* (Washington, DC: U.S. Department of Justice, 1995).

143. Dennis Overbye, "When Student-Adviser Tensions Erupt, The Results Can Be Fatal," *New York Times*, March 27, 2007, accessed July 23, 2010, http://www.nytimes.com/2007/03/27/science/27murd.html; "Widow of Slain Professor Speaks Out," *Los Angeles Times*, October 5, 1985, accessed July 23, 2010, http://articles.latimes.com/1985-10-05/local/me-1109_1_gory-details-theodore-streleski-stanford-university-mathematics-professor; Associated Press, "Killer Refuses Parole a 3rd Time," *Los Angeles Times*, March 8, 1985, accessed July 23, 2010, http://articles.latimes.com/1985-03-08/news/mn-32279_1.

Chapter 13

1. B. J. Casey, Rebecca M. Jones, and Todd A. Hare, "The Adolescent Brain," *The Annals of the New York Academy of Sciences*, 1124 (2008): 111–126. doi:10.1196/annals.1440.010.

2. Patricia Torbet and Linda Szymanski, "State Legislative Responses to Violent Juvenile Crime: 1996–1997 Update," *Juvenile Justice Bulletin* (Washington, DC: Office of Juvenile Justice and Delinquency Prevention, 1998).

3. Ibid. 1.

4. H. Preston Elrod and Scott R. Ryder, *Juvenile Justice: A Social, Historical, and Legal Perspective*, 4th ed. (Burlington, MA: Jones and Bartlett Learning, 2013).

5. Hannah Simpson, "Florida Bill Aims to Decriminalize Teen "Sexting," *Miami Herald*, April 14, 2010, accessed April 20, 2010, http://www.miamiherald.com/2010/03/13/1578155/bill-aims-to-decriminalize-teen.html.

6. Randye Hoder, "Study Finds Most Teens Sext before They're 18," *Time*, July 3, 2014, accessed April 18, 2017, http://time.com/2948467/chances-are-your-teen-is-sexting/.

7. Simpson, op. cit.

8. Angel Zhang, "U.S. Age Boundaries of Delinquency," JJGPS StateScan, (Pittsburgh, PA: National Center for Juvenile Justice, 2016).

9. Elrod and Ryder, op. cit.

10. Edwin M. Lemert. *Social Pathology: A Systematic Approach to the Theory of Sociopathic Behavior* (New York: McGraw-Hill, 1951).

11. Zhang, op. cit.

12. Howard N. Snyder and Joseph Mulako-Wangota, Bureau of Justice Statistics, Arrests per 100,000 in Age Group, generated using the Arrest Data Analysis Tool at www.bjs.gov, January 10, 2017.

13. American Psychological Association, *Developing Adolescents: A Reference for Professionals* (Washington, DC: APA, 2002).

14. Lloyd D. Johnston, Patrick M. O'Malley, Richard A. Miech, Jerald G. Bachman, and John E. Schulenberg, *Monitoring the Future National Survey Results on Drug Use: 1975–2015: Overview of Key Findings on Adolescent Drug Use* (Ann Arbor: Institute for Social Research, The University of Michigan, 2016).

15. Brady E. Hamilton, Joyce A. Martin, Michelle J. K. Osterman, Sally C. Curtin, and T. J. Mathews, "Births: Final Data for 2014," *National Vital Statistics Reports* 64, no. 12 (Hyattsville, MD: National Center for Health Statistics, 2015).

16. Casey, et al., op. cit.

17. *OJJDP Statistical Briefing Book*, accessed January 10, 2017, http://www.ojjdp.gov/ojstatbb/crime/qa05102.asp?qaDate=2014.

18. Howard N. Snyder and Joseph Mulako-Wangota, Bureau of Justice Statistics, Arrests rates of Juveniles for All Offenses, generated using the Arrest Data Analysis Tool at www.bjs.gov, January 10, 2017.

19. William J. Bennett, John J. DiIulio, Jr., and John P. Walters, *Body Count: Moral Poverty ... And How to Win America's War Against Crime and Drugs* (New York: Simon and Schuster, 1996); John J. DiIulio, "The Coming of the Super-Predators," *Weekly Standard*, November 1995.

20. Franklin Zimring, *The Great American Crime Decline* (New York: Oxford University Press, 2007).

21. Howard N. Snyder and Joseph Mulako-Wangota, Bureau of Justice Statistics, Arrest Rates by Gender, generated using the Arrest Data Analysis Tool at www.bjs.gov, January 10, 2017.

22. Meda Chesney-Lind and Lisa J. Pasko, *The Female Offender: Girls, Women, and Crime*, 3rd ed. (Thousand Oaks, CA: Sage Publications, 2013).

23. Ibid.

24. Darrell Steffensmeier, Jennifer Schwartz, Hua Zhong, and Jeff Ackerman, "An Assessment of Recent Trends in Girls' Violence Using Diverse Longitudinal Sources: Is the Gender Gap Closing?" *Criminology* 43 (2005): 355?405.

25. Howard N. Snyder and Joseph Mulako-Wangota, Bureau of Justice Statistics, Arrests Rates by Race, generated using the Arrest Data Analysis Tool at www.bjs.gov, January 10, 2017.

26. Coalition for Juvenile Justice, *Disproportionate Minority Contact (DMC) Facts and Resources*, (Washington, DC: Author, 2010).

27. Charles Puzzanchera and Sarah Hockenberry, *National Disproportionate Minority Contact Databook*, (Washington, DC: Office of Juvenile Justice and Delinquency Prevention, 2013).

28. National Council on Crime and Delinquency, *And Justice for Some: Differential Treatment of Youth of Color in the Justice System* (Oakland, CA: National Council on Crime and Delinquency, 2007), www.nccd-crc.org/nccd/pubs/2007jan_jus-tice_for_some.pdf.

29. National Research Council, *Reforming Juvenile Justice: A Developmental Approach* (Washington, DC: The National Academies Press, 2013), doi: 10.17226/14685.

30. Ibid.; Office of Juvenile Justice and Delinquency Prevention, *Disproportionate Minority Contact* (NCJ 228306), (Washington, DC: U.S. Department of Justice, 2009).

31. National Council on Crime and Delinquency, op. cit.

32. The W. Haywood Burns Institute, "What Happens When the Bargain of Civil Society Is Breached?" April 21, 2015, http://www.burnsinstitute.org/blog/what-happens-when-the-bargain-of-civil-society-is-breached/.

33. Tom R. Tyler, *Why People Obey the Law: Procedural Justice, Legitimacy, and Compliance* (New Haven, CT: Yale University Press, 1990).

34. Heidi M. Hsia, "OJJDP Formula Grants Program," *Juvenile Justice Bulletin* (Washington, DC: Office of Juvenile Justice and Delinquency Prevention, 1999).

35. Emily R. Cabaniss, James M. Frabutt, Mary H. Kendrick, and Margaret B. Arbuckle, "Reducing Disproportionate Minority Contact in the Juvenile Justice System: Promising Practices," *Aggression and Violent Behavior* 12 (2007): 393–401.

36. Michael Lieber, Donna Bishop, and Mitchell Chamlin, "Juvenile Justice Decision-Making Before and After the Implementation of the Disproportionate Minority Contact (DMC) Mandate," *Justice Quarterly*, 28, no. 3 (2011): 460–492; Chenelle Jones, "Is Disproportionate Minority Contact Improving? An Exploratory Analysis of the Arrest, Confinement, and Transfer Stages in Rural and Urban Settings," *Journal of Ethnicity in Criminal Justice* 14, no. 1 (2016): 40–57.

37. Robert M. O'Brien, *Crime and Victimization Data* (Beverly Hills, CA: Sage, 1986).

38. Delbert Elliott, Suzanne Ageton, David Huizinga, Brian Knowles, and Rochelle Canton, "Prevalence and Incidence of Delinquent Behavior: 1976–1980. National Estimates of Delinquent Behavior by Sex, Race, Social Class and Other Selected Variables," *National Youth Survey Report No. 26* (Boulder, CO: Behavioral Research Institute, 1983).

39. Johnston et al., op. cit.

40. Marvin D. Krohn, Terence P. Thornberry, Chris L. Gibson, and Julie M. Baldwin, "The Development and Impact of Self-Report Measures of Crime and Delinquency," *Journal of Quantitative Criminology* 26 (2010): 509–525.

41. Richard F. Catalano, and J. David Hawkins, "The Social Development Model: A Theory of Antisocial Behavior," in *Delinquency and Crime: Current Theories*, ed. J. David Hawkins (New York, NY: Cambridge University Press, 1996): 149–197.

42. See, for example, David P. Farrington, "The Development of Offending and Antisocial Behavior from Childhood: Key Findings from the Cambridge Study in Delinquent Development," *Journal of Child Psychology and Psychiatry* 36 (1995): 929–964; Gerald R. Patterson, Marion S. Forgatch, Karen L. Yoerger, and Mike Stoolmiller, "Variables that Initiate and Maintain an Early-Onset Trajectory for Juvenile Offending," *Development and Psychopathology* 10 (1998): 531–547; Elizabeth B. K. Kim, Amanda B. Gilman, Karl G. Hill, and J. David Hawkins, "Examining Protective Factors against Violence among High-Risk Youth: Findings from the Seattle Social Development Project," *Journal of Criminal Justice* 45 (2016): 19–25.

43. Catalano and Hawkins, op. cit.

44. Barry Krisberg and James F. Austin, *Reinventing Juvenile Justice* (Thousand Oaks, CA: Sage Publications, 1993).

45. Ibid.

46. Elrod and Ryder, op. cit.

47. Krisberg and Austin, op. cit.

48. Ibid.

49. The Center on Juvenile and Criminal Justice, *Juvenile Justice History*, accessed January 12, 2017, http://www.cjcj.org/education1/juvenile-justice-history.html.

50. Elrod and Ryder, op. cit.

51. Krisberg and Austin, op. cit.

52. Alexander W. Pisciotta, "Saving the Children: The Promise and Practice of *Parens Patriae*, 1838–1898," *Crime and Delinquency* 28, (1982): 410–425.

53. Sanford J. Fox, "Juvenile Justice Reform: An Historical Perspective," *Stanford Law Review* 22, no. 6 (1970): 1187–1239; *Ex parte Crouse*, 4 Wharton 9, 11 (Pa. 1838).

54. Pisciotta, op. cit.

55. Elrod and Ryder, op. cit.

56. Marilyn I. Holt, *The Orphan Trains: Placing Out in America* (Lincoln, NE: University of Nebraska Press, 1993).

57. Fox, op. cit.

58. Ibid.

59. *People ex rel O'Connell v. Turner*, 55 Ill. 280, 283–84, 287 (1870).

60. Tony Platt, *The Child Savers*, 2nd ed. (Chicago: University of Chicago Press, 1977); Randall G. Shelden and Lynn T. Osborne, "'For Their Own Good': Class Interests and the Child Saving Movement in Memphis, Tennessee, 1900–1917," *Criminology* 27, no. 4 (1989): 747–767.

61. Shelden and Osborn, op. cit., 754.

62. Ibid.

63. Tony Platt, "Contemporary Comments: The Child Savers Reconsidered," *Current Issues in Criminal Justice* 20, no. 1 (2008): 123–138, 123.

64. See, for example, Steven L. Schlossman, *Love and the American Delinquent: The Theory and Practice of "Progressive" Juvenile Justice, 1825–1920* (Chicago: University of Chicago Press, 1977); Lawrence Friedman, *Crime and Punishment in American History* (New York: Basic Books, 1994).

65. Platt, *Contemporary Comments*, (2008), 124.

66. Sheldon and Osborn, op. cit., 764.

67. Robert E. Shepherd, Jr., "The Juvenile Court at 100 Years: A Look Back," *Juvenile Justice Journal* 6, no. 2 (1999): https://www.ncjrs.gov/html/ojjdp/jjjournal1299/2.html.

68. Ibid.

69. "The Illinois Juvenile Court Act of 1899," *Juvenile* & Family *Court* Journal 49, no. 4 (1998): 1–5.

70. Krisberg and Austin, op. cit.

71. *Commonwealth v. Fisher*, 213 Pennsylvania 48 (1905).

72. Schlossman, op. cit.

73. Michael D. Reisig, Scott E. Wolfe, and Kristi Holtfreter, "Legal Cynicism, Legitimacy, and Criminal Offending: The Non-Confounding Effect of Low Self-Control," *Criminal Justice and Behavior* 38 (2011): 1265–1279; Tyler, op. cit.

74. Elrod and Ryder, op. cit.

75. Stephanie A. Wiley and Finn-Aage Esbensen, "The Effect of Police Contact," Crime & Delinquency 62, no. 3 (2016): 283–307.

76. Terrie Moffitt, "Adolescence-Limited and Life-Course-Persistent Anti-Social Behavior: A Developmental Taxonomy," *Psychological Review* 100 (1993): 674–701.

77. John T. Whitehead and Steven P. Lab, *Juvenile Justice: An Introduction*, 8th ed. (New York: Routledge, 2015).

78. Robert E. Worden and Robin L. Shepard, "Demeanor, Crime, and Police Behavior: A Reexamination of the Police Services Study Data," *Criminology* 34, no. 1 (1996): 83–105.

79. Whitehead and Lab, op. cit.

80. Robert A. Brown, Kenneth J. Novak, and James Frank, "Identifying Variation in Police Officer Behavior between Juveniles and Adults," *Journal of Criminal Justice* 37 (2009): 200–208.

81. Jennifer L. Schulenberg and Deirdre Warren, "Police Discretion with Apprehended Youth: Assessing the Impact of Juvenile Specialization," *Police Practice and Research* 10, no. 1 (2009): 3–16.

82. Ibid.

83. Jodi L. Viljoen ad Ronald Roesch, "Competence to Waive Interrogation Rights and Adjudicative Competence in Adolescent Defendants: Cognitive Development, Attorney Contact, and Psychological Symptoms," *Law and Human Behavior* 29, no. 6 (2005): 723–742; Heather Zelle,

Christina L. Riggs Romaine, and Naomi E. S. Goldstein, "Juveniles' *Miranda* Comprehension: Understanding, Appreciation, and Totality of Circumstances Factors," *Law and Human Behavior* 39, no. 3 (2015): 281–293.

84. Barry C. Feld, "Police Interrogation of Juveniles: An Empirical Study of Policy and Practice," *Journal of Criminal Law and Criminology* 97, no. 1 (2006): 219–316; Haley D. Cleary and Sarah Vidal, "*Miranda* in Actual Juvenile Interrogations: Delivery, Waiver, and Readability," *Criminal Justice Review* 41, no. 1 (2016): 98–115.

85. *Fare v. Michael, C.*, 442 U.S. 707 (1979).

86. *J.D.B. v. North Carolina*, 131 S. Ct. 2394, 2399 (2011).

87. *Thompson v. Keohane*, 516 U.S. 99, 112 (1995) as cited in John M. P. Wesley. "Age of Intimidation: Why the Supreme Court Got It Right," New England Journal on Criminal & Civil Confinement 39, no. 1 (2013): 269–292.

88. *J.D.B. v. North Carolina*, 131 S. Ct. 2394, 2399 (2011), as cited in Wesley op. cit.

89. Christine S. Scott-Hayward, "Explaining Juvenile False Confessions: Adolescent Development and Police Interrogation," *Law & Psychological Review* 31 (2007): 53–76.

90. Feld, op. cit.; Hayley M. D. Cleary and Todd C. Warner, "Police Training in Interviewing and Interrogation Methods: A Comparison of Techniques Used with Adult and Juvenile Suspects," *Law and Human Behavior* 40, no. 3 (2015): 270–284.

91. Buffie Brooke Merryman, "Arguments against Use of the Reid Technique for Juvenile Interrogation," *Communication Law Review* 10, no. 2 (n.d.): http://commlawreview.org/Archives.

92. Feld, op. cit.

93. *Michael Crowe v. County of San Diego*, (2010): http://caselaw.findlaw.com/us-9th-circuit/1497387.html.

94. Merryman, op. cit.

95. Cleary and Warner, op. cit.

96. Cody Stoddard, Benjamin Steiner, Jacqueline Rohrbach, Craig Hemmens, and Katherine Bennett, "All the Way Home: Assessing the Constitutionality of Juvenile Curfew Laws," *American Journal of Criminal Law* 42, no. 3 (2015): 177–211.

97. David B. Wilson, Ajima Olaghere, and Charlotte Gill, "Juvenile Curfew Effects on Criminal Behavior and Victimization: A Campbell Collaboration Systematic Review," *Journal of Experimental Criminology* 12 (2016): 167–186.

98. Ibid.

99. Whitehead and Lab, op. cit.

100. Wilson et al., op. cit.

101. David McDowall and Colin Loftin, "Impact of Youth Curfew Laws on Juvenile Crime Rates," *Crime & Delinquency* 46, no. 1 (2000): 76–91.

102. Ibid.; Wilson et al., op. cit.; Ken Adams, "Effectiveness of Juvenile Curfews at Crime Prevention," *Annals of the American Academy* 587, no. 1 (2003): 136–159.

103. D.A.R.E. America, accessed on January 18, 2017, http://www.dare.org/about-d-a-r-e/.

104. Dennis P. Rosenbaum, "Just Say No to D.A.R.E.," *Criminology & Public Policy* 6, no. 4 (2007): 815–824.

105. Ibid.

106. Ibid.

107. C. A. Gruber, "A Positive Evaluation of DARE," *Law and Order* 46, no. 4 (1998): 52.

108. Joseph F. Donnermeyer, “Educator Perceptions of the D.A.R.E. Officer,” *Journal of Alcohol and Drug Education* 44, no. 1 (1998): 1–17.

109. Wayne L. Lucas, “Parents’ Perceptions of the Drug Abuse Resistance Education Program (DARE),” *Journal of Child & Adolescent Substance Abuse* 17, no. 4 (2008): 99–114.

110. Lucinda Grey and Laurie Lewis, “*Public School Safety and Discipline: 2013–14,*” U.S. Department of Education, (Washington, DC: National Center for Education Statistics, 2015): http://nces.ed.gov/pubsearch.

111. Benjamin Thomas, Laura Towvim, John Rosiak, and Kellie Anderson, “School Resource Officers: Steps to Effective School-Based Law Enforcement,” *National Center Brief* (Washington, DC: National Center for Mental Health Promotion and Youth Violence Prevention, 2013).

112. Maurice Canady, Bernard James, and Janet Nease, *To Protect and Educate: The School Resource Officer and the Prevention of Violence in Schools* (Hoover, AL: National Association of School Resource Officers, 2012).

113. American Bar Association, “Law-Related Education Network,” accessed January 23, 2017, http://www.americanbar.org/groups/public_education/resources/law_related_education_network.html.

114. Canady et al., op. cit.

115. Ibid.

116. Kyle Ramey, “Partners for Safety,” *American School Board Journal* (2004): 71–72.

117. Matthew T. Theriot, “School Resource Officers and the Criminalization of Student Behavior,” *Journal of Criminal Justice* 37 (2009): 280–287.

118. Sara Rimer, “Unruly Students Facing Arrest Not Detention,” *New York Times*, January 4, 2004, 1.

119. Paul J. Hirschfield, “Preparing for Prison? The Criminalization of School Discipline in the USA,” *Theoretical Criminology* 12 (2008): 79–101; Matthew T. Theriot and Matthew J. Cuellar, “School Resource Officers and Students’ Rights,” *Contemporary Justice Review* 19, no. 3 (2016): 363–379.

120. Ibid.

121. Ibid.

122. According to the U.S. Supreme Court ruling in *New Jersey v. T.L.O.*, school officials only need to have reasonable suspicion to search a student, because schools have a responsibility to maintain order and establish a safe environment.

123. National Center for Juvenile Justice, *Juvenile Offenders and Victims: 2014 National Report* (Washington, DC: Office of Juvenile Justice and Delinquency Prevention, 2014).

124. Sarah Hockenberry and Charles Puzzanchera, *Juvenile Court Statistics 2013* (Pittsburgh, PA: National Center for Juvenile Justice, 2015).

125. Ibid.

126. Whitehead and Lab, op. cit.

127. *Schall v. Martin*, 467 U.S. 253 (1984).

128. National Center for Juvenile Justice, op. cit., 94.

129. Hockenberry and Puzzanchera, op. cit., 32.

130. Barry Holman and Jason Ziedenberg, *The Dangers of Detention: The Impact of Incarcerating Youth in Detention and Other Secure Facilities* (Washington, DC: Justice Policy Institute, 2006).

131. He Len Chung, Michelle Little, and Laurence Steinberg, “The Transition to Adulthood for Adolescents in the Juvenile Justice System: A Developmental Perspective,” in *On Your Own Without a Net: The Transition to Adulthood for Vulnerable Populations*, eds. D. W. Osgood, E. M. Foster, C. Flanagan, and G. R. Ruth, (Chicago, IL: University of Chicago Press, 2005), 68–91.

132. Charles E. Frazier and John C. Cochran, "Detention of Juveniles: Its Effects on Subsequent Juvenile Court Processing Decisions," *Youth and Society* 17, no. 3 (1986): 286–305.

133. Hockenberry and Puzzanchera, *Juvenile Court Statistics*, 2.

134. Elrod and Ryder, op. cit.

135. Daniel P. Mears, Joshua J. Kuch, Andrea M. Lindsey, Sonja E. Siennick, George B. Pesta, Mark A. Greenwald, and Thomas G. Blomberg, "Juvenile Court and Contemporary Diversion: Helpful, Harmful, or Both?" *Criminology & Public Policy* 15 (2016): 953–981.

136. Brenda Vose and Kelly Vannan, "A Jury of Your Peers: Recidivism of Teen Court Participants," *Journal of Juvenile Justice* 3, no 1 (2013): 97–109.

137. Elrod and Ryder, op. cit.

138. Mears et al., op. cit.

139. Robert D. Hoge and Holly A. Wilson, "The Effects of Youth Diversion Programs on Recidivism: A Meta-Analytic Review," *Criminal Justice & Behavior* 40, no. 5 (2013): 497–518.

140. Elrod and Ryder, op. cit.

141. Juvenile Law Center, "Commonly Used Terms," accessed January 27, 2017, http://www.jlc.org/news-room/media-resources/glossary.

142. Hockenberry and Puzzanchera, op. cit.

143. National Center for Juvenile Justice, op. cit., 94.

144. Whitehead and Lab, op. cit.

145. George W. Burruss and Kimberly Kempg-Leonard, "The Questionable Advantage of Defense Counsel in Juvenile Court," *Justice Quarterly* 19, no. 1 (2002): 37–69; Lori Guevara, Cassia Spohn, and Denise Herz, "Race, Legal Representation, and Juvenile Justice: Issues and Concerns," *Crime and Delinquency* 50, no. 3 (2004): 344–371.

146. Whitehead and Lab, op. cit.

147. Hockenberry and Puzzanchera, op. cit.

148. Juvenile Law Center, op. cit.

149. Hockenberry and Puzzanchera, op. cit.

150. Hockenberry and Puzzanchera, op. cit.

151. National Center for Juvenile Justice, op. cit.

152. Ibid.

153. Ian Urbina, "Despite Red Flags about Judges, a Kickback Scheme Flourished," *New York Times*, March 27, 2009, accessed Mary 5, 2010, http://www.nytimes.com/2009/03/28/us/28judges.html.

154. Juvenile Law Center, "Luzern County Kids-for-Cash Scandal," accessed January 28, 2017, http://jlc.org/luzerne-county-kids-cash-scandal.

155. Justice Law Center, "Luzerne County: Federal Criminal Charges," accessed January 28, 2017, http://jlc.org/luzerne_federal_criminal_charges.

156. Juvenile Law Center, "Luzern County Kids-for-Cash Scandal."

157. H. N. Snyder and Melissa Sickmund, *Juvenile Offenders and Victims: 2006 National Report* (Washington, DC: Office of Juvenile Justice and Delinquency Prevention, 2006).

158. David C. May, Kevin L. Minor, Rick Ruddell, and Betsy A. Matthews, *Corrections and the Criminal Justice System*, (Sudbury, MA: Jones and Bartlett Publishers, 2007).

159. *Kent v. United States*, 383 U.S. 541 (1966).

160. *In re Gault*, 387 U.S. 1 (1967).

161. *In re Winship*, 397 U.S. 358 (1970).

162. *McKeiver v. Pennsylvania*, 403 U.S. 528 (1971).

163. May, et al., *Corrections and the Criminal Justice System.*

164. Sickmund and Puzzanchera, op. cit., 97.

165. Patrick Webb, "Privacy of Publicity: Media Coverage and Juvenile Proceedings in the United States," *International Journal of Criminal Justice Sciences* 3, no. 1 (2008): 1–14.

166. Ibid.

167. Sickmund and Puzzanchera, op. cit.

168. Ibid.

169. Ibid.

170. *Smith v. Daily Mail Publishing Co.*, 443 U.S. 97 (1979).

171. Rolando V. del Carmen, *Briefs of Leading Cases in Juvenile Justice* (Cincinnati, OH: Anderson Publishing Co., 1998).

172. Alecia Humphrey, "The Criminalization of Survival Attempts: Locking Up Female Runaways and Other Status Offenders," *Hasting Women's Law Journal* 15 (2004): 165–172.

173. National Center for Juvenile Justice, op. cit.

174. Hockenberry and Puzzanchera, op. cit.

175. Coalition of Juvenile Justice, *Deinstitutionalization of Status Offenders: Facts and Resources* (Washington, DC: Coalition of Juvenile Justice, 2011).

176. Juvenile Justice and Delinquency Prevention Act (Pub. L. No. 93-415, 1974), accessed January 30, 2017, https://www.ojjdp.gov/about/jjdpa2002titlev.pdf.

177. Coalition of Juvenile Justice, op. cit.

178. Ibid.

179. Patricia J. Arthur and Regina Waugh, "Status Offenses and the Juvenile Justice and Delinquency Prevention Act: The Exception Swallowed the Rule," *Seattle Journal for Social Justice* 7, no. 2 (2009): 555–576.

180. National Center for Juvenile Justice, op. cit.

181. Ibid.

182. Terry Aguayo, "Youth Who Killed at 12 Will Return to Prison, But Not for Life," *New York Times*, March 2, 2006, http://www.nytimes.com/2006/03/02/us/youth-who-killed-at-12-will-return-to-prison-but-not-for-life.html.

183. Brandon L. Bang, Brianne Posey, and Craig Hemmens, "Juvenile Waiver 2014: A Review of State Statutes," *Juvenile and Family Court Journal* 67, no. 2 (2016): 5–48.

184. Sarah Hockenberry and Charles Puzzanchera, *Delinquency Cases Waived to Criminal Court, 2011*, National Report Series (Washington, DC: Office of Juvenile Justice and Delinquency Prevention, 2014).

185. Melissa Sickmund, Anthony Sladky, and W. Kang, "Easy Access to Juvenile Court Statistics: 1985–2013," 2015, http://www.ojjdp.gov/ojstatbb/ezajcs/.

186. Hockenberry and Puzzanchera, *Delinquency Cases Waived to Criminal Court.*

187. Donna M. Bishop, Charles E. Frazier, and John C. Henretta, "Prosecutorial Waiver: Case Study of a Questionable Reform," *Crime & Delinquency* 35 (1989); Richard E. Redding, "The Effects of Adjudicating and Sentencing Juveniles as Adults: Research and Policy Implications," *Youth Violence & Juvenile Justice* 128 (2003): 128–155.

188. M. A. Bortner, "Traditional Rhetoric, Organizational Realities: Remand of Juvenile to Adult Court," *Crime & Delinquency* 32 (1996): 53–73; Eric J. Fritsch, Craig Hemmens, and Tory J. Cacti,

"Violent Youth in Juvenile and Adult Court: An Assessment of Sentencing Strategies in Texas," *Law & Policy* 18 (1996): 115–136.

189. Donna Bishop, C. E. Frazier, L. Lanza-Kaduce, and L. Winner, "The Transfer of Juveniles to Criminal Court: Does It Make a Difference?" *Crime & Delinquency* 42 (1996): 171–191; David L. Myers, "The Recidivism of Violent Youths in Juvenile and Adult Court: A Consideration of Selection Bias," *Youth Violence & Juvenile Justice* 18, no. 1/2 (2003): 115–137.

190. Benjamin Steiner and Emily Wright, "Assessing the Relative Effects of State Direct File Waiver Laws on Violent Juvenile Crime: Deterrence or Irrelevance?" *The Journal of Criminal Law and Criminology* 94, no. 4 (2006): 1451–1477.

191. Amy Linn, *History of Death Penalty for Juvenile Offenders*, Juvenile Justice Information Exchange, 2016, Accessed January 28, 2017, http://jjie.org/2016/02/13/history-of-death-penalty-for-juvenile-offenders/.

192. Victor L. Streib, "The Juvenile Death Penalty Today: Death Sentences and Executions for Juvenile Crimes, January 1, 1973–February 28, 2005," (Ada, OH: Ohio Northern University Claude W. Pettit College of Law, 2005): http://www.deathpenaltyinfo.org/files/pdf/juvdeathstreib.pdf.

193. Lynne Cothern, "Juveniles and the Death Penalty," *Coordinating Council on Juvenile Justice and Delinquency Prevention*, (Washington, DC: Office of Juvenile Justice and Delinquency Prevention, 2000).

194. *Thompson v. Oklahoma*, 487 U.S. 815 (1988).

195. Ibid.

196. *Roper v. Simmons* 543 U.S. 551 (2005).

197. Ibid.

198. Amy Linn, "History of Death Penalty for Juvenile Offenders," (Juvenile Justice Information Exchange, 2016): http://jjie.org/2016/02/13/history-of-death-penalty-for-juvenile-offenders/.

199. Joshua Rovner, "Juvenile Life without Parole: An Overview," (Washington, DC: The Sentencing Project, 2016).

200. *Graham v. Florida*, 130 S. Ct. 2011 (2010).

201. Rovner, op. cit., 2.

202. *Miller v. Alabama* and *Jackson v. Hobbs*, 132 S. Ct. 2455 (2012).

203. *Montgomery v. Louisiana* 577 U.S. ___ (2016).

204. Ibid.

205. Ashley Nellis, "The Lives of Juvenile Lifers: Findings from a National Survey," (Washington, DC: The Sentencing Project, 2012).

206. Ibid.

207. Sarah Hockenberry, Andrew Wachter, and Anthony Sladky, *Juvenile Residential Facility Census, 2014: Selected Findings* (Washington, DC: Office of Juvenile Justice and Delinquency Prevention, 2016).

208. Ibid.

209. Elrod and Ryder, op. cit.

210. Alfiee M. Breland-Noble, Elizabeth M. Z. Farmer, Melanie S. Dubs, Elizabeth Potter, and Barbara J. Burns, "Mental Health and Other Service Use by Youth in Therapeutic Foster Care and Group Homes," *Journal of Child and Family Studies* 14, no. 2 (2005): 167–180.

211. Richard P. Barth, Johanna K. P. Greeson, S. Guo, R. L. Green, and S. Hurley, "Outcomes for Youth Receiving Intensive In-Home Therapy or Residential Care: A Comparison Using Propensity Scores," *American Journal of Orthopsychiatry* 77, no. 4 (2007): 497–505.

212. Bethany R. Lee and Ronald Thompson, "Comparing Outcomes for Youth in Treatment Foster Care and Family-Style Group Care," *Children and Youth Services Review* 30, no. 7 (2008): 746–757.

213. Rajeev Ramchand, Andrew R. Morral, and Kirsten Becker, "Seven-Year Life Outcomes of Adolescent Offenders in Los Angeles," *American Journal of Public Health* 99, no. 5 (2009): 863–870.

214. Sigrid James, "What Works in Group Care? A Structured Review of Treatment Models for Group Homes and Residential Care," *Child Youth Services Review* 33, no. 2 (2011): 308–321.

215. Ronald W. Thompson, Gail L. Smith, D. Wayne Osgood, Thomas P. Dowd, Patrick C. Friman, and Daniel L. Daly, "Residential Care: A Study of Short- and Long-Term Educational Effects," *Children and Youth Services Review* 18, no. 3 (1996): 221–242.; Kathryn A. Kirigin, Curtis J. Braukmann, Jay D. Atwater, and Montrose M. Wolf, "An Evaluation of Teaching-Family (Achievement Place) Group Homes for Juvenile Offenders," *Journal of Applied Behavior Analysis* 15 (1982): 1–16.

216. Hockenberry, Wachter, and Sladky, op. cit.

217. National Center for Juvenile Justice, op. cit.

218. Ibid.

219. Elrod and Ryder, op. cit.

220. Edward K. Morris and Curtis J. Braukmann, *Behavioral Approaches to Crime and Delinquency: A Handbook of Application, Research, and Concepts* (New York: Plenum Press, 2007).

221. Frank S. Pearson, Douglas S. Lipton, Charles M. Cleland, and Dorline S. Yee, "The Effects of Behavioral/Cognitive-Behavioral Programs on Recidivism," *Crime & Delinquency* 48, no. 3 (2002): 476–496.

222. Virginia Department of Juvenile Justice, "Juvenile Recidivism in Virginia," *DJJ Research Quarterly* 3 (2005): 1–12.

223. Michelle Inderbitzen, "A Look from the Inside: Balancing Custody and Treatment in a Maximum-Security Facility," *International Journal of Offender Therapy and Comparative Criminology* 51, no. 3 (2007): 348–362.

224. Ibid.

225. R. C. Cronin, *Boot Camps for Adult and Juvenile Offenders* (Washington, DC: U.S. Department of Justice, National Institute of Justice, 1994).

226. Melissa Sickmund, *Juvenile Residential Facility Census 2002: Selected Findings*, Juvenile Offenders and Victims National Report Series (Washington, DC: Office of Juvenile Justice and Delinquency Prevention, 2006).

227. Jamie E. Muscar, "Advocating the End of Juvenile Boot Camps: Why the Military Model Does Not Belong in the Juvenile Justice System," *UC Davis Journal of Juvenile Law & Policy* 12, no 1 (2008): 1–50.

228. Doris L. MacKenzie, David B. Wilson, Gaylene S. Armstrong, and Angela R. Gover, "The Impact of Boot Camps and Traditional Institutions on Juvenile Residents: Perceptions, Adjustment, and Change" *Journal of Research in Crime and Delinquency* 38 (2001): 279–313.

229. David B. Wilson, Doris L. MacKenzie, and Fawn Ngo Mitchell, "Effects of Correctional Boot Camps on Offending," *Campbell Systematic Reviews* (Campbell Collaboration, 2005): www.campbell collaboration.org/lib/download/3/.

230. Muscar, op. cit.

231. S. Brady Calhoun "Update: No Federal Charges in Boot Camp Case," *News Herald* (Panama City, FL), April 16, 2010, accessed May 15, 2010: http//www.newsherald.com/articles/class-83103-div-morning.html.

232. Muscar, op. cit., 22

233. Ibid.

234. National Center for Juvenile Justice, op. cit.

235. E. Ann Carson and Elizabeth Anderson, "Prisoners in 2015," *Prisoners Series* (Washington, DC: Bureau of Justice Statistics, 2016).

236. Martin Forst, Jefferey Fagan, and T. Scott Vivona, "Youth in Prisons and Training Schools: Perceptions and Consequences of the Treatment-Custody Dichotomy," *Juvenile and Family Court Journal* 40 (1989): 1–14.; Jodi Lane, Lonn Lanza-Kaduce, Charles E. Frazier, and Donna M. Bishop, "Adult Versus Juvenile Sanctions: Voices of Incarcerated Youths," *Crime and Delinquency* 48, (2002): 431–455.

237. Aaron Kupchik, "The Correctional Experiences of Youth in Adult and Juvenile Prisons," *Justice Quarterly* 24, no. 2 (2007): 247–270.

238. Forst, et al., op. cit.

239. Barry Glick and William Sturgeon, *No Time to Play: Youthful Offenders in Adult Correctional Systems* (Lanham, MD: American Correctional Association, 1998).

240. Richard E. Redding, "Juvenile Transfer Laws: An Effective Deterrent to Delinquency?" *OJJDP Juvenile Justice Bulletin* (Washington, DC: Office of Juvenile Justice and Delinquency Prevention, 2010); Kareem L. Jordan and David L. Myers, "Juvenile Transfer and Deterrence: Re-examining the Effectiveness of a 'Get-Tough' Policy," *Crime and Delinquency* 57, no. 2 (2011): 247–270.

241. Whitehead and Lab, op. cit., 237.

242. Kupchik, op cit.

243. Mark W. Lipsey, David B. Wilson, and Lynne Cothern, "Effective Intervention for Serious Juvenile Offenders," *Juvenile Justice Bulletin* (Washington, DC: Office of Juvenile Justice and Delinquency Prevention, 2000).

244. National Center for Juvenile Justice, op. cit.

245. Jodi Lane, Susan Turner, Terry Fain, and Amber Sehgal, "Evaluating an Experimental Intensive Juvenile Probation Program: Supervision and Official Outcomes," *Crime & Delinquency* 51, no. 1 (2005): 26–52.

246. David M. Altschuler and Rachel Brash, "Adolescent and Teenage Offenders Confronting the Challenges and Opportunities of Reentry," *Youth Violence and Juvenile Justice* 2, no. 1 (2004): 72–87.

247. Jamie J. Fader, "You Can Take Me Outta the Hood, but You Can't Take the Hood Outta Me: Youth Incarceration and Reentry," in *Against the Wall: Poor, Young, Black and Male*, ed. E. Anderson (198–217). (Philadelphia, PA: University of Pennsylvania Press, 2008).

248. Steve V. Geis, "Aftercare Services," *Juvenile Justice Bulletin* (Washington, DC Office of Juvenile Justice and Delinquency Prevention, 2003).

249. Megan Kurlychek and Cynthia Kempinen, "Beyond Boot Camp: The Impact of Aftercare on Offender Reentry," *Criminology & Public Policy* 5, no. 2 (2006): 363–388; Ronald W. Thompson, Jay L. Ringle, Mona Way, Jeffery Peterson, and Jonathan C. Huefner, "After-Care for a Cognitive-Behavioral Program for Juvenile Offenders: A Pilot Investigation," *Journal of Behavior Analysis of Offender and Victim Treatment and Prevention* 2, no. 3 (2010): 198–211; James B. Wells, Kevin I. Minor, Earl Angel, and Kevin D. Stearman, "A Quasi-Experimental Evaluation of a Shock Incarceration and Aftercare Program for Juvenile Offenders," *Youth Violence and Juvenile Justice* 4, no. 3 (2006): 219–233.

250. Don A. Andrews, James D. Bonta, and Robert D. Hoge, "Classification for Effective Rehabilitation: Rediscovering Psychology," *Criminal Justice and Behavior* 17 (1990): 19–52; Lipsey, et al., op. cit.

251. Andrews, et al., op. cit.

252. Mark Lipsey, "The Primary Factors that Characterize Effective Interventions with Juvenile Offenders: A Meta-Analytic Overview," *Victims & Offenders*, 4, no. 2 (2009): 124–147.

253. Andrews et al., op. cit.; Lipsey, op. cit.

254. James Bonta and Don A. Andrews, *The Psychology of Criminal Conduct* (Cincinnati, OH: Anderson, 2016).

255. Ibid.

256. Ibid.

257. Bonta and Andrews, op. cit.

258. Meda Chesney-Lind and Randall G. Shelden, *Girls, Delinquency and Juvenile Justice*, 4th ed. (Hoboken, NJ: Wiley-Blackwell, 2014).

259. Don Andrews, "Enhancing Adherence to Risk-Need-Responsivity: Making Quality a Matter of Policy," *Criminology and Public Policy* 5 (2006): 595–602; Elizabeth K. Drake, Steve Aos, and Marna G. Miller, *Evidence-Based Public Policy Options to Reduce Crime and Criminal Justice Costs: Implications in Washington State Public Policy Options* (Washington State Institute for Public Policy, 2010).

260. Andrews, op. cit.

261. Drake, et al., op. cit.

262. Patricia Chamberlain, Joe Price, Leslie D. Leve, Heidemarie Laurent, John A. Landsverk, and John B. Reid, "Prevention of Behavior Problems for Children in Foster Care: Outcomes and Mediation Effects," *Prevention Science* 9, no. 1 (2008): 17–27; Patricia Chamberlain and Sharon F. Mihalic, *Blueprints for Violence Prevention, Book 8: Multidimensional Treatment Foster Care* (Boulder, CO: Center for the Study and Prevention of Violence, 1998): http://www.ncjrs.gov/pdffiles1/Digitization/174201NCJRS.pdf.

263. Patricia Chamberlain and John B. Reid, "Comparison of Two Community Alternatives to Incarceration for Chronic Juvenile Offenders," *Journal of Consulting and Clinical Psychology* 66, no. 2 (1998): 624–33; Patricia Chamberlain, Leslie D. Leve, and David S. DeGarmo, "Multidimensional Treatment Foster Care for Girls in the Juvenile Justice System: 2-Year Follow-Up of a Randomized Clinical Trial," *Journal of Consulting and Clinical Psychology* 75 (2007): 187–93.

264. James Alexander, Christie Pugh, and Bruce V. Parsons, "Functional Family Therapy," in *Blueprints for Violence Prevention (Book 3)*, ed. Delbert S. Elliott (Boulder, CO: Center for the Study and Prevention of Violence, Institute of Behavioral Science, University of Colorado, 1998).

265. Thomas L. Sexton and Charles W. Turner. "The Effectiveness of Functional Family Therapy for Youth With Behavioral Problems in a Community Practice Setting," *Journal of Family Psychology* 24, no. 3 (2010): 339–48.

266. Scott Henggeler, "Treating Serious Antisocial Behavior in Youth: The MST Approach," *Juvenile Justice Bulletin* (Washington, D.C.: U.S. Department of Justice, Office of Juvenile Justice and Delinquency Prevention, 1997): http://www.ncjrs.gov/pdffiles/165151.pdf.

267. Scott W. Henggeler, Gary B. Melton, and Linda A. Smith, "Family Preservation Using Multisystemic Therapy: An Effective Alternative to Incarcerating Serious Juvenile Offenders," *Journal of Consulting and Clinical Psychology* 60, no. 6 (1992): 953–61; Charles M. Borduin, Barton J. Mann, Lynn T. Cone, Scott W. Henggeler, Bethany R. Fucci, David M. Blaske, and Robert A. Williams, "Multisystemic Treatment of Serious Juvenile Offenders: Long-Term Prevention of Criminality and Violence," *Journal of Consulting and Clinical Psychology* 63, no. 4 (1995): 569–78.

268. Jane Timmons-Mitchell, Monica B. Bender, Maureen A. Kishna, and Clare C. Mitchell, "An Independent Effectiveness Trial of Multisystemic Therapy with Juvenile Justice Youth," *Journal of Clinical Child and Adolescent Psychology* 35 (2006): 227–36.

269. Barry Glick and John C. Gibbs, *Aggression Replacement Training®: A Comprehensive Intervention for Aggressive Youth (Third Edition—Revised and Expanded)* (Champaign, IL: Research Press, 2011).

270. Washington State Institute for Public Policy, *Outcome Evaluation of Washington State's Research-Based Programs for Juvenile Offenders*. (Olympia, Wash.: Washington State Institute for Public Policy, 2004): http://www.wsipp.wa.gov/rptfiles/04-01-1201.pdf.

271. Knut K. Gundersen and Frode Svartdal, "Aggression Replacement Training in Norway: Outcome Evaluation of 11 Norwegian Student Projects," *Scandinavian Journal of Education Research* 50, no. 1 (2006): 63–81.

272. National Institute of Justice, *Restorative Justice* (Washington, DC: Author, 2007). https://www.nij.gov/topics/courts/restorative-justice/Pages/welcome.aspx.

273. Drake, et al., op. cit.

Chapter 14

1. Memorable Quotes for *Back to the Future* (1985), The Internet Movie Data Base, accessed July 21, 2010, http://www.imdb.com/title/tt0088763/quotes.

2. Edith E. Flynn, "International Terrorism and the United States," in *Visions for Change: Crime and Justice in the Twenty-First Century*, eds. Roslyn Muraskin and Albert R. Roberts (Upper Saddle River, NJ: Prentice Hall, 1996).

3. The Free Dictionary, "Enemy Combatant," accessed July 21, 2010, http://legal-dictionary.thefreedictionary.com/Enemy+Combatant.

4. Paul Elias, "American Taliban Seeks Reduced Sentence," *Washington Post*, April 5, 2007, accessed July 21, 2010, http://www.washingtonpost.com/wp-dyn/content/article/2007/04/05/AR2007040500200_pf.html.

5. Richard A. Serrano, "'Shoe Bomber' Reid Given 3 Life Terms," *Los Angeles Times*, January 31, 2003, accessed July 21, 2010, http://articles.latimes.com/2003/jan/31/nation/na-reid31.

6. Jerry Markon and Timothy Dwyer, "Jurors Reject Death Penalty for Moussaoui," *Washington Post*, May 4, 2006, accessed July 21, 2010, http://www.washingtonpost.com/wp-dyn/content/article/2006/05/03/AR2006050300324.html.

7. *Rasul v. Bush*, 542 U.S. 466 (2004).

8. *Hamdi v. Rumsfeld*, 542 U.S. 507 (2004).

9. Holder v. Humanitarian Law Project, 561 U.S. ___ (2010).

10. James Vicini, "Supreme Court Upholds Terrorism Support Law," Reuters, June 21, 2010, accessed July 21, 2010, http://www.reuters.com/article/idUSTRE65K4B420100621—The issue in the case was "whether 18 U.S.C. 2339B(a)(1), which prohibits the knowing provision of 'any ... service, ... training, [or] expert advice or assistance,' to a designated foreign terrorist organization, is unconstitutionally vague; Whether the criminal prohibitions in 18 U.S.C. § 2339B(a)(1) on the provision of 'expert advice or assistance' 'derived from scientific [or] technical' knowledge and 'personnel' are unconstitutional with respect to speech that furthers only lawful, nonviolent activities of proscribed organizations."

11. James Barrett, "A Complete List of Radical Islamic Terror Attacks on U.S. Soil under Obama," *Daily Wire*, December 7, 2016, accessed April 12, 2017, http://www.dailywire.com/news/11410/complete-list-radical-islamic-terror-attacks-us-james-barrett.

12. Committee on Oversight and Government Reform, Hearing on Radicalization: Social Media and the Rise of Terrorism, Hearing before the Subcommittee on National Security, U.S. House of Representatives, October 28, 2015, accessed April 11, 2017, https://oversight.house.gov/hearing/radicalization-social-media-and-the-rise-of-terrorism/.

13. Brian McManus, "An Expert Explains How Social Media Can Lead to the 'Self-Radicalization' of Terrorists," *Vice*, December 7, 2015, accessed April 11, 2017, https://www.vice.com/en_us/article/we-asked-an-expert-how-social-media-can-help-radicalize-terrorists.

14. Michael Harriot, "The Ku Klux Klan's Big Recruiting Weekend," *The Root*, June 20, 2017, accessed October 4, 2017, https://www.theroot.com/the-ku-klux-klans-big-recruiting-weeked-1796260626.

15. Al Baker and Marc Santora, "San Bernardino Attackers Discussed Jihad in Private Messages, F.B.I. Says," *New York Times*, December 16, 2015, accessed April 11, 2017, https://www.nytimes.com/2015/12/17/us/san-bernardino-attackers-discussed-jihad-in-private-messages-fbi-says.html.

16. Matt Hamilton, Kate Mather, James Queally, and Richard A. Serrano, "The Man Who Bought the Rifles: Who Is Enrique Marquez?" *Los Angeles Times*, December 9, 2015, accessed April 11, 2017, http://www.latimes.com/local/lanow/la-me-ln-enrique-marquez-rifles-20151209-story.html.

17. David Hopper, "The Psychology of Radicalization," *The Academic Minute*. January 23, 2017, accessed April 11, 2017, https://academicminute.org/2017/01/arie-kruglanski-university-of-maryland-the-psychology-of-radicalization/.

18. Terry Gross, "Who Are America's 'Homegrown Terrorists?" *NPR*, interview of Peter Bergen, February 2, 2016, accessed April 11, 2017, http://www.npr.org/2016/02/02/465257993/who-are-americas-homegrown-terrorists; See also Ryan Hunter and Daniel Heinke, "Radicalization of Islamist Terrorists in the Western World," *FBI Law Enforcement Bulletin* 2011, accessed April 11, 2017, https://leb.fbi.gov/2011/september/perspective-radicalization-of-islamist-terrorists-in-the-western-world.

19. Jeremy G. Carter and David L. Carter, "Law Enforcement Intelligence: Implications for Self-Radicalized Terrorism," *Police Practice and Research*, 2012, accessed April 11, 2017, https://scholarworks.iupui.edu/bitstream/handle/1805/3857/Carter-2012-Law-Enforcement-Intelligence.pdf.

20. Gary Cox, personal communication, January 27, 2017.

21. Harvard Law Review "The Supreme Court and the New Police," *Harv. L. Rev.* 122 (April 2009).

22. See "The Threat to *Miranda*," editorial, *New York Times*, May 16, 2010, WK9.

23. Stephen Thomas Erlewine, "Merle Haggard Biography," All Music, 2010, accessed July 25, 2010, http://www.allmusic.com/cg/amg.dll?p=amg&sql=11:3ifrxql5ldse~T1.

24. Merle Haggard, Think Exist, "Merle Haggard Quotes," accessed July 24, 2010, http://thinkexist.com/quotation/in-when-i-came-out-of-prison-as-an-ex-convict-i/402153.html.

25. Emma Lazarus, "The New Colossus," in *The Poetry of Freedom* 431 (William R. Benet & Norman Cousins eds., 1945) (1883) in Jennifer M. Hansen The Inaugural Symposium on Immigration: Comment: Sanctuary's Demise: The Unintended Effects of State and Local Enforcement of Immigration Law, 10 Scholar 289, *St. Mary's Law Review on Minority Issues* (2008): 289.

26. Kimberly Jantz, Symposium Issue: What about Federalism? States' Rights and the New State Immigration Laws: Comment: The Boiling Point: Does Oklahoma Have a Role to Play in Creating Immigration Law or a Responsibility to Allow the Federal Government to Independently Manage Reform, Borders, and Treaties? *Tulsa J. Comp. & Int'l L.* 15 (Spring 2008): 243.

27. Jens Manuel Krogstad, Jeffrey S. Passel, and D'Vera Cohn, "5 Facts about Illegal Immigration in the United States," *Pew Research Center*, November 3, 2016, accessed April 16, 2017, http://www.pewresearch.org/fact-tank/2016/11/03/5-facts-about-illegal-immigration-in-the-u-s/.

28. Serena Marshall, "Obama Has Deported More People than Any Other President," ABC News, August 29, 2016, accessed April 17, 2017, http://abcnews.go.com/Politics/obamas-deportation-policy-numbers/story?id=41715661.

29. Maria Sacchetti, "ICE Immigration Arrests of Noncriminals Double Under Trump, *The Washington Post*, April 16, 2017, accessed October 4, 2017, https://www.washingtonpost.com/local/immigration-arrests-of-noncriminals-double-under-trump/2017/04/16/98a2f1e2-2096-11e7-be2a-3a1fb24d4671_story.html?utm_term=.b1a4af20f6d4.

30. Ron Nixon and Liz Robbins, "Office to Aid Crime Victims Is Latest Step in Crackdown on Immigrants," *New York Times*, April 26, 2017, accessed May 4, 2017, https://www.nytimes.com/2017/04/26/us/politics/trump-voice-immigrants-crime.html?_r=0.

31. David Pike, "Texas Immigration Detention Requests Surged in February," *The Brownsville Herald*, April 10, 2017, accessed April 16, 2017, http://www.brownsvilleherald.com/news/article_6236e522-1e2b-11e7-b7c8-a3ed3feb3f26.html.

32. Steven Rosenfeld, "ICE Reopening Private Prisons and Adding Beds at County Jails to Expand Deportation Machinery," *ALTERNET*, February 24, 2017, accessed April 16, 2017, http://www.alternet.

org/print/immigration/ice-reopening-shuttered-private-prisons-and-adding-beds-county-jails-expand-deportation.

33. Maya Rhodan, "Attorney General Jeff Sessions Brings Tough Talk on Immigration to the Mexican Border," *Time* April 11, 2017, accessed April 17, 2017, http://time.com/4734956/jeff-sessions-immigration-mexico-border-nogales-speech/.

34. Catherine E. Shoichet, Susannah Cullinance, and Tal Kopan, U.S. Immigration: DACA and Dreamers Explained, September 5, 2017, accessed October 4, 2017, https://www.washingtonpost.com/local/immigration-arrests-of-noncriminals-double-under-trump/2017/04/16/98a2f1e2-2096-11e7-be2a-3a1fb24d4671_story.html?utm_term=.b1a4af20f6d4.

35. Rory Caroll, Robin Respaut, and Andy Sullivan, "The U.S. Sanctuary Cities Face Roughly $2.27 Billion in Cuts by Trump Policy," Reuters, January 26, 2017, accessed April 16, 2017, http://www.reuters.com/article/us-usa-trump-sanctuarycities-idUSKBN1592V9.

36. Gail Ablow, "Sanctuary Cities, Explained," *Moyers and Company* April 25, 2017, accessed April 26, 2017, http://billmoyers.com/story/sanctuary-cities-explained/.

37. Fox News, "NJ Mayor: Trump Makes Sanctuary Cities 'Fugitive Slave Catchers,'" Fox News Insider, April 3, 2017, accessed May 6, 2017, http://insider.foxnews.com/2017/04/03/newark-mayor-ras-baraka-says-sanctuary-cities-are-fugitive-slave-holders-trump.

38. Rory Caroll, Robin Respaut, and Andy Sullivan, op. cit.

39. Alan Gomez, "Federal Judge Blocks Trump Plan to Punish 'Sanctuary Cities,'" *USA Today*, April 25, 2017, accessed April 26, 2017, https://www.usatoday.com/story/news/nation/2017/04/25/california-judge-blocks-trump-order-sanctuary-city-money/100897066/.

40. James Barragan, "Gov. Greg Abbott Signs 'Sanctuary Cities' Ban into Law on Facebook Live," *The Dallas Morning News*, May 7, 2017, accessed May 10, 2017, https://www.dallasnews.com/news/texas-politics/2017/05/07/abbott-signs-sanctuary-cities-ban-law.

41. Catherine E. Stoichet, "Kate Steinle Case: Judge Dismisses Claim over 'Sanctuary City' Policy," CNN, January 10, 2017, accessed April 26, 2017, http://www.cnn.com/2017/01/10/politics/kate-steinle-wrongful-death-suit/.

42. Jonathan H. Adler, "The Outrage Over the Steinle Verdict is Misplaced," *The Washington Post*, December 2, 2017, accessed December 16, 2017, https://www.washingtonpost.com/news/volokh-conspiracy/wp/2017/12/02/the-outrage-over-the-steinle-verdict-is-misplaced/?utm_term=.79a32ad75c91.

43. Jennifer M. Hansen, op. cit.

44. Ibid., 327.

45. Hansen, op. cit., 330.

46. Ibid., 330, 331.

47. John Marks, Jr., personal communication, July 28, 2010.

48. Jantz, op. cit., 279.

49. Randall G. Shelley, "If You Want Something Done Right ...: *Chicanos Por La Causa v. Napolitano* and the Return of Federalism to Immigration Law," *Akron L. Rev.* 43 (2010): 603, 637.

50. Eugene Robinson, "Arizona's New Immigration Law Is an Act of Vengeance," *Washington Post*, April 27, 2010, accessed July 25, 2010, http://www.washingtonpost.com/wp-dyn/content/article/2010/04/26/AR2010042602595.html.

51. David Nakamura, "Trump Administration Announces End of Immigration Protection for 'Dreamers,'" *The Washington Post*, September 5, 2017, accessed December 16, 2017, https://www.washingtonpost.com/news/post-politics/wp/2017/09/05/trump-administration-announces-end-of-immigration-protection-program-for-dreamers/?tid=a_inl&utm_term=.22c2b727baf7; Melissa Macaya, "As the Battle Over DACA Intensifies, the Fight to Save the Program is Especially Personal for these Congressional Interns," *The Washington Post*, December 15, 2017, accessed December 16, 2017, https://www.washing-

tonpost.com/news/post-nation/wp/2017/12/15/as-the-battle-over-daca-intensifies-in-congress-the-fight-to-save-the-program-is-especially-personal-for-these-congressional-interns/?utm_term=.927f71f8806e.

52. Risdon N. Slate, W. Wesley Johnson, and Sharla S. Colbert, "Police Stress: A Structural Model," *Journal of Police and Criminal Psychology* 22 (2007): 102–112.

53. Risdon N. Slate and W. Wesley Johnson, "A Comparison of Federal and State Probation Officer Stress Levels," presented at the Academy of Criminal Justice Sciences 2008 Annual Meeting, Cincinnati, Ohio.

54. Risdon N. Slate, Terry L. Wells, and W. Wesley Johnson, "Opening the Manager's Door: State Probation Officer Stress and Perceptions of Participation in Workplace Decision Making," *Crime & Delinquency* 49, no. 4 (October 2003): 519–541.

55. Chastity Blankenship and Risdon N. Slate, "Factors Influencing Federal and State Probation Officer Turnover Intention," *Corrections: Policy, Practice and Research* 1, no. 4 (2016): 293–319.

56. Risdon N. Slate and Ronald E. Vogel, "Participative Management and Correctional Personnel: A Study of the Perceived Atmosphere for Participation in Correctional Decision Making and Its Impact on Employee Stress and Thoughts about Quitting," *Journal of Criminal Justice* 25, no. 5 (1997): 397–408; Risdon N. Slate, Terry L. Wells, and W. Wesley Johnson, "Opening the Manager's Door: State Probation Officer Stress and Perceptions of Participation in Workplace Decision Making," *Crime & Delinquency* 49, no. 4 (October 2003): 519–541.

57. Christina Maslach, *Burnout: The Cost of Caring* (Englewood Cliffs, NJ: Prentice Hall, Inc., 1982).

58. Brian Garrett, personal communication, July 23, 2010.

59. Corey Williams, "Boy 11, Hangs Himself after Social Media Prank," *The Ledger* (Lakeland, Florida), April 8, 2017, A4.

60. Georgia Diebelius, "In Full: Chilling Texts from Girl Who 'Encouraged Boyfriend to Kill Himself,'" *Metro*, August 1, 2016, accessed April 13, 2017, http://metro.co.uk/2016/08/01/in-full-chilling-texts-from-girl-who-encouraged-boyfriend-to-kill-himself-6042041/.

61. Garin Flowers, "Woman Live-streams Herself While Drunk Driving," *USA Today*, October 13, 2015, accessed April 13, 2017, https://www.usatoday.com/story/news/nation-now/2015/10/13/woman-live-streams-herself-while-drunk-driving/73858228/.

62. Mike McPhate, "Teenager Is Accused of Live Streaming a Friend's Rape on Periscope," *New York Times*, April 18, 2016, accessed April 14, 2017, https://www.nytimes.com/2016/04/19/us/periscope-rape-case-columbus-ohio-video-livestreaming.html.

63. David Schaper, "Should Viewers of Facebook Live Face Gang Rape Charges?," *NPR*, April 4, 2017, accessed April 13, 2017, http://www.npr.org/2017/04/04/522574666/should-viewers-of-facebook-live-gang-rape-face-charges.

64. Charles Hayes, Nancy Loo, and Julian Crews, "4 Charged with Hate Crime and Kidnapping in Facebook Live Torture of Man with Special Needs," WGNTV-Chicago, January 5, 2017, accessed April 14, 2017, http://wgntv.com/2017/01/05/4-charged-with-hate-crime-in-facebook-live-torture-of-man-with-special-needs/; See also Emanuella Grinberg, "Chicago Torture: Facebook Live Video Leads to 4 Arrests," CNN, January 5, 2017, accessed April 14, 2017, http://www.cnn.com/2017/01/04/us/chicago-facebook-live-beating/.

65. Drew Harwell, "Cleveland Police Seek Suspect in Facebook Homicide Video," *Washington Post*, April 16, 2017, accessed April 17, 2017, https://www.washingtonpost.com/national/cleveland-police-seek-suspect-in-facebook-live-homicide-video/2017/04/16/83ff3f56-22ea-11e7-a1b3-faff0034e2de_story.html?hpid=hp_hp-more-top-stories_ap-cleveland-630pm%3Ahomepage%2Fstory&tid=ptv_rellink&utm_term=.3fa0896e2ed9.

66. Alina Selyukh, "As We Leave More Digital Tracks, Amazon Echo Factors in Murder Investigation," *NPR*, December 28, 2016, accessed April 14, 2017, http://www.npr.org/sections/alltechconsidered/2016/12/28/507230487/as-we-leave-more-digital-tracks-amazon-echo-factors-in-murder-investigation.

67. Mitch Smith, "Fatal 'Swatting' Episode in Kansas Raises Quandary: Who Is to Blame?" *The New York Times*, Dcember 31, 2017, accessed January 11, 2018, https://www.nytimes.com/2017/12/31/us/wichita-swatting-barriss.html; Avi Selk and Eli Rosenberg, "A Twitter user claims to have made the 'swatting' call that led police to kill a man," The Washington Post, December 30, 2017, accessed January 11, 2018, https://www.washingtonpost.com/news/post-nation/wp/2017/12/30/why-a-twitter-user-claims-to-have-made-the-swatting-call-that-led-police-to-kill-a-man/?utm_term=.818a1285ccca.

68. Alene Tchekmedyian, "Woman is Sentenced to 5 Years in Prison for Framing Husband's Ex-Fiancee in Craigslist Rape Fantasy Plot," *Los Angeles Times*, October 18, 2017, accessed January 11, 2018, http://www.latimes.com/local/lanow/la-me-ln-craigslist-sentence-20171018-story.html.

69. DeeDee Correll, "Former Boyfriend Used Craigslist to Arrange Woman's Rape, Police Say" *Los Angeles Times*, January 11, 2010, accessed January 11, 2018, http://articles.latimes.com/2010/jan/11/nation/la-na-rape-craigslist11-2010jan11.

70. *City of California v. Quon*, 560 U.S. ___, (2010)—* It should be noted that the U.S. Supreme Court in *City of Ontario, California v. Quon* (2010) held that the search of a police officer's work-issued pager that uncovered sexually explicit personal text messages did not constitute a privacy violation. This decision has far-reaching implications for employees who are utilizing electronic means of communication supplied by their employers.

71. Kamika Dunlap, "California First Time DUI Offenders Get Interlock Devices," FINDLAW BLOTTER, June 18, 2010, accessed July 27, 2010, http://blogs.findlaw.com/blotter/2010/06/ca-first-time-dui-offenders-get-interlock-devices.html.

72. Kamika Dunlap, "OnStar Technology Leads to Accused Murderer's Arrest," FINDLAW BLOTTER, June 21, 2010, accessed July 27, 2010, http://blogs.findlaw.com/blotter/2010/06/onstar-technology-leads-to-accused-murderers-arrest.html.

73. ABC News, "Blood from Mosquito Traps Finnish Suspect," December 23, 2008, accessed July 27, 2010, http://www.abc.net.au/news/stories/2008/12/22/2453342.htm.

74. Emily Friedman, "A Different Kind of Bling: Bracelet Tracks Alcohol Consumption, Monitoring Device Like Lohan's Samples Sweat, Records Ethanol Levels," ABC News, July 17, 2007, accessed July 27, 2010, http://abcnews.go.com/US/story?id=3383679&page=1.

75. "DNA," Answers.com, Dictionary, accessed July 27, 2010, http://www.answers.com/topic/dna.

76. Becca Hutchinson, "DNA, Future of Criminal Justice Addressed," UDaily, University of Delaware, November 8, 2004, accessed July 27, 2010, http://www.udel.edu/PR/UDaily/2005/oct/dna110804.html.

77. Ryan W. Miller, "Police: Man Left DNA in Toilet During Burglary," *USA Today*, August 8, 2017, accessed October 6, 2017, https://www.usatoday.com/story/news/nation/2017/08/08/police-man-left-dna-toilet-during-burglary/551268001/.

78. German Lopez, "Drug Overdose Deaths Skyrocketed in 2016—and Traditional Opioid Painkillers Weren't the Cause," *Vox*, September 5, 2017, accessed December 16, 2017, https://www.vox.com/policy-and-politics/2017/9/5/16255040/opioid-epidemic-overdose-death-2016

79. Warren Richey, "Supreme Court to Hear California Prison Overcrowding Case," *The Christian Science Monitor*, June 14, 2010, accessed July 28, 2010, http://www.csmonitor.com/USA/Justice/2010/0614/Supreme-Court-to-hear-California-prison-overcrowding-case. See also Adam Liptak, "Justices, 5–4, Tell California to Cut Prisoner Population, *The New York Times*, May 23, 2011, accessed October 4, 2017, http://www.nytimes.com/2011/05/24/us/24scotus.html.

80. Dustin Gardiner, "Arizona Shuts Down Speed Cameras on Freeways," *The Arizona Republic*, July 16, 2010, accessed July 28, 2010, http://www.azcentral.com/news/articles/2010/07/16/20100716arizona-turns-off-speed-cameras.html.

81. Rick Rousos, "City Dips into Red-Light Fines for FSC," *The Lakeland Ledger*, June 22, 2010, B1–2.

82. Steve Andrews, "Polk Undercover Drug Investigators Play Wii During Raid," News Channel 8, (Tampa, FL), September 21, 2009, accessed July 27, 2010, also, see video at http://www2.tbo.com/content/2009/sep/21/undercover-drug-investigators-embarrass-polk-sheri.

83. Robert Moore, *Cybercrime: Investigating High-Technology Computer Crime* (Cincinnati, OH: Lexis Nexis Group, 2005).

84. Richard P. Seiter, *Corrections: An Introduction*, 3rd ed. (Upper Saddle River, NJ: Prentice Hall, 2011).

85. Bob Orr, "Predator Drones Shift from Battlefield to Border," CBS Evening News, November 9, 2010, accessed November 14, 2010, http://www/cbsnews.com/stories/2010/11/09/eveningnews/main7038641.shtml.

86. Hope Reese, "Police Are Now Using Drones to Apprehend Suspects and Administer Non-lethal Force: A Police Chief Weighs In," *Tech Republic*, November 25, 2015, accessed April 14, 2017, http://www.techrepublic.com/article/police-are-now-using-drones-to-apprehend-suspects-and-administer-non-lethal-force-a-police-chief/.

87. The Times Editorial Board, "Police the Sheriff's Drones," *The Los Angeles Times*, January 26, 2017, accessed April 14, 2017, http://www.latimes.com/opinion/editorials/la-ed-sheriff-drones-20170125-story.html.

88. Governing the States and Localities, "Law Enforcement Agencies Using Drone List, Map: Current as of 2013," 2017, accessed April 15, 2017, http://www.governing.com/gov-data/safety-justice/drones-state-local-law-enforcement-agencies-license-list.html.

89. Craig Whitlock and Craig Timberg, "Border-Patrol Drones Being Borrowed by Other Agencies More Often than Previously Known," *Washington Post*, January 14, 2014, accessed April 15, 2017, https://www.washingtonpost.com/world/national-security/border-patrol-drones-being-borrowed-by-other-agencies-more-often-than-previously-known/2014/01/14/5f987af0-7d49-11e3-9556-4a4bf7bcbd84_story.html?utm_term=.4eef25a855f9.

90. Jack Nicas, "Criminals, Terrorists Find Use for Drones, Raising Concerns," *Wall Street Journal*, January 28, 2015, accessed April 15, 2017, https://www.wsj.com/articles/criminals-terrorists-find-uses-for-drones-raising-concerns-1422494268.

91. Ben Popper, "The Teenager behind the Drone Gun Now has a Drone-Mounted Flamethrower," *The Verge*, December 8, 2015, accessed April 26, 2017, http://www.theverge.com/2015/12/8/9871732/drone-flamethrower-austin-haughwout.

92. Jo Ciavaglia, "How PA Handles Prison Medical Care," The Real Cost of Prisons Weblog, March 23, 2009, accessed July 28, 2010, http://realcostofprisons.org/blog/archives/2009/03/how_pa_handles.html.

93. "Video Teleconferencing Equipment for Visitation and Arraignments," Corrections Community, A Place Where Corrections Professionals Can Interact and Collaborate, accessed July 28, 2010, http://community.nicic.gov/forums/p/6937/13759.aspx—message board cites like these are likely to be more prevalent in the future so criminal justice professionals may communicate and share information.

94. Inside Edition, "High Infidelity: Man Uses Drone to Catch Wife of 18 Years Who He Says Is Cheating, Broadcasts Video on Internet," November 15, 2016, accessed April 15, 2017, http://www.insideedition.com/headlines/19908-high-infidelity-man-uses-drone-to-catch-wife-of-18-years-who-he-says-is.

95. Raju Chebium, "N.J. Lawmakers Introduce Anti-Bullying Act," *USA Today*, November 19, 2010, accessed November 23, 2010, http://www.usatoday.com/news/nation/2010-11-19-new-new-jersey-bully-bill-N.htm; Audrey Harvin, "Sen. Lautenberg Introduces College Anti-Bullying Bill," *Burlington County Times*, November 19, 2010, accessed November 23, 2010, http://www.phillyburbs.com; James Kleimann and Nicholas Loffredo, "Clementi Family Grateful as Anti-Bullying Bill Sails through Legislature," Wyckoff Patch, accessed November 22, 2010, http://www.wyckoff.patch.com; see Bullying Information Center Website, accessed November 22, 2010, http://www.education.com/topic/school-bullying-teasing.

96. Legal Action Center, "Public Opinion Favors Criminal Justice and Drug Policy Reform, Making Now the Time to Act," *Newsroom*, 2017, accessed April 16, 2017, https://lac.org/public-opinion-favors-criminal-justice-and-drug-policy-reform-making-now-the-time-to-act/.

97. Gallup, "Death Penalty," October 5–9, 2016, accessed April 16, 2017, http://www.gallup.com/poll/1606/death-penalty.aspx.

98. Mark Berman, "Judges Block Arkansas from Carrying out Series of Executions," *Washington Post*, April 15, 2017, accessed April 16, 2017, https://www.washingtonpost.com/news/post-nation/wp/2017/04/14/arkansas-judge-prohibits-state-from-using-lethal-injection-drug-blocking-scheduled-executions/?utm_term=.79cddfa0fb29.

99. Risdon N. Slate, W. Wesley Johnson, and Sharla Colbert, "Police Stress: A Structural Model," *Journal of Police Science and Criminal Psychology* 22 (2007): 102–112.

100. State Attorney 10th Judicial Circuit of Florida, "Full Text of State Attorney Investigative Report on LPD Officers," June 25, 2013, accessed April 15, 2017, https://archive.org/stream/717538-fdle-investigative-report-on-lpd-officers-6-25-13/717538-fdle-investigative-report-on-lpd-officers-6-25-13_djvu.txt.

101. Steve Miller, "In Florida, Cops Flout the Law and Continue Working," *Miami New Times*, June 7, 2016, accessed April 15, 2017, http://www.miaminewtimes.com/news/in-florida-cops-flout-the-law-and-continue-working-8506418.

102. See James Queally, "Disgust and Dismay over Oakland Police Sex Scandal as Department Is Called 'A Cesspool,'" *Los Angeles Times*, June 19, 2016, accessed April 16, 2017, http://www.latimes.com/local/lanow/la-me-ln-oakland-police-sex-scandal-20160619-snap-story.html; Phillip M. Bailey, "Louisville Police Sex Abuse Scandal: Here's What We Know," *Courier-Journal*, March 8, 2017, accessed April 16, 2017, http://www.courier-journal.com/story/news/local/2017/03/18/louisville-police-sex-abuse-scandal-heres-what-we-know/99325946/.

103. See Risdon N. Slate and W. Wesley Johnson, *Criminalization of Mental Illness: Crisis and Opportunity for the Justice System* (Durham, NC: Carolina Academic Press, 2008); Adam Serwer, "Beyond Bars," *The American Prospect*, December 14, 2009, accessed July 28, 2010, http://www.prospect.org/cs/articles?article=beyond_bars.

104. Serwer, op. cit.; see also our discussion on chronic offenders in Chapter 6.

105. Ibid.

106. Ibid. see also Steven F. Messner and Richard Rosenfeld about prison union contributions to Governor Pataki in *Crime and the American Dream*, 4th ed. (Belmont, CA: Wadsworth, 2007).

107. Victor A. Kowalewski, "Police Training and Education toward a Critical Professionalism" in *The Future of Criminal Justice*, ed. Gene Stephens (Cincinnati, OH: Anderson Publishing, 1982).

108. Risdon N. Slate and W. Wesley Johnson, *Criminalization of Mental Illness: Crisis and Opportunity for the Justice System* (Durham, NC: Carolina Academic Press, 2008).

109. Ken Kerle, personal communication, July 27, 2009; see Ed Wolahan, National Institute of Corrections, "Crisis Intervention Teams: An Effective Response to Mental Illness in Corrections," U.S. Department of Justice, Live Satellite/INTERNET Broadcast, July 29, 2010, accessed July 28, 2010, http://www.ncjrs.gov/notices/nic-images/CIT-flier.pdf.

110. See Drug Court Monitoring, Evaluation, and Management Information Systems: National Scope Needs Assessment Monograph, Bureau of Justice Assistance, U.S. Department of Justice, Office of Justice Programs, February 2003, accessed July 27, 2010, http://www.ncjrs.gov/pdffiles1/bja/195077.pdf.

111. Collaborative Justice, "Homeless Courts, Judicial Council of California," 2010, accessed July 27, 2010, http://www.courtinfo.ca.gov/programs/collab/homeless.htm.

112. Nicholas Riccardi, "These Courts Give Wayward Veterans a Chance," *The Los Angeles Times*, March 10, 2009, accessed July 27, 2010, http://articles.latimes.com/2009/mar/10/nation/na-veterans-court10.

113. Ibid., 132.

114. Slate and Johnson, op. cit.

115. Erik Roskes, personal communication, April 26, 2017.

116. Slate and Johnson, op. cit., 247–249.

117. Kristina Rogosta, "Maine Becomes 44th State to Reform Mental Illness Treatment Laws," Treatment Advocacy Center, Arlington, Virginia, April 14, 2010, accessed July 28, 2010, http://www.treatmentadvocacycenter.org/storage/tac/documents/tac—maine_bill_signed_news_release_final—_04-14-2010.pdf.

118. Preventable Tragedies Database, Treatment Advocacy Center, Arlington, Virginia, accessed July 28, 2010, http://www.treatmentadvocacycenter.org/index.php?option=com_wrapper&Itemid=251.

119. Virginia Tech Review Panel, *Mass Shootings at Virginia Tech, April 16, 2007,* Report of the Review Panel Presented to Governor Kaine, Commonwealth of Virginia, August 2007, accessed July 28, 2010, http://www.governor.virginia.gov/TempContent/techPanelReport-docs/FullReport.pdf; Mass Shootings at Virginia Tech: A 210 page Addendum to the Report of the Review Panel was Presented to Governor Timothy M. Kaine, November 2009, accessed July 28, 2010, http://graphics8.nytimes.com/packages/pdf/us/20091204vatech.pdf.

120. J. Richards, personal communication, April 30, 2007.

121. Ibid., 1.

122. Leanne F. Alarid and Philip L. Reichel, *Corrections: A Contemporary Introduction* (New York: Pearson Education, Inc., 2008); Nancy M. Ritter, *Preparing for the Future: Criminal Justice in 2040,* National Institute of Justice, November 2006, accessed July 28, 2010, http://www.ojp.usdoj.gov/nij/journals/255/2040.html.

123. Lawrence W. Sherman's *Ideas in American Policing: Evidence-Based Policing,* Police Foundation, 1, accessed July 26, 2010, http://www.policefoundation.org/pdf/Sherman.pdf.

124. See James J. Willis, Stephen D. Mastrofski, and David Weisburd, *COMPSTAT in Practice: An In-Depth Analysis of Three Cities,* Police Foundation, 2003, accessed July 28, 2010, http://www.policefoundation.org/pdf/compstatinpractice.pdf.

125. Henry J. Steadman, Foreword in Slate and Johnson, op. cit.

126. Associated Press, "Santa-Suit Killer Lost Wife, Job before Attack," December 27, 2008, accessed July 23, 2010, http://www.msnbc.msn.com/id/28385277; Jezebel, "Santa Claus Killer Murders 8 in L.A. Tragedy," December 26, 2008, accessed July 23, 2010, http://jezebel.com/5118404/santa-claus-killer-murders-8-in-la-tragedy; Sky News, "Santa Massacre: Killer's Hit List," December 30, 2008, accessed July 23, 2010, http://news.sky.com/skynews/Home/World-News/California-Santa-Killer-Bruce-Pardo-Planned-To-Kill-More-Than-His-Nine-Victims/Article/200812415195535?f=rss.

127. *Los Angeles Times,* "Las Vegas Shooting Updates: Portraits of the Victims Emerge, October 4, 2017, accessed October 4, 2017, http://www.latimes.com/nation/la-las-vegas-shooting-live-updates-carnage-concert-leaves-50-dead-100-injured-20171002-htmlstory.html; Rebecca Hersher, "Sheer Number of Casualties Makes Las Vegas Count Difficult," *NPR,* October 4, 2017, accessed October 6, 2017, http://www.npr.org/sections/health-shots/2017/10/04/555584905/sheer-number-of-casualties-makes-las-vegas-count-difficult.

128. "On Easter Sunday of 1873 in Colfax, La., white citizens gunned down and hung perhaps as many as 150 African Americans. On Dec. 29, 1890, U.S. Army soldiers killed 200 Lakota Native Americans with machine guns at South Dakota's Wounded Knee Creek. And some historians now believe that more than 300 people died in Tulsa, Okla., between May 31 and June 1, 1921, when whites torched the area's African-American neighborhoods, driving out victims like Mary J. Parrish, who described fleeing with her baby daughter in hand "amidst showers of bullets from the machine gun," from Olivia B. Waxman, "Las Vegas was the Deadliest Shooting in Modern U.S. History. Here's

Why 'Modern' is so Important," *Time*, October 4, 2017, accessed October 6, 2017, http://time.com/4968108/las-vegas-deadliest-shooting-modern-us-history/.

129. Williams, F. P., & McShane, M. D. (2004). *Criminological Theory* (4th ed). Upper Saddle River, NJ: Prentice-Hall.

130. *District of Columbia v. Heller*, 554 U.S. 570 (2008); *McDonald v. Chicago*, 561 U.S. 742 (2010).

131. Jenn Jacques, "Polk County Sheriff's Office Steps Up to Launch Florida's First Sentinel Program," *Bearing Arms*, June 22, 2017, accessed October 7, 2017, https://bearingarms.com/jenn-j/2017/06/22/polk-county-sheriffs-office-steps-launch-floridas-first-sentinel-program/.

132. Audra D.S. Burch and Patricia Mazzei, "Death Toll is at 17 and Could Rise in Shooting," *New York Times*, February 14, 2018, accessed March 1, 2018, https://www.nytimes.com/2018/02/14/us/parkland-school-shooting.html.

133. Mark Berman and Kevin Sullivan, "Red Flags. Warnings. Cries for Help. How a System Built to Stop the Parkland School Shooter Repeatedly Broke Down," *The Washington Post*, February 23, 2018, accessed March 1, 2018, https://www.washingtonpost.com/national/red-flags-warnings-cries-for-help-how-a-system-built-to-stop-the-parkland-school-shooter-broke-down/2018/02/23/3ccff52c-18d9-11e8-b681-2d4d462a1921_story.html?utm_term=.fd7635f5fc50

134. Ranker, "Celebrities Who Were Arrested in 2017," *Celebrity Events*, accessed October 4, 2017, https://www.ranker.com/list/celebrities-arrested-in-2017/celebrity-events.

135. Tadd Haislop, "End of 2017 Offseason Eases Fear of NFL Player Arrests," *Sporting News*, July 17, 2017, accessed October 4, 2017, http://www.sportingnews.com/ca/nfl/news/nfl-arrests-2017-domestic-violence-marijuana-weed-assault-charges/1axpb44wef1ef1tum5qmkyeo8l.

136. Bruce J. Vila in Nancy M. Ritter, op. cit.

137. Ritter, op. cit.

138. Johnnie L. Cochran, Speech at Florida Southern College, Branscomb Auditorium, Lakeland, Florida, March 31, 1996.

139. Stephen R. Covey, "Seven Habits of Highly Effective People," July 13, 2002, accessed July 23, 2010: http://www.leaderu.com/cl-institute/habits/habit5.html.

140. John Stuart Mill, *On Liberty* (London: Longman, Roberts & Green, 1869); Bartleby.com, 1999, accessed July 24, 2010, http://bartleby.com/br/130.html.

141. Gene Stephens, *The Future of Criminal Justice* (Cincinnati, OH: Anderson Publishing Co., 1982), 1; 17.

142. Victor Hugo, Brainy Quote, accessed July 24, 2010, http://www.brainyquote.com/quotes/quotes/v/victorhugo104893.html.

About the Authors

Risdon N. Slate, Ph.D.

Risdon N. Slate earned his degrees in criminal justice from the Claremont Graduate School (Ph.D.) in Claremont, California, the University of South Carolina (M.C.J.), and the University of North Carolina at Charlotte (B.S.). He has prior work experience as administrative assistant to the warden at a medium/maximum security, death row prison and as a United States Probation Officer in Columbia, South Carolina.

Dr. Slate is currently Professor of Criminology at Florida Southern College. He has also taught at California State University Long Beach, University of Maine at Augusta, and St. Leo University.

Dr. Slate has published a number of scholarly articles. His research interests include criminal justice practitioner stress, and he is co-author of the book *Criminalization of Mental Illness: Crisis and Opportunity for the Justice System.* He has served as a trainer for police, judicial, detention, and correctional personnel concerning the impact of persons with mental illness on the criminal justice system and testified on that subject before Congress.

Patrick R. Anderson, Ph.D.

Dr. Anderson received the Ph.D. in Criminology from Florida State University. He earned the Bachelor of Arts degree from Furman University where he attended on a track scholarship, and the Master of Divinity degree from Southwestern Baptist Theological Seminary. He worked as a juvenile probation caseworker and casework supervisor in Ft. Worth, Texas.

Dr. Anderson has taught at Louisiana State University, Florida Community College at Jacksonville, University of North Florida, and Wake Forest University. His published books include *Introduction to Criminal Justice, Expert Witnesses: Criminologists in the Courtroom*, and *A Prototypical State Male Correctional Facility*. He has published numerous articles in scholarly journals and has written many opinion columns for major newspapers.

Dr. Anderson has served as a consultant for criminal justice agencies and as an expert witness in numerous court cases regarding police procedure, custody deaths, police pursuit, and transportation of prisoners. He is now Emeritus Professor of Criminology at Florida Southern College.

Lisa M. Carter, Ph.D.

Dr. Lisa Carter joined the Florida Southern College faculty in August of 2012 as an assistant professor in the Criminology department. She also teaches courses for the Women and Gender Studies program at the college. She earned her B.A in Sociology with a specialization in deviant behavior from the University of Kentucky, and her M.S. in Corrections and Juvenile Justice Studies from Eastern Kentucky University. She completed her Ph.D. in Criminology at Indiana University of Pennsylvania.

Dr. Carter has also taught courses at Eastern Kentucky University, St. Francis University, and Penn State Altoona. Her research interests include: female criminality and gender-specific programming, corrections and rehabilitation, reintegration, and death penalty issues. She is the co-editor of the book titled, *Female Offenders and Reentry: Pathways and Barriers to Returning to Society.*

In her spare time, Dr. Carter enjoys cycling, running, cooking, discussions with her book club, volunteering, and spending time with her husband and pug.

Name Index

Subject Index